# Financial Deregulation and Integration in East Asia

NBER–East Asia Seminar on Economics
Volume 5

National Bureau of Economic Research
Korea Development Institute
Chung-Hua Institution for Economic Research
Tokyo Center of Economic Research

# Financial Deregulation and Integration in East Asia

Edited by

Takatoshi Ito and
Anne O. Krueger



The University of Chicago Press

*Chicago and London*

TAKATOSHI ITO is senior advisor in the Research Department of the International Monetary Fund and a research associate of the National Bureau of Economic Research. ANNE O. KRUEGER is professor of economics at Stanford University and a research associate of the National Bureau of Economic Research.

The University of Chicago Press, Chicago 60637
The University of Chicago Press, Ltd., London

Printed in the United States of America
05 04 03 02 01 00 99 98 97 96   1 2 3 4 5
ISBN: 0-226-38671-6 (cloth)

Library of Congress Cataloging-in-Publication Data

Financial deregulation and integration in East Asia / edited by Takatoshi Ito and Anne O. Krueger.
p. cm.—(NBER–East Asia seminar on economics; v. 5)
"Contains edited versions of papers presented at the NBER–East Asia Seminar on Economics fifth annual conference, held in Singapore, June 15–17, 1994"—Acknowl.
Includes bibliographical references and index.
1. Financial institutions—Deregulation—East Asia—Congresses. 2. Capital market—Deregulation—East Asia—Congresses. 3. Fiscal policy—East Asia—Congresses. 4. East Asia—Economic integration—Congresses. I. Itō, Takatoshi. II. Krueger, Anne O. III. NBER–East Asia Seminar on Economics (5th:1994:Singapore) IV. Series: NBER–East Asia seminar on economics (Series); v. 5.
HG187.E37F548 1996
332.1′0954—dc20   95-25306
CIP

♾ The paper used in this publication meets the minimum requirements of the American National Standard for Information Sciences—Permanence of Paper for Printed Library Materials, ANSI Z39.48-1984.

Since this volume is a record of conference proceedings, it has been exempted from the rules governing critical review of manuscripts by the Board of Directors of the National Bureau (resolution adopted 8 June 1948, as revised 21 November 1949 and 20 April 1968).

# Contents


| | | |
|---|---|---|
| | Acknowledgments | xi |
| | **Introduction**<br>Takatoshi Ito and Anne O. Krueger | 1 |
| 1. | **Credible Liberalizations and International Capital Flows: The "Overborrowing Syndrome"**<br>Ronald I. McKinnon and Huw Pill<br>*Comment:* Francisco de Asis Nadal De Simone<br>*Comment:* Chong-Hyun Nam | 7 |
| 2. | **Japanese and U.S. Exports and Investment as Conduits of Growth**<br>Jonathan Eaton and Akiko Tamura<br>*Comment:* Chong-Hyun Nam<br>*Comment:* V. V. Bhanoji Rao | 51 |
| 3. | **Foreign Direct Investment in China: Sources and Consequences**<br>Shang-Jin Wei<br>*Comment:* Pakorn Vichyanond<br>*Comment:* Wing Thye Woo | 77 |
| 4. | **Interdependence through Capital Flows in Pacific Asia and the Role of Japan**<br>Akira Kohsaka<br>*Comment:* Toshihiko Kinoshita<br>*Comment:* Ya-Hwei Yang | 107 |

5. **The Structural Determinants of Invoice Currencies in Japan: The Case of Foreign Trade with East Asian Countries** 147
Shin-ichi Fukuda
*Comment:* Akira Kohsaka

6. **An Evaluation of Japanese Financial Liberalization: A Case Study of Corporate Bond Markets** 167
Akiyoshi Horiuchi
*Comment:* Won-Am Park

7. **The Role of Macroeconomic Policy in Export-Led Growth: The Experience of Taiwan and South Korea** 193
Kenneth S. Lin, Hsiu-Yun Lee, and Bor-Yi Huang
*Comment:* Amina Tyabji

8. **Money and Prices in Taiwan in the 1980s** 229
Ya-Hwei Yang and Jia-Dong Shea
*Comment:* Kenjiro Hirayama
*Comment:* Muthi Samudram

9. **Financial Liberalization: The Korean Experience** 247
Won-Am Park
*Comment:* Shin-ichi Fukuda
*Comment:* Huw Pill

10. **The Principal Transactions Bank System in Korea and a Search for a New Bank-Business Relationship** 277
Sang-Woo Nam
*Comment:* Akiyoshi Horiuchi
*Comment:* Shang-Jin Wei

11. **Monetary Autonomy in the Presence of Capital Flows: And Never the Twain Shall Meet, Except in East Asia?** 307
Wing Thye Woo and Kenjiro Hirayama
*Comment:* Ronald I. McKinnon
*Comment:* Basant K. Kapur

12. **Interest Parity and Dynamic Capital Mobility: The Experience of Singapore** 335
Tse Yiu Kuen and Tan Kim Song
*Comment:* Ngiam Kee Jin

| | | |
|---|---|---|
| 13. | **Singapore as a Financial Center: New Developments, Challenges, and Prospects**<br>Ngiam Kee Jin<br>*Comment:* Sang-Woo Nam<br>*Comment:* Pakorn Vichyanond | 359 |
| | Contributors | 387 |
| | Author Index | 391 |
| | Subject Index | 395 |

# Acknowledgments

This volume contains edited versions of papers presented at the NBER–East Asia Seminar on Economics fifth annual conference, held in Singapore, June 15–17, 1994.

We are indebted to Chong-Hyun Nam and Tzong-shian Yu, who served as members of the program committee, for organizing the conference and to Martin Feldstein and Geoffrey Carliner for their support of the conference series. We also thank Kirsten Foss Davis for her tireless efforts in making conference arrangements, and Deborah Kiernan for overseeing the editorial work in preparing the volume for publication.

Our special thanks goes to Basant Kapur and the Department of Economics and Statistics, National University of Singapore, who hosted the conference this year. All participants praised the host for organizing an efficient but hospitable conference.

The National Bureau of Economic Research provided logistical support, for which we are grateful. We are also indebted to the Chung-Hua Institution, the Korea Development Institute, the National Bureau of Economic Research, and the Tokyo Center of Economic Research (TCER) for their financial assistance.

Takatoshi Ito and Anne O. Krueger

# Introduction

Takatoshi Ito and Anne O. Krueger

One of the striking trends in the international economy over the past several decades has been the increased mobility and volume of capital flows. It is estimated that the *daily* volume of international financial transactions now exceeds the annual value of global GNP.

Increased financial mobility has been both a cause and a result of increasing financial integration of the global economy. With greater integration, domestic financial markets are increasingly affected by world events. Dialogue among the major countries' governments increasingly focuses on the appropriateness of each others' policy stances with regard to monetary, interest rate, and exchange rate policy.

Capital flows motivated by interest rate differentials used to be limited to industrial countries. However, in the 1990s, some developing countries, now called "emerging markets," became a popular destination for direct and portfolio investment from industrial countries. For example, net capital flows from industrial countries to developing countries are estimated to have increased from less than $15 billion in 1990 to more than $100 billion in 1993. There are at least three reasons for this rapid change. First, those developing countries with high growth and current account surpluses obviously became attractive investment opportunities because of their high potential capital gain and likely currency appreciation. Second, industrial countries suffered recessions, and their interest rates came down substantially. Third, large institutional investors in the United States started to diversify into international investment opportunities.

Simultaneously, regulation of domestic financial markets, which in earlier

Takatoshi Ito is senior advisor in the Research Department of the International Monetary Fund and a research associate of the National Bureau of Economic Reasearch. Anne O. Krueger is professor of economics at Stanford University and a research associate of the National Bureau of Economic Research.

years appeared both feasible and consistent with efficient economic performance, has been greatly affected. Decisions regarding changes in interest rates in any large national capital have immediate effects on financial conditions in all other countries; efforts to control interest rates in such circumstances can lead to large financial flows between countries. That, in turn, can limit the efficacy of monetary policy instruments aimed at domestic macroeconomic balances.

In part because earlier types of regulation no longer effectively achieve their intended result because of increased financial integration, and in part because those regulations that appeared to serve their purpose earlier now appear to impinge on the efficient functioning of financial markets, countries around the world have been engaged in widespread financial deregulation.

Nowhere has this trend been more pronounced than in the countries of East Asia. Japan has assumed its role as a major creditor nation only within the past two decades. Moreover, with its large current account surpluses, the challenges of managing of its own domestic macroeconomic aggregates have changed greatly. Simultaneously, the East Asian newly industrialized economies (NIEs), which began their rapid development in an era when capital markets were less integrated, have faced the dual task of liberalizing their markets in response to their own growth as well as to the changing international economy.

Deregulation itself has proved challenging, both because of increased interdependence and because deregulation inevitably affects the functioning of the macroeconomy in ways that are not well understood. In a number of cases, deregulation has affected the behavior of exchange rates, interest rates, and capital flows in unanticipated ways.

As deregulation spreads to emerging markets, these countries start to enjoy the benefits and pay the costs of being linked to the world capital market. As the economic prospects of a country become brighter, capital suddenly flows into the country and may provide scarce resources for more investment and growth. However, the capital flows may appreciate the currency so that the competitiveness of export industries suffers, or may cause expansions of domestic credit that result in inflation. Integration in the world capital market makes the policy options very different from before.

The fifth NBER–East Asia Seminar on Economics focused on financial deregulation and integration in the East Asian region, with a view to understanding how deregulation is affecting those markets and to improving knowledge of the ways in which financial integration is affecting responses to various policies in the countries of the region.

The papers presented at the conference, which are collected in this volume, cover a wide variety of aspects of this topic—deregulation per se, exchange rate behavior under alternative regimes, responses of capital flows to deregulation and integration, behavior of individual types of capital flows (such as direct foreign investment), and so on. As a group, the papers demonstrate both the widespread nature of deregulation and the challenges that deregulation presents, especially because of the mobility of capital between countries.

The first two chapters in this volume focus on the interrelationship between domestic financial changes and the international economy more generally. As already mentioned, deregulation and integration have been global phenomena, affecting countries in Europe, North America, South America, as well as Asia. Some of the phenomena are general, and lessons from other parts of the world are applicable to Asia as well.

In chapter 1, McKinnon and Pill consider a problem associated with a number of policy reform efforts, that is, what they term "excessive" capital inflows. When policy reforms are credible, people may want immediately to increase their consumption in anticipation of higher future real incomes, and the result is a sharp deterioration in the savings-investment balance, financed by a large increase in capital inflows (which would not have happened in earlier years when there was little capital mobility). McKinnon and Pill believe that it is financial market failures that do not brake these large inflows, so that there has been financing even for very risky projects and a sharp deterioration in banks' balance sheets. This situation is intensified when (implicit or explicit) deposit insurance for banks creates a moral hazard problem. The authors believe that the authorities should not deregulate controls over capital flows or financial institutions at too early a stage of the policy reform process because of these problems and should seek ways to reduce capital inflows to appropriate levels.

Chapters 2, 3, and 4 examine various aspects of the determinants of capital flows between countries. In chapter 2, Eaton and Tamura examine the roles of the United States and Japan in trading with and investing in various countries in the Asia-Pacific region. They use a gravity model to ascertain the determinants of U.S. and Japanese flows, using variables such as population, factor endowments, per capita incomes, and distance. They find that Japan and the United States relate to other countries in the region in similar ways, although Japan's lack of natural resources affects trading patterns and the U.S. current account deficit has limited the U.S. role as a provider of capital.

Wei, in chapter 3, examines the origins and the effects of foreign direct investment (FDI) in China. A first finding is that FDI comes overwhelmingly from overseas Chinese, and not from the countries that have been suppliers of foreign capital to other economies in the region. He then proceeds to relate differences in growth rates of Chinese cities to the magnitudes of capital inflows and finds that they contribute significantly to cross-city differences in growth rates and also the rate of growth of Chinese exports.

Kohsaka's analysis in chapter 4 focuses on the capital flow links among the countries of Asia. He finds that there has been considerably greater financial integration among countries in the region in recent years. Moreover, both foreign direct and portfolio investment into Southeast Asian countries grew rapidly during the 1980s, but the major source of increase was from the NIEs of

East Asia, rather than from Japan, although Japan remained a large supplier of capital to the region. The turnabout in the role of the NIEs from capital recipients to capital suppliers is the major structural change that took place with respect to capital flows in Asia in the 1980s.

Chapters 5 and 6 focus on particular aspects of Japanese financial markets. Fukuda investigates the determinants of the invoice currencies of Japanese exports and imports. He finds that there is a very low fraction of Japanese exports where invoices are denominated in yen, even in transactions in East Asia, contrasted with practices in Europe and the United States. Using sectoral data on invoice currencies, Fukuda relates this practice to Japanese exporters' strategy of pricing-to-market, absorbing exchange rate risk so that they do not lose market share when the yen increases in value. On the import side, the low fraction of yen-invoiced goods is attributable to the high fraction of primary commodities, such as oil, in Japan's imports and the practice of pricing those commodities in U.S. dollars.

Horiuchi analyzes some aspects of Japanese financial liberalization in his paper. He examines liberalization of the corporate bond market, which reduced the reliance of Japanese firms on bank financing. Horiuchi shows that the manner in which liberalization was carried out created a new distortion in the financial system. The distortion was the restriction of the right to issue convertible bonds to large well-established firms, thus preventing some firms that could have employed additional capital with a high rate of return from obtaining it, and permitting managers of the large established firms to enjoy additional perquisites.

Lin, Lee, and Huang, in chapter 7, use the experiences of both Korea and Taiwan to investigate the macroeconomic policy implications of export-led growth. The paper contends that monetary, fiscal, and exchange rate policies were influenced and in fact disciplined by the pursuit of an export-led growth strategy. Sound fiscal policy, however, is identified as an important way to give more freedom to other policy instruments within the overall goal of keeping export industries competitive. Although the central banks in Taiwan and South Korea were legally "independent," they accommodated the need for development funds; thus inflation rates were relatively high during the years of high economic growth.

In chapter 8, Yang and Shea begin by noting that Taiwan's rate of inflation was very low—3 percent, on average—during the 1980s despite average annual growth of the money supply of around 20 percent. They develop and test a quarterly model, incorporating money demand for stock and real estate trading and the level of imports (itself a function of the appreciation of the NT dollar) and conclude that these two phenomena explain the relative stability of Taiwanese prices.

Chapters 9 and 10 analyze the financial liberalization of the Korean economy. In chapter 9, Park provides a survey of financial policies and liberalization in Korea since the early 1980s. He shows that, to date, the impact of financial deregulation in Korea has been primarily on nonbank financial institutions. He examines the savings-investment balance and interest parity conditions in an effort to ascertain the degree to which Korean financial markets have become integrated with the rest of the world and concludes that there is still significant capital immobility. Park's analysis suggests that the barrier to increased financial efficiency in Korea is now the banking system itself, and that its deregulation could result in significant increases in efficiency.

In chapter 10, Nam examines the bank-business relationship in Korea. He argues that while the "principal transactions" bank system in Korea helped carry out credit controls and avoided excessive concentration of banks, it also hampered the autonomous development of bank-business cooperation, of the type that occurs in Japan's main bank system. Nam predicts that with the liberalization of Korean bank credits, the largest corporations will have bargaining power with the banks, while smaller established companies will be restricted to an exclusive relationship with one bank. While Korean industrial groups are quite similar in structure to their Japanese counterparts, the relationship between a group and a bank in Korea is very different from that in Japan, affecting the outcome of liberalization processes.

Chapters 11, 12, and 13 examine aspects of financial liberalization in Singapore and its neighboring countries. In chapter 11, Woo and Hirayama examined the possible reasons for the freedom in interest rate policy, namely, deviations of the domestic interest rate from the U.S. dollar interest rate. Three episodes of government interventions in the foreign exchange markets in Indonesia, Malaysia, and Singapore at various times are cited for creating enough uncertainties to cause risk premia, a wedge between the domestic and foreign interest rates. In chapter 12, Tse and Tan use the interest parity condition between Singapore and the Eurodollar market to test the effect of deregulation. They find that deregulation was associated with a marked reduction in the divergence of interest rates from uncovered interest parity, which is consistent with the view that the degree of capital mobility increased as deregulation progressed.

In the final chapter, Ngiam surveys the process of deregulation of the Singapore financial market, including the evolution of SIMEX, the Asian Dollar Market, the Singapore stock market, the Asian Dollar Bank Market, and Forex. He then evaluates the prospects for Singapore's emergence as a financial center for the region. While financial deregulation has made Singapore more competitive as a financial center, the fact that Hong Kong and Japan are also deregulating means that competition to become the financial center of the region is increasing.

This volume provides a good picture of the overall status of financial markets in Japan, China, Korea, Taiwan, and Singapore. All countries in the region—as in much of the rest of the world—are in the process of financial deregulation, and none has completed the transition. Both the analysis and the empirical results provide evidence of the complexity of the process of financial deregulation and the challenges it poses for policymakers everywhere.

# 1 Credible Liberalizations and International Capital Flows: The "Overborrowing Syndrome"

Ronald I. McKinnon and Huw Pill

When undertaking reform and stabilization programs, countries are prone to excessive foreign borrowing that ultimately proves unsustainable. This paper outlines a model in which short-run deviations from sustainable behavior are caused by financial market failure. Because banks fail as efficient information conduits between depositors and borrowers, excessively optimistic expectations about the success of the reform are created among domestic residents, international investors, and the policy authorities. Initially, improved economic performance and large inflows of foreign capital justify such optimism. Only later do the sustainability conditions bind so that the economy collapses into a recession, financial crisis, and capital flight.

Recent events in Mexico have again highlighted the vulnerability to the "overborrowing syndrome" of economies undertaking liberalization programs (McKinnon 1993, chap. 10). Financial stabilization and real economic reform with NAFTA membership in prospect stimulated vast inflows of short-term capital—"hot money"—into Mexico in the late 1980s and early 1990s. Such inflows caused a dramatic collapse in domestic private saving (see table 1.1) and generated an ultimately unsustainable credit-driven consumption boom that finally collapsed into forced devaluation and financial crisis in December 1994. The implications of this episode for the real economy are not yet apparent. They are unlikely to be positive.

Unfortunately, this phenomenon is not unique. Examples abound across geographical and temporal dimensions. Memories of the Latin American debt crises of the early 1980s are still reasonably fresh, the most prominent cases occurring in the Southern Cone nations—Chile (see table 1.2), Argentina, and Uruguay. Moreover, the history of South America during the last two centuries is punctuated by episodes of excessive borrowing followed by financial crisis

Ronald I. McKinnon is the William Eberle Professor of International Economics at Stanford University. Huw Pill is assistant professor of business administration at Harvard Business School.

**Table 1.1** **Savings and the Current Account in Mexico, 1989–93 (% of GDP, except where stated)**

| | Average of Three Prior Years | Year Prior to Episode | Inflow Episode | | | |
|---|---|---|---|---|---|---|
| | | | Year 1 | Year 2 | Year 3 | Year 4 |
| Real GDP growth (%) | −0.3 | 1.2 | 3.3 | 4.4 | 3.6 | 2.6 |
| Savings | 21.1 | 21.6 | 21.5 | 22.4 | 21.8 | 21.9 |
| Public sector | 3.8 | 0.4 | 3.2 | 7.4 | 6.6 | 7.3 |
| Private sector | 15.1 | 17.8 | 15.5 | 11.2 | 10 | 7.7 |
| Current account | −0.5 | −2.2 | −3 | −3.2 | −4.7 | −7.1 |

*Source:* Schadler et al. (1993).

**Table 1.2** **Chile's Overborrowing Experience, 1978–82 (% of GDP)**

| | 1978 | 1979 | 1980 | 1981 | 1982 |
|---|---|---|---|---|---|
| Investment | 16.5 | 19.6 | 23.9 | 23.9 | 9.6 |
| Consumption | 72.4 | 71.1 | 70.5 | 76.2 | 76.1 |
| Budget deficit | 0.8 | −1.7 | −3.1 | −1.6 | 2.4 |
| Current account deficit | 7.7 | 5.7 | 7.2 | 14.6 | 9.4 |
| GDP growth (% per annum) | 8.2 | 8.3 | 7.8 | 5.5 | −14.1 |

*Source:* Dornbusch (1985).

and default. Writing in 1937, the Royal Institute of International Affairs concluded that "the history of investment in South America throughout the last century has been one of confidence followed by disillusionment, of borrowing cycles followed by widespread defaults" (Dornbusch 1985).

The Southern Cone experiences—especially the Chilean episode in 1978–82—have become textbook classics (Edwards and Edwards 1987; Bosworth, Dornbusch, and Labán 1994). Well-engineered supply-side fiscal and trade reforms undertaken after 1973 had, by 1978, generated enthusiastic expectations about lower inflation and increased future income. Facing enormous inflows of foreign financial capital during 1978–81, however, Chile's foreign exchange and banking systems failed to cope adequately with the problem of disinflating. By 1982–83, exchange overvaluation triggered widespread bankruptcy in heavily indebted industry and agriculture causing a severe downturn in national product. In addition to devaluing the currency under pressure from capital flight, the government was forced to reintervene in the banking system to payoff both foreign and domestic depositors.

Many other liberalizing economies have suffered similar episodes of boom-time "overborrowing"—with the domestic banking system being the principal intermediary between foreign lenders (depositors) and domestic borrowers—followed by financial crisis and bust. Uruguay and Argentina paralleled Chile in the late 1970s. Examples are not confined to Latin America. Turkey and Sri Lanka suffered in the early 1980s. In December 1993, the International Monetary Fund (IMF) published *Recent Experiences with Surges in International Capital Flows* (Schadler et al. 1993). This paper outlined several more recent episodes of overborrowing, including Egypt beginning in 1991–92 and Thailand in 1988, as well as Chile (in 1990, following recovery from its earlier debacle), Colombia, and Mexico (for summary data of these episodes, see table 1.3). An updated list might include India, Malaysia, Estonia, and Argentina in the 1990s. Even subsequently successful East Asian "tigers" have not been immune to such problems. After successful structural and financial reforms in 1964–65, Korea overborrowed in the late 1960s, lost domestic monetary control, and rekindled inflation (McKinnon 1973). A second and ultimately successful stabilization program was required in the early 1980s to restore Korea's financial stability.

Even mature industrialized economies are vulnerable. In Britain, the Thatcher government undertook apparently successful industrial restructuring and fiscal consolidation during the early 1980s. However, attempts to disinflate by exchange rate stabilization, beginning with Chancellor Lawson's famous "shadowing of the Deutsche Mark," touched off a credit-led consumption and property market boom in 1988–89 associated with large inflows of foreign capital through the British banking system. After a crash in asset values and a downturn in Britain's economy in 1990–91, capital flight forced sterling devaluation in 1992—with Britain leaving the European Exchange Rate Mechanism. Similar cycles have been observed in Spain (another of the Schadler et al. [1993] examples), Sweden (Berg 1994), and the antipodes (Fischer and Reisen 1993; Lattimore 1994). Several authors analyzed the European cases in terms of the "Walters critique" (Walters 1986, 1990; Giavazzi and Spaventa 1990) by highlighting the problems of exchange rate management per se rather than by recognizing the magnitude of the international capital flows themselves as a problem—an omission corrected by Pill (1993). Australia and New

**Table 1.3** **Recent Capital Flows in Selected Countries (billion dollars; % of GDP in parentheses)**

| | | Inflow Episode | | | |
|---|---|---|---|---|---|
| Country (Year of Episode) | Average of Three Prior Years | Year 1 | Year 2 | Year 3 | Year 4 |
| Chile (1990) | 1 | 3 | 1.1 | 3.1 | – |
| | (4.5) | (10.6) | (3.5) | (8.1) | |
| Colombia (1991) | 0.4 | 2 | 1.3 | – | – |
| | (0.9) | (4.8) | (2.7) | | |
| Mexico (1989) | −0.4 | 4.9 | 11 | 20.8 | 24.7 |
| | (−0.2) | (2.4) | (4.6) | (7.4) | (7.6) |
| Spain (1987) | −1.8 | 10.9 | 9.2 | 14.6 | 14.5 |
| | (−1.1) | (3.8) | (2.7) | (3.8) | (3.1) |
| Thailand (1988) | 1.4 | 3.1 | 6.7 | 9.3 | 11.8 |
| | (3.3) | (5.2) | (9.7) | (11.4) | (12.6) |

*Source:* Schadler et al. (1993).

Zealand suffered from overborrowing in the absence of explicit exchange rate pegs, suggesting the problem is broader than the existing exchange management literature has assumed.

This paper investigates the macroeconomic forces driving the overborrowing phenomenon, highlighting the interactions among successful real-side reform, flows of international financial capital, and possible market failure in the domestic banking and financial system as it is liberalized. Why have some countries embarking on otherwise apparently well-designed stabilization programs suffered from the overborrowing syndrome? How did the successful East Asian economies (Japan, Taiwan, and Singapore in the 1960s) avoid such problems? What lessons do such episodes have for liberalizing economies in East Asia and elsewhere? What policy implications come from a systematic analysis of the problem?

Most previous analyses of the overborrowing phenomenon have focused on the credibility of the reform program (Mussa 1986; Calvo 1987; Daveri 1991). A belief that the elimination of trade restrictions on consumer imports is merely temporary may provoke an unsustainable consumption spending spree, fueled by excessive borrowing, as domestic residents exploit the "window of opportunity" presented by the relaxation of controls. Such excessive borrowing will include borrowing from abroad if the capital account of the balance of payments is left open. This "lack of credibility" hypothesis *may* be consistent with the Chilean data from the late 1970s, which shows heavy spending on consumer durables combined with a sharp fall in private saving.

However, overborrowing has typically financed increased expenditure on nontraded goods; this would not be precluded by the reimposition of trade restrictions in the aftermath of a policy reversal. Moreover, in many cases, the industries most dramatically affected by the "boom-bust" cycle were construction and real estate—the quintessential nontradable sectors. Empirical work reported in a recent IMF study (Reinhart and Végh 1993) uses simulation methods to suggest that—for plausible parameter values—the magnitude of the capital inflows during overborrowing episodes is too great to be explained by this lack-of-credibility or "temporariness" hypothesis. Moreover, the most prominent explanations of the European Walters critique variant of the overborrowing phenomenon (Miller and Sutherland 1991; King 1990, 1994) have attributed a decisive role to excess, rather than insufficient, credibility—the complete opposite of the explanation used for developing nations.

In the light of such research and observation, this paper focuses on credible reform and stabilization programs. In many cases, when they were introduced the policies adopted by reformist governments appeared highly credible to individuals and firms in the countries in question. Observers seemed genuinely enthusiastic about the reforms' chances of success, generating optimistic expectations of future income. In the extensive documentation on Chile in 1978–82, a number of prominent Chilean economists have highlighted the prevailing mood of "triumphalism" about the success of the reform program (e.g.,

Schmidt-Hebbel 1987). Political speeches from that period (although hardly objective) are laced with the same sentiments:

> [Chile] in ten years will be a developed nation . . . where 70% of the population have colour TVs. (Labor Minister Jose Piñera, 1980; reported in Conley and Maloney 1995)

> The economy is growing in such a way that in eleven years income per capita will double in contrast to past circumstances where this would only have been achieved after forty-six years. (Economy Minister Sergio de Castro, 1980; reported in Conley and Maloney 1995)

The reaction of the international capital markets and consequent rapid growth of capital inflows were themselves seen as further evidence of the success of the reforms. The way in which capital inflows feed off themselves in a self-sustaining cycle is central to our analysis of overborrowing. This feature is probably even more apparent in more recent cases, especially in Mexico, given the susceptibility of fund managers and other participants in the international capital markets to "emerging markets' mania."

Therefore, for analytical purposes, we start with the premise that real-side reform—such as trade liberalization, utility privatization, or domestic deregulation—is fully credible in the eyes of the private sector. Reforms raise the potential productivity of new investment above the levels attainable before the reform. To take advantage of these new opportunities to increase disposable income in the future, at least some economic participants must undertake discrete new investments that are large relative to their initial endowments. If the returns to such investment are certain in real terms, it is easy to design a financial system to intermediate funds between borrowers and lenders. In the absence of risk, domestic money and foreign exchange become a "veil"—the whole analysis can be collapsed into a simple two-period Fisherian model of intertemporal consumption and investment. The simple geometry of this framework, both when the capital account is open and when it is closed, is developed below. As intuition would lead one to expect, welfare is unambiguously raised when it is possible to borrow abroad at a fixed world interest rate. This relaxes credit constraints, allowing firms to undertake new investment and households to smooth consumption. Nevertheless, the effect of reform on domestic saving remains an interesting issue.

If the payoff to investing in new technology is uncertain, how financial intermediaries evaluate risk becomes important. Instead of a pure model of real borrowing and lending à la Fisher, the precise character of the monetary, credit, and foreign exchange regimes must eventually be specified. However, a simple extension of the Fisherian model, focusing on the nature of the domestic financial system, is proposed below and offers a limited approach to analyzing some of these problems.

One remarkable feature of the consumption booms associated with overborrowing episodes is the surprise their existence and magnitude aroused.

Conventional macroeconomic theory (as embodied, e.g., in large-scale macroeconometric models) failed to forecast—and subsequently has failed to explain—either the nature of the initial consumption boom or the depth and length of the subsequent recession (for a discussion of the British experience, see Church, Smith, and Wallis 1994). This failure has prompted considerable research into the role of financial systems in the macroeconomy (Gertler and Gilchrist 1992; Kashyap, Stein, and Wilcox 1993). A growing associated macroeconomic literature suggests that banks are "special" in some economically important sense (Bernanke and Blinder 1988). In developing nations (and, to a lesser extent, in industrialized economies), they dominate domestic borrowing and lending, especially to small firms and households. Moreover, they are often the major conduit for short-term ("hot") money flows through the foreign exchanges.

As yet, this finance and macroeconomic research has had little impact on our understanding of the episodes discussed in this paper (for an exception, see Pill 1993). This paper uses a variant of the Fisherian framework (first introduced by McKinnon 1973). Because of a discontinuity in the production technology, the financial system and supply of credit play an important role in determining real economic outcomes. This allows us to address the role of the domestic financial system during overborrowing episodes.

Because the liabilities of commercial banks are monies or near monies, deposits—both foreign and domestic—may be guaranteed by the authorities in an attempt to preserve the integrity of the payments system. This will give private monetary institutions (commercial banks) a strong comparative advantage as financial intermediaries. The very fact of (often implicit) deposit insurance (which allows depositors to believe they will be bailed out if the reform goes awry) implies that lenders might excessively discount the lower tail of possible outcomes of the real-side reforms from the point of view of the economy as a whole. Unless otherwise restricted, domestic private saving could fall too far, and foreign indebtedness build up too much, in response to a real-side reform that increases expected future income *and its variance.*

## 1.1 Some Stylized Facts

Although we do not claim that these are universally associated with overborrowing problems, recent surveys of the macroeconomic consequences of large capital inflows on recipient countries (Schadler et al. 1993; Fischer and Reisen 1993) agree that the main distinguishing features of an overborrowing episode include:

- *Rapid growth of domestic credit,* largely financed out of capital inflows intermediated through the domestic banking system, leading to higher levels of domestic consumption
- *Widening of any current account deficit* on the balance of payments, as

greater availability of financing from abroad eases the external constraint

- *Weaker domestic monetary control* and rising or sustained *high domestic price inflation,* typically associated with problems in attempting to sterilize the capital inflows
- *Appreciation of the real exchange rate,* appropriately defined, with higher inflation concentrated in the nontradable goods sector; prices of domestic assets, especially real estate or house prices, typically increase
- A large proportion of the capital inflow in the form of *overseas deposits placed with the domestic banking system,* increasing pressure on the government to broaden the base of insured deposits
- *Greater vulnerability* to adverse shocks and increased likelihood that the stabilization program will be derailed and thrown into reverse
- *Culmination in a financial crisis, capital flight, and recession,* often forcing an uncontrolled, deep devaluation of the currency, with a resurgence of inflation

A recurrent theme of the Schadler et al. (1993) paper is the correlation of fiscal consolidation with the capital inflow surge (see table 1.4). One would generally expect independent implementation of such policies to reduce inflows of capital as the total public borrowing requirement falls and less public debt is sold abroad. Instead, fiscal consolidation apparently acts as a signal to international investors that the overall reform program is credible—as if the government was indeed getting the order of economic liberalization "right" (McKinnon 1982, 1993). As such, it is a stimulus to the capital inflows we discuss below. Pill (1993) discusses why fiscal consolidation may be a necessary precondition for large capital inflows to occur.

Note that under the temporariness hypothesis, it is hard to understand why an improvement in the public finances is a precondition for overborrowing. Often, one associates fiscal deficits with government borrowing abroad. Instead, fiscal consolidation would seem to signal the commitment of the policy authorities and thus add to the credibility of the reform program, rather than suggest that it will be abandoned in the future. This further justifies our focus on credible policy programs.

## 1.2 The Simple Fisherian Two-Period Model

The simple structural framework presented in this section extends the Fisherian two-period model of intertemporal investment and consumption introduced by McKinnon (1973), as refined by Krugman (1979). The central feature of this model is the existence of two potential production technologies—a "traditional" production process, $f(\cdot)$, which exhibits decreasing returns to scale over all possible levels of production, and a "modern" production technology, $g(\cdot)$, which has increasing returns over some range but requires a large initial

**Table 1.4** **Fiscal Policy during a Capital Inflow Episode (government surplus as % of GDP)**

| Country (Year of Episode) | Average of Three Prior Years | Year Prior to Episode | Inflow Episode Year 1 | Year 2 | Year 3 | Year 4 |
|---|---|---|---|---|---|---|
| Chile (1990) | 2.8 | 5.3 | 3.8 | 2.3 | 3.2 | – |
| Colombia (1991) | −1.5 | −0.6 | −0.2 | −0.4 | – | – |
| Egypt (1991) | −16 | −17.2 | −5 | – | – | – |
| Mexico (1989) | | | | | | |
| Operational balance | −1.4 | −4.5 | −1.7 | 2.6 | 2.3 | 3.3 |
| Primary balance | 4.4 | 6 | 8.1 | 7.8 | 5.5 | 5.6 |
| Spain (1987) | −6.2 | −6 | −3.1 | −3.3 | −2.8 | −4 |
| Thailand (1988) | −4.2 | −1.6 | 1.3 | 4.1 | 4.7 | 3.9 |

*Source:* Schadler et al. (1993).

fixed investment, *F*. The former mode of production has existed for a long time so that no major start-up investments are required. In contrast, adopting the postreform technology does require major investment or reequipment decisions. Although the new technology is potentially more productive, access to credit is required to overcome the indivisibility in the production process implied by the start-up cost. Credit plays an important role in the determination of real output by overcoming technological indivisibilities.

The economy consists of a large number (*N*) of identical, risk-neutral firm-households. These are free to choose between adopting the new technology or retaining traditional manufacturing methods. They maximize utility—represented by a utility function $U(c_1, c_2)$—with respect to the available production techniques and an initial endowment ($m$), taking prices (the real interest rate, $r$) as given. We assume a single composite commodity good that is freely traded with the rest of the world. In this context, it is plausible to believe that the utility function of all firm-households is homothetic over consumption in each period. Because all firm-households are identical and have the same opportunity set, in equilibrium they must all achieve the same level of utility.

Initially, we assume a world of perfect certainty. In this world, the role of the financial system is passive—complications introduced by the detailed institutional structure of the financial mechanism can safely be ignored. Although credit plays an important role in the solution to the model by overcoming indivisibilities in investment, the way credit is intermediated is initially of little importance. Later, uncertainty is introduced into the model, and the structure of the financial system then plays a central role.

Exploiting the simple Fisherian two-period framework generates two significant practical advantages. First, the solution to the model can be illustrated by straightforward geometry, relegating the detailed algebraic solution to an appendix. Second, the optimization problem facing firm-households can be conveniently split into two parts: an investment decision, maximizing firm wealth (value) subject to technological constraints and the real interest rate, and a consumption decision, maximizing utility for given wealth and the same real interest rate.

The government undertakes a reform of the real economy. Typically, a liberalization of the current account of the balance of payments, with the abolition of tariffs and other trade restrictions, is the starting point. Other potential reforms include privatization, deregulation, and domestic structural reforms, such as weakening of trade union powers through labor legislation. Measures of this type are common to all the liberalization and stabilization programs discussed in the introduction to the paper. These reforms are modeled analytically as follows. Prior to liberalization, all firm-households were constrained to use the traditional production technique, $f(\cdot)$ in figure 1.1. The reform allows access to the "modern" technology described above,[1] as represented by $g(\cdot)$ in figure 1.1.

Should this structural reform be undertaken in the presence of administrative controls on the cross-border movement of financial capital? If so, what form should these controls take? Drawing on earlier work (Pill 1993), we initially characterize two polar states for the economy: the *domestically liberalized economy* (DLE) and the *internationally liberalized economy* (ILE). In the former, inflows of international capital are not permitted and all domestic investment must be financed out of domestic saving. In the latter, domestic residents are free to borrow as they wish from a perfectly elastic pool of international capital at a constant world interest rate ($r^*$).

The subsequent sections solve our simple intertemporal model in these two environments using a geometric approach. A formal algebraic derivation is presented in appendix A. A useful benchmark for comparison is the prereform equilibrium, which, following McKinnon (1973), we call the *financially repressed economy* (FRE). If all firm-households are confined to the same traditional technology, no capital market will exist. Because preferences and endowments are identical (by assumption), all households will make the same consumption and production decisions; if one wishes to borrow, they all would and there would be no supply of savings to lend. Thus households maximize utility with respect to the production opportunity set defined by the traditional technology, with production equal to consumption in each period. Both production and consumption occur at $Q^{FRE} = C^{FRE}$ in figure 1.1.

## 1.3 Domestically Liberalized Economy

In order to exploit the new technological possibilities introduced by the reform process, however, suppose now that firm-households may borrow in the first period to cover the initial fixed investment while maintaining positive con-

1. This is consistent with the large endogenous growth literature (e.g., Romer 1990), which formally demonstrates Adam Smith's proposition that "specialization is limited by the size of the market." Once access to the large (possibly perfectly elastic) world market is attained, entrepreneurs can invest in modern techniques rather than the "small-scale" traditional modes of production.

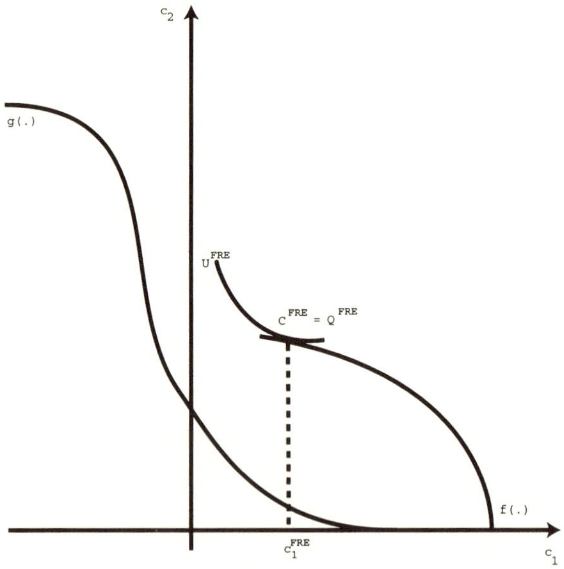


**Fig. 1.1 Financially repressed economy**

sumption. Financial intermediaries are able to raise funds from those domestic firms that continue to employ traditional production techniques and can thus extend credit to other firms that wish to make discrete investments in the modern, postreform technology.

Two conditions must be satisfied in equilibrium. First, because all firm-households are identical, they must achieve the same utility level (Krugman 1979). All households must have the same consumption opportunity set, as defined by their intertemporal budget constraint. The constraint is defined by a line tangent to the production function, with slope reflecting the real interest rate (see fig. 1.2). With firm-households confined to using one or other of the production technologies, the budget constraint must simultaneously be tangent to both production functions. Therefore, the slope of the constraint—and thus the equilibrium real interest rate, $r^{\mathrm{DLE}}$—is entirely determined by technological factors: the gap in average productivity between the postreform investment technology and the traditional one.

With the real interest rate determined in this manner, firm-households continuing to use the traditional technology will choose to produce at point $Q_{\mathrm{T}}^{\mathrm{DLE}}$, where real income is maximized. They consume at point $C^{\mathrm{DLE}}$. This implies consumption $c_1^{\mathrm{DLE}}$ out of production income $x_1^{\mathrm{T}}$, the difference being saved as deposits with the banking system. In effect, the higher postreform interest rate induces these firm-households to invest less in the traditional technology in order to support lending in the capital market.

Firm-households exploiting the modern, postreform technology also con-

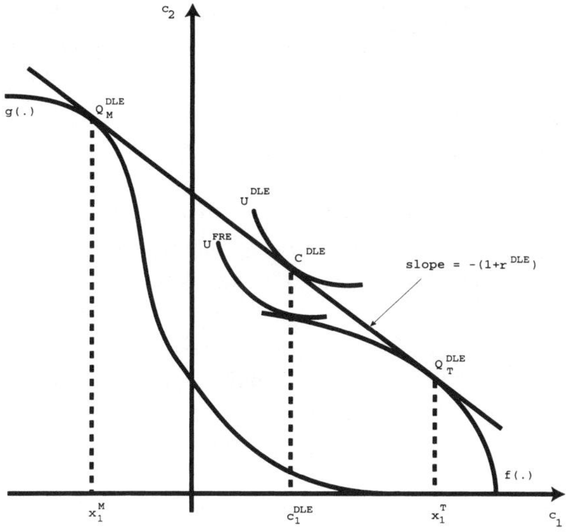


**Fig. 1.2 Domestically liberalized economy**

sume at $C^{\mathrm{DLE}}$—the identical consumption profiles imply a common level of utility. However, their intertemporal income-maximizing production decision involves producing at $Q_{\mathrm{M}}^{\mathrm{DLE}}$, implying a potentially negative cash flow (endowment less consumption and real investment) in the first period ($x_1^{\mathrm{M}}$). Therefore, firm-households employing the modern technology must borrow $c_1^{\mathrm{DLE}} - x_1^{\mathrm{M}}$ in the first period from the domestic banking system.

Second, the credit market must clear. As we have seen, the real interest rate is technologically determined and thus cannot vary to clear the market. Only changes in the proportion of firm-households that continue with the traditional technology (and thus save) and the proportion that adopt the modern technique (and thus borrow) can be the equilibrating mechanism. Therefore, the credit-market–clearing condition, $N_{\mathrm{M}}(c_1^{\mathrm{DLE}} - x_1^{\mathrm{M}}) = N_{\mathrm{T}}(x_1^{\mathrm{T}} - c_1^{\mathrm{DLE}})$, will determine how many firm-households adopt the modern technology ($N_{\mathrm{M}}$) and how many continue to use traditional techniques ($N_{\mathrm{T}}$).

Since income and substitution effects counteract each other, the relationship between first-period consumption in the DLE and that which would obtain in the absence of trade reform is unclear. In figure 1.2, first-period consumption in the DLE is arbitrarily drawn to be identical to that in the FRE; slight changes in the nature of technology or preferences could move the DLE consumption equilibrium in either direction. However, consumption in the second period will be much higher in the DLE because of the higher productivity of the new technology. With indivisibilities in the postreform technology, one cannot draw unambiguous conclusions about the behavior of current savings when liberalization occurs. This contrasts with the conclusion reached by Conley and Maloney (1995), who showed that, in the absence of technological indivisibilities, reform would necessarily lower current domestic saving. Nevertheless, over the two periods, the reform produces an unambiguous improvement in welfare as the opportunity set expands in the DLE.

## 1.4 Internationally Liberalized Economy

Once restrictions on the capital account of the balance of payments have been abolished, domestic residents are able to borrow freely from the perfectly elastic international capital market. In equilibrium, the domestic real interest rate must equal the exogenous world real interest rate ($r^*$ in fig. 1.3). This is the meaningful definition of perfect capital market integration (Frankel 1992). Using foreign savings intermediated through the domestic financial system, *all* domestic firm-households now choose to borrow so as to adopt the modern production process, producing at $Q^{\mathrm{ILE}}$, where intertemporal real income is maximized (see fig. 1.3). Not only does welfare improve relative to that obtainable prior to the initiation of the real-side reform, but it is unambiguously greater than that attainable in the DLE—where capital controls constrain the expansion of the consumption opportunity set even as trade is liberalized (this is an issue to which we return later; it is illustrated in fig. 1.6).

In the ILE, consumption occurs at $C^{\mathrm{ILE}}$. Even starting with a very low or "repressed" implicit deposit rate in the prereform era at $C^{\mathrm{FRE}}$, figure 1.3 shows that consumption in the first period, $c_1^{\mathrm{ILE}}$, becomes higher because of the dominant income effect. Current saving falls relative to that in the prereform era.[2] Given the higher permanent income available to them following the successful implementation of structural real reform, domestic residents borrow from the perfectly elastic capital market in order to smooth their consumption. Moreover, current savings in the ILE are unambiguously lower than in the DLE equilibrium (again because substitution and income effects reinforce each other).

The counterpart of the capital inflow needed to finance domestic borrowing is a current account deficit, $\mathrm{CA} = -N\,(c_1^{\mathrm{ILE}} - x_1^{\mathrm{ILE}})$ in figure 1.3. The country consumes more than it has produced in the first period. Sustainability of the balance of payments in this certain world is guaranteed by the subsequent trade surplus in the second period, $N\,(x_2^{\mathrm{ILE}} - c_2^{\mathrm{ILE}})$—the investment in modern technology pays off in the second period, allowing future production to exceed consumption.

In a world of complete certainty, the advantage of liberalizing the capital account of the balance of payments prior to, or concurrently with, the implementation of a real-side reform is clear. A fall in domestic saving in response to a trade reform is likely to be intertemporally optimal. Households should

2. Even if, in the repressed state, the domestic interest rate had (accidentally) been at the international level, the income effect of economic reform would still dominate: current consumption would still increase.

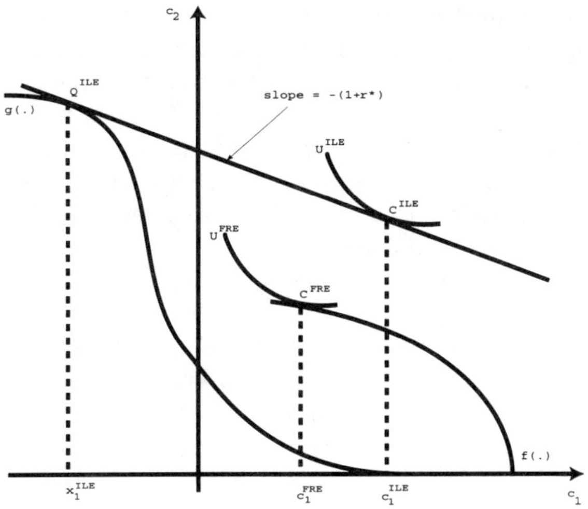


**Fig. 1.3 Internationally liberalized economy**

consume more in the first period in order to smooth their intertemporal consumption path given a higher level of permanent income.

In contrast, in the DLE—where all investment is domestically financed—any incipient fall in saving drives up real interest rates and "crowds out" some new investment, while limiting current consumption. However, in the ILE, the fall in domestic saving is met by inflows of international capital that can maintain the new higher level of investment. Extensive borrowing from the rest of the world is the optimal solution—overborrowing cannot arise.

## 1.5 Introducing Uncertainty and an Explicit Financial System

In order to introduce the possibility of overborrowing, we now relax the assumption of perfect certainty. This immediately introduces an active role for the domestic financial system. We first describe how uncertainty is modeled within our Fisherian analytical framework and then describe the institutional nature of the financial system.

Uncertainty is introduced by making the productivity of the modern production technique a random variable (the modern technology production function becomes $g'(\cdot) = (a + \varepsilon)\, g(\cdot)$, where $a$ and $\varepsilon$ are orthogonal). The variability of $a$ represents macroeconomic risk—the uncertainty about how successful the implementation of real-side reform will be. It is assumed that the number of firm-households is sufficiently large and their experience is sufficiently diverse that any firm-specific idiosyncratic risk $\varepsilon$ can be eliminated by efficient risk management of the banks' asset portfolio. Firm-specific risk is ignored in what follows. The banking system faces only irreducible "market" or macroeconomic risk. The productivity of the traditional production process remains certain.

The domestic capital market is viewed as synonymous with indigenous deposit-taking commercial banks. The implications of relaxing this assumption are discussed below. Subsequently, we show that, in the presence of certain common market interventions by the authorities, the banks may enjoy a comparative advantage that allows them to dominate alternative financial intermediaries. The preeminent role of the banking system as a conduit for hot money flows—one of the stylized facts of overborrowing episodes noted above—is thus endogenous to our framework.

Uncertainty is resolved in two stages. At the beginning of the first period, a value $\hat{a}$—representing privileged prior knowledge about the productivity shock—is drawn from a probability distribution, $H_1(\hat{a})$. The outcome of this drawing is known to the banks, but all other economic actors in this economy—the government, the domestic firm-households, and overseas investors—only know the distribution function from which it is drawn. At the beginning of the second period, the value of $a$—the productivity shock itself—is realized. This information is common knowledge. The final realization of $a$ is drawn from a distribution $H_2(a)$ with mean $\hat{a}$.

This framework gives the banks an informational advantage. They have extra information about the likely final realization of $a$ when consumption and investment decisions are being made. This informational advantage is a simple formalization of the notion that "banks are special," an idea that is prominent in recent macroeconomic literature (Bernanke and Blinder 1988; Kashyap et al. 1993) and in earlier work in finance and development (Shaw 1973; McKinnon 1973). The other participants in this economy rely on the banking system to convey implicitly the relevant information about the magnitude of $\hat{a}$—the mean of the distribution—through the credit conditions and real interest rates they choose to offer to the market.

With a large number of atomistic firm-households and international investors, no individual has an incentive to incur the costs of assessing macroeconomic risks, since these costs would not be faced by competing firms. Competitors would gain a cost advantage. Moreover, the variance of market or macroeconomic risk may be small compared to the variance of firm-specific risk for any individual firm. Firm-households have a greater incentive to monitor idiosyncratic risk than do banks, which (given efficient portfolio management of their balance sheet) only face macroeconomic risk. The efficient solution requires the competitive banking system to undertake the assessment of macroeconomic risks and each individual firm-household to concentrate on firm-specific or local risks, inferring the macroeconomic information for their investment and consumption decisions from the resulting market credit conditions and interest rates.

The role of the banking system is central to this discussion. However, if banks are "well behaved"—in the sense that they act as efficient conduits of financial flows from savers to borrowers—the solutions to our simple analytical model are identical to those discussed in the case of certainty for both the

DLE and ILE (at least ex ante) in figures 1.2 and 1.3, respectively. In each case, the outcome will be efficient given the information available at the beginning of the first period (including the private information of the banking system). Moreover, the ILE outcome Pareto dominates the DLE outcome—ex ante, it remains preferable to implement the structural reform program without controls on international capital flows.[3] This is the sense in which a well-behaved financial system simply operates as a veil behind which efficient real economic decisions are being made.

Of course, ex post the outcome may not be efficient. Indeed, for some realizations, it is possible that the DLE outcome may Pareto dominate the ILE outcome. Domestic residents may have borrowed more than would have been desirable given the eventual realization of $a$. However, with the informational structure of the model as we have assumed, it is not possible to intervene to prevent these outcomes. The government would require better knowledge of the effects of the implementation of the structural reform program—and our model does not have this form. As Conley and Maloney (1995) demonstrate, to provide a rationale for government intervention and the maintenance of capital controls, the authorities must have risk preferences different from those of the risk-neutral domestic residents. While there are plausible political economy justifications of this structure, it does not sit easily with the assumption of identical firm-households (which permits use of representative agent analysis) and our implicit assumption that the government acts in the interests of its constituents. To say simply that the government is "more risk averse" masks what the underlying problems might be.

Accounting for downside risk that is intrinsic to the reform process offers a reasonable explanation of countries' reluctance to simultaneously and fully liberalize all markets including the capital account. However, for this rationale to be fully convincing, it is necessary to explain why the private sector is unable to account for the riskiness of the reform program itself. We set about trying to explain why the private sector proves unable to solve this risk management problem. Our explanation centers on market failure in the financial system. Market failure interacts with the special informational role of the banking system to generate an environment of excessively optimistic private sector expectations. In contrast, the policy authorities make their economically important decisions before this environment is created and ought to be less susceptible to "bootstrap" effects that allow excessive optimism to feed on itself, leading to overborrowing. Unfortunately, short-term political considerations may foster triumphalist private sector expectations rather than restrain them. This offers a role for external monitors—international organizations such as the IMF—in pressuring governments to avoid excessive capital inflows.

3. A sufficient, but not necessary, condition for this result is our earlier assumption that all firm-households are risk neutral.

## 1.6 Deposit Insurance and Financial Market Failure

We have shown that, even in the presence of uncertainty, it is optimal to implement real structural reforms in the absence of administrative controls on the cross-border movement of international capital, provided the domestic banks are well behaved. However, market failure and poor risk management in banking systems are common phenomena, especially when the banking system is exposed to novel forms and magnitudes of risk by the ongoing process of domestic economic liberalization and financial innovation. The nature and magnitude of the capital inflows themselves might further aggravate the problem.

To understand how capital inflows affect the solvency of banks, let us briefly describe how they change the risks faced by the banking sector. When large inflows of foreign financial capital enter the newly liberalized domestic banking system, risk is likely to multiply rapidly. We can categorize the risks in the following manner:

- *Credit risk*—exposure to the failure of a borrower to repay a loan—will increase as bank lending rises. A sudden increase in the availability of loanable funds through capital inflows may encourage greater investment in risky prospects such as lending to real estate or securities market participants.
- *Foreign exchange exposure* is dramatically increased if the inflows are foreign currency denominated while the banks enjoy a comparative advantage (informational or otherwise) in domestic lending in local currency. Lack of experience and the absence of derivatives markets may make managing such risks more problematic in less-developed countries (LDCs) than in developed nations.
- *Real exchange rate risk* rises because the profitability of traded goods industries is lowered as more capital flows in.
- *Settlement risk* rises if the payments system is incapable of dealing with the magnitude or direction of cross-border settlements.
- *Liquidity risk* will rise if the size of the capital inflows is large relative to that of domestic securities markets. If banks attempt to invest the inflows in domestic markets (say real estate) they may simply bid up the price of housing, helping to create bubbles in real estate and equity prices and inducing destabilizing "herding" or "fad" behavior among market participants (Shiller 1991).
- Risks arise from the *supervisory and regulatory framework:* regulators face larger and different challenges in assessing the risks borne by the institutions they supervise when capital inflows are considerable and the risks described above multiply. For example, regulations may be inappropriate for the new policy regime: banks may not identify prob-

lem assets, thus making it impossible to measure the quality of their portfolios.

- All of the above effects can lead to greater *systemic risk:* the chances of contagion between different banks will rise as credit, liquidity, and settlement risks rise.

Here, we focus on the interaction between regulatory failure and the role of (possibly implicit) government-backed deposit insurance schemes. In order to preserve the integrity of the payments system, the monetary authorities may feel compelled to offer a public guarantee of banks' deposit liabilities. As has been well documented in the finance and development literature (reviewed in World Bank 1990), this is likely to introduce moral hazard into the banking system's behavior. This is but one of many potential examples of market failure.

When the government insures deposits against adverse macroeconomic outcomes, it alters how the banking system views the risks associated with making loans. Therefore, the banks' behavior changes as they exploit the authorities' guarantee—this is the essence of the moral hazard problem (McKinnon 1993, chap. 7). In our simple analytical framework, this process can be formalized as follows. The banks know the magnitude of $\hat{a}$ and thus the distribution from which the ultimate realization of $a$ will be drawn. However, because of deposit insurance, the banks' depositors are protected from outcomes in the lower tail of this distribution. Banks therefore base their lending and interest rate decisions on the value $\hat{a}'$, the mean of this truncated distribution, rather than $\hat{a}$, the mean of the true underlying distribution of $a$.

Necessarily, $\hat{a}'$ is greater than $\hat{a}$. The banking system therefore behaves as if their private knowledge suggested better future economic performance following the liberalization process than is actually likely given the true realization of $\hat{a}$ (these ideas are formalized in appendix B). The consequences of this market failure depend on the capital account regime.

In the DLE, the effect is to raise the domestic interest rate (see fig. 1.4). Using the same approach as outlined above, a well-behaved financial system would set a market real interest rate $r^E$, based on the expected productivity shock realization $\hat{a}$. Recall that real interest rates are entirely determined by technological factors in the DLE. If the banking system suffers from moral hazard induced by deposit insurance, they will base their behavior on a productivity shock $\hat{a}'$ rather than $\hat{a}$. The implicit signal offered by credit conditions will be that the likely outcome of the liberalization process is more favorable. Therefore, more of the firm-households will wish to adopt the modern technology, in the belief that it will be highly productive. However, this will induce excess demand for credit that can only be met by raising the real interest rate until it is once again tangent to both the traditional technology schedule and that associated with modern technology under the realization $\hat{a}'$—that is, a higher real interest rate $r^F$. In equilibrium, the amount of borrowing undertaken

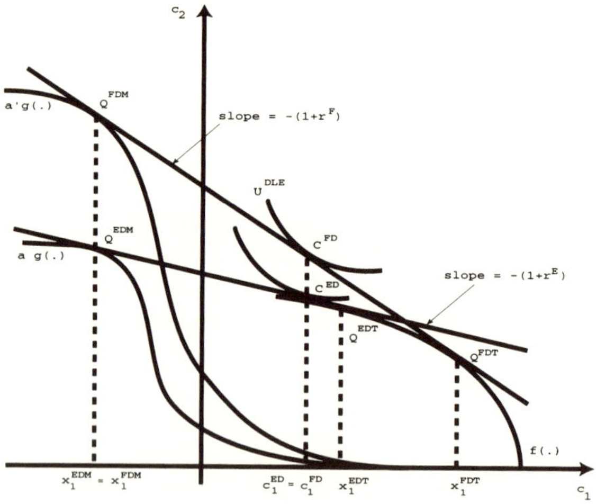


**Fig. 1.4 Market failure in the DLE**

may be higher or lower than if the financial system were well behaved. There is no guarantee that overborrowing will occur. While first-period surplus output beyond internal investment for those firm-households that continue to employ the traditional (denoted T) production technique ($x_1^{FDT}$, where F denotes market failure in the financial system and D denotes the DLE) will necessarily be higher than would be the case with an efficient (denoted E) banking system ($x_1^{EDT}$), first-period consumption ($c_1^{FD}$ and $c_1^{ED}$ in the market failure and efficient cases, respectively) and investment in the modern (denoted M) technology (determined by $x_1^{FDM}$ and $x_1^{EDM}$ in the two cases) could be higher or lower. The effect on the savings rate and aggregate borrowing of market failure in the DLE is therefore ambiguous.[4] Financial market failure is reflected in higher financial yields; the effects on financial quantities—specifically credit aggregates—are uncertain.

In the ILE, the interest rate $r^*$ is determined in the perfectly elastic international capital market. It cannot rise as in the DLE and therefore cannot be indicative of market failure in the financial system. Instead, moral hazard in the banking system manifests itself through excessive capital inflows (see fig. 1.5). The excessively optimistic reporting of prospective productivity gains by the banking system (i.e., the erroneous indication, implicitly signaled through credit conditions, that the expected productivity shock is $\hat{a}'$ rather than $\hat{a}$) encourages domestic residents to invest more heavily in the new technology than

4. In fig. 1.4, we draw the knife-edge case where $x_1^{FDM} = x_1^{EDM}$ and $c_1^{FD} = c_1^{ED}$: consumption and investment in the new technology are unchanged. Different assumptions about the relative magnitude of the offsetting income and substitution effects could result in higher or lower levels for either consumption or investment.

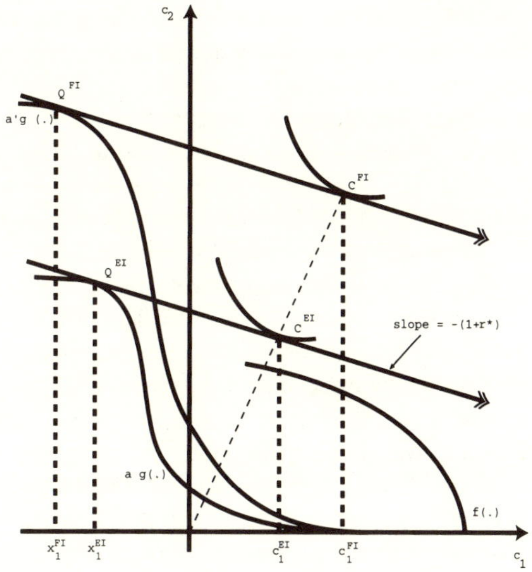


**Fig. 1.5 Market failure in the ILE: the overborrowing syndrome**

is appropriate for the actual expected productivity realization (at $Q^{\mathrm{FI}}$ rather than $Q^{\mathrm{EI}}$, where I denotes the ILE). Moreover, domestic residents will overconsume in the first period (at $c_1^{\mathrm{FI}}$ instead of $c_1^{\mathrm{EI}}$) in anticipation of higher future incomes than are likely to emerge. Both overconsumption and overinvestment are financed in part by excessive borrowing from the rest of the world, beyond that which would maximize welfare ex ante in the absence of market failure. With financial failure, aggregate borrowing by the liberalizing economy $N(c_1^{\mathrm{FI}} - x_1^{\mathrm{FI}})$ is unambiguously greater than the desired level of aggregate borrowing when the financial system is well behaved, namely, $N(c_1^{\mathrm{EI}} - x_1^{\mathrm{EI}})$. This is the essence of the overborrowing syndrome.

## 1.7 Rational Beliefs and Rational Expectations

Note that, in the first period, the behavior of the economy with a well-functioning capital market (figs. 1.2 and 1.3) is identical to that of an economy with a poorly functioning financial system and a lower realization of $\hat{a}$ (known only to the banks) (figs. 1.4 and 1.5). Ex ante, for either the DLE or the ILE, these two situations are observationally equivalent. It is precisely this feature of the model that allows us to capture a phenomenon we believe is central to understanding overborrowing episodes.

The "deep" productivity parameters in this model are not directly observable ex ante. Participants in the economy have to base their decisions on imperfect information inferred from the behavior of the economy as a whole and specifically—given the special role of the banking system as a gatherer of, and conduit for, information concerning macroeconomic risks—the state of domestic credit conditions. However, as mentioned above, there are two possible models of the economy that are consistent with the same values for all observables in the first period. If participants wrongly attribute the initial boom to a favorable realization of $\hat{a}$ when in fact it is due to market failure in the financial system, overborrowing can arise. While such behavior turns out to have been inefficient ex post, there is nothing irrational about the private decisions being made ex ante. It is not irrational to be wrong if one could not detect one's error on the basis of observable information. The most plausible explanation of how this could arise comes from uncertainty about the authorities' information set. If the authorities have the same information set as the banks, they ought to be able to supervise and regulate the financial system so as to prevent market failure. The nonbank domestic private sector, overseas investors, and even other policymakers may trust that regulation of the banking system is sufficient to ensure a well-behaved financial system. When policy credibility—including the credibility of bank regulation—is high, overoptimism can emerge because nonbank private actors believe the financial system is well regulated and thus well behaved, when in practice it may not be (see the discussion of bank regulation in the next section).

The rational expectations paradigm cannot deal with a multiplicity of potential models that are indistinguishable ex ante. Central to the rational expectations approach to economic theorizing is the existence of a common structural model of the economy that all participants share. This structure is believed to be correct in an *objective* sense. Our framework does not correspond to this view. We find it useful to draw on the concept of "rational beliefs," introduced by Kurz (1990). He proposed a wider notion that both encompasses and extends that of rational expectations. The rational beliefs approach permits individuals to hold different views about the structure of the economy, provided the models implicit in these views are not refutable by observed or observable data. This structure allows the economy to deviate from "sustainable" paths in the short run—which could last for an extended period—until observed data demonstrate that the structural model implying this ex post unsustainable behavior was incorrect. This approach has been applied to U.S. stock market data (Kurz 1993). We believe it is even more applicable in the current context.

The rational beliefs structure closely resembles our view of how overborrowing emerges. Ex ante, domestic firm-households believe the real economic reform program is credible and the financial system is well behaved; this is their Bayesian prior. Consequently, they will respond to the signals offered by the domestic financial system through real interest rates and credit conditions. Their confidence in the success of the reform program will be bolstered by the economic "boom" observed in the first period. Indeed, their prior beliefs are apparently confirmed by the performance of the economy (and the associated vast inflows of capital that occur in the ILE case). This is true whether or not the financial system is genuinely well behaved. It is precisely this initial improvement in economic performance that engenders the triumphalist assessment of the reform process that we identified in the introduction to this paper. Triumphalism itself breeds even greater confidence in the liberalization program—the process creates a self-sustaining momentum of its own.

Only when the true realization of the productivity shock is observed in the second period will the alternative models be distinguishable to the nonbank sectors. In some—unfortunately rare—cases, the triumphalist beliefs are are borne out.[5] More frequently, they prove unfounded. It is financial market failure that has been driving domestic credit expansion rather than genuine improvements in structural economic performance. Ex post, domestic residents have overborrowed and participants in the international capital market have overlent. However, ex ante, there was nothing irrational about such decisions. They were justified on the basis of the model participants in the economy had in mind when the decisions were being made, a model that was consistent with and could not be falsified by observed data.

Our previous work (Pill 1993) using macroeconomic modeling techniques similar to those proposed in the British context by Muellbauer and Murphy (1990)—which would be dismissed by many as ad hoc theorizing devoid of microeconomic foundations—has been criticized for failing to take into account the sustainability conditions implied by forward-looking agents. Once we move to the rational beliefs approach outlined above, economic behavior is entirely consistent with sustainability and forward-looking formation of expectations *under the model of the economy the market participants themselves implicitly believe.* This model turns out to be incorrect, but this was not apparent ex ante when investment and consumption decisions were made because the model held by participants and the "true" (bank market failure) model were *observationally equivalent.*[6]

This framework therefore captures the intuition we discussed in the opening of this paper. Rather than being associated with lack of credibility of the reform program, overborrowing arises when domestic residents become excessively optimistic about the economy's prospects following the implementation of reform. These optimistic expectations are generated by market failure of some form—in our case, that induced in the banking system by deposit insurance—but the existence of such failures is obscured until it is too late for their effects to be accounted for. Consumption and investment decisions have already been made, and overborrowing has occurred—this is likely to ultimately prove highly costly to correct.

5. This implicitly makes an assumption about the distribution $H_2(\cdot)$, namely, that it is symmetric and concentrated close to the mean. Of course, it is possible that ex ante excessive borrowing will turn out to be justified ex post by an unexpectedly favorable realization of the productivity shock.

6. Even if foreign depositors realized the potential for financial market failure and the likelihood that banks will misrepresent $\hat{a}$, they still have little incentive to impose market discipline on the banks by removing their deposits while they believe the deposit insurance scheme will bail them out.

Our earlier macroeconomic models (e.g., Pill 1993) ignore the long-run sustainability issues raised by intertemporal choices. This has been criticized as ad hoc. Once we move to a rational beliefs framework, such criticism rings hollow. The behavior described by our macroeconomic models need not ignore the transversality conditions imposed by intertemporal optimization problems. It is simply that the agents are using what ultimately turns out to be the wrong economic model. Their behavioral decisions may be consistent with long-run sustainability constraints in the context of the implicit economic model they believe. Unfortunately, this model proves to be a poor description of the true underlying economic structure because it does not encompass market failures in the banking system. Clearly, further work is required to marry the macroeconomic modeling more closely to the microfoundations offered by the rational beliefs framework.

## 1.8 Policy Responses to Overborrowing

What are the appropriate policy responses to overborrowing of this form? Before returning to the simple structural model outlined above, it is illuminating to draw some parallels with Keynes's policy prescriptions for the Depression. Central to Keynes's explanation of the Depression (Keynes 1936) was the self-sustaining nature of low private sector economic confidence and real activity. If the private sector's "animal spirits" were negative, economic activity was discouraged. But the lack of economic activity merely reinforced the negative sentiment. Keynes argued that a government-led economic stimulus could break the self-sustaining vicious circle of low confidence and low activity.

The overborrowing syndrome has similar features. The triumphalist animal spirits associated with the initiation of economic reform stimulate economic activity that, in turn, reinforces optimism about the liberalization program, which seems to be generating immediate tangible rewards. Rather than to stimulate real activity as in the Keynesian case, government intervention may be required to restrain positive animal spirits and the self-sustaining excesses of the initial boom phase of the reform program.

In describing the appropriate policy response to potential overborrowing, one should respect the informational constraints on the authorities imposed by the information structure of the model. Specifically, the government is unaware of the realization of $\hat{a}$, the privileged information obtained by the banking system. Uncertainty about whether the authorities know this privileged information is a cause of the potential for observationally equivalent equilibria described above.

The most straightforward policy response—and the first-best solution—would be to eliminate the market failure in the banking system altogether. As we saw above, the nonbank sectors could then rely on the financial system to offer correct signals about real macroeconomic shocks and an ex ante efficient outcome would result. If the government withdrew its guarantee of bank deposits, there would be no moral hazard for the banks to exploit. In principle, the banking system would then behave efficiently and give the correct information signals to the market as a whole. Unfortunately, the effects of such a policy are unlikely to be so positive. The authorities face a time consistency problem. Ex ante, it is clearly in their interest to disavow any responsibility for bank deposits in the hope of imposing the correct market discipline on the banking system. However, ex post—in the event of financial crisis—the government and central bank will be compelled to bail out at least the core of the financial system in order to protect the integrity of the payments and settlement system and maintain at least the semblance of international confidence. Banks are special, not because they are financial intermediaries, but because they are custodians of the monetary system. The banks will realize this at the outset and thus behave as if there is deposit insurance because of the authorities de facto or implicit deposit insurance scheme. The government's rejection of deposit insurance is unlikely to be credible.[7]

If deposit insurance (whether explicit or implicit) is de facto almost inevitable, one could attempt to limit its effects by creating of a small number of "narrow banks" to form the core of the payments system. These would be more heavily regulated and restricted than the generality of peripheral banks that, in principle, would be allowed to fail in the event of financial crisis since their collapse would not threaten the integrity of the settlement system.[8] However, it is probably more difficult to "ring fence" the payments system than this simple outline describes. Contagion and systemic risk are likely to breach the rather artificial distinction between core "narrow" banks and peripheral banks. It is likely the government would be faced with the same time consistency issue as described above.

One solution to the moral hazard problem would be to regulate the banks sufficiently closely that they could not exploit the consequent creation of moral hazard. In our framework, if the authorities have the necessary information, regulation will be perfect and overborrowing cannot arise. If the authorities lack the privileged information, their attempts at regulation may be misguided. It is precisely the confidence of the nonbank private sector in the efficiency of banking supervision and regulation that leads domestic firm-households to hold Bayesian priors that the financial system is well behaved. Of course, even when the authorities have imperfect knowledge of macroeconomic shocks, there is considerable scope for improvement in bank regulation, especially in

7. This phenomenon was demonstrated in the seminal Chilean example. Initially the authorities pursued a "free banking" policy, with no intervention in the financial or banking system and no explicit deposit insurance scheme. However, it is apparent that market failure in the banking sector was endemic by 1982 as banks exploited the moral hazard generated by the inevitable implicit deposit insurance.

8. This is a possible characterization of the U.K. system in which the "Big Four" retail, clearing banks (plus the main Scottish banks and possibly a couple of others) are simply "too big to fail." Although their designation as "narrow banks" is unofficial, they act in concert with the Bank of England to avoid large commercial risks.

LDCs, where existing systems are generally primitive. However, as suggested above, the very fact of large capital inflows is itself likely to undermine the regulatory system since it will increase the magnitude of intermediation to be assessed and introduce new forms of risk (such as exchange risk, risks arising from cross-national differences in legal systems, or cross-border settlement risk). Improvements in bank regulation are desirable but are unlikely to be a completely effective policy response to potential overborrowing.

Conley and Maloney (1995) have investigated whether the optimal policy response to potential overborrowing is to open the capital account of the balance of payments and allow international financial capital unfettered access to domestic financial institutions or to keep the capital account completely closed. This prejudges the issue of whether it is appropriate to consider only polar extremes—perfect capital mobility (the pure ILE) and complete absence of cross-border capital flows (the pure DLE). Where trade-offs exist, economics generally suggests interior solutions are optimal.

We have already shown that, should the banking system be well behaved, the market solution is efficient and there is no scope for policy intervention. The optimal policy is to allow unrestricted cross-border movement of capital; a polar solution is first-best. However, the authorities do not know ex ante whether the banking system is well behaved or suffers from market failure. Nevertheless, if they did, simply communicating the information to the private sector (both domestic residents and potential foreign investors) would solve the problem of itself. It is central to our rational beliefs framework that the two situations are indistinguishable ex ante both to the nonbank private sector and to the policy authorities.

This is a strict interpretation of the rational beliefs equilibrium. Using a weaker solution concept—which might be called a "pseudorational beliefs" equilibrium—one could envisage such an announcement being insufficient to correct the problem. Depositors, both domestic and foreign, would be protected by deposit insurance and would have no incentive to withdraw their savings from the banking system. Similarly, on the asset side of the banks' balance sheet, adverse selection from the macroeconomic risk could imply continued excessive borrowing for high-risk projects (McKinnon 1993, chap. 7). However, the problem of adverse selection is beyond the scope of the simple model presented in this paper.

Remember that the authorities are forced to choose a capital account regime before any of the uncertainty in our model is resolved. That is, they cannot infer from the banks' lending and interest rate decisions whether (given the government's knowledge of $H_1(\hat{a})$) it is more likely that there is market failure in the banking system or that there will be a good outcome for the probability shock. The banks' choice of credit supply will depend on the choice of capital regime; one has already been chosen before any information can be inferred. Although the information available to the nonbank private sector and the policy authorities is identical at any point in time, the two groups make their economically important decisions in different information environments. The nonbank private sector makes its consumption and investment decisions taking the macroeconomic environment—most importantly, credit conditions—as given. It is precisely this timing that allows triumphalist sentiment about the reform program to be generated and the problems of overborrowing to emerge. There are spillovers or externalities between private sector agents—the optimism of one firm-household helps to generate macroeconomic conditions which foster optimism among others—that are mutually reinforcing.

In contrast, the government's decision about policy regime is taken before macroeconomic conditions are observed; indeed, determination of the latter depends vitally on the former. Rather than taking macroeconomic conditions as given, the authorities ought to be aware of their ability to affect them. Moreover, the authorities should not prove susceptible to the spillover effects generated through optimistic expectations. As already noted, to the extent that they are absorbed in triumphalist euphoria, external monitors such as the IMF should step in to calm the excessive optimism and maintain macroeconomic stability.

The government's choice of welfare-maximizing capital account regime is therefore based on a productivity shock given by the expected value of $\hat{a}$, which we denote $\ddot{a}$. Moreover, the authorities should entertain the possibility that market failure may occur in the financial system. Those countries that have suffered most extensively from overborrowing problems have either assumed away such problems (as in the Chilean "free banking" experiment during 1978–82) or have been complacent about the omniscience or ability of their bank regulators (as in the United Kingdom in the late 1980s).

McKinnon (1973, 1993) has argued that deposits held by foreign residents at domestic banks should be subject to the same level of reserve requirements as domestic deposits. Note that non–interest-bearing reserve requirements are an implicit tax on financial intermediation. In the absence of such requirements, there is a bias toward capital inflows that, as we have seen, can prove destabilizing.

In our framework, the international capital market is perfectly elastic. The public finance literature suggests that the burden of the tax—although nominally a reserve requirement on deposits—will fall entirely on borrowers, who are all domestic residents. Foreign depositors require a market rate of return, and therefore the reserve requirement tax on them must be zero. Moreover, a natural extension of Pigovian taxation theory would suggest that the implicit reserve requirement tax could be larger than that applied to domestic deposits to account for the macroeconomic externalities introduced by the instability caused by overborrowing.

Our model supports these conclusions. It may well be preferable to have no capital controls rather than to have completely exclusionary capital controls because, ex ante, the ILE solution is likely to Pareto dominate the DLE solution whether the financial system is well behaved or not (see figs. 1.6*A* and

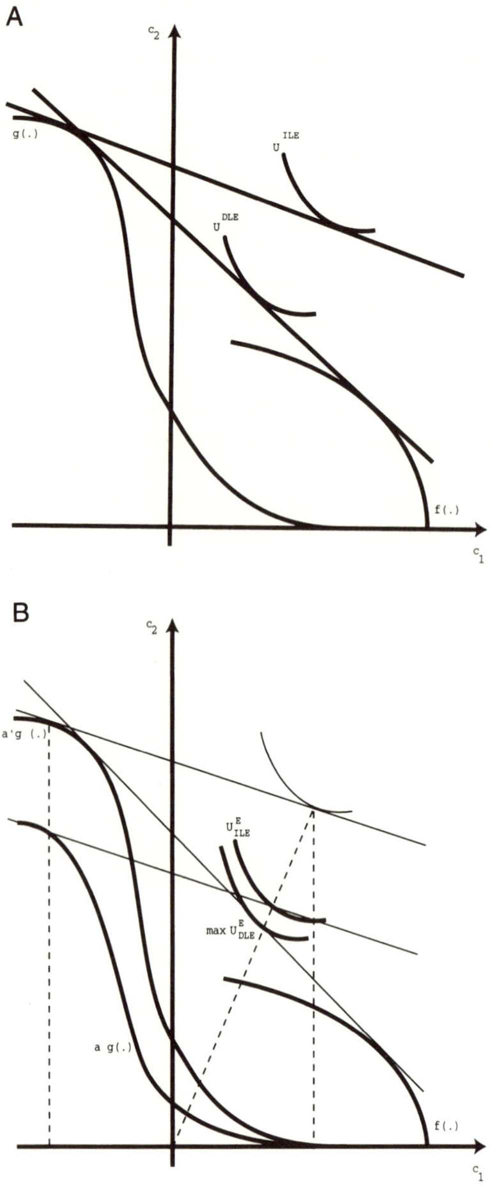


**Fig. 1.6** (*A*) Welfare comparison in absence of market failure; (*B*) Welfare comparison with market failure

1.6*B*). The former is straightforward to interpret; the latter requires more explanation (see appendix C). Problems arise because those firm-households that continue to use the traditional technology in the market failure DLE will attain a different welfare level from those that adopt the modern technology. This may prevent Pareto comparisons with the ILE when there is financial market failure. As figure 1.6*B* is drawn here, the expected utility of firm-households in the ILE exceeds the maximum attainable utility of any firm-household in the DLE. Therefore, ex ante, the ILE Pareto dominates the DLE. The potential for overborrowing to occur does not justify the imposition of controls completely excluding the inflow of foreign capital.

Nevertheless, ex ante, an interior solution with limited capital controls will Pareto dominate both polar outcomes. If one could impose different requirements on borrowing intended for investment purposes and on borrowing for consumption purposes, then the Pigovian tax reserve requirements could replicate the first-best outcome achieved in the absence of market failure (provided the tax revenue could be costlessly redistributed to all domestic firm-households in a nondistortionary way; i.e., lump-sum transfers are possible) (see fig. 1.7). As figure 1.7 is drawn here, a higher reserve requirement is needed on borrowing for consumption. This arises from the implicit assumptions about the nature of technology and preferences embodied in the way we have drawn the production function and indifference curves. The representation used here corresponds to our earlier discussion of the stylized facts of overborrowing episodes. These facts suggested that the problem manifests itself largely through excessive consumption rather than excessive investment. While this does not necessarily imply a higher reserve requirement on consumer borrowing,[9] intuition would suggest such an outcome is likely.

By imposing an implicit tax on foreign deposits, in the form of a reserve requirement, the effective real interest rate for domestic borrowers is raised; the budget constraints have slope *tt* for investment and *t′t′* for consumption. In the market failure model, this will reduce both first-period investment and first-period consumption toward their optimal levels (from $x_1^{FI}$ toward $x_1^{EI}$ and from $c_1^{FI}$ toward $c_1^{EI}$, respectively). Such a policy will reduce the extent of overborrowing and improve ex ante welfare for all firm-households. As noted above, with differential reserve requirements for investment and consumption borrowing and lump-sum transfers, an ex ante first-best solution can be obtained, even in the presence of financial market failure. Unfortunately, achieving this result imposes very strong information requirements on the government that are difficult to attain.

Obviously, in the well-behaved banking sector model, such reserve require-

9. Since the world real interest rate is exogenous in our model, it is income, rather than substitution, effects that will determine the relative magnitude of overborrowing for consumption and investment purposes. In contrast, the magnitude of the optimal reserve requirement will be determined solely by substitution effects because, with lump-sum transfers, expected real income is unchanged.

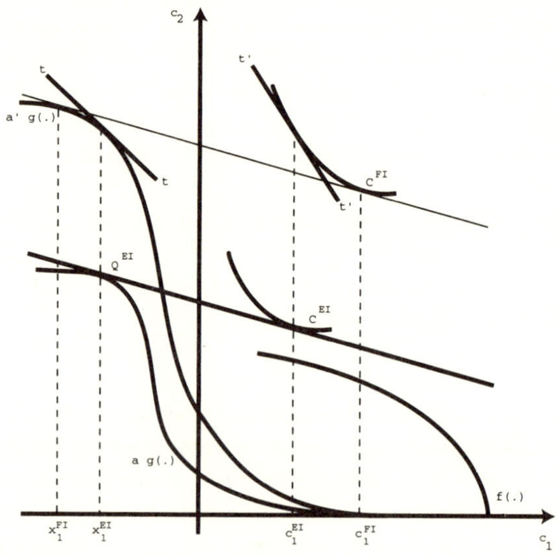


**Fig. 1.7 Policy responses to overborrowing**

ments introduce an inefficient distortion. However, since the government internalizes the potentially large macroeconomic costs of overborrowing and subsequent financial crisis in a way that private individual firm-households do not, the policy authorities may view the imposition of such controls as welfare improving ex ante. Even for relatively small probabilities that the financial market failure model is objectively true, the potential costs of financial crisis following an overborrowing episode are large enough to justify a small efficiency loss should the financial system turn out to be well behaved.

The public finance literature generally assumes a second-best world, in which lump-sum transfers cannot be made and the redistribution of tax revenue is costly in terms of efficiency. Moreover, it would be difficult to enforce differential reserve requirements for consumption and investment lending. There would be incentives for the private sector to organize between the two markets for borrowing and to extract supernormal rents. In a plausible, practical setting, only much blunter policy tools are available. A single reserve requirement (except in pathological cases) will not be able to precisely replicate the first-best solution, although the outcome will still Pareto dominate the polar extremes.[10] If the marginal rate of intertemporal substitution is greater than the marginal rate of intertemporal transformation over the relevant ranges, then additional controls on consumption borrowing, beyond the reserve requirement tax on investment borrowing, may be justified.

10. Strictly, it will always dominate the perfect capital mobility pole that, in turn, almost always dominates the zero capital mobility pole.

## 1.9 Conclusions: Policy Implications

How should policymakers respond to the possibility of overborrowing in the course of an otherwise successful liberalization program? Improved banking regulation with higher capital and reserve requirements could help. However, such measures are unlikely to prove fully effective, given the banking industry's inherently asymmetric information structure. The authorities may wish to impose other financial controls to limit the potential for damage should overborrowing arise. Controls on cross-border movements of financial capital are one appropriate tool. This summary of policy options draws on the experience of East Asian countries that have successfully liberalized.

- *Restrain short-term capital flows,* particularly those intermediated through the domestic banking system (as in Japan in the 1950s and 1960s). The preferred policy instrument is probably reserve requirements rather than direct administrative controls. These level the playing field between domestic and foreign sources of funds and are harder to evade. Marginal reserve requirements could be increased if capital controls become unduly large.
- *Be more liberal with "direct" investment,* perhaps in the form of joint ventures with domestic partners. Direct investment brings new technology into the economy and by-passes the banking system—thus avoiding the market failure problems discussed above.
- *Limit organized consumer borrowing*—say on bank credit cards—and *restrict access to mortgage finance* (as in Japan and Taiwan through the 1970s). Such measures should help to prevent the runaway excess demand for consumer durables and nontraded services that may reignite domestic price inflation.
- *Consolidate compulsory social security contributions into a Singapore-style provident fund.* A fully funded compulsory saving program—geared to preventing the dramatic falls in private saving seen during overborrowing episodes—should be considered earlier rather than later in the liberalization process.

After its overborrowing debacle in the late 1970s through 1981, all of these measures were subsequently introduced into Chile during the 1980s. During Chile's successful recovery in the 1990s, these measures have helped to sustain domestic saving and prevent exchange rate overvaluation when pressure from capital inflows—now largely incipient—again become very great.

The example of several successful East Asian economies in avoiding the overborrowing problem during their liberalization programs in the 1960s and 1970s suggests the policy conclusions of our analysis are appropriate in the context of stabilization and liberalization policies currently being introduced in Latin America, India, Egypt, and elsewhere.

# Appendix A

To algebraically solve for the DLE outcomes, we can exploit two of the main advantages of the Fisherian two-period framework, namely, that the real interest rate is purely technologically determined and that investment and consumption decisions are separable. In order to find the equilibrium real interest rate, we solve for firm investment decisions as a function of the interest rate.

Firms maximize the present value of their net worth (a measure of firm value or wealth) taking the real interest rate as given. For those firms adopting the modern technology,

$$\text{(A1)} \qquad \max_{i} W = \left[\frac{g(i)}{1 + r}\right] - (i - m),$$

where $W$ is wealth, $i$ is investment inclusive of fixed costs, and $m$ is the initial endowment. The resulting first-order condition, where $i_{\mathrm{M}}$ is optimal investment in the modern technique, is

$$\text{(A2)} \qquad g(i_{\mathrm{M}}) = 1 + r.$$

Equating the marginal rate of transformation to the gross real interest rate, we can solve this implicit function for investment as a function of the interest rate, substitute it back into the production function for modern technology, and differentiate to find the marginal rate of transformation as a function of the interest rate:

$$\text{(A3)} \qquad \mathrm{MRT}_{\mathrm{M}}(r) = g'(i_{\mathrm{M}}(r)).$$

Repeating this analysis for the traditional technology results in an expression for the marginal rate of transformation in the original production process. The equilibrium condition requires the marginal rate of transformation to be equated across production techniques. We therefore have an equation that can be solved for the equilibrium DLE real interest rate:

$$\text{(A4)} \qquad \mathrm{MRT}_{\mathrm{M}}(r) = \mathrm{MRT}_{\mathrm{T}}(r) \quad \Rightarrow \quad r_{\mathrm{DLE}}.$$

Substituting the equilibrium real interest rate and the implied level of investment in the original maximized expression, we find wealth. Consumption decisions are now made, maximizing utility for given wealth and real interest rate. The problem gives the equilibrium levels of consumption, $c_1$ and $c_2$ (which are common to all households regardless of which production techniques they use):

$$\text{(A5)} \qquad \max_{c_1 c_2} U(c_1, c_2) \quad \text{subject to} \quad c_1 + \frac{c_2}{1 + r} \leq W.$$

These consumption and investment levels define the equilibrium level of borrowing (by the firms that adopt modern technology) and financial saving (by those which retain the original production technique). Market clearing in the credit market is described by the following expression, which also pins down the proportion of firm-households that choose either the traditional technique (T) or the modern technique (M):

$$\text{(A6)} \qquad N_M[(i_M + c_1) - m] = N_T[m - (c_1 + i_T)],$$
$$N = N_T + N_M.$$

In the ILE, the real interest rate is determined by the perfectly elastic international capital market. As we have seen, with the world real rate lower than the DLE equilibrium rate, all domestic residents adopt the modern technology. The solution procedure is then straightforward: simply substitute the world rate, $r^*$, into the expressions for investment (A3), wealth (A1), and consumption (A5) for the modern production technique firms derived above.

## Appendix B

In this appendix, we present a simple formal model of deposit-insurance–induced market failure in the banking system. For the purposes of the exposition in the main text, all we require is that banks discount outcomes in the lower tail of the probability distribution. This would appear to be an implication of any plausible formalization of moral hazard caused by government guarantees of the banks' deposit liabilities.

However, to pursue a more formal analysis, we aim to endogenize the results of the market failure. Specifically, we attempt to encompass how changes induced in bank behavior by the existence of deposit insurance alter the choices made by the nonbank private sector. In principle, this can affect the welfare ranking of potential capital account regimes.

The point is essentially as follows. Deposit insurance encourages banks to ease credit conditions. The domestic nonbank private sector reacts to such easing by increasing the amount it borrows to invest and consume. The higher gearing this implies makes bankruptcy more likely, and thus increases the potential worth of the deposit insurance scheme to the banking system.

As this discussion suggests, we have a simultaneous system that has to be solved to find the relevant market failure distortion. In the main text, we assumed that the market failure results in banks' using a realization of the distribution for the probability shock $\hat{a}'$, when the true realization is $\hat{a}$. These two are related as follows: $\hat{a}'$ is the expected value of $a'$, where $a'$ is defined as:

$$\text{(B1)} \qquad a' = a \quad \text{if} \quad a \in (\bar{a}, \infty)$$
$$a' = \bar{a} \quad \text{if} \quad a \in (-\infty, \bar{a}),$$

and $\bar{a}$ is the true realization of $a$ at which the average private sector firm (i.e., the firm with idiosyncratic shock $\varepsilon = 0$) will go bankrupt.

Whether a firm-household goes bankrupt depends on the amount of borrowing it does in the first period. This, in turn, is related to the signals offered by the banking system about the success of the reform program through the market credit conditions. The private sector—if it believes the banking system is well behaved—will choose to invest according to the schedules derived in appendix A. The argument presented here applies only to the ILE; this is the simpler case, because real interest rates are exogenously determined. Similar intuition applies to the DLE, but the derivation is harder because one has to account for the effect of market failure on the equilibrium interest rate, which also affects consumption, investment, and borrowing decisions.

We showed in appendix A that in the ILE, investment will be determined by equating the marginal rate of transformation to the real interest rate. We now augment this expression to include the expected value of the stochastic productivity shock, where this expectation is flawed because of the market failure (denoted by F) in the banking system.

(B2) $$\hat{a}'\, g'(i) = 1 + r^* \quad \Rightarrow \quad i_{MF} = i_{MF}(\hat{a}').$$

This investment decision will imply an expected level of wealth, which itself is an argument of the consumption function derived from utility maximization. This implies that borrowing, $b$, is a function of $\hat{a}'$ for two reasons: first, it increases the borrowing undertaken for investment since the returns available seem greater, and second, it raises consumption borrowing since higher returns imply higher wealth:

(B3) $$b(\hat{a}') = m - [i(\hat{a}') + c_1(\hat{a}')].$$

The firm household will go bankrupt if, after paying off its creditors out of its period-two output, there is no residual for consumption. Therefore, $\bar{a}$ is defined as follows:

(B4) $$\bar{a}g(i(\hat{a}')) - (1 + r^*)\, b(\hat{a}') = 0.$$

This gives $\bar{a}$ as a function of $\hat{a}'$ and therefore allows us to find the simultaneous solution of equations (B4) and (B2).

# Appendix C

This appendix briefly describes how to interpret figure 1.6*B,* which offers an ex ante welfare comparison of the DLE and ILE when there is market failure in the financial system. Figure 1.6*A* has already clearly demonstrated that, in the absence of such market failure, the ILE is Pareto superior to the DLE.

Therefore, if the ILE also welfare dominates the DLE when market failure exists, then policymakers should undertake their liberalization and real reform programs even if appropriate controls on capital inflows cannot be secured.

As discussed in the main text, if banks are subject to market failure they will set credit conditions such that the nonbank private sector assumes the expected productivity shock will be $\hat{a}'$, rather than its true magnitude $\hat{a}$. As shown in figure 1.4, in the DLE this implies consumption at $C^{FD}$ and production either at $Q^{FDT}$ (for the firm-households continuing to use the traditional technology) or at $Q^{FDM}$ (for those adopting the modern technology). Similarly, figure 1.5 shows consumption at $C^{FI}$ and production at $Q^{FI}$ (for *all* firm-households) in the ILE.

What implications does this have for welfare analysis? As external observers, we know that the true magnitude of the expected productivity shock is $\hat{a}$; therefore, we should base our ex ante analysis on this productivity level.

Consider first the DLE. A complication arises here because there are two groups of firm-households (one continuing to use the traditional technology, the other exploiting the postreform production process) that achieve different levels of utility. Although (as we showed in the main text) there is no presumption that consumption or investment in the modern technology will be too high or too low with financial market failure in the DLE, because the equilibrium real interest rate is higher than would be the case if the banking system were efficient, borrowers will have to pay more interest and are thus worse off. In contrast, depositors with the banking system—that is, those firm-households continuing to employ the traditional technology—enjoy higher interest payments, guaranteed by the deposit insurance scheme. They will actually be better off than if there were no market failure. In figure 1.6*B*, we simply draw the utility level achieved by the depositors; this is the maximum utility attainable by a firm-household in the DLE market failure equilibrium (max $U^E_{DLE}$).

Now consider the ILE. First-period consumption and investment decisions by the nonbank private sector are based on the expected productivity shock $\hat{a}'$. These are irreversible when the realization of the true value of $a$ is apparent. For the actual magnitude of the expected productivity shock $\hat{a}$, the intertemporal budget constraint will be represented by the lower line. This has slope $-(1 + r^*)$ and goes through the "true" expected production function at $x_1^{FI}$ (note that this is *not* a point of tangency since firms are maximizing with respect to the *anticipated* productivity shock $\hat{a}'$ rather than the "true" expected productivity shock $\hat{a}$). With consumption in the first period already determined at $c_1^{FI}$, this implies an expected welfare level $U^E_{ILE}$ (again, the indifference curve is *not* tangent to the budget constraint because consumption decisions are being made in anticipation of the better productivity shock rather than the true expected productivity shock).

Figure 1.6*B* has $U^E_{ILE} > \max U^E_{DLE}$. The expected utility in the market failure ILE is greater than the maximum attainable utility in the market failure DLE.

With our simplifying assumption of risk neutrality, this is sufficient to establish that the ILE Pareto dominates the DLE in the presence of financial market failure as well as when the banking system is efficient. (Obviously, such an assumption is not necessary. Modest levels of risk aversion would not materially affect the result.) In this case, the ILE welfare dominates the DLE unambiguously. If the authorities are forced to adopt a polar capital account regime, one with no impediments to the cross-border movement of international capital is preferable.

This result depends on how the diagram is drawn; one could envisage cases (with different preferences, technologies, or world real interest rates) in which $U^{E}_{ILE} < \max U^{E}_{DLE}$. Clearly, this is insufficient to reverse the policy implication. Even if the depositors in the DLE (those firm-households continuing to employ the traditional technology) are better off than would be the case in the ILE, there remain those firm-households that have adopted the modern, postreform production process. The latter group are necessarily worse off in the market failure DLE than they would be in the market failure ILE. In such a case, the two capital account regimes are simply not Pareto rankable.

Simply because there is potential market failure in the financial system, one cannot conclude that it is preferable to implement the liberalization and reform program while excluding foreign capital. The benefits arising from consumption smoothing may dominate the costs of overborrowing. However, as shown in the main text, partial capital controls can help mitigate the latter problem while not ruling out exploitation of the benefits of the former.

## References

Berg, L. 1994. Household savings and debts: The experience of the Nordic countries. *Oxford Review of Economic Policy* 10(2): 42–53.

Bernanke, B. S., and A. S. Blinder. 1988. Credit, money and aggregate demand. *American Economic Review* 78(2): 435–39.

Bosworth, B. P., R. Dornbusch, and R. Labán. 1994. *The Chilean economy: Policy lessons and challenges.* Washington, D.C.: Brookings Institution.

Calvo, G. 1987. On the costs of temporary policy. *Journal of Development Economics* 27: 147–69.

Church, K., P. Smith, and K. Wallis. 1994. An econometric evaluation of consumers' expenditure equations. *Oxford Review of Economic Policy* 10(2): 71–85.

Conley, J. P., and W. F. Maloney. 1995. Optimal sequencing of credible reforms with uncertain outcomes. *Journal of Development Economics* 48, no. 1 (October).

Daveri, F. 1991. How expectations affect reform dynamics in developing countries. Policy and Research Affairs Working Paper. Washington, D.C.: World Bank.

Dornbusch, R. 1985. Over-borrowing: Three case studies. In *International debt and the developing countries,* ed. G. W. Smith and J. T. Cuddington. Washington, D.C.: World Bank.

Edwards, S., and A. C. Edwards. 1987. *Monetarism and liberalism: The Chilean experiment.* Cambridge, Mass.: Ballinger.

Fischer, B., and H. Reisen. 1993. *Liberalising capital flows in developing countries: Pitfalls, prerequisites and perspectives.* Development Centre Study. Paris: Organisation for Economic Co-operation and Development.

Frankel, J. A. 1992. Measuring international capital mobility: A review. *American Economic Review* 82(2); 197–202.

Gertler, M., and S. Gilchrist. 1992. Monetary policy, business cycles and the behavior of small manufacturing firms. New York University. Mimeograph.

Giavazzi, F., and L. Spaventa. 1990. The new EMS. In *The European Monetary System in the 1990s,* ed. P. deGrauwe and L. Papademos. London: Longman.

Kashyap, A. K., J. C. Stein, and D. W. Wilcox. 1993. Monetary policy and credit conditions: Evidence from the composition of external finance. *American Economic Review* 82(1): 78–98.

Keynes, J. M. 1936. *The general theory.* London: Macmillan.

King, M. A. 1990. Comment on Muellbauer and Murphy. *Economic Policy,* no. 11: 385–89.

———. 1994. Debt deflation: Theory and evidence. *European Economic Review* 38 (3/4): 419–45.

Krugman, P. 1979. Interest rate ceilings, efficiency and growth: A theoretical analysis. Massachusetts Institute of Technology. Mimeograph.

Kurz, M. 1990. On the structure and diversity of rational beliefs. Stanford University. Mimeograph.

———. 1993. Asset prices with rational beliefs. Stanford University. Mimeograph.

Lattimore, R. 1994. Australian consumption and saving. *Oxford Review of Economic Policy* 10(2): 54–70.

McKinnon, R. I. 1973. *Money and capital in economic development.* Washington, D.C.: Brookings Institution.

———. 1982. The order of economic liberalization: Lessons from Chile and Argentina. *Carnegie-Rochester Series on Public Policy* 17:159–86.

———. 1993. *The order of economic liberalization: Financial control in the transition to a market economy,* 2d ed. Baltimore: John Hopkins University Press.

Miller, M., and A. Sutherland. 1991. The Walters' critique of the EMS: A case of inconsistent expectations? *Manchester School* 59(Supp.): 23–37.

Muellbauer, J., and A. Murphy. 1990. The U.K. current account deficit. *Economic Policy,* no. 11: 347–95.

Mussa, M. 1986. The adjustment process and timing of a trade liberalization. In *Economic liberalization in developing countries,* ed. A. Choski and D. Papgeoriou. Oxford: Blackwell.

Pill, H. 1993. The Walters' critique: Over-borrowing lessons from the EMS? Stanford University. Mimeograph.

Reinhart, C. M., and C. A. Végh. 1993. Nominal interest rates, consumption booms and lack of credibility: A quantitative examination. Washington, D.C.: International Monetary Fund. Mimeograph.

Romer, P. 1990. Endogenous technological change. *Journal of Political Economy* 98:71–125.

Schadler, S., M. Carkovic, A. Bennett, and R. Kahn. 1993. Recent experiences with surges in capital inflows. Occasional Paper no. 108. Washington, D.C.: International Monetary Fund.

Schmidt-Hebbel, K. 1987. Consumo e inversion in Chile (1974–1983): Una interpretacion "real" del boom. In *Del auge a la crisis de 1982,* Instituto Interamericano de Mercades de Capital. Georgetown, Santiago, Chile: ILADES.

Shaw, E. S. 1973. *Financial deepening in economic development.* Oxford: Oxford University Press.

Shiller, R. J. 1991. *Market volatility.* Cambridge: MIT Press.

Walters, A. A. 1986. *Britain's economic renaissance.* Oxford: Oxford University Press.
———. 1990. *Sterling in danger.* London: Fontana.
World Bank. 1990. *Financial systems and development.* Washington, D.C.: World Bank.

## Comment Francisco de Asis Nadal De Simone

McKinnon and Pill's paper presents a model that tries to capture what is referred to as the "overborrowing" syndrome that follows macroeconomic stabilization and real-side reform. This syndrome comprises an inflow of "excessive" foreign capital that produces an excess of domestic demand, inflation in nontradables, loss of monetary control, and, finally, the likely reversal of the reform process.

If reforms are credible, if there is certainty and perfect information, and if contracts can be enforced easily, the structure of the financial system is neutral even without capital account restrictions. Overborrowing does not arise. If those assumptions do not hold, however, the overborrowing syndrome appears because the financial system is no longer neutral: banks are "special." Banks are unique because of institutional features, such as deposit insurance schemes, that induce market participants to take relatively higher risks. This fact together with the credit rationing that results from less than perfect information are the sources of excessive capital inflows. As those capital inflows endanger the reform process, some restrictions on credit expansion must be put in place and some capital controls must remain.

The paper, therefore, produces a conceptual framework for analyzing the overborrowing syndrome in the context of a small open economy that has undertaken a disinflation program using the exchange rate as nominal anchor, together with a successful liberalization of current account transactions. Cases both without and with free capital mobility are considered. However, it is the combination of disinflation with free capital flows that most interests us because this is the policy mix that leads to overborrowing.

The paper focuses on credible reform and stabilization programs. I shall deal with four issues: (1) empirical regularities observed in disinflation programs, (2) reasons why the explanation of the capital inflows cannot be dissociated from the credibility issue, (3) reasons why banks, if truly "special," deserve a more explicit modeling than undertaken in the paper, and (4) features that a model trying to explain the boom-bust or the bust-boom cycle should have.

### Empirical Regularities

Countries using either exchange-rate–based (EB) anchors or money-based (MB) anchors have experienced a slow convergence of the inflation rate to the

Francisco de Asis Nadal De Simone is an adviser to the Economics Department of the Reserve Bank of New Zealand.

devaluation rate, or to the rate of growth of the relevant money aggregate. As a result, they have experienced an appreciation of the real exchange rate—in many cases, quite substantial.

However, the choice of the nominal anchor seems to matter for the path of economic activity. EB programs have been observed to produce an initial rise in consumption and in real activity followed by a contraction; the reverse is true of MB programs. Most important for our concern here, however, is the behavior of the external accounts and the real interest rate.

Under EB programs, the current account has always deteriorated as suggested in the paper. The real interest rate fell in the "tablita" program of the late 1970s in Argentina, in the Austral plan in Argentina (1985), in the Cruzado plan in Brazil (1986), and in the Israeli plan (1985), all programs based on an exchange rate anchor. The interest rate has risen, however, in the heterodox programs of the mid-1980s.

In MB programs, the current account has not shown a clear pattern and, if anything, has seemed to show some short-run improvement. The interest rate has tended to rise sharply. This was the case in Chile in 1975 and in Argentina and Brazil in 1990, for example.

**Credibility of the Reform and Stabilization Programs**

The paper discards too quickly, I believe, the role of credibility. I was surprised to see that Reinhart and Végh's quantitative analysis is mentioned to support the view that credibility is not enough to explain the facts mentioned above. In that paper, however, less than full credibility is assumed. The same assumption is made in a more recent paper by Calvo and Végh (1992), where the IMF study is also quoted in support of the view that in the cases mentioned we are dealing with less than fully credible reforms. I think that McKinnon and Pill's paper belongs more to that framework than the authors admit. This results in tension between the text, the model, and the empirical regularities.

1. The disinflation and reform programs mentioned in the paper are less than fully credible as the persistence of inflation shows. This has been attributed in the literature to backward indexation or to nonsynchronized price setting. At a policy level, it has motivated the use of some heterodox policies such as price and wage controls. Interestingly enough, the result has been that heterodox and orthodox programs have shared similar characteristics, suggesting that these measures cannot solve the fundamental problem of lack of credibility.

If the foreign inflation rate is zero as assumed in the model, the domestic rate of inflation must converge to zero as well. The fact that it does not is more consistent with a less than fully credible reform and stabilization program.

Note that the success of the fiscal reform seems to be unrelated to the dynamics discussed. Thus, a successful fiscal reform, although necessary, is clearly not sufficient. What is necessary is to convince market participants that the overall program is both economically and politically sustainable.

2. Another factor that makes me think that it would be better to view the EB program as less than fully credible is the fall in the real exchange rate. If the

program were fully credible, we should instead expect inflation to fall immediately to its new equilibrium, consistent with the new steady state, given by the lower rate of devaluation. The real exchange rate would not change or would rise.

In a truly dynamic model where the equilibrium real exchange rate is modeled explicitly and agents have rational expectations, it could be shown that credible liberalization will lead economic agents to expect a higher equilibrium real exchange rate. Thus, the expected rate of return on foreign asset holdings will also be higher tomorrow, and agents will spend less today. This will produce an excess supply of nontraded goods that will be removed via a reduction of their price, a depreciation of the real exchange rate. This will depend on the share of nontraded goods in domestic expenditure, the relative price elasticity of the excess demand for traded goods, the influence of the difference between the rate of time preference and the real interest rate on the desired excess of domestic spending over domestic income. If the liberalization is not credible, domestic spending will increase today in anticipation of the reversal of the liberalization measures, a fact consistent with most Latin American countries experience with trade liberalization. The real exchange rate will appreciate making further adjustment more difficult.

3. I think that the fact that a large proportion of capital inflows is in the form of overseas deposits placed with the domestic banking sector is not related solely to implicit deposit insurance. It is instead most likely another aspect of the short-term view adopted by foreign capital and therefore an argument in favor of thinking that the market does not view reforms as sustainable. The purpose of the capital inflow is to profit from the expected real exchange rate appreciation. This is another consequence of the noncredibility of the program.

4. Moreover, it is argued in the paper that the market perceives the increase in income following the successful real-side reform as permanent. In a truly intertemporal framework—using some version of the permanent-income hypothesis of consumption, for example—permanent increases in income are not likely to affect the current account. This is not what the stylized facts show. Temporary changes in income or anticipated future changes in permanent income can be associated with changes in savings and in the current account.

A related matter is that overborrowing is the result of domestic financial market inefficiencies. This sort of Ponzi scheme is most likely to be associated with transient changes in economic policy.

5. In the model, once excess demand is generated via the inflow of foreign capital, it should be followed by inflation in the nontradable sector together with a current account deficit. This is consistent with a less than fully credible EB program. If the public expects a higher rate of devaluation to be resumed in the future (it is now zero), the fall in the nominal lending interest rate is perceived as temporary. As this reduces the cost of present consumption with respect to future consumption, there is excess demand: output expands, and

there is a current account deficit. The overheated economy keeps the rate of inflation above that of devaluation, and the real exchange rate appreciates. Over time, the real exchange rate appreciation reduces excess aggregate demand for home goods, and output declines.

Policymakers have noticed that the increase in liquidity is dangerous. For this reason, some programs have also implemented higher reserve requirements, a higher discount rate, or tightened controls on short-term capital flows. These measures largely explain the sharp increase in real interest rates, as in Israel in 1985.

### Financial Market Imperfections and "Special" Banks

First a naive comment: in most countries of the world some form of deposit insurance exists, and it is difficult to see why it should play such a crucial role when a stabilization program is undertaken, or, in other words, why it should not play a more pervasive role in international capital markets. Now let me comment on the imperfections suggested in the text of the paper but not fully incorporated in the model.

As hinted already, the belief that deposit insurance may actually be responsible for the kind of boom-bust or bust-boom cycle studied here seems somewhat exaggerated. Many industrialized nations provide some form of deposit insurance, with some exceptions. The Australian central bank has the authority to take over a troubled institution, although there is no formal deposit scheme. In Luxembourg, small-depositor insurance does not appear to be guaranteed. In New Zealand, it is expressly prohibited. In Canada, Switzerland, and the United Kingdom, insurance is provided by the banking authorities. In Japan and Belgium, banks and the authorities operate insurance facilities jointly. In France, Italy, Germany, and Sweden, it is the banking industry that administers deposit insurance. Within the European Union, the 1986 Banking Directive recommended that deposit insurance schemes cover all credit institutions.

Given the extent of deposit insurance, namely in countries over all the spectrum of capital mobility, it seems somewhat exaggerated to single out this institution as the factor responsible for overborrowing.

Moreover, the model is truly more representative of a less developed country: no primary securities, equity concentrated in families, no bond market, and so on. It takes a great leap of faith to use the case of the pound sterling's departure from the Exchange Rate Mechanism for empirical support. In the model, the fiscal deficit is money financed, and the stabilization plan is aimed at eliminating this inflation. The model really better fits a Latin American country and a less than fully credible EB program.

Another market imperfection suggested is asymmetric information. This results in credit rationing in the model: firms and people are financially constrained in production (working capital) and demand (liquidity). From the famous article by Stiglitz and Weiss (1981) on credit rationing, it is obvious that monetary policy affects investment through credit availability and not through the interest rate because the interest rate not only conveys information on relative scarcities but also on different qualities of borrowers. If for a given interest rate a risk-neutral borrower is indifferent between two projects, an increase in the interest rate will make him prefer the riskier project, the project with the higher probability of bankruptcy. As the expected return to the bank in that case is lower, credit rationing occurs. It is not clear from the model why banks should increase loans without taking into account the effects of this increase on the expected return to the loans. The model really needs much more structure here so as to take into account how banks use the interest rates they charge to sort potential borrowers and affect the actions of borrowers. There are interest rates in this case that equate supply and demand, but they are not equilibrium ones.

If credit rationing occurs instead because of interest rate ceilings on lending institutions, then interest rates are below the equilibrium levels. Notice that in this case of credit rationing the interest rate that equates supply and demand is most likely to be an equilibrium interest rate. The distinction between these cases seems to me very important. Again the model really needs to much more explicitly identify the source of the financial market inefficiency.

Finally, the real deposit rate rises in the internationally liberalized economy because the elimination of the fiscal deficit reduces the need to extract financing from the banking system. The abolition of reserve requirements eliminates the wedge between deposit and lending rates and thus allows deposit rates to rise even when the lending rate is falling. This policy shock should also be made explicit in the model. Presumably, in a dynamic discussion these effects should be made explicit. Otherwise, there is tension in the model as the increase in net foreign official reserves via the capital inflow becomes exogenous to the model (although it is endogenous in the discussion).

Banks are special. However, the behavior of the banking industry, especially its demand for reserves, is not modeled explicitly in the uncertainty environment suggested in the paper.

### Some Necessary Features of a Dynamic Model of Reform and Stabilization

*The equilibrium real exchange rate.* In a fully credible stabilization and reform program, the equilibrium real exchange rate is not likely to remain constant: both commercial policy and capital controls affect its equilibrium level. Similarly, because many successful fiscal reforms require a change in the composition of government expenditures—not only a change in their share in GDP—they will also affect the equilibrium real exchange rate.

Trade liberalization makes available new investment opportunities and allows not only a move along the production possibility frontier but also access to a new technology. This is another source of change of the equilibrium real exchange rate.

*Banks' supply of funds.* In the model, the exchange rate peg is believed to hold into the indefinite future. The authorities are said to be forced to control their policy instrument, the narrow money supply, so as to keep the domestic nominal interest rate consistent with uncovered interest parity. Notice that the money supply measure should not be considered a policy instrument because, in a truly fixed exchange rate system such as the one assumed in the paper, the stock of the money supply is endogenously determined by the balance of payments. The central bank passively purchases and sells foreign exchange at the pegged rate. If the foreign currency is purchased from banks, as is assumed here, those banks will find themselves with enlarged holdings of domestic monetary reserves, which will induce an expansion of the country's money stock. This capital inflow should be modeled which will require more structure to explain banks' supply of funds.

*Expectations.* The issue of how expectations are modeled also seems important. If some backward price indexing exists, or if rigidities such as nonsynchronized price setting are highlighted, then there is likely to be a group of agents who have extrapolative and destabilizing expectations as they forecast for shorter periods. Those forecasting for longer planning horizons tend to have stabilizing expectations instead. This has been shown to matter for the dynamics of the system, for example, in a simulation of the effects of financial liberalization of the Italian economy by Gandolfo and Padoan (1990).

In McKinnon and Pill's paper, adequate modeling of expectations could show that less than perfect credibility results from agents' anticipating that capital account liberalization without domestic financial market reforms is bound to lead the economy into an explosive path.

## Conclusions

I agree that capital market imperfections, asymmetric information, and the like, are present in most if not all of the countries that undertook stabilization programs. The fact that the boom-bust cycle is related to both a capital account surplus and a current account deficit seems to me, however, to point to causes other than those suggested in the paper. A most fundamental force must explain these phenomena. I suggest that most stabilization programs seem to run into a basic sustainability syndrome motivated by dynamic inconsistency.

Credibility of the reform process is essential, in particular for the well functioning of domestic financial markets. However, credibility takes time to build. Credibility requires two elements. First, the *overall* program must be feasible, not just the fiscal adjustment. Second, policy commitments must not be subject to a time inconsistency problem. Simple and not excessively state-contingent rules are to be preferred to discretion. Tying the hands of policymakers guarantees that a better equilibrium ensues. This can be done by introducing a series of constraints on discretion in policy making. First, a signal that an irreversible change in regime is going to take place raises the political cost of policy reversals and thereby promotes credibility. This is an internal political constraint. Second, effective checks on the various branches of the policy-making apparatus, such as creating an independent central bank or introducing the legal prohibition of deficit monetization, increase the credibility of reform. These are internal legal constraints. External legal constraints such as the prohibition on quotas or increases in bound tariffs in WTO also raise the credibility of the reform. Finally, external economic constraints such as adopting an economic program supported by a multilateral agency also provide credibility to the reform. It is suspected, however, that none of these measures, even not all of them adopted simultaneously, are likely to be a perfect substitute for the actual path followed by the reform process.

Trade liberalization demonopolizes the economy and improves the allocation of resources by better price signaling. However, adjustment requires the use of credit. Without access to the credit market, even sound projects will not be undertaken, and sound firms may go out of the market. Thus current account convertibility requires a functioning financial system. It is clear that the quality of money and capital markets influences the benefits that can be obtained from real-sector reform. Trade liberalization also requires some capital inflows to finance the adjustment costs as well. However, capital inflows are not a substitute for fiscal reform as they appreciate the exchange rate and offset the depreciation of the equilibrium real exchange rate that is likely to result from trade liberalization. But a successful fiscal reform is just the beginning of a lengthy process aiming at a lasting change of market participant expectations.

In the literature about the sequencing of reforms it has already been suggested that domestic financial market reform must be undertaken before any liberalization of the capital account is attempted. McKinnon has also argued this in the past. From this point of view, the paper does not add much new.

After living for 25 years in a country which is a textbook case of unsound macroeconomic policy and failed stabilization programs, I remain unconvinced by the "overborrowing syndrome" hypothesis.

## References


Calvo, Guillermo A., and Carlos A. Végh. 1992. Currency substitution in developing countries: An introduction. *Revista de Analisis Economico* 7:3–27.

Gandolfo, Giancarlo, and Pier Paolo Padoan. 1990. Perfect capital mobility and the Italian economy. In *Exchange rate regimes and currency union,* ed. Ernst Baltensperger and Hans-Werner Sinn, 36–61. Frankfurt: St. Martins.

Stiglitz, Joseph E., and Andrew Weiss. 1981. Credit rationing in markets with imperfect information. *American Economic Review* 71:393–410.

## Comment Chong-Hyun Nam

McKinnon and Pill have written an excellent paper that is full of insights and provides very useful messages to policymakers in both developing and developed nations. The paper is especially interesting to me because Korea is currently involved in liberalizing its capital account, and the possibility of excessive capital inflow has recently become an acute issue.

The highlight of McKinnon and Pill's paper is the demonstration of why and how some economic reform programs can lead to excessive capital inflows when the capital account is open. For that, the paper provides models as well as some factual evidence. The paper also examines the effects of a country's trade reform on its investment and saving patterns, using a Fisherian type of model. Finally, the paper suggests some policy prescriptions to mitigate potential damage due to overborrowing.

I have two major comments on the paper: one is on the relevancy to reality of the Fisherian type of model, and the other concerns the practicality of the policy prescriptions suggested. Both comments will be made in the light of Korean experiences.

First, using a Fisherian two-period model, the paper shows that some real-side reforms, such as trade reform, can raise income and consumption in both periods when the capital market is open, and more important, it shows that domestic private saving could fall sharply as a consequence. Indeed, the Mexican experience seems to confirm this argument. As shown in table 1.1, the private saving rate in Mexico declined sharply from 15.5 to 7.7 percent in the three-year period following an economic reform plan put into action in 1989. This drop was accompanied by a sharp rise in foreign capital inflow which took place during the same period as shown in table 1.3.

It seems, however, that the Korean experience provides a contrasting case. The Korean economy, for instance, underwent a rapid liberalization period during the 1980s on almost all fronts, real as well as financial. Following a view generally held by economists on sequencing of economic liberalization, Korea undertook trade reform first and pursued it much more quickly and more extensively than financial reform. In particular, a very conservative step-by-step approach was taken toward the liberalization of the capital account of the balance of payments. Nonetheless, steady and significant progress was made in opening up the capital account during the 1980s.

An important consequence of all of these liberalization efforts undertaken in Korea may be found in a rapid rise in both income and the domestic saving rate: between 1981 and 1991, real income grew at an annual rate of nearly 10 percent, and the domestic saving rate rose to greater than 36 percent from less than 22 percent.

An interesting question then is, Why is Korea's saving pattern so different

Chong-Hyun Nam is professor of economics at Korea University.

from Mexico's? McKinnon and Pill may argue that Korea's capital account had been less open than Mexico's. That may have some truth in it. But I have a couple of other hunches. One is that the domestic saving rate may depend much more on income level and its growth rate than on the domestic real interest rate. In fact, many econometricians, including Nam (1988), seem to support this view, at least when the Korean economy is concerned. My other hunch has to do with the role of the real exchange rate, in that an overvalued currency can encourage consumption of imported goods and may lead to less domestic savings. I do not know much about the Mexican experience with real exchange rates, but I do know that Korea has been rather successful in maintaining a stable real exchange rate over time at a realistic level (Nam 1995). So I wonder what different results McKinnon and Pill's model would produce if modifications were made so that saving or consumption is a function of real income rather than of real interest rate.

Now let me turn to the policy recommendation part of the paper. I fully share McKinnon and Pill's view that the potential damage due to overborrowing can be real when economic reform plans are implemented with the capital account open or the capital account being opened up simultaneously. In that case, therefore, some kind of safeguards or precautionary measures may be needed.

For that purpose, McKinnon and Pill suggest a list of *do*'s and *don't*'s, such as restricting consumer access to credits, restraining short-term capital flow itself, and setting up a system something like Singapore's provident fund. I think these measures may be of help in mitigating the potential damage, but I wonder whether these measures are workable. I also wonder whether such compulsory measures as suggested above can be consistent with the concept of economic liberalization. It is quite conceivable that these measures may also produce undesirable side effects.

In any case, I think it would be better to take a gradual approach to opening up the capital account, controlling the speed and scope. But I am not sure how much "gradualness" would be optimal. I recall that Robert Mundell (1992) recently came to Korea and expressed his views on the Korean case. He suggested that Korea, with a saving rate already over 35 percent, can afford to forget entirely about relying on foreign capital for its economic development. This is certainly an another extreme view.

## References

Mundell, Robert. 1992. Stabilization policies and capital imports in semi-open economies. Paper presented at conference on Money and Finance in the Open Economy, Institute of Economic Research, Korea University, Seoul, November.

Nam, Chong-Hyun. 1995. The role of trade and exchange rate policy in Korea's growth. In *Growth theories in light of the East Asian experience,* ed. Takatoshi Ito and Anne O. Krueger. Chicago: University of Chicago Press.

Nam, Sang-Woo. 1988. The determinants of national saving in Korea: A sectoral approach. Working Paper no. 8821. Seoul: Korea Development Institute, December.

# 2 Japanese and U.S. Exports and Investment as Conduits of Growth

Jonathan Eaton and Akiko Tamura

## 2.1 Introduction

Japan and the United States are two major sources of technological innovation in the world economy. These two countries employ the largest number of research scientists and engineers among the OECD nations and are major patenters of innovations throughout the world (see, e.g., Eaton and Kortum 1994). The dissemination of this innovation around the world takes several forms. One is through the export of new products or of existing products at lower cost. Another is through direct foreign investment (DFI).

Our purpose here is to examine the roles of Japanese and U.S. exports and DFI as conduits of new technology. We first develop a theoretical model of technology diffusion in which one country, the source of innovation, develops new inputs into the production process at a regular rate. A fraction of these innovations are potentially useful in another country, which we call the destination. When these ideas are potentially useful, the innovating firm can introduce them into the destination country either by producing them at home and exporting them there or by investing in the destination country to produce them locally. We compare the desirability of these alternatives. Our model identifies country characteristics that determine the extent to which innovators will use one method or the other to take advantage of their ideas abroad.

The analysis has several implications for the relationship between export and DFI levels, on the one hand, and characteristics of the destination country, on the other. One is that innovators will tend to exploit new ideas in smaller countries relatively more by exporting there, and in larger countries through DFI. For many parameter values our model implies that DFI will be most sig-

Jonathan Eaton is professor of economics at Boston University and a research associate of the National Bureau of Economic Research. Akiko Tamura is a graduate student in economics at Boston University.

nificant for middle-income destination countries: At low levels of income market size is too small to support much DFI, while high wages in high-income countries deter it. Factors that reduce the fixed cost of DFI, such as a high level of education, obviously encourage it, while factors that raise the opportunity cost of labor, such as a high natural resource endowment, discourage it.

Our model implies that bilateral trade and investment flows can be captured by a modified "gravity model" that relates exports and DFI to destination country characteristics reflecting market size, the cost of direct investment, the level of development, and transportation costs. In the second part of our analysis we estimate such a model for annual Japanese and U.S. exports and outward DFI to a panel of 72 and 76 countries, respectively, during the period 1985–90. Our aim is to identify the characteristics of a country that are significant in determining how much Japan and the United States export and invest there.[1]

Several implications of the theoretical model find empirical support in the export and DFI patterns of both countries: First, distance, as a measure of transport costs, inhibits trade much more than it inhibits DFI. The negative effect of distance on trade exceeds that on DFI for both countries. Second, market size, as measured by population, favors DFI relative to investment: population elasticities for both Japanese and U.S. exports and DFI are less than one but closer to one for DFI than for exports. Third, a high level of human capital, which we interpret as indicative of lower overhead investment costs, is associated with a larger DFI position (although human capital also has a positive, but less substantial, effect on exports from both countries as well).

While these results are common to both Japanese and U.S. trade and investment patterns, others are not. The prediction that the importance of DFI relative to exports peaks for middle-income countries is satisfied by the United States but not by Japan. While population density, which we interpret as implying lower labor costs, is associated with more DFI from the United States, it brings in less from Japan. A possible explanation is that much Japanese DFI occurs to exploit natural resources that are processed for export to Japan (a possibility not captured by our theoretical model).

We estimate the model both with and without regional effects. Except for the role of distance, the basic implications are not very sensitive to the inclusion of

1. Leamer (1984) is the standard reference on the empirical implementation of factor endowments theory to trade flows. Helpman (1987) applies a model of imperfect competition and scale economies to the estimation of trade flows. Our analysis here combines elements of these two approaches. Less work has been done on the empirical specification of investment flows. Mundell (1957), Purvis (1972), and Markusen (1983) model the relationship between trade and investment flows. Helpman (1984) and Markusen (1984) provide models of DFI. The analysis here builds on earlier empirical work of Eaton and Tamura (1994),who analyze regional patterns of Japanese and U.S. trade and investment flows. The current paper develops a theoretical framework for modeling trade and investment flows as well as pursuing an empirical analysis. Moreover, different issues are considered. In particular, here we examine the role of distance and of potential nonlinearities in the relationship between trade and investment, on the one hand, and the level of development, on the other.

regional effects. We do not undertake a lengthy discussion of regional trade and investment patterns here, which was the purpose of Eaton and Tamura (1994). One finding that is worth reporting, however, is that, correcting for distance and other national features, Japan imports more from the United States than does any other region of the world except East Asia.

We present our theoretical framework in section 2.2. Section 2.3 reports our results on Japanese and U.S. exports and DFI positions. We offer some conclusions in section 2.4.

## 2.2 A Model of Trade, Investment, and Growth

Our theoretical model focuses on two countries. One, which we call the source, constantly generates innovations for production. The other, the destination, eventually adopts these innovations, but with a lag. The number $n$ of innovations available in the source summarizes the state of technology there, while the size of the subset $m$ of these innovations available to the destination summarizes its state of technology. We first describe the equilibrium at any moment when $m$ and $n$ are given and then turn to what happens as $m$ and $n$ grow over time.

### 2.2.1 The Static Equilibrium

At any moment the source country can produce a homogeneous, costlessly tradable final output (which serves as numeraire) with a variety of $n$ intermediate inputs according to the standard Dixit-Stiglitz (Dixit and Stiglitz 1977) production relationship:

$$Q = \left(\int_0^n x_i^{\rho} di\right)^{1/\rho}, \quad \rho \in (0,1).$$

Here $Q$ represents final output and $x_i$ denotes the amount of input $i$. The implied cost of producing an amount $Q$ is

$$C(p,Q) = \left(\int_0^n p_i^{\rho/(\rho-1)} di\right)^{(\rho-1)/\rho} Q,$$

where $p_i$ is the price of input $i$. The destination has the technology to use a subset $m$ of these inputs to produce the same final output. Intermediates are produced with one unit of labor in either country.

The technology to produce each intermediate $i$ is owned by a firm in the source, which takes the wages in each country, $w_s$ and $w_d$ in the source and destination, respectively, as given, as well as the prices charged by other input producers in either country. Inputs can be exported, but exporting one unit of any input requires the use of $\tau$ workers in the exporting country. Owners of individual input technologies face the decision of where to produce. Inputs in principle can be produced in each market for local production or in one market to service both (or through some combination of the two). To make the analysis less taxonomic we will assume that exporting inputs from country d to country s is so costly that it is unprofitable. (As the reader will see, even with simple assumptions things get complicated.) Hence the $n - m$ inputs that have not been absorbed into the destination's technology are solely produced in country s for use in s. Owners of the $m$ inputs common to both countries must decide whether to serve the destination market by exporting there or by producing there. Exporting a unit requires $\tau$ country-s workers, while producing in country d at all requires employing $F$ country-d overhead workers on an ongoing basis.

Since producers of all inputs, whether they export or produce locally, set the prices of their individual inputs taking all other input prices as given, to maximize profit individual producers will charge a markup $1/\rho$ over marginal cost. Hence producers selling in the local market of the source country will always set a price $p_s = w_s/\rho$, while those exporting to country d will set a c.i.f. price $p_X = w_s(1 + \tau)/\rho$ and those producing locally in country d will charge $p_D = w_d/\rho$.

*The Source*

Since the source produces all of its own inputs, we can take care of it quickly. From the cost function implied by the production function, zero profits in the production of the final (numeraire) good require that $p_s = n^{(1-\rho)/\rho}$ or a wage in the source country of

$$w_s = \rho n^{(1-\rho)/\rho}. \tag{1}$$

Hence as $n$ grows, allowing for greater division of labor in country s, so does the wage there.

*The Destination*

In the destination country, however, there are two potential sources of input supply, so that things are more complicated.

Denote by $\lambda^D$ the fraction of the $m$ inputs that have been absorbed into country d's technology that producers choose to produce in country d (so that the remaining $1 - \lambda^D$ are exported from country s). The cost of producing a unit of final output in country d is then

$$c_D = \{m[(1 - \lambda^D)\upsilon_X + \lambda_D\upsilon_D]\}^{(p-1)/\rho},$$

where $\upsilon_X = p_X^{\rho/(\rho-1)} = (1 + \tau)^{\rho/(\rho-1)}/n$ and $\upsilon_D = p_D^{\rho/(\rho-1)}$. For country d to compete in the world market for the final good requires that local production be competitive, or that

$$1 = c_D = \{m[(1 - \lambda^D)\upsilon_X + \lambda^D\upsilon_D]\}^{(\rho-1)/\rho}. \tag{2}$$

In order for any domestic production of inputs to occur it must be the case that the marginal cost of producing locally is less than that of importing (since the first requires a fixed cost while the second does not). Thus $\upsilon_D > \upsilon_X$. Hence the zero-profitability condition (2) implies a negative relationship between $\lambda^D$ and $\upsilon_D$.

The profit earned from producing an input in country d is

$$\pi_D = (1 - \rho)\{m[(1 - \lambda^D)\upsilon_X + \lambda^D\upsilon_D]\}^{-1/\rho}\upsilon_D Q_d - w_d F,$$

where $Q_d$ is the amount of the final good produced in country d, while the profit earned from exporting to country d is

$$\pi_X = (1 - \rho)\{m[(1 - \lambda^D)\upsilon_X + \lambda^D\upsilon_D]\}^{-1/\rho}\upsilon_X Q_d.$$

For $\lambda_D \in (0,1)$, then, requires that $\pi_X = \pi_D$ or, incorporating the zero profitability of final production condition (2), that

$$\upsilon_D - \upsilon_X = \frac{\rho\upsilon_D^{(\rho-1)/\rho}F}{(1 - \rho)Q_d}. \tag{3}$$

If the left-hand side of equation (3) exceeds the right, then $\lambda_D = 1$, while if the right-hand side exceeds the left, then $\lambda_D = 0$.

If there are $L_d$ workers available to direct foreign investors in country d, then $L_d - \lambda^D mF$ of them will be available for final production of inputs. These will divide themselves evenly among the $\lambda^D m$ inputs that are locally produced. Hence the amount of each locally produced input will be $x_D = L_d/(\lambda^D m) - F$. The production of final output in country d is therefore

$$Q_d = \frac{(m\lambda^D)^{(1-\rho)/\rho}L_d - (m\lambda^D)^{1/\rho}F}{[1 - (1 - \lambda^D)m\upsilon_X]^{1/\rho}}. \tag{4}$$

Hence equation (1) determines $w_s$ and (hence $p_s = w_s/\rho$, $p_X = w_s(1 + \tau)/\rho$, and $\upsilon_X = p_X^{\rho/(\rho-1)}$) as a function of $n$, the state of technology in country s, as well as the production parameter $\rho$ and the transport cost $\tau$. Equations (2), (3), and (4) then determine the wage in country d, $w_d$ (and thus $p_D$ and $\upsilon_D$), the fraction of inputs produced in country d, $\lambda^D$, and output in country d, $Q_d$, as functions of the wage in s, the labor force in d, $L_d$, the number of inputs that can be used in d, $m$, and the production function parameter $\rho$ and the number of overhead workers $F$.

Solving the four equations, the equilibrium fraction of inputs produced locally turns out to be

$$\lambda^D = \min[\tilde{\lambda}^D, 1],$$

where

$$\tilde{\lambda}^D = \frac{x}{2\rho}\left[-1 + \sqrt{1 + \frac{4(1 - \rho)\rho}{x}\frac{L}{Fn\sigma}}\right] \tag{5}$$

and where $\sigma = m/n$, the fraction of inputs that country d can use, $x = (1 - \sigma\tau')/\sigma\tau'$, and $\tau' = (1 + \tau)^{\rho/(\rho-1)}$. Note that $\lambda^D$ increases with the ratio of the labor force to the required number of overhead workers $L/(Fn\sigma)$ and with the transport cost $\tau$ and decreases with the fraction of inputs $\sigma$ that country d can use.

### 2.2.2 Dynamics

Our concern is with a situation in which the countries grow over time. We model this as the process of $n$ and $m$ growing at a common rate $g$.[2] Obviously, if the number of overhead workers required to produce a good locally remains constant, without any growth in the labor force eventually almost all inputs in the destination country will be imported. Since the ratio of the volume of trade to output seems to have remained roughly constant over time, even as the division of labor has increased, technical progress must have occurred in overhead as well. To allow for a steady state in which the proportion of trade to production remains constant even as the world economy grows we let the fixed cost of DFI fall in proportion as the number of available inputs increases. We also want to allow for the possibility that more advanced countries, that is, destination countries that are better able to absorb new foreign technologies, might also provide overhead services more efficiently. To capture these effects we set $F = f/(\sigma^{\mu}n)$, where $f$ is a positive constant and $\mu$ is a (presumably positive) parameter capturing the effect of relative productivity on the efficiency with which overhead services can be provided.

Incorporating this expression for $F$ into equation (5) we get a share of DFI (if it is interior) of

$$(6)\qquad \tilde{\lambda}^D = \frac{x}{2\rho}\left[-1 + \sqrt{1 + \frac{4(1-\rho)\rho}{x}\frac{L\sigma^{\mu-1}}{f}}\right],$$

which is independent of the current state of technology $n$. Under these assumptions output in the two countries will grow at a common rate $(1 - \rho)g/\rho$, with the relative productivity of the destination depending on $\sigma$. The fraction of inputs produced locally will remain constant over time.

It remains the case that countries that are larger relative to the fixed cost parameter $f$, and countries that are more expensive to export to, will have relatively more investment. Depending on the parameter $\mu$, however, the share of products produced locally might rise or fall with the destination's relative productivity as reflected by the ratio $\sigma$.

To illustrate what the model implies for the relationship between a country's

2. Krugman (1979) provides a growth model in which the steady state has this property. Here, as in Krugman, new products erupt in the source country spontaneously and trickle down to the destination. Our model could accommodate an endogenous R&D process as in Grossman and Helpman (1991), but since our focus is on how technologies are transmitted rather than how they are developed we treat innovation as exogenous.

ability to absorb technology and how much DFI it attracts relative to exports, table 2.1 reports values of $\lambda^D$ and the ratio of exports to output ($X/Q$) for values of $\sigma$ between .1 and 1 (at intervals of .1). In our base case, reported in the first pair of columns, $L/f = 5$, $\rho = .75$, $\rho = 0.5$, and $\mu = 2$. Our choice of $\mu$ implies that overhead requirements fall more than in proportion to the number of inputs that the country can use. The chosen value of $\rho$ implies an elasticity of substitution between inputs of 4 and a markup over the marginal cost of production of 33 percent. Transport costs are 5 percent of the marginal cost of production in the source. Given these other parameter values, our choice of the ratio of the fixed cost parameter to the labor force implies a ratio of overhead to production workers of between 5 and 10 percent.

We also report the implications of (1) dropping $\mu$ to 1 (so that overhead requirements in more advanced countries are exactly inversely proportional to their ability to adopt inputs), (2) dropping $\rho$ to .5 (so that the elasticity of substitution between inputs is 2), (3) raising $\tau$ to .1, and (4) doubling the labor force.

Several things are worth noting in table 2.1: First, doubling the population raises the fraction of inputs produced locally, with more effect in richer countries. The model thus predicts that DFI will tend to increase more than in proportion to the destination country's size while exports will increase in less than proportion. At the same time an increase in population acts to reduce the ratio of exports to output. Hence the model predicts nonhomogeneity in the relationship between country size, on the one hand, and exports and DFI, on the other, with an increase in country size leading to a less than proportional increase in exports but a more than proportional increase in DFI.

Second, the relationship between the destination's ability to absorb technology and the extent to which source country innovators will exploit their ideas through DFI can be nonmonotonic. In all but the case in which $\mu = 1$ it is an "inverted U" relationship, with the fraction of inputs provided through invest-

**Table 2.1** **Simulated DFI and Export Shares**

| | Base | | $\mu = 1$ | | $\rho = .5$ | | $\tau = .1$ | | $L/f = 10$ | |
|---|---|---|---|---|---|---|---|---|---|---|
| $\sigma$ | $\lambda^D$ | $X/Q$ | $\lambda^D$ | $X/Q$ | $\lambda^D$ | $X/Q$ | $\lambda^D$ | $X/Q$ | $\lambda^D$ | $X/Q$ |
| .1 | .12 | .08 | 1.00 | 0 | .25 | .07 | .12 | .07 | .25 | .07 |
| .2 | .24 | .13 | 1.00 | 0 | .47 | .10 | .24 | .11 | .47 | .09 |
| .3 | .34 | .17 | .99 | 0 | .66 | .10 | .35 | .15 | .64 | .09 |
| .4 | .43 | .20 | .92 | .03 | .80 | .08 | .44 | .17 | .77 | .08 |
| .5 | .49 | .22 | .84 | .07 | .89 | .05 | .51 | .18 | .84 | .07 |
| .6 | .53 | .25 | .77 | .12 | .93 | .04 | .56 | .20 | .88 | .06 |
| .7 | .54 | .28 | .70 | .18 | .91 | .06 | .59 | .22 | .87 | .08 |
| .8 | .53 | .33 | .62 | .27 | .85 | .12 | .60 | .24 | .83 | .11 |
| .9 | .49 | .40 | .53 | .37 | .72 | .24 | .59 | .28 | .76 | .19 |
| 1.0 | .42 | .50 | .41 | .50 | .45 | .52 | .55 | .33 | .63 | .32 |

ment peaking for middle-income countries. The share of DFI rises between the poorest and middle-income countries because the fixed cost falls, but for richer countries this effect is overshadowed by the higher labor costs in the more advanced country. When $\mu = 1$ the first effect is inoperative so that only the second manifests itself, so that the share of inputs provided through DFI falls as $\sigma$ rises.

Third, despite the nonmonotonicity in the relationship between the fraction of inputs provided through DFI and output, exports tend to rise with $\sigma$. The reason is that as $\sigma$ rises so does the wage and the cost of production in the destination country relative to the cost of production in the source. Since the elasticity of substitution between inputs exceeds 1, an increased relative cost of production and, hence, through the fixed markup, an increased price, implies a lower expenditure on the input. Hence a poor country tends to use a much larger amount of a domestically produced input, relative to an imported input, than a richer country. Notice that when the elasticity of substitution falls to 2 the tendency of exports to rise with $\sigma$ is much less pronounced.

Fourth, doubling transport costs, not surprisingly, reduces exports and raises the fraction of inputs produced locally. The effect is greater for richer countries. The model predicts, then, that innovators will tend to exploit their ideas in more distant countries via DFI and in closer countries through export.

## 2.3 Japanese and U.S. Exports and DFI

We use the model as a basis for examining Japanese and U.S. exports and outward DFI positions with a balanced panel of 72 countries in the case of Japan and 76 countries in the case of the United States, using annual data for the period 1985–90. Our model implies that exports to a country and DFI positions in that country will be determined by (1) the labor force available for employment by direct foreign investors in that country relative to the cost of investing there, (2) the country's ability to adopt technologies from the source country, and (3) the cost of exporting goods there.

### 2.3.1 Econometric Specification and Variables

To capture the effect of the country's available labor force relative to investment costs we relate Japanese and U.S. exports $X_{it}$ and outward DFI $O_{it}$ at time $t$ to partner $i$'s population $\text{POP}_{it}$. Our model implies that exports and DFI are potentially nonhomogeneous in size. Hence we introduce a specification that allows for nonhomogeneity. We capture the effect of a country's ability to absorb technology from the source through income per capita $\text{YPC}_{it}$. Since our model implies that the effect of $\sigma$ on the relative importance of DFI and exports might be nonmonotonic, we introduce both a linear and quadratic measure of income per capita. Also, the ability of a country to make use of Japanese and U.S. ideas might depend on its factor endowments. We use the destination's population density $\text{DEN}_{it}$ as an inverse measure of natural resource endowments and a measure of the average years of schooling per worker $HK_i$ to capture human capital.[3] Finally we use distance $d_i$ from Japan or the United States to capture transport costs.[4] Different regions of the world might have unobserved characteristics (such as different policies toward imports and DFI) other than those which we have taken into account. Hence in one set of estimates we include dummy variables for the region of the destination country $\delta_{Ri}$ (assigned as indicated in the appendix, table 2A.1). We also include dummy variables to take into account systematic effects of time $\delta_T$.

As the subscripts indicate, we have annual data for the variables POP, YPC, and DEN. Our measure of human capital, taken from Kyriacou (1991), is available only at five-year intervals. Hence we use the measure for 1985 for all years.[5] Table 2A.3 in the appendix indicates sources of data.

Our specification embodies elements of both the standard gravity and factor endowments specifications of trade patterns extended to explain DFI positions as well as trade flows.[6] In contrast to these approaches, our model implies potential nonhomogeneity in the relationship between our dependent and explanatory variables. To accommodate these, we assume that for each dependent variable $V(V = X, O)$, the explanatory variables are linear homogeneous in $a_V + V_{it}$, where $a_V$ is a threshold parameter that we estimate. A positive value of $a_V$ implies that the function of the explanatory variables explaining $V$ must achieve a minimum threshold value before strictly positive values of $V$ occur. A negative value of $a_V$ means that a minimum level of $V$ occurs independently of the explanatory variables.

For Japan and the United States separately, then, we estimate the equations:

$$V_{it} = \max[-a_V + C_V \mathrm{POP}_{it}^{\alpha_V} \mathrm{YPC}_{it}^{\beta_V + \beta'_V \ln \mathrm{YPC}_{it}} \mathrm{DEN}_{it}^{\gamma_V} \mathrm{HK}_{it}^{\epsilon_V} d_i^{\eta_V}$$
$$\exp(D_T \delta_{VT} + D_R \delta_{VR} + u_{it}), 0]$$

for $V = X, O$. Here $u_{Vit}$ is a normal error term associated with dependent variable $V$ and $\delta_{VT}$ is the column vector of coefficients of dummy variables for time and $\delta_{VR}$ is the column vector of dummy variables for region. For each depen-

3. These measures also might reflect aspects of labor force availability relative to the cost of investment. A high level of human capital might, other things equal, reduce the cost of overhead, while a high natural resource endowment might reduce the labor force available for producing in the manufacturing sector (to which our model is more appropriate).

4. Distances are between major cities. Table 2A.2 reports the cities chosen and the distances between them for the cities in our sample. Distance might also raise the overhead requirement for DFI.

5. Kyriacou (1991) constructs a measure of the average level of human capital from official data on schooling using a perpetual inventory method. We thank Mark Spiegel for making the data available to us.

6. Deardorff (1984) discusses the "gravity" approach to modeling trade flows econometrically. It has its origins in the work of Tinbergen (1962) and Poyhonen (1963). The framework has recently been applied to regional trade issues by Frankel and Wei (1993). Drysdale and Garnaut (1982) provide a very thorough survey of the approach. Leamer (1974), as we do here, estimates a model that encompasses the factor endowments and gravity approaches.

dent variable $V$ we estimate the intercept $a_V$, the constant $C_V$, the population coefficient $\alpha_V$, the per capita income coefficients $\beta_V$ and $\beta'_V$, the density coefficient $\gamma_V$, the human capital coefficient $\epsilon_V$, and the distance coefficient $\eta_V$. Note that we allow for a nonconstant elasticity of income per capita.

We estimate the equations by maximum likelihood. To derive the maximum likelihood function we rearrange this relationship and take natural logarithms of each side to obtain

$$\begin{aligned}\ln(a_V + V_{it}) &= C_V + \alpha_V \ln \text{POP}_{it} + \beta_V \ln \text{YPC}_{it} \\ &\quad + \beta'_V(\ln \text{YPC}_{it})^2 + \gamma_V \ln \text{DEN}_{it} + \epsilon_V \ln \text{HK}_i \\ &\quad + \eta_V di_i + D_{VT}\delta_T + D_{VR}\delta_R + u_{Vit} \\ &\equiv Z'_{Vit}\theta_V + u_{it}.\end{aligned}$$

The density function for $V_{it}$ is

$$f(V_{it}) = f(u_{it})\left|\frac{\partial u_{it}}{\partial V_{it}}\right| = f(u_{it})\frac{1}{V_{it} + a_V}.$$

We assume that $u_{it} \sim N(0, \sigma^2)$. Hence,

$$f(V_{it}) = \frac{1}{a_V + V_{it}} \cdot \frac{1}{(2\pi\sigma^2)^{1/2}} \exp\left\{-\frac{[\ln(V_{it} + a_V) - Z'_{it}\theta_V]^2}{2\sigma^2}\right\}$$

and the log-likelihood function is

$$\ln L(V,Z';\theta_V,a_V) =$$
$$\left\{-\ln(V_{it} + a_V) - \frac{1}{2}(\ln 2\pi + \ln \sigma^2) - \frac{1}{2\sigma^2}[\ln(V_{it} + a_V) - Z'_{it}\theta_V]^2\right\}.$$

The maximum likelihood estimates of $a_V$ and $\theta_V$ maximize $\ln L(V,Z';\theta_V,a_V)$.

Tables 2.2 and 2.3 report the estimated equations for Japan and the United States, respectively. The numbers in parentheses below the estimated coefficients are Eicker-White standard errors (see White 1982). Defining $\pi_V = \{\theta_V, a_V\}$ as the vector of parameters, these are the square roots of the diagonal elements of the matrix

$$\text{Var}(\pi_V) = A^{-1}(\pi_V)B(\pi_V)A^{-1}(\pi_V),$$

where

$$A(\pi_V) = \frac{1}{NT}\sum_{t=1}^{T}\sum_{i=1}^{N}\frac{\partial^2 \ln f(V_{it},Z'_{it},\theta_V,a_V)}{\partial\pi_V\partial\pi'_V},$$

$$B(\pi_V) = \frac{1}{NT}\sum_{t=1}^{T}\sum_{i=1}^{N}\left[\frac{\partial \ln f(V_{it},Z'_{it},\theta_V,a_V)}{\partial\pi_V} \cdot \frac{\partial \ln f(V_{it},Z'_{it},\theta_V,a_V)}{\partial\pi'_V}\right].$$

**Table 2.2** **Japan: Trade and Investment Equations (maximum likelihood, Tobit estimates)**

| | V = Export | | V = DFI Out | |
|---|---|---|---|---|
| Variable | (1) | (2) | (3) | (4) |
| *N* | 432 | 432 | 432 | 432 |
| Log-likelihood | −3,015.62 | −3,098.43 | −2,749.42 | −2,906.23 |
| *a* | −2.428 | −2.713 | 1.484 | 2.121 |
| | (0.266) | (0.153) | (0.076) | (0.082) |
| C | 21.746 | 8.920 | 21.386 | 6.334 |
| | (3.842) | (3.957) | (7.568) | (9.634) |
| ln POP | 0.716 | 0.699 | 0.837 | 0.779 |
| | (0.025) | (0.032) | (0.048) | (0.074) |
| ln YPC | −6.352 | −3.200 | −6.985 | −2.965 |
| | (0.879) | (0.914) | (1.728) | (2.177) |
| $(\ln \text{YPC})^2$ | 0.409 | 0.234 | 0.417 | 0.210 |
| | (0.048) | (0.050) | (0.097) | (0.118) |
| ln DEN | 0.053 | 0.106 | −0.050 | −0.046 |
| | (0.028) | (0.034) | (0.068) | (0.088) |
| ln HK | 0.730 | 0.755 | 1.140 | 1.040 |
| | (0.153) | (0.151) | (0.271) | (0.307) |
| ln JDIST | −0.022 | −0.166 | 0.354 | −0.093 |
| | (0.027) | (0.012) | (0.045) | (0.028) |
| DR1:W. Europe | −0.376 | | −0.943 | |
| | (0.166) | | (0.254) | |
| DR2:C. America | −0.105 | | −1.423 | |
| | (0.350) | | (0.568) | |
| DR3:S. America | −0.775 | | −3.167 | |
| | (0.229) | | (0.362) | |
| DR4:Middle East | −0.935 | | −4.513 | |
| | (0.236) | | (0.518) | |
| DR5:E. Asia | 1.774 | | 4.102 | |
| | (0.295) | | (0.495) | |
| DR6:S. Asia | −0.185 | | −1.471 | |
| | (0.312) | | (0.565) | |
| DR7:Africa | −0.842 | | −2.855 | |
| | (0.249) | | (0.383) | |
| DR8:Oceania | 0.525 | | 2.075 | |
| | (0.180) | | (0.327) | |

*Equation:* $\ln(a + V) = \max\,[Z'b + u, \ln a]$.

*Notes:* Numbers in parentheses are Eicker-White standard errors. Time dummies (DT1–DT5) are included in all regressions. $Z' = \{C$, constant; POP, population; YPC, per capita GNP; DEN, density; HK, human capital; JDIST, distance from Japan; DR1–DR8, region dummies$\}$.

Because of the intercepts $a_V$, the coefficients $\alpha_V$, $\beta_V$, $\beta'_V$, $\gamma_V$, $\epsilon_V$, and $\eta_V$ converge only asymptotically to the elasticity of the dependent variable with respect to the corresponding independent variable as the independent variable approaches infinity. Table 2.4 reports the actual elasticities calculated at the mean values of the dependent variables.

**Table 2.3** **United States: Trade and Investment Equations (maximum likelihood, Tobit estimates)**

| | V = Export | | V = DFI Out | |
|---|---|---|---|---|
| Variable | (1) | (2) | (3) | (4) |
| *N* | 456 | 456 | 456 | 456 |
| Log-likelihood | −3,333.44 | −3,461.19 | −3,341.37 | −3,418.73 |
| *a* | 3.648 | 0.947 | 8.176 | 8.438 |
| | (0.782) | (0.434) | (1.661) | (2.057) |
| *C* | −0.819 | −23.623 | 13.116 | 4.862 |
| | (3.631) | (4.599) | (6.239) | (6.569) |
| ln POP | 0.746 | 0.778 | 0.927 | 0.828 |
| | (0.027) | (0.033) | (0.055) | (0.054) |
| ln YPC | −0.944 | 3.537 | −5.022 | −3.285 |
| | (0.808) | (1.023) | (1.405) | (1.457) |
| $(\ln \text{YPC})^2$ | 0.120 | −0.118 | 0.339 | 0.251 |
| | (0.045) | (0.056) | (0.078) | (0.079) |
| ln DEN | 0.087 | 0.138 | 0.108 | 0.055 |
| | (0.029) | (0.036) | (0.053) | (0.050) |
| ln HK | 0.378 | 0.395 | 1.368 | 1.428 |
| | (0.118) | (0.141) | (0.281) | (0.288) |
| ln UDIST | −0.129 | −0.069 | −0.055 | −0.055 |
| | (0.016) | (0.014) | (0.031) | (0.020) |
| DR1:W. Europe | −1.305 | | −0.974 | |
| | (0.180) | | (0.319) | |
| DR2:C. America | −0.632 | | 0.002 | |
| | (0.198) | | (0.414) | |
| DR3:S. America | −1.102 | | −0.546 | |
| | (0.169) | | (0.332) | |
| DR4:Middle East | −0.995 | | −2.909 | |
| | (0.356) | | (0.666) | |
| DR5:E. Asia | 0.528 | | 0.022 | |
| | (0.255) | | (0.507) | |
| DR6:S. Asia | −1.241 | | −2.890 | |
| | (0.274) | | (0.550) | |
| DR7:Africa | −1.319 | | −1.222 | |
| | (0.210) | | (0.508) | |
| DR8:Oceania | 0.109 | | 0.904 | |
| | (0.269) | | (0.540) | |
| DR10:Japan | 0.123 | | −1.003 | |
| | (0.209) | | (0.378) | |

*Equation:* $\ln (a + V) = \max [Z'b + u, \ln a]$.

*Notes:* Numbers in parentheses are Eicker-White standard errors. Time dummies (DT1–DT5) are included in all regressions. $Z' = \{C$, constant; POP, population; YPC, per capita GNP; DEN, density; HK, human capital; UDIST, distance from United States; DR1–DR8, DR10, region dummies$\}$.

**Table 2.4** **Trade and Investment Elasticities**

| | With Region Dummies | | Without Region Dummies | |
|---|---|---|---|---|
| | Export | DFI Out | Export | DFI Out |
| Japan | | | | |
| Population | 0.715 | 0.837 | 0.699 | 0.780 |
| Income per worker | 1.085 | 0.583 | 1.056 | 0.854 |
| Density | 0.053 | −0.050 | 0.106 | −0.046 |
| Human capital | 0.729 | 1.141 | 0.754 | 1.041 |
| Distance from Japan | −0.022 | 0.354 | −0.166 | −0.093 |
| United States | | | | |
| Population | 0.747 | 0.929 | 0.778 | 0.830 |
| Income per worker | 1.225 | 1.110 | 1.397 | 1.259 |
| Density | 0.087 | 0.108 | 0.138 | 0.055 |
| Human capital | 0.378 | 1.371 | 0.395 | 1.432 |
| Distance from U.S. | −0.130 | −0.055 | −0.069 | −0.055 |

### 2.3.2 Results

We discuss effects of population, per capita income, factor endowments, and distance in turn.

*Population*

Consistent with the theory we find that population has a nonhomogeneous effect both on exports and DFI. Moreover, consistent with the model we find that the population elasticity for imports tends to be lower than that for DFI, so that large countries do tend to receive more DFI than exports compared with small countries. While our estimates of population elasticities for exports are less than 1, as our theory would predict, they are also less than 1 for DFI, in contrast with what our theoretical model predicted. The results thus suggest that larger countries are more closed overall than smaller countries, but relatively less closed to DFI than to exports.

*Per Capita Income*

The U.S. results confirm the model's prediction of an elasticity of exports with respect to the level of development above 1. The elasticity for Japan is very close to 1, however. Our estimates imply that increases in relative per capita income increase DFI at an accelerating rate. The effect on exports differs between the Japan and the United States, however. The effect of income per capita on imports from Japan also tends to accelerate, while its effect on imports from the United States is sensitive to the inclusion of region dummies. Figures 2.1*A* and 2.1*B* illustrate (for Japan) and 2.2*A* and 2.2*B* (for the United States) the effects of increases in the destination country's income per capita on DFI and exports from the two countries, with and without the inclusion of regional dummies. A rough impression is that, for Japan, exports tend to replace DFI as income grows, with the opposite the case for the United States. This result suggests that Japan's cost of DFI tends to be relatively lower in poor countries compared with the United States.

*Factor Endowments*

We find that increased density acts to increase exports from both countries. An explanation is that, given per capita income, countries with less in the way of natural resources absorb more technology from the two countries and hence import more. We find less tendency for more densely populated countries to absorb more DFI. In the case of Japanese DFI the relationship is negative. One explanation, not accounted for in our theoretical model, is that some Japanese DFI is undertaken to exploit natural resources.

Increases in human capital have a significant effect on both exports and DFI from both countries, suggesting that once other factors are taken into account, countries with more human capital tend to absorb more technology from Japan and the United States. Moreover, the elasticity with respect to DFI is much larger than with respect to exports. A plausible explanation consistent with our model is that a high level of human capital reduces the fixed cost of undertaking DFI.

*Distance*

The effects of distance on exports and DFI, unlike the effects of most of our other explanatory variables, are quite sensitive to the inclusion of regional effects. This sensitivity is not surprising given the multicolinearity between the two. We find, however, that distance always has an inhibiting effect on exports (as a standard gravity specification would predict). Moreover, as our model would predict, distance reduces trade more than it reduces DFI. Except for the case of Japan, when regional dummies are included, we find that distance also tends to inhibit DFI, but by less than it inhibits exports. Hence Japan and the United States tend to trade relatively more close by and to invest relatively more far away.[7]

*Regional Effects*

Eaton and Tamura (1994) discuss the regional concentration of Japanese and U.S. trade and DFI patterns. This earlier work did not include distance as a separate explanatory variable, incorporating the effect of distance through the regional effects. A primary finding there was that, correcting for size, per capita income, and factor endowments, Japan imported more from the United

7. Brainard (1993a, 1993b) provides evidence on the role of distance in trade and DFI decisions from firm-level data. She also finds a tendency for firms to rely more on domestic production than on exports to serve more distant markets.

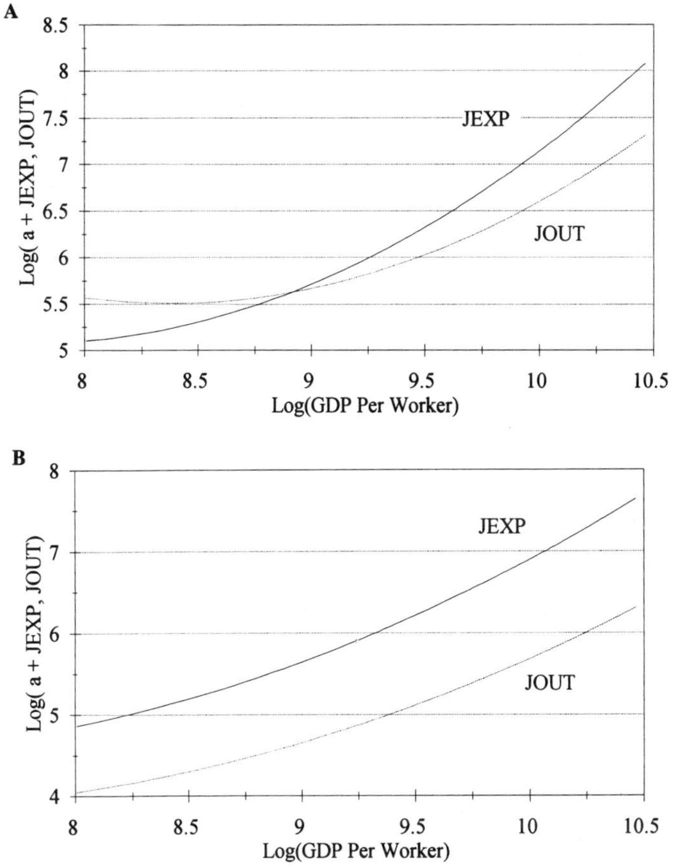


**Fig. 2.1 Japan regression: export and DFI out (*A*) with region dummies and (*B*) without region dummies**

States than the typical country in Western Europe. Our results here strengthen this finding significantly. We find that, once distance as well as these other factors are taken into account, Japan imports more from the United States than any other region except East Asia, including not only Western Europe but North and Central America as well. We still find Japan to be more closed than Western Europe to U.S. DFI, but only slightly so. We also continue to find Oceania and East Asia to be highly open to both exports and DFI from both countries.

## 2.4 Conclusion

Japan and the United States are not only the two largest economies in the world; measures of research activity and patenting indicate that they are also

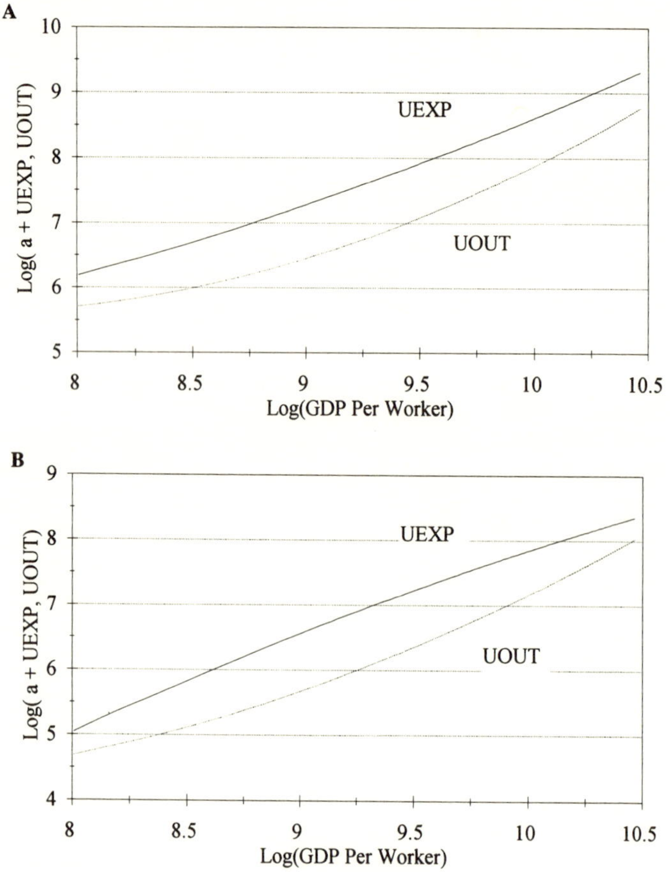


**Fig. 2.2 U.S. regression: export and DFI out (*A*) with region dummies and (*B*) without region dummies**

the two largest sources of technological innovation in the world. Exports and DFI are two major conduits for transferring technology abroad.

In this paper we have developed a simple model for the decision whether to exploit a technology abroad via export or via DFI. The model points to country size, technological sophistication, and distance as important factors. Moreover, it suggests that the effects of these variables may be not only nonhomogeneous but nonmonotonic as well.

We use the model as a basis for specifying a model of Japanese and U.S. export and DFI patterns around the world. The implications of some but not all aspects of the model are confirmed. We do find, for example, that the importance of DFI relative to exports tends to grow with country size, but that DFI as well as exports tend to increase less than in proportion to country size while our model predicts that DFI should increase more than in proportion. Consistent with our model we also find that distance tends to inhibit DFI much less than it inhibits exports. Both Japan and the United States tend to export relatively more close by and to invest relatively more far away. The model predicts that the relationship between exports and DFI, on the one hand, and a country's ability to absorb technology, on the other, can be very nonmonotonic. We find some tendency for Japanese exports to rise relative to DFI as countries become more advanced, with U.S. exports and DFI exhibiting the opposite tendency.

A striking finding, reinforcing a major result in Eaton and Tamura (1994), is that Japan is relatively open to U.S. exports compared with other regions of the world, taking into account size, income, and factor endowments. Here we find that taking distance into account sharply accentuates this result: once distance as well as these other factors are corrected for Japan is more open to U.S. exports than any region except East Asia.

Our empirical work has focused very narrowly on exports and DFI, taking the background of innovation and diffusion as given. A task for future research is the integration of the issues considered here with an analysis of the factors determining the rate of innovation in the world economy.

# Appendix

**Table 2A.1** **Region Definitions and Samples**

| | |
|---|---|
| **North America** | |
| United States | (Japan) |
| Canada | (Japan, U.S.) |
| Mexico | (Japan, U.S.) |
| **Western Europe** | |
| United Kingdom | (Japan, U.S.) |
| Austria | (Japan, U.S.) |
| Belgium-Luxembourg | (Japan, U.S.) |
| Denmark | (Japan, U.S.) |
| France | (Japan, U.S.) |
| Germany | (Japan, U.S.) |
| Italy | (Japan, U.S.) |
| Netherlands | (Japan, U.S.) |
| Norway | (Japan, U.S.) |
| Sweden | (Japan, U.S.) |
| Finland | (Japan, U.S.) |
| Greece | (Japan, U.S.) |
| Iceland | (Japan, U.S.) |
| Ireland | (Japan, U.S.) |
| Portugal | (Japan, U.S.) |
| Spain | (Japan, U.S.) |
| Turkey | (Japan, U.S.) |
| **Central America** | |
| Costa Rica | (Japan, U.S.) |
| Dominican Republic | (U.S.) |
| El Salvador | (Japan, U.S.) |
| Guatemala | (Japan, U.S.) |
| Honduras | (Japan, U.S.) |
| Panama | (Japan, U.S.) |
| Trinidad and Tobago | (Japan, U.S.) |
| **South America** | |
| Argentina | (Japan, U.S.) |
| Bolivia | (Japan, U.S.) |
| Brazil | (Japan, U.S.) |
| Chile | (Japan, U.S.) |
| Colombia | (Japan, U.S.) |
| Ecuador | (Japan, U.S.) |
| Paraguay | (Japan, U.S.) |
| Peru | (Japan, U.S.) |
| Uruguay | (Japan, U.S.) |
| Venezuela | (Japan, U.S.) |
| Guyana | |

*(continued)*

**Table 2A.1** (continued)

| | | | |
|---|---|---|---|
| **Middle East** | | Ivory Coast | (Japan, U.S.) |
| Israel | (Japan, U.S.) | Kenya | (Japan, U.S.) |
| Jordan | (Japan, U.S.) | Madagascar | (Japan, U.S.) |
| Syria | (Japan, U.S.) | Malawi | (U.S.) |
| Egypt | (Japan, U.S.) | Mauritania | (Japan) |
| **East Asia** | | Mauritius | (U.S.) |
| Taiwan | (Japan, U.S.) | Morocco | (Japan, U.S.) |
| Hong Kong | (Japan, U.S.) | Mozambique | (Japan, U.S.) |
| Indonesia | (Japan, U.S.) | Nigeria | (Japan, U.S.) |
| Korea | (Japan, U.S.) | Zimbabwe | (U.S.) |
| Malaysia | (Japan, U.S.) | Rwanda | (Japan, U.S.) |
| Philippines | (Japan, U.S.) | Senegal | (Japan, U.S.) |
| Singapore | (Japan, U.S.) | Sierra Leone | (U.S.) |
| Thailand | (Japan, U.S.) | Sudan | (Japan, U.S.) |
| **South Asia** | | Tunisia | (Japan, U.S.) |
| Bangladesh | (Japan, U.S.) | Burkina Faso | (Japan) |
| India | (Japan, U.S.) | Zambia | (Japan, U.S.) |
| Pakistan | (Japan, U.S.) | **Oceania** | |
| **Africa** | | Australia | (Japan, U.S.) |
| Algeria | (U.S.) | New Zealand | (Japan, U.S.) |
| Burundi | (U.S.) | Fiji | (Japan) |
| Cameroon | (Japan, U.S.) | Papua New Guinea | (Japan, U.S.) |
| Central African Republic | (U.S.) | **Japan** | |
| Gabon | (Japan, U.S.) | Japan | (U.S.) |
| Gambia | (Japan) | | |

*Note:* Sample(s) in which country is included given in parentheses.

**Table 2A.2** **Distance Data in the Sample**

| Country | City | JDIST[a] | UDIST[b] |
|---|---|---|---|
| United States | Chicago | 10,140 | 0 |
| United Kingdom | London | 9,562 | 6,378 |
| Austria | Vienna | 9,131 | 7,553 |
| Belgium | Brussels | 9,456 | 6,678 |
| Denmark | Copenhagen | 8,696 | 6,855 |
| France | Paris | 9,717 | 6,677 |
| Germany, West | West Berlin | 8,933 | 7,098 |
| Italy | Rome | 9,864 | 7,770 |
| Netherlands | Amsterdam | 9,292 | 6,624 |
| Norway | Oslo | 8,664 | 6,685 |
| Sweden | Stockholm | 8,173 | 6,895 |
| Canada | Ottawa | 10,333 | 1,049 |
| Japan | Tokyo | 0 | 10,140 |
| Finland | Helsinki | 7,824 | 7,143 |
| Greece | Athens | 9,515 | 8,761 |
| Iceland | Reykjavik | 8,800 | 4,769 |
| Ireland | Dublin | 9,591 | 5,899 |
| Portugal | Lisbon | 11,150 | 6,438 |

Table 2A.2 (continued)

| Country | City | JDIST[a] | UDIST[b] |
|---|---|---|---|
| Spain | Madrid | 10,768 | 6,742 |
| Turkey | Ankara | 8,768 | 9,137 |
| Australia | Canberra | 7,955 | 15,106 |
| New Zealand | Wellington | 9,275 | 13,440 |
| Argentina | Buenos Aires | 18,359 | 9,003 |
| Bolivia | La Paz | 16,533 | 6,789 |
| Brazil | Brasilia | 17,686 | 7,602 |
| Chile | Santiago | 17,230 | 8,547 |
| Colombia | Bogota | 14,306 | 4,340 |
| Costa Rica | San Jose | 13,171 | 3,560 |
| Dominican Republic | Santo Domingo | 13,233 | 3,094 |
| Ecuador | Quito | 14,430 | 4,754 |
| El Salvador | San Salvador | 12,493 | 3,126 |
| Guatemala | Guatemala City | 12,323 | 3,033 |
| Honduras | Tegucigalpa | 12,601 | 3,081 |
| Mexico | Mexico City | 11,309 | 2,705 |
| Panama | Panama | 13,547 | 3,707 |
| Paraguay | Asuncion | 18,007 | 8,083 |
| Peru | Lima | 15,492 | 6,091 |
| Uruguay | Montevideo | 18,570 | 9,112 |
| Venezuela | Caracas | 14,169 | 4,028 |
| Guyana | Georgetown | 12,522 | 2,568 |
| Trinidad and Tobago | Port-of-Spain | 14,402 | 4,302 |
| Israel | Jerusalem | 9,155 | 9,972 |
| Jordan | Amman | 9,085 | 10,001 |
| Syria | Damascus | 8,956 | 9,887 |
| Egypt | Cairo | 9,578 | 9,899 |
| Bangladesh | Dacca | 4,897 | 12,727 |
| Taiwan | Taipei | 2,105 | 11,998 |
| Hong Kong | Hong Kong | 2,886 | 12,546 |
| India | New Delhi | 5,848 | 12,043 |
| Indonesia | Jakarta | 5,789 | 15,807 |
| Korea, Republic of | Seoul | 1,164 | 10,525 |
| Malaysia | Kuala Lumpur | 5,330 | 14,938 |
| Pakistan | Islamabad | 5,977 | 11,404 |
| Philippines | Manila | 3,007 | 13,099 |
| Singapore | Singapore | 5,325 | 15,089 |
| Thailand | Bangkok | 4,612 | 13,788 |
| Algeria | Algiers | 10,806 | 7,454 |
| Burundi | Bujumbura | 12,070 | 12,480 |
| Cameroon | Yaounde | 13,071 | 10,488 |
| Central African Republic | Bangui | 12,461 | 11,022 |
| Gabon | Libreville | 13,509 | 10,577 |
| Gambia | Banjul | 14,030 | 7,463 |
| Ivory Coast | Abidjan | 14,099 | 9,097 |
| Kenya | Nairobi | 11,262 | 12,896 |
| Madagascar | Antananarivo | 11,416 | 15,109 |

(*continued*)

**Table 2A.2** (continued)

| Country | City | JDIST[a] | UDIST[b] |
|---|---|---|---|
| Malawi | Lilongwe | 12,339 | 13,643 |
| Mauritania | Nouakchott | 13,498 | 7,217 |
| Mauritius | Port Louis | 10,639 | 15,971 |
| Morocco | Casablanca | 11,604 | 6,853 |
| Mozambique | Maputo | 13,135 | 14,358 |
| Nigeria | Lagos | 13,485 | 9,628 |
| Zimbabwe | Harae | 12,813 | 13,698 |
| Rwanda | Kigali | 11,907 | 12,427 |
| Senegal | Dakar | 13,926 | 7,300 |
| Sierra Leone | Freetown | 14,337 | 8,094 |
| Sudan | Khartoum | 10,486 | 11,183 |
| Tunisia | Tunis | 10,425 | 7,959 |
| Burkina Faso | Ouagadougou | 13,304 | 8,788 |
| Zambia | Lusaka | 12,924 | 13,296 |
| Fiji | Suva | 7,240 | 11,650 |
| Papua New Guinea | Port Moresby | 5,083 | 13,590 |

[a]Distance from Japan (Tokyo) in kilometers.
[b]Distance from United States (Chicago) in kilometers.

**Table 2A.3** **Data Sources**

| Variable | Source |
|---|---|
| Exports | *Direction of Trade Statistics Yearbook* (Washington, D.C.: International Monetary Fund, various issues) |
| DFI out | |
| Japan | *Zaisei-Kinyu Tokei Geppou* (Fiscal/Financial Statistics Monthly) (Tokyo: Ministry of Finance, various issues) |
| United States | *Survey of Current Business* (Washington, D.C.: Department of Commerce, various issues) |
| Population | Penn World Table (Mark 5.6) (see Summers and Heston 1991) |
| GDP per capita | Penn World Table (Mark 5.6) (see Summers and Heston 1991) |
| Surface area | *Statistical Yearbook* (New York: Statistical Office United Nations, various issues) |
| Human capital | Kyriacou (1991) |
| Distance (from Tokyo; from Chicago) | Software Toolworks World Atlas v. 5.0 (The Software Toolworks Inc.) |

# References

Brainard, S. Lael. 1993a. An empirical assessment of the factor proportions explanation of multinational sales. NBER Working Paper no. 4583. Cambridge, Mass.: National Bureau of Economic Research.

———. 1993b. An empirical assessment of the proximity-concentration tradeoff between multinational sales and trade. NBER Working Paper no. 4580. Cambridge, Mass.: National Bureau of Economic Research.

Deardorff, Alan V. 1984. Testing trade theories and predicting trade flows. In *The handbook of international economics,* ed. Ronald W. Jones and Peter B. Kenen. Amsterdam: North-Holland.

Dixit, Avinash, and Joseph E. Stiglitz. 1977. Monopolistic competition and optimum product diversity. *American Economic Review* 67:297–308.

Drysdale, Peter, and Ross Garnaut. 1982. Trade intensities and the analysis of bilateral trade flows in a many-country world: A survey. *Hitotsubashi Journal of Economics* 22:62–84.

Eaton, Jonathan, and Samuel Kortum. 1994. International patenting and technology diffusion. NBER Working Paper no. 4931. Cambridge, Mass.: National Bureau of Economic Research.

Eaton, Jonathan, and Akiko Tamura. 1994. Bilateralism and regionalism in Japanese and U.S. trade and direct foreign investment patterns. *Journal of the Japanese and International Economies* 8:478–510.

Frankel, Jeffrey A., and Shang-Jin Wei. 1993. Trade blocs and currency blocs. NBER Working Paper no. 4335. Cambridge, Mass.: National Bureau of Economic Research.

Grossman, Gene M., and Elhanan Helpman. 1991. *Innovation and growth in the world economy.* Cambridge: MIT Press.

Helpman, Elhanan. 1984. A simple theory of international trade with multinational corporations. *Journal of Political Economy* 92:451–71.

———. 1987. Imperfect competition and international trade: Evidence from fourteen industrial countries. *Journal of the Japanese and International Economies* 1:62–81.

Krugman, Paul R. 1979. A model of innovation, technology transfer, and the world distribution of income. *Journal of Political Economy* 87:253–66.

Kyriacou, George. 1991. Level and growth effects of human capital. C. V. Starr Center Working Paper no. 91–26. New York: New York University.

Leamer, Edward E. 1974. The commodity composition of international trade in manufactures. *Oxford Economic Papers,* Ser. C 26:350–74.

———. 1984. *Sources of international comparative advantage.* Cambridge: MIT Press.

Markusen, James R. 1983. Factor trade and commodity trade as complements. *Journal of International Economics* 15:341–56.

———. 1984. Multinational, multi-plant economies, and the gains from trade. *Journal of International Economics* 16:205–26.

Mundell, Robert A. 1957. International trade and factor mobility. *American Economic Review* 47:321–37.

Poyhonen, Pentti. 1963. A tentative model for the volume of trade between countries. *Weltwirtschaftliches Archiv* 90:93–99.

Purvis, Douglas D. 1972. Technology, trade, and factor mobility. *Economic Journal* 82:991–99.

Summers, Robert, and Alan Heston. 1991. The Penn World Tables (Mark 5): An expanded set of international comparisons, 1950–1988. *Quarterly Journal of Economics* 106:327–69.

Tinbergen, Jan. 1962. Shaping the world economy: Suggestions for an international policy. New York: Twentieth Century Fund.
White, Halbert. 1982. Maximum likelihood estimation of misspecified models. *Econometrica* 50:1–26.

## Comment Chong-Hyun Nam

This is an excellent piece of empirical work. The empirical part of the paper relies on a rich set of data, and estimation results by and large confirm commonsense expectations. The highlight is Eaton and Tamura's confirmation that country characteristics such as population, income level, land abundance, human capital, and locational distance are all important determinants not only of bilateral trade flows but also of bilateral direct foreign investment. The paper also develops a simple model to determine whether a country will grow as a capital importer or exporter. I have only a couple of short comments on the paper: one concerns the structure of the estimated equations, and the other concerns interpretation of some estimation results.

First, I felt that it would have been very useful if Eaton and Tamura had explained at the outset why the estimation equations were constructed as shown in the paper and, in particular, why the same structural equation could be used for explaining both bilateral trade flows and bilateral direct foreign investment flows.

In estimating bilateral trade flows, the paper seems to have included most of the important explanatory variables, but they may not be sufficient. For instance, it seems that some price variables, such as exchange rates, and some protection measures may also work as good explanatory variables for bilateral trade flows.

As for bilateral direct foreign investment flows, still more explanatory variables may be conceivable, depending on the purpose of direct foreign investment. For instance, Korea's outbound direct foreign investment is often intended to take advantage of wage rate differentials, to circumvent protection measures, or to develop and secure a stable supply of raw materials. So, it may be worthwhile to examine some variables or proxies corresponding to these purposes.

Second, the elasticity of export or import with respect to a country's population size was estimated to be significantly less than 1. Eaton and Tamura conjecture that this is so because large countries tend to be more protectionist than small countries. They further argue that if this conjecture is correct, an implication is that the formation of a trading bloc would mean less trade be-

Chong-Hyun Nam is professor of economics at Korea University.

tween the member countries in the bloc collectively and Japan or the United States.

I am not convinced by this line of argument. First, I do not find any strong a priori reasons to believe large countries would tend to be more protectionist than small countries, or vice versa. Instead, the low trade elasticity with respect to country size could be more due to the fact that largeness in economic size allows greater exploitation of scale economies in production and a greater degree of economies of scope in products which leads to lower trade elasticity. I also think that the mere formation of a trading bloc would not necessarily reduce trade between the bloc and another country outside the bloc, unless the member countries of the bloc become more protectionistic against outsiders than before the bloc was formed.

## Comment V. V. Bhanoji Rao

Eaton and Tamura's paper is very rich in statistical results. However, it appears to be somewhat unfinished because in many instances there is insufficient interpretation and explanation, as my comments below will indicate. I follow the headings in section 2.3 of the Eaton-Tamura paper for my comments.

### Econometric Specification and Variables

To explain the bilateral trade and investment of Japan and the United States with a number of countries in the Asia-Pacific region, the variables used are: population of the country, per capita income, population density, years of schooling of an average worker, distance between Japan or the United States and the country, and time dummies. The selection of variables takes into account gravity models and factor intensity explanations of trade flows. One cannot but agree with the selection of variables in regard to explaining trade flows. The paper, however, lacks a discussion of the applicability of these variables to investment flows. Such a discussion would greatly improve the authority and authenticity of the paper.

Factor endowments are proxied by per capita income (proxy for capital-labor ratio), population density (proxy for labor-land ratio), and the average years of schooling of the labor force (human capital). Since the last variable, in fact, refers to the quality of the labor force, we have here capital intensity, land intensity, and quality intensity of labor. Is there some anomaly here? What is the rationale for this special treatment of labor? An explanation is needed.

As for the methodology, it would be useful to provide a short explanatory

V. V. Bhanoji Rao is associate professor of economics and senior fellow (Public Policy Programme) at the National University of Singapore.

statement on why the maximum likelihood method is preferred to standard regression analysis.

**Results**

*Population.* Trade elasticities with respect to population are less than unity indicating that small countries are relatively more and large countries relatively less trade oriented. According to the authors, "The results thus suggest that larger countries are more closed overall than smaller countries." A more important explanation may be that large countries, by virtue of their market size, find that a wide variety of enterprises are viable in catering to domestic demands. This is the case of natural import substitution that goes on all the time. Furthermore, in the case of commodities where the large countries in the region may have a comparative advantage (e.g., rice, sugar, and textiles), it may be that protectionism in Japan and the United States is the real factor behind the relatively low trade elasticities. The authors should build into their explanation all the plausible factors rather than limit themselves to just one.

Eaton and Tamura also found that the larger countries tend to have relatively lower per capita direct foreign investment (DFI) from either Japan or the United States. This is also explained by the suggestion that large countries are more closed than small countries. The authors should recognize that in some instances, protectionism may lead to greater DFI to tap the domestic markets (e.g., the automobile sector in Indonesia), although this is not what is implied by their results. The authors should also examine more closely whether population size matters at all in regard to *per capita* DFI flows.

*Per capita income.* With reference to per capita income, Japan's export elasticities are slightly higher than the U.S. elasticities. Both countries, however, have either unitary or higher than unitary elasticities. DFI elasticities have the same pattern as the export elasticities. On the import side, Japan's elasticities are lower than the U.S. elasticities and somewhat lower than unity. Interpreting these patterns, the authors note that Japan buys more from poor countries and sells more to rich countries. In regard to DFI elasticities, which are close to 1 or greater than 1, the differences between Japan and the United States are relatively less pronounced, though Japan's DFI elasticities are slightly higher than the U.S. elasticities. Japan, thus, tends to invest more in and export more to countries with relatively higher per capita purchasing power. Could it be because foreign policy and human rights considerations play a relatively larger role in U.S. trade and investment policies? There is a need to probe into and explain the patterns of the elasticities and expand the discussion.

*Factor endowments.* The authors' finding is that land-scarce Japan tends to import significantly less from high-density countries, while the land-abundant United States tends to import more from such countries. This finding is in accordance with a priori expectations. Both the United States and Japan, however, tend to export to countries with greater population densities. This finding has been left unexplained.

The authors note that a high level of education in a country significantly reduces Japan's involvement in any form with that country. This finding too requires some explanation.

*Distance.* The findings confirm that distance inhibits trade. The interesting findings, however, are that U.S. trade is more inhibited by distance than Japan's and that distance also inhibits U.S. DFI, but not Japanese DFI. Could it be that the findings are evidence of the Japanese drive for markets and investment outlets in contrast to the historical U.S. drive to promote political and other noneconomic interests? The paper should add a brief explanatory statement.

## Concluding Observation

The Eaton-Tamura paper in its present form remains a statistical exercise on the determinants of the trading and investment relationships of Japan and the United States individually with a group of countries. The paper's use and significance would have been greatly enhanced if the authors had interpreted and explained the results and drawn useful policy conclusions, if any.

# 3 Foreign Direct Investment in China: Sources and Consequences

Shang-Jin Wei

Whether it is a white cat or a black cat, it is a good one if it catches mice.

Deng Xiaoping

## 3.1 Introduction

China used to be one of the most closed economies in terms of policy toward foreign investment and external debt. Starting from virtually no foreign-owned firms on Chinese soil before 1979, China has now become one of the largest developing host countries for foreign investment with the flow of foreign direct investment (FDI) reaching $26 billion (U.S.) in 1993 (China State Statistics Bureau 1994). This dramatic change is part of the overall Chinese effort that began about 15 years ago to reform the economic system and open up to the outside world. The credo of Deng Xiaoping (and his comrades) is measured pragmatism, as the epigraph indicates. Foreign investors may have greed as their motive, but they are welcome in China nevertheless, as long as their presence helps China to grow.

This paper has two objectives. First, it seeks to examine FDI in China from an international perspective. In particular, it asks whether China has received "enough" FDI from major source countries after controlling for key economic characteristics. Second, the paper studies several consequences of FDI in China, particularly FDI's contribution to China's rapid growth, its exports, and its reform effort.

The paper is organized as follows: In section 3.2, I provide an overview of foreign-invested firms in China. In section 3.3, I attempt to put China's hosting of FDI in an international perspective. Using data on outward investment from the five largest source countries, I estimate the average amount of FDI in a host country as a function of several economic characteristics. China's actual receipt of investment from these countries is compared with the model predic-

Shang-Jin Wei is assistant professor of public policy at the Kennedy School of Government, Harvard University, and a faculty research fellow of the National Bureau of Economic Research.

The author thanks Chen Huaxuen, Esther Drill, and especially Jungshik Kim for efficient research and editorial assistance. The author also thanks Jeffrey Frankel, Pakorn Vichyanond, Wing Thye Woo, and seminar participants for thoughtful comments. The author alone is responsible for any errors that remain.

tion. In section 3.4, I examine several economic consequences of FDI in the Chinese economy. A data set covering 434 cities over 1988–90 is employed to quantify these effects. Section 3.5 concludes the paper.

## 3.2 General Features of Foreign Investment in China

Before 1979, virtually no foreign-owned firms operated in China, nor did China have many external loans. Chinese leaders used to take pride in this fact. Indeed, even foreign aid volunteered by foreign governments or international organizations was viewed with suspicion. For example, after the great 1976 earthquake in Tangshang (which registered about 8 on the Richter scale and caused millions of deaths), the Chinese government refused an aid offer from the International Red Cross. This attitude toward foreign money took a dramatic turn in 1979 when Deng Xiaoping introduced economic reform and initiated the "open door policy."

Several factors contributed to this change. Two primary ones are (1) the disastrous economic performance under rigid central planning before 1979 and (2) the glittering examples of Japan and the four Asian "tigers," particularly Hong Kong and Taiwan.

Foreign capital going into China mainly takes the form of loans. In 1991, the value of FDI was slightly more than 60 percent of that of loans. Over the period 1990–91, the single fastest growing item in non-FDI foreign capital inflow was, in fact, portfolio investment (Chinese bonds and equities purchased by foreigners). The growth rate was 3,551.5 percent. This is probably not as astonishing as it may sound because China started from an extremely low position. Even with that exponential growth, the total amount of bonds and equities issued in 1991 was only $108.45 million.

This paper focuses on the sources and economic consequences of direct investment. Two types of data on direct investment are typically reported in Chinese statistics: contractual value and realized amount. "Contractual value" is supposedly the amount foreign investors plan or intend to invest in China (over a period of time) at the time the investment application is approved by the Chinese government. The actual investment is not bound by this contractual amount and is typically much smaller. Indeed, the reported contractual amount may even inflate the planned or intended investment because local government officials may have an incentive to announce (or to lure foreign investors to agree on) a large number. For all practical purposes, only the realized amount, or what is sometimes called "actual utilization," is economically meaningful. All data on foreign investment below will be realized values unless noted otherwise.

The growth of FDI in China truly has been exponential (table 3.1). During 1979–81, the average annual inflow of FDI (excluding "compensation trade" and export processing) was less than $0.25 billion (Kueh 1992, table 2b). By 1991, the total amount of realized FDI in China was already $4.37 billion. And the realized foreign capital in 1992 and 1993 reached $19.2 billion and $36.7

**Table 3.1** **Realized FDI in China, 1983–93 (billion U.S. dollars)**

| Year | China | All Developing Countries |
|---|---|---|
| 1983 | 0.64 | 16.29 |
| 1984 | 1.26 | 16.13 |
| 1985 | 1.66 | 12.25 |
| 1986 | 1.88 | 13.24 |
| 1987 | 2.31 | 18.33 |
| 1988 | 3.19 | 25.33 |
| 1989 | 3.39 | 31.13 |
| 1990 | 3.49 | 28.65 |
| 1991 | 4.37 | – |
| 1992 | 11.20 | – |
| 1993 | 25.76 | – |

*Sources:* Data for 1983–90 are from Amirahmadi and Wu (1994, table 2); the original source that the authors cite is *Balance of Payment Statistics Yearbook* (Washington, D.C.: International Monetary Fund, 1990 and 1991). Data for 1991–93 are from China State Statistics Bureau (1994).

billion, respectively; the one-year growth rate was 91.5 percent. The realized FDI in these two years was $11.2 billion and $25.76 billion, respectively, with a growth rate of 130 percent. By the end of 1993, the total number of registered foreign-invested/managed firms reached 167,500, of which 83,100 (or 49.6 percent of the total) were newly established in 1993 (China State Statistics Bureau 1994).

Foreign direct investment takes one of the following four forms: equity joint ventures, contractual joint ventures, wholly owned foreign firms, and joint exploration (mainly for offshore oil). The values of the four forms of FDI during 1990–91 are reported in table 3.2. In terms of percentage shares of total value in 1991, joint ventures and wholly owned foreign firms accounted for the lion's shares of FDI (52.7 and 26.0 percent, respectively). The wholly owned foreign firm has been the fastest growing form of FDI in recent years. In 1991, it had grown 66.10 percent over the 1990 value, after having a growth rate of 83.93 percent in 1990 over 1989.

In Chinese statistics, there is a third category of foreign capital aside from loans and FDI. The third category, called "other foreign investment" in official statistics, has three subcategories: leasing, compensation trade, and export processing/assembly. The values of these categories in 1991 were $6.89 million, $208.25 million, and $85.13 million, respectively. Altogether, other foreign investment is about 7 percent (300.27/4,366.34) as large as FDI. The biggest subcategory of the three, compensation trade, in which foreign firms provide machines or product designs to Chinese firms and obtain part of the output as payment, is no longer as popular as it was at the beginning of the open door policy reform.[1]

1. See Kueh (1992) for an analysis of the evolution of FDI in China up to 1990, and particularly for his summary of the role of foreign investment in the development of Chinese coastal areas.

**Table 3.2 Realized Foreign Capital Going into China, 1990–91 (million U.S. dollars)**

| | 1990 | | 1991 | |
|---|---|---|---|---|
| Capital | Amount | Change over 1989 (%) | Amount | Change over 1990 (%) |
| *Total* | 10,289.39 | 2.29 | 11,554.17 | 12.29 |
| *External loans* | 6,534.52 | 3.96 | 6,887.56 | 5.40 |
| Loans from foreign governments | 2,523.57 | 17.43 | 1,809.85 | −28.28 |
| Loans from international financial institutions | 1,065.59 | −1.73 | 1,364.77 | 28.08 |
| Export credit | 898.43 | 39.99 | 1,161.97 | 29.33 |
| Commercial bank loans | 2,043.96 | −9.94 | 2,442.52 | 19.50 |
| Bonds and equity shares issued abroad | 2.97 | −97.89 | 108.45 | 3,551.5[a] |
| *Direct foreign investment* | 3,487.11 | 2.79 | 4,366.34 | 25.21 |
| Joint ventures | 1,886.07 | −7.42 | 2,298.96 | 21.88 |
| Contractual joint ventures | 673.56 | −10.41 | 763.60 | 13.37 |
| Wholly owned foreign firms | 683.17 | 83.93 | 1,134.74 | 66.10 |
| Joint exploration | 244.31 | 5.22 | 169.04 | −30.81 |
| *Other foreign investment* | 267.76 | −29.70 | 300.27 | 12.14 |
| International leasing | 30.45 | −52.31 | 6.89 | −77.37 |
| Compensation trade | 158.74 | −39.25 | 208.25 | 31.19 |
| Export processing/assembly | 78.57 | 40.96 | 85.13 | 8.35 |

*Source:* China Ministry of Foreign Economic Relations and Trade (1992, 1993).

[a]The percentage change reported in the original source (551.52 percent) appears to be an error.

## 3.3 Sources of Foreign Investment from an International Perspective

This section discusses FDI in China from an international perspective. To accomplish this, I will first estimate a gravity-type model to establish a "norm" for inward investment from major source countries and then determine whether China is an underachiever or overachiever as a host to FDI from these countries.

Worldwide FDI more than doubled in nominal terms between 1975 and 1985, and quadrupled between 1980 and 1990 to reach a record high of $200 billion in 1989 and $234 billion in 1990 (United Nations 1992, 1993). To keep our discussion about FDI in China in perspective, we note that FDI is largely a "north-north" phenomenon. The developed countries accounted for 97 percent of all FDI outflows in the 1980s, reaching $226 billion in 1990. An overwhelming proportion of FDI also goes into developed countries. In terms of FDI inflows, the developed countries accounted for 83 percent in the 1985–90 period (United Nations 1993).

Of the FDI that does go into developing countries, the Asia-Pacific share has been increasing over time, from about 30 percent in 1980 to over 50 percent by 1989. In 1989, for example, of the $30 billion or so of FDI that went into the developing world, about $17 billion went into the Asia-Pacific region. Between 1980–82 and 1986–88, FDI had increased by a factor of three in the newly industrializing economies in the region and the ASEAN nations, and by a factor of 13 in China (United Nations 1992). The rapid increase in the case of China certainly reflects its originally low base.

The distribution of FDI in China in terms of major source countries for 1990–91 is summarized in table 3.3. In 1991, Hong Kong was the dominant supplier. Of the total FDI of $4.4 billion, Hong Kong contributed $2.4 billion, or about 55 percent. This is a typical pattern. Hong Kong's share in total FDI in China has been above 50 percent for all but one year since the beginning of the open door policy in 1979. One should note, however, that part of the reported Hong Kong investment is actually Taiwanese investment in disguise (to avoid political inconvenience with the Taiwanese government). Another (small) part of the reported Hong Kong investment is really mainland Chinese capital in disguise (to take advantage of the preferential treatment accorded to foreign capital by the mainland).

Japan is the second largest source country. With an investment of $532.50 million in 1991, it accounted for 12.2 percent of the total. The next two major

**Table 3.3 Source Country Distribution of FDI in China: Flow Data (million U.S. dollars)**

| Country | 1991 | 1990 |
|---|---|---|
| Total | 4,366.34 | 3,487.11 |
| Hong Kong | 2,405.25 | 1,880.00 |
| Japan | 532.50 | 503.38 |
| United States | 323.20 | 455.99 |
| Germany | 161.12 | 64.25 |
| Macao | 81.62 | 33.42 |
| Singapore | 58.21 | 50.43 |
| Britain | 35.39 | 13.33 |
| Italy | 28.21 | 4.10 |
| Thailand | 19.62 | 6.72 |
| Australia | 14.91 | 24.87 |
| Switzerland | 12.31 | 1.48 |
| Canada | 10.76 | 8.04 |
| France | 9.88 | 21.06 |
| Bermuda | 8.00 | – |
| Netherlands | 6.67 | 15.98 |
| Norway | 6.05 | 2.23 |
| Philippines | 5.85 | 1.67 |
| Panama | 3.56 | 6.76 |
| Ireland | 2.50 | – |
| Indonesia | 2.18 | 1.00 |
| Malaysia | 1.96 | 0.64 |

*Source:* China Ministry of Foreign Economic Relations and Trade (1993).

suppliers are the United States and Germany, accounting for 7.4 and 3.7 percent, respectively. It is worth noting that other East Asian economies, particularly those with a large Chinese diaspora, such as Macao, Singapore, Thailand, and Indonesia, have also supplied a significant amount of direct investment to China.

The primitive and imperfect legal regime in China is one important reason for the lopsided distribution of the supply of FDI. On the one hand, investors from the United States and other large home countries of multinational corporations are wary about the security and stability of their investment in China. On the other hand, the overseas Chinese (particularly those residing in Hong Kong) can use their cultural and linguistic links to help reduce information and contractual costs. To contribute to the skewed source country distribution, some regions in China offer explicit or implicit preferential policies to overseas Chinese who trace their ancestry to those regions.

There is another distinct characteristic of investment from overseas Chinese that may be worth noting. The average size of investment from an overseas Chinese investor is much smaller than that from non–ethnic Chinese. One explanation is simply that overseas Chinese tend to have small or medium-sized firms (either for cultural reasons or because the industries they typically operate in have small optimal scales). The other explanation, which I find at least as plausible as the first, is a transaction cost story associated with China's primitive legal system. Other things equal, imperfect legal protection implies a high transaction cost for firms in China because learning ill-defined customs and vague operating rules is costly. Overseas Chinese can largely circumvent this problem by using their linguistic and cultural advantage or personal connections. Hence, non–ethnic Chinese investors may perceive a higher transaction cost than overseas Chinese. Suppose this transaction cost is basically fixed (i.e., does not depend on the size of investment), then small projects may not be worth enough to overcome this cost and are never implemented. The minimum amount of investment for non–ethnic Chinese is thus larger than for overseas Chinese.[2]

### 3.3.1 Toward an Empirical Model of FDI Distribution

A norm for bilateral investment is notoriously difficult to establish because FDI is likely to be influenced by a long list of factors, many of which are difficult to measure or observe. I consider a reduced-form specification for bilateral investment (flow or stock). Let $I_{ij}$ be direct investment from country $i$ to country $j$. We have

$$I_{ij} = f(X_i, Y_j, Z_{ij}).$$

I will explain the three categories of determinants in turn. We take $X_i$ to be a vector of variables that influence the measured size of the overall magnitude

2. I thank Chongen Bai for suggesting this interpretation.

of outward investment from country *i;* it includes legal restrictions on or incentives for capital outflow, including country *i*'s corporate tax schedule and the treatment of foreign affiliate tax payment to host country governments. The key feature of variables in this vector is that they are common to all outward investments of country *i,* irrespective of destination. (In our sample, most countries' outward direct investment is realized investment, but some countries such as Japan report only government approval data. Our $X$ vector should include an indicator for the deviation of country *i*'s measurement method from the "normal" definition of FDI in the sample.) Our statistical specification in the later part of the paper allows us to be less specific about this vector.

The quantity $Y_j$ is a vector of variables related to the overall attractiveness of country *j* to FDI. I will divide the factors into two subcategories. The first group includes macroeconomic characteristics of the host country, such as size (measured by GNP), level of development, and level of human capital.[3] The second subcategory includes all restrictions on and incentives for inward foreign investment. Many countries grant tax holidays or reduced taxes on foreign companies' profits. This provides incentives for certain source countries to direct their outward-going capital to such host countries.

Finally, $Z_{ij}$ is a vector of variables that are specific to the *ij* pair and that influence the incentives or disincentives for investment going from country *i* to country *j.* One principal variable in this vector is a bilateral treaty between countries *i* and *j* that includes offering country *i*'s investors a more favorable tax treatment in country *j* relative to investors from other countries.[4] The other important variable in this vector is ethnic, linguistic, or historical ties that serve to reduce information costs for business transactions taking place between nationals of countries *i* and *j.* This variable is not easy to measure. As a proxy, geographic distance is used. In particular, this paper computes the "great circle distance" between major cities (usually the capitals) of a given pair of countries.

To implement the FDI function, I assume a linear specification of the following form:

$$\log \text{FDI}_{ij} = \alpha_i + \beta_1 \log \text{GNP}_j + \beta_2 \log \frac{\text{GNP}_j}{\text{Pop}_j} + \beta_3 \log \text{Distance}_{ij} + \beta_4 \text{Literacy}_j + \mu_{ij}.$$

### 3.3.2 Data

The basic data set for this part of the paper is outward FDI from the five largest source countries in the 1987–90 period. The source is United Nations

3. Recent work on "new" growth theory implies that human capital in the host country plays an important role in FDI decisions (see Lucas 1990).

4. See Hines and Wilard (1992) for an interesting analysis of the determinants in reaching bilateral tax treaties.

(1992). I will also make use of GNP, per capita GNP, and literacy data from World Bank (1992).

The five largest source countries for direct investment over the period 1987–90 were Japan, the United Kingdom, the United States, France, and Germany (United Nations 1992). Their annual average outflows of investment during the period were $36.5, $30.5, $23.9, $19.5, and $17.1 billion, respectively. The total investment outflow from the five accounted for about 70.5 percent of all outward investment from the developed countries.

### 3.3.3 Basic Results

Table 3.4 reports the basic regression results for the flow of FDI. Column (1) reports the result of a fixed-effects regression assuming source-country–specific intercepts. The coefficient for the GNP variable is positive and significant as expected. A 1 percent increase in the size of a host country is associated with a 0.53 percentage point increase in FDI. A 1 percent increase in per capita GNP is associated with a 0.42 percentage point increase in FDI flow. Furthermore, geography matters: a 1 percent increase in distance is associated with a 0.39 percentage point reduction in FDI. This confirms our casual impression that outward foreign investment is highly regionalized.[5] Investment is, to some extent, a neighborhood event. It is worth pointing out that, in spite of a less rigorous microfoundation for the specification, the adjusted $R^2$ of over 0.50 is reasonably large for a cross-country regression.

A competing specification for the panel data set is what is called the random-effects model. In such a model, the source-country–specific intercept is assumed to be a random draw from a common distribution that is uncorrelated with the error term of the regression (Hsiao 1986). Strictly speaking, since the five source countries are not randomly drawn from the pool of all source countries, but rather are chosen deliberately because they are the largest source countries, the fixed-effects model is the appropriate model to use. On the other hand, because a random-effects model can often result in drastically different coefficient estimates (Hsiao 1986, 41–42), it is performed here purely as a robustness check of our fixed-effects model. The result is reported in column (2). Luckily, for our data set, the random-effects specification produces essentially the same estimates as the fixed-effects model.

It may be useful to comment a bit more on the positive sign of the coefficient of the per capita GNP term. One often hears the hypothesis that direct investment seeks countries with low labor costs. Since wage level should be highly correlated with per capita GNP, one would expect a negative sign for the per capita GNP term. Why do we obtain a statistically significant positive sign? One explanation is that per capita GNP is positively correlated with a country's

5. Hufbauer, Lakdawalla, and Malani (1994) have estimated a gravity-type model for outward investment from the United States, Japan, and Germany and reported, among other things, a geographic bias in FDI.

**Table 3.4** **Norm of Inward FDI: Flow**

| Variable | Fixed Effect (1) | Random Effect[a] (2) | Fixed Effect (3) | Random Effect[b] (4) |
|---|---|---|---|---|
| Constant | | −1.61 | | −1.40 |
| | | (1.41) | | (1.45) |
| log $GNP_j$ | 0.53** | 0.53** | 0.49** | 0.49** |
| | (0.06) | (0.06) | (0.07) | (0.07) |
| log $PCGNP_j$ | 0.42** | 0.43** | 0.31* | 0.33** |
| | (0.09) | (0.09) | (0.12) | (0.12) |
| log $Distance_{ij}$ | −0.38** | −0.37** | −0.40** | −0.39** |
| | (0.11) | (0.11) | (0.11) | (0.11) |
| $Literacy_j$ | | | 1.57# | 1.54# |
| | | | (0.86) | (0.87) |
| $N$ | 237 | 237 | 204 | 204 |
| Standard error of regression | 1.59 | 1.61 | 1.51 | 1.53 |
| $R^2$ | 0.50 | 0.52 | 0.53 | 0.54 |
| Adjusted $R^2$ | 0.49 | 0.51 | 0.51 | 0.53 |

*Equation:* $\log \text{FDI-flow}_{ij} = \alpha_i + \beta_1 \log GNP_j + \beta_2 \log PCGNP_j + \beta_3 \log Distance_{ij} + \beta_4 Literacy_j + \mu_{ij}$.

*Note:* Numbers in parentheses are standard errors.

[a]Variance of $\mu_{ij}$ = 2.5574, variance of $\alpha$ = 0.30320, implied differencing factor = 0.11808.

[b]Variance of $\mu_{ij}$ = 2.3180, variance of $\alpha$ = 0.34868, implied differencing factor = 0.10962.

#Significant at the 10 percent level.

*Significant at the 5 percent level.

**Significant at the 1 percent level.

level of human capital. Recent theories of economic growth that emphasize the importance of human capital accumulation (e.g., Lucas 1990) predict that inward foreign investment is positively correlated with the stock of human capital in the host country. Hence, per capita GNP can be positively correlated with inward investment.

To investigate this possibility, I adopt the adult literacy ratio as a crude measure of average human capital.[6] (In the sample, the simple correlation between per capita GNP and adult literacy is 0.56.) Columns (3) and (4) of table 3.4 report the results with the literacy variable as an additional regressor. The point estimate for the variable is positive and statistically significant at the 10 percent level. According to the estimate in the fixed-effects regression, a 1 percent increase in the literacy ratio is associated with a 1.57 percentage point higher inward FDI. The qualitative features of the estimates for the other variables do

6. The data are converted from adult illiteracy ratios from World Bank (1992, table 1). No data are reported for high-income economies. But they are noted in the table as having less than 5 percent illiteracy according to Unesco. Hence, a value of 2.5 percent illiteracy is assigned for all high-income economies.

not change (the point estimates for the GNP and per capita GNP terms become somewhat smaller).

The flow data on FDI may reflect the peculiarity of year-to-year fluctuation in the spatial distribution of foreign investment. For example, during 1989–90, FDI going into China was greatly reduced as a result of the international reaction to the Tiananmen Square Incident. In addition, the stock of FDI is more important than the flow variable for many calculations, including the contribution of foreign investment to host country production capacity. For these reasons, I also look at the spatial distribution of the stock of FDI.

Table 3.5 reports the basic regression results for the FDI stock data. The crucial result is the estimates of the fixed-effects model. The coefficient on the GNP variable is 0.74 (somewhat larger than the flow regression) and significant at the 1 percent level. It suggests that larger economies tend to host more foreign investment, although the increment in foreign investment is less than proportional to the increase in the size of the host country. The coefficient on per capita GNP is 0.29 and significant. Again, the stock of foreign investment tends to be distributed among rich countries. As with the flow data, part of the reason for this may be that the average level of human capital is an important

**Table 3.5 Norm of Inward FDI: Stock**

| Variable | Fixed Effect (1) | Random Effect[a] (2) | Fixed Effect (3) | Random Effect[b] (4) |
|---|---|---|---|---|
| Constant | | −1.40 | | −0.93 |
| | | (1.40) | | (1.29) |
| log $GNP_j$ | 0.74** | 0.74** | 0.72** | 0.72** |
| | (0.06) | (0.06) | (0.06) | (0.06) |
| log $PCGNP_j$ | 0.29** | 0.29** | 0.18# | 0.18 |
| | (0.08) | (0.08) | (0.10) | (0.10)# |
| log $Distance_{ij}$ | −0.38** | −0.36** | −0.43** | −0.42** |
| | (0.12) | (0.12) | (0.10) | (0.10) |
| $Literacy_j$ | | | 1.57* | 1.56* |
| | | | (0.67) | (0.68) |
| $N$ | 323 | 323 | 272 | 272 |
| Standard error of regression | 1.77 | 1.78 | 1.48 | 1.49 |
| $R^2$ | 0.51 | 0.52 | 0.60 | 0.61 |
| Adjusted $R^2$ | 0.50 | 0.51 | 0.59 | 0.60 |

*Equation:* $\log \text{FDI-stock}_{ij} = \alpha_i + \beta_1 \log \text{GNP}_j + \beta_2 \log \text{PCGNP}_j + \beta_3 \log \text{Distance}_{ij} + \beta_4 \text{Literacy}_j + \mu_{ij}$.

*Note:* Numbers in parentheses are standard errors.

[a]Variance of $\mu_{ij}$ = 3.1747, variance of $\alpha$ = 0.24515, implied differencing factor = 0.13496.

[b]Variance of $\mu_{ij}$ = 2.2200, variance of $\alpha$ = 0.35987, implied differencing factor = 0.84390E−01.

#Significant at the 10 percent level.

*Significant at the 5 percent level.

**Significant at the 1 percent level.

determinant of the marginal value of physical capital and the former is correlated with per capita GNP.

In columns (3) and (4), the adult literacy variable is again added to the regressions as a measure of average human capital. The coefficient for the new variable is positive and significant at the 1 percent level. A 1 percent rise in the adult literacy level is associated with a 1.57 percentage point increase in the stock of foreign investment. As expected, the point estimate on the per capita GNP variable is reduced (to 0.18), although it remains positive and significant.

### 3.3.4 Comparing China and Asia to the "Norm"

The statistical model in the last section has effectively established a "norm" for inward foreign investment (from the five largest source countries) as a function of a host country's size, level of development, level of human capital, and geographic location. Against this empirical norm, we can then investigate whether China, or any other country, has attracted "enough" foreign capital.

I will examine the difference between actual foreign investment and the model predictions for China, India, and the four Asian newly industrialized economies (NIEs). The basic economic characteristics of the six economies are summarized in table 3.6. The computed differences of inward investment relative to the norm are reported in table 3.7. Column (1) refers to FDI flow, and column (2) to FDI stock.

Despite the fact that China was one of the largest developing host countries for FDI by the end of the 1980s, it may still not be hosting enough FDI after one adjusts its FDI volume by its size and other characteristics. This appears to be the case. In terms of flow of FDI in 1989–90, China does not seem to have attracted enough investment from four of the major source countries (the United States, Germany, France, and the United Kingdom).[7] For example, it received 88 percent less investment from Germany than it should have based on its economic characteristics ($\exp(-2.145) - 1$). The FDI that China hosts from Japan is an exception to this pattern. The actual Japanese investment going into China in 1990 was actually 25 percent more than the model prediction ($\exp(0.229) - 1$). The Japanese investment in China will probably stay high. As was revealed in two surveys of Japanese firms conducted by Japan's Export-Import Bank in 1992 and 1993, China was believed to be the most promising destination for Japanese FDI in the medium-term (i.e., three years following the survey years; Kinoshita 1994).

Chinese underachievement in attracting FDI in 1990 could partly be due to source country reaction to the Tiananmen Square Incident. But the stock of FDI should be less affected by this. The discrepancy between actual and predicted values of the FDI stock is given in column (2). As expected, the extent of underachievement is less than for the flow data in all cases. Nevertheless, China has attracted less than normal investment from four of the five major

7. A blank entry in table 3.7 means that the recorded actual investment is zero.

**Table 3.6 Country Indicators, 1990**

| Country | GNP per Capita ($) | GNP (million $) | Literacy Rate |
|---|---|---|---|
| China | 370 | 419,469 | 0.73 |
| Hong Kong | 11,490 | 66,642 | 0.77 |
| India | 350 | 297,325 | 0.48 |
| Korea | 5,400 | 231,120 | 0.975 |
| Singapore | 11,160 | 33,480 | 0.88 |
| Taiwan | 7,284 | 147,384 | 0.932 |

*Source:* World Bank (1992).

source countries even according to the stock data. For example, the U.S. investment that China hosts falls short of its potential by almost 89 percent ($\exp(-2.20) - 1$).

Part of the reason for China's underachievement is its late entry into the game. The open door policy was only a decade old in 1990. The more important reason for the underachievement is the imperfect legal protection that China still offers to foreign investors. Luckily, overseas Chinese appear less concerned about the legal environment and have made stakes in the country in large numbers. The investment from overseas Chinese perhaps makes up for much of the shares lost from the major source countries in the world.

We should note that the GNP and per capita GNP variables may have substantially underestimated China's true size and level of development. After adjusting for purchasing power, the World Bank and International Monetary Fund found that China's per capita GNP was likely to be on the order of $2,000 rather than $370 as reported in table 3.6. A more conservative measure by Lardy (1994) put the estimate at $1,000. This would still increase the magnitude of China's GNP and per capita GNP by a factor of 1.7 relative to the exchange-rate–based measure. If PPP-adjusted values were used in estimating the FDI model, one would expect even greater underachievement by China in attracting FDI from the major source countries.

(On the other hand, the reported literacy rate may overestimate the average level of human capital. If secondary school enrollment or other variables were used as a measure of human capital, the magnitude of Chinese underachievement would become somewhat smaller.)

India has many similarities with China, in terms of size, level of development, as well as history of policy toward FDI. In terms of stock of FDI, India has hosted too little FDI from all major source countries except Britain. (Being a former British colony helps in this case.) But in terms of recent flow of FDI, India is catching up fast, particularly with FDI from the United States.[8]

The four Asian NIEs are all well known to be very open in terms of their

8. See Reddy (1994) for a more detailed discussion.

**Table 3.7 Actual − Predicted FDI**

| Host Country and Source Country | Flow (I) | Stock (II) |
|---|---|---|
| China | | |
| France | – | −0.027536154 |
| Germany | −2.14538 | −1.339597464 |
| Japan | 0.229325 | 0.483750194 |
| United States | – | −2.200443029 |
| Hong Kong | | |
| France | −0.919753075 | 0.407244235 |
| Germany | – | 1.134640694 |
| United Kingdom | – | 2.18819952 |
| Japan | 1.749702215 | 2.524893761 |
| United States | 1.098459721 | 1.643532038 |
| India | | |
| Germany | −1.32010806 | −0.04662088 |
| United Kingdom | 0.303903848 | 0.158203423 |
| Japan | −1.23166192 | −1.08397329 |
| United States | 0.563331068 | −0.69884843 |
| Korea | | |
| Germany | −0.123430409 | −0.937957704 |
| United Kingdom | −1.471476436 | −2.741689682 |
| Japan | −1.155126452 | 0.210981429 |
| United States | 0.016230347 | −0.660793841 |
| Singapore | | |
| France | −0.07105872 | 0.916713536 |
| Germany | 1.350871801 | 1.719693422 |
| United Kingdom | 2.42726016 | 2.614859104 |
| Japan | 1.418084502 | 2.717613697 |
| United States | 2.023788452 | 1.559094071 |
| Taiwan | | |
| Germany | −0.685266376 | −1.07056284 |
| United Kingdom | −0.454679817 | – |
| Japan | −0.266864061 | 0.354950696 |
| United States | −0.265043318 | −0.181538507 |

*Specification of models:* I, $\log \text{FDI-flow}_{ij} = \alpha_i + \beta_1 \log \text{GNP}_j + \beta_2 \log \text{PCGNP}_j + \beta_3 \log \text{Distance}_{ij} + \beta_4 \text{Literacy}_j + \mu_{ij}$; II, $\log \text{FDI-stock}_{ij} = \alpha_i + \beta_1 \log \text{GNP}_j + \beta_2 \log \text{PCGNP}_j + \beta_3 \log \text{Distance}_{ij} + \beta_4 \text{Literacy}_j + \mu_{ij}$

trade policies. However, their policies toward FDI differ markedly. On one extreme, Singapore and Hong Kong are very open to foreign investment. Both have hosted a substantially greater stock of FDI than an average economy in the world with similar economic and geographic characteristics. On the other extreme, Taiwan and Korea are much more cautious toward foreign-invested firms on their territories. Both host less than average direct investment from the four major source countries (the United States, Germany, France, and the United Kingdom).

To summarize, in contrast to its reception of vast investment from overseas Chinese, China so far has not attracted enough direct investment from the United States and European source countries. However, this is not drastically different from the situations in Taiwan and Korea.

## 3.4 Economic Consequences of Foreign Capital in China

In the second half of the paper, I will discuss several consequences of foreign investment in China. Specifically, I will concentrate on three aspects of foreign investment: (1) its contribution to overall rapid growth, (2) its contribution to the rapid growth of China's exports, and (3) its contribution to the expansion of the nonstate sector in China. Much of my evidence is derived from a statistical analysis of a city-level data set covering the period 1988–90.[9]

In an earlier paper (Wei 1995), I reviewed the evolution of China's open door policy and discussed the contribution of export activity and foreign investment to China's rapid growth. The following discussion differs from the earlier paper in several important aspects. First, new questions are asked, particularly in terms of the connection between foreign investment and the expansion of the nonstate sector. Second, the treatment of foreign investment is more refined. In the previous paper, only the flow of FDI was used in the statistical analysis, whereas here the stock of foreign capital is computed and analyzed. Furthermore, a measure of the stock of aggregate city-level physical capital is added so that the statistical specification corresponds better with the economic theory.

I will first sketch a theoretical model that will be the basis of my statistical investigation. After an explanation of the data set, I will present the main statistical results and draw economic inferences.

### 3.4.1 A Minimalist Model

To guide later statistical analyses, a parsimonious specification will be sufficient. Let city $j$ operate with the following production function:

$$Y_j = A_j L_j^{\alpha} K_j^{\beta} H_j^{\gamma}$$

where $L$, $K$, and $H$ are the city's labor force, stock of physical capital, and stock of human capital, respectively, and $A$ is a productivity shift parameter.

The productivity shift parameter can be conceptually decomposed into national and city-specific components. For simplicity, assume that

$$A_j = S_n S_j,$$

9. For recent analyses of the relationship between FDI and home economies and of other issues, see Feldstein (1995), Lipsey (1995), and Froot (1993).

where $S_n$ and $S_j$ are the national and city-specific components of the productivity shift parameter.

Use $g$ to denote any growth rate. The above specification can be translated into growth terms.

$$g_{Y_j} = g_{S_n} + g_{S_j} + \alpha g_{L_j} + \beta g_{K_j} + \gamma g_{H_j}.$$

The central focus for the second half of the paper is on the impact of foreign investment. Foreign investment in city $j$ could affect the city's output in three ways. First, it may raise growth of the city's overall capital stock, $g_{K_j}$. Second, it may increase city $j$'s overall productivity growth, $g_{S_j}$. Third, if beneficial effects spill over to other cities in the country, it may raise the growth of the national productivity level, $g_{S_n}$.

Foreign investment can raise productivity through a number of channels. First, many foreign firms bring new technology ("software," such as product design, as well as "hardware," such as machinery) to the host country. Second, and perhaps more important in the Chinese context, foreign firms bring modern management concepts, marketing techniques, and work discipline. Third, even domestic firms that do not directly receive foreign investment may benefit from it by learning and mimicking the management, marketing, or production techniques of foreign-owned firms. This spillover effect from foreign-owned to domestic firms stems from the fact that learning is greatly helped by physical proximity and human interactions.

If foreign investment in city $j$ raises the growth of national productivity, $g_{S_n}$, through cross-city spillover, it will merely enlarge the intercept term in a cross-city regression. Hence, our identification of the contribution of the foreign investment falls on $g_{S_j}$. In actual implementation, I will assume that $g_{S_j}$ is a linear function of the stock of FDI in city $j$ and that the functional form is the same for all cities.

### 3.4.2 Data

The data set employed here covers 434 cities over the period 1988–90 (China State Statistics Bureau 1989, 1991). The 434 cities constituted the entire universe of cities in China in 1988. Moreover, the data cover areas surrounding each city (greater city area) rather than just the metropolitan area. This helps to avoid certain sample selection biases, such as uncovering a relationship that is peculiar to the coastal areas or the special economic zones.

A few general features of the data set should be noted to put the subsequent regression results in perspective. During 1988–90, the average growth rate of gross industrial output across the cities was 39.8 percent (and the output-weighted average was close to this as well). Note also that these two years were a relatively slow growing period in a fast-growing decade.

It may be interesting to note the growth rate of foreign-invested firms relative to other types of firms. Table 3.8 reports the (nominal) growth rates by ownership type.[10] The first three types, individual-owned firms (INDs), township and village enterprises (TVEs), and foreign-invested firms (FORs) constitute over half of the nonstate sector in China.[11] All three categories grew faster than the average growth rate of total output. But the foreign-invested firms grew the fastest. The two-year growth rate was an astonishing 119.4 percent. (The combined two-year inflation rate during the period was about 18 percent. So the real two-year growth rate for the foreign-invested firms was about 100 percent.)

Although foreign-invested firms were growing quickly, they were tiny in terms of their share in total industrial output (table 3.9). In 1988, foreign-invested firms accounted for less than 1 percent of total output. The share almost doubled to 1.71 percent by the end of 1990. In contrast, the state sector shrank rapidly in relative terms. The state sector lost almost 5 percentage points in share of total output over a two-year period. Most of this lost ground was gained by the TVEs.

What makes the subsequent regression analysis interesting is the tremendous variation across the cities. For example, the share of foreign-invested firms in total output ranges from 0 to 62.1 percent in 1988. (About 115 cities in 1988 had a positive stock of foreign investment.) The growth rates of foreign-invested firms also vary tremendously, from −92 percent (exp(−2.821) − 1) to 11,050 percent (exp(4.714) − 1)!

### 3.4.3 Foreign Investment and Total Output Growth

We start our analysis with the contribution of foreign investment to China's overall industrial growth. The benchmark results are reported in table 3.10. The dependent variable in all four regressions is the city's growth rate in gross industrial output.

In the first regression, the growth rates of capital stock and labor force are the only two regressors other than the intercept. Both variables are statistically significant at the 10 percent level. The point estimates for capital growth and labor growth are 0.17 and 0.25, respectively. The apparent decreasing returns to scale could reflect the technical inefficiency of many Chinese firms, especially the state-owned firms.

I introduce foreign investment into the regression in two ways. First, I use the beginning-of-sample (i.e., 1988) share of the stock of foreign capital in the city's total capital. Second, I use the beginning-of-sample share of foreign-invested firm output in the city's total output.

There are two variations in the first approach depending on the assumption

10. For simplicity, I will refer to wholly foreign-owned, equity or contractual joint ventures, and joint explorations as "foreign-invested firms."

11. The other category within the nonstate sector is "urban collectives," which I do not have data on. For a detailed discussion of the four categories of the nonstate sector, see Wei and Lian (1993).

**Table 3.8** **Two-Year Growth Rates of Gross Industrial Output, 1988–90 (434 Chinese cities)**

| | IND | TVE | FOR | "State" | Total |
|---|---|---|---|---|---|
| Simple average | 1.137 | 0.492 | 1.194 | 0.305 | 0.398 |
| Minimum | −0.993 | −0.730 | −2.821 | −2.505 | −0.304 |
| Maximum | 38.366 | 12.383 | 4.714 | 3.442 | 7.739 |
| *N* | 343 | 348 | 115 | 334 | 363 |

**Table 3.9** **Share in Industrial Output by Type of Firms, 1988–90 (434 Chinese cities)**

| | IND | TVE | FOR | "State" |
|---|---|---|---|---|
| 1988 | | | | |
| Simple average | 1.10 | 20.20 | 0.99 | 78.1 |
| Minimum | 0.01 | 0.45 | 0.00 | 26.4 |
| Maximum | 29.70 | 66.40 | 62.10 | 99.3 |
| *N* | 351 | 348 | 341 | 340 |
| 1990 | | | | |
| Simple average | 1.18 | 25.20 | 1.71 | 73.30 |
| Minimum | 0.01 | 0.11 | 0.00 | 8.98 |
| Maximum | 22.30 | 85.23 | 65.90 | 99.80 |
| *N* | 408 | 422 | 398 | 398 |

**Table 3.10** **Foreign Investment and City's Total Output Growth, 1988–90 (434 Chinese cities)**

| Variable | (1) | (2) | (3) | (4) |
|---|---|---|---|---|
| GPop | .168# | .168# | .167# | .114 |
| | (.098) | (.098) | (.098) | (.118) |
| GCap | .251* | .248* | .247* | .249* |
| | (.041) | (.043) | (.042) | (.043) |
| FDI88d/Cap88 | | .072 | | |
| | | (.062) | | |
| FDI88nd/Cap88 | | | .065## | |
| | | | (.043) | |
| YFor88/Y88 | | | | .317* |
| | | | | (.122) |
| *N* | 355 | 347 | 347 | 337 |
| SEE | .132 | .128 | .128 | .125 |
| Adjusted $R^2$ | .197 | .217 | .219 | .225 |

*Notes:* Dependent variable is growth rate of gross industrial output during 1988–90. See the appendix for definitions of independent variables. Numbers in parentheses are heteroskedasticity-consistent standard errors. All regressions have an intercept which is not reported.

##Significant at the 15 percent level.

#Significant at the 10 percent level.

*Significant at the 5 percent level.

of the depreciation of foreign capital. In the first variation, a 10 percent depreciation rate is assumed when accumulating the annual flow of FDI into a stock measure. (The official exchange rate in 1988 of 3.72 yuan/dollar is used to convert the dollar value of FDI stock into Chinese yuan.) The result is reported in column (2). We observe that the foreign capital share variable has a positive coefficient (0.072), which would be consistent with the hypothesis that foreign investment raises city-specific productivity. Unfortunately, it is not statistically significant at the 10 percent level.

Because the annual flows of FDI are in nominal U.S. dollar terms, a 10 percent nominal depreciation rate implies a greater real depreciation rate (10 percent plus the annual inflation rate). Furthermore, the reported city capital stock is likely to assign an insufficient depreciation rate to capital stock in Chinese firms. This could further underestimate the true ratio of foreign capital to the city's total capital stock. Partly as a correction to this problem, I also use the second variation, in which a zero nominal rate of depreciation is assumed for FDI (i.e., the real rate of depreciation is approximately equal to the U.S. inflation rate). This assumption gives the regression result in column (3). This time, the estimate is statistically significant at the 15 percent level. A 1 percent increase in the share of foreign capital in the city's capital stock in 1988 is associated with a 0.065 higher growth rate of industrial output in the subsequent two-year period. Although the positive sign is consistent with a productivity-lifting role for FDI, the point estimate is not terribly big.

The uncertainty about the depreciation rate (and, to a lesser extent, the exchange rate used to convert FDI from dollar values into yuan values) means that the foreign capital share variable probably has serious measurement problems. The measurement error could introduce a downward bias into the measured estimate of the contribution of FDI stock to overall growth.

An alternative measure of the significance of foreign capital is the share of foreign-invested firm output in a city's total output. This variable is much easier to measure and should circumvent the difficulties in properly measuring the stock of FDI. The regression result with this variable is in column (4) of table 3.10. This share variable is positive and statistically significant at the 5 percent level. Holding the growth of inputs constant, a 1 percent increase in the share of foreign-invested firms in output in 1988 is associated with a 0.32 percent higher growth rate in output during 1988–90. This is a more significant number. In table 3.9, we found that the difference between the cities with the highest and those with an average share of foreign firms in output was 61 percent. This could produce an almost 20 (61*0.32) percentage point difference in the growth rate of output.

### 3.4.4 Introducing Human Capital and Coastal Areas

One omission from the regressions in section 3.4.3 is a measure of the stock of human capital. Human capital plays a central role in (one branch of) the new growth theory. I will add to the basic regression the share of skilled labor in a city's labor force as a measure of the average level of a city's human capital.

Table 3.11 replicates the key regressions in table 3.10 with the additional variable, GHumCap, the growth of the average human capital level. The added variable is not significant for the first two regressions but is significant (at the 10 percent level) for the regression that includes the share of foreign firm output in total output. The feature to notice, however, is that the qualitative characteristics of FDI remain the same as before. In particular, in columns (2) and (3), FDI exhibits a positive and statistically significant association with growth in total output.

One may think that one important impetus for rapid growth in certain parts of China is a favorable policy environment. A priori, a combination of the following three things could together explain the observed pattern: (1) Localized reform experiments promote growth. (2) Foreign investment does not contribute to growth beyond contribution to the capital stock. (3) Foreign investment happens to be concentrated in cities with many localized reform experiments. In other words, the apparent positive association between foreign investment and high growth could be a spurious result of not having a measure of localized reform experiments in the regression.

To investigate this possibility, I will identify subsets of cities that may have had intensive reform experiments. The "special economic zones" (SEZs) are

**Table 3.11 Foreign Investment, Human Capital, and City's Total Output Growth, 1988–90 (434 Chinese cities)**

| Variable | (1) | (2) | (3) |
|---|---|---|---|
| GPop | .171# | .170# | .110 |
| | (.099) | (.099) | (.117) |
| GCap | .242* | .241* | .243* |
| | (.042) | (.042) | (.042) |
| FDI88d/Cap88 | .076 | | |
| | (.059) | | |
| FDI88nd/Cap88 | | .067# | |
| | | (.041) | |
| YFor88/Y88 | | | .310* |
| | | | (.128) |
| GHumCap | .026 | .026 | .034# |
| | (.021) | (.021) | (.020) |
| *N* | 346 | 346 | 336 |
| SEE | .128 | .128 | .125 |
| Adjusted $R^2$ | .220 | .221 | .231 |

*Notes:* Dependent variable is growth rate of gross industrial output during 1988–90. See the appendix for definitions of independent variables. Numbers in parentheses are heteroskedasticity-consistent standard errors. All regressions have an intercept which is not reported.

##Significant at the 15 percent level.

#Significant at the 10 percent level.

*Significant at the 5 percent level.

one such subset. Four cities (Shenzhen, Zhuhai, Shantou, and Xiamen) were declared SEZs in 1980. The entire island province of Hainan was made to be an SEZ ("special area open to foreign investment" in official terms) in 1983. In an SEZ, tax concessions and fewer restrictions on foreign exchange and land use are deployed to attract foreign investment. But a large quantity of domestic investment has been stimulated in SEZs by the same or similarly beneficial environments.

The 14 "open coastal cities" are the second such subset. An open coastal city can offer much the same benefits to foreign (and often to domestic) investors that SEZs do. Its income tax is less favorable than in an SEZ but more favorable than in the rest of the country.

The third subset of special cities is the group of 72 "comprehensive reform experimenting cities," designated by either the central or provincial government. The governments of these cities are supposed to have greater authority in managing firms inside their city boundaries, and greater access to the revenue originating in them, and can take over certain firms previously managed directly by the ministries in Beijing.

I create two dummies to investigate possible special effects of these cities. The first dummy, Open, is for SEZs and open coastal cities. The second, Reform, is for the 72 comprehensive reform experimenting cities. In my previous paper (Wei 1996), I found that an open coastal city or an SEZ does grow faster than the national average by about 18 percentage points if one only controls for labor force growth, but not for capital stock growth. The 72 reform experimenting cities did not grow any faster than an average city in the sample after controlling for the growth of the labor force.

We now have a measure of the growth in capital stock as well. Table 3.12 reports regression results with these two dummies. This time, even the coastal open cities and SEZs do not seem to be more special than an average city after controlling for capital stock growth. Indeed, the point estimate is slightly negative (but insignificantly different from zero). In other words, the unconditionally high growth rates in these cities can be entirely accounted for by higher than average input growth. These cities are special because of their ability to accumulate (or attract) capital and labor inputs at a rapid rate.

The qualitative features of foreign capital measures in the last three regressions are similar to the previous results. Indeed, the point estimates tend to become slightly larger with marginally increased significance levels.

### 3.4.5 Foreign Investment and Exports

It has been widely commented that foreign-invested firms in China have helped to increase China's exports to the outside world. The importance of foreign-invested firms in China's exports has grown rapidly. Its share increased from about 1 percent in the mid-1980s to 27.5 percent in 1993 (Lardy 1994, 72, table 3.9).

The high and increasing export propensity of foreign-invested firms relative

**Table 3.12 Foreign Investment, Coastal Cities, and Growth, 1988–90 (434 Chinese cities)**

| Variable | (1) | (2) | (3) | (4) |
|---|---|---|---|---|
| GPop | .162# | .155# | .153# | .095 |
| | (.098) | (.100) | (.101) | (.122) |
| GCap | .252* | .248* | .248* | .253* |
| | (.041) | (.043) | (.043) | (.044) |
| FDI88d/Cap88 | | .107# | | |
| | | (.057) | | |
| FDI88nd/Cap88 | | | .094* | |
| | | | (.039) | |
| YFor88/Y88 | | | | .415* |
| | | | | (.143) |
| Reform | −.014 | −.010 | −.010 | −.007 |
| | (.015) | (.014) | (.014) | (.014) |
| Open | −.014 | −.040 | −.042 | −.047 |
| | (.038) | (.038) | (.039) | (.039) |
| *N* | 355 | 347 | 347 | 337 |
| SEE | .132 | .128 | .128 | .125 |
| Adjusted $R^2$ | .195 | .218 | .219 | .226 |

*Notes:* Dependent variable is growth rate of gross industrial output during 1988–90. See appendix for definitions of independent variables. Numbers in parentheses are heteroskedasticity-consistent standard errors. All regressions have an intercept which is not reported.

##Significant at the 15 percent level.

#Significant at the 10 percent level.

*Significant at the 5 percent level.

to Chinese firms has much to do with the export performance criteria that the Chinese government imposes on them. But before we conclude that China's overall export level has been raised by the presence of foreign-invested firms, we must entertain some other possibilities.

Foreign-invested firms could *displace* exports by Chinese firms. This may happen if foreign-invested firms compete head to head with Chinese firms and possibly drive them out of export-related activities. Depending on how much Chinese exports are displaced by foreign-invested firms, overall Chinese exports could be lower than without foreign firms. Alternatively, foreign-invested firms could *promote* export activities among Chinese firms. This may happen, for example, when the foreign-invested firms pass on, intentionally or not, marketing know-how to Chinese firms which otherwise may not be able to sell in the world market. If this happens, overall Chinese exports can be raised by more than the exports of the foreign-invested firms.

The point is that the net effect of foreign investment on China's exports depends on the way the foreign investment and the export activities of Chinese firms interact. With city-level data on exports by state trading corporations (the bulk of non–foreign-firm exports), I can investigate this interaction.

In various regressions, I find that the cross-city differences in export activity are not statistically related to either the difference in the growth of FDI or the difference in the initial stock of foreign capital. (The results are not reported to save space.) Thus, I conclude that foreign-invested firm exports do not displace Chinese firm exports. They may help to promote Chinese exports if enough marketing know-how is spilled over to other cities in the country (and thus not related to city-level exports).

### 3.4.6 Foreign Investment and the Expansion of the TVE Sector

The rapid growth of the Chinese economy and the success of Chinese economic reform is largely due to the rapid expansion of the nonstate sector, including foreign-invested firms. Here I would like to examine the interaction between foreign investment and other parts of the nonstate sector, in particular, the TVEs.

As we observed in tables 3.8 and 3.9, the TVEs are the giants in the nonstate sector. Starting de nova in 1979, they already accounted for 20.2 percent of total industrial output by 1988 and gained 5 percentage points in share over the 1988–90 period. The two-year growth rate in TVE output was 64 percent (exp(0.492) − 1). Is the expansion of the TVE sector helped or curbed by the presence of foreign-invested firms?

Table 3.13 reports some rudimentary regressions that may provide a suggestive (but speculative) answer to the question. The dependent variable in all regressions is the growth rate in output by the TVEs. The regressors are the three ways of measuring the relative importance of foreign capital in cities. The coefficients are all positive and, for the last two measures, statistically

**Table 3.13 Foreign Investment and Growth of the TVE Sector, 1988–90**

| Variable | (1) | (2) | (3) |
|---|---|---|---|
| Intercept | .313* | .313* | .313* |
| | (.018) | (.018) | (.018) |
| FDI88d/Cap88 | .185 | | |
| | (.137) | | |
| FDI88nd/Cap88 | | .169# | |
| | | (.094) | |
| YFor88/Y88 | | | .764* |
| | | | (.283) |
| *N* | 339 | 339 | 339 |
| SEE | .319 | .319 | .326 |
| Adjusted $R^2$ | .003 | .005 | .010 |

*Notes:* Dependent variable is growth rate of gross industrial output by TVEs during 1988–90. See appendix for definitions of independent variables. Numbers in parentheses are heteroskedasticity-consistent standard errors.

##Significant at the 15 percent level.

#Significant at the 10 percent level.

*Significant at the 5 percent level.

significant at the 10 percent level. For example, a city with a 1 percent higher share of foreign firm output in total output in 1988 is likely to have a 0.76 percentage point higher growth rate for its TVE sector.

This positive association could come from the additional competition that the presence of foreign-invested firms provides for TVEs. But I think that it more likely results from certain positive externalities from the foreign firms to domestic TVEs. One important externality is technological spillover. The other, possibly more important one, is modern management techniques, marketing, and work discipline that foreign-invested firms exhibit to the TVEs. Whatever the channels, the presence of foreign-invested firms appears to be helpful to the further expansion of the nonstate sector.

## 3.5 Concluding Remarks

Foreign investment in China comes disproportionately from overseas Chinese, particularly those residing in Hong Kong. An empirical norm of inward FDI is established as a function of the host country's size, development level, literacy, and geographic location and source country characteristics based on data about geographic distribution of the outward FDI of the five largest source countries. Relative to an "average" host country, China appears to host too little foreign investment from all the major source countries (the United States, Germany, France, and the United Kingdom) except Japan.

The paper also attempts to assess several economic consequences of FDI in China. Based on city-level data, it finds statistically significant evidence that FDI is positively associated with cross-city differences in growth rates, after taking into account the growth of labor, physical, and human capital. Foreign-invested firms have higher export propensity than average Chinese firms. The paper tests and concludes that foreign-invested firms do not displace exports by Chinese firms. Hence, their contribution to overall Chinese exports is at least the amount of their direct exports. Finally, the paper examines the interaction of FDI and the nonstate sector in China. There is some tentative evidence supporting the hypothesis that foreign-invested firms contribute positively to the rapid expansion of the township and village enterprises.

# Appendix

## *Variable Acronyms in the Statistical Tables*

GPop—growth rate of nonagricultural population.
GCap—growth rate of the net value of capital ("fixed asset").
FDI88d/Cap88—ratio of the stock of foreign capital to net value of capital in 1988, where a 10 percent depreciation rate is assumed for foreign capital and

the official exchange rate in 1990 (3.72 yuan/dollar) is used to convert the dollar value of FDI into the *renminbi* (RMB) value.

FDI88nd/Cap88—ratio of the stock of foreign capital to net value of capital in 1988, where zero depreciation is assumed for foreign capital and the official exchange rate in 1990 (3.72 Yuan/dollar) is used to convert the dollar value of FDI into the RMB value.

YFor88/Y88—share of foreign-invested/managed firms in total city output in 1988.

GHumCap—growth rate of the average level of human capital, where average human capital is measured as share of skilled labor in the total nonagricultural labor force.

Reform—dummy for the 72 "comprehensive reform experimenting cities."

Open—dummy for either 14 "coastal open cities" or 4 "special economic zones."

## References

Amirahmadi, Hooshang, and Weiping Wu. 1994. Foreign direct investment in developing countries. *Journal of Developing Areas* 28:167–90.

China Ministry of Foreign Economic Relations and Trade. 1992, 1993. *Almanac of China's foreign economic relations and trade 1992/93.* Beijing: China Ministry of Foreign Economic Relations and Trade.

China State Statistics Bureau. 1989, 1991. *Chinese urban statistics yearbook.* Beijing: China State Statistics Bureau.

———. 1994. Statistical report on national economy and social development in 1993. *People's Daily* (overseas edition), March 2.

Feldstein, Martin. 1995. The effects of outbound foreign direct investment on the domestic capital stock. In *The effects of taxation on multinational corporations,* ed. M. Feldstein, J. Hines, and R. G. Hubbard, 43–63. Chicago: University of Chicago Press.

Froot, Kenneth A. 1993. *Foreign direct investment.* Chicago: University of Chicago Press.

Hines, James, Jr., and Kristen L. Wilard. 1992. Trick or treaty? Bargains and surprises in international tax agreements. Harvard University and Princeton University.

Hsiao, Cheng. 1986. Analysis of panel data. Econometrics Society Monograph no. 11. Cambridge: Cambridge University Press.

Hufbauer, Gary, Darius Lakdawalla, and Anup Malani. 1994. Determinants of direct foreign investment and its connection to trade. Manuscript.

Kinoshita, Toshihiko. 1994. Japan's foreign direct investment in East and Southeast Asia: The current situation and the prospect for the future. Report. Tokyo: Research Institute for International Investment and Development, Export-Import Bank of Japan.

Kueh, Y. Y. 1992. Foreign investment and economic change in China. *China Quarterly* 131:637–90.

Lardy, Nicholas R. 1994. *China in the world economy.* Washington, D.C.: Institute for International Economics.

Lipsey, Robert E. 1995. Outward direct investment and the U.S. economy. In *The effects of taxation on multinational corporations,* ed. M. Feldstein, J. Hines, and R. G. Hubbard, 7–33. Chicago: University of Chicago Press.

Lucas, Robert. 1990. Why doesn't capital flow from rich to poor countries? *American Economic Review: Papers and Proceedings* 80:92–96.

Reddy, J. Mahender. 1994. United States investment in India. Paper presented at sixth biennial conference on U.S.-Asia Economic Relations, sponsored by American Committee on Asian Economic Studies and Asia Pacific Center of Brandeis University, Brandeis University, June 16–18.

United Nations. 1992. *World investment directory 1992.* Vol. 1, *Asia and the Pacific.* New York: United Nations.

———. 1993. *World investment directory 1992.* Vol. 3, *Developed countries.* New York: United Nations.

Wei, Shang-Jin. 1995. The open-door policy and China's rapid growth: Evidence from city-level data. In *Growth theories in light of the East Asian experience,* ed. Takatoshi Ito and Anne O. Krueger. Chicago: University of Chicago Press.

Wei, Shang-Jin, and Peng Lian. 1993. Love and hate: State and nonstate firms in transition economies. Kennedy School of Government Faculty Research Working Paper Series, R93–40. Cambridge: Harvard University, November.

World Bank. 1988. *China: External trade and capital.* Washington, D.C.: World Bank.

———. 1992. *World development report 1992: Development and the environment.* New York: Oxford University Press.

———. 1994. *China: Foreign trade reform.* Washington, D.C.: World Bank.

## Comment Pakorn Vichyanond

On sources of foreign direct investment (FDI), I have three observations. First, in the equations explaining stocks and flows of FDI, it is notable that labor cost is left out. This factor is crucial as it strongly influenced numerous Japanese corporations to relocate their production plants to China, Vietnam, and Southeast Asia. Instead, the included variable is literacy, which is definitely less significant than relative wages as a determinant of FDI.

Second, another important variable that was neglected is exchange rate fluctuation. This particular factor was very meaningful in inducing Japanese FDI in Thailand because exchange rate levels and volatility affect not only the costs but also the revenue or profits of private corporations. Therefore, exchange rate should be included as another prominent explanatory variable.

Third, investment privileges given to tap FDI, such as tax exemptions or allowances, constitute another important determinant of FDI so they should be specifically treated.

On consequences of FDI, my worries concern the host country or recipient of FDI, not cross-city differences. Thus, the following questions are raised concerning the impact of FDI in a national context.

First, it is usually unquestionable that FDI spurs economic growth in host

Pakorn Vichyanond is a senior research fellow at the Thailand Development Research Institute.

countries. The robust Thai economy in 1988–90, for instance, was strongly stimulated by investment, of which FDI constituted a growing portion. What deserves to be asked is, How sustainable is it to rely on FDI as a means to accelerate economic growth? Over time, labor cost grows higher and exchange rates vary; consequently, the attractions to FDI subside, so do the sizes of the markets of or in host countries.

Second, the favorable impact of FDI on exports of host countries is similar to the impact on economic growth. What should be investigated is how long export promotion can be achieved via FDI (e.g., privileges given to FDI with a prerequisite of a minimum level of exports within certain years) because most export promotion measures are now deemed to be trade distortions. The GATT conclusions reached in Morocco, for instance, were distinctly against agricultural subsidies, and those subsidies are to be terminated or reduced markedly within a specific time frame.

Third, some negative repercussions of FDI should be recognized and addressed. Examples of such adverse effects are transfer pricing and environmental degradation. The drug industry in Thailand suffered severely from the problem of transfer pricing in the past.

Finally, the merits of FDI may be questioned in several respects. For instance, historically FDI deserves attention or privileges because it naturally brings with it supporting capital funds, accommodating markets for commodities to be produced, and technology from abroad. But in the current scenario where globalism prevails in most regards, those merits of FDI may not be deemed valuable anymore. Capital funds can be tapped worldwide. Accommodating markets can be found in newly opened countries, for example, China, Eastern Europe, and Indochina. And technology transfer has become more available on a commercial basis, or not necessarily tied to FDI. Therefore, it is not surprising that at present several developing countries have changed their viewpoints on FDI from the conventional perspective. In other words, FDI is not always heaven anymore. It is formidably challenged by numerous alternatives that do not have the adverse effects of FDI.

## Comment Wing Thye Woo

In this brilliant paper, Wei presents three propositions: (1) FDI has positive effects on growth; (2) FDI promotes growth of the nonstate sector; and (3) FDI has come disproportionately from the Chinese diaspora.

Wing Thye Woo is professor of economics and head of the Pacific Studies Program at the Institute of Governmental Affairs at the University of California, Davis.

## FDI Promotes Economic Growth

Wei's proof comes from estimating

$$Y = F(K, L, \text{FDI}) \tag{1}$$

across cities and finding that FDI is significantly positive for two of the three proxies used. A quick inspection of tables 3.10 and 3.11 reveals two troubling features. First, equation (1) is a serious misspecification of the production function because the dependent variable is *gross* industrial output and intermediate input is not included as a regressor. Second, we have the anomalous situation in which the theoretically preferred proxy (FDI88d/Cap88) is insignificant but the theoretically flawed proxy (FDI88nd/Cap88) is significant. The former assumes a 10 percent depreciation of the foreign-owned capital stock, while the latter assumes zero depreciation.

I do not doubt that FDI promotes growth, but I think that Wei's empirical procedures are likely to have greatly overstated its contribution. My reservations are based on the position that the fundamental reason for Chinese economic growth is the liberalization and hence marketization of the command economy. We must be sensitive to the fact that FDI has occurred most in the cities where FDI has been legally allowed to occur, that is, the 5 special economic zones (SEZs), the 14 open coastal cities (OCCs), and the 72 comprehensive reform experimenting cities (CRECs). However, being allowed to liberalize and actually implementing liberalization are two different matters. Because not all local leaders are equally enthusiastic about introducing capitalist-style measures to boost economic development, local leaders differ considerably in their receptivity to FDI. My conjecture is that the regional distribution of FDI reflects to a considerable extent the degree of liberalization actually implemented across the various cities. This means that one major reason why FDI has an output effect beyond its expansion of the capital stock is that in general FDI occurred in the cities that have liberalized the most and hence have raised their growth potential the most. In short, FDI is correlated with total factor productivity (TFP) growth because FDI is a good proxy for the degree of economic liberalization and the greater the liberalization, the higher TFP growth.

Hereby, we also have the explanation for why the Reform and Open dummies (used to differentiate the SEZs, the OCCs, and the CRECs from the cities legally unfriendly to FDI) are statistically insignificant when they are added to equation (1). These dummies represent the formal granting of liberalization authority to certain cities, whereas FDI represents the actual implementation of liberalization in the cities that have permission to do so. Since the continuous distribution of FDI is a better proxy of the regional degree of economic liberalization than the 0/1 dummies, the insignificance of the Reform and Open dummies only shows that the inclusion of FDI has robbed these dummies of their statistical function.

It is likely that the statistical significance of FDI is also due to its also being a proxy for favored access to intermediate inputs. Price liberalization is most advanced in the cities where FDI is most concentrated, and since prices of intermediate inputs are the highest in these cities, they suffer no shortage of intermediate inputs. Simply put, FDI is more likely to flow to cities with no power shortages than to cities with chronic power shortages.

**FDI Promotes Growth of the Nonstate Sector**

Wei's proof of this proposition consists of regressing

(2) $$Y \text{ of TVEs} = f(\text{FDI})$$

and finding that two of the three proxies for FDI are statistically significant (see table 3.13). We note that equation (2) is a greater misspecification of the production function than equation (1) because it has no input variables as regressors.

We also note that since FDI is a proxy for the degree of economic liberalization, it should be natural that it is positively correlated with the output growth of the nonstate sector, another by-product of economic liberalization. It is therefore somewhat surprising that one of the FDI proxies failed to be significant in such a favorable setting. Perhaps, gross misspecification has a role in the unexpected result.

**How Big Is FDI's Contribution to Growth?**

The facts are: Poland is more marketized than China, China has more FDI than Poland, and China has grown faster than Poland. These facts, however, do not show that FDI is a better promoter of growth than marketization, just as the Chinese experience does not show that gradual reform is superior to Polish-style rapid and comprehensive reforms.

The high growth of China, the great amount of FDI in China, and the explosive growth of the town and village enterprise (TVE) sector are all products of the marketization of a labor-surplus peasant economy (see Sachs and Woo 1994). In 1978, over three-quarters of the Chinese labor force were engaged in subsistence farming, the peasants were kept down on the farms by the Household Registration System, and the official estimate was that one-third of the farm labor force was surplus labor. The high aggregate growth rate and the growth of TVE output are the results of the absorption of surplus agricultural labor and the absence of the need to reduce the state industrial sector to release labor for the growth of the TVEs. The inflow of FDI to China is the natural response to the low wages of the surplus labor economy.

FDI doubtlessly increases TFP directly by technological transfers and indirectly by providing an efficient management style to be emulated by the Chinese enterprises. However, Wei's estimated contribution of FDI to TFP growth is an overstatement of these direct and indirect effects because of the close correlation between FDI and the degree of economic liberalization.

## A Disproportionate Amount of FDI Is from the Chinese Diaspora

The bulk of the empirical work in the paper involves estimating an international norm of investment (see tables 3.3–3.7). This may seem a somewhat puzzling exercise. What is the policy implication of finding that Western Europe and the United States are underinvesting in China unless China can imperiously demand that the laggards double their FDI efforts? One is therefore left wondering about the role and importance of section 3.3 in this excellent paper.

I think that section 3.3 implies a very important hypothesis that should not be overlooked (and that should be tested by the author in a future paper)—a point more important to Eastern Europe and Russia than to China. As most FDI in China has been from the Chinese diaspora, this means that the other transition economies (except for Vietnam) that do not have large diasporas are unlikely to experience significant income growth from FDI.

## Reference

Sachs, Jeffrey, and Wing Thye Woo. 1994. Structural factors in the economic reforms of China, Eastern Europe, and the Former Soviet Union. *Economic Policy* 18:101–45.

# 4 Interdependence through Capital Flows in Pacific Asia and the Role of Japan

Akira Kohsaka

Pacific Asia has been one of the most dynamic cases of outward-oriented development in the world in the past two decades. In light of the emerging trend toward "institutional" regional integration, as in Europe 1992 and NAFTA, it has been widely discussed whether Pacific Asia's development has enhanced regional economic interdependence or "natural" integration through trade flows (see, e.g., Eaton and Ho 1993; Frankel 1992; Frankel and Wei 1994; Petri 1993; Saxonhouse 1993).

It would be natural, then, to ask whether we can also find regional integration through capital, as through trade. Before discussing integration issues, however, we should realize what is going on in both inter- and intraregional capital flows in Pacific Asia. Nevertheless, there are fewer studies of capital flows than of trade (e.g., Yuan 1986; Frankel 1992; Kohsaka 1993). Thus we must first examine the changing patterns of capital flows and the degree of interdependence through capital in the region.

There is a vast literature on the general trend in capital flows to developing countries, provided by multilateral financial institutions (such as the International Monetary Fund [IMF] 1994; the World Bank 1993c; Bank for International Settlements [BIS] 1994; International Finance Corporation 1992). Based on these studies, this paper will review the changing pattern and nature of capital flows in Pacific Asia since the 1980s, to identify underlying fundamental factors that not only have contributed to these changes but also are unique to the region. We will then clarify intraregional interdependence through capital, and the role of Japan in it, by investigating multilateral aspects of these flows within the region.

Akira Kohsaka is professor of economics at the Osaka School of International Public Policy, Osaka University.

The author is grateful for helpful comments by Toshihiko Kinoshita, Anne O. Krueger, Ya-Hwei Yang, and other seminar participants.

Capital flows consist of such components as grants, official loans, suppliers and export credits, commercial bank loans, foreign direct investment, and portfolio investment. Significant changes in the pattern of external finance to developing countries during the last two decades can be found in table 4.1.

Table 4.1 shows that "the 1970s and 1980s were the boom-and-bust years of commercial bank finance to developing countries" (World Bank 1993b). In 1981 more than seven times as much long-term capital rushed into developing countries as a decade earlier, while the flow increased by less than 30 percent over the next decade. Accompanying shifts in the composition of flows were dominated by changes in the role of commercial bank loans. In 1981, commercial bank loans made up the largest share of total external finance to developing countries, followed by official loans and then by foreign direct investment; in 1991 commercial bank loans had fallen to second largest, far behind official loans and closely followed by foreign direct investment.

As will be shown below, external finance to Pacific Asia—comprising China, Hong Kong, Indonesia, Korea (South), Malaysia, the Philippines, Singapore, Taiwan, and Thailand—has also followed this trend, but to a limited degree. In addition, the region will be shown to have intensified natural integration through intraregional capital flows, as it had through trade flows in the late 1980s.

Previous studies found the following changing pattern of capital flows in the region up to the early 1980s: First, capital flows from developed economies in the Pacific Basin increased in importance. Second, the importance of Japan in particular was magnified across all components of capital flows. Third, private flows played a more significant role than official flows. The 1980s saw quite dynamic changes in the region, however, so it is not difficult to imagine that this pattern no longer holds.

Furthermore, the early 1990s is said to have seen a radical shift in the pattern of capital flows to developing countries "from debt to equity financing and

**Table 4.1 External Finance to Developing Countries: Gross Long-Term Flows (% of total)**

| Component | 1971 | 1981 | 1991 |
|---|---|---|---|
| Official flows | 39.9 | 33.3 | 45.3 |
| Grants | 9.0 | 7.3 | 14.5 |
| Official loans | 30.9 | 26.0 | 30.8 |
| Suppliers and export credits | 10.8 | 11.0 | 12.3 |
| Commercial bank loans | 35.7 | 46.1 | 17.4 |
| Foreign direct investment | 12.3 | 8.3 | 16.5 |
| Portfolio investment | 1.2 | 1.3 | 8.5 |
| Total (billion $) | 19.5 | 156.9 | 205.3 |

*Source:* World Bank (1993b).

from bank to nonbank sources" (World Bank 1993b). This shift partly reflects the improved economic climate in some Latin American countries. Can we find similar development in Pacific Asia?

This paper is organized as follows: Section 4.1 demonstrates differences in patterns of external finance between Asia and Latin America in order to show regional diversity of recent developments in capital flows. Recent changes in the structure of foreign capital inflow and local capital outflow, rather than of net flows, are examined in section 4.2 for both Pacific Asia as a whole and individual countries in the region. Since Pacific Asian countries have diverse structures of external finance, we suggest that regional aggregation may obscure or distort the size and direction of capital flows. Section 4.3 attempts to identify underlying factors that not only have helped realize these changes but also are unique to the region. We suggest that changes in macroeconomic balances provide the fundamental mechanism that has determined structural changes in net capital flows. In Section 4.4, we scrutinize changes in the geographical distribution of these capital flows and indicate that the changes suggest increasing regional interdependence through capital flows, resulting in a sophisticated network of multilateral flows in the region, which would magnify the "regional aggregation bias" mentioned above. Then, section 4.5 examines the role of Japan as one of the key players in the region with respect to capital flows and finds some important changes there. Some conclusive remarks will be made at the end of the paper.

## 4.1 Regional Patterns of External Finance

Recent trends in capital flows to developing countries contrast sharply with those of the mid-1980s with respect to not only amount but composition. Annual average net flows declined from $31 billion for the years 1977–82 to $9 billion for 1983–89 and then rebounded to $92 billion for 1990–93 (see table 4.2 below for the developing countries' total net flow). Among the components of capital flows, the dominant one has been foreign direct investment (FDI), with portfolio investment showing remarkable growth, while long-term loans were actually flowing *out.*

The amount of foreign capital inflow net of amortization is sometimes called "net resource flows."[1] Figure 4.1 shows the amount and composition of long-term net resource flows to all developing countries, to East Asia and the Pacific, and to Latin America and the Caribbean during the period 1982–94 (World Bank 1994).[2] It is obvious that the above-mentioned general trend in gross

1. Net resource flows here consist of the net flow of long-term debt excluding IMF credits, direct foreign investment (net), and grants (excluding technical cooperation). Net resource flows minus grants correspond to changes in liabilities in the long-term capital account of the balance of payments.

2. In addition to Pacific Asia, East Asia and the Pacific includes Fiji, Laos, Papua New Guinea, Solomon Islands, Tonga, Vanuatu, and Western Samoa.

A

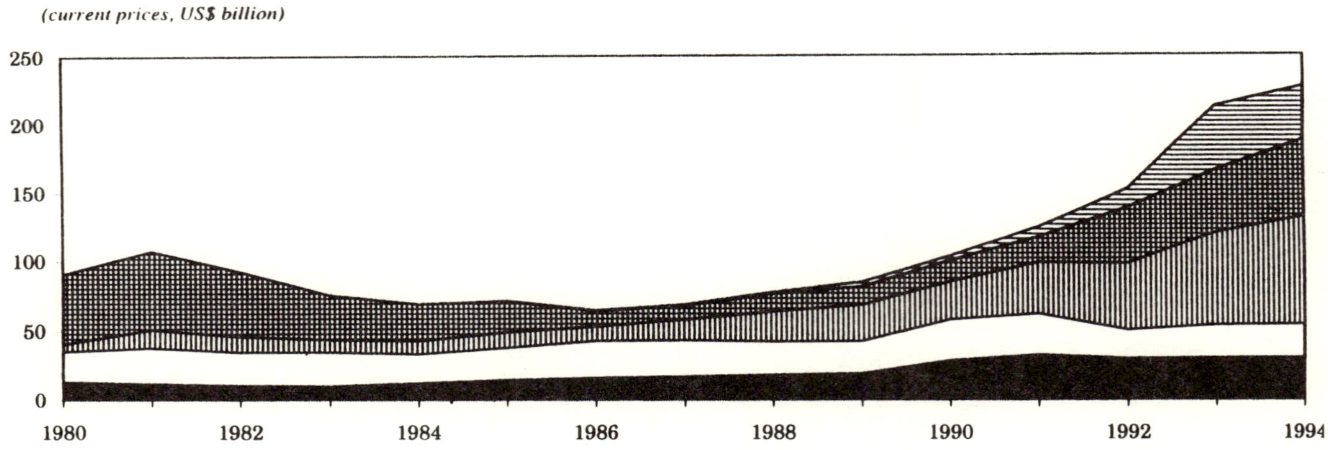
(current prices, US$ billion)
250
200
150
100
50
0
1980
1982
1984
1986
1988
1990
1992
1994

B

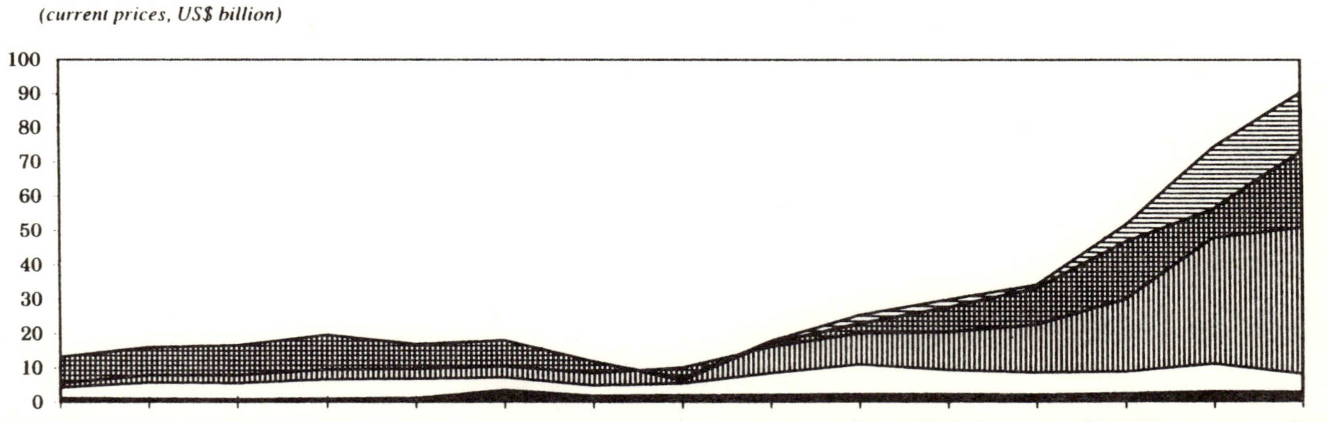
(current prices, US$ billion)
100
90
80
70
60
50
40
30
20
10
0

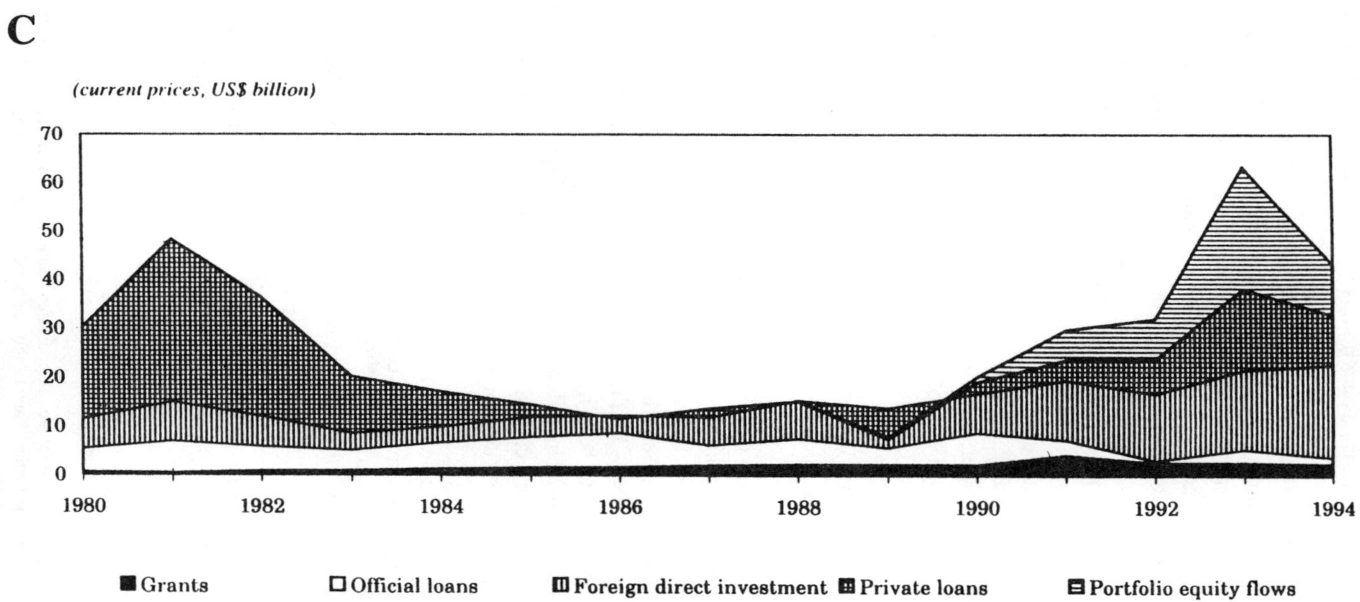


**Fig. 4.1 Net resource flows by region: (*A*) all developing countries; (*B*) East Asia and the Pacific; (*C*) Latin America and the Caribbean**

*Source:* World Bank (1995).

capital flows to developing countries as a whole is not necessarily identical to those of individual regions.

In Latin America and the Caribbean (fig. 4.1*C*), total net flows sharply declined from a peak of $50 billion in 1981, remained low at around $10-$20 billion during 1983–88, and then rebounded to eventually surpass the previous peak in 1993. During this process, the composition of capital flows changed dramatically. The flow of private loans (mostly commercial bank loans) disappeared and then turned negative (i.e., flowed out) in the mid-1980s. In its place, FDI became the most important form of capital flow, and in 1993, portfolio equity flows became the next most important form; private loans came back, not as bank loans, but as bond issues.

In contrast, East Asia and the Pacific never saw as significant a decline in net capital flows as Latin America, even in the early 1980s (fig. 4.1*B*). Total net flows remained stable during 1980–85 at around $15-$20 billion. The major form of capital was commercial bank loans, and the second was official loans. There then appeared a vigorous surge in total net capital flows, especially after 1986; this time, FDI was far more significant than in the early 1980s, while commercial bank loans resumed its growth as a major component, and portfolio equity flows surged starting in the early 1990s. Now, if we turn to the capital account figures of the balance of payments (see table 4.2), we can ascertain more striking contrasts between these two regions.

In the Western Hemisphere, foreign capital *outflow* in Other long-term flows (mainly commercial bank loans) continued not only in 1983–89 under the "debt overhang" but even in 1990–93, the most recent period listed. Note that this outflow forced the region to be a net capital exporter, instead of an importer, in the 1980s, which has been called the "lost decade." Under these circumstances, the surge of foreign capital inflow in the 1990s took, primarily, the form of portfolio investment (i.e. bonds and equities) and, then, the form of FDI.

On the other hand, Asia continued to receive a significant amount of foreign loans, although FDI caught up to and then exceeded this amount, and portfolio investment was catching up toward the 1990s.[3] More important, one notable fact is that local capital outflow (the assets flows in table 4.2) in Asia has become significant in each component of capital transactions, namely, FDI, portfolio investment, and loans. In fact, these annual average outflows amounted to about one-third of the corresponding foreign capital inflows for the period 1990–93. This will be shown to reflect increasing capital interdependence in Pacific Asia.

3. In addition to Pacific Asia, "Asia" includes Afghanistan, Bangladesh, Fiji, India, Kiribati, Laos, Maldives, Myanmar, Nepal, Pakistan, Papua New Guinea, Solomon Islands, Sri Lanka, Tonga, Vanuatu, Western Samoa, and "Asia not specified."

**Table 4.2** **Capital Account: Asia and Western Hemisphere (annual averages)**

| | Amount (billion U.S. $) | | | | Share (%) | | | |
|---|---|---|---|---|---|---|---|---|
| Net Flow | 1973–76 | 1977–82 | 1983–89 | 1990–93 | 1973–76 | 1977–82 | 1983–89 | 1990–93 |
| *Developing countries total* | | | | | | | | |
| FDI | 3.7 | 11.3 | 13.3 | 34.1 | 24.2 | 26.4 | 94.3 | 63.3 |
| Assets | −0.3 | −0.9 | −3.4 | −10.2 | 3.5 | 5.2 | 100.0 | 34.8 |
| Liabilities | 4 | 12.2 | 16.7 | 44.3 | 16.7 | 20.3 | 95.4 | 53.2 |
| Portfolio | −5.6 | −10.5 | 6.5 | 26.8 | −36.6 | −24.5 | 46.1 | 49.7 |
| Assets | −6.4 | −13.1 | 3.6 | −13 | 74.4 | 75.7 | −105.9 | 44.4 |
| Liabilities | 0.8 | 2.6 | 2.9 | 39.8 | 3.3 | 4.3 | 16.6 | 47.8 |
| Other LT | 17.2 | 42 | −5.7 | −7 | 112.4 | 98.1 | −40.4 | −13.0 |
| Assets | −1.9 | −3.3 | −3.5 | −6.1 | 22.1 | 19.1 | 105.9 | 20.8 |
| Liabilities | 19.1 | 45.3 | −2.1 | −0.9 | 79.9 | 75.4 | −12.0 | −1.1 |
| LT total | 15.3 | 42.8 | 14.1 | 53.9 | 103.4 | 139.9 | 160.2 | 58.9 |
| Assets | −8.6 | −17.3 | −3.4 | −29.3 | 50.0 | 38.5 | 27.2 | 99.0 |
| Liabilities | 23.9 | 60.1 | 17.5 | 83.2 | 74.7 | 79.6 | 82.2 | 68.7 |
| ST Capital | −0.5 | −12.2 | −5.3 | 37.6 | −3.4 | −39.9 | −60.2 | 41.1 |
| Assets | −8.6 | −27.6 | −9.1 | −0.3 | 50.0 | 61.5 | 72.8 | 1.0 |
| Liabilities | 8.1 | 15.4 | 3.8 | 37.9 | 25.3 | 20.4 | 17.8 | 31.3 |
| Total net | 14.8 | 30.6 | 8.8 | 91.5 | 100.0 | 100.0 | 100.0 | 100.0 |
| Assets | −17.2 | −44.9 | −12.5 | −29.6 | 100.0 | 100.0 | 100.0 | 100.0 |
| Liabilities | 32 | 75.5 | 21.3 | 121.1 | 100.0 | 100.0 | 100.0 | 100.0 |
| *Asia* | | | | | | | | |
| FDI | 1.3 | 2.7 | 5.2 | 19.8 | 23.2 | 20.3 | 36.4 | 53.5 |
| Assets | −0.1 | −0.2 | −2.6 | −7.0 | 50.0 | 28.6 | 46.4 | 45.1 |
| Liabilities | 1.4 | 2.9 | 7.8 | 27.7 | 24.1 | 20.7 | 39.2 | 50.8 |
| Portfolio | 0.2 | 0.6 | 1.4 | 7.2 | 3.6 | 4.5 | 9.8 | 19.5 |
| Assets | 0 | −0.1 | −0.9 | −3.4 | 0.0 | 14.3 | 16.1 | 19.4 |
| Liabilities | 0.2 | 0.7 | 2.3 | 10.6 | 3.4 | 5.0 | 11.6 | 19.4 |
| Other LT | 4.1 | 10.0 | 7.7 | 10 | 73.2 | 75.2 | 53.8 | 27.0 |
| Assets | −0.1 | −0.4 | −2.1 | −6.2 | 50.0 | 57.1 | 37.5 | 35.4 |
| Liabilities | 4.2 | 10.4 | 9.8 | 16.2 | 72.4 | 74.3 | 49.2 | 29.7 |
| LT total | 5.6 | 13.3 | 14.3 | 37 | 82.4 | 84.2 | 85.6 | 79.4 |
| Assets | −0.2 | −0.7 | −5.6 | −17.5 | 20.0 | 20.6 | 52.8 | 62.3 |
| Liabilities | 5.8 | 14 | 19.9 | 54.5 | 74.4 | 72.9 | 72.9 | 73.0 |
| ST Capital | 1.2 | 2.5 | 2.4 | 9.6 | 17.6 | 15.8 | 14.4 | 20.6 |
| Assets | −0.8 | −2.7 | −5 | −10.6 | 80.0 | 79.4 | 47.2 | 37.7 |
| Liabilities | 2 | 5.2 | 7.4 | 20.2 | 25.6 | 27.1 | 27.1 | 27.0 |
| Total | 6.8 | 15.8 | 16.7 | 46.6 | 100.0 | 100.0 | 100.0 | 100.0 |
| Assets | −1 | −3.4 | −10.6 | −28.1 | 100.0 | 100.0 | 100.0 | 100.0 |
| Liabilities | 7.8 | 19.2 | 27.3 | 74.7 | 100.0 | 100.0 | 100.0 | 100.0 |
| *Western Hemisphere* | | | | | | | | |
| FDI | 2.2 | 5.3 | 4.4 | 11.1 | 19.1 | 18.2 | −40.7 | 58.7 |
| Assets | −0.1 | −0.2 | −0.3 | −1.2 | 12.5 | 14.3 | 75.0 | 17.9 |
| Liabilities | 2.3 | 5.5 | 4.7 | 12.3 | 18.7 | 18.0 | −45.2 | 48.0 |
| Portfolio | 0.2 | 1.6 | −1.2 | 17.6 | 1.7 | 5.5 | 11.1 | 93.1 |

(*continued*)

**Table 4.2** (continued)

| | Amount (billion U.S. $) | | | | Share (%) | | | |
|---|---|---|---|---|---|---|---|---|
| Net Flow | 1973–76 | 1977–82 | 1983–89 | 1990–93 | 1973–76 | 1977–82 | 1983–89 | 1990–93 |
| Assets | −0.1 | −0.2 | −0.4 | −7.4 | 12.5 | 14.3 | 100.0 | 110.4 |
| Liabilities | 0.3 | 1.8 | −0.8 | 25 | 2.4 | 5.9 | 7.7 | 97.7 |
| Other LT | 9.1 | 22.2 | −14 | −9.8 | 79.1 | 76.3 | 129.6 | −51.9 |
| Assets | −0.6 | −1 | 0.3 | 1.9 | 75.0 | 71.4 | −75.0 | −28.4 |
| Liabilities | 9.7 | 23.2 | −14.3 | −11.7 | 78.9 | 76.1 | 137.5 | −45.7 |
| LT total | 11.5 | 29.1 | −10.8 | 18.9 | 88.5 | 110.6 | 65.1 | 79.1 |
| Assets | −0.8 | −1.4 | −0.4 | −6.7 | 22.2 | 13.7 | −66.7 | 51.9 |
| Liabilities | 12.3 | 30.5 | −10.4 | 25.6 | 74.1 | 83.6 | 60.5 | 69.6 |
| Other ST | 1.5 | −2.8 | −5.8 | 5 | 11.5 | −10.6 | 34.9 | 20.0 |
| Assets | −2.8 | −8.8 | 1 | −6.2 | 77.8 | 86.3 | 166.7 | 48.1 |
| Liabilities | 4.3 | 6 | −6.8 | 11.2 | 25.9 | 16.4 | 39.5 | 30.4 |
| Total | 13 | 26.3 | −16.6 | 23.9 | 100.0 | 100.0 | 100.0 | 100.0 |
| Assets | −3.6 | −10.2 | 0.6 | −12.9 | 100.0 | 100.0 | 100.0 | 100.0 |
| Liabilities | 16.6 | 36.5 | −17.2 | 36.8 | 100.0 | 100.0 | 100.0 | 100.0 |

*Source:* IMF (1994).

## 4.2 Capital Flows in Pacific Asia

### 4.2.1 Individual Patterns of Capital Flow

We have seen some differences in regional patterns of capital flow by comparing Asia with Latin America. Regionally aggregated capital flows, however, may not be very useful in grasping the changing nature and pattern of these flows in individual economies within the region, or rather, may obscure important differences between these economies. This is true for the case of Pacific Asia. Table 4.3 shows capital accounts of the balance of payments in Pacific Asia in aggregate as well as for individual economies. Overall, there appears to be little difference between Asia in table 4.2 and Pacific Asia in table 4.3. However, if we look into individual economies, table 4.3 suggests two points. First, during the period 1986–89, both Korea and Malaysia had huge net outflows of foreign loans, of which a significant part was premature amortization. This was not an involuntary outflow due to the drying-up of new loans as in the case of Latin America, but a voluntary outflow due to these countries' remarkably improved external balances. In this case, it should be noted that regional aggregation tends to understate the significance of loan capital in the other economies in the region because Korea's and Malaysia's outflows offset other countries' "other" flows (liabilities) for the period 1986–89.

Second, the geographical distribution of local capital outflow shows high concentration in the Asian newly industrializing economies (ANIEs). That is, in Pacific Asia, there seem to have been broadly two types of economies in terms of

**Table 4.3** **Long-Term Capital Account: Pacific Asia (annual averages)**

| | Amount (million U.S. $) | | | Share (%) | | |
|---|---|---|---|---|---|---|
| Net Flow | 1982–85 | 1986–89 | 1990–92 | 1982–85 | 1986–89 | 1990–92 |
| *Pacific Asia* | | | | | | |
| Total | 15,328 | 6,216 | 20,924 | 100.0 | 100.0 | 100.0 |
| Assets | −5,795 | −12,344 | −19,889 | 100.0 | 100.0 | 100.0 |
| Liabilities | 21,123 | 18,560 | 40,813 | 100.0 | 100.0 | 100.0 |
| FDI | 3,665 | 5,425 | 13,889 | 23.9 | 87.3 | 66.4 |
| Assets | −533 | −4,237 | −6,789 | 9.2 | 34.3 | 34.1 |
| Liabilities | 4,198 | 9,662 | 20,677 | 19.9 | 52.1 | 50.7 |
| Portfolio | 2,112 | 1,137 | 1,712 | 13.8 | 18.3 | 8.2 |
| Assets | −227 | −518 | −1,943 | 3.9 | 4.2 | 9.8 |
| Liabilities | 2,339 | 1,655 | 3,655 | 11.1 | 8.9 | 9.0 |
| Other | 9,552 | −346 | 5,323 | 62.3 | −5.6 | 25.4 |
| Assets | −5,035 | −7,590 | −11,157 | 86.9 | 61.5 | 56.1 |
| Liabilities | 14,587 | 7,244 | 16,480 | 69.1 | 39.0 | 40.4 |
| *China* | | | | | | |
| Total | 2,020 | 5,700 | 3,679 | 100.0 | 100.0 | 100.0 |
| Assets | −1,043 | −1,205 | −4,635 | 100.0 | 100.0 | 100.0 |
| Liabilities | 3,063 | 6,906 | 8,314 | 100.0 | 100.0 | 100.0 |
| FDI | 771 | 2,013 | 4,422 | 38.2 | 35.3 | 120.2 |
| Assets | −225 | −681 | −1,914 | 21.6 | 56.5 | 41.3 |
| Liabilities | 996 | 2,694 | 6,336 | 32.5 | 39.0 | 76.2 |
| Portfolio | 0 | 829 | −21 | 0.0 | 14.5 | −0.6 |
| Assets | −30 | −210 | −340 | 2.9 | 17.4 | 7.3 |
| Liabilities | 227 | 1,039 | 319 | 7.4 | 15.0 | 3.8 |
| Other | 1,052 | 2,859 | −722 | 52.1 | 50.2 | −19.6 |
| Assets | −789 | −314 | −2,380 | 75.6 | 26.1 | 51.4 |
| Liabilities | 1,841 | 3,173 | 1,658 | 60.1 | 45.9 | 19.9 |
| *Indonesia* | | | | | | |
| Total | 4,229 | 3,198 | 5,495 | 100.0 | 100.0 | 100.0 |
| Assets | 0 | 0 | 0 | 0.0 | 0.0 | 0.0 |
| Liabilities | 4,229 | 3,198 | 5,495 | 100.0 | 100.0 | 100.0 |
| FDI | 262 | 475 | 1,450 | 6.2 | 14.9 | 26.4 |
| Assets | 0 | 0 | 0 | 0.0 | 0.0 | 0.0 |
| Liabilities | 262 | 475 | 1,450 | 6.2 | 14.9 | 26.4 |
| Portfolio | 160 | −23 | −64 | 3.8 | −0.7 | −1.2 |
| Assets | 0 | 0 | 0 | 0.0 | 0.0 | 0.0 |
| Liabilities | 160 | −23 | −64 | 3.8 | −0.7 | −1.2 |
| Other | 3,807 | 2,746 | 4,109 | 90.0 | 85.9 | 74.8 |
| Assets | 0 | 0 | 0 | 0.0 | 0.0 | 0.0 |
| Liabilities | 3,807 | 2,746 | 4,109 | 90.0 | 85.9 | 74.8 |
| *Korea* | | | | | | |
| Total | 2,764 | −4,952 | 5,649 | 100.0 | 100.0 | 100.0 |
| Assets | −755 | −1,799 | −4,985 | 100.0 | 100.0 | 100.0 |
| Liabilities | 3,519 | −3,153 | 10,634 | 100.0 | 100.0 | 100.0 |
| FDI | 35 | 479 | −281 | 1.3 | −9.7 | −5.0 |
| Assets | −86 | −187 | −1,075 | 11.3 | 10.4 | 21.6 |
| Liabilities | 121 | 666 | 794 | 3.4 | −21.1 | 7.5 |

(*continued*)

**Table 4.3** (continued)

| | Amount (million U.S. $) | | | Share (%) | | |
|---|---|---|---|---|---|---|
| Net Flow | 1982–85 | 1986–89 | 1990–92 | 1982–85 | 1986–89 | 1990–92 |
| Portfolio | 380 | −81 | 3,223 | 13.7 | 1.6 | 57.1 |
| Assets | 0 | −20 | −48 | 0.0 | 1.1 | 1.0 |
| Liabilities | 380 | −61 | 3,271 | 10.8 | 1.9 | 30.8 |
| Other | 2,350 | −5,350 | 2,707 | 85.0 | 108.0 | 47.9 |
| Assets | −670 | −1,592 | −3,862 | 88.7 | 88.5 | 77.5 |
| Liabilities | 3,019 | −3,759 | 6,569 | 85.8 | 119.2 | 61.8 |
| *Malaysia* | | | | | | |
| Total | 3,138 | −306 | 4,695 | 100.0 | 100.0 | 100.0 |
| Assets | −279 | −483 | 168 | 100.0 | 100.0 | 100.0 |
| Liabilities | 3,418 | 178 | 4,527 | 100.0 | 100.0 | 100.0 |
| FDI | 1,038 | 825 | 3,508 | 33.1 | −270.0 | 74.7 |
| Assets | 0 | 0 | 0 | 0.0 | 0.0 | 0.0 |
| Liabilities | 1,038 | 825 | 3,508 | 30.4 | 464.0 | 77.5 |
| Portfolio | 1,080 | −96 | −398 | 34.4 | 31.5 | −8.5 |
| Assets | 0 | 0 | 0 | 0.0 | 0.0 | 0.0 |
| Liabilities | 1,080 | −96 | −398 | 31.6 | −54.1 | −8.8 |
| Other | 1,021 | −1,034 | 1,585 | 32.5 | 338.5 | 33.8 |
| Assets | −279 | −483 | 168 | 100.0 | 100.0 | 100.0 |
| Liabilities | 1,300 | −551 | 1,417 | 38.0 | −309.8 | 31.3 |
| *Philippines* | | | | | | |
| Total | 1,179 | 597 | 2,700 | 100.0 | 100.0 | 100.0 |
| Assets | −4 | −4 | −43 | 100.0 | 100.0 | 100.0 |
| Liabilities | 1,183 | 602 | 2,743 | 100.0 | 100.0 | 100.0 |
| FDI | 36 | 483 | 434 | 3.0 | 80.9 | 16.1 |
| Assets | 0 | 0 | 0 | 0.0 | 0.0 | 0.0 |
| Liabilities | 36 | 483 | 434 | 3.0 | 80.3 | 15.8 |
| Portfolio | 3 | 91 | 33 | 0.2 | 15.2 | 1.2 |
| Assets | −4 | −4 | −43 | 100.0 | 100.0 | 100.0 |
| Liabilities | 6 | 95 | 77 | 0.5 | 15.8 | 2.8 |
| Other | 1,141 | 24 | 2,233 | 96.8 | 3.9 | 82.7 |
| Assets | 0 | 0 | 0 | 0.0 | 0.0 | 0.0 |
| Liabilities | 1,141 | 24 | 2,233 | 96.5 | 3.9 | 81.4 |
| *Singapore* | | | | | | |
| Total | 1,763 | 340 | 4,197 | 100.0 | 100.0 | 100.0 |
| Assets | −1,855 | −4,627 | −2,925 | 100.0 | 100.0 | 100.0 |
| Liabilities | 3,618 | 4,967 | 7,122 | 100.0 | 100.0 | 100.0 |
| FDI | 1,101 | 2,397 | 3,811 | 62.4 | 705.0 | 90.8 |
| Assets | −171 | −347 | −1,286 | 9.2 | 7.5 | 44.0 |
| Liabilities | 1,271 | 2,744 | 5,098 | 35.1 | 55.2 | 71.6 |
| Portfolio | −14 | −166 | −1,103 | −0.8 | −48.8 | −26.3 |
| Assets | −194 | −284 | −1,511 | 10.4 | 6.1 | 51.7 |
| Liabilities | 180 | 118 | 409 | 5.0 | 2.4 | 5.7 |
| Other | 676 | −1,891 | 1,488 | 38.3 | −556.2 | 35.5 |
| Assets | −1,490 | −3,997 | −128 | 80.4 | 86.4 | 4.4 |
| Liabilities | 2,166 | 2,106 | 1,616 | 59.9 | 42.4 | 22.7 |

**Table 4.3** (continued)

| | Amount (million U.S. $) | | | Share (%) | | |
|---|---|---|---|---|---|---|
| Net Flow | 1982–85 | 1986–89 | 1990–92 | 1982–85 | 1986–89 | 1990–92 |
| *Taiwan* | | | | | | |
| Total | −1,686 | −1,204 | −5,364 | 100.0 | 100.0 | 100.0 |
| Assets | −1,730 | −4,151 | −7,342 | 100.0 | 100.0 | 100.0 |
| Liabilities | 45 | 2,947 | 1,978 | 100.0 | 100.0 | 100.0 |
| FDI | 148 | −2,059 | −1,499 | −8.8 | 171.0 | 27.9 |
| Assets | −51 | −2,960 | −2,366 | 2.9 | 71.3 | 32.2 |
| Liabilities | 199 | 901 | 867 | 443.6 | 30.6 | 43.8 |
| Portfolio | 0 | 0 | 0 | 0.0 | 0.0 | 0.0 |
| Assets | 0 | 0 | 0 | 0.0 | 0.0 | 0.0 |
| Liabilities | 0 | 0 | 0 | 0.0 | 0.0 | 0.0 |
| Other | −1,834 | 855 | −3,866 | 108.8 | −71.0 | 72.1 |
| Assets | −1,680 | −1,191 | −4,976 | 97.1 | 28.7 | 67.8 |
| Liabilities | −154 | 2,046 | 1,111 | −343.6 | 69.4 | 56.2 |
| *Thailand* | | | | | | |
| Total | 1,920 | 2,842 | 9,995 | 100.0 | 100.0 | 100.0 |
| Assets | −129 | −75 | −126 | 100.0 | 100.0 | 100.0 |
| Liabilities | 2,049 | 2,917 | 10,121 | 100.0 | 100.0 | 100.0 |
| FDI | 275 | 813 | 2,044 | 14.3 | 28.6 | 20.4 |
| Assets | −1 | −61 | −148 | 1.0 | 81.7 | 116.9 |
| Liabilities | 276 | 874 | 2,191 | 13.5 | 30.0 | 21.7 |
| Portfolio | 307 | 583 | 41 | 16.0 | 20.5 | 0.4 |
| Assets | 0 | 0 | 0 | 0.0 | 0.0 | 0.0 |
| Liabilities | 307 | 583 | 41 | 15.0 | 20.0 | 0.4 |
| Other | 1,339 | 1,446 | 7,910 | 69.7 | 50.9 | 79.1 |
| Assets | −128 | −14 | 121 | 99.0 | 18.3 | −16.9 |
| Liabilities | 1,466 | 1,460 | 7,888 | 71.6 | 50.0 | 77.9 |

*Source:* IMF (various years [a]).

capital flows since the latter half of the 1980s: one type with not insignificant two-way flows and the other type with mostly foreign capital inflow. Korea, Singapore, and Taiwan (and, probably, Hong Kong, for which balance of payments data are not available) are the former, and Indonesia and the Philippines are the latter; Malaysia and Thailand appear to be joining the former group.

For individual countries in Pacific Asia, the local and foreign flows in the main components of capital since the 1980s can be summarized as follows (see table 4.3). In three ANIEs, Korea, Singapore, and Taiwan, either current accounts have tended to run a surplus or local outflow has exceeded foreign inflow at least in some components of capital. Taiwan has been an extreme case in that, since the latter half of the 1980s, local capital outflow has overwhelmed foreign capital inflow in direct investment, portfolio investment, and other long-term capital. Singapore has become a net overseas portfolio investor since the late 1980s while remaining a net host country in terms of direct investment.

Korea has become a net overseas direct investor since the late 1980s while having been an important portfolio "investee" since the early 1990s.

In complete contrast to Taiwan, Indonesia and the Philippines have both remained one-way capital absorbers. Between these two groups, Malaysia, Thailand, and China have begun to send capital abroad as either direct investment (in the cases of Thailand and China) or portfolio investment (in the cases of Malaysia and China), while all three countries have been important destinations for the recent explosion of FDI from Japan and the Asian NIEs.

### 4.2.2 Individual Patterns of Foreign Capital Inflow

The most recent developments in foreign capital inflow are shown in table 4.4. The steadily increasing share of FDI in foreign capital inflow has been the most salient feature. In China, Malaysia, and Singapore, FDI has been the most important component of capital inflow. FDI literally rushed into China; the average share of FDI in total net long-term flows exceeded 50 percent over 1990–93.

The growing prominence of FDI reflects increased intraregional trade and intraregional division of labor under the global production, sourcing, and marketing strategies pursued by international businesses, as well as local market growth and deregulation. Indeed, we note that there is not only geographical concentration of FDI but also shifts in FDI even within Pacific Asia, which seems to result at least somewhat from "regulatory arbitrage" on the part of international businesses.

Meanwhile, in Korea, Malaysia, and Thailand, portfolio investment has grown rapidly very recently. In particular, in Korea more than 80 percent of net resource inflow in 1990–93 was portfolio investment.

Foreign investment in bonds includes both international issues, such as Eurodollar bonds, and direct purchases of local securities, which virtually started to expand in 1993 in Pacific Asia (see OECD, various issues); Hong Kong, Korea, Malaysia, and Thailand have been main recipients. Portfolio equity investment, on the other hand, includes international issues (including depository receipts) and direct purchases in local markets; China, Korea, Malaysia, and Thailand are the main recipients.

Finally, "official debt," or official loans, remained significant, though relatively smaller, in China, Indonesia, and the Philippines. Its role was reduced sharply in Malaysia and Thailand, however. This will be discussed in section 4.4 in more detail.

## 4.3 Macroeconomic Development in Pacific Asia

### 4.3.1 Factors in the Recent Developments in Capital Flows

We have observed that significant changes have occurred in capital flows to developing countries in general, as well as to Pacific Asia. What drove these

Table 4.4 **Capital Inflow: Pacific Asia (annual averages)**

| Flow | Amount (million U.S. $) 1986–89 | Amount (million U.S. $) 1990–93 | Share (%) 1986–89 | Share (%) 1990–93 |
|---|---|---|---|---|
| *China* | | | | |
| Net resource flow | 8,855 | 21,211 | 98.6 | 92.7 |
| Net LT debt flow | 5,933 | 8,683 | 67.0 | 40.9 |
| Official debt | 1,356 | 2,682 | 15.3 | 12.6 |
| Private bonds | 896 | 400 | 10.1 | 1.9 |
| Other loans | 3,681 | 5,601 | 41.6 | 26.4 |
| FDI | 2,694 | 11,952 | 30.4 | 56.3 |
| Portfolio equity | 0 | 1,031 | 0.0 | 4.9 |
| Grants | 229 | −456 | 2.6 | −2.1 |
| ST debt flow | 122 | 1,660 | 1.4 | 7.3 |
| Net total flow | 8,977 | 22,871 | 100.0 | 100.0 |
| *Indonesia* | | | | |
| Net resource flow | 3,301 | 6,185 | 91.4 | 78.8 |
| Net LT debt flow | 2,590 | 3,748 | 78.4 | 60.6 |
| Official debt | 2,342 | 2,788 | 70.9 | 45.1 |
| Private bonds | −42 | 143 | −1.3 | 2.3 |
| Other loans | 290 | 818 | 8.8 | 13.2 |
| FDI | 475 | 1,589 | 14.4 | 25.7 |
| Portfolio equity | 50 | 730 | 1.5 | 11.8 |
| Grants | 187 | 117 | 5.6 | 1.9 |
| ST debt flow | 312 | 1,660 | 8.6 | 21.2 |
| Net total flow | 3,613 | 7,844 | 100.0 | 100.0 |
| *Korea* | | | | |
| Net resource flow | −3,299 | 5,556 | 93.4 | 90.3 |
| Net LT debt flow | −3,996 | 2,343 | 121.1 | 42.2 |
| Official debt | −907 | −61 | 27.5 | −1.1 |
| Private bonds | −16 | 2,483 | 0.5 | 44.7 |
| Other loans | −3,074 | −80 | 93.2 | −1.4 |
| FDI | 666 | 724 | −20.2 | 13.0 |
| Portfolio equity | 29 | 2,484 | −0.9 | 44.7 |
| Grants | 2 | 5 | −0.1 | 0.1 |
| ST debt flow | −233 | 600 | 6.6 | 9.7 |
| Net total flow | −3,532 | 6,156 | 100.0 | 100.0 |
| *Malaysia* | | | | |
| Net resource flow | −308 | 4,877 | 74.9 | 80.7 |
| Net LT debt flow | −1,243 | −55 | 403.5 | −1.1 |
| Official debt | −205 | 52 | 66.6 | 1.1 |
| Private bonds | −74 | −101 | 24.0 | −2.1 |
| Other loans | −964 | −5 | 312.8 | −0.1 |
| FDI | 825 | 3,788 | −267.8 | 77.7 |
| Portfolio equity | 71 | 1,095 | −22.9 | 22.4 |
| Grants | 40 | 49 | −12.8 | 1.0 |
| ST debt flow | −103 | 1,170 | 25.1 | 19.3 |
| Net total flow | −411 | 6,046 | 100.0 | 100.0 |

(*continued*)

**Table 4.4** (continued)

| Flow | Amount (million U.S. $) | | Share (%) | |
|---|---|---|---|---|
| | 1986–89 | 1990–93 | 1986–89 | 1990–93 |
| *Philippines* | | | | |
| Net resource flow | 1,196 | 1,913 | 100.7 | 87.6 |
| Net LT debt flow | 317 | 766 | 26.5 | 40.0 |
| Official debt | 634 | 1,035 | 53.0 | 54.1 |
| Private bonds | −149 | 289 | −12.4 | 15.1 |
| Other loans | −168 | −558 | −14.0 | −29.2 |
| FDI | 483 | 516 | 40.4 | 27.0 |
| Portfolio equity | 63 | 354 | 5.3 | 18.5 |
| Grants | 332 | 278 | 27.8 | 14.5 |
| ST debt flow | −8 | 271 | −0.7 | 12.4 |
| Net total flow | 1,188 | 2,185 | 100.0 | 100.0 |
| *Thailand* | | | | |
| Net resource flow | 1,897 | 4,976 | 72.3 | 59.4 |
| Net LT debt flow | 370 | 1,652 | 19.5 | 33.2 |
| Official debt | −2 | 113 | −0.1 | 2.3 |
| Private bonds | −13 | 533 | −0.7 | 10.7 |
| Other loans | 385 | 1,007 | 20.3 | 20.2 |
| FDI | 874 | 2,244 | 46.1 | 45.1 |
| Portfolio equity | 515 | 903 | 27.1 | 18.1 |
| Grants | 139 | 177 | 7.3 | 3.6 |
| ST debt flow | 728 | 3,407 | 27.7 | 40.6 |
| Net total flow | 2,625 | 8,383 | 100.0 | 100.0 |

*Source:* World Bank (1994).

developments? Both domestic and international influences must have been at work (see, e.g., Fernandez-Arias 1994; Ghosh and Ostry 1993; Gooptu 1994).

The increasing share of FDI in both foreign capital inflow and local capital outflow has been the most salient feature of Pacific Asia. Consensus, however, has not yet been achieved on what exactly determines FDI. Such factors as low labor cost and product life cycle have become relatively less important because of technological changes. Taxation and other policy measures in the home country of multinational firms have become more crucial in determining FDI.

Nevertheless, changes in the international economic environment do play a crucial role in determining the size and direction of FDI. Remember that the FDI boom of the 1980s, mentioned above, was triggered by the major currency realignment due to the Plaza Accord in 1985, which brought drastic changes in international competitiveness among manufacturing exporters. The growing protectionist atmosphere in developed countries is another factor that could explain the relocation of production sites from developed to developing countries.

In contrast to FDI, portfolio investment requires a rather well arranged domestic capital market, which rarely exists in developing countries. Furthermore, although portfolio investment to some developing economies has expanded sharply in recent years, it may reflect only temporary favorable international economic conditions. Accordingly, it is not yet clear whether portfolio investment could be a sustainable source of external finance to developing countries.

International influences consist of both cyclical and structural factors. As with an upsurge in banking capital inflow to developing countries in the latter half of the 1970s, a cyclical downturn in industrial countries and a resulting decline in their interest rates played a significant role in the surge of portfolio investment in "emerging markets" in the early 1990s—as well as its recent reversal due to higher interest rates. Structural factors include institutional and technological developments in investor countries, which have enhanced competition in capital markets, increased capital mobility by lowering the transaction costs of market access, and widened the range of both investors and financial instruments. It has recently been observed that there has been increased international diversification of portfolio investment along with an broadened investor base.[4]

For host countries, the basic determinants of foreign investment include sound macroeconomic management, a well-qualified labor force, an efficient private sector, and an adequate regulatory system and policy framework. These factors are not necessarily sufficient but are crucial preconditions for attracting foreign capital that are well within the control of developing countries.

Now, supposing that developing economies share international developments in common, we will focus on domestic developments in Pacific Asia, which has attained remarkable results as distinct from other regions. More specifically, remembering that one of the key roles of capital flows is as investment finance, we will concentrate on the macroeconomic development of the Pacific Asian countries. As for regulatory and policy frameworks, all these countries significantly opened up their capital accounts during the mid-1980s, though it is beyond the scope of this paper to discuss the changing regulatory systems and policy frameworks for foreign capital flows and to assess their impact.[5]

4. In the 1990s we have seen a wider range of financial assets and a greater weight of institutional investors. These are both a cause and a result of increased global capital market integration. Technological advances and financial deregulation in developed countries, as well as financial asset accumulation, also constitute fundamental factors explaining these developments.

5. We give a cursory review of policy changes toward capital flows: Taiwan has been relatively generous to foreign capital in the manufacturing sector, but restrictive on overseas investment. In the 1980s, Taiwan worried about a persistent external surplus and eroded international competitiveness in export sectors, so it opened sectors further and allowed overseas portfolio and direct investment in the 1980s. FDI in Taiwan and Taiwanese overseas investment have both shown remarkable growth since 1987.

In contrast to Taiwan, Korea restricted incoming FDI in the 1970s and, instead, introduced commercial loans and allocated them at government discretion. But, once a medium-term external surplus was achieved in the mid-1980s, Korea seriously began trying to open capital transactions

### 4.3.2 Structural Changes in Macroeconomic Balances

Macroeconomic stability has often been regarded as one of the conditions necessary to attract foreign capital by demonstrating the manageability and creditworthiness of host countries. In this context, table 4.5 compares several macroeconomic indicators for "high-inflow" countries in Asia and in Latin America—those countries that attracted relatively high foreign capital inflow during 1990–93.

One of the interesting findings from table 4.5 is that there appears to be no association between macroeconomic stability and net capital inflow. By any measure of macroeconomic performance—real economic growth, domestic inflation, current account imbalance, or external debt indicators—the high-inflow economies in Asia were superior to those in Latin America. Openness as measured by the ratio of exports to GDP was also higher in Asia than in Latin America, and became more so, which naturally led to lower debt service ratios in Asia than in Latin America. In fact, high-inflow countries in Asia attracted foreign capital inflow through the three most recent periods, while those in Latin America all but lost access to the international capital market during 1983–89.

Of course, we could say that the macroeconomic performance during 1977–82 was the *cause* of the "debt crisis" and that during 1983–89 was the *result,* so that these periods could be regarded as a learning process for both international investors and host countries over their reckless behaviors in the past. But how then can we reconcile this with developments in the recent period?

More striking differences between the two country groups can be found in such structural measures as ratios of private investment and consumption to GDP. First, the average investment ratio in the Asian group was significantly higher than in the Latin American group, and became more so over the years. In fact, the ratio for 1990–93 was more than 1.5 times higher in Asia than in Latin America. Second, in Asia the investment ratio increased and the consumption ratio decreased through the three most recent periods, while in Latin America the consumption ratio showed significantly larger increases than the investment ratio from 1973–76 to 1977–82 and again from 1983–89 to 1990–93. In other words, we can see that, as is often observed, positive net foreign capital inflow was used for investment finance in Asia and for consumption finance in Latin America. Put differently, capital inflow *augmented* domestic

both inward and outward in a gradual manner. Increasing overseas direct investment and portfolio investment in the domestic market reflect the accelerated pace of this recent development.

The ASEAN4 nations—Indonesia, Malaysia, the Philippines, and Thailand—made efforts in the early 1980s to attract export-oriented foreign manufacturing corporations; these efforts were fully realized in the late 1980s. Recently, however, the rapid increase in FDI has led to bottlenecks of infrastructure so that, for example, preferential policies for FDI were partly "retrenched" in Malaysia in 1991.

**Table 4.5** **Macroeconomic Indicators: High-Inflow (1990–93) Asia and Western Hemisphere (annual averages; % of GDP unless otherwise noted)**

| Indicators | 1973–76 | 1977–82 | 1983–89 | 1990–93 |
|---|---|---|---|---|
| *Asia high inflows (1990–93)* | | | | |
| Real GDP[a] | 4.7 | 6.2 | 7.9 | 7.5 |
| Consumer prices[a] | 8.8 | 7.7 | 7.5 | 7.4 |
| Private investment | 27.3 | 27.9 | 31.4 | 33.5 |
| Private consumption | 73.8 | 73.6 | 69.1 | 66.4 |
| Exports | 12.7 | 15.2 | 16.6 | 21.8 |
| Imports | 13.3 | 16.2 | 18.1 | 22.9 |
| Current account balance | −0.3 | −1.2 | −0.9 | −1.2 |
| Fiscal deficit | −1.1 | −3.0 | −3.1 | −2.2 |
| Debt | 12.1 | 15.8 | 24.1 | 26.8 |
| Debt service | 9.0 | 11.7 | 17.0 | 12.8 |
| Real effective exchange rate[a,b] | – | 0.7 | −6.3 | −6.8 |
| Total net capital inflow | 1.6 | 2.1 | 1.8 | 3.6 |
| *Western Hemisphere high inflows (1990–93)* | | | | |
| Real GDP[a] | 6.2 | 4.3 | 2.4 | 2.1 |
| Consumer prices[a] | 30.0 | 43.6 | 143.7 | 250.3 |
| Private investment | 22.7 | 23.5 | 20.0 | 20.5 |
| Private consumption | 73.1 | 77.5 | 76.2 | 78.8 |
| Exports | 9.3 | 10.4 | 14.7 | 12.1 |
| Imports | 9.9 | 10.9 | 10.3 | 11.2 |
| Current account balance | −3.0 | −4.6 | −0.6 | −2.0 |
| Fiscal deficit | −2.4 | −4.3 | −5.3 | −0.1 |
| Debt | 19.9 | 31.8 | 50.2 | 35.4 |
| Debt service | 30.5 | 47.9 | 42.5 | 30.9 |
| Real effective exchange rate[a,b] | – | 3.2 | −2.2 | 2.2 |
| Total net capital inflow | 4.0 | 4.2 | −2.4 | 2.9 |

*Source:* IMF (1994).

*Note:* To define high- and low-inflow groups, countries within each region were ranked on the basis of average net capital inflow during 1990–93. Small countries with purchasing-power-parity (PPP) shares less than 0.1 percent in each region were excluded.

[a]Annual percentage change. Entry for 1973–76 reflects 1974–76.

[b]Data available only from 1979 onward. Entry for 1977–82 reflects 1980–82.

savings to finance investment in Asia, while it *substituted* for them in Latin America.

If we look at individual countries in Pacific Asia, we can find more dramatic structural changes in macroeconomic balances from the 1980s onward. Developing economies are generally thought of as being short of domestic savings and, as a result, likely to run a persistent external deficit. This is no longer the case in Pacific Asia. Table 4.6 shows domestic investment, national savings, the ratio of the saving-investment gap to GDP, and real economic growth in Pacific Asia since 1978.

In the ANIEs—Hong Kong, Korea, Singapore, and Taiwan—savings ratios

**Table 4.6** **Macroeconomic Balances: Pacific Asia (% of GDP and % growth rates)**

| Balance | 1978–81 | 1982–85 | 1986–89 | 1990–93 |
|---|---|---|---|---|
| *Indonesia* | | | | |
| Investment (I) | 23.0 | 27.7 | 31.6 | 34.9 |
| Savings (S) | 25.3 | 25.0 | 28.3 | 31.8 |
| S-I gap | 2.2 | −2.7 | −3.3 | −3.1 |
| GDP growth | 8.0 | 4.0 | 6.1 | 6.6 |
| *Korea* | | | | |
| Investment (I) | 32.6 | 29.1 | 31.0 | 36.7 |
| Savings (S) | 23.6 | 25.1 | 35.0 | 34.8 |
| S-I gap | −9.0 | −4.0 | 4.1 | −1.9 |
| GDP growth | 5.5 | 8.9 | 10.5 | 7.0 |
| *Malaysia* | | | | |
| Investment (I) | 30.2 | 34.1 | 26.0 | 34.4 |
| Savings (S) | 28.9 | 26.0 | 28.8 | 29.4 |
| S-I gap | −1.3 | −8.0 | 2.8 | −5.1 |
| GDP growth | 7.6 | 4.7 | 6.0 | 8.7 |
| *Philippines* | | | | |
| Investment (I) | 29.1 | 23.7 | 18.5 | 22.5 |
| Savings (S) | 25.2 | 21.7 | 19.1 | 18.2 |
| S-I gap | −3.9 | −2.0 | 0.6 | −4.2 |
| GDP growth | 5.0 | −2.4 | 5.1 | 0.9 |
| *Singapore* | | | | |
| Investment (I) | 43.8 | 46.7 | 37.3 | 40.4 |
| Savings (S) | 34.9 | 43.9 | 42.0 | 48.3 |
| S-I gap | −8.3 | −2.8 | 4.7 | 7.9 |
| GDP growth | 9.3 | 5.4 | 8.0 | 7.7 |
| *Thailand* | | | | |
| Investment (I) | 27.0 | 24.5 | 29.6 | 41.1 |
| Savings (S) | 21.4 | 19.6 | 27.2 | 33.4 |
| S-I gap | −5.6 | −4.9 | −2.4 | −7.7 |
| GDP growth | 6.7 | 5.5 | 9.9 | 8.9 |
| *Taiwan* | | | | |
| Investment (I) | 31.1 | 22.5 | 21.0 | 23.7 |
| Savings (S) | 33.1 | 32.9 | 37.4 | 29.5 |
| S-I gap | 2.0 | 10.5 | 16.4 | 5.8 |
| GDP growth | 11.8 | 6.9 | 9.7 | 6.2 |
| *Hong Kong* | | | | |
| Investment (I) | 34.0 | 26.3 | 26.6 | 28.3 |
| Savings (S) | 29.8 | 27.4 | 32.6 | 31.7 |
| S-I gap | −4.2 | 1.1 | 6.0 | 3.4 |
| GDP growth | 10.4 | 4.7 | 9.0 | 4.7 |
| *China* | | | | |
| Investment (I) | 35.3 | 38.1 | 43.8 | 35.2 |
| Savings (S) | 35.5 | 37.4 | 41.2 | 38.0 |
| S-I gap | 0.2 | −0.7 | −2.6 | 2.3 |
| GDP growth | 7.7 | 11.4 | 8.2 | 10.0 |

*Sources: International Financial Statistics Yearbook* (Washington, D.C.: IMF, 1994); *Key Indicators of Developing Asian and Pacific Countries* (Manila: Asian Development Bank, 1994).

have shown a steady upward trend in the last two decades and remained or become high enough that saving-investment differences have been positive or close to positive since the mid-1980s. Now, capital flows in the NIEs can increase on both the asset and liability sides, which makes the picture of capital flows in the region more complex than before; this situation will be discussed in section 4.4.

Unless the NIEs accumulate official foreign reserves indefinitely, their positive saving-investment differences imply negative net capital inflows or positive outflows, which may or may not be directed toward Pacific Asia. Of course, this does not mean that the ANIEs have become immune to external deficits. The point here is that some economies in the region have already "graduated" from the savings-shortage situation that is typical of developing economies so that financing the saving-investment gap is no longer their first priority for capital flows.

While this is not yet the case in the other economies in the region, savings ratios in Indonesia, Thailand, and China have also been relatively high and/or showing steady upward trends (the Philippines has been under economic stress since the debt crisis). Indeed, we should note that domestic savings have played a far more important role in investment finance than foreign savings and will do so in the future. These high and growing domestic savings reflect macroeconomic discipline and could support self-sustained growth through internal investment finance.[6] This growth would help maintain foreign capital inflow to augment domestic savings, even when these countries suffer from cyclical downturns. Here we see the major difference between Latin America and Pacific Asia. As far as domestic factors are concerned, the sustainability of external finance depends not only on short-term macroeconomic stability but also on longer-term macroeconomic-balance structures.

## 4.4 Interdependence through Capital Flows

From the analysis in section 4.3, we learned that both the financing needs of saving-investment gaps and the components of capital flows have changed and diversified over time and across economies in Pacific Asia since the 1980s. Until now, however, our observations have been limited to bilateral aspects of capital flows in countries and/or regions. Here we will try to extend our discussion to a multilateral network of capital flows in the region. We will discuss official capital flows, direct investment, and bank loans, in turn.

### 4.4.1 Official Capital Flows

Net official flows had been or turned negative in several rapidly growing economies (the ANIEs, Malaysia, and Thailand) in the late 1980s, while the other economies (China, Indonesia, and the Philippines) are still more or less

6. Causality appears to go from income growth to savings ratio (see World Bank 1993a).

dependent on official flows as a major financial source (table 4.4). But, note that these official flows did not change evenly across their components.

Official capital flows are divided into two components—official development assistance (ODA) and other official flows (OOF)—according to their "grant elements." OOF is likely to be "retrenched" faster than ODA in rapidly growing economies because it is rational to obtain and hold less costly loans and to repay more costly ones first. Table 4.7 shows net official flows of Pacific Asian economies by component and by creditor in dollar terms and in percentage shares.

Table 4.7 shows that Korea, Malaysia, and Thailand seemed to enter the net repayment "phase" of relatively costly OOF in the latter half of the 1980s. However, Malaysia and Thailand still depend on less costly ODA to a significant degree, while Korea has "graduated" and ceased to depend on official financial resources.

The relative contributions of some major creditors are also found in table 4.7. Regarding ODA, Japan's role remains dominant (with a greater than 50 percent share) and is still increasing in Malaysia. But this is no longer the case with respect to OOF. The role of the United States in ODA was modest and has diminished (with a less than 5 percent share). Multilateral institutions as a whole have been more important than the United States, but far less so than Japan.

On the other hand, table 4.7 gives a different picture of official flows to Indonesia, the Philippines, and China. All three have been receiving still-increasing amounts of ODA *as well as OOF.* For Indonesia and the Philippines, Japan's contribution was significant (with a greater than 50 percent share of ODA) and even expanded. For the Philippines, the United States has been a more important official creditor than multilateral institutions as a whole. For China, though, in both ODA and OOF, Japan's share is declining relative to that of multilateral institutions.

In keeping with the recent global trend, the importance of official flows as a source of external finance has somewhat declined in Pacific Asia. But this should be attributed to the "graduation" of several high-growth members in the region, rather than to the geographical redistribution of official development finance after the end of the Cold War as is generally claimed (e.g., see World Bank 1993b).

As for official capital flows, Japan has played a key role in enhancing regional interdependence in capital flows, but its role has changed significantly with the dynamic growth in the region. Japan's contribution to both ODA and OOF to the ANIEs has become modest, and this is also the case at least for OOF to the higher-income ASEAN4. But, for the rest of the region, Japan's role not only has remained significant but has grown.[7]

7. Most recently, ANIEs and some ASEAN members began to provide official financial assistance to neighboring low-income countries. We are going to observe two-way flows not only in FDI but in official flows in this region.

Table 4.7 **Net Official Flows: Pacific Asia (annual averages)**

| | Amount (million U.S. $) | | | | Share (%) | | | |
|---|---|---|---|---|---|---|---|---|
| Net Flow | Japan | United States | Multi-national | Total | Japan | United States | Multi-national | Total |
| *China* | | | | | | | | |
| ODA | | | | | | | | |
| 1981–85 | 304.8 | 0.0 | 244.5 | 681.8 | 44.7 | 0.0 | 35.9 | 100.0 |
| 1986–90 | 655.8 | 0.0 | 627.8 | 1,762.8 | 37.2 | 0.0 | 35.6 | 100.0 |
| 1990–92 | 786.4 | 0.0 | 789.2 | 2,379.8 | 33.0 | 0.0 | 33.2 | 100.0 |
| OOF | | | | | | | | |
| 1981–85 | 60.2 | 9.4 | 81.6 | 177.0 | 34.0 | 5.3 | 46.1 | 100.0 |
| 1986–90 | 124.7 | 30.6 | 419.8 | 688.3 | 18.1 | 4.4 | 61.0 | 100.0 |
| 1990–92 | 105.5 | 34.0 | 552.6 | 1,008.1 | 10.5 | 3.4 | 54.8 | 100.0 |
| *Indonesia* | | | | | | | | |
| ODA | | | | | | | | |
| 1981–85 | 231.8 | 71.8 | 126.8 | 780.4 | 29.7 | 9.2 | 16.2 | 100.0 |
| 1986–90 | 773.2 | 33.2 | 127.8 | 1,435.0 | 53.9 | 2.3 | 8.9 | 100.0 |
| 1990–92 | 1,096.7 | 16.0 | 132.7 | 1,908.7 | 57.5 | 0.8 | 7.0 | 100.0 |
| OOF | | | | | | | | |
| 1981–85 | 13.8 | 30.4 | 610.6 | 709.0 | 2.0 | 4.3 | 86.1 | 100.0 |
| 1986–90 | 407.4 | −10.2 | 1,214.4 | 1,666.0 | 24.5 | −0.6 | 72.9 | 100.0 |
| 1990–92 | 327.5 | 40.7 | 1,023.3 | 1,609.9 | 20.3 | 2.5 | 63.6 | 100.0 |
| *Korea* | | | | | | | | |
| ODA | | | | | | | | |
| 1981–85 | 48.1 | −9.6 | 7.6 | 65.5 | 73.4 | −14.7 | 11.6 | 100.0 |
| 1986–90 | 19.4 | −27.2 | 3.5 | 21.5 | 90.1 | −126.4 | 16.4 | 100.0 |
| 1990–92 | 36.1 | −33.3 | 1.6 | 36.8 | 98.3 | −90.7 | 4.4 | 100.0 |
| OOF | | | | | | | | |
| 1981–85 | 1.8 | 232.2 | 417.7 | 671.4 | 0.3 | 34.6 | 62.2 | 100.0 |
| 1986–90 | −1.2 | −314.4 | −462.1 | −786.8 | 0.2 | 40.0 | 58.7 | 100.0 |
| 1990–92 | −2.0 | −64.3 | −266.8 | −399.1 | 0.5 | 16.1 | 66.9 | 100.0 |
| *Malaysia* | | | | | | | | |
| ODA | | | | | | | | |
| 1981–85 | 120.6 | 0.4 | 14.6 | 202.2 | 59.6 | 0.2 | 7.2 | 100.0 |
| 1986–90 | 158.2 | −0.6 | 12.0 | 253.8 | 62.4 | −0.2 | 4.7 | 100.0 |
| 1990–92 | 243.2 | 0.0 | 16.7 | 322.3 | 75.4 | 0.0 | 5.2 | 100.0 |
| OOF | | | | | | | | |
| 1981–85 | 10.5 | 7.4 | 86.5 | 140.8 | 7.4 | 5.3 | 61.4 | 100.0 |
| 1986–90 | −23.5 | −12.0 | 18.6 | −17.8 | 131.8 | 67.4 | −104.3 | 100.0 |
| 1990–92 | 40.3 | 0.0 | 49.7 | 65.4 | 61.6 | 0.0 | 76.0 | 100.0 |
| *Philippines* | | | | | | | | |
| ODA | | | | | | | | |
| 1981–85 | 178.7 | 102.2 | 52.5 | 404.3 | 44.2 | 25.3 | 13.0 | 100.0 |
| 1986–90 | 480.7 | 231.6 | 88.2 | 936.6 | 51.3 | 24.7 | 9.4 | 100.0 |
| 1990–92 | 712.4 | 233.7 | 180.8 | 1,349.5 | 52.8 | 17.3 | 13.4 | 100.0 |
| OOF | | | | | | | | |
| 1981–85 | 44.0 | 13.8 | 401.1 | 484.3 | 9.1 | 2.8 | 82.8 | 100.0 |
| 1986–90 | 117.3 | 101.4 | 190.0 | 473.0 | 24.8 | 21.4 | 40.2 | 100.0 |

*(continued)*

Table 4.7 (continued)

| Net Flow | Amount (million U.S. $) | | | | Share (%) | | | |
|---|---|---|---|---|---|---|---|---|
| | Japan | United States | Multi-national | Total | Japan | United States | Multi-national | Total |
| 1990–92 | 140.3 | 116.7 | 396.0 | 751.4 | 18.7 | 15.5 | 52.7 | 100.0 |
| *Thailand* | | | | | | | | |
| ODA | | | | | | | | |
| 1981–85 | 225.8 | 24.6 | 86.3 | 436.4 | 51.7 | 5.6 | 19.8 | 100.0 |
| 1986–90 | 366.2 | 27.6 | 73.3 | 616.4 | 59.4 | 4.5 | 11.9 | 100.0 |
| 1990–92 | 412.9 | 23.7 | 79.4 | 763.8 | 54.1 | 3.1 | 10.4 | 100.0 |
| OOF | | | | | | | | |
| 1981–85 | 22.4 | −13.4 | 364.9 | 425.8 | 5.3 | −3.1 | 85.7 | 100.0 |
| 1986–90 | 83.8 | −9.6 | −125.9 | −40.7 | −205.8 | 23.6 | 309.2 | 100.0 |
| 1990–92 | 218.8 | 15.0 | −244.0 | 93.8 | 233.2 | 16.0 | −260.1 | 100.0 |

*Source: Geographical Distribution of Financial Flows to Developing Countries* (Paris: OECD, various issues).

### 4.4.2 Foreign Direct Investment

There are no reliable comprehensive data available on the geographical distribution of private capital flows within Pacific Asia. But, for direct investment, we can make a good conjecture about the general tendency of its movement by compiling figures on individual host economies for stocks of direct investment by investor country as shown in table 4.8.

Note that each economy's figures for FDI are not exactly comparable (see Japan External Trade Organization 1993). Some are on approval basis, and others are on disbursement basis. Benchmark years for the accumulation of investment figures are different across the economies. Some figures are totals of all industries; others cover only manufacturing. And FDI from the ANIEs and other developing economies are often unavailable separately, which would lead to an underestimation of FDI by the ANIEs and the ASEAN4 countries here.

Despite these shortcomings, we can safely obtain a general picture of changes in the amount, pace, and direction of FDI in the region from table 4.8 as follows:

First, throughout the period 1982–93, FDI increased vigorously in the region. Total FDI in the region increased by 1.7 times during 1982–86, 2.5 times during 1986–90, and 1.9 times during 1990–93 (see the bottom three rows in table 4.8). Especially since the latter half of the 1980s, the rate of increase has accelerated.

Second, this acceleration in FDI increase was mainly because of FDI to China and the ASEAN4 excluding the Philippines. FDI to the ANIEs grew rapidly, but without much acceleration. (FDI to China and the ASEAN4 increased by 3.1 and 2.7 times, respectively, during 1986–90 and by 3.1 and 1.9 times during 1990–93, as against a 1.4 times increase in FDI to the ASEAN4

**Table 4.8** **FDI Stocks: Pacific Asia (% share of total stock in each host country)**

| | Destination | | | | | | | | | | | |
|---|---|---|---|---|---|---|---|---|---|---|---|---|
| Source | Hong Kong | Singapore | Taiwan | Korea | NIEs | Indonesia | Malaysia | Philippines | Thailand | ASEAN4 | China | Total |
| *United States* | | | | | | | | | | | | |
| 1982 | 46.7 | 32.3 | 30.3 | 29.1 | 32.9 | 5.6 | 9.9 | 48.3 | 8.5 | 11.1 | n.a. | 18.1 |
| 1986 | 41.2 | 36.7 | 29.2 | 29.5 | 33.5 | 7.7 | 8.7 | 57.0 | 19.1 | 15.5 | 15.6 | 21.5 |
| 1990 | 30.6 | 37.4 | 24.9 | 28.7 | 30.3 | 5.7 | 5.6 | 53.6 | 11.6 | 9.4 | 11.2 | 15.1 |
| 1993 | 28.1 | 39.2 | 24.7 | 29.3 | 30.8 | 5.5 | 11.2 | 50.2 | 14.0 | 10.9 | 8.1 | 13.9 |
| *European Community* | | | | | | | | | | | | |
| 1982 | 14.2 | 36.7 | 9.2 | 13.1 | 21.9 | 11.7 | 18.1 | 9.8 | 23.2 | 15.5 | n.a. | 17.6 |
| 1986 | 10.9 | 30.0 | 12.9 | 9.5 | 17.9 | 12.0 | 24.9 | 12.2 | 15.8 | 14.5 | 7.2 | 14.8 |
| 1990 | 10.9 | 27.2 | 15.6 | 15.5 | 18.8 | 12.3 | 15.2 | 11.1 | 7.4 | 11.3 | 5.0 | 12.3 |
| 1993 | 12.4 | 25.7 | 14.8 | 23.1 | 19.9 | 13.0 | 17.6 | 17.7 | 10.1 | 13.0 | 3.2 | 12.0 |
| *Japan* | | | | | | | | | | | | |
| 1982 | 30.1 | 16.8 | 20.9 | 47.1 | 23.8 | 36.9 | 21.8 | 18.0 | 23.4 | 29.8 | n.a. | 27.9 |
| 1986 | 20.5 | 24.0 | 25.2 | 52.3 | 29.5 | 33.2 | 19.4 | 13.7 | 20.5 | 26.3 | 15.1 | 26.0 |
| 1990 | 31.5 | 28.2 | 29.3 | 48.2 | 33.2 | 24.9 | 25.2 | 15.2 | 35.4 | 27.8 | 13.6 | 27.2 |
| 1993 | 34.1 | 28.2 | 28.9 | 41.0 | 31.8 | 20.6 | 22.3 | 15.5 | 23.8 | 21.9 | 8.6 | 20.6 |
| *Hong Kong* | | | | | | | | | | | | |
| 1982 | | n.a. | 8.3 | 0.0 | 2.7 | 10.1 | 3.2 | 5.9 | 3.4 | 7.2 | n.a. | 5.7 |
| 1986 | | n.a. | 5.8 | 3.6 | 2.6 | 11.9 | 3.7 | 6.0 | 3.2 | 8.0 | 53.6 | 11.5 |
| 1990 | | n.a. | 4.6 | 2.9 | 2.3 | 9.6 | 3.4 | 6.8 | 5.9 | 7.2 | 59.7 | 13.6 |
| 1993 | | n.a. | 6.3 | 0.0 | 2.2 | 8.4 | 2.6 | 5.2 | 15.2 | 9.5 | 63.6 | 20.9 |
| *Singapore* | | | | | | | | | | | | |
| 1982 | 1.7 | | 0.0 | n.a. | 0.2 | 0.0 | 6.6 | n.a. | 3.6 | 1.6 | n.a. | 1.1 |
| 1986 | 1.4 | | 0.0 | n.a. | 0.2 | 2.0 | 9.0 | n.a. | 2.8 | 2.8 | 0.4 | 1.7 |
| 1990 | 1.0 | | 1.0 | n.a. | 0.6 | 2.6 | 7.8 | n.a. | 3.7 | 3.8 | 1.1 | 2.6 |
| 1993 | 2.3 | | 2.6 | n.a. | 1.1 | 5.8 | 6.4 | 1.9 | 4.2 | 5.2 | 1.4 | 3.6 |

(*continued*)

**Table 4.8** (continued)

| Source | Destination | | | | | | | | | | | |
|---|---|---|---|---|---|---|---|---|---|---|---|---|
| | Hong Kong | Singapore | Taiwan | Korea | NIEs | Indonesia | Malaysia | Philippines | Thailand | ASEAN4 | China | Total |
| *Taiwan* | | | | | | | | | | | | |
| 1982 | 1.3 | n.a. | | n.a. | 0.1 | 0.0 | 1.4 | n.a. | 6.8 | 2.2 | n.a. | 1.5 |
| 1986 | 0.0 | n.a. | | n.a. | 0.0 | 0.9 | 1.8 | n.a. | 6.2 | 2.5 | n.a. | 1.4 |
| 1990 | n.a. | n.a. | n.a. | | n.a. | 4.8 | 2.3 | n.a. | 0.6 | 2.9 | n.a. | 1.7 |
| 1993 | n.a. | n.a. | n.a. | | n.a. | 5.4 | 3.5 | 1.9 | 0.0 | 3.0 | n.a. | 1.8 |
| *NIEs* | | | | | | | | | | | | |
| 1982 | 3.0 | 0.0 | 8.3 | 0.0 | 3.1 | 10.1 | 11.6 | 5.9 | 14.0 | 11.0 | n.a. | 8.4 |
| 1986 | 1.4 | 0.0 | 5.8 | 3.7 | 2.8 | 16.2 | 15.4 | 6.0 | 12.3 | 14.0 | 54.0 | 15.0 |
| 1990 | 1.7 | 0.0 | 5.6 | 3.6 | 3.0 | 23.0 | 36.7 | 6.8 | 17.2 | 23.1 | 60.7 | 23.3 |
| 1993 | 2.6 | 0.0 | 8.9 | 3.0 | 4.0 | 25.5 | 31.3 | 9.3 | 24.9 | 25.9 | 65.0 | 31.1 |
| *ASEAN4* | | | | | | | | | | | | |
| 1982 | 0.0 | 0.0 | 0.0 | 0.0 | 0.0 | 2.5 | 8.0 | 0.0 | 2.0 | 2.5 | n.a. | 1.7 |
| 1986 | 0.0 | 0.0 | 0.0 | 0.0 | 0.0 | 0.0 | 4.4 | 0.0 | 2.3 | 1.1 | 0.5 | 0.7 |
| 1990 | 0.9 | 0.0 | 0.0 | 0.0 | 0.1 | 0.0 | 4.0 | 0.0 | 0.9 | 1.0 | 0.4 | 0.7 |
| 1993 | 1.8 | 0.0 | 0.0 | 0.0 | 0.2 | 0.0 | 4.4 | 0.0 | 0.0 | 0.9 | 0.9 | 0.8 |
| *Total (million $)* | | | | | | | | | | | | |
| 1982 | 1,245 | 4,492 | 3,495 | 1,436 | 10,668 | 11,777 | 1,600 | 2,228 | 6,819 | 22,424 | n.a. | 33,092 |
| 1986 | 2,506 | 6,421 | 5,893 | 3,633 | 18,453 | 15,809 | 3,217 | 2,722 | 9,076 | 30,824 | 6,538 | 55,815 |
| 1990 | 3,971 | 11,547 | 13,215 | 7,873 | 36,606 | 38,678 | 15,610 | 3,303 | 25,687 | 83,278 | 20,452 | 140,336 |
| 1993 | 5,287 | 16,607 | 17,667 | 10,552 | 50,113 | 67,625 | 31,233 | 4,897 | 54,738 | 158,493 | 64,180 | 272,786 |
| *Ratio of year-end stocks* | | | | | | | | | | | | |
| 86/82 | 2.01 | 1.43 | 1.69 | 2.53 | 1.73 | 1.34 | 2.01 | 1.22 | 1.33 | 1.37 | n.a. | 1.69 |
| 90/86 | 1.58 | 1.80 | 2.24 | 2.17 | 1.98 | 2.45 | 4.85 | 1.21 | 2.83 | 2.70 | 3.13 | 2.51 |
| 93/90 | 1.33 | 1.44 | 1.34 | 1.34 | 1.37 | 1.75 | 2.00 | 1.48 | 2.13 | 1.90 | 3.14 | 1.94 |

*Source:* Calculated from national statistics.

during 1982–86.) Recall that FDI from the ANIEs is likely to be underestimated.

Third, with increasing FDI in the region, Japan's share as an investor was larger than the U.S. and EC shares and stayed almost constant throughout the 1980s (26–28 percent), unlike the declining shares of the United States and European Community. Japan's share rose slightly in 1986–90 but fell to 21 percent in 1990–93, mainly because of its cyclical downturn.

Fourth, the share of the ANIEs as investors has dramatically expanded throughout the entire period covered, from 8 percent (1982) to 31 percent (1993), the most remarkable new development in the region since the early 1980s. This is particularly the case for the ASEAN4 in the late 1980s as well as in China since then. Two movements are notable: one is Hong Kong's investment in China, and the other is, to a lesser degree, Taiwan's in the ASEAN4.[8]

Fifth, FDI in the region grew rapidly and accelerated, and during the process, the share of intraregional FDI (from Japan plus the NIEs) increased from less than 40 percent (1982) to more than 50 percent (1990). A notable point is that the increased intraregional direct investment proceeded hand in hand with increased intraregional trade.

The developments in FDI in Pacific Asia, outlined above, undoubtedly have some structural factors in common with FDI in the global context, though somewhat magnified. First, there is a general trend of expansion in worldwide production, sourcing, and marketing strategies by international businesses. This "globalization" trend of international business has been shared and strengthened by those in rapidly growing developing economies in the region. We can confirm this by noting the accelerating intraregional trade and proliferating horizontal and/or vertical international division of labor found in manufacturing industries. Second, other domestic factors must have contributed—for example, local economic growth and deregulation of capital movements in the region, both of which have been, again, particularly salient in Pacific Asia.

### 4.4.3 International Banking Flows

Finally, we will deal with banking flows, that is, the cross-border claims and liabilities of banks, a component of private capital flows whose geographical distribution is most difficult to trace. We note that, outside the BIS reporting area, Asia was the only region during 1985–93 in which cross-border lending by BIS-reporting banks continued to grow (see table 4.9). The distribution of

8. Hong Kong's FDI to China includes Chinese domestic investment via Hong Kong in pursuit of the preferential treatment of FDI in China, called "round-tripping" of Chinese capital. Thus, note that Hong Kong's FDI to China is to some extent inflated by this round-tripping. See World Bank (1993c).

**Table 4.9** **Distribution of International Bank Lending outside the Reporting Area by BIS-Reporting Banks (end of year)**

| | Positions (billion U.S. $) | | | | Share (%) | | | |
|---|---|---|---|---|---|---|---|---|
| Country | 1985 | 1990 | 1992 | 1993[a] | 1985 | 1990 | 1992 | 1993[a] |
| All countries | 583.6 | 664.8 | 689.7 | 687.7 | 100.0 | 100.0 | 100.0 | 100.0 |
| Developed countries | 112.3 | 161.2 | 149.1 | 142.7 | 19.2 | 24.2 | 21.6 | 20.8 |
| Latin America | 236.5 | 184.8 | 187.4 | 189.8 | 40.5 | 27.8 | 27.2 | 27.6 |
| Asia | 94.3 | 135.4 | 167.7 | 183.5 | 16.2 | 20.4 | 24.3 | 26.7 |

*Source: The Maturity, Sectoral and Nationality Distribution of International Bank Lending, Second Half 1993* (Basel: BIS, 1993).

[a]Preliminary figures for 1993.

**Table 4.10** **International Claims outside the Reporting Area by Nationality of BIS-Reporting Banks**

| | | Share (%) | | | |
|---|---|---|---|---|---|
| Claims on: | Total (million U.S. $) | Japan | United States | United Kingdom | Germany |
| All countries | 687,720 | 20.5 | 12.9 | 10.6 | 15.9 |
| Pacific Asia | 165,247 | 40.9 | 9.6 | 8.1 | 6.3 |
| China | 32,538 | 39.7 | 2.2 | 6.7 | 5.5 |
| Indonesia | 29,866 | 54.9 | 8.1 | 5.9 | 5.4 |
| Korea | 40,295 | 29.9 | 10.4 | 10 | 7 |
| Malaysia | 12,607 | 41.1 | 9.8 | 13.8 | 7.4 |
| Philippines | 5,633 | 16.6 | 44.1 | 10.3 | 2.7 |
| Taiwan | 15,185 | 26.8 | 16.1 | 9.7 | 8.5 |
| Thailand | 29,123 | 55.2 | 7.9 | 5.7 | 6.2 |
| Offshore centers | 338,214 | 62.8 | 3.1 | 6 | 8.3 |
| Hong Kong | 186,856 | 66.1 | 3 | 4.9 | 7.3 |
| Singapore | 151,358 | 58.8 | 3.3 | 7.3 | 9.6 |

*Source: The Maturity, Sectoral and Nationality Distribution of International Bank Lending, Second Half 1993* (Basel: BIS, 1993).

bank lending by the nationality of the reporting banks indicates the dominance of Japanese banks in Pacific Asia, particularly in its offshore financial centers, Hong Kong and Singapore (table 4.10).[9] In the case of Japanese banks, despite Japanese boom and bust, their long-term foreign-currency external lending increased solely in Asia during 1990–93 (Ministry of Finance 1994).

9. Similar geographical concentration could be found in the case of U.S. banks lending to Latin America and German banks to Eastern Europe, but their degrees of dominance are not as great as Japan's.

One could correctly point out that it is impossible and useless to try too hard to trace multilateral banking flows. In fact, the existence of growing offshore financial markets makes simply infeasible the construction of a matrixlike table for bank loans within the region. Also, international financial transactions can no longer be regional because of developments in telecommunications and other technical innovations.

When we look at the cross-border claims and liabilities of banks and nonbanks, we recognize how widely and how deeply each economy is linked to the international financial market. The claims and liabilities of the two international financial centers, Hong Kong and Singapore, grew remarkably during the 1980s, and those of Japan started to expand vigorously in 1985. In fact, Japan, Hong Kong, and Singapore increased cross-border claims and liabilities as a ratio to GDP two to four times during the 1980s.[10] Note that growth has been mainly in interbank transactions.[11]

Table 4.11 illustrates the key role of Hong Kong in international financial transactions by reporting external bank claims and liabilities. The most conspicuous fact is, of course, that the position of Japanese banks as financial intermediaries has become paramount. Table 4.11 also indicates that, aside from the financial giant, Japan, a financial network through interbank transactions has steadily widened and deepened in Pacific Asia by such players as China, Taiwan, and Singapore vis-à-vis Hong Kong.

Financial interrelation has been promoted vigorously through three financial centers in the region, Tokyo, Hong Kong, and Singapore. Their market sizes as ratios to GDP increased by two to four times during the 1980s. Unlike the cases of official flows and FDI, Japan's role in banking flows has become huge since the 1980s. In fact, in the Hong Kong market, intraregional claims and liabilities amounted to 80 percent of the total. Although the other two ANIEs, Taiwan and Korea, are still cautious in opening up, their liberalizations of capital transactions are now on the time table. Closer interdependence through capital has been also found in cross-border banking.

10. Cross-border claims by banks are (as a percentage of GDP)

| Country | 1981 | 1990 |
|---|---|---|
| Japan | 7 | 32 |
| Hong Kong | 161 | 662 |
| Singapore | 549 | 1,058 |

*Source:* IMF (various years [b]).

11. Malaysia and then Thailand became more closely linked with the international arena in the latter half of the 1980s in terms of cross-border claims and liabilities. Although the liberalization of their capital accounts will change the situations in Taiwan and Korea, this has not happened yet. A relatively thin link to the international market is also found in Indonesia and the Philippines.

Table 4.11 External Bank Liabilities and Claims: Hong Kong

| Country | Amount (million U.S. $) | | | | Share (%) | | | |
|---|---|---|---|---|---|---|---|---|
| | 1980 | 1985 | 1990 | 1993 | 1980 | 1985 | 1990 | 1993 |
| *Liabilities* | | | | | | | | |
| United States | 2,156 | 6,593 | 12,792 | 11,990 | 6.6 | 7.9 | 3.2 | 2.7 |
| Japan | 1,797 | 10,731 | 258,273 | 286,679 | 5.5 | 12.9 | 64.1 | 65.4 |
| China | 191 | 2,821 | 14,939 | 20,056 | 0.6 | 3.4 | 3.7 | 4.6 |
| Korea | 414 | 1,364 | 1,039 | 1,525 | 1.3 | 1.6 | 0.3 | 0.3 |
| Taiwan | 104 | 1,215 | 951 | 827 | 0.3 | 1.5 | 0.2 | 0.2 |
| Singapore | 8,223 | 20,162 | 29,881 | 34,967 | 25.2 | 24.2 | 7.4 | 8.0 |
| Indonesia | 531 | 906 | 660 | 1,505 | 1.6 | 1.1 | 0.2 | 0.3 |
| Malaysia | 171 | 139 | 185 | 223 | 0.5 | 0.2 | 0.0 | 0.1 |
| Thailand | 138 | 155 | 402 | 1,267 | 0.4 | 0.2 | 0.1 | 0.3 |
| Philippines | 682 | 646 | 870 | 680 | 2.1 | 0.8 | 0.2 | 0.2 |
| European Community | 12,019 | 24,368 | 55,666 | 59,635 | 36.8 | 29.2 | 13.8 | 13.6 |
| Grand total | 32,658 | 83,399 | 402,952 | 438,632 | 100.0 | 100.0 | 100.0 | 100.0 |
| *Claims* | | | | | | | | |
| United States | 2,035 | 6,655 | 14,558 | 15,722 | 5.9 | 6.6 | 3.1 | 3.0 |
| Japan | 1,984 | 13,320 | 309,419 | 334,326 | 5.7 | 13.2 | 66.7 | 64.5 |
| China | 1,490 | 3,919 | 15,486 | 25,221 | 4.3 | 3.9 | 3.3 | 4.9 |
| Korea | 2,726 | 8,286 | 6,642 | 9,062 | 7.9 | 8.2 | 1.4 | 1.7 |
| Taiwan | 1,274 | 1,268 | 3,591 | 7,661 | 3.7 | 1.3 | 0.8 | 1.5 |
| Singapore | 3,528 | 14,462 | 28,192 | 22,569 | 10.2 | 14.3 | 6.1 | 4.4 |
| Indonesia | 1,364 | 1,725 | 2,832 | 4,063 | 3.9 | 1.7 | 0.6 | 0.8 |
| Malaysia | 466 | 938 | 830 | 1,717 | 1.3 | 0.9 | 0.2 | 0.3 |
| Thailand | 810 | 1,583 | 3,510 | 8,596 | 2.3 | 1.6 | 0.8 | 1.7 |
| Philippines | 2,408 | 2,934 | 1,551 | 639 | 7.0 | 2.9 | 0.3 | 0.1 |
| European Community | 6,440 | 24,628 | 36,836 | 38,160 | 18.6 | 24.3 | 7.9 | 7.4 |
| Grand total | 34,585 | 101,262 | 464,087 | 518,022 | 100.0 | 100.0 | 100.0 | 100.0 |

*Source: Monthly Digest of Statistics* (Hong Kong: Census and Statistics Department, Hong Kong Monetary Authority, various issues).

## 4.5 The Role of Japan in the Region

Finally, we examine the role of Japan as a major capital supplier as well as a financial intermediary in Pacific Asia. Japan's total long-term capital outflow reached its peak of $192 billion in 1989, which coincided with the peak of its "bubble economy," or financially inflated boom. After the bubble burst, along with the economic downturn, its capital outflow declined sharply and hit the bottom at $58 billion in 1992. Among the components of capital, portfolio investment, the most significant since the mid-1980s, makes up more than 50 percent of the total outflow, FDI 20 percent, and loans 10 percent. After 1992, FDI and loans shrank more than portfolio investment (see table 4.12).

Although data on bilateral capital flows between Japan and Pacific Asia are

**Table 4.12** **Long-Term Capital Account by Region: Japan (annual averages)**

A. World

| | Amount (million U.S. $) | | | | Share (%) | | | |
|---|---|---|---|---|---|---|---|---|
| Net Flow | 1983–85 | 1986–88 | 1989–91 | 1992–94 | 1983–85 | 1986–88 | 1989–91 | 1992–94 |
| Total | −43,958 | −132,974 | −31,925 | −62,884 | 100.0 | 100.0 | 100.0 | 100.0 |
| Assets | −57,010 | −138,269 | −144,777 | −80,517 | 100.0 | 100.0 | 100.0 | 100.0 |
| Liabilities | 13,052 | 5,295 | 112,852 | 17,633 | 100.0 | 100.0 | 100.0 | 100.0 |
| FDI | −4,994 | −22,434 | −40,271 | −15,002 | 11.4 | 16.9 | 126.1 | 23.9 |
| Assets | −5,343 | −22,736 | −40,960 | −16,216 | 9.4 | 16.4 | 28.3 | 20.1 |
| Liabilities | 349 | 302 | 689 | 1,213 | 2.7 | 5.7 | 0.6 | 6.9 |
| Trade credits | −3,434 | −3,123 | 195 | 4,867 | 7.8 | 2.3 | −0.6 | −7.7 |
| Assets | −3,448 | −3,103 | 202 | 4,873 | 6.0 | 2.2 | −0.1 | −6.1 |
| Liabilities | 13 | −20 | −7 | −7 | 0.1 | −0.4 | 0.0 | 0.0 |
| Loans | −10,321 | −13,639 | 12,425 | −4,311 | 23.5 | 10.3 | −38.9 | 6.9 |
| Assets | −10,258 | −13,561 | −19,258 | −7,845 | 18.0 | 9.8 | 13.3 | 9.7 |
| Liabilities | −63 | −78 | 31,683 | 3,535 | −0.5 | −1.5 | 28.1 | 20.0 |
| Securities investment[a] | −24,724 | −87,307 | 2,639 | −45,932 | 56.2 | 65.7 | −8.3 | 73.0 |
| Assets | −35,531 | −92,228 | −75,722 | −56,546 | 62.3 | 66.7 | 52.3 | 70.2 |
| Liabilities | 10,807 | 4,921 | 78,360 | 10,614 | 82.8 | 92.9 | 69.4 | 60.2 |
| Other | −485 | −6,471 | −6,913 | −2,505 | 1.1 | 4.9 | 21.7 | 4.0 |
| Assets | −2,430 | −6,641 | −9,039 | −4,783 | 4.3 | 4.8 | 6.2 | 5.9 |
| Liabilities | 1,946 | 170 | 2,126 | 2,277 | 14.9 | 3.2 | 1.9 | 12.9 |

B. ANIEs

| | Amount (million U.S. $) | | | Share (%) | | |
|---|---|---|---|---|---|---|
| Net Flow | 1988–89 | 1990–91 | 1992–93 | 1988–89 | 1990–91 | 1992–93 |
| Total | −2,739 | 36,219 | 8,585 | 100.0 | 100.0 | 100.0 |
| Assets | −3,616 | −3,907 | 1,217 | 100.0 | 100.0 | 100.0 |
| Liabilities | 878 | 40,126 | 7,368 | 100.0 | 100.0 | 100.0 |
| FDI | −2,689 | −1,774 | −272 | 98.2 | −4.9 | −3.2 |
| Assets | −2,749 | −1,820 | −455 | 76.0 | 46.6 | −37.4 |
| Liabilities | 61 | 46 | 183 | 6.9 | 0.1 | 2.5 |
| Trade credits | −189 | 2 | 1,142 | 6.9 | 0.0 | 13.3 |
| Assets | −189 | 2 | 1,144 | 5.2 | 0.0 | 94.0 |
| Liabilities | −1 | 0 | −2 | −0.1 | 0.0 | 0.0 |
| Loans | 5,535 | 33,169 | 9,548 | −202.1 | 91.6 | 111.2 |
| Assets | −190 | −1,886 | 473 | 5.3 | 48.3 | 38.9 |
| Liabilities | 5,725 | 35,054 | 9,075 | 652.4 | 87.4 | 123.2 |
| Securities investment[a] | −5,121 | 4,701 | −2,089 | 187.0 | 13.0 | −24.3 |
| Assets | −213 | −309 | −166 | 5.9 | 7.9 | −13.6 |
| Liabilities | −4,909 | 5,010 | −1,924 | −559.4 | 12.5 | −26.1 |
| Other | −275 | 122 | 256 | 10.0 | 0.3 | 3.0 |
| Assets | −276 | 107 | 221 | 7.6 | −2.7 | 18.1 |
| Liabilities | 2 | 16 | 36 | 0.2 | 0.0 | 0.5 |

*(continued)*

**Table 4.12** (continued)

C. Other Asia

| | Amount (million U.S. $) | | | Share (%) | | |
|---|---|---|---|---|---|---|
| Net Flow | 1988–89 | 1990–91 | 1992–93 | 1988–89 | 1990–91 | 1992–93 |
| Total | −6,020 | −5,534 | −2,987 | 100.0 | 100.0 | 100.0 |
| Assets | −6,324 | −6,212 | −5,782 | 100.0 | 100.0 | 100.0 |
| Liabilities | 304 | 678 | 2,795 | 100.0 | 100.0 | 100.0 |
| FDI | −1,720 | −2,346 | −1,982 | 28.6 | 42.2 | 66.3 |
| Assets | −1,697 | −2,343 | −1,985 | 26.8 | 37.7 | 34.3 |
| Liabilities | −23 | −4 | 3 | −7.4 | −0.5 | 0.1 |
| Trade credits | 19 | −29 | 682 | −0.3 | 0.5 | −22.8 |
| Assets | 19 | −29 | 688 | −0.3 | 0.5 | −11.9 |
| Liabilities | 0 | 0 | −6 | 0.0 | 0.0 | −0.2 |
| Loans | −5,236 | −3,830 | −3,475 | 87.0 | 69.2 | 116.3 |
| Assets | −5,236 | −3,832 | −3,482 | 82.8 | 61.7 | 60.2 |
| Liabilities | 0 | 2 | 8 | 0.0 | 0.2 | 0.3 |
| Securities investment[a] | 549 | 751 | 2,565 | −9.1 | −13.6 | −85.9 |
| Assets | 189 | −82 | −224 | −3.0 | 1.3 | 3.9 |
| Liabilities | 361 | 833 | 2,789 | 118.6 | 122.9 | 99.8 |
| Other | 368 | −80 | −778 | −6.1 | 1.4 | 26.0 |
| Assets | 402 | 74 | −779 | −6.4 | −1.2 | 13.5 |
| Liabilities | −34 | −153 | 1 | −11.2 | −22.6 | 0.0 |

*Source:* Bank of Japan (various issues).

[a]Securities investment is identical to portfolio investment.

not available, table 4.12 shows long-term capital flows between Japan and two subregions in Asia, namely, the ANIEs and "other Asia," the latter dominated by the ASEAN4 and China with respect to capital flows.[12] According to table 4.12, parallel with the general trend of flows, Japan's capital outflow to the ANIEs fell sharply after 1990, while its outflow to "other Asia" remained relatively steady and significant.

For the ANIEs, the main declining components were loans and trade credits, and then direct investment. In fact, in 1992–93 loans flew *back into* Japan from Hong Kong, Korea, and Singapore partly because of a "stock adjustment" after the Japanese bubble burst.[13] The focus of Japanese FDI shifted away from the ANIEs after 1990 because these countries have lost their major advantages of cheap labor costs and undervalued exchange rates. On the other hand, loan inflow from the ANIEs to Japan was significant throughout 1988–93, in partic-

12. "Other Asia" includes, in addition to Pacific Asia, Afghanistan, Bangladesh, Bhutan, Brunei, East Timor, India, Macao, Maldives, Myanmar, Nepal, Pakistan, and Sri Lanka.

13. Long-term loans by Japanese banks and insurance companies to Asian countries, particularly to Hong Kong, Korea, Singapore, and Thailand, once again expanded, reaching $13 billion in 1994 (Bank of Japan, various issues).

ular during 1990–91 mainly vis-à-vis Hong Kong and Singapore. Note also that there was significant ANIE portfolio investment in Japan in 1990–91, again mainly through Hong Kong and Singapore.

For "other Asia," the recent retrenchment in Japan's capital flows, described above, has hardly been felt (table 4.12). In fact, total net capital outflow declined, but only slightly from $6.3 billion (1988–89) to $5.8 billion (1992–93). As for the composition of capital, loans and direct investment have remained the largest and second largest components (60 and 35 percent shares, respectively). Meanwhile, long-term capital inflow from "other Asia" to Japan has been negligible.

This is not the whole story about capital flows between Japan and Asia, however, because we have not yet examined short-term capital flows and these flows are crucially important in discussing Japan's role in capital flows in Pacific Asia. Because of data unavailability on multilateral flows from short-term monetary transactions, however, we cannot deal directly with their intraregional flows. Instead, we can only make some conjectures based on investment income data. Figure 4.2 shows Japan's investment income flows by region since 1983. Investment income includes not only direct investment income but loan interest and other income accrued to Japan's total external assets and liabilities.[14]

Figure 4.2 shows that investment income flows between Japan and the ANIEs have been huge compared with those between Japan and the United States and the European Community. Note in particular that Japan paid more investment income to the ANIEs than to the United States during 1988–92. This may seem puzzling because the United States has invested longer and more in Japan than have the ANIEs and capital flows between Japan and the ANIEs have declined significantly recently. The answer is given by figure 4.3, which illustrates Japan's total external assets and liabilities outstanding by capital flow component.

Figure 4.3 shows that Japan's external assets consist mainly of securities investment and short-term monetary assets, plus some direct investment and loans, and that its external liabilities are constituted primarily by short-term monetary liabilities and then by securities investment. Thus, we see the significance of short-term monetary transactions, which appeared, not in long-term capital flows, but in investment income by region.

In other words, the hidden factor in the puzzle is short-term monetary flows between Japan and the ANIEs, in particular Hong Kong and Singapore. Although international bank loans relatively declined on a net basis in Pacific Asia, as elsewhere, international interbank claims and liabilities expanded on a gross basis rather rapidly through international financial centers, and this general trend enhanced and deepened international banking flows within the region. Japan's role in intraregional capital flows appears to reside in its key relationship with Hong Kong and Singapore.

14. Investment income comprises direct investment income, interest on trade credit, loans, bank loans and deposits, and external bonds, and interest and dividends on securities.

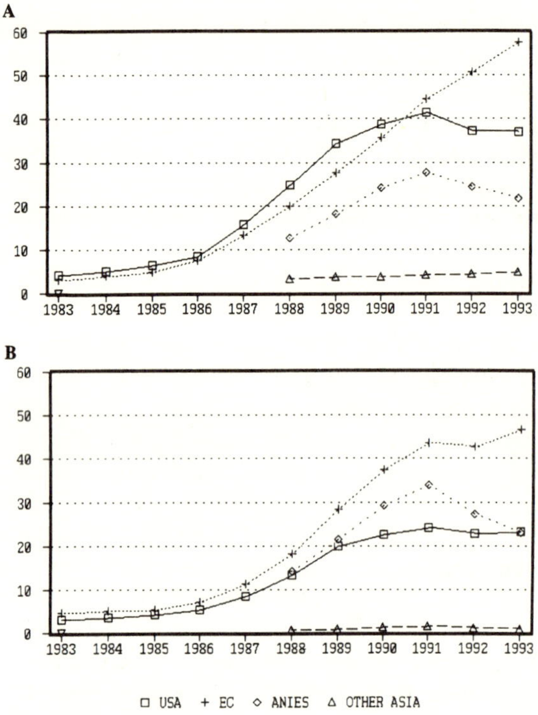


**Fig. 4.2 Japanese investment income by region, 1983–93: (*A*) credit (billion U.S.$); (*B*) debit (billion U.S.$)**
*Source:* Bank of Japan (various issues).

## 4.6 Concluding Remarks

We have examined developments in capital flows in Pacific Asia since the early 1980s. The regional pattern of external finance has been different from those of other developing regions. First, Pacific Asia did not suffer from such a severe decline in foreign capital inflow in the 1980s as did other developing regions. Second, some countries in Pacific Asia became "source countries" of capital either overall or of a specific component of capital.

However, Pacific Asia also displays some features in its changing pattern of external finance in common with other developing countries. FDI has begun to play a more significant role in capital flows. Portfolio investment has shown steady growth as an important new form of capital flows, though its sustainability remains in question.[15]

15. On the recent upsurge in portfolio investment flows to developing countries and its macroeconomic impact, see Claessens (1995a, 1995b), IMF (1994), World Bank (1993c), Calvo, Leiderman, and Reinhart (1993), Frankel (1994), Corbo and Hernandez (1994), Schadler et al. (1993), and Mathieson and Rojas-Suarez (1993).

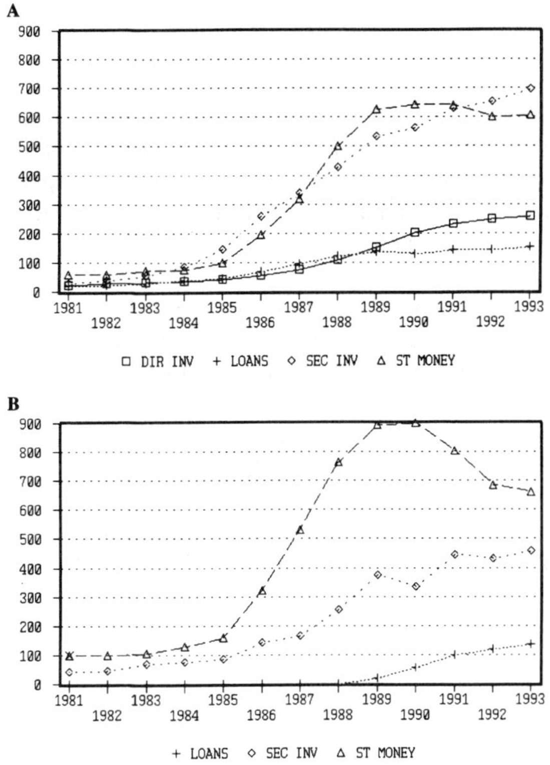


**Fig. 4.3 Japan: (*A*) external assets (billion U.S.$); (*B*) external liabilities (billion U.S.$)**
*Source:* Bank of Japan (various issues).

The ANIEs have appeared as far more important capital suppliers in the region since the 1980s. This has generated a greatly diversified and sophisticated network of capital flows in Pacific Asia. This is obviously one of the reasons for the relative decline of EC and U.S. capital in the region during that period.

One of the fundamental factors in this change in capital flows was the structural development in macroeconomic balances of these economies in the process of their dynamic growth in the 1980s. Indeed, some of them "graduated" from the stage of persistent domestic saving shortages typical of developing countries; this "graduation" in turn caused a significant change in the size and direction of capital flows.

Even though long-term international bank loans have appeared to shrink on a net basis, cross-border bank claims and liabilities have shown a great increase relative to domestic economic activities, especially through the international financial centers. This has widened and deepened international capital transactions among economies in the region.[16]

As a result, Japan's role as a capital supplier has remained large, although not larger than in the early 1980s. Its role has become limited to a specific category of lower-income countries in the region. In fact, Japan's role in capital flows in Pacific Asia has been changing across various components of capital flows. It is no longer the dominant capital supplier in the region, though it has become the most important financial intermediary.

After realizing the importance of structural changes in macroeconomic balances and enhanced regional interdependence through capital flows, we should be more cautious in using regional aggregation. In such a dynamic region as Pacific Asia, aggregation across diverse economies sometimes gives misleading information about amounts as well as directions of those flows that may cancel one another within the region. This may not only be the case for capital flows.

Finally, we should note that, in the background of these shared developments, various preconditions for foreign investment were provided by host countries in Pacific Asia. They created the conditions necessary for increasing capital flows in order to help finance macroeconomic imbalances on one hand and tap technological spillovers on the other, while changes in the international economic climate as well as in the source countries may have created sufficient conditions.

## References

Bank of Japan. Various issues. *Balance of payments monthly.* Tokyo: Bank of Japan.

BIS (Bank for International Settlements). 1994. *Annual report 1994.* Basel: Bank for International Settlements.

Calvo, Guillermo A., Leonardo Leiderman, and Carmen M. Reinhart. 1993. Capital inflows and real exchange rate appreciation in Latin America: The role of external factors. *IMF Staff Papers* 40 (March): 32–52.

Claessens, Stijn. 1995a. The emergence of equity investment in developing countries: Overview. *World Bank Economic Review* 9, no. 1 (January): 1–17.

———. 1995b. Portfolio capital flows: Hot or cold? *World Bank Economic Review* 9, no. 1 (January): 153–74.

Corbo, V., and L. Hernandez. 1994. Macroeconomic adjustment to capital inflows: Latin American style versus East Asian style. Policy Research Working Paper no. 1377. Washington, D.C.: World Bank.

Eaton, Jonathan, and Corrinne Ho. 1993. Trade and investment in the North-America-Pacific region: Does NAFTA matter? In *Asian economic dynamism and new Asia-Pacific economic order.* Proceedings of Kyushu University International Symposium. Fukuoka: Kyushu University.

16. In fact, there is evidence that capital mobility and interest rate linkage among the economies has increased (see Glick and Hutchison 1990; Frankel 1992; Haque and Montiel 1990; Montiel 1994).

Fernandez-Arias, Eduardo. 1994. The new wave in private capital flows: Push or pull? Policy Research Working Paper no. 1312. Washington, D.C.: World Bank.

Frankel, Jeffrey A. 1992. Is Japan creating a yen bloc in East Asia and the Pacific? NBER Working Paper no. 4050. Cambridge, Mass.: National Bureau of Economic Research, April.

———. 1994. Sterilization of money inflows: Difficult (Calvo) or easy (Reisen). IMF Working Paper. Washington, D.C.: International Monetary Fund.

Frankel, Jeffrey A., and Shang-Jin Wei. 1994. Yen bloc or dollar bloc? Exchange rate policies of the East Asian economies. In *Macroeconomic linkage: Savings, exchange rates, and capital flows,* ed. Takatoshi Ito and Anne O. Krueger. Chicago: University of Chicago Press.

Ghosh, Atish R., and Jonathan Ostry. 1993. Do capital flows reflect economic fundamentals in developing countries? IMF Working Paper no. 93/34, Washington, D.C.: International Monetary Fund, April.

Glick, Reuven, and Michael Hutchison. 1990. Financial liberalization in the Pacific Basin: Implications for real interest rate linkages. *Journal of the Japanese and International Economies* 4:36–48.

Gooptu, Sudarshan. 1994. Are portfolio flows to emerging markets complementary or competitive? Policy Research Working Paper no. 1360. Washington, D.C.: World Bank.

Haque, Nadeem Ul, and Peter J. Montiel. 1990. How mobile is capital in developing countries? *Economic Letters* 33 (August): 1391–98.

IMF (International Monetary Fund). 1993. Private market financing for developing countries. Washington, D.C.: International Monetary Fund, December.

———. 1994. *World economic outlook.* Washington, D.C.: International Monetary Fund, October.

———. Various years (a). *Balance of payments statistics yearbook.* Washington, D.C.: International Monetary Fund.

———. Various years (b). *International financial statistics yearbook.* Washington, D.C.: International Monetary Fund.

International Finance Corporation. 1992. *Emerging stock markets: Factbook 1992.* Washington, D.C.: International Finance Corporation.

Kohsaka, Akira. 1993. Economic interdependence in capital flows in East Asia. In *Regional integration and its impact on developing countries,* ed. K. Ohno. Tokyo: Institute of Developing Economies.

Japan External Trade Organization. 1993. *Sekai to Nihon no Kaigai Chokusetsu Toshi* (Foreign direct investment of the world and Japan). JETRO White Paper. Tokyo: Japan External Trade Organization.

Mathieson, Donald J., and Liliana Rojas-Suarez. 1993. Liberalization of the capital account. IMF Occasional Paper no. 103. Washington, D.C.: International Monetary Fund, March.

Ministry of Finance (Japan). 1994. *Annual report of International Finance Bureau.* Tokyo: Ministry of Finance.

Ministry of International Trade and Industries, Japan. 1993. *Tsusho Hakusho* (White paper on international trade).

Montiel, Peter J. 1994. Capital mobility in developing countries: Some measurement issues and empirical estimates. *World Bank Economic Review* 8, no. 3 (September).

OECD (Organisation for Economic Co-operation and Development). Various issues. *Financial statistics monthly.* Paris: Organisation for Economic Co-operation and Development.

Petri, Peter A. 1993. The East Asian trading bloc: An analytical history. In *Regionalism and rivalry: Japan and the United States in Pacific Asia,* ed. Jeffrey A. Frankel and Miles Kahler. Chicago: University of Chicago Press.

Saxonhouse, Gary R. 1993. Pricing strategies and trading blocs in East Asia. In *Regionalism and rivalry: Japan and the United States in Pacific Asia,* ed. Jeffrey Frankel and Miles Kahler. Chicago: University of Chicago Press.

Schadler, S., M. Carkovic, A. Bennet, and R. Kahn. 1993. Recent experiences with surges in capital inflows. IMF Occasional Paper no. 108. Washington, D.C.: International Monetary Fund.

World Bank. 1993a. *East Asian miracle.* New York: Oxford University Press.

———. 1993b. *Global economic prospects and the developing countries.* Washington, D.C.: World Bank.

———. 1993c. *World debt tables,* vol. 1. Washington, D.C.: World Bank.

———. 1994. *World debt tables,* vol. 1. Washington, D.C.: World Bank.

———. 1995. *World debt tables,* vol. 1. Washington, D.C.: World Bank.

Yuan, Tsao. 1986. Capital flows among Pacific Basin economies. In *Pacific growth and financial interdependence,* ed: Augustine H. H. Tan and Basant Kapur. London: Allen and Unwin.

## Comment Toshihiko Kinoshita

Kohsaka's paper gives an updated and well-balanced overview of capital flows both into and out of Pacific Asia and will no doubt benefit those who are interested in this subject. Its coverage of all types of capital flows in this area is quite informative. Features of capital flow in Pacific Asia are made quite understandable through the comparison with Latin America. In that sense, it is a good paper. However, it seems to me that the description dwells too much on the phenomenon—though the analysis of savings-investment gaps as related to capital flow is well written.

Broadly speaking, capital flows can be classified in two categories. One is determined by the market. The other—official development finance (ODA plus OOF except export credit)—is determined by the policies of donor governments. The rise and fall of private capital flows, or the first category of flow, may well be explained by factors influencing the market. Kohsaka stresses in his paper the significance of vigorously growing foreign direct investment (FDI) in this region. Then, the logic of the recent rise and fall of FDI from Japan and elsewhere must be further explained. Such explanation is necessary in order to have a better idea of what might happen in the future.

There must be factors both in host countries and on the investors' side that influence the rise and fall of FDI. On the host country side in this region, we can easily find such factors: deregulation policies, such as the open door and reform policies of China and Vietnam; a growing domestic (or regional) market; and competition among host countries to induce more FDI, in particular, export-oriented FDI. On the investors' side, let me illustrate my interpretation

Toshihiko Kinoshita is executive director and head of research at the Institute for International Investment and Development, Export-Import Bank of Japan, and former visiting scholar at the National Bureau of Economic Research.

of the mechanism that expanded Japan's FDI in the 1980s and the reverse mechanism that decreased it in the early 1990s (see figs. 4C.1 to 4C.4). The increase in FDI by Taiwan and Korea could be explained by the appreciation of their currencies vis-à-vis the U.S. dollar, a domestic labor shortage, and a fast-growing technological backlog.

Now, let me return to officially supported capital flow. As Kohsaka contends, it comprises ODA and OOF. Japan's ODA, for instance, has shown fast growth. That of the United States has not in the past decade. This difference reflects the differing policies of the two countries. It may be worth mentioning.

As for OOF, there exist two basic flows—one multilateral, the other bilateral. Let me add some facts. The former comprises the capital flows of the World Bank and the Asian Development Bank (ADB). The ADB will be more sensitive to a country-to-country balance in the region and the World Bank to a region-to-region balance (e.g., Asia vs. Africa). Bilateral OOF flows consist of officially supported suppliers' and buyers' credit and untied loans, which is more prevalent in this region, or such loans as have been massively supplied by the Export-Import Bank of Japan. Export credit as a whole is relatively less policy-based. It can be regarded as rather passive finance, particularly when the recipient is very creditworthy. Should exporters of country A fail in an international tender on a specific project, country A's export credit agency is not requested to provide financing.

The above-mentioned officially supported untied loans are one of the financial menus used in the new policy of the Japanese government, since 1987, to flow more Japanese capital to developing countries in a harmonious way. The main borrowers have been governments or governmental agencies, which sometimes relend to local private banks. These are my comments. Now let me ask one question.

Kohsaka classifies countries in the region into three groups. China is classified as a country that outflows capital somewhat and inflows capital at the same time. Will China's pattern of two-way capital flow continue into the twenty-first century?

## Comment Ya-Hwei Yang

Kohsaka's paper gives an overview of the recent trend of capital flows both into and out of the Pacific Asia. Kohsaka finds that some countries in the region have become source countries of capital. Foreign direct investment has come to play a more significant role. Portfolio investment appears to have shown steady growth. The author mentions that the fundamental factors which have

Ya-Hwei Yang is research fellow and director of the Taiwan Economy Division at Chung-Hua Institution for Economic Research.

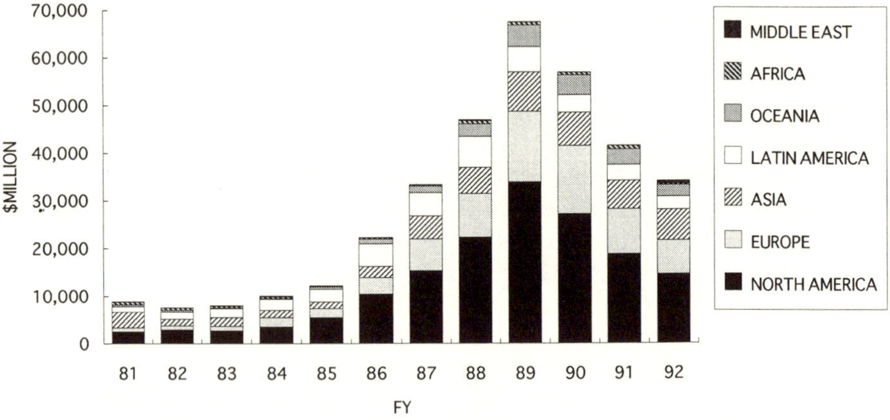


**Fig. 4C.1 Trends in Japan's outward FDI by region**
*Source:* Prepared by Export-Import Bank of Japan with statistics from Ministry of Finance.

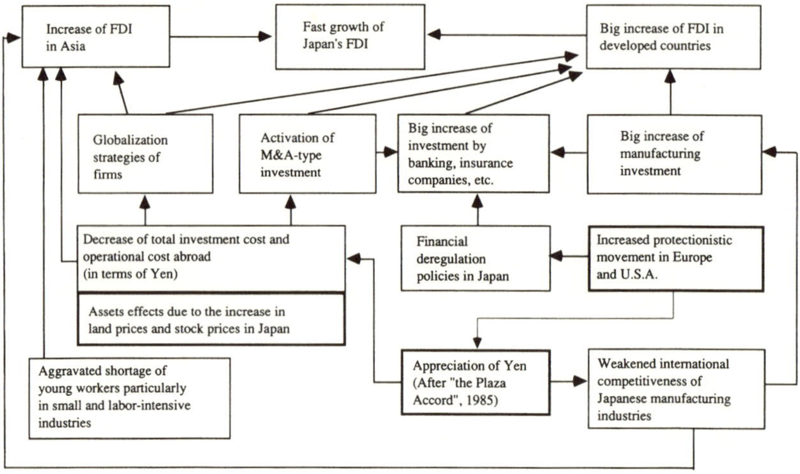


**Fig. 4C.2 Expansion mechanism of Japan's outward FDI in the latter half of the 1980s**

generated this change in capital flow are structural developments. Some of the countries have graduated from the stage of persistent domestic savings shortage. In addition, the role of Japan as a capital supplier has remained important, but not so dominant as before.

I have learned a great deal from this paper. It provides valuable information on the above-mentioned issues. I would like to add some complementary points here. Some of the issues need further study, if enough data are available. First, if this paper were able to give more explanation for each important phe-

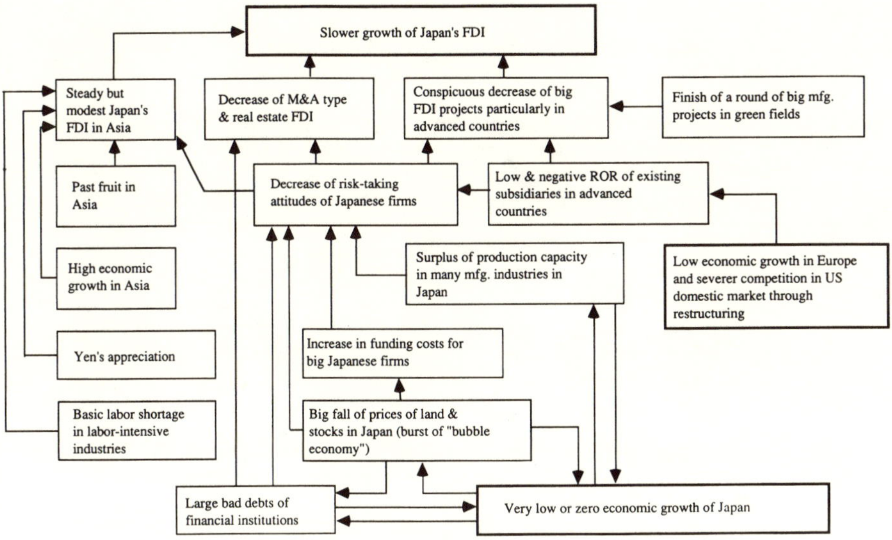


**Fig. 4C.3 Change in expansion mechanism of Japan's outward FDI since the early 1990s**

nomenon, it would be more comprehensive. For example, why have the net capital flows in the relationship between Japan and the NIEs changed? In addition, if the capital movement between any two countries were identified, it would be more informative. I understand that data availability is a problem that cannot be solved at present.

Because I am from Taiwan, I will give a brief synopsis of the case of Taiwan in related issues. Taiwan is one of the NIEs, also one of the four "tigers" in Asia. It has maintained a high growth rate and stable price levels. In recent years, many Taiwanese businesses have moved to other countries, especially to mainland China and Southeast Asia. The reason for this phenomenon is that traditional labor-intensive goods made in Taiwan are not as competitive as before. Labor in Taiwan has become more expensive because labor shortage is a serious problem. Land prices are increasing greatly, as well. Therefore, these traditional industries must invest abroad to search for cheaper labor and cheaper land, instead of staying in Taiwan. In the past five years, much Taiwanese capital has gone to mainland China. In the past three years, some Southeast Asian countries, such as Vietnam, seem to be more attractive to Taiwanese investments. In each of these Southeast Asian countries, Taiwan is usually ranked among the top three investor countries. When Taiwanese firms move outward, their primary capital fund sources are their head offices in Taiwan. Capital outflows generally follow the direction of overseas investment. Therefore, there is a large amount of capital flowing out of Taiwan. However, the offshore banking center of Taiwan is not yet matured and advanced. Therefore,

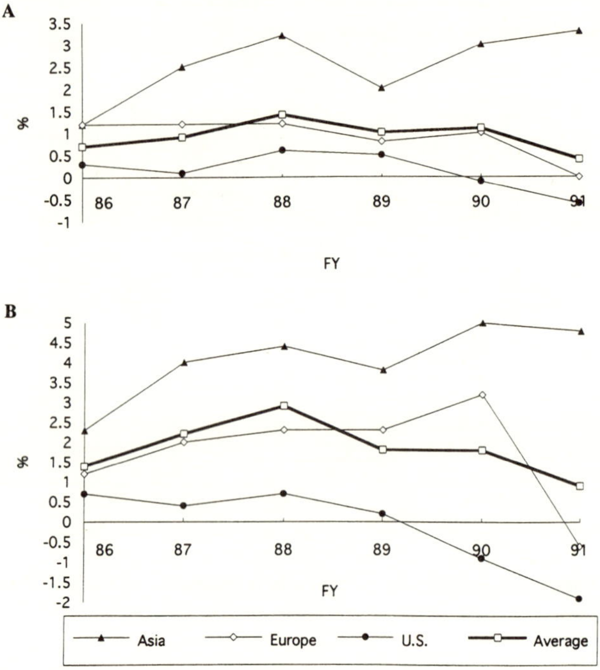


**Fig. 4C.4 Operational profit ratio of Japanese affiliates vis-à-vis total sales: (*A*) all industries; (*B*) manufacturing sector**

*Source: Wagakuni Kigyo No Kaigai Jigyo Katsudo* (Ministry of International Trade and Industry), no. 22 (1993).

much of this capital movement passes through the underground economy, instead of through official financial channels. In addition, the trade and capital flow patterns between Japan and Taiwan have not changed much so far. Although Taiwan has been an export-oriented country, it still has the same big trade deficit with Japan that it has had for decades. Most machines and key parts of manufactured goods are imported from Japan to Taiwan. Therefore, the capital flow relationship between the two has not changed much.

Different countries have different stories, and I have provided Taiwan's case as a reference for Kohsaka's paper.

# 5 The Structural Determinants of Invoice Currencies in Japan: The Case of Foreign Trade with East Asian Countries

Shin-ichi Fukuda

## 5.1 Introduction

During the past decade, Japan's share as a trading partner of East Asian countries increased substantially. In addition, in the late 1980s, direct investment from Japan to most East Asian countries rose significantly. However, despite these growing roles for Japan, the internationalization of the Japanese yen has not increased as rapidly as Japan's economic power in East Asia. For example, Frankel (1991) and Frankel and Wei (1994) showed that East Asian governments were less tempted to link their currencies to the yen than to the dollar. To the extent that reducing exchange rate volatility can reduce trade risk, it is natural to suppose that East Asian governments will try to link their currencies to the Japanese yen unless a costless hedge through a perfect forward/futures market is possible. However, Frankel and Wei's results imply that this is not the case in East Asian countries and that the U.S. dollar still has the dominant weight in East Asian currency baskets. In addition, they pointed out that the U.S. dollar continues to be the dominant invoicing currency among East Asian countries.

Table 5.1 reports time-series data of invoice currency ratios in Japan's exports and imports. Yen-invoiced ratios, which were negligible in 1970, jumped to 40 percent of exports and 20 percent of imports in 1993. However, the shares of the U.S. dollar are still significant not only in Japan's total exports and imports but also in Japan's trade with East Asian countries. In addition, compared to other developed countries, Japan still lagged in the use of its own currency. Table 5.2 reports domestic invoice currency ratios in 1976, 1980, and 1988

Shin-ichi Fukuda is associate professor at the Institute of Economic Research, Hitotsubashi University.

The author thanks J. Eaton, A. Kohsaka, T. Ito, and other seminar participants for their helpful comments on an earlier draft of this paper.

**Table 5.1** **Invoice Currency Ratios in Japanese Exports and Imports (%)**

| | Exports | | | | Imports | | | |
|---|---|---|---|---|---|---|---|---|
| | In Yen | | In U.S. Dollar | | In Yen | | In U.S. Dollar | |
| Year | World | East Asia | World | East Asia | World | East Asia | World | East Asia |
| 1969 | 0.6 | – | 90.1 | – | – | – | – | – |
| 1970 | 0.9 | – | 90.5 | – | 0.3 | – | 80.0 | – |
| 1971 | 2.0 | – | 90.4 | – | – | – | – | – |
| 1972 | 8.6 | – | 82.8 | – | – | – | – | – |
| 1973 | 11.3 | – | 81.0 | – | – | – | – | – |
| 1974 | 15.0 | – | 77.7 | – | – | – | – | – |
| 1975 | 17.0 | – | 78.5 | – | 0.9 | – | 89.9 | – |
| 1976 | 19.4 | – | 76.3 | – | – | – | – | – |
| 1977 | 18.8 | – | 76.9 | – | – | – | – | – |
| 1978 | 19.8 | – | 75.4 | – | 1.6 | – | – | – |
| 1979 | – | – | – | – | – | – | – | – |
| 1980 | 28.9 | – | 66.3 | – | 2.4 | – | 93.1 | – |
| 1981 | 31.8 | 29.8 | 62.8 | 68.9 | – | – | – | – |
| 1982 | 33.8 | – | 60.9 | – | – | – | – | – |
| 1983 | 40.5 | 48.0 | 50.2 | – | 3.0 | 2.0 | – | – |
| 1984 | 39.5 | – | 53.1 | – | – | – | – | – |
| 1985 | 39.3 | 47.3 | 52.2 | 51.3 | 7.3[a] | – | – | – |
| 1986 | 35.5 | 37.5 | 53.5 | – | 9.7 | 9.2 | 82.1[b] | 88.6[b] |
| 1987 | 33.4 | 41.1 | 55.2 | 56.5 | 10.6 | 11.5 | 81.7 | 87.6 |
| 1988 | 34.3 | 41.2 | 53.2 | 56.0 | 13.3 | 17.5 | 78.5 | 86.9 |
| 1989 | 34.7 | 43.5 | 52.4 | 53.6 | 14.1 | 19.5 | 77.3 | 79.0 |
| 1990 | 37.5 | 48.9 | 48.8 | 48.1 | 14.5 | 19.4 | 75.5 | 78.8 |
| 1991 | 39.4 | 50.8 | 46.7 | 45.9 | 15.6 | 21.6 | 75.4 | 76.5 |
| 1992 | 40.1[c] | – | 46.6[c] | – | 17.0[c] | – | 74.5[c] | – |
| 1993 | 40.7[c] | – | 48.6[c] | – | 21.6[c] | – | 72.1[c] | – |

*Sources:* Exports: Until 1982, *Yushutsu Shinyojyo Toukei* by Bank of Japan; between 1983 and 1991, *Export Confirmation Statistics* by Ministry of International Trade and Industry (MITI); for 1992, *Kessai Tuka Douko* by MITI.

Imports: Until 1980, *Yushutsu Syonin Todokede Houkokusho* by MITI; between 1981 and 1985, *Houkokusyorei Ni Motoduku Houkoku* by Ministry of Finance; between 1986 and 1991, *Import Reporting Statistics* by MITI; for 1992, *Kessai Tuka Douko* by MITI; for 1993, *Yusyutu (Yunyu) Houkokusyo Douko* by MITI.

*Note:* Unless specified, data are averaged annually.

[a]Figures for fiscal year.

[b]Figures for December 1986.

[c]Figures for September.

among major OECD countries. In the United States and Germany, almost all exports were invoiced by their own currencies. However, domestic invoice currency ratios in Japan were very small, the lowest among these countries in both exports and imports.

The purpose of this paper is to investigate why yen-invoiced ratios are so

**Table 5.2** **Domestic Invoice Currency Ratios among Major OECD Countries (%)**

| | Export | | | Import | | |
|---|---|---|---|---|---|---|
| Country | 1976 | 1980 | 1988 | 1976 | 1980 | 1988 |
| Japan (world trade) | 19.4 | 28.9 | 34.3 | 0.9[a] | 2.4 | 13.3 |
| Japan (East Asian trade) | – | 29.8[b] | 41.2 | – | – | 17.5 |
| France | 68.3 | 62.5 | 58.5 | 31.5 | 33.1 | 48.9 |
| Germany | 86.9 | 82.3 | 81.5[c] | 43.0 | 43.0 | 52.6 |
| Italy | – | 36.0 | 38.0 | – | 18.0 | 27.0[c] |
| Sweden | 66.1 | – | – | 25.8 | – | – |
| Denmark | 54.0 | – | – | 23.0 | – | – |
| Austria | 54.7[a] | – | – | 24.7 | – | – |
| Netherlands | 50.2 | – | – | 31.4 | – | – |
| Belgium | 47.7[d] | – | – | 25.4[d] | – | – |
| United Kingdom | 73.0[e] | 76.0 | 57.0 | – | 38.0 | 40.0 |
| United States | – | 97.0 | 96.0 | – | 85.0 | 85.0 |

*Sources:* Data for 1976, *Annual Report* (Tokyo: MITI, 1979); data for 1980 and 1988, Tavlas and Ozeki (1991).

[a]Figure for 1975.

[b]Figure for 1981.

[c]Figure for 1987.

[d]Figure for January to September 1976.

[e]Figure for October to November 1976.

low in Japan's foreign trade with East Asian countries and the United States. Related issues have already been investigated by several authors (see, among others, Hamada and Horiuchi 1987; Tavlas and Ozeki 1992; Kawai 1992, 1994; Takeda and Turner 1992; Ito 1993; Taguchi 1994). Most of these studies, however, have focused on general aspects of the internationalization of the Japanese yen. Extending some results in the existing literature, this paper focuses on more specific aspects of invoice currencies and investigates how Japan's trade structures affected the choice of the invoice currencies.

The first part of the paper investigates the determinants of invoice currencies in Japan's exports. Focusing on the heavy reliance of Japan's exports on the United States, we show that the "pricing-to-market" (PTM) behavior of Japanese exporters may well explain the choice of invoice currency.[1] One noteworthy result in the paper is that although most Japanese exports to East Asia are still invoiced in the U.S. dollar, the Japanese yen is becoming the dominant invoice currency when exporting TVs, VCRs, and automobiles to East Asia.

1. PTM models were originally presented by Krugman (1987) and others. Several authors have investigated the PTM behavior of Japanese exporters (e.g., Giovannini 1988; Ohno 1989; Marston 1990; Saxonhouse 1993). All of these studies were based on the data set of domestic and export price indexes for disaggregated commodities. However, except for Saxonhouse (1993), these studies did not focus on export price discrimination among different foreign countries. The following analysis is in marked contrast with these studies in that we use a data set that classifies export prices by both commodity and country bases.

The reason is that for these commodities, product differentiation may make price arbitrage among different markets very difficult. Hence, the PTM theory implies that Japan's exporting firms, which have relatively strong market power in East Asian markets, tend to choose the Japanese yen as an invoice currency in the exports of these product-differentiated commodities.

The second part of the paper considers other structural determinants of invoice currencies. In the analysis, we focus on invoice currency ratios in Japan's imports and on the relation between invoice ratios and trade dependency. We show that low yen-invoiced ratios are caused mainly by the large shares of oil and raw materials in Japan's imports. We also show that recent changes in Japanese invoice currency ratios are due to East Asia's changing trade dependency on the United States.

The paper is organized as follows: Based on the PTM theory, section 5.2 considers the determinants of invoice currency and presents our hypothesis. Section 5.3 explains the characteristics of invoice currency ratios in Japan's exports. Section 5.4 empirically examines how the PTM theory can explain the choice of invoice currency by Japanese exporters. Section 5.5 discusses invoice ratios in Japan's imports, and section 5.6 investigates the relation between invoice ratios and trade dependency. Section 5.7 summarizes our main results and discusses their implications.

## 5.2 Determinants of Invoice Currencies in Japan's Exports

In explaining the determinants of invoice currencies in Japan's exports, several previous studies have pointed out four factors. The first is the heavy reliance of Japan's exports on the United States. Since only a small fraction (16 percent in 1991) of Japanese exports to the United States are invoiced in the yen and since a large fraction of Japanese exports go to the United States, the structure of Japan's exports leads to relatively low yen-denominated invoice currency ratios in Japan's total exports. The second factor is inertia due to the previous economic power of the United States. It is well known that once a country's currency is established as an invoice currency, a large change in economic environment is necessary to replace it, even if the relative economic power of that country has declined in world trade (see Krugman 1980; Matsuyama, Kiyotaki, and Matsui 1993). Thus, although Japan's economic power in world trade has risen, it will take a long time for the yen to become the key currency in world trade. The third factor is the relatively small size of the short-term capital market in Japan. Although its volume has been increasing recently, the size of the treasury bill market in Japan is still much smaller than in the United States. Since the short-term capital market would be where foreign investors would park their yen-denominated funds, its limited size reduces the invoice currency ratio of the yen in trade. The fourth factor is the role of Japan's large trading companies, which handle the bulk of Japanese exports and imports. Since these companies have a relative advantage in avoiding foreign exchange risks, their existence may lead to relatively low yen-denominated invoice currency ratios in Japan's total exports.

The first factor indicates that low invoice ratios are caused by some structural problem in Japanese exports. However, it does not necessarily show why only a small fraction of Japan's exports to the United States are invoiced in the Japanese yen. In addition, it cannot explain why most exports to East Asian countries are invoiced in the U.S. dollar. The following analysis looks into this and shows that PTM models may explain why yen invoice ratios are low in Japanese exports.

Authors such as Ito (1993) have conjectured that the issue of invoice currency may be related to the PTM behavior of Japanese exporters. In addition, Giovannini (1988) has shown theoretically that firms set their export prices in foreign currency if profits are a concave function of the exchange rate while they set their export prices in home currency if profits are a convex function of the exchange rate. Fukuda and Ji (1995) have applied Ito's and Giovannini's results and presented a rigorous empirical study of the relationship between PTM behavior and the choice of invoice currency in Japanese exports.

The basic idea of these studies is that invoice prices in contracts cannot be changed easily when the exchange rate fluctuates. To the extent that the foreign market is highly competitive and exporters cannot control market prices for their own products, a rise in selling price will mean a loss of market share in the foreign market. Thus, Japanese manufacturers, who maximize their long-run profits, will choose to invoice their exports in terms of the importer's currency. The following analysis examines the validity of this idea empirically. We consider the following hypothesis:

HYPOTHESIS: When invoicing in the foreign currency, the export price in terms of the domestic currency is positively correlated with the exchange rate in terms of the domestic currency. When invoicing in the domestic currency, the correlation between the export price and the exchange rate is ambiguous in terms of the domestic currency.

This hypothesis implies that the choice of invoice currency may be revealed by the correlation between the export price and the exchange rate.[2] The basic reason is that invoicing exports in the foreign currency can eliminate unexpected selling price fluctuations caused by unexpected exchange rate fluctuations. Thus, exports are invoiced in the foreign currency if the exporters prefer stabilizing the selling price in the foreign market. Since the export price is positively correlated with the exchange rate in terms of the domestic currency when the selling price is stabilized in the foreign market, the hypothesis follows. In sections 5.3 and 5.4, we examine this hypothesis empirically.

2. For a formal proof of this hypothesis, see Giovannini (1988) and Fukuda and Ji (1995). A similar hypothesis was originally proposed by McKinnon (1979, chap. 4) in a less formal framework.

## 5.3 Invoice Currency Ratios of Japanese Exports

In order to examine the validity of our hypothesis, this section first investigates invoice currency ratios in Japan's exports to the United States and East Asian countries.[3] Table 5.3 lists average invoice currency ratios by U.S. dollar and Japanese yen for each commodity in 1991, and table 5.4 lists yen-invoiced ratios for each commodity in 1983. The tables show two noteworthy features.

First, for commodities such as textiles, chemicals, and metal products, the U.S. dollar is the dominant export invoice currency both for the United States and for East Asia. In 1983, yen-invoiced ratios were negligible among all of these commodities. Even in 1991, almost all exports of steel were invoiced in the U.S. dollar, and only one-fourth of chemical exports were invoiced in the yen both for the United States and East Asian countries.

Second, for electric machines and automobiles, invoice currency ratios showed marked differences between the United States and East Asian countries. When we look at exports to the United States, more than 90 percent were invoiced in the U.S. dollar. However, when we look at exports to East Asian countries, yen-invoiced ratios were relatively high. This implies that for these specific commodities, the yen is becoming the dominant export-invoicing currency in East Asian countries (see also table 5.5).

One possible explanation for this implication is the increase in intrafirm trade in recent years. Because the intrafirm trade of Japanese companies tends to be invoiced in the yen, recent increases of yen-invoiced ratios may be attributable to increases in intrafirm trade in these commodities. However, Tables 5.4 and 5.5 show that, except for TV exports, yen-invoiced ratios in these exports were already high in 1983 and 1987, when the size of Japan's direct investment in East Asia was limited. In addition, since intrafirm trade has similarly increased in other industries and to other areas, it cannot explain why the yen is becoming the dominant currency only in exports of electric machines and automobiles to East Asian countries.

For commodities such as TVs, VCRs, and automobiles, product differentiation may make price arbitrage among different markets very difficult. Thus, for these commodities, Japan's exporting firms tend to choose different invoice currencies in different foreign markets depending on their preference for price stabilization. On the other hand, for commodities such as textiles, chemicals, and metal products, the degree of product differentiation will be limited. Thus, for these relatively homogeneous commodities, the PTM theory is less relevant, and their selling prices tend to be quoted in the international currency, that is, the U.S. dollar.

To the extent that our hypothesis holds true, the above results imply that

3. East Asia includes the following 17 countries: Korea, Taiwan, Hong Kong, Thailand, Singapore, Malaysia, the Philippines, Indonesia, India, Brunei, Cambodia, Laos, Myanmar, Pakistan, Sri Lanka, Nepal, and Bhutan.

**Table 5.3** **Invoice Currency Ratios in Japanese Exports, 1991 (%)**

| | To United States | | | To East Asia | | | To World | | |
|---|---|---|---|---|---|---|---|---|---|
| Commodity | U.S. Dollar | Yen | Misc.[a] | U.S. Dollar | Yen | Misc.[a] | U.S. Dollar | Yen | Misc.[a] |
| All commodities | 83.4 | 16.5 | 0.1 | 45.9 | 50.8 | 3.3 | 46.8 | 39.4 | 13.8 |
| Foodstuffs | 76.3 | 23.6 | 0.0 | 55.7 | 42.5 | 1.8 | 55.6 | 41.2 | 3.2 |
| Textiles | 80.1 | 19.5 | 0.4 | 71.0 | 28.5 | 0.5 | 63.0 | 32.5 | 4.5 |
| Chemicals | 74.8 | 25.0 | 0.2 | 78.6 | 20.1 | 1.2 | 63.0 | 26.2 | 10.8 |
| Nonmetal mineral | 78.8 | 21.1 | 0.1 | 61.3 | 36.7 | 1.9 | 53.5 | 40.5 | 6.0 |
| Metal products | 89.3 | 10.6 | 0.0 | 78.8 | 19.9 | 1.3 | 76.8 | 19.5 | 3.7 |
| Steel | 99.1 | 0.9 | 0.0 | 88.6 | 10.9 | 0.5 | 87.7 | 9.4 | 2.9 |
| Machines | 83.3 | 16.6 | 0.1 | 33.2 | 62.6 | 4.2 | 42.2 | 42.8 | 15.0 |
| Generators | 83.2 | 16.6 | 0.1 | 25.9 | 67.5 | 6.6 | 40.7 | 48.8 | 10.5 |
| TVs | 91.4 | 8.3 | 0.3 | 19.9 | 74.8 | 5.3 | 35.0 | 56.6 | 8.4 |
| VCRs | 91.4 | 8.6 | 0.1 | 27.7 | 62.3 | 10.0 | 42.1 | 39.7 | 18.2 |
| Automobiles | 86.1 | 13.9 | 0.0 | 19.1 | 69.8 | 11.1 | 44.2 | 35.3 | 20.5 |
| Ships | 97.6 | 2.4 | 0.0 | 22.8 | 77.2 | 0.1 | 13.7 | 86.2 | 0.1 |
| Heavy electric | 73.3 | 26.6 | 0.1 | 45.4 | 51.7 | 2.9 | 41.0 | 51.5 | 7.5 |
| Other | 86.5 | 13.3 | 0.1 | 58.7 | 39.4 | 1.9 | 52.7 | 30.4 | 16.9 |

*Source: Export Confirmation Statistics* (Tokyo: MITI, 1991).

[a]Invoice ratios for other miscellaneous currencies.

**Table 5.4** **Yen-Invoiced Ratios in Japanese Exports, 1983 (%)**

| Commodity | To United States | To East Asia | To World |
|---|---|---|---|
| All commodities | 13 | 48 | 40 |
| Textiles | 0 | 9 | 31 |
| Chemicals | – | 20 | 12 |
| Metal products | 1 | 6 | 14 |
| General machinery | 27 | 70 | 53 |
| Electric machines | 6 | 75 | 41 |
| Tape recorders | 2 | 85 | 32 |
| Automobiles | 18 | 83 | 46 |
| Motorcycles | – | 89 | 26 |
| Ships | – | 100 | 90 |
| Optical instruments | 14 | 8 | 47 |

*Source: Annual Report of the International Finance Bureau* (Tokyo: Ministry of Finance, 1984).

selling prices of TVs, VCRs, and automobiles are stable in U.S. markets but unstable in East Asian markets. In other words, for TVs, VCRs, and automobiles, we can expect that the exchange rate in terms of the yen is positively correlated with the yen-denominated export prices to U.S. markets and is less correlated with those to East Asian markets. The following section investigates the validity of this implication empirically.

**Table 5.5** **Invoice Currency Ratios in Japanese Exports to East Asian Countries (%)**

| | 1987 | | 1988 | | 1989 | | 1990 | | 1991 | |
|---|---|---|---|---|---|---|---|---|---|---|
| Commodity | June | December | June | December | June | December | June | December | June | December |
| *Invoiced in the Japanese yen* | | | | | | | | | | |
| All commodities | 45.1 | 41.1 | 42.0 | 42.8 | 42.6 | 47.9 | 49.2 | 52.0 | 51.5 | 52.2 |
| Machines | 58.0 | 53.1 | 53.7 | 55.0 | 53.8 | 58.6 | 60.6 | 63.7 | 63.1 | 63.8 |
| Generators | 72.0 | 56.1 | 59.7 | 60.4 | 73.9 | 65.3 | 70.3 | 68.8 | 70.0 | 64.7 |
| TVs | 37.9 | 41.8 | 43.4 | 41.5 | 58.4 | 67.1 | 74.7 | 77.1 | 70.5 | 78.0 |
| VCRs | 53.8 | 63.0 | 39.6 | 49.0 | 44.0 | 48.8 | 64.8 | 64.9 | 60.7 | 63.6 |
| Automobiles | 73.6 | 71.7 | 68.4 | 69.5 | 66.7 | 68.4 | 65.3 | 65.3 | 69.4 | 72.4 |
| Ships | 39.2 | 4.4 | 59.2 | 86.8 | 42.9 | 95.9 | 88.0 | 97.0 | 99.2 | 97.7 |
| Heavy electric | 30.4 | 34.4 | 41.2 | 43.9 | 34.9 | 51.5 | 43.9 | 50.2 | 48.2 | 58.4 |
| *Invoiced in the U.S. dollar* | | | | | | | | | | |
| All commodities | 52.6 | 56.3 | 55.2 | 54.2 | 54.4 | 49.3 | 48.1 | 44.3 | 45.6 | 44.2 |
| Machines | 39.4 | 43.7 | 42.6 | 41.2 | 42.2 | 37.8 | 35.9 | 31.5 | 33.3 | 31.7 |
| Generators | 27.1 | 33.0 | 39.9 | 37.6 | 25.8 | 34.3 | 28.9 | 22.9 | 28.8 | 20.7 |
| TVs | 55.7 | 49.5 | 47.8 | 51.1 | 39.0 | 27.0 | 22.3 | 14.4 | 21.9 | 14.5 |
| VCRs | 36.4 | 30.9 | 46.6 | 40.0 | 46.1 | 41.6 | 25.2 | 27.9 | 31.6 | 26.1 |
| Automobiles | 22.6 | 27.4 | 24.7 | 24.2 | 25.1 | 24.4 | 28.7 | 28.1 | 21.9 | 17.8 |
| Ships | 60.8 | 95.6 | 40.8 | 13.2 | 57.1 | 4.1 | 12.0 | 3.0 | 0.8 | 2.3 |
| Heavy electric | 58.8 | 61.0 | 57.9 | 54.6 | 61.9 | 46.3 | 54.2 | 45.7 | 50.3 | 39.7 |

*Source: Export Confirmation Statistics* (Tokyo: MITI, various issues).

## 5.4 Empirical Results

Using highly disaggregated data sets of Japanese export prices, this section investigates how the PTM behavior of Japanese exporters can explain the choice of invoice currency.[4] Specifically, we examine how the prices of TVs, VCRs, and automobiles are correlated with the yen-dollar exchange rate in exports to the United States and East Asian countries.

Before this investigation, however, we must first mention that East Asian currencies have traditionally been tied more to the U.S. dollar than to the Japanese yen.[5] If stabilizing the selling price in East Asian markets is desirable, the strong link between East Asian currencies and the U.S. dollar will imply that Japanese exporters will achieve more effective selling price stabilization by invoicing in the dollar than by invoicing in the yen. On the other hand, if invoice ratios of the U.S. dollar are low, we can conjecture that Japanese exporters may have less incentive to stabilize their selling prices in East Asian markets. We apply this conjecture to exports of TVs, VCRs, and automobiles, and examine the validity of our hypotheses.

In the following empirical analysis, data on export prices are based on Japan Tariff Association (various issues). These trade statistics report the quantity and value of Japanese exports by both commodity and country. Each export value is based on f.o.b. value in terms of the yen.[6] Since commodity classifications are highly disaggregated, dividing each export value by its export quantity leads to the approximate export price of each commodity to each country.

All data are monthly. The sample period of estimations is January 1988 to December 1992. We chose this sample period because the commodity classifications in *Japan Export and Imports (Commodity by Country)* changed at the beginning of 1988. The sample period almost corresponds to the period for which the invoice ratios of Japanese exports are available on a commodity and country basis. In addition, the yen-dollar exchange rate showed relatively mild fluctuations during this sample period.

We ran the following regression:

$$(1) \qquad \mathrm{dEP}(i,j)_t = \text{constant} + \sum_{k=0}^{2} a_k * \mathrm{dS}_{t-k},$$

where $\mathrm{dEP}(i,j)_t$ is the first difference of the logarithm of the relative price of commodity *i*'s export to country *j* at time *t*, and $\mathrm{dS}_t$ is the first difference of the logarithm of the U.S. dollar exchange rate in terms of the yen at time *t*. The

4. Empirical results in this section are based on Fukuda and Ji (1995).

5. Among East Asian countries, Hong Kong pegs its currency to the U.S. dollar. On the other hand, most other East Asian currencies have adopted the basket system to peg their currencies. Although the composition of the basket is not officially announced, it is well known that the weight of the yen has not been significant.

6. When exports are invoiced in the foreign currency, export prices are transformed to yen-denominated prices by using some announced exchange rate. Although the announced exchange rate is not equal to the actual exchange rate, it is highly correlated with the actual exchange rate.

relative price of commodity *i*'s export was calculated by dividing the export price of commodity *i* by the corresponding domestic price indexes.

We estimated equation (1) by the ordinary least squares method. Since East Asian currencies are highly correlated with the U.S. dollar, we used only the (monthly averaged) yen-dollar exchange rate as an exchange rate variable. We also allowed lagged exchange rate effects by the Almon lag method.

We estimated the above equation for TVs, VCRs, and automobiles.[7] Although various kinds of data are available for these commodities, we used data on commodities that have a significant amount of exports both to the United States and to East Asian countries (see the appendix for details). To be consistent with tables 5.3 and 5.4, we included the 17 countries listed in footnote 3 as the East Asian countries.

As we examined in the last section, our hypothesis implies that the exchange rate in terms of yen will be positively correlated with the yen-denominated prices of exports to U.S. markets but will be less correlated with those of exports to East Asian markets. Thus, we expect the sum of estimated coefficients, $\Sigma a_k$, in equation (1) to be significantly positive in exports to U.S. markets but to be less statistically significant in those to East Asian markets.

Table 5.6 reports the regression results. The table shows two noteworthy results. First, in the case of exports to the United States, all estimates of $\Sigma a_k$ are significantly positive. In particular, except for TVs, the estimated values of $\Sigma a_k$ lie between zero and one and are close to one.[8] This result implies that when exporting to the United States, Japanese exporters largely adjust their yen-denominated export prices to exchange rate fluctuations in order to keep their selling prices constant in terms of the U.S. dollar.

Second, in the case of exports to East Asian countries, the estimated values of $\Sigma a_k$ are small and not significantly different from zero. This implies that when exporting to East Asian countries, Japanese exporters do not adjust their yen-denominated export prices to exchange rate fluctuations.

Noting that most exports to the United States are invoiced in the U.S. dollar and that most exports to East Asian countries are invoiced in the yen, the above two results are consistent with our hypothesis. In particular, we conjecture that Japan's export price behavior differs markedly between U.S. and East Asian markets.

## 5.5 Determinants of Invoice Currencies in Japan's Imports

As we explained in the introduction, the yen-invoiced ratios in Japan's imports are still very low. This is true not only in comparison to other OECD

7. Although Japan's exports of automobiles were voluntarily restricted, the restriction was not binding during our sample period.

8. Even the estimated result for exports of TVs may be consistent with our hypothesis because their dollar-invoiced ratios were unstable over time (94.4 percent in 1987, 77.6 percent in 1989, and 91.4 percent in 1991).

**Table 5.6 Regressions of Export Prices on Exchange Rates**

| Commodity and Destination | Estimates of $\Sigma a_k$ | $R^2$ | D-W |
|---|---|---|---|
| TV | | | |
| United States | 2.56 (1.28)** | 0.07 | 2.87 |
| East Asia | 0.15 (0.70) | 0.03 | 1.51 |
| VCR | | | |
| United States | 0.86 (0.45)** | 0.27 | 2.90 |
| East Asia | −0.08 (0.47) | 0.09 | 2.57 |
| Automobiles (type 1) | | | |
| United States | 0.95 (0.34)** | 0.17 | 2.42 |
| East Asia | 0.32 (0.57) | 0.09 | 2.77 |
| Automobiles (type 2) | | | |
| United States | 0.98 (0.28)** | 0.22 | 2.45 |
| East Asia | 0.30 (0.51) | 0.01 | 2.72 |

*Sources:* See appendix.
*Note:* Numbers in parentheses are standard errors.
**Significant at 2.5 percent level.

countries but also in comparison to ratios in Japan's exports. As in exports, inertia due to the previous economic power of the United States as well as the relatively small size of the short-term capital market in Japan may be somewhat responsible for the low ratios. However, in the case of Japan's imports, it has been stressed that almost negligible yen-invoiced ratios in oil and raw material imports are more important.[9]

Table 5.7 reports invoice currency ratios for each commodity in Japan's imports by commodity and country bases. A salient feature in this table is that yen-invoiced ratios are almost negligible in mineral and other raw material imports. In particular, crude oil imports are almost always invoiced in the U.S. dollar. The reason is that products of crude oil and other raw materials are traded in well-established international markets. Because trades denominated in the U.S. dollar dominate these international markets, dollar invoice ratios are dominant in mineral and other raw material imports.

Noting that Japan's import structure is heavily weighted toward minerals and other raw materials,[10] it is easy to see that these high dollar-invoiced ratios lead to low yen-invoiced ratios in Japan's total imports. In fact, if we confine our attention to the imports of manufactured goods, yen-invoiced ratios are significantly higher. In particular, in imports from East Asian countries, more than 30 percent of manufactured goods are yen-invoiced on average (see table 5.7). In addition, more than 30 percent of imports from Korea and Taiwan were yen-

9. Ito (1993) showed that the rise in Japan's yen-invoiced imports over the decade was due to the recent decline in the share of oil and raw materials in Japan's imports.

10. E.g., the proportion of food, fuel, and raw materials in Japan's total imports was 53 percent in 1988, while that in German total imports was 25 percent.

**Table 5.7** **Invoice Currency Ratios in Japanese Imports by Commodity, 1991 (%)**

| | Origin of Imports | | | | | | | | |
|---|---|---|---|---|---|---|---|---|---|
| | Total | | United States | | East Asia | | European Community | | |
| Commodity | U.S. Dollar | Yen | U.S. Dollar | Yen | U.S. Dollar | Yen | U.S. Dollar | Yen | Deutsche Mark |
| All commodities | 75.4 | 15.6 | 88.7 | 11.2 | 76.5 | 21.6 | 15.9 | 31.4 | 29.5 |
| Foodstuffs | 72.4 | 22.2 | 85.1 | 14.8 | 73.1 | 26.3 | 22.2 | 40.3 | 7.1 |
| Raw material and fuel | 97.2 | 1.9 | 98.5 | 1.5 | 97.4 | 2.4 | 50.0 | 22.1 | 5.8 |
| Textiles | 77.4 | 12.5 | 99.9 | 0.1 | 79.9 | 19.7 | 53.9 | 19.6 | 6.2 |
| Ore and scrap metal | 98.1 | 1.2 | 99.0 | 1.0 | 97.1 | 2.4 | 88.2 | 2.7 | 1.5 |
| Other raw material | 91.8 | 5.9 | 97.8 | 2.2 | 90.5 | 8.9 | 32.2 | 29.0 | 7.1 |
| Mineral and fuel | 99.5 | 0.3 | 99.9 | 0.1 | 99.7 | 0.3 | 73.9 | 16.9 | 4.8 |
| Crude oil | 100.0 | 0.0 | 100.0 | 0.0 | 100.0 | 0.0 | 100.0 | 0.0 | 0.0 |
| Manufactured | 60.0 | 23.7 | 87.2 | 12.6 | 63.8 | 32.8 | 13.5 | 30.4 | 33.8 |
| Chemicals | 51.7 | 32.5 | 84.6 | 15.1 | 69.8 | 28.0 | 12.3 | 58.5 | 21.4 |
| Machines | 52.5 | 22.5 | 87.4 | 12.4 | 49.5 | 43.9 | 7.3 | 17.9 | 59.3 |
| Other | 66.9 | 21.9 | 88.1 | 11.6 | 68.5 | 29.0 | 21.5 | 26.9 | 12.6 |

*Source: Import Reporting Statistics* (Tokyo: MITI, various issues).

invoiced in recent years, although most imports from ASEAN countries were invoiced in the U.S. dollar (see table 5.8).

This feature is true even if we confine our attention to imports of intermediate goods. Table 5.9 reports the results of the survey conducted by the Economic Planning Agency of the Japanese government in 1993. The survey asked Japan's major manufacturers about invoice ratios in their intermediate goods imports. The results show that in pulp and paper products, petroleum and coal products, and metal products, almost all imports of intermediate goods are invoiced in the U.S. dollar. In addition, in these industries, the shares of imports are very high among their inputs of intermediate goods. On the other hand, in general machinery, electrical machinery, and transportation equipment and precision instruments, less than half of intermediate goods imports are invoiced in the U.S. dollar. However, in these industries, most intermediate goods are purchased inside Japan.

The above results imply that low yen-invoiced ratios are mainly due to Japan's import structure. That is, yen-invoiced ratios are high in the imports of manufactured goods and some intermediate goods. However, the weight of these imports is very small in Japan's total imports. On the other hand, dollar-invoiced ratios are very high in the imports of raw materials. Since raw materi-

**Table 5.8** **Invoice Currency Ratios in Japanese Imports by Country, 1991 (%)**

| | 1987 | | 1988 | | 1989 | | 1990 | | 1991 | |
|---|---|---|---|---|---|---|---|---|---|---|
| Country | U.S. Dollar | Yen | U.S. Dollar | Yen | U.S. Dollar | Yen | U.S. Dollar | Yen | U.S. Dollar | Yen |
| World | 81.7 | 10.6 | 78.5 | 13.3 | 77.3 | 14.1 | 75.9 | 14.4 | 75.4 | 15.6 |
| United States | 90.6 | 9.2 | 85.9 | 8.8 | 89.5 | 10.2 | 80.9 | 11.6 | 88.7 | 11.2 |
| East Asia (average) | 87.6 | 11.5 | 81.2 | 17.5 | 79.0 | 19.5 | 78.8 | 19.4 | 76.5 | 21.6 |
| Korea | 72.8 | 27.2 | 62.9 | 37.0 | 60.5 | 39.3 | 61.8 | 38.1 | 59.7 | 39.8 |
| Taiwan | 85.2 | 14.8 | 77.4 | 22.5 | 71.9 | 27.7 | 67.8 | 31.6 | 66.3 | 33.1 |
| ASEAN | 94.7 | 4.2 | 91.7 | 6.6 | 90.3 | 7.9 | 89.0 | 9.1 | 85.7 | 12.1 |
| West Asia | 98.7 | 1.1 | 98.2 | 1.8 | 98.4 | 1.5 | 98.8 | 1.1 | 98.5 | 1.4 |
| European Community | 19.5 | 27.3 | 21.0 | 26.9 | 19.5 | 27.7 | 16.3 | 26.9 | 15.9 | 31.4 |

*Source: Import Reporting Statistics* (Tokyo: MITI, various issues).

**Table 5.9** **Invoice Currency Ratios in the Imports of Japanese Manufacturers, 1993 (%)**

| Industry | Invoice Ratios of U.S. Dollar | Share of Imports in Material Costs | Share of Material Costs in Sale Prices |
|---|---|---|---|
| Foodstuffs | 53.4 | 30.5 | 45.6 |
| Textile products | 76.5 | 27.1 | 45.3 |
| Lumber and wood | 71.3 | 45.0 | 66.3 |
| Pulp and paper | 97.5 | 27.2 | 55.3 |
| Chemicals | 66.7 | 21.4 | 45.2 |
| Petroleum and coal | 99.8 | 55.6 | 79.1 |
| Iron and steel | 82.5 | 37.9 | 61.9 |
| Nonferrous metals | 90.7 | 30.9 | 66.5 |
| General machinery | 10.0 | 3.5 | 46.2 |
| Electrical machinery | 36.3 | 8.2 | 52.6 |
| Trans & precision[a] | 16.5 | 3.0 | 45.0 |
| Other | 65.7 | 45.4 | 53.5 |
| Average | 63.3 | 23.1 | 52.0 |

*Source:* Unpublished report by Economic Planning Agency.
[a]Trans & precision = transportation equipment and precision instrument.

als account for a relatively large share of Japan's imports, average yen-invoiced ratios become very low in Japan's total imports.

## 5.6 What Structural Changes Can Increase Yen-Invoiced Ratios?

In previous sections, we discussed the proposition that relatively low invoice ratios of the Japanese yen are due to the structure of Japan's foreign trade. The purpose of this section is to investigate whether recent structural changes in

Japan's foreign trade have affected yen-invoiced ratios in East Asian countries. In the analysis, we focus on the degree of trade dependency of East Asian countries on Japan and the United States. One simple-minded conjecture is that an East Asian country will increase yen-invoiced ratios when its degree of trade dependency on Japan increases and that on the United States decreases because a country that has a large share in foreign trade will have relatively strong bargaining power in deciding its invoice currency.

In order to investigate the validity of this conjecture, we regressed the invoice ratios in Japan's foreign trade on East Asian trade dependency ratios and estimated the following equations:

$$\text{(2a)} \qquad \text{MY} = a_1 + c_2{*}MY_{-1} + c_1{*}XJ + c_2{*}XUS\,,$$

$$\text{(2b)} \qquad \text{MD} = a_3 + c_4{*}MD_{-1} - c_1{*}XJ - c_2{*}XUS\,,$$

$$\text{(3a)} \qquad \text{XY} = b_1 + b_2{*}XY_{-1} + d_1{*}MJ + d_2{*}MUS\,,$$

$$\text{(3b)} \qquad \text{XD} = b_3 + b_4{*}XD_{-1} - d_1{*}MJ - c_2{*}MUS\,,$$

where MY = yen-invoiced ratios in Japan's imports from East Asia, MD = dollar-invoiced ratios in Japan's imports from East Asia, XY = yen-invoiced ratios in Japan's exports to East Asia, and XD = dollar-invoiced ratios in Japan's exports to East Asia. In addition, XJ = the East Asian export dependency ratio on Japan, XUS = the East Asian export dependency ratio on the United States, MJ = the East Asian import dependency ratio on Japan, and MUS = the East Asian import dependency ratio on the United States.

All data are quarterly. The sample periods are from the first quarter of 1986 to the fourth quarter of 1991 in the case of Japanese imports and from the first quarter of 1987 to the fourth quarter of 1991 in the case of Japanese exports. The estimation is based on the maximum likelihood method, with the constraints that the effects of trade dependency ratios on the yen- and dollar-invoiced ratios are opposite but of the same magnitude. To the extent that our conjecture is correct, we expect that $c_1$ and $d_1$ are significantly positive and that $c_2$ and $d_2$ are significantly negative.

Table 5.10 reports the estimation results. The estimates of $c_2$ and $d_2$ are significantly negative, as expected. However, no estimates of $c_1$ and $d_1$ are significant. These results imply that although yen-invoiced ratios tend to increase when the degree of trade dependency on the United States decreases, they change little even when the degree of trade dependency on Japan increases. In other words, at least in our sample period, Japan's invoice currency ratios are affected by changing trade dependency on the United States and not by changing trade dependency on Japan.

In previous sections, we showed that Japan's exporters tend to choose the U.S. dollar as an invoice currency in order to keep market share in foreign markets. We also pointed out that Japan's importers tend to invoice in the U.S. dollar because most of their imports are traded in terms of the U.S. dollar in

**Table 5.10** **Effects of Trade Dependency Ratios on Invoice Currency Ratios**

| | Imports[a] | Exports[b] |
|---|---|---|
| Dependency on Japan | 0.08 | 0.02 |
| (estimates of $c_1$ and $d_1$) | (0.26) | (0.47) |
| Dependency on United States | −0.41** | −0.57** |
| (estimates of $c_2$ and $d_2$) | (−3.39) | (−2.22) |
| $R^2$ in eq. (2a) or (3a) | 0.86 | 0.96 |
| $R^2$ in eq. (2b) or (3b) | 0.86 | 0.97 |

*Source:* Except for Taiwan, the data of each region's trade dependency ratios are from *Direction of Trade Statistics* (Washington, D.C.: International Monetary Fund, various issues).

*Note:* Numbers in parentheses are *t*-values.

[a]Estimated equations (2a) and (2b).

[b]Estimated equations (3a) and (3b).

**Signifiant at 2.5 percent level.

well-established international markets. The results in this section are consistent with these views because they can be interpreted to mean that Japan's exporters and importers are passive (or reluctant) to change their choice of invoice currencies.

## 5.7 Concluding Remarks

We have investigated the determinants of invoice currencies in Japan's foreign trade with East Asian countries. We showed that the Japanese yen is becoming the dominant invoice currency in exports of TVs, VCRs, and automobiles to East Asia. We also pointed out that in imports of manufactured products from East Asian countries, Japan tends to invoice in the yen. However, since the weights of these commodities have been relatively small in Japan's total foreign trade, neither of these two factors was enough to increase average yen-invoiced ratios in Japan's exports and imports. In addition, Japan's exporters and importers are relatively passive in changing their invoice currency from the U.S. dollar to the yen.

Aside from the choice of invoice currencies, there is recent evidence that the use of the yen is prevailing among East Asian countries. For example, table 5.11 reports the currency composition of external debt among selected East Asian countries. It shows that in these countries yen-denominated external debt increased greatly in the latter half of the 1980s. Probably these increases occurred partly because the yen's appreciation raised nominal debt after 1985 and partly because official development assistance from Japan increased yen-denominated loans in these countries.

However, when we look at invoice currency ratios in the late 1980s, the yen's ratios in Japan's exports decreased. In addition, the yen's ratios in Japan's imports were still low, although they had gradually increased throughout the

**Table 5.11** **Currency Composition of East Asian External Debt (%)**

| Country | 1980 U.S. Dollar | 1980 Yen | 1983 U.S. Dollar | 1983 Yen | 1986 U.S. Dollar | 1986 Yen | 1989 U.S. Dollar | 1989 Yen |
|---|---|---|---|---|---|---|---|---|
| Indonesia | 43.5 | 20.0 | 42.3 | 23.3 | 26.0 | 33.9 | 19.5 | 35.2 |
| Korea | 53.5 | 16.5 | 64.4 | 12.5 | 49.4 | 22.0 | 35.1 | 26.6 |
| Malaysia | 38.0 | 19.0 | 65.8 | 14.2 | 30.4 | 45.0 | 34.2 | 36.6 |
| Philippines | 51.6 | 22.0 | 51.2 | 20.0 | 48.1 | 25.5 | 36.9 | 32.6 |
| Thailand | 39.7 | 25.5 | 32.5 | 27.3 | 20.6 | 39.9 | 23.6 | 40.9 |
| Aggregate of above | 47.3 | 19.5 | 53.2 | 18.5 | 38.5 | 29.3 | 28.1 | 35.7 |

*Source:* Tavlas and Ozeki (1992).

1980s. An implication of this paper is that without substantial changes in Japan's trade structure, the low invoice ratios of the Japanese yen may not change in the near future.

# Appendix

The data on export prices are based on Japan Tariff Association (various issues). In the estimation, we used the following four kinds of commodities: (1) TV = color television receivers incorporating cathode-ray television picture tubes, for broadcasting, other than chassis and kits; (2) VCR = video-recording or reproducing apparatus of magnetic tape type; (3) automobiles (type 1) = motor cars and other motor vehicles principally designed for the transport of persons with spark-ignition internal combustion reciprocating piston engines, with cylinder capacity exceeding 1,000 cc but not exceeding 1,500 cc, excluding those unassembled or disassembled; and (4) automobiles (type 2) = motor cars and other motor vehicles principally designed for the transport of persons with spark-ignition internal combustion reciprocating piston engines, with cylinder capacity exceeding 1,500 cc but not exceeding 2,000 cc, excluding those unassembled or disassembled.

# References

Frankel, Jeffrey A. 1991. Is a yen bloc forming in Pacific Asia? In *Finance and the international economy,* ed. R. Obrien and S. Hewin. New York: Oxford University Press.

Frankel, Jeffrey A., and Shang-Jin Wei. 1994. Yen bloc or dollar bloc: Exchange rate policies of the East Asian economies. In *Macroeconomic linkage: Savings, exchange rates, and capital flows,* ed. T. Ito and A. O. Krueger, 295–329. Chicago: University of Chicago Press.

Fukuda, Shin-ichi, and Ji Cong. 1995. On the choice of invoice currency by Japanese exporters: The PTM approach. *Journal of the Japanese and International Economies* 8:511–29.

Giovannini, Alberto. 1988. Exchange rates and traded goods prices. *Journal of International Economics* 24:45–68.

Hamada, Koichi, and Akiyoshi Horiuchi. 1987. Monetary, financial, and real effects of yen internationalization. In *Real-financial linkages among open economies,* ed. S. W. Arndt and J. D. Richardson, 167–91. Cambridge: MIT Press.

Ito, Takatoshi. 1993. The yen and the international monetary system. In *Pacific dynamism and the international economic system,* ed. C. F. Bergsten and N. Noland, 299–322. Washington, D.C.: Institute of International Economics.

Japan Tariff Association. Various issues. *Japan exports and imports (commodity by country).* Tokyo: Japan Tariff Association.

Kawai, Masahiro. 1992. Internationalization of the yen (in Japanese). In *Current status of international finance,* ed. T. Ito, 275–326. Tokyo: Yuhikaku.

———. 1994. The international use of the Japanese yen: Currency invoicing of Japanese trade. Paper presented at annual meeting of the Japan Association of Economics and Econometrics, Nanzan University, Nagoya, September 23–24.

Krugman, Paul R. 1980. Vehicle currencies and the structure of international exchange. *Journal of Money, Credit, and Banking* 12:513–26.

———. 1987. Pricing to market when the exchange rate changes. In *Real-financial linkages among open economies,* ed. S. W. Arndt and J. D. Richardson, 49–70. Cambridge: MIT Press.

Marston, Richard C. 1990. Pricing to market in Japanese manufacturing. *Journal of International Economics* 29:217–36.

Matsuyama, Kiminori, Nobuhiro Kiyotaki, and Akihiko Matsui. 1993. Toward a theory of international currency. *Review of Economic Studies* 60:283–307.

McKinnon, Ronald I. 1979. *Money in international exchange: The convertible currency system.* Oxford: Oxford University Press.

Ohno, Kenichi. 1989. Export pricing behavior of manufacturing: A U.S.-Japan comparison. *IMF Staff Papers* 36:550–79.

Saxonhouse, Gary R. 1993. Pricing strategies and trading blocs in East Asia. In *Regionalism and rivalry,* ed. J. A. Frankel and M. Kahler, 89–119. Chicago: University of Chicago Press.

Taguchi, Hiroo. 1994. On the yen bloc. In *Macroeconomic linkage: Savings, exchange rates, and capital flows,* ed. T. Ito and A. O. Krueger, 335–55. Chicago: University of Chicago Press.

Takeda, Masahiko, and Philip Turner. 1992. *The liberalisation of Japan's financial markets: Some major themes,* BIS Economic Paper no. 34. Basel: Monetary and Economic Department, Bank of International Settlements.

Tavlas, George S., and Yuzuru Ozeki. 1992. *The Japanese yen as an international currency.* IMF Occasional Paper no. 90. Washington, D.C.: International Monetary Fund.

## Comment Akira Kohsaka

Fukuda intends to identify determinants of currency invoicing ratios and their changes in Japanese external trade. More specifically, he tries to explain the apparently modest role of the Japanese yen as an invoice currency. He concludes by emphasizing the role of strategic pricing policies on the export side and commodity composition on the import side. The first half of the paper on the export side is relatively well argued, but the latter half does not seem very convincing and, in fact, seems tautological in explaining the small share of yen invoicing.

Turning to the export side, the paper links currency invoicing to exporter pricing strategies. By looking at the impact of yen-dollar exchange rate changes on export prices by commodity and by region, it is shown that for selected machinery products there is a significant positive correlation between yen-dollar exchange rates and relative export prices for Japanese exports to the United States but that there is no such correlation for exports to East Asia. This is claimed to suggest that Japanese exporters use pricing strategies to stabilize dollar prices in the United States and do not use such strategies in East Asia. Thus, as far as Japanese manufacturing exports to the United States are concerned, the paper confirms at least partially Saxonhouse's (1993) observation that the large share of dollar invoicing can be attributed to Japanese exporter pricing behavior.

I have several comments and questions at this point. First, I wonder whether we can truly identify currency invoicing with strategic price stabilization denominated in that currency. Noting that invoice currency ratios vary greatly both by commodity and by trading partner, as shown in tables 5.3, 5.4, 5.7, and 5.8, export prices are determined in diverse ways depending not only on market structures such as openness, competitiveness, and so on, but also on product characteristics such as degree of product differentiation. Thus it might be more appropriate to claim that the strategic price-setting behavior of exporters constitutes only a part of the story in explaining levels and changes in invoice currency ratios.

Second, although it is true that local currencies in East Asia have been more or less linked to the U.S. dollar, the author seems to put too much emphasis on their close linkage. In fact, in East Asia, a few Asian newly industrialized economies have had sharp appreciation of their currencies against the U.S. dollar since the latter half of the 1980s, and others have been through a series of devaluations during the same period. Despite this, the paper does not seem to pay due attention to the differences between yen-dollar and yen–local-currency exchange rates. If this were properly taken into account, its impact on export prices in terms of *local currencies in East Asia* could give some

Akira Kohsaka is professor of economics at the Osaka School of International Public Policy, Osaka University.

results different from those obtained in the paper. Until then, we cannot tell for sure whether Japanese exporter pricing policy is consistent with the pricing-to-market theory in East Asia.

In addition, a few minor points about equation (1) need clarification. The Japanese export price is partly converted from dollar denomination using a certain "official conversion rate," which is known to be fairly different from actual rates. Does this affect the result obtained, and to what extent? The author supposes price adjustment to be symmetric between upward and downward movements. Is it likely that yen depreciation will make Japanese exporters increase their yen export prices? In the case of differentiated manufacturing goods such as TVs and VCRs, the content of Japanese exports could differ between those to the United States and those to East Asia. If this is the case, can we distinguish between pricing-to-market and "pricing-to-product"?

On the import side, the author ascribes the low yen-invoicing ratio to import concentration or "bias" toward low yen-invoiced items or regional concentration on low yen-invoiced imports from the United States. This seems to be a tautology, however, and would never constitute reasoning or explanation for why the yen-invoicing ratio is low. Rather we would like to know the reasons for differences in invoice currency ratios for the same items and/or the same trading partners between Japan and other developed economies, (if such differences exist).

Finally, although the author concludes that "without substantial changes in Japan's trade structure, the low invoice ratios of the Japanese yen may not change in the near future," it is too hasty to draw this kind of conclusion from this paper.

First, even *without* changes in the Japanese trade structure, exchange rate changes against the U.S. dollar and the yen in the currencies of non-U.S. trade partners (especially East Asia) and changes in their market structures could increase yen-invoicing ratios.

Second, and more important, since we have observed rapid changes in Japan's trade structure since the 1970s across both regions and commodities along with increasing yen-invoicing ratios, there is no reason we will no longer see this kind of development for the near future. Accordingly, yen-invoicing ratios are likely to increase in time, unless the recent trend is unexpectedly reversed.

## Reference

Saxonhouse, Gary R. 1993. Pricing strategies and trading blocs in East Asia. In *Regionalism and rivalry: Japan and the United States in Pacific Asia,* ed. Jeffrey A. Frankel and Miles Kahler, 89–119. Chicago: University of Chicago Press.

# 6 An Evaluation of Japanese Financial Liberalization: A Case Study of Corporate Bond Markets

Akiyoshi Horiuchi

## 6.1 Introduction

Since the late 1970s, the Japanese financial system has been gradually but steadily liberalized. Japan entered the "era of financial liberalization" in the 1980s. As will be explained to some extent in this paper, foreign exchange transactions were greatly liberalized, thereby spurring the internationalization of Japanese financial markets. Full-scale liberalization of interest rates, which used to be covered by the Temporary Law of Interest Rate Adjustment (1947), was started in 1984 when the Japanese government placed the deregulation of interest rates on the agenda for the U.S.-Japan Yen-Dollar Committee.[1] By 1993 almost all bank deposit rates except for small-denominated and demand deposits had been liberalized. In October 1994 the remaining regulations on deposit interest rates were removed, except for that on "current deposits" (*toza-yokin*).[2] The Japanese financial system is far more market-oriented than it was in the high-growth period from the early 1950s to the beginning of the 1970s, and it seems certain that financial liberalization has improved the efficiency of the Japanese economy.

Akiyoshi Horiuchi is professor of economics at the University of Tokyo.

The author thanks Takatoshi Ito, Anne Krueger, Kenneth Lin, Won-Am Park, and the other seminar participants for their helpful comments and suggestions. He also thanks Jean-Michel Paul, John Stachurski, and Noriyuki Yanagawa for their comments on an earlier version of this paper. Hyon-Gak Shin and Shinya Uesaki provided the author with excellent assistance in processing statistics.

1. See Frankel (1984) for a detailed explanation of the agreement of the Yen/Dollar Committee. The primary objective of this committee was to realign the Japanese yen, which was regarded as substantially undervalued. But, as Frankel points out, it was ambiguous whether the liberalization of Japanese financial markets and other "structural policies" included in the agreement were effective in amending the undervaluation of the yen.

2. Regarding the recent process of interest deregulation, see Federation of Bankers Associations of Japan (1994, 86–94).

However, it is noteworthy that Japan's financial liberalization has been characterized by "gradualism." The monetary authorities have been in part skeptical about the efficiency of the market mechanism and in part worried about the anticipated "destructive impact" of free market mechanisms on the status quo in the financial system. Therefore, they have controlled its implementation so as to avoid radical changes in the conventional framework of the financial system, and to preserve the equilibrium attained among various vested interests in the financial sector. For example, despite the apparent process of liberalizing interest rates, most Japanese financial markets, particularly the bank deposit market, seem to be far from "contestable" because the regulatory segregation of various financial businesses from one another effectively prevents full-scale competition. Therefore, the benefits of interest rate liberalization have not yet been fully realized. The remaining regulation via financial segregation symbolizes the gradualism of Japan's financial liberalization.[3]

This gradualism may have contributed to superficially stabilizing the Japanese financial system, as the authorities intended. It should be noted, however, that this gradualism gives a distorted nature to the financial liberalization, which can be regarded as the cost of liberalization in Japan. In order to evaluate Japan's financial liberalization since the early 1980s, we should not neglect the cost of gradualism. The purpose of this paper is to investigate the cost by focusing on the process of liberalization in the Japanese corporate bond market.

Japanese corporate finance was dominated by indirect finance centered on bank lending for the nearly 40 years between the early 1940s and the late 1970s. However, figure 6.1 and table 6.1 indicate that its structure has undergone remarkable changes since the late 1970s. The most conspicuous changes were a steady decrease in major firms' reliance on borrowing from banks and a corresponding increase in the amount of bond issues. We might say that Japanese corporate finance has been substantially "securitized" during the last decade. In particular, major Japanese companies issued convertible bonds intensively to raise funds in the latter half of the 1980s. According to figure 6.2, almost half of all corporate bonds were issued in the form of convertible bonds during this period. Thus, the securitization of Japan's corporate finance during the last decade was accompanied by a surge in convertible bond issues.[4]

The policy of liberalizing the corporate bond market accounts for this process of securitization. As will be seen in section 6.2, the ability of Japanese firms to issue corporate bonds has been strictly controlled since the 1930s. But the internationalization of financial markets exerted great pressure on domestic bond markets in the early 1980s, thereby promoting their liberalization. The restrictive control of corporate bond issues has since been relaxed, and the

3. The Financial System Reform Law of 1992 enforced in April 1993 allows financial institutions to compete in each other's spheres via subsidiaries. However, the entry of various financial institutions into other spheres has been controlled by the MOF. The MOF determines which financial institutions are allowed entry into other spheres at what time.

4. Hoshi (1993) shows that Japan's major firms tended to decrease borrowing from banks by issuing convertible bonds during the 1980s.

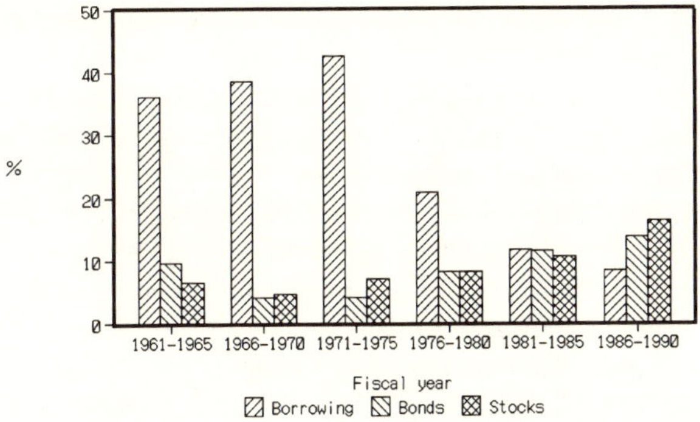


**Fig. 6.1 Composition of fund-raising by major companies, F.Y. 1969–92**
*Source*: BOJ (various years).

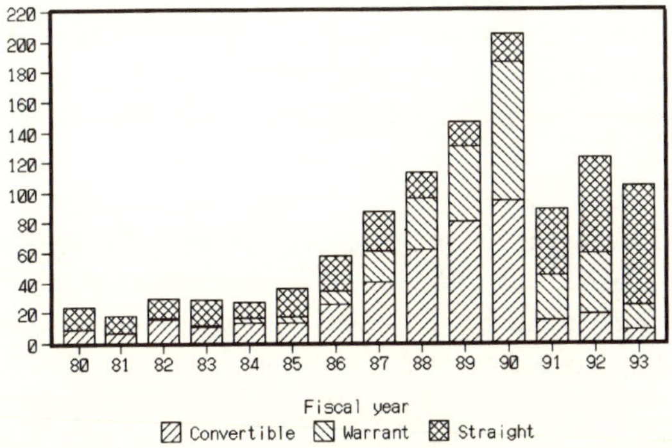


**Fig. 6.2 Corporate bonds issued by Japanese firms, F.Y. 1979–92**
*Source: Koshasai Yoran* (Handbook of Japanese Bonds) (Tokyo: Nomura Research Institute, various years).

**Table 6.1 Components of Fund-Raising by Major Companies[a] in Japan (average %)**

| Period | Stocks | Bonds | Loans | Internal Funds | Other | Total |
|---|---|---|---|---|---|---|
| 1961–70 | 6.1 | 5.6 | 37.7 | 32.4 | 18.4 | 100.0 |
| 1971–75 | 4.0 | 7.0 | 42.6 | 33.8 | 12.6 | 100.0 |
| 1976–80 | 8.0 | 8.1 | 20.9 | 50.7 | 12.4 | 100.0 |
| 1981–85 | 11.4 | 10.5 | 11.7 | 61.2 | 5.3 | 100.0 |
| 1986–92 | 11.6 | 17.6 | 8.4 | 51.0 | 11.4 | 100.0 |

*Source:* BOJ (various issues).

[a]"Major companies" refers to about 600 firms chosen from the group of listed companies whose book value of equity capital is more than ¥1.0 billion. Financial institutions are not included among major companies.

number of big firms allowed to issue bonds in domestic markets has gradually been increased.

Thus, the surge in bond issues in the 1980s may seem to be a natural response by Japanese corporations to liberalization in the bond markets. The standard theory of corporate finance, however, cannot sufficiently account for this phenomenon. In this paper, we propose a hypothesis to explain the surge in convertible bond issues in the late 1980s. The hypothesis relates the active issue of convertible bonds by Japanese firms to the combination of an imperfect mechanism of corporate governance and the distorted or half-finished nature of the corporate bond market liberalization.

First, it can be argued that the possibility of issuing convertible bonds mitigated the constraints of bankruptcy for corporate managers, thus encouraging them to issue convertibles. According to our hypothesis, the rapid increase in convertible and warrant bond issues in the late 1980s was related to imperfect corporate governance in Japan.

Second, the process of liberalizing the domestic corporate bond market was distorted during the 1980s in the sense that only well-established major companies were allowed to issue convertible and other equity-related bonds. In theory, such instruments are most useful for small and relatively newly established enterprises, in order to overcome the agency problem due to asymmetric information. However, such firms were effectively excluded from domestic corporate bond markets during the recent gradual process of liberalization. This paper will argue that the distortion due to the gradualism of liberalization led to the surge in equity-related bond issues by major companies in Japan under conditions of imperfect corporate governance.

This paper is organized as follows: In section 6.2, we present a rough sketch of the evolution of Japanese corporate bond markets from the early postwar period to the late 1980s. In particular, we explain the process of relaxing eligibility requirements for corporate bond issues and emphasize its distorted nature. In section 6.3, we take up the question of why equity-related bonds, and convertibles in particular, were issued so actively during the second half of the 1980s. We propose a simple hypothesis of imperfect corporate governance. This hypothesis predicts that managers of well-established firms will be eager to issue convertibles with a view to extending their opportunity to enjoy perquisites, and that they will increase the volume of convertible issues when the market holds strong expectations of a rise in their firms' stock prices. In the latter half of section 6.3, we investigate statistically whether these predictions were actually observable during the late 1980s in Japan on the basis of companies' financial data. We summarize our discussion in section 6.4.

## 6.2 Liberalization of Japan's Corporate Bond Markets

In this section, we discuss the process of liberalization in corporate bond markets in postwar Japan. We emphasize that until the mid-1980s, restrictive rules regarding eligibility were imposed on firms that wanted to issue bonds in the domestic market. Then, we discuss how the restrictive eligibility requirements have been relaxed in response to a "hollowing" of domestic corporate bond markets.

### 6.2.1 The Process of Controlling Corporate Bond Issues

It is well known that during the post–World War II years, and particularly during the 1950s and 1960s, Japanese corporations depended heavily on borrowing from banks, as table 6.1 suggests. In contrast, bond finance was relatively more important for Japanese corporations in the 1920s and 1930s. According to Net Supply of Industrial Funds data prepared by the Bank of Japan (BOJ), even in 1931 bonds provided 21.7 percent of external corporate funding and bank loans only 15.2 percent.

But in 1933, when Japan's financial system was suffering from serious turmoil caused by international financial disorder, with the support of the Ministry of Finance (MOF) and the Industrial Bank of Japan (IBJ), around 30 of the largest private bond-underwriting companies and banks established the Kisai Kondan Kai, or the Bond Issue Arrangement Committee (BIAC), in order to restore stability and soundness to the securities markets. At the heart of the BIAC were eight private banks, headed by the IBJ. Therefore, the interests of private banks, particularly big banks, were reflected in the workings of the BIAC. For example, the banks succeeded in structuring BIAC regulations so that only "trustee banks" were allowed to manage relevant collateral until the maturity of a bond, in return for a fee. Thus, although securities companies participated as underwriting members of the BIAC, only banks could earn the collateral fee. It should also be noted that the BIAC was a semipublic organization in which the MOF could exert strong influence on specific processes of decision making. We can safely say that the MOF regulated Japanese corporate bond markets through the BIAC in tight collaboration with big private banks.[5]

Precisely, the BIAC was in charge of controlling the straight bond market. The markets of "equity-related bonds," such as convertible bonds, were controlled, not by the BIAC, but by another organization consisting only of underwriting securities companies. However, this organization, like the BIAC, was closely monitored by the MOF, and therefore, its way of controlling convertible bond issues was quite similar to the BIAC approach to straight bonds. For example, the principle of collateral, which will be explained in the following,

5. The BIAC group met monthly throughout the high-growth period to determine the volume of new private sector debt issues, the firms that would be permitted to issue, and the specific terms of each issue. During the forced "low interest rate" period from about 1955 to 1970, the IBJ was in a most strategic position, given its status as the only permanent, nonrotating private sector member of the BIAC. But, as Calder (1993) describes in great detail, the IBJ's role was not "top-down" allocation but more mediation. The convention of the BIAC was to react to specific requests to issue rather than to formulate general guidelines; the IBJ organized a case-by-case consensus on these requests by private firms.

was applied not only to straight bond issues but also to convertible issues, and the eligibility requirements for convertibles were determined and adjusted in parallel with those for straight bonds. We will also explain the eligibility requirements for corporate bond issues in detail below.

One of the most important roles of the BIAC was to establish the principle of collateral, which prohibited Japanese firms from issuing corporate bonds without sufficient collateral, usually in the form of real estate or specified government bonds. The organization that controlled convertible bond issues followed the BIAC and adopted this principle as well. The principle of collateral persisted until 1979 when Sears Roebuck Tokyo issued uncollateralized bonds. Collateral requirements urged by the powerful private banks after the panic of 1927 thus played a crucial role in destroying the Japanese corporate bond market; by the late 1930s corporations issued virtually no bonds at all. Equity continued, however, to be a major source of corporate finance, constituting over half of corporate funding every year from 1934 through the onset of the Sino-Japanese War in 1937 (table 6.2). It was the sudden expansion of heavy industrial investment demand under the pressure of war with China, and the onset of patriotic savings drives by the banks to provide funds to meet this demand, coupled with the uncertainties a wartime environment created for capital markets, that led to the decline of equity and to heavy corporate reliance on debt.

In spite of radical structural change in the Japanese economy immediately after World War II, the dominant position of the banking sector in corporate finance was kept intact. Article 65 of the Securities Exchange Act, which was instituted in April 1948 following the U.S. Glass-Steagall Act, precluded banks from underwriting bonds for public placement, but it did uphold the principle of collateral for all corporate bond issues. Unlike the U.S. banks, Japanese banks were not prohibited from being shareholders of their client firms, although the Anti-Trust Law specifies the maximum proportion of each firms's shares that banks are allowed to hold.[6] Thus, Article 65 of the Securities Exchange Act did not decrease the dominance of the banking sector in postwar Japan's financial system. The BIAC, the long-term credit banks, and the extensive legal controls introduced in mobilizing the Japanese financial system for World War II also survived, creating a debt-oriented, bank-dominated financial system with a strong bias toward the status quo. Since the banking sector, which had a vested interest in preserving the overwhelming importance of bank loans in the financial system, was so influential in arranging corporate bond issues, it is hardly surprising that corporate bond markets were prevented from fully developing in postwar Japan.[7]

6. At present, this maximum proportion is 5 percent. Banks can be among the largest shareholders of large Japanese companies by holding just a few percent of their shares.

7. During the high-growth period, the underdeveloped nature of corporate bond markets did not seem an obstacle to rapid industrial development. The intimate relationship developed between

**Table 6.2** **Composition of Industrial Funds (average %)**

| Period | Stocks | Bonds | Loans[a] | Total |
|---|---|---|---|---|
| 1931–40 | 49.1 | 6.9 | 44.0 (43.3) | 100.0 |
| 1941–50 | 13.3 | 3.7 | 83.1 (72.5) | 100.0 |
| 1951–60 | 14.2 | 4.4 | 81.4 (72.7) | 100.0 |
| 1961–70 | 9.4 | 3.5 | 87.1 (78.9) | 100.0 |
| 1971–75 | 5.7 | 3.9 | 90.4 (81.7) | 100.0 |
| 1976–80 | 7.1 | 4.3 | 88.7 (75.2) | 100.0 |
| 1981–85 | 7.7 | 3.5 | 88.8 (80.4) | 100.0 |

*Source: Economic Statistics Annual* (Tokyo: BOJ, various years). The BOJ stopped publishing this data in 1986.

*Note:* This table covers the net supply of external funds to all industrial firms in Japan and, therefore, does not show very clearly the structural changes that have occurred in major company financing since the mid-1970s (cf. table 6.1).

[a]Numbers in parentheses are component ratios of loans from private financial institutions.

### 6.2.2 Eligibility Requirements for Corporate Bond Issues

Credit allocation through domestic corporate bond markets was based on both the principle of collateral and eligibility requirements for bond issues. The eligibility requirements were basically requirements for sufficient net worth (book value), amount of dividend per share, profit rates (both per share and as a ratio to total capital), and equity-capital ratio (ratio of equity to total assets). Unless they were able to satisfy these requirements, firms were not allowed to issue bonds at all. Table 6.3 shows an example of the eligibility requirements for convertible bond issues with collateral as of May 1985. These specific requirements were less severe than those in the 1970s and early 1980s, and as will be explained in the following section, they were substantially relaxed during the second half of the 1980s.

Moreover, the eligibility requirements for bond issuing effectively worked to crowd out small and medium-size firms from corporate bond markets, as such firms did not possess sufficiently large net wealth. This mechanism corresponds to the collateral principle in the sense that the possibility of default was kept to a minimum in the bond markets. Although, this regulation may have been effective in stabilizing Japan's bond market, it hindered the development of a flexible price mechanism in the corporate bond market and, in turn, strengthened the system of indirect finance based on the banking sector. Even

banks and borrower firms worked sufficiently well to help industrial sectors finance their large investment expenditures. See, e.g., Hoshi, Kashyap, and Scharfstein (1991) and Prowse (1990). But, as this paper insists, the immature corporate bond market has become a weak point in the mechanism of corporate governance since the banking sector has lost its dominance in the financial system.

**Table 6.3** **Example of Eligibility Requirements for Issuing Convertible Bonds (as of May 1985)**

A. The book value of net wealth must be more than ¥10.0 billion.
B. The amount of dividend must be no less than ¥5.0 per share.
C. The after-tax profit per share must be either no less than ¥7.0 or the current profit must be positive immediately before the year and the after-tax profit per share must be expected to be no less than ¥7.00 in the coming year.
D. The value of net wealth must be more than 1.2 times as much as equity capital.
E. The equity capital ratio must be more than 15 percent.
F. The profit rate per total capital must be more than 4 percent.

*Source: Koshasai Yoran* (Handbook of Japanese Bonds) (Tokyo: Nomura Research Institute, 1987), 428–30.

*Note:* A firm had to satisfy A, B, and C and more than one among D, E, and F before being permitted to issue convertible bonds with collateral. The eligibility requirements for issuing convertible bonds without collateral were much stricter. For example, firms with less than ¥33.0 billion net wealth were not permitted to issue convertibles without collateral at all as of 1985.

after 1988, when a rating system was introduced for determining eligibility requirements, the system appears to have been utilized as a means of excluding firms with a low rating from the bond markets.[8]

### 6.2.3 Internationalization and Pressures from Abroad

The Foreign Exchange and Foreign Trade Control Law (FEFTCL) of 1948 and the Foreign Investment Law of 1950 prohibited in principle all foreign exchange transactions unless specifically permitted by the government. These laws conferred on regulatory authorities great discretion in mediating between the domestic financial system and its global environment and provided the basic legislative framework that governed foreign exchange transactions for more than a generation, until December 1980.

The December 1980 revisions of the long-standing FEFTCL did not initiate or result in any categorical relaxation of Japanese foreign exchange controls. Other incremental steps had been taken previously. Furthermore, important provisions for exchange controls to be invoked in times of financial crisis remained even after the revised FEFTCL came into effect (MOF 1993, 139). But the de facto removal of controls during normal times helped ratify and accelerate the historical movement of Japanese corporate finance away from the reliance on domestic bank loans that had been the essence of the indirect financing mechanisms of the high-growth period.

Most important, the erosion of exchange controls that began during the 1970s and was accelerated by revision of the FEFTCL let Japanese companies

8. In 1990 the system of eligibility requirements was radically changed in that traditional requirements such as minimum net wealth were all abolished and instead a system of rating was introduced. Specifically, firms with rating BBB can issue straight bonds for public placement. Those with a rating higher than A can issue straight bonds without collateral.

issue straight and convertible bonds overseas, particularly in the Euromarkets. There, the absence of collateral requirements and mandatory prospectus issues, together with the broad range of financial instruments, swaps, and exchange rate hedging mechanisms not available in Japan, made raising funds cheaper and often quicker and more convenient than in Japan itself.

Starting in 1961 with Sumitomo Metals and Kawasaki Steel, Japanese corporations had periodically issued bonds abroad during the high-growth era. But the total amount raised was small: during the early 1970s the Euromarkets accounted for only 1.7 percent of Japanese corporate financing, although the share had risen by the late 1970s to 19.6 percent, mainly to finance offshore operations. In the early 1980s reliance on offshore finance began to rise even more sharply, primarily through large-scale corporate bond issues in the Euromarkets, with the Japanese surge abroad driven by both expectations of a strong yen (in the case of foreign-currency–denominated issues) and the more flexible issuing conditions available outside Japan. In 1979 the value of corporate bonds issued by Japanese corporations in domestic markets totaled over ¥2.4 trillion, more than three times the value of offshore issues; but by 1985 total Japanese corporate bond issues offshore had risen by ¥3.3 trillion, more than 25 percent greater than the total for Japanese corporate issues within Japan (table 6.4). Total Euromarket financial issues, with terms dictated by markets rather than by bureaucratic fiat, supplied over half of all Japanese corporate bond financing and one-third of total corporate finance, despite the low cost of capital to domestic issuers within Japan.

The higher bond issuance fees compelled Japanese firms to issue bonds abroad in the 1980s, and the de facto buyers of the bonds were mostly Japanese investors, thereby giving rise to a "hollowing" of domestic corporate bond markets. The MOF has tried to prevent this hollowing by regulating Japanese investors' purchase of Eurobonds issued by Japanese firms. Specifically, Japanese investors are forbidden to buy such corporate bonds within three months of the bonds' issuance. But this regulation seems to have been ineffective because underwriting securities companies in London could circumvent it by selling the Eurobonds issued by Japanese firms to Japanese investors by subscription. This subscription system has helped the underwriters to minimize the cost of mediation between Japanese firms and Japanese investors in the Eurobond markets.

Offshore financing by Japanese corporations exerted pressure to relax issuing restrictions, especially collateral requirements (which incidentally did not exist in many of the Euromarkets where Japanese firms were active in raising funds). Banks had long opposed any relaxation of collateral requirements within the domestic bond market because the stringent rules had allowed them to reap considerable fee income and, more important, had prevented the full-scale development of financing methods substitutable for bank loans. The existence of these fees caused the total bond-issuing cost in the domestic market

**Table 6.4** **"Hollowing" of the Domestic Corporate Bond Market (billion yen)**

| | Amount of Corporate Bonds Issued by Japanese Firms | | |
|---|---|---|---|
| Fiscal Year | (A) Total | (B) Issued Abroad | B/A (%) |
| 1977 | 1,781 | 378 | 21.2 |
| 1978 | 2,253 | 563 | 26.1 |
| 1979 | 2,403 | 751 | 31.3 |
| 1980 | 1,791 | 701 | 39.1 |
| 1981 | 2,945 | 1,130 | 38.4 |
| 1982 | 2,887 | 1,375 | 47.6 |
| 1983 | 3,479 | 1,918 | 55.1 |
| 1984 | 5,130 | 2,795 | 54.5 |
| 1985 | 5,838 | 3,254 | 55.7 |
| 1986 | 8,670 | 4,118 | 47.5 |
| 1987 | 11,310 | 5,340 | 47.2 |
| 1988 | 14,635 | 6,891 | 47.1 |
| 1989 | 20,412 | 11,129 | 54.5 |
| 1990 | 8,809 | 5,437 | 61.7 |
| 1991 | 12,280 | 8,193 | 66.7 |
| 1992 | 10,396 | 6,001 | 57.7 |

*Source: Monthly Report of Japanese Bonds* (Tokyo: Association of Securities Underwriters, various issues).

*Note:* Corporate bonds include straight, convertible, and warrant bonds.

to be significantly higher than in Euromarkets.[9] Japanese banks began to reassess this situation during the mid-1980s, as the rush offshore cut back their share of corporate financial business.[10]

The MOF took important steps toward market orientation in the regulation of corporate bond issues, which made the control-minded policies of the BIAC more difficult. As we saw earlier, collateral had in principle been required for all Japanese corporate bond issues between 1933 and the early 1970s. In December 1972, under the MOF's guidance, underwriting securities companies and trustee banks determined the rules for "noncollateralized convertibles," and according to this new rule Mitsubishi Trading Company issued noncollateralized convertibles in 1973 for the first time in Japan. In reality, this 1972 rule did not imply an introduction of full-scale "noncollateralization" into con-

9. As Takeda and Turner (1992, 77–78) point out, bond issuance fees were significantly higher in the Japanese domestic market than in Euromarkets mainly because banks intervene intensively in bond issues in the domestic market.

10. The hollowing of domestic corporate bond markets does not seem to have been mitigated in spite of the liberalization of domestic markets. According to table 6.4, the relative importance of corporate bonds issued by Japanese firms abroad has increased since 1990. The MOF reportedly introduced the March 1993 regulation forbidding securities companies to sell by subscription Eurobonds issued by Japanese firms to domestic investors in order to stop the hollowing phenomenon.

**Table 6.5 Process of Liberalizing Noncollateralized Convertibles: Changes in the Eligibility Requirement of Minimum Value of Net Wealth and Number of Eligible Firms**

| Date | Minimum Value of Net Wealth (billion ¥) | Changes in Number of Eligible Firms |
|---|---|---|
| March 1979[a] | 150 | 2 |
| January 1983 | 110 | 11 → 25 |
| April 1984 | 55 | 26 → 97 |
| July 1985 | 33 | 111 → 175 |
| February 1987 | 20[b] | 180 → 330[c] |
| November 1988 | 20[d] | 130 → 500[c] |

*Source: Annual Report of Securities Bureau* (Tokyo: MOF, various issues).

[a]The eligibility requirements for noncollateralized convertible bonds were first determined in March 1979.

[b]The rating criterion was introduced. A firm rated A or higher became eligible irrespective of minimum net wealth and other requirements. A firm rated BBB or higher was eligible if its net wealth was no less than ¥55.0 billion.

[c]Presented in round numbers.

[d]A firm rated BBB became eligible if its net wealth was no less than ¥33.0 billion.

vertible bond issues because issuing firms were still required to hold specific assets as a sort of security.

In March 1979 Sears Roebuck became Japan's first noncollateralized convertible bond issuer, followed the next month by Matsushita Corporation and by 21 other firms during 1979–84. This time, the bonds were truly noncollateralized. Although in the early 1980s the eligibility requirements for noncollateralized convertible issues were so strict as to permit only a few firms of recognized credibility to issue them, the requirements were steadily relaxed during the latter half of the 1980s. As a result, the number of the firms eligible to issue noncollateralized convertibles greatly increased (table 6.5). This liberalization surely contributed to the remarkable increase in the volume of convertibles issued in the domestic market during the latter half of the 1980s. As table 6.6 indicates, the rapid increase in convertible bond issues in the domestic market during this period was primarily due to the surge in noncollateralized convertibles.[11]

It is noteworthy, however, that small-scale enterprises were in effect excluded from the convertible bond market even in the late 1980s. The amount of convertibles issued by firms listed on the over-the-counter market, which are typical of small-scale businesses, was ¥84.5 billion from 1977 to 1989, just less than 0.3 percent of the total amount of convertibles issued in the domestic market during the same period.

11. In January 1985 TDK undertook the first unsecured straight bond issue in the domestic market since 1932; by February 1987 more than 350 other firms had also been authorized to do so. In 1985 the MOF's Securities Exchange Council proposed the eventual abolition of the collateral rule, a change facilitating the flow of capital toward consumer- and service-oriented firms at the expense of by-now capital-rich heavy industry.

Table 6.6 Convertible Bonds Issued by Japanese Firms in the Domestic Market (billion yen)

| Fiscal Year | Noncollateralized | With Reservation of Assets | With Collateral | Total |
|---|---|---|---|---|
| 1970 | – | – | 108(19) | 108(19) |
| 1971 | – | – | 62(10) | 62(10) |
| 1972 | – | 85(6) | 169(43) | 254(49) |
| 1973 | – | 185(18) | 210(63) | 395(81) |
| 1974 | – | 117(13) | 163(41) | 279(54) |
| 1975 | – | 171(12) | 160(29) | 330(41) |
| 1976 | – | 0(0) | 56(14) | 56(14) |
| 1977 | – | 35(3) | 128(23) | 163(26) |
| 1978 | – | 145(5) | 232(22) | 377(27) |
| 1979 | 50(1) | 150(7) | 154(23) | 354(31) |
| 1980 | 0(0) | 40(1) | 57(11) | 97(12) |
| 1981 | 60(1) | 208(15) | 258(36) | 526(52) |
| 1982 | 45(1) | 182(12) | 191(33) | 418(46) |
| 1983 | 50(2) | 604(29) | 208(36) | 861(67) |
| 1984 | 856(34) | 364(31) | 382(60) | 1,611(125) |
| 1985 | 665(29) | 376(29) | 545(84) | 1,586(142) |
| 1986 | 2,342(95) | 291(18) | 836(91) | 3,468(204) |
| 1987 | 4,322(204) | 228(21) | 505(77) | 5,055(302) |
| 1988 | 6,335(252) | 136(17) | 524(64) | 6,995(333) |
| 1989 | 7,022(245) | 128(13) | 490(37) | 7,640(295) |
| 1990 | 853(40) | 20(3) | 39(4) | 911(47) |
| 1991 | 1,151(69) | 71(13) | 57(4) | 1,279(86) |
| 1992 | 534(30) | 27(7) | 14(2) | 575(39) |

*Source: Koshasai Yoran* (Handbook of Japanese Bonds) (Tokyo: Nomura Research Institute, various issues).

*Note:* Numbers in parentheses are number of convertible bond issues.

## 6.3 Convertible Bond Issues and the Structure of Corporate Governance

As has been explained, the most conspicuous structural change in Japan's corporate finance during the 1980s was the surge in equity-related bond issues and decline in the relative importance of bank borrowing. In particular, Japanese firms actively issued convertible bonds in the late 1980s. The restrictive rules on bond issues managed by the BIAC and other organizations were gradually relaxed during this period, so that well-established firms gained easier access to the convertible bond market. Therefore, it may seem natural for such firms to have increased the amount of convertibles issued during the late 1980s. For them the convertible bond is a close substitute for bank credit as a means of fund-raising. From the viewpoint of standard corporate finance theory, however, it is difficult to explain why they preferred issuing convertibles to bank loans, as will be discussed later.

In this section we will propose a hypothesis to explain the surge in convertible bonds in the late 1980s. This hypothesis is related both to a particular characteristic of liberalization in the corporate bond market and to the mechanism of corporate governance in Japan. As was explained in section 6.2, an important characteristic of the liberalization of Japanese bond markets was the favorable treatment of major well-established companies. For those firms' managers, convertible bond issues were not a means of overcoming the agency problem due to asymmetric information, but a means of increasing their perquisite expenditure. This is in essence the hypothesis advocated in this paper.

### 6.3.1 Standard Theory of Convertible Bond Issues

The standard theory of corporate finance provides two reasons to issue convertible bonds. In either case imperfect information plays an essential role. First, firms' managers or shareholders would issue convertible bonds to signal their incentive to avoid risky projects that may entail large losses for their creditors under the rule of limited liability. Issuing convertible bonds implies that, even if a risky project goes well and realizes extraordinary returns, current shareholders must yield most of the returns to investors who hold convertibles. Thus, convertible bonds are thought to be effective in mitigating the agency problem existing between shareholders and creditors (debtholders) emphasized by Jensen and Meckling (1976).

Second, according to Stein (1992), some firms, particularly medium-quality ones, have incentives to issue convertible bonds in order to obtain funding conditions different from those available to low-quality firms. High-quality firms with good prospects of returns are able to issue straight bonds or to borrow from banks without endangering default risk. On the other hand, low-quality firms with poor prospects of returns are forced to issue stock instead of straight bonds because the latter incurs serious default risk. As Stein (1992) shows, medium-quality firms with adequately good prospects may be able to differentiate themselves from low-quality firms by issuing convertible bonds in the capital market.

In either of these cases, convertible bonds are instrumental for firms who suffer from the agency problem caused by asymmetric information. Therefore, these theories predict that firms that are newly established or have not yet achieved excellent performance should be more active in issuing convertible bonds than well-established firms.[12] According to Brealey and Myers, "convertibles tend to be issued by the smaller and more speculative firms" (1991, 549).

### 6.3.2 Another Hypothesis

It is doubtful whether the standard theories about convertible bonds are applicable to the situation in Japan during the latter half of the 1980s. Although the eligibility requirements for convertible bonds became less and less restric-

12. Hitachi issued U.S. dollar–denominated convertible bonds in September 1962. At that time Hitachi could not choose a straight bond issue because the company was not well known among U.S. investors. This case can be clearly understood from the viewpoint of the standard theory.

tive during the 1980s, only relatively large scale firms were allowed to issue convertibles. Overwhelmingly important issuers of convertibles were major companies that were previously established in the Japanese economy. For them, the agency problem due to asymmetric information emphasized by the standard theories seems to be irrelevant.

It may be said that outside investors overrated stock prices of industrial firms during the late 1980s. If managers and current shareholders understood the overvaluation of their stock prices in the capital market, they would have been induced to issue shares and convertible bonds to outsiders in order to exploit the excess profits due to asymmetric information. Can this hypothesis of outsider overvaluation be relevant to Japan's capital markets in the latter half of the 1980s? If this hypothesis were true, current shareholders (insiders) would reduce their equity positions as much as possible in order to press stocks overrated from their viewpoint on outside investors. In reality, however, current shareholders did not seem to reduce their equity positions. In particular, in the late 1980s, Japanese firms did not reduce the share of internal funds in the total amount of fund-raising.[13] It would be irrational for current shareholders to increase the amount of retained profits when outsiders overrate their firms' stock value because it means missing a chance to take excess profits by issuing convertibles and stocks to ignorant outside investors. Thus, the relatively high importance of internal funds in Japanese corporate finance in the late 1980s weakens the hypothesis of outsider overvaluation.

Why then were big Japanese companies so eager to issue convertible bonds in the late 1980s? Managers of those firms reportedly explained that convertibles were preferable to bank loans and other means of raising funds because convertibles could be issued at extremely low coupon rates when investors had strong bullish expectations about the firms' stock prices.[14] But this explanation is not convincing from the viewpoint of shareholders of those firms because low coupon rates on convertibles imply a high probability that shareholders will be forced in the near future to yield some valuable shares in their firms to bond investors. Extraordinarily bullish expectations, such as those observed in the stock market during the latter half of the 1980s, would not necessarily induce firms to issue convertibles if their concern was purely that of maximizing profits on behalf of their current shareholders.

If managers are not sufficiently constrained by the principle of maximizing shareholder profits, however, incentives may exist for them to issue convertible bonds and reduce borrowing from banks. In particular, bullish expectations

13. The importance of internal funds (i.e., depreciation and retained profits) was very low during the high-growth period in Japan. The proportion of internal funds in the total amount of funds raised by major companies was 30.2 and 42.4 percent in the 1960s and 1970s, respectively. However, internal funds have relatively increased since the early 1970s. From 1980 to 1984, the average proportion of internal funds was 56.4 percent. From 1985 to 1989, the proportion did not significantly decrease, remaining at 53.6 percent (BOJ, various issues).

14. E.g., it was widely known that many Japanese firms could issue convertible bonds in Switzerland at zero coupon rates in 1989.

of stock prices may more strongly induce corporate managers to issue more convertibles than otherwise. We explain this by introducing a simple two-period model.

### 6.3.3 A Simple Model

We assume here that there is no problem of asymmetric information between insiders and outside investors of the sort considered, for example, by Jensen and Meckling (1976) and Stein (1992). Therefore, if they are perfectly disciplined to maximize current shareholder profits, incumbent managers have no particular reason to prefer issuing convertibles to borrowing from banks. Furthermore, managers are assumed to be constrained by the extremely high penalty of bankruptcy. In other words, it is assumed that they want to avoid default at any expense because in bankruptcy they incur huge pecuniary and psychological costs. The assumptions both of no asymmetric information and of the constraints of bankruptcy costs on managers are plausible in the case of Japan's well-established firms. The managers of those companies have accumulated intangible assets embodied in themselves whose value will be totally lost should their firms go bankrupt.

A firm is assumed to have an investment opportunity with positive net present value. The amount of external funds that must be raised to proceed with this investment opportunity is denoted $I$. When this investment is carried out, the value of the firm will in the next period be $X_H$ with probability $P$, and $X_L (X_H > X_L)$ with probability $1 - P$. We assume that the managers of the firm can enjoy a perquisite or a "pet" investment represented by $Z$ in addition to the normal investment $I$. The managers raise $I + Z$ either by borrowing from banks or by issuing convertible bonds. For simplicity, we assume that all agents are risk-neutral and the equilibrium interest rate is zero.[15]

*The case of borrowing from banks.* When the firm borrows from a bank, the maximum amount of funds will be denoted $X_L$ because of the assumption of prohibitive bankruptcy costs. Thus,

$$1 + Z \leqq X_L . \tag{1}$$

The present value of the firm's stock $V$ is given by the following equation:

$$\begin{aligned} V &= P(X_H - I - Z) + (1 - P)(X_L - I - Z) \\ &= PX_H + (1 - P)X_L - I - Z \\ &= V_0 - Z, \end{aligned}$$

15. In practice, it is difficult to identify perquisite expenditure by incumbent managers. But, e.g., we may regard various investment expenditures in order to preserve and/or increase job opportunities for present employees as typical perquisite expenditure. Many Japanese firms engaged in financial investment called *zai-tech* during the late 1980s. Those financial activities may also be perquisites because they were associated with an undue increase in the risk from the viewpoint of shareholders.

where $V_0$ is the firm's share value when the managers do not take any perquisite at all. We assume an efficient capital market here, so that managers' expenditure on perquisite $Z$ leads to a decline in the firm's value $V$.

*The case of issuing convertible bonds.* To raise funds $I + Z$, the firm could issue convertible bonds whose total face value is $F$. The bonds will be converted into $100C$ percent of the firm's shares in the future when its stock value turns out to be $X_H$. But when the stock value is $X_L$ in the second period, they will not be converted into shares, so that the managers will have to repay $F$ to bondholders. The constraint of bankruptcy costs assumed above requires that $F$ be no larger than $X_L$; that is,

$$F \leqq X_L .$$

The present value of the convertible bond $I + Z$ is

$$I + Z = PCX_H + (1 + P)F .$$

Therefore, the maximum amount of $I + Z$ is given by the following condition:

$$I + Z \leqq PCX_H + (1 - P)X_L = X_L + P(CX_H - X_L) . \tag{2}$$

As theoretical consistency requires $CX_H > X_L$, the maximum value of $I + Z$ can be larger than $X_L$ when the firm issues convertibles. The assumption of an efficient capital market ensures that the present stock value of the firm $V$ is equal to $V_0 - Z$.

If the firm is allowed to freely change the conversion ratio $C$, it can increase the maximum amount of perquisite expenditure $Z$ by offering a higher ratio $C$ to investors. But the present rules governing the issuing of convertibles prevents managers from manipulating $C$ in Japan. Under the present institutional framework, we can assume this conversion ratio to be exogenously given.[16]

By comparing inequalities (1) and (2), we can see that the managers can increase the amount expended on the "pet" investment $Z$ by issuing convertibles. An increase in $Z$ will lead to capital loss for the firm's current shareholders. Therefore, if shareholders are able to instill sufficient discipline in managers so as to maintain profit maximization as their only goal, there is no

16. The ratio $C$ is equal to the face value $F$ of the convertible bond divided by the conversion price. In Japan the conversion price is determined by

$$(1 + S) \times (\text{the standardized stock price}) \times (\text{the number of stock shares}),$$

where $S$ is institutionally determined by self-regulation among securities companies. The standardized stock price of an issuing firm is determined as an average of the firm's stock price over several days immediately before the issuing data. Thus, the conversion ratio $C$ given by the following formula can be regarded as a constant:

$$C = F/[(1 + S) \times (\text{the standardized stock price}) \times (\text{the number of stock shares})].$$

particular incentive for managers to issue convertibles. If incumbent managers are to some extent free from the discipline of maximizing shareholder profits, however, they have incentives to increase expenditure $Z$ by issuing convertibles at the expense of present shareholders. In this primitive model, investors' bullish expectations are presented by a higher value of either $P$ or $X_H$. Thus, equation (2) shows that when investors have more bullish expectations of the firm's value, as during the late 1980s, managers' incentives to issue convertibles become stronger, other things being constant.

Our model assumes imperfect corporate governance in Japan in the sense that corporate managers have latitude more or less to direct firms' resources to satisfy their own (and probably employees') preference for perquisite expenditure. On the basis of this assumption, we can explain the surge in convertibles issues during the latter half of the 1980s. The liberalization of the convertible bond market that started in the early 1980s weakened the severity of bankruptcy constraints for corporate managers and thereby increased their perquisite expenditure. The sharp rise in stock prices during the second half of the 1980s produced optimistic expectations of future stock prices, which helped managers expand the latitude of perquisite investment as equation (2) suggests. In contrast, since 1990, when pessimistic expectations began to prevail in the stock market, Japanese firms have lost their enthusiasm for issuing convertibles. The amount of convertible bond issues has substantially decreased since 1990 as figure 6.2 shows.[17]

### 6.3.4 Evidence Supporting the Hypothesis

We can derive two propositions from our hypothesis of imperfect corporate governance. The first proposition is that the active issuance of convertibles by a firm tends to increase its perquisite expenditure, thereby deteriorating the firms' performance from the shareholders' viewpoint. The second is that the more optimistic the stock market is, the more strongly stimulated managers are to issue convertibles to increase perquisite expenditure. In the following, we consider whether statistical evidence supports these propositions.

*Responses of stock prices to convertible bond issues.* The most straightforward statistical test of the first proposition is to examine the responses of individual firms' stock prices to issues of convertible bonds. This is an event study. According to our hypothesis of imperfect corporate governance, issuing convertible bonds signals to the stock market the managers' intent to increase perquisite expenditure. Thus, provided that the stock market is efficient, the stock price would respond negatively to the announcement of a convertible bond

17. As was explained in section 6.2, the eligibility requirements for domestic convertible bond issues have been substantially eased since the late 1980s. This mitigation has extended opportunities for small-scale businesses to issue convertible bonds. Thus, the number of firms listed on the over-the-counter market that issued convertibles increased in the early 1990s.

issue. On the other hand, under the standard theory of corporate finance, issuing convertibles is good news for outside investors, who suffer from imperfect information about corporate management. Therefore, stock prices would respond positively to the announcement of a convertible bond issue.

We test the response of stock prices to issues of convertible bonds in Japan's domestic market from 1985 to 1991. Specifically, we examine changes in the rate of return on shares in issuing firms compared with the average rate of return on shares in their peer firms. If an issue of convertibles is bad news for outside investors, the announcement of such an issue will decrease the stock price and thereby reduce its rate of return.

It is essential for our test to identify when news of a convertible issue is made public by an issuing firm. When the managers of a firm want to issue a convertible bond, they must submit an application to an underwriting securities company at least four months before the scheduled date of the bond issue. The underwriter introduces the application to the regular meeting organized by major underwriters to examine the feasibility of the proposed issue. After the regular meeting has decided that the proposed issue is feasible, the firm's board of directors officially determines to issue convertibles with specific issuing conditions and releases the decision to the press. At the same time, the firm is required to submit a securities registration statement to the MOF following the stipulation of the Securities Exchange Act.

Although the length of the time lag between the press release and the day when the bonds are actually issued varies from case to case, it is usually several weeks. We can identify the precise date of announcement of individual issues by consulting newspapers. We select convertible bond issues announced to the press from January to December 1988, when Japanese firms most actively issued convertibles. The number of sample firms thus collected is a little less than 300. We had to exclude from our sample firms not listed on the Tokyo Stock Exchange because the data on holding period return on their stocks are not available to us. The total number of sample firms is 262: 188 cases issuing in the domestic market and 74 issuing in foreign markets.

If an issue of convertibles is bad (good) news for investors, the press release of the plan to issue bonds will decrease (increase) the firm's stock price immediately, and the holding period rate of return on the stock will be lower (higher) than those of peer firms during the specific month. The holding period rate of return $R_i(t)$ of firm $i$ in the month $t$ when the firm announces the plan of issuing convertibles and the industrial average of holding period return $R_I(t)$ can be obtained from the Japan Securities Research Institute. Table 6.7 summarizes the average $\Sigma_i[R_i(t) - R_I(t)]/n$ of estimated responses in holding period return on issuing firms' stocks, where $n$ is the size of the sample. Our concern is whether the average is significantly negative as the hypothesis of imperfect corporate governance predicts. If this hypothesis is true, the holding period returns on issuing firms' stocks are on average lower than the industrial averages over the three months preceding their issues of convertibles.

The result in table 6.7 is, unfortunately, ambiguous. In total, the average of

**Table 6.7** **Relative Rate of Return on Stock When a Firm Decides to Issue Convertible Bonds Compared with Industrial Average, January to December 1988 (%)**

| | Number of Firms | Average | Standard Errors |
|---|---|---|---|
| Domestic issues | 188 | 0.24 | 0.48 |
| Foreign issues | 74 | −0.88 | 0.81 |
| Total | 262 | −0.07 | 0.41 |

*Sources: Koshasai Yoran* (Handbook of Japanese Bonds) (Tokyo: Nomura Research Institute, 1989); *Kabushiki-toshi Shuekiritu* (Rates of Return on Common Stocks) (Tokyo: Japan Securities Research Institute, 1990).

*Note:* The basic data are holding period returns (from the end of the previous month to the end of the current month) on stock, when issuing firms announced their issuing plans, minus the average of industries' holding period return. The sample consists of all firms that announced a plan to issue convertibles from January to December 1988. Our sample excludes those firms not listed on the Tokyo Stock Exchange, because data on their holding period returns were not available in our data source. There were some cases in which a firm issued a few convertible bonds on the same day to raise a large amount of funds. In this table, we do not treat the multiple issues separately. Therefore, the number of issuing firms in this table is smaller than the number of issues recorded in table 6.6.

holding period returns is slightly negative compared with the industrial average. But it is not statistically significant at all. In the case of foreign issues, the stock prices seem to show a slightly stronger negative response to the announcement. But it is not significant either.

Therefore, our event study does not give clear-cut support to the hypothesis of imperfect corporate governance. The standard hypothesis of convertible bond issues, which expects a positive response of stock prices to the announcement, is not supported either. However, we need to mention a caveat. The validity of our event study depends crucially on the presumption that the stock market is efficient in Japan. This presumption is problematic. We have not yet reached any unambiguous conclusion concerning the efficiency of the Japanese stock market (see, e.g., Hoshi 1987). However, in my understanding, there is a lot of casual evidence that casts doubt on the validity of the efficiency hypothesis in Japan. Therefore, we should refrain from deriving a definite conclusion based on the event study summarized in table 6.7.

*Profitability after convertible bond issues and the influence of stock price increases on convertible bond issues.* In the following, we examine the relevancy of the hypothesis of imperfect corporate governance by using statistical methods alternative to the event study we explained above. Specifically, on the basis of panel data from the mid-1980s to early 1990s, we test whether the firms that issued convertible bonds systematically experienced deterioration of their profit rates after the issue, compared with peer firms in the same industries. The sample is 509 Japanese firms. They are major firms, and until the late 1980s they had been eligible to issue convertibles without collateral. In other words, they had been given the widest range of options in their fund-raising until the late 1980s. The dependent variable, PRG($t$), is the profit rate of each firm compared with the average profit rate of peer firms belonging to the same industry. Independent variables are the lagged profit rate compared with the industrial average, PRG($t-1$), and the amount of convertibles issued each year divided by total assets with suitable lags, CB($t-i$) for $i = 1, \dots, 4$. The sample period is the seven years from 1985 to 1991.

The result of the panel-data estimation is summarized in table 6.8. The result clearly shows that an increase in convertible issues significantly decreased the profit rate of issuing firms with two or three years' lag. This suggests that managers of major companies tend to issue convertibles in order to pursue their own objectives rather than profit maximization on behalf of current shareholders.

The second proposition derived from our model is that an increase in expected stock prices will induce incumbent managers to issue convertibles because it mitigates the constraint of bankruptcy for them. We examine whether this prediction was true during the late 1980s. We choose the amount of convertibles issued each year divided by total assets as a dependent variable (CB($t$)). Independent variables are lagged variables CB($t-1$) and CB($t-2$), lagged stock prices ST($t-1$) and ST($t-2$), and lagged profit rates PR($t-1$) and PR($t-2$). We introduce lagged variables CB($t-1$) and CB($t-2$) because rules concerning convertible issues in Japan have greatly influenced the pattern of issuing behavior of individual firms.[18] The lagged stock prices are introduced on the assumption that they essentially determine investor expectations of the stock prices. We are particularly interested in the statistical significance of these lagged stock prices in the following investigation. We choose the Tobit model to test the proposition because the frequency with which the dependent variable CB($t$) takes the value zero is rather high—nearly 80 percent of dependent variable values are zero. The estimated result is summarized in table 6.9.

The result shows that higher stock prices induced firms to issue larger amounts of convertible bonds in the following year. Since we may suppose that an increase in stock prices positively influences the market expectations of stock prices, the result suggests that the higher level of expected prices stimulated convertible issues during the late 1980s. The result in table 6.9 thus supports our hypothesis that bullish expectations in the stock market will induce corporate managers to issue convertible bonds. This suggests that corporate governance has been inefficient in Japan from the viewpoint of shareholders.

### 6.3.5 A Discussion

We can summarize our investigation concerning the relationship between the surge of convertible bond issues and liberalization in the bond market dur-

18. Since 1973, the self-regulatory rule determined by the group of underwriting securities companies has restricted the length of intervals between issues of convertibles so that firms are in effect required to take an interval of at least one year to reissue convertibles.

**Table 6.8** **Profit Rates and Convertible Bond Issues, 1985–91 (panel-data estimation; random-effects method)**

| Variable | Estimation |
|---|---|
| PRG ($t-1$) | 0.60100 (50.19) |
| CB($t$) | −0.00379 (−0.49) |
| CB($t-1$) | −0.01362 (−1.81) |
| CB($t-2$) | −0.03833 (−4.79) |
| CB($t-3$) | −0.03616 (−4.16) |
| CB($t-4$) | −0.01777 (−1.86) |
| Constant | 0.00725 (11.17) |
| Mean of dependent variable | 0.00821 |
| Sum of squared residuals | 1.55409 |
| Standard error of regression | 0.02258 |
| Adjusted $R^2$ | 0.3126 |

*Source: NIKKEI NEEDS. TS. COMPANY* (Tokyo: Nihon Kezai Shimbun, Division of Datebank, 1994).

*Notes:* Dependent variable is PRG($t$) = the operating profit rate (per total assets) of each firm minus the average profit rate of the industry. CB($t$) = the amount of convertible bonds issued by each firm divided by total assets. Numbers in parentheses are $t$-values.

**Table 6.9** **Stock Prices and Convertible Bond Issues, 1985–91 (Tobit estimation)**

| Variable | Estimation |
|---|---|
| Constant | −0.19034 (−15.73) |
| CB($t-1$) | −0.16596 (−2.11) |
| CB($t-2$) | 0.32382 (4.20) |
| ST($t-1$) | 0.02374 (3.35) |
| ST($t-2$) | 0.00170 (0.26) |
| PR($t-1$) | 0.96481 (5.83) |
| PR($t-2$) | −0.48500 (−2.05) |
| Log of likelihood function | −735.923 |
| Percent of positive observations | 0.20236 |

*Source: NIKKEI NEEDS. TS. COMPANY* (Tokyo: Nihon Kezai Shimbun, Division of Datebank, 1994).

*Notes:* Dependent variable is CB($t$). ST($t$) = stock price at end of year $t$, standardized by setting stock prices at 1991 year-end to 100.0. PR($t$) = profit rate per total assets in year $t$. Numbers in parentheses are $t$-values.

ing the 1980s in Japan. The liberalization stimulated Japanese firms to issue a large amount of convertible bonds, thereby reducing their reliance on bank loans. Although this impact of liberalization in the bond market seems remarkable, it is doubtful whether the impact was genuinely productive. Convertible bonds and other equity-related bonds, such as warrant bonds, are instrumental for firms facing serious agency problems because they have just started business or because they have not yet achieved excellent performance and more important because they do not enjoy favorable treatment resulting from a long-term relationship with their main banks. In theory, such bonds would not be so attractive for firms that have established themselves in the Japanese economy because they are not confronted with agency problems caused by asymmetric information.

The liberalization in the Japanese corporate bond market has allowed more and more firms to utilize convertibles and warrants as a means of fund-raising. But the eligibility requirements confined the possible use of those instruments to relatively large scale and well-established firms during the 1980s. The requirement excluded from the corporate bond market those firms that most needed the instruments. For example, firms registered on the over-the-counter market, most of which were promising small and medium-sized companies, are not allowed to issue warrants at all and find stricter constraints imposed on them when issuing convertibles, compared to well-established firms.

It should be noted that these small-scale firms have rarely participated in the traditional main bank relationships that are supposed to weaken pressure from capital markets on incumbent managers. Managers of small firms cannot afford to abuse the freedom of issuing convertible bonds for the purpose of increasing perquisite expenditure instead of reducing agency costs as suggested by the standard theory.

Therefore, the liberalization in corporate bond markets brought forth only superficial consequences in the 1980s. Most managers in Japan's big companies enthusiastically welcomed the liberalization because it widened the possibility of increasing their perquisite expenditure by mitigating the constraint of bankruptcy. Our statistical examination confirms that the surge in issues of convertibles tended to be associated with increases in perquisite expenditure during the latter half of the 1980s in Japan.

We may conclude that financial liberalization in Japan's corporate bond markets has been conducted in a distorted manner. The process indicates how timid or distrustful the related parties, including the monetary authorities, are about the productivity of the full-scale corporate bond market mechanism. They should acknowledge that the firms with a significant possibility of default can be efficiently treated in the market. In other words, corporate bond markets do not play a meaningful role when only blue-chip firms without any risk of default are permitted to issue various instruments. There remain serious obstacles for small-scale and venture businesses in Japanese corporate bond markets. The surge of convertible issues in the late 1980s and the subsequent deteriorating performance of issuing companies in the early 1990s suggest the remaining weakness of Japanese capital markets.

## 6.4 Concluding Remarks

In this paper, we investigated the process of liberalization in Japanese bond markets during the 1980s and its consequences in the late 1980s. The domestic bond market has been greatly liberalized since the early 1980s, mainly because of pressure from abroad associated with internationalization of financial markets. But the process of liberalization was distorted and imperfect in the sense that only well-established firms were permitted wide opportunities in choosing various bonds as a means of fund-raising, and small-sized and relatively newly established firms were not allowed access to such instruments. In theory, firms of the latter type would have had genuine need for convertibles and other equity-related bonds. The consequence of the distorted liberalization was an increase in perquisite expenditure by well-established firms because convertible bonds mitigated the constraint of bankruptcy they had confronted during the high-growth era.

This paper provides two lessons. First, Japan should more boldly accept the market-oriented consequences of financial liberalization. Many Japanese, particularly the Japanese monetary authorities, are still skeptical about the efficiency of market mechanisms in the financial system and have an irresolute attitude toward full-scale liberalization. There appears to be a somewhat self-congratulatory attitude in their belief that their "careful" and conservative policy of liberalizing the financial system in Japan ("gradualism" in this paper) has contributed to stability in spite of drastic structural changes since the mid-1970s. We should, however, pay enough attention to the negative effects of their conservative policy, such as those we have emphasized in this paper.

Second, the present situation of corporate governance in Japan deserves further careful investigation. In this paper we discussed the possibility that the nature of governance, which is imperfect from the shareholders' viewpoint, resulted in inefficient expenditure by corporations in the late 1980s. Many people might claim that the present structure of corporate governance actually stimulated rapid industrial development in the Japanese economy. Mutual shareholding among major corporations has protected incumbent managers from capital market pressures, thereby promoting managerial decision making from a long-term perspective. At the same time, the main bank relationship between banks and borrower firms is regarded as efficiently monitoring and disciplining managers to pursue efficient management, in place of capital markets.[19]

However, our recent experience indicates that we have not yet established the perfect structure of corporate governance in Japan. During the high-growth era, the primary objective of corporate managers was to exploit the abundant opportunities of rapid growth. The Japanese corporate structure, which give

19. See, e.g., Aoki, Patrick, and Sheard (1994). There are some empirical studies which support the hypothesis that Japanese corporate governance led to efficient management, particularly through the monitoring and disciplining provided by the main bank relationship. See Hoshi, Kashyap, and Scharfstein (1990a, 1990b, 1991), Lichtenberg and Pushner (1992), Morck and Nakamura (1992), and Prowse (1990). Most of their analyses are confined to the period up to the late 1980s. If they had considered the structural changes in Japanese industry from the late 1980s to the early 1990s, they might have obtained more pessimistic results on the efficiency of current Japanese corporate governance.

wide discretionary power to incumbent managers and current employees, did not lead to serious losses for the other stakeholders mainly because the rapid growth of corporations covered up potential conflicts of interest between different stakeholders. When an industry is confronted with severe structural changes, however, the Japanese way of promoting wide discretion of incumbent managers and employees may have the weakness of delaying the restructuring of corporations. As Boot (1992) exemplifies, insiders of corporations tend to resist fundamental structural changes in order to preserve their own vested interests.

Full-scale financial liberalization is expected to strengthen the capital market monitoring of corporate management, thereby building an efficient mechanism of corporate finance in Japan that is somewhat different from the traditional one that has dominated Japan's corporate sector for more than four decades. Thus, we should be much more positive in liberalizing Japanese capital markets.

## References

Aoki, Masahiko, Hugh Patrick, and Paul Sheard. 1994. The Japanese main bank system: An introductory overview. In *The Japanese main bank system: Its relevancy for developing and transforming economies,* ed. Masahiko Aoki and Hugh Patrick, 3–50. Oxford: Oxford University Press.

BOJ (Bank of Japan). Various issues. *Financial statements of principal enterprises.* Tokyo: Bank of Japan.

Boot, Arnoud W. 1992. Why hang on to losers?: Divestitures and takeovers. *Journal of Finance* 47:1401–23.

Brealey, Richard A., and Stewart C. Myers. 1991. *Principles of corporate finance,* 4th ed. New York: McGraw-Hill.

Calder, Kent E. 1993. *Strategic capitalism: Private business and public purpose in Japanese industrial finance.* Princeton, N.J.: Princeton University Press.

Federation of Bankers Associations of Japan. 1994. *The banking systems in Japan.* Tokyo: Federation of Bankers Association (Zenginkyo).

Frankel, Jeffrey A. 1984. *The yen/dollar agreement: Liberalizing Japanese capital markets.* Policy Analysis in International Economics no. 9. Washington, D.C.: Institute for International Economics.

Hoshi, Takeo. 1987. Stock market rationality and price volatility: Tests using Japanese data. *Journal of the Japanese and International Economies* 1:441–62.

———. 1993. Financial deregulation and corporate financing in Japan. La Jolla: Graduate School of International Relations and Pacific Studies, University of California. Mimeograph.

Hoshi, Takeo, Anil Kashyap, and David Scharfstein. 1990a. Bank monitoring and investment: Evidence from the changing structure of Japanese corporate banking relationships. In *Asymmetric information, corporate finance, and investment,* ed. R. Glenn Hubbard, 105–26. Chicago: University of Chicago Press.

———. 1990b. The role of banks in reducing the costs of financial distress in Japan. *Journal of Financial Economics* 27:67–88.

———. 1991. Corporate structure, liquidity and investment: Evidence from Japanese panel data. *Quarterly Journal of Economics* 106:33–60.

Jensen, Michael, and William Meckling. 1976. Theory of the firm: Managerial behavior, agency costs and ownership structure. *Journal of Financial Economics* 3:302–60.

Lichtenberg, Frank R., and George M. Pushner. 1992. Ownership structure and corporate performance in Japan. NBER Working Paper no. 4092. Cambridge, Mass.: National Bureau of Economic Research.

MOF (Ministry of Finance). 1993. *Annual report of the Bureau of International Finance.* Tokyo: Ministry of Finance.

Morck, Randall, and Masao Nakamura. 1992. Banks and corporate control in Japan. Faculty of Business, University of Alberta. Mimeograph.

Prowse, Stephen D. 1990. Institutional investment patterns and corporate financial behavior in the U.S. and Japan. *Journal of Financial Economics* 27:43–66.

Stein, Jeremy C. 1992. Convertible bonds as backdoor equity financing. *Journal of Financial Economics* 32:3–21.

Takeda, Masahiko, and Philip Turner. 1992. The liberalization of Japan's financial markets: Some major themes. BIS Economic Paper no. 34. Basel: Bank of International Settlements.

## Comment Won-Am Park

Horiuchi argues quite interestingly that the active issue of convertible bonds by well-established Japanese firms during the financial liberalization in the 1980s created distortions. This happened because the managers of well-established firms tended to utilize convertibles to increase their perquisite expenditures instead of requisite expenditures, while small firms were not allowed to issue convertible bonds. The author thinks that small firms should have been allowed to issue convertible bonds to mitigate the agency problem existing between shareholders and creditors (debtholders).

These arguments, unfortunately, are not entirely convincing. First, imperfect information will not accord with full-scale financial liberalization as shown in the credit-rationing literature. In contrast, the author seems to argue that fuller financial liberalization, particularly in corporate finance, is desirable because of asymmetric information and easily misguided corporate governance. The author must clarify why imperfect information does not support credit rationing but requires fuller financial liberalization.

Second, the author does not provide a consistent explanation for perquisite expenditure or "pet" investment by managers of well-established firms. It appears that managers of those firms were eager to reap large capital gains by issuing convertible bonds at extremely low coupon rates when investors had strong bullish expectations about the firms' stock prices. This is the asymmetric information problem between insiders and outsiders. Then the paper reads

Won-Am Park is professor of economics at Hong-Ik University and a research associate of the Korea Development Institute.

as if this would not explain Japanese capital markets in the latter half of the 1980s because shareholders did not concurrently reduce their equity positions nor did Japanese firms reduce the share of internal funds in the total amount of funds. The author should explain this conflicting evidence in a consistent way.

Third, the panel-data econometric studies are shown in table 6.7 to confirm that convertible bond issues financed perquisite expenditure. However, the econometric investigation in table 6.7 needs to be refined. The panel data could be rearranged to remove too many zeros in convertible bond issues (it has been said that nearly 80 percent of convertible bond issue data are zeros). The fixed-effect regression, as well as the random-effect regression, should be done as a robustness check. In addition, time dummy variables or time-varying coefficient estimation should be included because eligibility requirements for convertible bonds issues have been loosened gradually (table 6.5). The finding that more convertible bond issues led to lower profit rates may not be evidence that convertible bond issues financed perquisite expenditures. Even if convertible bond issues financed requisite investments, operating profit rates could have gone down in the beginning as new equipment was installed. Considering all these aspects, it will be better to investigate whether more convertible bond issues led to lower stock prices.

The author does not carry out empirical tests on the responses of stock prices of individual firms to issues of convertible bonds for some ambiguous reasons. My hunch is that more convertible bond issues by well-established firms were associated with higher stock prices because outside investors had bullish expectations of stock prices in the latter half of the 1980s, and because most shareholders were outsiders who care about stock prices. In this situation, managers of well-established firms, as insiders, would issue more convertible bonds to finance both requisite and perquisite investments at low coupon rates. The asymmetric information between insiders and outsiders would create distortions in the capital market. However, the distortions did not seem severe enough to bring about significant changes in equity positions and less reliance on internal finance. This is my explanation for the conflicting evidence on the profit-seeking activities of the managers of well-established firms.

Overall, the conclusions drawn in this paper could change with a more balanced view of the Japanese experience with corporate bond market liberalization. Managers of well-established firms might behave as insiders. If this is true in the case of well-established firms, it will also be true in the case of small firms. Managers of small firms will take advantage of their insider position once they are allowed to issue convertible bonds. As long as outside investors have bullish expectations of stock prices, the agency problem of small firms will not be cured by the issuance of convertible bonds. Actually convertible bond issues by small firms will emphasize the insider-outsider problem. Viewed in this way, one can justify Japan's gradual approach to corporate bond market liberalization.

# 7 The Role of Macroeconomic Policy in Export-Led Growth: The Experience of Taiwan and South Korea

Kenneth S. Lin, Hsiu-Yun Lee, and Bor-Yi Huang

## 7.1 Introduction

Inflation, unemployment, and budget deficits have long been the focus of macroeconomic policy. Recently, macroeconomists turned their attention to growth and development. One remarkable result in the new endogenous growth theory is that government policy can affect the steady state growth rate. Empirical analysis of the effect of macroeconomic policy on long-run growth has so far produced mixed results.

The purpose of this paper is to characterize the role of macroeconomic policy in the export-led growth experience of Taiwan and South Korea. Argentina, Chile, Taiwan, and South Korea all started their postwar economic development with an import-substitution approach in the 1950s. However, after three decades, Argentina and Chile, unlike Taiwan and South Korea, showed mediocre macroeconomic performance with erratic GDP growth and high inflation (Lin 1988). One fundamental difference is that Taiwan and South Korea switched to an export-led approach in the 1960s. What is the role of macroeconomic policy in successful export-led growth, a causal factor or an inevitable choice?

For a country adopting an export-led approach, we argue that international competition forces households, firms, and government in this country to react to external shocks optimally, and their decisions and policies are endogenous.

Kenneth S. Lin is professor of economics at National Taiwan University. Hsiu-Yun Lee is associate professor of economics at the Graduate Institute of International Economics, National Chung Cheng University. Bor-Yi Huang is associate professor of finance at Shih Chien College, Taipei.

The authors thank participants in the NBER seminar and in the economics group seminar at Victoria University of Wellington, Tsong-Min Wu of National Taiwan University, and Kun-Hong Kim of Victoria University of Wellington for helpful comments, Woo-Kyu Park of the Korea Development Institute for providing the South Korean data used in section 7.4, and Jiing-Ting Jong for excellent research assistance.

It is natural that any pattern of correlation between macroeconomic policy and economic growth is possible, depending on the underlying external shocks. The correlation patterns under export-led regimes are also unlikely to dominate the outcomes of cross-country growth regressions, so the empirical results obtained in cross-country growth regressions may not be useful in revealing the role of macroeconomic policy in export-led growth.

Since the ultimate goal of any economic policy of export-led growth is maintaining and enhancing the international competitiveness of the country's export goods, this goal in turn disciplines macroeconomic policy that prevents the adoption of any measure hurting export growth. Even though there are many instruments available for implementing macroeconomic policy, not all of them are free instruments in achieving such a particular objective. For Taiwan and South Korea, we found that sound fiscal policy gives the set of available instruments the maximum degree of freedom. For example, suppose that government is under pressure to offer greater fiscal incentives to compensate exporting firms for profit losses caused by temporary external shocks. The governments that can offer such incentives by running a temporarily high level of budget deficits are those that have sound fiscal discipline.

It is through the conduct of monetary and exchange rate policies that the central bank has its most profound influence on inflation, interest rates, exchange rates, and the balance of payments. The central bank in developed countries has been designed as the monetary authority whose primary responsibility is to maintain price stability. However, the central bank in most developing countries has difficulty in achieving the goal of price stability because of the two roles it plays: First, its development bank role requires the central bank to use exchange rate management and to provide interest rate subsidies or preferential loans to promote growth. Second, its fiscal support role requires the central bank to generate inflation tax revenues for the government. Even though the central banks in Taiwan and South Korea are not independent compared to their counterparts in developed countries our case study indicates that sound fiscal policy allows these central banks to play a more active role in promoting exports without immediately jeopardizing price stability. However, as the importance of the export-led approach as a source of growth declines, it is more likely that government spending becomes an important fiscal instrument in stimulating economic growth. A less independent central bank will be a cause of concern since it makes inflationary finance easier. Therefore, designing an independent central bank could be crucial for both countries' future macroeconomic performance.

The remainder of the paper is organized as follows: In section 7.2, we present some stylized facts on macroeconomic policy and economic growth. When macroeconomic policy and aggregate variables such as inflation rate, investment, and exports all respond to external shocks, virtually any pattern of correlation between macroeconomic policy and economic variables can be obtained. This makes regression results difficult to interpret regarding the links between macroeconomic policy and aggregate variables. In section 7.3, we use a case study to evaluate the role of macroeconomic policy in export-led growth. First, we construct two indexes of central bank independence for Taiwan; we do not find a negative association between inflation and central bank independence in Taiwan or South Korea. In searching for the explanation, we focus on the relation between fiscal discipline and moderate inflation. In section 7.4, we use the special loan policy to address the point that the macroeconomic policy adopted by a government is highly influenced by the structure of the domestic economy. In section 7.5, we look at current account and exchange rate management and argue that the export success of Taiwan and South Korea is not a product of aggressive devaluations. Section 7.6 offers some concluding remarks.

## 7.2 Macroeconomic Policy and Growth: Some Stylized Facts

In this section, we present some stylized facts on macroeconomic policy and growth. The most crucial link between macroeconomic policy and long-run growth is that a higher investment-GDP ratio leads to better GDP growth. Table 7.1 shows that the associations between them for both Taiwan and South Korea are not positive across all subperiods.[1] Taiwan had a sharp decrease in investment-GDP ratio without any negative impact on growth rate between the periods 1981–85 and 1986–90, while South Korea experienced a sharp increase in investment-GDP ratio without an increase in growth rate between the periods 1971–75 and 1976–80. This suggests that a higher (lower) investment-GDP ratio does not necessarily lead to rapid (slow) economic growth. Recently, Fischer (1991) found that a sharp increase in investment between the periods 1960–73 and 1973–80 did not lead to an increase in the growth rate in regions like Latin America, Asia, and Africa. Dervis and Petri (1987) also reported that investment is not well correlated with growth in their study of the seven most rapidly growing countries (Taiwan, South Korea, Brazil, Thailand, Portugal, Greece, and Yugoslavia) for the 1965–85 period. The evidence here confirms this cross-regional empirical regularity.

What are the factors that account for the less clear positive relationship? Taiwan decided to pursue an industrial targeting policy after the first oil shock. Since most private enterprises were uninterested in joining the heavy and chemical industry development plan, the government and state-owned enterprises had to carry out most of the plan. As a result, the ratio of investment by state-owned enterprises to GDP rose to 9.1 percent in the 1976–80 period (see table 7.1).[2] Those state-owned enterprises, however, are known for inefficiency and mass corruption in undertaking investment projects. As a result, higher investment spending did not lead to higher real capital stock and higher pro-

1. Here investment is measured by fixed capital formation.

2. An enterprise is state-owned if the government has more than half of the ownership. According to Young's (1993) calculation, Taiwan's state-owned enterprises accounted for, on average, 46 percent of machinery and equipment investment during the 1951–91 period.

**Table 7.1** **Basic Statistics of Taiwanese and South Korean Development**

| Period | Taiwan | South Korea |
|---|---|---|
| | *Per Capita Real GDP Growth Rate* | |
| 1961–65 | 6.7 | 3.5 |
| 1966–70 | 6.3 | 7.3 |
| 1971–75 | 6.6 | 6.7 |
| 1976–80 | 8.2 | 5.7 |
| 1981–85 | 4.9 | 6.7 |
| 1986–90 | 7.2 | 8.7 |
| | *Inflation Rate (Implicit GDP deflator/CPI)* | |
| 1961–65 | 2.7/1.6 | 17.5/15.9 |
| 1966–70 | 4.6/3.9 | 14.7/11.8 |
| 1971–75 | 10.6/11.1 | 17.9/14.2 |
| 1976–80 | 8.5/8.6 | 19.1/15.9 |
| 1981–85 | 3.6/3.8 | 7.0/6.9 |
| 1986–90 | 2.3/2.2 | 5.4/5.3 |
| | *Ex Post Real Interest Rate* | |
| 1961–65 | 3.3 | −1.5 |
| 1966–70 | 1.5 | 12.2 |
| 1971–75 | −3.4 | −1.8 |
| 1976–80 | −0.7 | −1.2 |
| 1981–85 | 3.8 | 4.4 |
| 1986–90 | 3.4 | 4.6 |
| | *Investment-GDP Ratio* | |
| 1961–65 | 15.6 (4.2) | 13.1 |
| 1966–70 | 21.1 (6.0) | 23.4 |
| 1971–75 | 26.3 (8.7) | 22.9 |
| 1976–80 | 27.6 (9.1) | 30.1 |
| 1981–85 | 23.5 (6.9) | 28.5 |
| 1986–90 | 20.5 (4.4) | 30.8 |
| | *Export-GDP Ratio* | |
| 1961–65 | 17.0 | 6.0 |
| 1966–70 | 25.1 | 12.5 |
| 1971–75 | 41.7 | 23.9 |
| 1976–80 | 50.9 | 31.0 |
| 1981–85 | 53.1 | 35.4 |
| 1986–90 | 53.7 | 37.0 |
| | *Government Expenditure–GDP Ratio* | |
| 1961–65 | 12.3 | 13.9 |
| 1966–70 | 13.0 | 17.1 |
| 1971–75 | 12.0 | 15.4 |
| 1976–80 | 12.9 | 16.3 |
| 1981–85 | 14.9 | 17.0 |
| 1986–90 | 14.2 | 16.1 |
| | *Deficit-GDP Ratio* | |
| 1961–65 | 0.93 | 0.63 |
| 1966–70 | 0.69 | 0.72 |
| 1971–75 | −1.20 | 1.76 |
| 1976–80 | −1.19 | 1.66 |
| 1981–85 | 0.75 | 1.34 |
| 1986–90 | −0.02 | −0.30 |

*Sources: International Financial Statistics* 1994 (Washington, D.C.: International Monetary Fund, various issues); Taiwan, *Central Government Budget Yearbook* (Taipei: Directorate-General of Budget, Accounting, and Statistics, Executive Yuan, Republic of China, various issues).

*Note:* Numbers in parentheses are ratios of investment by state-owned enterprises to GDP.

ductivity, and many projects turned out to be failures because of poor decisions. In the first half of the 1980s, as the number of investment projects undertaken by the government and state-owned enterprises declined, the investment-GDP ratio decreased but had no negative impact on economic growth.

About the same time, the South Korean government adopted an industrial targeting policy with similar objectives. But it emphasized fostering large-scale firms in the private sector through extensive state support and close cooperation between large firms (*chaebols*) and the government. In the heavy and chemical industry (HCI) program, the government provided very generous industry-specific incentives, including tax breaks, preferential loans, interest rate subsidies for participating firms, and import restrictions on targeted industries. Targeted industries were overinvested and had a substantial level of idle capacity. The *chaebols* instructed to undertake the investment projects were never blamed for any poor performance. Further, whenever an investment project failed, state-owned banks assumed full responsibility and defrayed the loss with inflationary tax revenues.

Because an increasing number of investment projects in Taiwan and South Korea were decided on the basis of strategic considerations, those projects could no longer be evaluated according to the efficiency of investment fund allocation. Allocative inefficiency could explain the absence of a clear positive association for Taiwan and South Korea.[3] Further, as displayed in figure 7.1, the peaks of investment-GDP ratio in Taiwan occurred in 1975 and 1980, which lagged behind the peak in South Korea about one year. To stay close to its chief rival, state-owned enterprises and government in Taiwan often rushed to undertake investment projects when Taiwan found itself lagging behind in the race. Finally, according to Dollar and Sokoloff (1989) and Lin and Chan (1992), although enormous effort and resources have been devoted to the industrial targeting policies, those policies failed to affect the aggregate performance of the two economies measured in terms of productivity growth, structural change, and aggregate performance of exports.

Concerning the relationship between macroeconomic policy and GDP growth, four findings are worth mentioning. First, unlike the cross-regional evidence for Latin America and Asia in table 7.2, a negative relationship does not exist between GDP growth and inflation for Taiwan and South Korea. In theory, higher inflation reduces the efficiency of exchange mechanism. Once more resources are devoted to transactions and cash management instead of to production in an inflationary environment, higher inflation increases the actual cost of capital goods and hence reduces investment.[4]

3. The Singaporean government has also pursued an active industrial targeting policy. This policy allowed the Singaporean economy to catch up and surpass Hong Kong's initial lead in manufacturing. However, Young (1992) argued that the massive investment rates under this industrial targeting policy have led to the low total factor productivity growth in Singapore.

4. This mechanism has been developed by Fischer (1983) in a neoclassical growth model and by De Gregorio (1992) in an endogenous growth model.

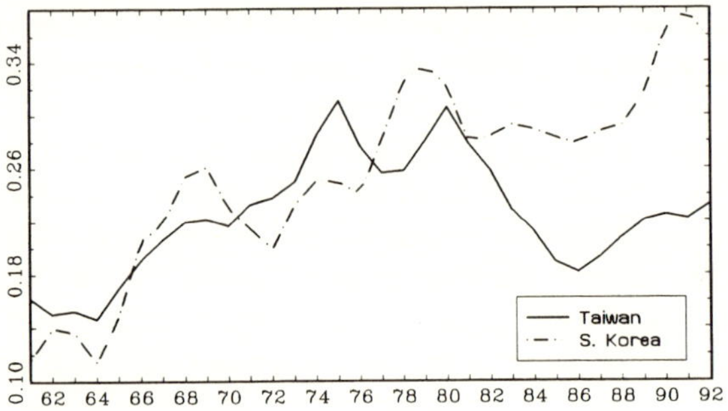


**Fig. 7.1 Investment-GDP ratio**
*Sources:* Taiwan, *Financial Statistics Monthly, Taiwan District, R.O.C.* (Taipei: Central Bank of China, various issues); South Korea, *International Financial Statistics* (Washington, D.C.: International Monetary Fund, various issues).

**Table 7.2 Inflation and Growth**

| Period | Per Capita Real GDP Growth Rate | Inflation Rate |
|---|---|---|
| | *Africa* | |
| 1965–73 | 1.1 | 5.2 |
| 1974–80 | 0.4 | 15.8 |
| 1981–90 | −1.0 | 18.9 |
| | *Asia* | |
| 1965–73 | 3.2 | 14.8 |
| 1974–80 | 3.7 | 8.9 |
| 1981–90 | 4.9 | 6.9 |
| | *Latin America* | |
| 1965–73 | 3.3 | 22.0 |
| 1974–80 | 2.5 | 53.0 |
| 1981–90 | −0.9 | 249.0 |
| | *Taiwan* | |
| 1965–73 | 8.0 | 4.3 |
| 1974–80 | 6.3 | 11.5 |
| 1981–90 | 6.1 | 3.0 |
| | *South Korea* | |
| 1965–73 | 6.9 | 10.9 |
| 1974–80 | 5.6 | 17.7 |
| 1981–90 | 7.7 | 6.1 |

*Source:* Africa, Asia, and Latin America numbers are taken from Fischer (1993). Taiwan and South Korea numbers are authors' calculation.

Second, table 7.1 shows that a less clear positive association exists between ex post real interest rates and per capita GDP growth rates in Taiwan than in South Korea. Markets for primary securities are generally underdeveloped in developing countries. Therefore, private financial savings are mainly currency and deposits. If the real rates of return on these assets become significantly negative as a consequence of inflationary finance or credit overexpansion, then private financial savings held in these claims will decrease and less saving can be channeled into productive investment through the formal banking system.[5] This could hurt economic growth. Taiwan has a significant informal (or unregulated) financial sector, which has been a major supplier of funds for small and medium-sized firms in Taiwan.[6] Although Taiwanese monetary authorities adopted a restrictive monetary policy, it is the informal financial sector that results in a less clear association. On the other hand, negative real interest rates in the periods 1961–65 and 1971–80 did not significantly hurt South Korean growth performance. When an economy has no access to international borrowing and lending, domestic saving becomes the only source of funds for investment. Negative real interest rates could hurt growth through a decrease in private financial saving. Since South Korea was able to borrow against its future trade surpluses in the international credit market, negative real interest rates had less impact on growth.

Third, a government that runs large budget deficits has bad macroeconomic policy if the budget deficits result from (1) an inefficient tax system and (2) out-of-control increases in government spending. According to table 7.1, GDP growth was negatively correlated with the budget deficit–GDP ratio for South Korea during the period 1961–80, while no such clear association exists for Taiwan during the period 1961–93. Taiwan's central government budget surpluses even stayed at the level of 1.2 percent of GDP in the 1970s, which provided cash reserves when the government ran huge deficits in the late 1980s (see fig. 7.2). The plots of the centered five-year moving averages of the GDP growth and budget deficit–GDP ratio in figure 7.3*D* suggest a positive association for Taiwan in the 1970s. That is, permanent low budget deficits do not necessarily lead to better growth performance, if they cause delays in the construction of infrastructure necessary for further growth.

Fourth, it is not the initial level of openness measured by the export-GDP ratio that accounts for the two-country difference in growth performance, a finding also supported by Dervis and Petri (1987). Further, the export-GDP ratios in Taiwan and South Korea rose sharply between 1963 and 1973, and then had a mild increase with volatile swings between 1974 and 1987. The subsequent decline made the two economies only slightly more open in 1991 than in 1973.

Both countries have encountered huge current account surpluses since the middle of 1980s. They were under pressure from the United States to reduce huge trade surpluses with the United States through structural adjustment. In response to this pressure, both countries adopted exchange rate appreciation

5. This mechanism was developed in the endogenous growth model by Roubini and Sala-i-Martin (1992).

6. According to Shea and Yang's (1990) estimate, private enterprises in Taiwan borrowed up to 34 percent of annual funds for investment and operations from the informal financial sector in the 1964–91 period.

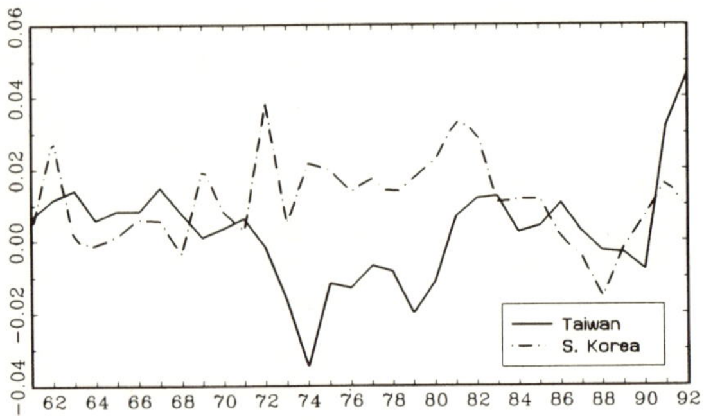


**Fig. 7.2 Government deficit–GDP ratio**

*Sources:* Taiwan, *Central Government Budget Yearbook* (Taipei: Directorate-General of Budget, Accounting, and Statistics, Executive Yuan, Republic of China, various issues); South Korea, *International Financial Statistics* (Washington, D.C.: International Monetary Fund, various issues).

and domestic spending expansion policies to downplay the importance of their export-led approaches. As displayed in figures 7.4 and 7.5, both export-GDP and current account–GDP ratios have steadily declined since 1987. When economic growth begins to rely more on domestic spending, the discipline on macroeconomic policy imposed by an export-led approach will be weaker. If our hypothesis is correct, then the decline in the export-GDP ratio will be a cause for concern about future macroeconomic performance because the government will lack external discipline in its policy making. Hence, imposing a sufficient set of constraints on both countries' policy making through the design of better institutions or the market mechanism will be crucial for their future growth.

Next we run the growth regressions for the period 1961–92. In general, the regression results in table 7.3 did not support the channels necessary to establish the link between macroeconomic policy and growth. The Durbin-Watson *d*-statistic has been argued to be a useful diagnostic tool for detecting misspecification in linear regression. According to the values of the Durbin-Watson *d*-statistics reported in table 7.3, it appears that most of the GDP growth regressions are not seriously misspecified. Several empirical findings emerged from the regression analysis.

First, unlike empirical results reported in Fischer (1991) and Levine and Renelt (1992), the investment-GDP ratio is not a significant factor in accounting for the per capita GDP growth rate over the past three decades in Taiwan and South Korea. Figures 7.3*B* and 7.6*B* plot the centered five-year moving averages of GDP growth rate and investment-GDP ratio since 1970. The plots exhibit a negative association between the two variables in each of the two decades, which is consistent with the assertion that a high investment-GDP ratio does not necessarily lead to better growth performance when investment does not have allocative efficiency.

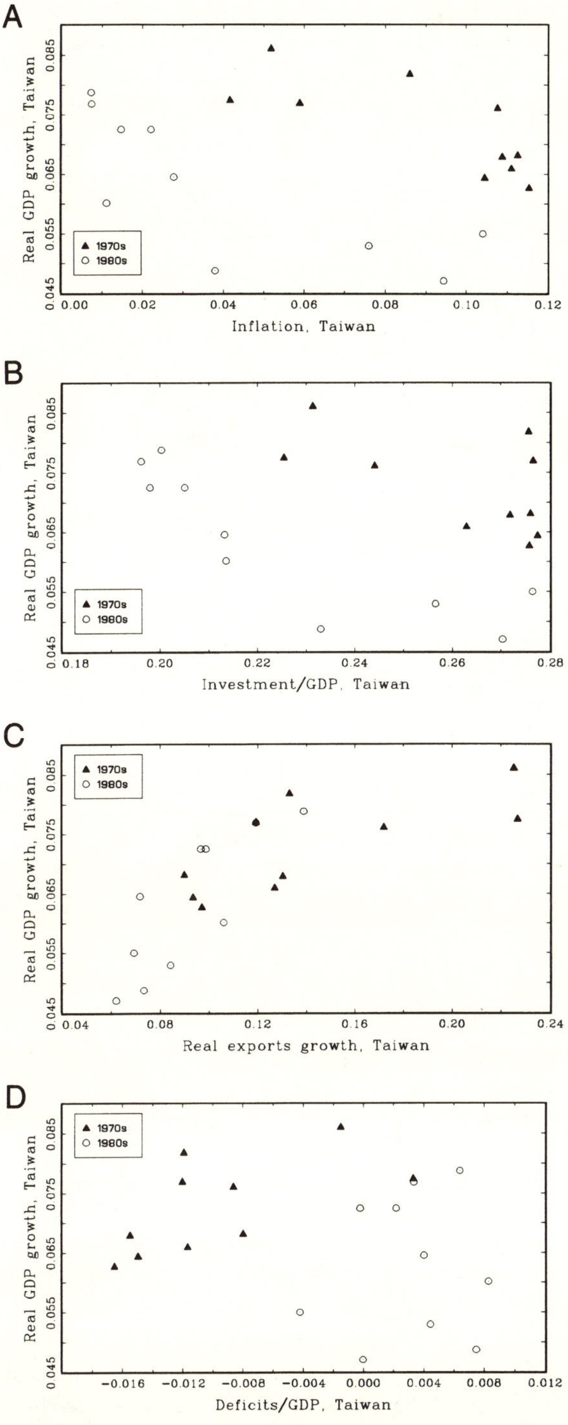


**Fig. 7.3 Taiwan: (*A*) inflation and GDP growth; (*B*) investment-GDP ratio and GDP growth; (*C*) Export growth and GDP growth; (*D*) government deficit–GDP ratio and GDP growth**

*Sources: A–C,* see sources for fig. 7.1; *D,* see sources for fig. 7.2.

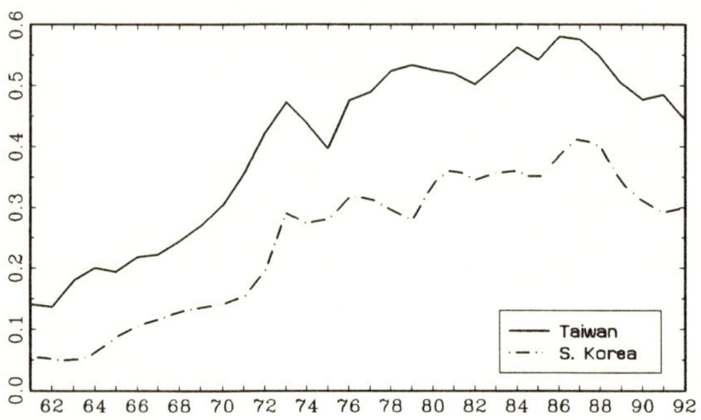


**Fig. 7.4 Export-GDP ratio**
*Sources:* See sources for fig. 7.1.

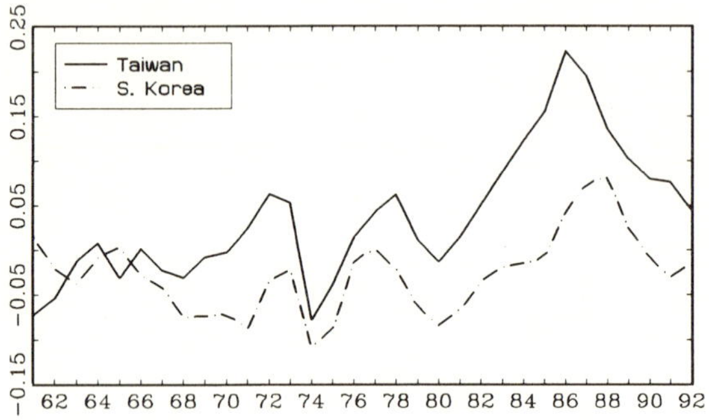


**Fig. 7.5 Current account–GDP ratio**
*Sources:* See sources for fig. 7.1.

Second, real export growth is the only consistently significant variable in all the GDP growth regressions. Exports played a key role in accelerating growth for the two countries. More precisely, both countries, like Hong Kong and Singapore, are fast-growing economies whose growth of exports outpaced that of GDP: Taiwan's (South Korea's) per capita real export growth rate of 14.9 percent (12.4 percent) accompanied an average annual growth rate of per capita real GDP of 6.5 percent (6.4 percent) over the 1961–92 period. Further, according to table 7.3, the statistical relationship between real export growth and GDP growth is more robust in Taiwan than it is in South Korea. As clearly indicated in the plots of the centered five-year moving averages of GDP growth and export growth in figures 7.3*C* and 7.6*C*, the fact that the relationship does not significantly shift over time generates a more robust statistical relationship for Taiwan. However, we cannot know how export growth led to such excellent growth performance without imposing and testing structural restrictions on export growth and GDP growth.

**Table 7.3** **Generalized Regressions of Per Capita GDP Growth Rates**

| Eq. | Constant | Inflation Rate | Investment/ GDP | Deficit/ GDP | Export/ GDP | Export Growth | Foreign Assets/GDP | D-W | $\bar{R}^2$ |
|---|---|---|---|---|---|---|---|---|---|
| | | | | *Taiwan (Sample period: 1961–92)* | | | | | |
| 1 | 0.08 | −0.19 | | | | | | 1.66 | 0.09 |
| 2 | 0.07 | −0.19 | 0.01* | | | | | 1.67 | 0.06 |
| 3 | 0.08 | −0.24 | | −0.27* | | | | 1.76 | 0.08 |
| 4 | 0.07 | −0.19 | | | 0.03* | | | 1.65 | 0.08 |
| 5[a] | 0.04 | −0.06* | | | | 0.26 | | 1.26 | 0.73 |
| 6 | 0.08 | −0.19 | | | | | −0.004* | 1.68 | 0.06 |
| 7 | 0.09 | −0.22 | −0.03* | −0.28* | | | | 1.75 | 0.05 |
| 8 | 0.07 | −0.17* | −0.06* | | 0.03* | | | 1.62 | 0.05 |
| 9[a] | 0.03* | −0.07* | 0.04* | | | 0.27 | | 1.26 | 0.73 |
| 10 | 0.07 | −0.20 | 0.02* | | | | −0.004* | 1.26 | 0.73 |
| 11 | 0.09 | −0.20 | −0.11* | −0.32* | −0.04* | | | 1.41 | 0.04 |
| 12[a] | 0.04 | −0.11 | −0.005* | −0.39 | | 0.27 | | 1.41 | 0.73 |
| 13 | 0.08 | −0.24 | −0.03* | −0.34* | | | −0.002* | 1.78 | 0.02 |
| 14[a] | 0.04 | −0.11 | | −0.38 | | 0.26 | | 1.41 | 0.74 |
| 15 | 0.09 | | −0.10* | | | | | 1.67 | 0.003 |
| 16 | 0.09 | | −0.12* | 0.06* | | | | 1.64 | −0.03 |
| 17 | 0.09 | | −0.18* | | 0.05* | | | 1.65 | 0.02 |
| 18[a] | 0.04 | | −0.02* | | | 0.27 | | 1.28 | 0.72 |
| 19 | 0.09 | | −0.12* | | | | 0.002* | 1.66 | −0.03 |
| 20 | 0.07 | | | 0.23* | | | | 1.60 | −0.03 |
| 21 | 0.06 | | | | 0.02* | | | 1.66 | −0.03 |
| 22[a] | 0.03 | | | | | 0.27 | | 1.28 | 0.73 |
| 23 | 0.07 | | | | | | −0.000* | 1.67 | −0.03 |
| | | | | *South Korea (Sample period: 1961–92)* | | | | | |
| 1 | 0.08 | −0.14 | | | | | | 1.90 | 0.04 |
| 2 | 0.06 | −0.11* | 0.07* | | | | | 1.89 | 0.02 |
| 3 | 0.09 | −0.09* | | −0.82 | | | | 1.80 | 0.11 |
| 4 | 0.06 | −0.09* | | | 0.07* | | | 1.93 | 0.05 |
| 5[a] | 0.07 | −0.13 | | | | 0.10 | | 2.09 | 0.14 |
| 6 | 0.09 | −0.09* | | | | | 0.02* | 1.94 | 0.07 |
| 7 | 0.06 | −0.05* | −0.10* | −0.95 | | | | 1.83 | 0.12 |
| 8 | 0.06 | −0.09* | −0.02* | | 0.08* | | | 1.93 | 0.02 |
| 9[a] | 0.05* | −0.12* | 0.05* | | | 0.11 | | 2.07 | 0.11 |
| 10 | 0.18 | −0.08* | −0.28* | | | | 0.08 | 2.07 | 0.16 |
| 11 | 0.06 | −0.02* | −0.02* | −1.04 | 0.10* | | | 1.92 | 0.14 |
| 12[a] | 0.04* | −0.06* | 0.12* | −1.00 | | 0.12 | | 2.05 | 0.17 |
| 13 | 0.16 | −0.04* | −0.19* | −0.78* | | | 0.06* | 1.97 | 0.16 |
| 14[a] | 0.08 | −0.09* | | −0.85 | | 0.09 | | 2.09 | 0.18 |
| 15 | 0.04 | | 0.10* | | | | | 1.81 | 0.006 |
| 16 | 0.04 | | 0.12* | −1.00 | | | | 1.81 | 0.14 |
| 17 | 0.04 | | −0.02* | | 0.10* | | | 1.88 | 0.03 |
| 18[a] | 0.03* | | 0.09* | | | 0.12 | | 1.85 | 0.08 |
| 19 | 0.18 | | −0.28* | | | | 0.08 | 2.01 | 0.12 |
| 20 | 0.07 | | | −0.90 | | | | 1.72 | 0.11 |
| 21 | 0.04 | | | | 0.09 | | | 1.87 | 0.06 |
| 22[a] | 0.05 | | | | | 0.10 | | 1.86 | 0.09 |
| 23 | 0.08 | | | | | | 0.03 | 1.88 | 0.08 |

[a]Sample period is 1964–92.

*Not significant at 10 percent level.

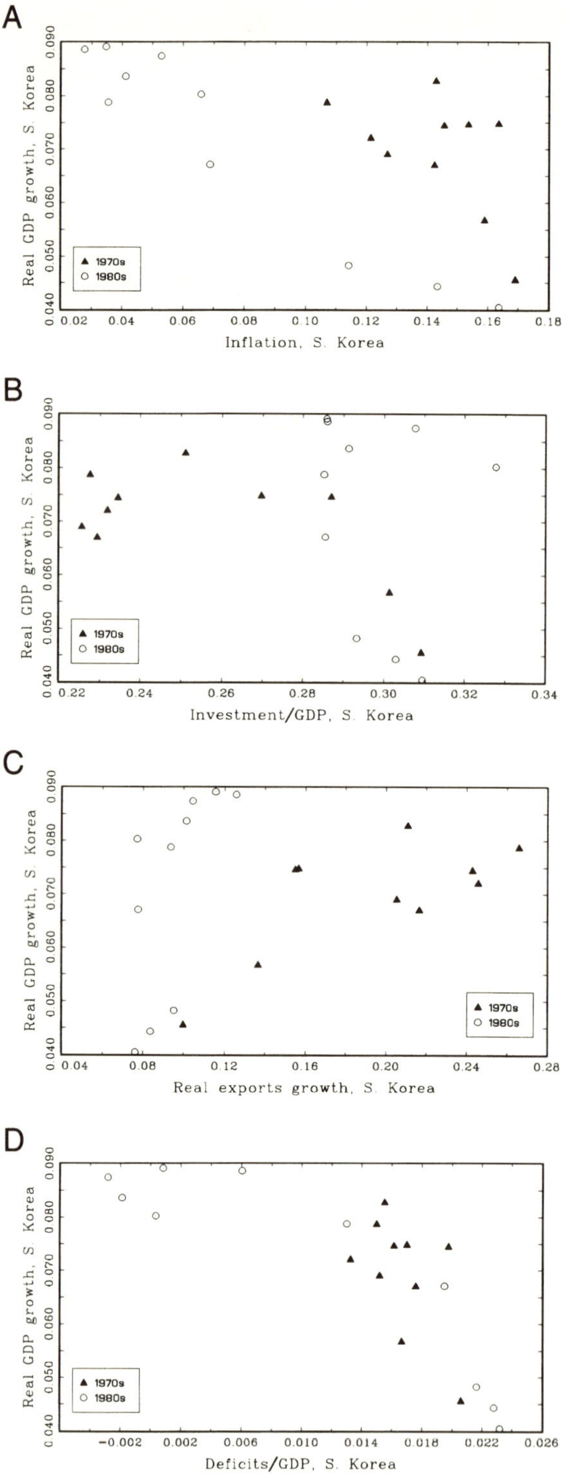


**Fig. 7.6 South Korea: (*A*) inflation and GDP growth; (*B*) investment-GDP ratio and GDP growth; (*C*) Export growth and GDP growth; (*D*) government deficit–GDP ratio and GDP growth**

*Sources: A-C,* see sources for fig. 7.1; *D,* see sources for fig. 7.2.

Third, the coefficient estimate for inflation rate has the expected sign in each GDP growth regression for both countries. However, the significance of inflation rate depends on the measurement of general price level used in the regressions. For example, suppose that the consumer price index was used to construct the inflation rate series. Then the coefficient estimate for inflation rate became insignificant when the per capita export growth rate was included in regressions. This suggests that export growth for Taiwan is a more significant factor in accounting for GDP growth than inflation rate is. This result does not hold for the implicit GDP deflator. While the use of the implicit GDP deflator has yielded less significant coefficient estimates in South Korea's regressions, the relationship between inflation and GDP growth is more robust, as displayed in figure 7.6*A* when the consumer price index was used to construct inflation rate. Recently, Fischer (1993) found that the high-inflation outliers in his cross-sectional growth regressions did not account for the overall negative relationship between inflation and growth. Rather, the negative relationship is stronger at low and moderate inflation than at high inflation. However, the two-country comparison between Taiwan and South Korea confirms Fischer's finding only when the implicit GDP deflator is used. Finally, the export-GDP ratio, which measures the openness of an economy, does not have a significant coefficient estimate in the whole period.

When international competition forces macroeconomic policy to be clearly set within the context of a commitment to growth through export promotion, it requires government to surrender its discretionary power in macroeconomic policy making. As a result, both macroeconomic policy variables and measures of growth performance become endogenous variables. The correlation between macroeconomic policy and GDP growth will not be stable across subperiods because such correlations merely reflect the predominance of some external shock in the period being considered. This explains why the regression outcomes fail to reveal any robust and significant statistical relationships. Recently, there have been disputes about the mechanism by which a causal factor affects the growth performance of the two countries. Some researchers emphasize macroeconomic policy as the mechanism, while others cite industrial policy. The unstable correlation patterns suggest that it would be difficult (if not impossible) to detect any meaningful causal factor using time-series data.

## 7.3 Fiscal Policy and Central Bank Independence

While the regression results indicate that export growth could account for GDP growth and that no clear correlation patterns exist between macroeconomic policy and growth performance, they do not tie down the channel of influence, nor the precise role of macroeconomic policy in export-led growth. One alternative approach would be imposing structural restrictions on growth and macroeconomic policy in econometric models. Then one can use those structural restrictions to identify the channel of influence. This approach also resolves the difficulty that a never-ending array of alternative plausible variables can be entered in the growth regressions.

The case study approach presents another, though less formal, method of characterizing the role of macroeconomic policy in export-led growth. Here we adopt this approach to describe the role of fiscal policy and the central bank in successful export-led growth. According to table 7.4, the Taiwanese and South Korean central banks receive relatively high scores of average legal independence compared to those in 16 industrial countries. But their average inflation rates in the period 1973–87 were higher than the rates of those countries for the following reason. For most developing countries, even though the law is explicit as to central bank independence, it cannot be fully implemented

**Table 7.4 Central Bank Independence and Aggregate Performance**

| Country | CBI Index[a] (LVAU) | Turnover Rate | Average Inflation (1973–88) | Standard Error Inflation (1973–88) | Per Capita Real GNP Growth Rate[b] (1973–87) |
|---|---|---|---|---|---|
| | | *Developed Countries* | | | |
| Switzerland | 0.68 | 0.13 | 3.1 | 2.1 | 1.4 |
| Germany | 0.66 | 0.10 | 3.4 | 2.0 | 1.8 |
| United States | 0.51 | 0.13 | 6.4 | 3.3 | 1.6 |
| Denmark | 0.47 | 0.05 | 8.6 | 3.3 | 1.1 |
| Canada | 0.46 | 0.10 | 7.2 | 2.8 | 2.8 |
| Netherlands | 0.42 | 0.05 | 4.3 | 3.2 | 1.1 |
| United Kingdom | 0.31 | 0.10 | 6.7 | 4.8 | 2.0 |
| Australia | 0.28 | n.a. | 9.5 | 2.7 | 1.4 |
| France | 0.27 | 0.15 | 8.2 | 3.5 | 1.5 |
| Sweden | 0.27 | 0.15 | 8.3 | 2.8 | 1.5 |
| New Zealand | 0.27 | 0.15 | 12.2 | 3.2 | 0.7 |
| Italy | 0.22 | 0.08 | 12.5 | 5.4 | 2.9 |
| Spain | 0.21 | 0.20 | 12.4 | 4.7 | 1.2 |
| Belgium | 0.19 | 0.13 | 6.0 | 3.4 | 1.5 |
| Japan | 0.16 | 0.20 | 4.5 | 4.1 | 2.6 |
| Norway | 0.14 | 0.08 | 8.2 | 2.4 | 3.0 |
| | | *Developing Countries* | | | |
| Chile | 0.49 | 0.45 | 51.8 | 59.1 | 0.7 |
| Argentina | 0.44 | 0.93 | 356.7 | 253.5 | −0.5 |
| Venezuela | 0.37 | 0.30 | 12.7 | 7.5 | −0.3 |
| Mexico | 0.36 | 0.15 | 50.2 | 39.3 | 1.2 |
| Taiwan | 0.34 | 0.23 | 7.2 | 9.9 | 6.5 |
| Malaysia | 0.34 | 0.13 | 5.1 | 4.4 | 3.7 |
| South Korea | 0.32 | 0.43 | 10.9 | 9.3 | 7.2 |
| Singapore | 0.27 | 0.37 | 5.4 | 7.9 | 6.1 |
| Brazil | 0.26 | n.a. | 273.3 | 203.9 | 2.4 |
| Thailand | 0.26 | 0.20 | 8.0 | 6.9 | 4.9 |

[a]LVAU = Unweighted aggregation of legal variables. Scores for central bank independence, except that for Taiwan, are from Cukierman (1992).

[b]Numbers in developing countries are per capita real GDP growth rates.

because the government tends to do things that may not be in strict accordance with the law. To reduce such bias, we use the actual turnover rate of the bank president proposed by Cukierman (1992) as an alternative measure. The turnover rates in both Taiwan and South Korea are higher than in the developed countries on the list in table 7.4, a result consistent with their inflationary performance.

A single index cannot characterize the dynamic relationship between central bank independence and the export-led approach, such as the ways in which the central bank resolves its conflicts with the executive branch when export-promoting policy affects price stability. According to Taiwanese central bank law, the objectives of central bank operations are (1) promoting financial stability, (2) ensuring the health of the banking system, (3) maintaining the stable purchasing power of its currency, and (4) assisting economic development without compromising the above three goals. Price stability is not the only objective.

The board of directors of Taiwan's central bank is responsible for the review of monetary and exchange rate policies. The ministers of finance and economic affairs are both permanent and voting members of the board, and the bank's president must attend the weekly cabinet meeting. Requests for more cooperation from the central bank in promoting export growth are often raised in the meetings. Even though central bank law requires the board to have regular meetings, the bank's president usually convenes the board meeting after important decisions on monetary and exchange rate policies have been made. The central bank's president occasionally testifies before the parliament at the request of a member of the parliament. The parliament has no say in the formulation and conduct of monetary and exchange rate policies, and the central bank does not hold any regular public hearings. These facts taken together put the central bank under the control of the executive branch of government.

Although central bank law did not explicitly ban government and state-owned enterprises from soliciting loans or advances from the central bank in Taiwan, the central bank did not extend such loans or advances after the great 1945–49 inflation.[7] However, the latest amendment of the central government bond issuance law in 1991 allows the central bank to directly purchase government bonds from their issuer, the Ministry of Finance (i.e., the monetization of public debts), with the parliament's approval.[8] This amendment has attracted attention because budget deficits have increased dramatically during recent years. If massive corruption in Taiwan's infrastructure construction and public

7. In the 1970s, the central bank even held a huge number of shares of a private company, Hwa-Long Polyester Co., after it rescued the company from bankruptcy using inflationary tax revenues under directives from some very high level government officials.

8. Initially, the executive branch wanted the amendment that the central bank can directly purchase government bonds without any consent from the parliament. However, this met with strong resistance from the opposition party. Both sides eventually compromised on this issue by adding the parliamentary approval precondition.

investment projects and the surge in civil service salaries continue, any future accelerating increase in budget deficits will put more pressure on the central bank to monetize the public debt.[9] In other words, fiscal policy is vital to the central bank's ability to maintain price stability.

On the other hand, South Korean central bank law explicitly states that one of the central bank's objectives is employing all feasible means to promote economic development. To assure this, the minister of finance not only presides over the monetary committee of the Bank of Korea, which is responsible for the design of monetary and credit policies, but also nominates the committee members. When a resolution of the committee is in conflict with the executive branch's position, the minister of finance can ask the committee to reconsider the resolution. Even if the committee refuses, the minister can bring the case to the country's president for the final decision. This puts the Bank of Korea under the direct control of the Ministry of Finance. The Bank of Korea is also allowed to directly purchase government bonds from the government, extend loans or advances to the government, and even hold government-guaranteed securities. The upper limit on the total balance of unpaid public debt, loans, and advances is set by the National Assembly.

Given that both central banks lack independence in operation, the most important factor that accounts for moderate and more stable inflation in both countries is the commitment to an export-led approach. For such an approach, the optimal policies are those maintaining and enhancing the international competitiveness of export goods. This commitment in turn imposes a set of constraints on macroeconomic policy that prevents the adoption of measures antithetical to export growth.[10] Other factors include the following: (1) the objectives in policy making must be well defined and easy to measure, (2) the costs of wrong policy making must be visible fairly rapidly, and (3) the degree of freedom in the feasible set of instruments must be sufficient for achieving any policy objective. When a decline in export growth is caused by significant mistakes in policy making, it makes the costs of mistakes highly visible to policymakers and private agents and therefore quickly puts pressure on government authorities to promptly adjust policy.

9. For example, the construction of the second northern Taiwan highway started in 1986 and is planned to be completed in 1997, with four years' delay. The original budget for this 120-km highway was NT$58.1 billion. However, the budget was inflated to an estimated NT$176.8 billion in 1993. During the period 1986–93, Taiwan did not experience very serious inflation problems, so inflation was not the reason for the surge in the budget. Massive corruption in the KuoMingTang (KMT) regime may be the explanation. Another example is the Taipei Mass Rail Transit System. The original estimate of NT$250 billion was nearly doubled to about NT$480 billion in 1993. Civil service salaries are also a major item of budgetary expenditure; they amounted to 31.8 percent of the total budget at all levels of governments in FY 1993. It has been difficult to cut this budgetary expenditure since civil servants and military personnel have been strong supporters of the KMT regime over the past four decades.

10. It is not clear why the governments in both countries decided to switch to an export-led approach in the 1960s. Balassa (1988) describes Taiwan's decision to adopt an export-led approach as an experiment.

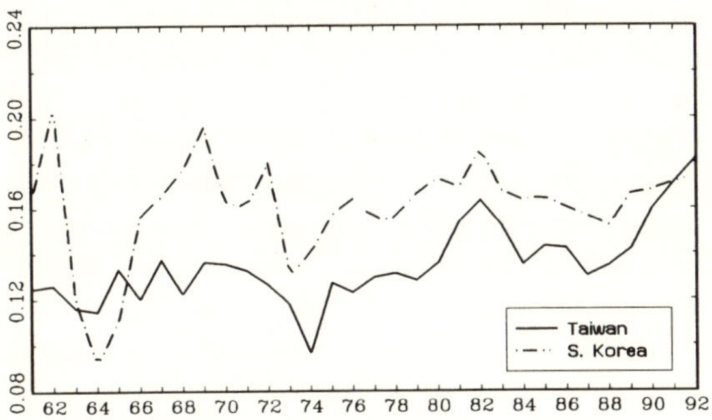


**Fig. 7.7 Government spending–GDP ratio**
*Sources:* See sources for fig. 7.2.

Figure 7.7 shows that government spending was kept under tight control in the period 1961–90, even with large budget surpluses in the 1970s for Taiwan.[11] South Korean budget deficits in the 1970s were mainly caused by generous tax breaks and fiscal incentives provided in its industrial targeting policy. The budget deficits returned to normal in the 1980s. On the other hand, both the six-year national development plan and the surge in civil service salaries contributed to huge budget deficits in Taiwan for FY 1990, 1991, and 1992. The government spending–GDP ratio began to climb in the 1980s, with a clearer upward trend in Taiwan. The upward trend shows that both countries began to use government spending as an instrument to stimulate the economy. Tight budgetary control means that governments do not have to resort to inflationary tax revenues as a source of funds.

For Taiwan and South Korea, sound fiscal discipline plays two roles in export-led growth: (1) It gives the set of instruments the maximum degree of freedom in achieving the export growth goal. (2) It allows the central bank to be more flexible in promoting exports without immediately jeopardizing price stability. The set of instruments for implementing macroeconomic policy includes monetary bases, interest rates, credit allocation, government spending, tax rates, and exchange rates. However, not all of them are free instruments in achieving any particular policy goal. The degree of freedom depends on the combination of monetary, fiscal, and exchange rate policies the government actually adopts. For example, if a government persistently runs budget deficits and the central bank collects inflationary tax revenues for the government, it is unlikely that government authorities can use export financing subsidies or fiscal incentives to maintain export profitability without generating higher gov-

11. Since both Taiwan and South Korea gave national security top priority in deciding their annual budgets, the national defense budgets occupied a significant portion of central government spending. Hence, the government expenditure–GDP ratio would not be as high as first thought once this factor is taken into account.

ernment deficits and inflation. That is, they cannot be free instruments in maintaining export profitability.

As argued in Sargent and Wallace (1981), for a given path of government budget deficits, tighter monetary policy lowers inflation today but at the cost of higher inflation in the future. That is, the central bank cannot effectively implement a tight monetary policy to bring inflation under control without considering the behavior of government budget deficits. On the other hand, Alesina (1989), Bade and Parkin (1985), and Parkin (1986) found that developed countries with independent central banks experience significantly lower inflation than developed countries whose central banks are under the control of the executive branch of government. As suggested in Alesina and Summers (1993), central bank independence might improve macroeconomic performance through two channels: (1) An independent central bank that is free from political pressure may behave more predictably, promoting economic stability and reducing risk premia in real interest rates. (2) To the extent that high inflation has adverse effects on economic performance either by creating distortions, encouraging rent-seeking activities, or raising risk premia, one would expect central bank independence to improve economic performance. The time inconsistency theory of inflation of the type developed in Kydland and Prescott (1977) also concludes that a more independent central bank could reduce the inflation rate.

Since the central bank has its most pervasive influence on inflation, interest rates, exchange rates, and the balance of payments, through the conduct of monetary and exchange rate policies, the main objective of most central banks in developed countries has been confined to maintaining price stability. As mentioned in the introduction, the two potentially conflicting roles of central banks in developing countries often make it difficult for them to maintain their independence. However, it is sound fiscal policy, not central bank independence, that accounted for moderate and more stable inflation in both Taiwan and South Korea.

As the export-GDP ratio continues to decline and the economy matures, government spending will become an important instrument because economic growth will rely more on domestic spending, and economic and social stability becomes the goal.[12] If higher government deficits are expected as a consequence of more aggressive government spending, a less independent central bank will be a cause of concern because a less independent central bank makes the monetization of public debt easier. Therefore, designing an independent central bank could be crucial for both countries' future economic performance.

12. Dervis and Petri (1987) also found that countries at the bottom end of the expenditure range in their cross-country sample generally increased their government spending, while countries at the top end decreased theirs.

## 7.4 Special Loan Policy

Although international competition imposes constraints on macroeconomic policy, optimal macroeconomic policy differs across the two countries, depending on the structure of the economy. The Taiwanese government has confined its role to providing infrastructure and other public goods. It used medium-term economic planning that set development targets, and those plans were generally indicative. The interactions between the economic bureaucracy and the private sector can be characterized as mutual adjustment rather than collaboration.

Even though small and medium-sized enterprises accounted for more than two-thirds of Taiwan's total exports, the government did not offer generous specific incentives to them. Since most of these firms cannot supply the information necessary to issue their own notes or publicly traded shares, the banking system and unregulated financial sector are their main sources of funds. Interest rate subsidies and preferential loans are probably the most important export-promoting instruments. The central bank offers export financing through state-owned commercial banks and specialized banks. Table 7.5 shows the significant difference between the rediscount rate on export loans and the regular rediscount rate. While export-financing policy increases the international competitiveness of exports by reducing borrowing costs, inflationary pressure is built up with export activities as long as funds for investment and business operations are scarce in the export sector and the export loan rate is lower than the market interest rate. As a result, a negative association exists between inflation rate and rediscount rate on export loans. When the economy encountered serious inflationary problems in 1974 and 1980, the central bank was forced to raise the rediscount rate on export loans. On the other hand, when the economy's export growth slows, the central bank lowers the rediscount rate on export loans to stimulate exports only if it will not immediately threaten price stability.

The central bank also set up a medium- and long-term credit special fund to finance infrastructure construction and investment projects in 1973. The source of funds is deposits of the postal saving system (PSS) at the central bank. Under the industrial targeting policy, the central bank extended preferential loans to qualified firms through commercial and specialized banks to promote machine imports. For example, it offered U.S.$600 million in preferential loans for financing major strategic export industries and technology-intensive industries in 1978. After extending those special loans, banks can apply for special rediscounts at the window of the central bank.

In the late 1970s and 1980s, huge trade surpluses and inappropriate exchange rate management forced the central bank to hold huge foreign exchange reserves. The special loan policy was criticized for its inflationary effects. When this policy posed a threat to price stability, the central bank abandoned

**Table 7.5 Principal Interest Rates on Central Bank Loans and Discounts (% per annum)**

| | Taiwan | | South Korea | | |
|---|---|---|---|---|---|
| Year | Rediscounts | Rediscounts on Export Loans | Discounts for Commercial Bills[a] | Loans for Exports[b] | Loans to Government |
| 1966 | – | – | 28.0 | 3.5 | 2.0 |
| 1967 | – | – | 28.0 | 3.5 | 2.0 |
| 1968 | – | – | 28.0–23.0 | 3.5 | 2.0 |
| 1969 | – | – | 23.0–22.0 | 3.5 | 2.0 |
| 1970 | – | – | 22.0–19.0 | 3.5 | 2.0 |
| 1971 | 9.25 | – | 19.0–16.0 | 3.5 | 2.0 |
| 1972 | 8.50 | – | 16.0–11.0 | 3.5 | 2.0 |
| 1973 | 10.75 | 8.75 | 9.0 | 3.5 | 2.0 |
| 1974 | 12.00 | 8.00 | 9.0 | 3.5 | 2.0 |
| 1975 | 10.75 | 6.00 | 9.0–13.0 | 3.5 | 2.0 |
| 1976 | 9.50 | 6.00 | 13.0 | 3.5 | 2.0 |
| 1977 | 8.25 | 5.50 | 9.0–14.0 | 3.5 | 2.0 |
| 1978 | 8.25 | 5.50 | 9.0–14.5 | 4.0 | 2.0 |
| 1979 | 11.00 | 9.50 | 14.5 | 4.0 | 2.0 |
| 1980 | 11.00 | 9.50 | 20.5–15.5 | 10.0 | 5.0 |
| 1981 | 11.75 | 10.00 | 14.5–10.5 | 10.0 | 5.0 |
| 1982 | 7.75 | 7.25 | 6.5–5.0 | 5.0 | 5.0 |
| 1983 | 7.25 | 7.00 | 5.0 | 5.0 | 5.0 |
| 1984 | 6.75 | 6.75 | 5.0 | 5.0 | 5.0 |
| 1985 | 5.25 | 5.25 | 5.0 | 5.0 | 5.0 |
| 1986 | 4.50 | 4.50 | 5.0–7.0 | 7.0 | 5.0 |
| 1987 | 4.50 | 4.50 | 7.0 | 7.0 | 5.0 |
| 1988 | 4.50 | 4.50 | 7.0–8.0 | 8.0 | 5.0 |
| 1989 | 7.75 | 7.75 | 8.0–7.0 | 7.0 | 5.0 |
| 1990 | 7.75 | 7.75 | 7.0 | 7.0 | 5.0 |
| 1991 | 6.25 | 6.25 | 7.0 | 7.0 | 5.0 |
| 1992 | 5.625 | 5.875 | 7.0 | 7.0 | 5.0 |
| 1993 | 5.50 | – | 5.0 | 5.0 | 5.0 |

*Sources: Monthly Statistical Bulletin* (Seoul: Bank of Korea, various issues); *Financial Statistics Monthly, Taiwan District, R.O.C.* (Taipei: Central Bank of China, various issues).

[a]Discounts on commercial bills from August 3, 1972, to March 29, 1982, are rates for prime enterprises.

[b]Includes loans for general exports and imports, loans for exports of construction and services, and loans for export preparation of agricultural and marine products.

it in the middle of 1989. Since a government budget deficit cannot have been a source of inflation during this period, export booms, together with this special loan policy, appear to account for moderate inflation in Taiwan.

On the other hand, South Korea established a powerful agency, the Korean Planning Board, that controls instruments for implementing economic planning and heavily intervened in the allocation of resources. The government provides domestic market protection, implements industrial targeting, issues permits of entry in many industries, and guarantees foreign loans for private firms. In general, the government acted as a partner in industrial targeting. "Korea, Inc." is an adequate description of the relation between government and big private enterprises.

In the 1980s, five large state-owned banks accounted for nearly all formal commercial credit. The banking system and the central bank were used to channel domestic and foreign savings or supply credits to the *chaebols*. The composition of special loans and discounts of the Bank of Korea in table 7.6 suggests a close partnership between government and the *chaebols*. Unlike the

**Table 7.6** **Special Loans and Discounts of Central Banks**

| | Taiwan (million NT dollars) | South Korea (billion won) | | |
|---|---|---|---|---|
| Year | Special Discounts[a] | Preferential Loans[b] | General Loans | Rediscounts on Commercial Bills |
| 1966 | 4,458 (44.1) | 4 | 0.3 | – |
| 1967 | 5,267 (45.2) | 8 | – | – |
| 1968 | 6,866 (49.3) | 14 | – | 1.2 |
| 1969 | 6,651 (46.1) | 32 | – | 2 |
| 1970 | 7,173 (49.7) | 48 | 21 | 16 |
| 1971 | 8,195 (49.9) | 71 | 6 | 23 |
| 1972 | 7,298 (43.0) | 100 | 34 | 39 |
| 1973 | 24,552 (57.8) | 216 | 8 | 44 |
| 1974 | 40,258 (60.9) | 308 | 214 | 90 |
| 1975 | 44,814 (57.2) | 380 | 167 | 102 |
| 1976 | 35,605 (35.3) | 461 | 127 | 73 |
| 1977 | 34,740 (21.6) | 457 | 131 | 75 |
| 1978 | 37,218 (15.5) | 775 | 153 | 82 |
| 1979 | 59,494 (21.1) | 1,002 | 620 | 168 |
| 1980 | 82,252 (28.6) | 1,533 | 396 | 297 |
| 1981 | 106,400 (55.7) | 1,713 | 870 | 593 |
| 1982 | 166,683 (73.6) | 1,750 | 1,210 | 960 |
| 1983 | 120,561 (66.5) | 1,739 | 2,258 | 955 |
| 1984 | 89,330 (73.2) | 1,786 | 3,976 | 1,063 |
| 1985 | 53,733 (93.7) | 2,044 | 5,463 | 1,321 |
| 1986 | 39,895 (74.1) | 1,927 | 6,116 | 1,292 |
| 1987 | 48,800 (84.6) | 1,133 | 7,144 | 1,620 |
| 1988 | 8,500 (92.0) | 527 | 6,417 | 1,862 |
| 1989 | 700 (0.6) | 639 | 5,921 | 2,588 |
| 1990 | – | 892 | 5,968 | 3,820 |
| 1991 | – | 986 | 6,093 | 5,488 |
| 1992 | – | 1,031 | 6,138 | 5,873 |
| 1993 | – | 1,055 | 6,570 | 5,178 |

*Sources: Monthly Statistical Bulletin* (Seoul: Bank of Korea, various issues); *Financial Statistics Monthly, Taiwan District, R.O.C.* (Taipei: Central Bank of China, various issues).

[a]Special discounts in Taiwan have been ceased in April 1989. Numbers in parentheses are special discounts as a percentage of total claims of the central bank on depository institutions.

[b]Preferential loans consist of loans for foreign trade and loans on collateral of export bills.

case in Taiwan, general loans extended by the Bank of Korea constituted the major component of its special loans and discounts. Those loans were allocated to specific borrowers under the industrial targeting policy. Table 7.5 also shows that commercial bank credit was offered at very low interest rates. Since the funds were strictly rationed, households and small and medium-sized businesses were forced into the informal financial sector, where lending rates exceeded bank loan rates by 20 percent or more.

Like most countries in the early stages of economic development, the gap between investment and domestic saving had to be filled with international borrowing. Nearly three-quarters of investment in the late 1950s and about half in the 1960s was financed from abroad. Before 1965, U.S. aid constituted a significant external financing source, which was channeled into private investment through government saving. As U.S. aid began to decline, the South Korean government first attempted to generate domestic saving as a main source of funds for investment finance. The government decided to undertake an interest rate reform in 1965 that was designed to channel household saving into investment finance through the regulated financial sector by offering positive real interest rates on deposits. The M2-GDP ratio rose substantially during the period 1965–72, reflecting an increase in the supply of funds through depository institutions. When the HCI program was launched in the 1970s, the South Korean government was under constant pressure from *chaebols* to lower real interest rates, and the country entered the negative interest rate era on August 3, 1972. The idea of channeling household saving into investment finance through depository institutions was then abandoned. The enormous difference in real interest rates between the regulated financial sector and its unregulated counterpart induced most household saving into the unregulated sector. The limited loanable funds in the regulated financial sector were strictly rationed to selected *chaebols* at negative real interest rates. As a result, the South Korean M2-GDP ratio has not risen since the middle of 1970s, and South Korea had to rely on international borrowing to finance its investment projects. South Korea's foreign borrowing assumed equal importance with government saving. Even though South Korea borrowed more extensively than Taiwan and other Asian developing countries, it maintained good control over its foreign debt. As shown in figure 7.8, Taiwan became a creditor in the late 1970s, while South Korea has been a debtor over the past three decades. However, net foreign asset–GDP ratios in both countries share similar trend properties.

To maintain negative real interest rates, the South Korean central bank had to tightly control the regulated financial sector. In the early 1980s, when the cost of capital rose abroad and foreign debt threatened to grow out of control, the South Korean government lifted the market entry restriction on contractual saving institutions to stimulate household and corporate saving. Those institutions, offering higher and safer returns than the unregulated financial sector, drew new funds into the regulated financial sector and evidently also increased the net flow of funds.

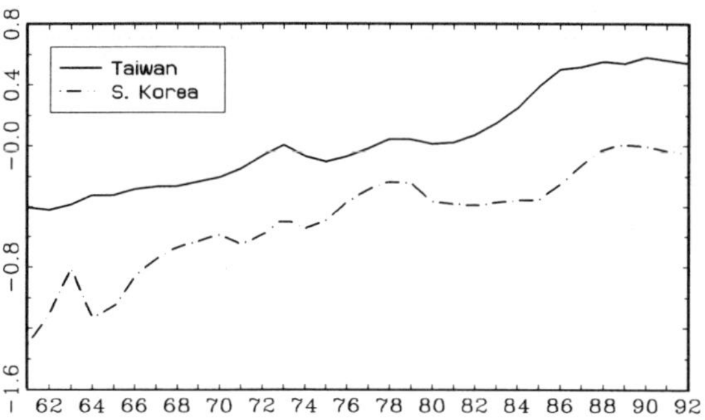


**Fig. 7.8 Foreign asset–GDP ratio**
*Sources:* See sources for fig. 7.1.

The special loan policies adopted by each of the two central banks reflects the difference in industrial organization between Taiwan and South Korea. Since firms in the Taiwanese export sector are small and medium-sized, the export financing policy, which was based solely on export activities, played an important role in the allocation of credit. Under this structure, direct intervention in allocating the funds for investment finance was not possible. This uniform incentive on the basis of export performance is a more efficient method of export promotion. Although Taiwan's planning agency cannot select technology with increasing returns, as its South Korean counterpart did, Taiwan's growth performance drew on a large pool of experienced entrepreneurs and human resources. For South Korea, the partnership between government and the *chaebols* created moral hazard problems. Under the industrial targeting in the 1970s, the *chaebols* were heavily leveraged with loan guarantees through state-owned banks, and the government in turn held responsibility for the failure of the *chaebols*' investment projects. The bailout certainty provided by the Bank of Korea through inflationary tax revenues induced excessive risk taking. Even after many efforts, the government has not been able to extricate itself from its relations with the *chaebols.*

## 7.5 Current Account and Exchange Rate Policy

The current account is the excess of saving over investment. Since saving and investment are outcomes of intertemporal decisions by households, firms, and government, current account behavior is best analyzed in an intertemporal macroeconomic model, and expectations of future events can be a decisive factor in determining its behavior.

Time-series data on saving, investment, and current account for Taiwan and South Korea are shown in Figures 7.9*A* and 7.9*B*. The current account–GDP ratio fluctuates around mean zero for South Korea, while it exhibits an upward trend for Taiwan. Different investment and saving behavior in the two countries

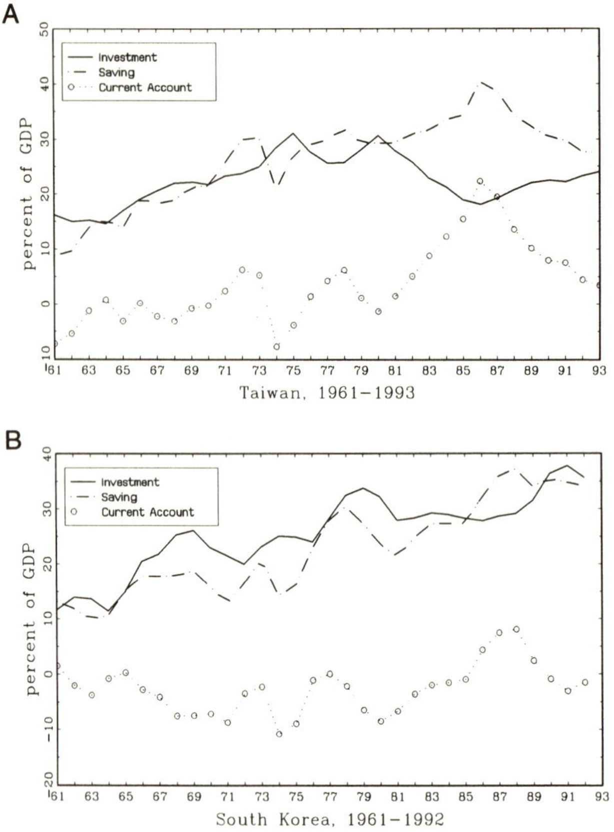


**Fig. 7.9 Investment, saving, and current account: (*A*) Taiwan; (*B*) South Korea**
*Sources:* See sources for fig. 7.1.

accounts for the difference: the investment-GDP and saving-GDP ratios move in concert for South Korea. But saving-GDP movement dominates current account–GDP movement for Taiwan.

Since most capital goods were imported in the early stages of economic development, domestic saving can be channeled into investment finance only to the extent that it can be translated into availability of foreign exchange. With limited capacity to repay their foreign debts, Taiwan and South Korea were forced to transform domestic saving into foreign exchange in the 1950s. But they demonstrated that rapid growth of manufactured exports was an alternative solution to the foreign exchange shortage in the early 1960s. Although the export-led approach emphasizes the importance of the "right" real exchange rate in promoting exports, the export success of these two countries was not a product of aggressive devaluations. That is, they performed well, not because they devalued aggressively to achieve the "right" real exchange rate, but rather because international competition disciplined macroeconomic policy so that the real exchange rate was “right” for export-led growth.

Taiwan and South Korea had different exchange rate policies because they took different approaches to domestic monetary policy. In the 1960s and 1970s, South Korea experienced inflation as a consequence of an improved balance of payments and an expansionary monetary policy. Once more rapid inflation at home than abroad decreased the real exchange rate, the government was forced to adopt an aggressive devaluation policy to offset the effects of inflation on the real exchange rates during 1960–80 as displayed in figure 7.10*B*. That is, exchange rate adjustment is not a free instrument under an expansionary domestic monetary policy. As a result, the exchange rate of won per U.S. dollar increased from 124.8 in 1961 to 607.4 in 1980. On the other hand, Taiwan adopted a restrictive monetary policy in the 1960s and 1970s.

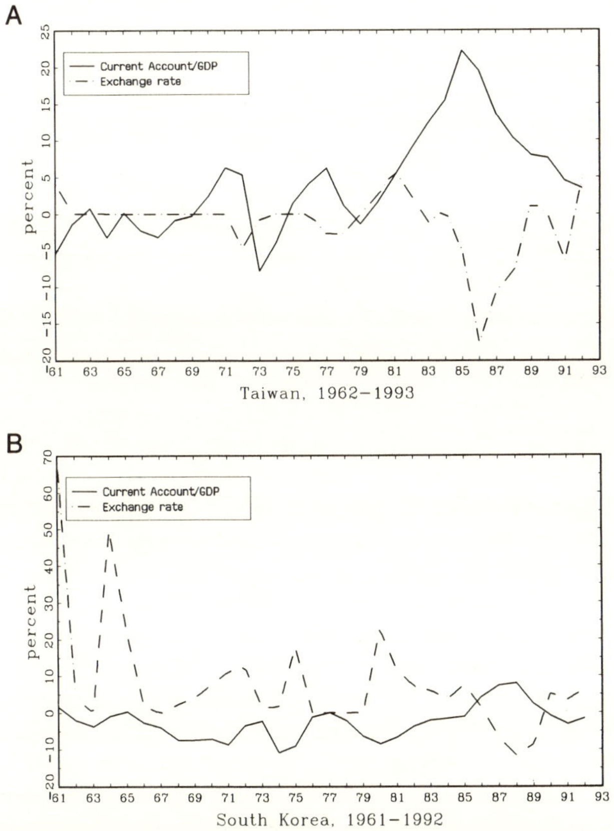


**Fig. 7.10 Current account and exchange rate change: (*A*) Taiwan; (*B*) South Korea**

*Sources:* See sources for fig. 7.1.

Figure 7.10*A* shows that when Taiwan encountered current account surplus problems in the period 1971–73 and 1976–79, only periodic adjustments of nominal exchange rates were necessary to maintain a realistic real exchange rate.

Even though the export-led approach takes advantage of opportunities for international trade, it also exposes the economy to external shocks. To insulate the domestic economy, most central banks hold foreign exchange reserves as an instrument to absorb the impact of external shocks on the economy. An appropriate level of foreign exchange reserves also enables the government to use better fiscal incentives to restore the external competitiveness of its exports when there is a temporary decrease in exports caused by external shocks.

For a small open economy with perfect mobility, investment, saving, and current account depend on the real interest rate in the world credit market. In theory, any pattern of correlation between investment and saving is possible, depending on shocks affecting the economy. However, this observation does not mean that investment is uncorrelated with saving over time. A prime instrument for a country to use in achieving its foreign reserve objectives is regulatory restriction of capital inflows and outflows. With imperfect capital mobility, a boom in investment opportunities will be financed less by foreign capital inflows and more by domestic saving induced by higher domestic interest rates. Hence, more imperfect capital mobility leads to a higher correlation between investment and saving. This may explain the positive correlation between investment and saving for South Korea, but offers no explanation for the almost zero correlation for Taiwan.

Overly large foreign reserves could cause a concern about the economy's long-run prospects when it results from imbalance between saving and investment. For example, when Taiwan's current account had huge surpluses in the 1980s, the central bank accumulated substantial foreign exchange reserves. As displayed in figures 7.5 and 7.11, the current account–GDP ratio increased from 1.5 percent in 1981 to 22.3 percent in 1986, while the foreign reserve–GDP ratio jumped from 17.0 percent in 1986 to 70.3 percent in 1987. Even the political uncertainties faced by Taiwan cannot justify the amount of foreign reserves held by the Taiwanese central bank in the 1980s (see fig. 7.11). Huge current account surpluses also signify serious misallocation of resources in the economy. Since private saving and private investment are outcomes of intertemporal decisions, the government can either change the decision environment in the private sector or use fiscal expansion to correct such misallocation.

The government in Taiwan began a series of adjustments, such as import liberalization, currency appreciation, government spending expansion, and the relaxation of outward exchange controls. Among them,currency appreciation is the most important adjustment measure taken by the government. Taiwan's central bank began to appreciate NT dollars in September 1985 under U.S. pressure. It ran a controlled crawling appreciation at a rate of NT$0.01 per day (about 7.8 percent per year) until December 1986. Then the adjustment took a

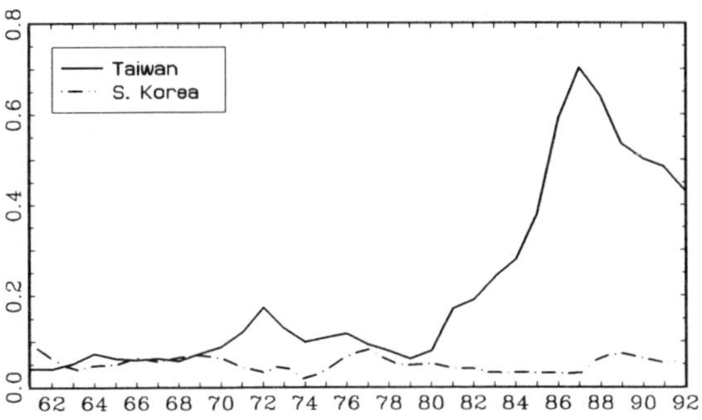


**Fig. 7.11 Foreign reserve–GDP ratio**
*Sources:* See sources for fig. 7.1.

less regular pace. Appreciation stopped for most of February 1987, but subsequent irregular appreciation brought the rate to NT$33.53 to U.S.$1 by the end of April 1987. Since the expected appreciation rate exceeded the 2 percent interest differentials in favor of the United States, the arbitrage opportunity attracted a flood of hot money despite tight controls still imposed on capital inflow. To maintain financial stability in Taiwan, the central bank imposed restrictions on the maximum amount of foreign liabilities that can be held by each bank in July 1987.[13] By the fourth quarter of 1989 the extent of appreciation had reached 26 percent. The nominal NT-U.S. dollar exchange rate appreciated from 29.9 in 1985 to 25.4 in 1992. Taiwan's nominal exchange rate had appreciated 60 percent in seven years. Although the central bank defended its appreciation policy on the grounds that small and medium-sized firms need longer periods of time to make necessary adjustments, the central bank under this policy incurred a huge capital loss in foreign reserves. As displayed in table 7.7, the central bank was the most profitable state-owned enterprise in Taiwan before 1986. Under this appreciation policy, the annual before-tax profit of the central bank shrank from NT$38.2 billion in FY 1986 to NT$1.7 billion in FY 1987. It is easy to conclude that currency appreciation is not optimal because (1) it is not an effective policy in changing the decision environment of the private sector, and (2) the capital loss and opportunity costs incurred in holding such huge foreign reserves are significant.

This substantial capital inflow handicapped the central bank in its pursuit of price stability. As clearly shown in table 7.8, the sharp increase in foreign reserves during the period 1980–88 caused increases in the monetary base (reserve money). To insulate the money supply from this increase in the monetary base, the central bank raised the reserve requirement for the banking sys-

13. More seriously, as hot money poured into the Taiwanese stock market, the Taiwan stock price index rapidly increased from 839.73 (base year 1966 = 100) in January 1986 to 12,495.34 in February 1990. During this period, about one-tenth of the population in Taiwan participated in stock market activities.

**Table 7.7** **Before-Tax Net Profit of Taiwan Central Bank (million NT dollars)**

| Fiscal Year | Central Bank | CPC | TPC |
|---|---|---|---|
| 1980 | 15,404 | −685 | 11,627 |
| 1981 | 17,458 | 2,784 | 17,232 |
| 1982 | 31,961 | 5,504 | 19,235 |
| 1983 | 38,541 | 8,138 | 17,234 |
| 1984 | 38,240 | 22,580 | 22,118 |
| 1985 | 47,844 | 19,470 | 32,543 |
| 1986 | 38,184 (10,000) | 30,668 | 27,987 |
| 1987 | 1,704 (43,560) | 52,204 | 34,733 |
| 1988 | 2,263 (47,873) | 59,954 | 35,964 |
| 1989 | 2,784 (64,774) | 64,874 | 33,784 |
| 1990 | 2,434 (62,480) | 33,822 | 29,263 |
| 1991 | 9,603 (41,367) | 22,483 | 31,150 |
| 1992 | 13,352 (26,104) | 23,367 | 33,741 |

*Sources: Yearbook of Financial Statistics, Taiwan District, R.O.C.* (Taipei: Central Bank of China, 1992); *Income Statement of Central Bank, Taiwan District, R.O.C.* (Taipei: Central Bank of China, 1993).

*Notes:* Numbers in parentheses are capital losses of foreign reserves. CPC: China Petroleum Co., Ltd. TPC: Taiwan Power Co., Ltd.

**Table 7.8** **Changes in Monetary Base (% per annum)**

| Year | Monetary Base | Net Foreign Asset | Net Domestic Asset |
|---|---|---|---|
| 1981 | 22.4 | 88.3 | −66.0 |
| 1982 | 8.5 | 16.6 | −8.1 |
| 1983 | 16.0 | 54.6 | −38.6 |
| 1984 | 13.4 | 53.9 | −40.0 |
| 1985 | 14.7 | 77.7 | −63.0 |
| 1986 | 28.9 | 234.9 | −196.0 |
| 1987 | 27.1 | 192.1 | −165.0 |
| 1988 | 26.5 | 5.3 | 21.2 |
| 1989 | 32.5 | −1.8 | 34.2 |
| 1990 | 0.2 | −10.1 | 10.3 |
| 1991 | 9.2 | 26.7 | −15.5 |

*Source: Financial Statistics Monthly, Taiwan District, R.O.C.* (Taipei: Central Bank of China, various issues).

tem in 1988 (table 7.9), and it increased open market operations in order to stabilize the level of monetary base. Another instrument used by the central bank were the deposits replaced by the PSS. For example, the deposits replaced by the PSS accounted for the 80 percent of total deposits in the PSS. It is not surprising that depository institutions held a large portion of their required reserves in T-bills, saving bonds, and certificates of deposit. Tables 7.8 and 7.9 indicated that those policies kept the monetary base under control.

Import protection was reduced in late 1986. For example, the complex sys-

**Table 7.9** **Reserve Requirements for Commercial Banks**

| | Demand Deposits | | Time Deposits | |
|---|---|---|---|---|
| | Taiwan | South Korea | Taiwan | South Korea |
| 1971 | 30 | 18 | 17 | 12 |
| 1972 | 30 | 19 | 17 | 14 |
| 1973 | 30 | 22 | 17 | 18 |
| 1974 | 30 | 19 | 14 | 15 |
| 1975 | 23 | 24 | 13 | 17 |
| 1976 | 23 | 24 | 13 | 17 |
| 1977 | 23 | 24 | 13 | 17 |
| 1978 | 28 | 27 | 13 | 20 |
| 1979 | 23 | 27 | 11 | 20 |
| 1980 | 23 | 14 | 11 | 10 |
| 1981 | 23 | 3.5 | 11 | 3.5 |
| 1982 | 21 | 5.5 | 11 | 5.5 |
| 1983 | 21 | 5.5 | 10 | 5.5 |
| 1984 | 21 | 4.5 | 10 | 4.5 |
| 1985 | 21 | 4.5 | 10 | 4.5 |
| 1986 | 21 | 4.5 | 10 | 4.5 |
| 1987 | 21 | 7.0 | 10 | 7.0 |
| 1988 | 23 | 10.0 | 11 | 10.0 |
| 1989 | 27 | 10.0 | 13 | 10.0 |
| 1990 | 26.5 | 11.5 | 12 | 11.5 |
| 1991 | 25.25 | 11.5 | 11.25 | 11.5 |
| 1992 | 25.25 | 11.5 | 10.875 | 11.5 |
| 1993 | 24.25 | 11.5 | 10.125 | 11.5 |

*Sources: Monthly Statistical Bulletin* (Seoul: Bank of Korea, various issues); *Financial Statistics Monthly, Taiwan District, R.O.C.* (Taipei: Central Bank of China, various issues).

*Note:* In 1988, the marginal reserve ratio for both demand and time deposits is 30 percent for South Korea, which is the ratio applied to the increment of each half-monthly average deposits compared with the first half-monthly average deposits of April 1989.

tem by which imports were valued for the purpose of assessing customs duties was simplified in August 1986, and the average tariff rate fell to 13.0 percent in 1988 and 10.3 percent in 1989. The Taiwanese government has planned further reductions in tariffs with the following goals: average tariff rates between 0 and 5 percent for raw materials, maximum 10 percent tariff rate on intermediate products, and about 20 percent on final goods.

Like Taiwan, South Korea relied on U.S. aid and military procurement to fill most of its foreign exchange requirements until the late 1950s. Because some U.S. payments were tied to local services valued in local currency, there was a strong incentive to overvalue the won. The won is estimated to have been overvalued by a factor of two. After the South Korean government adopted an export-led approach in the early 1960s, there were two devaluations to solve the overvaluation problem. Most effects of the first devaluation were offset by inflation, and the second devaluation was followed by the adoption of a managed float exchange system. This system remained in effect until 1974, when South Korea decided to undertake the HCI plan.

Unlike Taiwan, South Korean domestic saving was not sufficient to finance all investment projects, and hence extensive borrowing abroad was needed to accelerate Korea's development in the 1970s. In the first half of the 1980s, the international debt crisis raised the concern that South Korea might have overborrowed. Unlike the adjustment programs in most Latin American counterparts, the adjustment program implemented between 1980 and 1981 quickly restored growth, lowered the inflation rate, and reduced current account deficits. This adjustment program included a large devaluation and sharply contractionary monetary policy. The adjustment was successful because investment in the export sector generated the necessary capacity to repay foreign debt.

When a country experiences a temporary favorable external shock, the government of the country can choose between using current account surpluses to retire foreign debt or using the surpluses to acquire foreign reserves. Since Taiwan does not borrow extensively abroad or allow its citizens to hold foreign assets, the only option is to accumulate foreign reserves when a favorable temporary external shock occurs. On the other hand, since South Korea has a large foreign debt, it has the additional option of retiring foreign debt using current account surpluses. The South Korean government, under pressure, began to use exchange rate management to solve the problem of current account surpluses. The won appreciated only 5 percent against the U.S. dollar between the middle of 1986 and April 1987. But the won appreciated another 21 percent against the U.S. dollar before it depreciated again in 1989. Further, according to figure 7.10*B*, the exchange rate policy appears to partially account for current account–GDP movement in the 1980s. Other adjustments, such as import liberalization and expenditure expansion policies, also account for current account movement. For example, official figures indicate that the average tariff was lowered from 23.4 percent in 1983 to 19.3 percent in 1987, 18.1 percent in 1988, and 12.7 percent in 1989. The government planned further reductions in tariff rates by 1993. It also dismantled the import surveillance system that threatened protectionist action in the event that imports of certain commodities reached particular levels. As a result, the current account returned to deficit in 1990, while foreign exchange reserves stayed fairly stable without any significant trend.

## 7.6 Concluding Remarks

In this paper, we studied the role of macroeconomic policy in export-led growth. When a government adopts an export-led approach, international competition forces government policy to be clearly set within the context of a commitment to growth through exporting. Thus macroeconomic policy is forced to react optimally to any external shock. This may explain why regression results do not easily reveal any robust and significant statistical relationships between macroeconomic policy and growth for Taiwan and South Korea. Two issues remain to be resolved: first, the links between export growth and economic growth, and second, the mechanism under which a government is willing to fully commit itself to an export-led approach. One possible answer to the second issue is that once rapid growth begins, there is widespread acceptance of the export-led approach among private agents. This acceptance further enhances the credibility of the export-led approach.

In the case study, we argued that fiscal discipline not only gives macroeconomic policy instruments the maximum degree of freedom in achieving export growth goals but also allows the central bank to be more flexible in promoting exports without immediately jeopardizing its price stability goal. However, when the importance of the export-led approach as a source of growth begins to decline, government spending will become an important instrument because economic growth will depend more on domestic spending, and economic and social stability will become a social goal. A less independent central bank will be a cause of concern because it makes inflationary finance easier. Therefore, designing an independent central bank could be crucial for the future economic performance of both Taiwan and South Korea.

## References

Alesina, Alberto. 1989. Politics and business cycles in industrial democracies. *Economic Policy* 8 (Spring): 58–98.

Alesina, Alberto, and Lawrence H. Summers. 1993. Central bank independence and macroeconomic performance: Some comparative evidence. *Journal of Money, Credit and Banking* 25 (2): 151–62.

Bade, Robert, and Michael Parkin. 1985. Central bank laws and monetary policy. London: University of Western Ontario. Mimeograph.

Balassa, Bela. 1988. The lessons of East Asian development: An overview. *Economic Development and Cultural Change* 36 (3): S273–S290.

Cukierman, Alex. 1992. *Central bank strategy, credibility and independence: Theory and evidence.* Cambridge: MIT Press.

De Gregorio, Jose. 1992. Economic growth in Latin America. *Journal of Development Economics* 39:59–84.

Dervis, Kemal, and Peter Petri. 1987. The macroeconomics of successful development: What are the lessons? *NBER Macroeconomics Annual* 1:211–55.

Dollar, David, and Kenneth Sokoloff. 1989. Industrial policy, productivity growth, and structural change in the manufacturing industries: A comparison of Taiwan and South Korea. Paper presented at conference on *State Policy and Economic Development in Taiwan* Dec. 4–5, Taipei, Taiwan.

Fischer, Stanley. 1983. Inflation and growth. NBER Working Paper no. 1235. Cambridge, Mass.: National Bureau of Economic Research.

———. 1991. Macroeconomics, development and growth. *NBER Macroeconomics Annual* 5:329–64.

———. 1993. The role of macroeconomic factors in growth. *Journal of Monetary Economics* 32:485–512.
Kydland, Finn E., and Edward Prescott. 1977. Rules rather than discretion: The inconsistency of optimal plans. *Journal of Political Economy* 85 (3): 473–93.
Levine, Ross, and David Renelt. 1992. A sensitivity analysis of cross-country growth regressions. *American Economic Review* 82:942–63.
Lin, Ching-Yuan. 1988. East Asia and Latin America as contrasting models. *Economic Development and Cultural Change* 36 (3): S153–S197.
Lin, Kenneth S., and Vei-Lin Chan. 1992. Product quality, industrial organization and aggregate performance of exports. *Research in Asian Economic Studies* 4A:123–44.
Parkin, Michael. 1986. Domestic monetary institutions and deficits. In *Deficits,* ed. James M. Buchanan, Charles K. Rowley, and Robert D. Tollison. Oxford: Blackwell.
Roubini, Nouriel, and Xavier Sala-i-Martin. 1992. Financial repression and economic growth. *Journal of Development Economics* 39:5–30.
Sargent, Thomas J., and Neil Wallace. 1981. Some unpleasant monetarist arithmetic. *Federal Reserve Bank of Minneapolis Quarterly Review* 10, no. 3 (Fall): 1–17.
Shea, Jia-Dong, and Ya-Hwei Yang. 1990. Financial system and the allocation of investment funds. CIER Discussion Paper no. 9001. Taipei: Chung-Hua Institution for Economic Research.
Young, Alwyn. 1992. A tale of two cities: Factor accumulation and technical change in Hong Kong and Singapore. *NBER Macroeconomics Annual* 6:13–63.
———. 1993. The tyranny of numbers: Confronting the statistical realities of the East Asian growth experience. Working paper. Cambridge, Mass.: Sloan School of Management, MIT.

## Comment Amina Tyabji

This paper examines the role of macroeconomic policy in the successful export-led growth of two first-tier East Asian newly industrialized economies (NIEs), namely, Taiwan and South Korea (hereafter Korea). The main thrust of the argument rests on the premise that in order to maintain export competitiveness, the economy and polity must make optimal policy choices that "discipline macroeconomic policy." Sound fiscal policies, which are defined to include temporary budget deficits, are seen to be necessary because they permit the central bank to implement export-promoting policies without immediately jeopardizing price stability. Lin, Lee, and Huang also take up the issue of central bank independence and its link to inflation. The paper covers a broad range of issues, such as whether macroeconomic policies matter, which facets of these policies matter, and so on. My comments are organized according to the sections of the paper.

Section 7.2 presents some stylized facts on macroeconomic policy and growth in the two countries. Growth theories regard investment as a crucial link between macroeconomic policy and long-run growth. However, this asso-

Amina Tyabji is senior lecturer in the Department of Economics and Statistics, National University of Singapore.

ciation does not hold across subperiods for Taiwan and Korea. This is in conformity with the evidence reported in Fischer (1991) and Dervis and Petri (1987).

The authors attribute the above finding for Taiwan to increased investment by state-owned enterprises, well known for "inefficiency and massive corruption." For Korea, they attribute it to government targeting of heavy chemical industries, which led to substantial idle capacity and subsequent bailing out by state-owned banks. However, the lack of positive association could also be due to changes in incremental capital output ratio (which would seem to be the case in Korea) and to other structural changes.

The authors regard the industrial targeting policies of the two countries as failures when measured in terms of exports, productivity performance, and structural change. Does this imply that winners are more difficult to pick at more advanced stages of economic development? To put it differently, are the results of government intervention related to the stage of economic development? Do the type, form, and degree of intervention matter at different stages?

In addition to the above, there are four other findings:

1. Contrary to theoretical expectations and empirical findings for Latin America and Asia, a negative relationship does not exist between growth and inflation in Korea and Taiwan. There is also no clear association between ex post real interest rates and per capita GDP growth rates in different subperiods. This is attributed to the availability of alternative sources of finance, from the informal sector in Taiwan and from external borrowing in Korea.

2. Large budget deficits can be expected to exert a negative impact on GDP. The data show that this was true for Korea during 1961–80, but not to the same extent for Taiwan. It should be noted, however, that for both countries, deficits/surpluses are extremely low. Thus their impact is unlikely to be significant. How do government expenditure–GDP ratios or deficit/surplus-GDP ratios compare internationally? What about the composition of government spending? Would this make a difference?

3. The paper argues that sound fiscal policy matters for economic growth, and soundness is defined to include low budget deficits. Yet the authors write, "That is, permanent low budget deficits do not lead to better growth performance, if they cause delays in the construction of infrastructure necessary for further growth." It would seem, therefore, that it is not deficits per se, but rather the kind of government expenditure, that also matters.

4. The early fiscal discipline in these two countries has or is likely to weaken because of external pressure to reduce current account surpluses. The resultant currency appreciation, with its impact on exports, demands policy shifts to increase domestic spending, to be achieved through fiscal stimuli.

To verify the stylized facts, the writers run growth regressions for the period 1961–92. By and large the results are not very robust. This may be the consequence of model specification. The authors claim that a commitment to growth through exports endogenizes macropolicy variables and measures of economic growth. This according to them explains the poor results. In addition, their empirical findings are at odds with those of others, such as Fischer (1991) and Levine and Renelt (1992), regarding the link between investment and per capita GDP growth.

While real export growth does matter, the writers note that "we cannot know how export growth led to such excellent growth performance without imposing and testing structural restrictions on export growth and GDP growth." A nonrigorous mechanism is however explained in section 7.3 of the paper.

In section 7.3, macroeconomic policies, that is, fiscal and monetary policies, are examined in the context of central bank independence. On conceptual grounds it could be argued that central bank independence does have the potential to improve long-run inflationary performance. The empirical evidence, however, is far from compelling.

The authors, following Cukierman (1992), compute an index of central bank independence for Korea and Taiwan. While both received relatively high scores for average legal independence compared to 16 industrial countries (table 7.4), their average inflation rates in the period 1973–87 are among the highest for those countries. This they attribute to difficulty in implementing the relevant laws. As an alternative explanatory factor, they use the actual turnover rate of central bank presidents to explain the inflation rate. However, as can be observed from table 7.4, the evidence goes both ways.

Perhaps the real issue is not central bank independence per se, but rather the recognition of the need to coordinate fiscal and monetary policies if price level stability is to be preserved. There is an accompanying need to develop government securities markets as an alternative to financing from central banks.

Nevertheless, recent amendments to Taiwan's central bank legislation allow debt monetization, which when viewed in the light of recent increases in budget deficits could result in higher inflation.

Section 7.4, on special loan policies, examines the measures used to stimulate exports in the two economies. In the main these took the form of preferential credit to targeted industries and activities. This in any event is not unique. The difference, however, is that such credit was and is specifically targeted to export activities, with more direct measures being employed in Korea. Also in both countries, the main channels were state-owned commercial banks, although there is no reason why such policy cannot be executed where banks are privately owned—the case in many developing economies.

Policies of this nature smack of financial repression, a subject of a rather long-standing but inconclusive debate in the development literature. In Korea and Taiwan, subsidized credit was directed to growth sectors, specifically exports. As firms producing for the export market are more efficient than those producing for sheltered domestic markets, subsidized credit enhanced economic growth. Or as Stiglitz would put it, the social returns from such regulations exceeded the private returns.

Section 7.5 of the paper is concerned with current account and exchange rate policy. In the first part, it is argued that while the exports of manufactured goods yielded the necessary foreign exchange for economic growth, the robust export performance was not the result of aggressive devaluation. The second part is a chronology of policy changes and the problems of dealing with export success—current account surpluses. For Taiwan, the paper describes the monetary measures the country's central bank took to deal with the huge increase in foreign reserves. One of the measures cited is not very clear, "the deposits replaced by the PSS [postal saving system]." It would have been useful to explain this in greater detail and to compare it with other conventional measures.

In the early 1980s, together with other less-developed countries, Korea had a large external debt. Its success in dealing with that problem is attributed in this paper to devaluation and restrictive monetary policy. Undoubtedly, export orientation generated the necessary foreign exchange. However, fiscal policies which contribute to export and income growth also assist debt repayment. Since much of the focus of the paper is on the role of fiscal policy, it is surprising that the link is not explored here.

Since the mid-1980s both Taiwan and Korea have been under pressure to appreciate their currencies. Both have liberalized imports and employed other measures to stimulate domestic demand, both private and public. The paper does not mention the upsurge in their foreign direct investment to mitigate the dampening effects of the appreciation.

The first-tier East Asian NIEs, including Taiwan and Korea, relied on manufactured exports to fuel economic growth. This export promotion/orientation took place in a stable macroeconomic environment. By itself this would not have been enough. Nonmacroeconomic policies (which the paper does not mention), such as the trade and payments regime, labor market conditions and policies, infrastructure, the role and efficiency of the public sector, and human resource development, were equally important. All these nonmacroeconomic policies also involve government intervention. Where such intervention led to wealth creation instead of rent seeking and reduced distortions, its contribution was positive.

## References


Cukierman, Alex. 1992. *Central bank strategy, credibility and independence: Theory and evidence.* Cambridge: MIT Press.

Dervis, Kemal, and Peter Petri. 1987. The macroeconomics of successful development: What are the lessons? *NBER Macroeconomics Annual* 2:211–55.

Fischer, Stanley. 1991. Macroeconomics, development and growth. *NBER Macroeconomics Annual* 5:329–64.

Levine, Ross, and David Renelt. 1992. A sensitivity analysis of cross-country growth regressions. *American Economic Review* 82:942–63.

# 8 Money and Prices in Taiwan in the 1980s

Ya-Hwei Yang and Jia-Dong Shea

## 8.1 Introduction

Taiwan's experience with economic development has been unique and surprising in many respects. In the 1980s, another surprising phenomenon took place in Taiwan. As reported in table 8.1, the average annual growth rate of the money supply in the period 1981–89 was as high as roughly 20 percent, while the GDP deflator and CPI had grown only 2.99 and 3.10 percent, respectively, on average. The WPI had even fallen by an average rate of 0.49 percent annually. If we consider only the years 1986 and 1987, the difference between the growth rates of the money supply and those of prices is even more astonishing. In these two years, the M1A, M1B, and M2 supplies increased 39.24, 44.62, and 25.93 percent, respectively, on average, while the GDP deflator, WPI, and CPI increased merely 1.94, −3.30, and 0.84 percent.[1]

A high growth rate in the money supply accompanied by a low inflation rate was not a new experience in Taiwan. As table 8.1 shows, during the period 1962–80, the money supply in Taiwan increased by an average annual rate of around 21–24 percent, while domestic prices only grew by an average rate of

Ya-Hwei Yang is research fellow and director of the Taiwan Economy Division at Chung-Hua Institution for Economic Research. Jia-Dong Shea is research fellow and director of the Institute of Economics, Academia Sinica.

The authors appreciate comments from Takatoshi Ito, Anne Krueger, Kenjiro Hirayama, Muthi Samudram, Wing Woo, Daisy Day, A. L. Lin, T. Y. Lin, and J. F. Lin on the first draft of this paper. A discussion with Chung-Ming Kuan was especially valuable.

1. M1A includes currency outside monetary institutions, checking accounts, and passbook deposits. M1B includes M1A and passbook savings deposits. M2 includes M1B, time deposits, time savings deposits (including deposits replaced by the postal savings system), foreign currency deposits, foreign exchange proceeds deposits, foreign exchange trust funds, negotiable certificates of deposit, and foreign currency certificates of deposit of enterprises and individuals in monetary institutions; in addition, bank debentures issues, savings bonds, and Treasury bills–B issued by the central bank held by enterprises and individuals are included.

**Table 8.1** **Annual Growth Rate of Prices and Money Supply (%)**

| | Prices | | | Money Supply | | |
|---|---|---|---|---|---|---|
| Period or Year | GDP Deflator | WPI | CPI | M1A | M1B | M2 |
| 1962–70[a] | 3.62 | 1.86 | 2.92 | 17.21 | 18.15 | 21.10 |
| 1971–80[a] | 10.32 | 10.66 | 11.07 | 24.04 | 26.34 | 26.44 |
| 1962–80[a] | 7.14 | 6.49 | 7.21 | 20.80 | 22.46 | 23.91 |
| 1981–89[a] | 2.99 | −0.49 | 3.10 | 18.13 | 20.88 | 21.98 |
| 1981–93[a] | 3.22 | −0.46 | 3.31 | 13.97 | 17.01 | 19.90 |
| 1981 | 12.07 | 7.63 | 16.33 | 9.03 | 13.79 | 18.65 |
| 1982 | 3.43 | −0.19 | 2.96 | 5.91 | 14.60 | 24.29 |
| 1983 | 1.91 | −1.17 | 1.37 | 14.73 | 18.44 | 26.42 |
| 1984 | 0.89 | 0.46 | −0.03 | 5.75 | 9.25 | 20.06 |
| 1985 | 0.59 | −2.59 | −0.16 | 7.93 | 12.22 | 23.38 |
| 1986 | 3.38 | −3.34 | 1.16 | 46.14 | 51.42 | 25.29 |
| 1987 | 0.49 | −3.26 | 0.52 | 32.34 | 37.82 | 26.56 |
| 1988 | 1.07 | −1.56 | 1.29 | 23.41 | 24.37 | 17.86 |
| 1989 | 3.11 | −0.37 | 4.40 | 17.89 | 6.06 | 15.26 |
| 1990 | 3.80 | −0.61 | 4.13 | −9.45 | −6.62 | 9.86 |
| 1991 | 3.90 | 0.16 | 3.62 | 6.61 | 12.08 | 19.28 |
| 1992 | 3.72 | −3.67 | 4.47 | 8.34 | 12.43 | 16.60 |
| 1993 | 3.53 | 2.51 | 2.94 | 12.95 | 15.28 | 15.13 |

*Sources:* GDP deflator (PGDP), *Quarterly National Income Statistics in Taiwan Area, R.O.C.* (Taipei: Directorate-General of Budget, Accounting and Statistics [DGBAS], Executive Yuan, Republic of China, various issues); WPI and CPI, *Commodity-Price Statistics Monthly in Taiwan Area, R.O.C.* (Taipei: DGBAS, Executive Yuan, Republic of China); M1A, M1B, and M2, *Financial Statistics Monthly, Taiwan District, R.O.C.* (Taipei: Central Bank of China, various issues).

[a]Average annual value.

about 6.5–7.2 percent. Economists in Taiwan used to explain this phenomenon by pointing out that the income elasticity of money demand in Taiwan was as high as 1.2–1.5 and the economic growth rate was also quite high.[2] By multiplying the average economic growth rate of 1962–80, 9.8 percent, by the income elasticity, 1.5, they argued that economic growth alone had produced an increase in real money demand of 14.7 percent annually on average, which left a discrepancy of about 6–9 percent with the average annual growth rate of the money supply, 21–24 percent. This discrepancy is roughly equal to the average rate of increase in the deflator of 7.14 percent in this period.

2. Several scholars have put forward different views to explain this high income elasticity of money demand. Tsiang (1977) argues that import and export transactions create extra demand for money that is not taken care of by the national income variable. Shea (1983) shows that the processes of monetarization, financial development, and specialization in the production process have all contributed to the high income elasticity of money demand in Taiwan. Further, as Wing Woo pointed out during the discussion at the EASE conference in Singapore, Taiwanese residents were prohibited from holding foreign assets before the mid-1980s, so that a large proportion of accumulated wealth must have taken the form of money. This also helps to explain Taiwan's high income elasticity of money demand.

This line of argument explains the relationship between the money supply and prices during 1962–80 in Taiwan reasonably well. However, its power to explain the experience in the 1980s seems much weaker. In 1981–89, if the income elasticity of money demand remained at 1.5, an 8.0 percent average growth rate of real GDP should have increased real money demand by 12 percent. Subtracting from the average growth rate of the money supply of about 20 percent the average growth rate of real money demand and the average growth rate of the GDP deflator of about 3 percent, we obtain a significant discrepancy of 5 percent. Thus, we need other factors to explain why money demand in this period increased at a higher rate and created this discrepancy. Alternatively, we need to examine whether there were other factors beneficial to the stabilization of prices.

This issue has attracted the attention of numerous scholars in Taiwan. Many of them, such as Wu (1989), Huang and Ouyang (1989), Lin and Lee (1989), Shih (1990), Chiu and Hou (1993), and Wu and Shea (1993), emphasize that prosperous stock and real estate transactions in this period created a great deal of transactional demand for money.[3] Although there are no official data on the value of real estate transactions, table 8.2 shows that the total trading value of listed stocks increased drastically from NT$195.2 billion in 1985 to NT$25,408 billion in 1989.

It is generally believed that a large proportion of the investment in stocks and real estate in this period was motivated by speculation. In fact, this period, especially the latter half of the 1980s, can be called an era of speculation. In addition to speculative transactions in stocks and real estate, other gambling activities, such as the "everybody-happy lotto" (*ta-chia-lo*) in the first half of the 1980s and the "six-combination lotto" (*liou-her-tsai*) in the latter part of the 1980s, were also very popular. Although, again, official data are unavailable on the volume of these gambling activities, they absorbed an enormous amount of money balances.

In addition, since the mid-1980s, Taiwan's currency has been "locally internationalized" in the sense that it has been circulating in Southeast Asian countries and in part of mainland China, especially the newly developing southeastern provinces. There are also reports that some commodity or real estate transactions in mainland China between Taiwanese businessmen have been paid in Taiwanese money in Taiwan. These factors have also created additional demand for money in Taiwan.

3. Empirical evidence supporting the argument that the trading value of stocks would "absorb" money can also be found in Field (1984), Wenninger and Radecki (1986), Friedman (1988, appendix B), and Allen and Connolly (1989), all concerning the experience of the United States. As Friedman (1988) points out, there are several channels by which the stock market affects money demand. The transactional demand effect is just one of them. This paper will emphasize only the transactional demand effect. Empirical studies concerning the substitution effect of stock prices in Taiwan by regressing money demand or inflation rate on the expected increase rate of stock prices can be found in Liang (1989).

**Table 8.2 Factors Contributing to Price Stabilization**

| Year | Total Trading Value of Listed Stocks (billion NT$) | Exchange Rate at End of Year (NT$/U.S.$) | Effective Tariff Rate[a] (%) | Import Price Index (1991=100) | Export Price Index (1991=100) |
|---|---|---|---|---|---|
| 1980 | 162.1 | 36.01 | 8.88 | 131.13 | 110.34 |
| 1981 | 209.2 | 37.84 | 8.06 | 141.37 | 116.52 |
| 1982 | 133.9 | 39.91 | 7.85 | 139.80 | 117.73 |
| 1983 | 363.8 | 40.27 | 8.41 | 136.33 | 116.67 |
| 1984 | 324.5 | 39.47 | 8.68 | 135.13 | 116.91 |
| 1985 | 195.2 | 39.35 | 8.40 | 133.13 | 116.75 |
| 1986 | 675.7 | 35.00 | 8.44 | 115.79 | 111.80 |
| 1987 | 2,668.6 | 28.55 | 7.56 | 107.28 | 103.57 |
| 1988 | 7,868.0 | 28.17 | 6.12 | 106.22 | 100.82 |
| 1989 | 25,408.0 | 26.17 | 6.69 | 100.52 | 97.07 |
| 1990 | 19,031.2 | 27.11 | 5.74 | 102.89 | 99.46 |
| 1991 | 9,682.7 | 25.75 | 5.23 | 100.00 | 100.00 |
| 1992 | 5,917.1 | 25.42 | 5.40 | 93.08 | 94.62 |
| 1993 | 9,056.7 | 26.67 | 5.26 | 97.41 | 99.53 |

*Sources:* Total trading value of listed stocks, *Taiwan Stock Exchange Statistical Data* (Taipei: Taiwan Stock Exchange, various years); exchange rate, *Financial Statistics Monthly, Taiwan District, R.O.C.* (Taipei: Central Bank of China, various issues); tariff revenue, *Yearbook of Tax Statistics, R.O.C.* (Taipei: Department of Statistics, Ministry of Finance, Republic of China, various years); import value, *Monthly Statistics of Exports and Imports in Taiwan Area, R.O.C.* (Taipei: Department of Statistics, Ministry of Finance, Republic of China, various issues) (imports are recorded upon completion of all customs formalities); export price index and import price index, see source for WPI and CPI in table 8.1 (f.o.b. for export price index and c.i.f. for import price index).

[a]Effective tariff rate = Tariff revenue/(Import value − Tariff revenue).

As for price-stabilizing factors, the factors most often emphasized include the appreciation of the NT dollar, import decontrol, and the stabilization of international prices. These factors have all contributed to the lowering or stabilization of prices for traded goods. According to table 8.2, the exchange rate of the U.S. dollar relative to the NT dollar dropped steadily from 40.27 at the end of 1983 to 26.17 in 1989 and, after a short rebound, to 25.42 in 1992. The effective tariff rate, defined as the proportion of total revenue of customs duties relative to total import value, also fell, from 8.68 percent in 1984 to 5.23 percent in 1991. These factors pushed the import price index from 141.37 in 1981 to 100.52 in 1989 and, after a rebound in 1990, further to 93.08 in 1992. The export price index also dropped, from 117.73 in 1982 to 97.07 in 1989 and, after a two-year rebound, to 94.62 in 1992.

Since imported goods constitute a large proportion of the commodities covered by both the WPI and CPI measures and exported goods are also included in the measure of WPI, the lowering of the import price index and the export price index in the 1980s naturally had the effect of stabilizing the WPI and CPI. However, among the components of final demand on GDP, imports is a subtracting term. To argue that the lowering of import prices is beneficial to the stabilization of the GDP deflator therefore requires further theoretical justification.

Chen and Chen (1989) follow the quantity theory of money under an open economy to set up the following commodity market equilibrium condition

$$MV/P + T(Y, P_m/P) = Y,$$

where $M$ is the money supply, $V$ is the income velocity of money, $P$ is the GDP deflator, $T$ is the balance of trade, $P_m$ is import prices, $Y$ is real GDP, and $MV/P$ denotes domestic expenditure. Based on this equation, Chen and Chen show that money supply and import prices have positive impacts, while real GDP has a negative impact on the GDP deflator. Further, they show theoretically, as well as empirically with Taiwanese data from 1962 to 1986, that as the ratio of imports relative to GDP increases, the impact of import prices on the GDP deflator rises and the impact of the money supply falls. Their results therefore support the argument that the lowering of import prices in Taiwan in the 1980s helped stabilize the GDP deflator. Ou's (1991) empirical study covering the period from 1970.1 to 1990.4 also concludes that import prices had more influence than money supply on both the GNP deflator and the CPI, by comparing the accumulated impacts over eight quarters.

This paper intends to resolve the above-mentioned puzzle of how Taiwan could have a high growth rate of money supply and a low inflation rate at the same time in the 1980s, by adding stock trading value and import prices into the list of explanatory variables in the domestic price equation. Since the impact of import prices on the WPI and CPI is so apparent, we take the GDP deflator as the measure of domestic prices. Although, as mentioned above, several studies have stressed the extra money demand caused by stock and real estate transactions, Huang and Ouyang (1989) is the only one that takes price change rather than money demand as the dependent variable in the estimated equation and includes both stock transactions and import prices as explanatory variables. However, in that paper the price variable considered is the CPI, and no adequate theoretical foundation is given to justify the inclusion of both import prices and stock transactions as explanatory variables. This paper will first propose in section 8.2 a theoretical model that relates the GDP deflator to money supply, stock transactions, and import prices, as well as other traditional variables. In section 8.3, the actual data for Taiwan over the period from 1978.1 to 1993.2 are then applied to estimate the price equation. Section 8.4 summarizes the major findings of this paper.

## 8.2 The Model

In order to examine the money and price phenomenon in the 1980s, our model will incorporate the stock transaction and import price factors that played an important role in Taiwan then. To include the factors mentioned above as explanatory variables, we follow the tradition of equating money demand and money supply to determine the general price level, which is defined as the GDP deflator in this paper.

We break down the demand for money into transactions demand and portfolio demand. The former covers money that is held for the purpose of paying for domestic purchases of production factors, intermediate inputs, final products, and assets. The total payment for the purchase of production factors and intermediate inputs is closely related to the value of nominal GDP; the domestic purchase of final products is measured by total nominal domestic expenditures in national income accounting; and asset transactions can be proxied by the trading values of listed stock and real estate.

Assume the transaction velocities of circulation of money held for the above four categories of transactions differ among themselves and are all negatively related to the interest rate. Then, the transactions demand for money in nominal terms MT can be written as[4]

$$\text{MT} = f(\text{PGDP*GDP, PGDP*GDP} - \text{BT (GDP, PGDP, PM), S, RET, } r),$$

where PGDP is the GDP deflator; GDP is real GDP; PM is import prices; BT is the nominal balance of trade with $\partial\text{BT}/\partial\text{GDP} < 0$, $\partial\text{BT}/\partial\text{PGDP} < 0$, and $\partial\text{BT}/\partial\text{PM} > 0$ if the Marshall-Lerner condition holds; S is the total transaction value of listed stocks; RET is the value of real estate transactions; and $r$ is the interest rate.[5] The partial derivatives of this transactions demand equation with respect to the first four explanatory variables are all positive, and the partial derivative with respect to the interest rate is negative. Thus, the equation for the transactions demand for money can be reexpressed as

$$\text{(1)} \qquad \text{MT} = f(\overset{+}{\text{PGDP}}, \overset{+}{\text{GDP}}, \overset{+}{\text{S}}, \overset{+}{\text{RET}}, \overset{-}{\text{PM}}, \overset{-}{r}).$$

The plus or minus sign above each right-hand-side variable denotes the sign of the partial derivative of the left-hand-side variable with respect to that particular variable.

According to portfolio theory, the portfolio demand for money is a decreasing function of interest rate, expected inflation rate, and expected returns, including capital gains and dividends or rental of stock and real estate investments. Since the values of the expected inflation rate and the expected return on stocks and real estate are very difficult to measure, this paper omits these variables and simply defines the equation of portfolio demand for money MP as

4. Since each category of transaction applies a different price deflator, it is difficult to define an appropriate deflator for the demand for money, if we specify the money demand equation in real terms. Based on the same argument, Field (1984) and Wenninger and Radecki (1986) specify their money demand equations in nominal terms like ours when they incorporate asset transactions into their equations.

5. Note that PGDP*GDP − BT denotes total nominal domestic expenditures. Examples of relating nominal money demand to nominal domestic expenditures can be found in Dornbusch (1980, chap. 7) and Chen and Chen (1989).

(2) $$\mathrm{MP} = f(\overset{-}{r}) .$$

Let us equate money supply M and money demand $M^d$, which is the sum of transactions demand MT and portfolio demand MP:

(3) $$\mathrm{M} = \mathrm{M}^d = \mathrm{MT} + \mathrm{MP}.$$

We solve this equation for PGDP with the allowance of an one-period lag of influence of import price, yielding

(4) $$\mathrm{PGDP} = f(\overset{+}{\mathrm{M}}, \overset{-}{\mathrm{GDP}}, \overset{-}{\mathrm{S}}, \overset{-}{\mathrm{RET}}, \overset{+}{\mathrm{PM}(-1)}, \overset{+}{r}),$$

where PM($-1$) denotes import prices of the last period. This equation indicates that money supply, import prices of the last period, and interest rate all have positive effects on the GDP deflator of the current period, while real GDP and the total values of stock transactions and real estate transactions have negative effects on the GDP deflator.

The above four equations constitute the theoretical model in this paper. In macroeconomic theory, the price level or inflation is determined by a complete aggregate demand–aggregate supply (AD-AS) model. Our model of equating money demand and money supply presents only the LM equation in the complete AD-AS system. However, the relationship among macrovariables that holds in a complete macrosystem should also hold in each equation of the system. To avoid complicating the discussion by introducing other variables into the model, we stick to this simple LM equation rather than using a complete macromodel in the analysis, so that we can concentrate on the impacts of money supply, stock trading value, and import prices on the GDP deflator.

## 8.3 Empirical Results

We apply the actual data for Taiwan to estimate equation (4). However, since data for real estate transactions are not available and are very difficult to estimate accurately, the variable RET will be omitted in the estimation equation.[6] In addition, to make the estimated coefficients more meaningful, the logarithmic form is taken for all variables except interest rate. The period encompassing the 1980s is our key period of study. Quarterly data from 1978.1 to 1993.2 are analyzed. Both narrow and broad definitions of money, M1A, M1B, and M2, are used in this empirical study in logarithmic form, LM1A, LM1B, and LM2.

6. A general impression in the 1980s was that the value of real estate transactions usually moved closely with stock transactions. In other words, the value of real estate transactions was highly correlated with that of stock transactions. Therefore, omitting the variable RET in the equation estimation should not affect our results much.

We rewrite the empirical model as follows:

$$\text{LPGDP}_t = f(\text{LGDP}_t, r_t, \text{LM}_t, \text{LS}_t, \text{LPM}_{t-1}),$$

where LPGDP, LM, LGDP, LS, and LPM are the logarithmic forms of PGDP, M, GDP, S, and PM, respectively. It deserves mentioning that PM is expressed by an index transformed from NT dollars after tariff, therefore NT dollar appreciation and import decontrol are already taken into consideration. Data sources of variables are reported in the notes to tables 8.1, 8.2, and 8.5.

There is now much evidence that many macrovariables are nonstationary. We first examine the existence of unit roots using the augmented Dickey-Fuller test as shown in table 8.3. It is found that all the variables in logarithmic form have a unit root and that the first differences of these variables do not possess unit roots. In other words, these variables should be differenced once to obtain stationary variables.

Engle and Granger (1987) point out that nonstationary variables may be cointegrated in the sense that certain linear combinations of these variables are stationary and hence suggest some long-run equilibrium relationships. We

**Table 8.3 Augmented Dickey-Fuller *t*-Statistics**

| Variable | Level | First Difference |
|---|---|---|
| LPGDP | −2.3429 | −5.4023*** |
| LGDP | −2.3240 | −10.4494*** |
| *r* | −2.1168 | −3.3080* |
| LM1A | −1.1367 | −3.7300** |
| LM1B | −1.1590 | −3.6791** |
| LM2 | −0.6647 | −3.8373** |
| LPM | −2.6715 | −3.3530* |
| LS | −1.6548 | −4.1901*** |

*Note:* MacKinnon critical values: 1 percent, −4.1109; 5 percent, −3.4824; 10 percent, −3.1689.
*Significant at 10 percent level.
**Significant at 5 percent level.
***Significant at 1 percent level.

**Table 8.4 Engle-Granger Cointegration Test**

| | | | |
|---|---|---|---|
| Vector | LPGDP<br>LGDP<br>*r*<br>LPM(−1)<br>LS<br>LM1A | LPGDP<br>LGDP<br>*r*<br>LPM(−1)<br>LS<br>LM1B | LPGDP<br>LGDP<br>*r*<br>LPM(−1)<br>LS<br>LM2 |
| Dickey-Fuller *t*-statistic | −3.5373 | −3.7289 | −3.4625 |

*Note:* MacKinnon critical values: 1 percent, −6.0487; 5 percent, −5.3332; 10 percent, −4.9786.

execute the cointegration test and show the results in table 8.4. We found that there is no cointegration among these variables, regardless of the definition of money. Therefore, we take differences of all variables before we perform the regression analysis, so as to avoid the problem of spurious regression (Granger and Newbold 1974).

One other thing deserving attention is the structural change in stock trading. The stock market was stable before the mid-1980s. It started to rise around 1986, and the boom continued for several years. The stock price index rose almost steadily from 746 in 1985 to 8,616 in 1989. Then, the central bank adopted a contractionary monetary policy in 1989 by raising the rediscount rate and the required reserve ratio of deposits. This contractionary policy did have its effect. The stock market bubble burst in 1990. The stock price index fell almost 80 percent from its peak of 12,495 in February 1990 to a low of 2,560 in October. By March 1991, it had recovered to 5,000, and stock trading became stable again. Therefore, when we consider the influence of the stock market, the period between 1986 and 1991 should be taken into special consideration. In the regression equation, we add a dummy variable *T*, with the value of 1 for this period, and 0 out of this period, to capture the effect of this structural change.

We thus summarize the above factors to express the regression equation as the following:

$$(5) \qquad D(\text{LPGDP}) = f(D(\text{LGDP}), D(r), D(\text{LPM}(-1)), \\ T, D(\text{LS}), TD(\text{LS}), D(\text{LM})).$$

*D*(*X*) denotes the first difference of variable *X*. *T* is the dummy variable to capture the impact of structural change in the stock market on the constant term of the equation. *TD*(LS) is the product of *T* and *D*(LS), which is added to capture the impact on the coefficient for stock trading value.

The empirical results by ordinary least squares (OLS) are reported in table 8.5. It shows that all the estimated coefficients are correct in sign, although some are insignificantly different from zero.

As explained at the end of section 8.2, our model is just part of a complete macrosystem. In a complete system, real GDP, money supply, and interest rate should all be endogenous variables. Since the purpose of this paper is to study price behavior, a complete macromodel is not specified. However, to circumvent the simultaneous-equation bias problem, an estimation method such as two-stage least squares should be adopted.

To implement two-stage least squares estimation, we include LPM(−1) and the last two period values of endogenous variables as exogenous or instrumental variables. In addition, in a highly open economy like Taiwan's, the prosperity of foreign economies, measured by the aggregate industrial production index of industrialized countries, is a very important influence on exports, GDP, trade surplus, and consequently money supply. Real government consumption is also important in determining GDP as well. Thus, these variables are also

**Table 8.5** **Ordinary Least Squares Results**

| Variable | *D*(LPGDP) | *D*(LPGDP) | *D*(LPGDP) |
|---|---|---|---|
| Constant | 0.012*** | 0.009* | 0.004 |
| | (2.918) | (1.999) | (0.411) |
| *D*(LGDP) | −0.322*** | −0.315*** | −0.387*** |
| | (−3.184) | (−3.815) | (−4.430) |
| *D*(*r*) | 0.005 | 0.009** | 0.006 |
| | (1.375) | (2.237) | (1.332) |
| *D*(LPM(−1))[a] | 0.216** | 0.222*** | 0.220** |
| | (2.629) | (2.762) | (2.480) |
| *T* | −0.0005 | 0.0002 | 0.003 |
| | (−0.095) | (0.039) | (0.565) |
| *D*(LS) | 0.007 | 0.008 | 0.009 |
| | (1.153) | (1.351) | (1.394) |
| *TD*(LS) | −0.032*** | −0.032*** | −0.027** |
| | (−2.777) | (−2.858) | (−2.205) |
| *D*(LM1A) | 0.200*** | | |
| | (3.423) | | |
| *D*(LM1B) | | 0.232*** | |
| | | (3.792) | |
| *D*(LM2) | | | 0.300* |
| | | | (1.792) |
| Adjusted $R^2$ | 0.453 | 0.474 | 0.372 |
| *F* | 8.220*** | 8.867*** | 6.158*** |

*Sources:* GDP (real GDP at 1986 prices), *Quarterly National Income Statistics in Taiwan Area, R.O.C.* (Taipei: DGBAS, Executive Yuan, Republic of China, various issues); *r* (interest rate of three-month time deposits of First Commercial Bank), *Financial Statistics Monthly, Taiwan District, R.O.C.* (Taipei: Central Bank of China, various issues).

*Note:* Numbers in parentheses are *t*-values.

[a]PM = Import price index * (1 + Effective tariff rate).

*Significant at 10 percent level.

**Significant at 5 percent level.

***Significant at 1 percent level.

included as exogenous variables. Then, two-stage least squares estimation is implemented to derive table 8.6.

All the equations in tables 8.5 and 8.6 have a good fit, according to the *F*-statistics. The empirical results in the two tables are similar, except for a few differences in the significance of *t*-values. The following results are observed:

1. *D*(LGDP) has a negative and significant coefficient. It shows that higher income can result in lower inflation pressure. Higher income makes money demand higher, negatively influencing the price level.

2. The interest rate *r* has a positive coefficient. Thus, a rise in the interest rate pushes up the price level. The influence of interest rates on price levels is active through the money demand function.

3. The coefficients of *T* and *D*(LS) are insignificant. However, the coefficient of *TD*(LS) is significantly negative. This result indicates that the influence

**Table 8.6** **Two-Stage Least Squares Results**

| Variable | *D*(LPGDP) | *D*(LPGDP) | *D*(LPGDP) |
|---|---|---|---|
| Constant | 0.014** | 0.010 | −0.012 |
| | (2.266) | (1.469) | (−0.618) |
| *D*(LGDP) | −0.360** | −0.317* | −0.300 |
| | (−2.036) | (−1.684) | (−1,413) |
| *D*(*r*) | 0.012* | 0.014* | 0.017* |
| | (1.740) | (1.904) | (1.828) |
| *D*(LPM(−1)) | 0.175* | 0.193** | 0.216** |
| | (1.891) | (2.090) | (2.049) |
| *T* | −0.001 | −0.0004 | 0.005 |
| | (−0.208) | (−0.077) | (0.735) |
| *D*(S) | 0.009 | 0.009 | 0.011 |
| | (1.442) | (1.583) | (1.672) |
| *TD*(S) | −0.036*** | −0.035*** | −0.041** |
| | (−2.813) | (−2.863) | (−2.530) |
| *D*(LM1A) | 0.167* | | |
| | (1.937) | | |
| *D*(LM1B) | | 0.199** | |
| | | (2.166) | |
| *D*(LM2) | | | 0.606* |
| | | | (1.741) |
| Adjusted $R^2$ | 0.413 | 0.451 | 0.295 |
| *F* | 4.978*** | 5.061*** | 3.668*** |

*Sources:* GC (real government consumption expenditures at 1986 prices), *Quarterly National Economic Trends, Taiwan, R.O.C.* (Taipei: DGBAS, Executive Yuan, R.O.C., various issues); IP (aggregate industrial production index of industrialized countries), *International Financial Statistics* (IMF).

*Notes:* Numbers in parentheses are *t*-values. Instrumental variables: *D*(LPGDP(−1)), *D*(LPGDP(−2)), *D*(LGDP(−1)), *D*(LGDP(−2)), *D*(*r*(−1)), *D*(*r*(−2)), *D*(LPM(−1)), *D*(LIP(−1)), *D*(LGC(−1)), *T*, *D* (LS), *TD*(LS), *D*(LM(−1)), *D*(LM(−2)); LM = LM1A or LM1B or LM2.

*Significant at 10 percent level. **Significant at 5 percent level. ***Significant at 1 percent level.

of stock trading had a significant impact on prices only in the period 1986–91. The implication is that stock trading does absorb the influence of money supply on prices when the stock market is very active; but when stock market trading is stable, its negative influence on prices diminishes.

4. LPM(−1) has a significant positive coefficient. This result supports the argument that import prices (after considering the appreciation of the NT dollar and import decontrol) will influence domestic prices with a one-period time lag.

5. Most coefficients for money supply (LM1A, LM1B, and LM2) are significantly positive. This means that too great a money supply does create inflationary pressure.

After obtaining these results, we would like to make a comparison between our model and the traditional one. Traditionally, the money demand equation is written as

$$M^d = f(\text{GDP}, r, \text{PGDP}) .$$

By equating $M^d$ and money supply M, we can derive the price equation as follows:

$$\text{PGDP} = f(\text{GDP}, r, \text{M}) . \tag{6}$$

After considering partial adjustments and the logarithmic forms of the variables, we obtain the OLS regression results in table 8.7. We also apply two-stage least squares to estimate the traditional price equation, as our model does. The results are shown in table 8.8.

The relative performance of the different models can be measured by their predictive power. Four commonly used measures of predictive power, root mean square error, mean absolute error, mean absolute percentage error, and Theil's inequality coefficient, are calculated and reported in tables 8.9 and 8.10. These comparisons show that no matter which measure is used, and no matter which definition of money supply is considered, our model always has better forecasting performance than the traditional model.

## 8.4 Conclusions

Taiwan has maintained both a high growth rate and stable prices for decades. In the 1980s, a high money growth rate and a low inflation rate appeared at the same time. Explanations based on traditional money demand theory cannot be applied to explain this phenomenon well. This paper sets up a theoretical

**Table 8.7 Traditional Model by Ordinary Least Squares**

| Variable | *D*(LPGDP) | *D*(LPGDP) | *D*(LPGDP) |
|---|---|---|---|
| Constant | 0.014*** | 0.012*** | 0.012 |
| | (3.644) | (2.789) | (1.454) |
| *D*(LGDP) | −0.393*** | −0.383*** | −0.438*** |
| | (−4.299) | (−4.242) | (−4.782) |
| *D*(*r*) | 0.004 | 0.006 | 0.004 |
| | (0.871) | (1.486) | (0.880) |
| *D*(LM1A) | 0.122** | | |
| | (2.103) | | |
| *D*(LM1B) | | 0.156** | |
| | | (2.457) | |
| *D*(LM2) | | | 0.143 |
| | | | (0.872) |
| Adjusted $R^2$ | 0.330 | 0.346 | 0.288 |
| *F* | 10.993*** | 11.776*** | 9.214*** |

*Note:* Numbers in parentheses are *t*-values.
*Significant at 10 percent level.
**Significant at 5 percent level.
***Significant at 1 percent level.

**Table 8.8** **Traditional Model by Two-Stage Least Squares**

| Variable | *D*(LPGDP) | *D*(LPGDP) | *D*(LPGDP) |
|---|---|---|---|
| Constant | 0.015** | 0.013* | −0.0002 |
| | (2.419) | (1.870) | (−0.013) |
| *D*(LGDP) | −0.423** | −0.396* | −0.450** |
| | (−2.220) | (−1.938) | (−2.040) |
| *D*(*r*) | 0.012* | 0.013* | 0.018* |
| | (1.681) | (1.780) | (1.902) |
| *D*(LM1A) | 0.104 | | |
| | (1.178) | | |
| *D*(LM1B) | | 0.122 | |
| | | (1.281) | |
| *D*(LM2) | | | 0.419 |
| | | | (0.234) |
| Adjusted $R^2$ | 0.280 | 0.305 | 0.156 |
| *F* | 4.982* | 4.429*** | 4.027*** |

*Notes:* Numbers in parentheses are *t*-values. Instrumental variables: *D*(LPGDP(−1)), *D*(LPGDP(−2)), *D*(LGDP(−1)), *D*(LGDP(−2)), *D*(*r*(−1)), *D*(*r*(−2)), *D*(LIP(−1)), *D*(LGC(−1)), *D*(LM(−1)), *D*(LM(−2)); LM = LM1A or LM1B or LM2.

*Significant at 10 percent level.

**Significant at 5 percent level.

***Significant at 1 percent level.

**Table 8.9** **Forecasting Performance by Ordinary Least Squares**

| Money Supply | Root Mean Square Error | Mean Absolute Error | Mean Absolute Percentage Error | Theil's Inequality Coefficient |
|---|---|---|---|---|
| M1A | | | | |
| Our model | 0.0485 | 0.0378 | 0.8320 | 0.0053 |
| Traditional model | 0.1215 | 0.0938 | 2.0705 | 0.0135 |
| M1B | | | | |
| Our model | 0.0394 | 0.0306 | 0.6759 | 0.0043 |
| Traditional model | 0.1124 | 0.0858 | 1.8928 | 0.0125 |
| M2 | | | | |
| Our model | 0.0710 | 0.0583 | 1.2867 | 0.0078 |
| Traditional model | 0.1223 | 0.0981 | 2.1644 | 0.0136 |

model and executes an empirical study to analyze the phenomenon.

In the 1980s, stock market fever and real estate speculation were rampant; both constitute an important portion of the transactions demand for money. Therefore, inflationary pressure was eased. In addition, appreciation of the NT dollar and import decontrol contributed to price stability to some extent. In our theoretical model, the above-mentioned factors are included as influences on money demand. And by equating money demand and money supply, the GDP

**Table 8.10 Forecasting Performance by Two-Stage Least Squares**

| Money Supply | Root Mean Square Error | Mean Absolute Error | Mean Absolute Percentage Error | Theil's Inequality Coefficient |
|---|---|---|---|---|
| M1A | | | | |
| Our model | 0.0501 | 0.0417 | 0.9158 | 0.0056 |
| Traditional model | 0.1145 | 0.0914 | 2.0131 | 0.0127 |
| M1B | | | | |
| Our model | 0.0407 | 0.0329 | 0.7244 | 0.0045 |
| Traditional model | 0.1085 | 0.0861 | 1.8963 | 0.0120 |
| M2 | | | | |
| Our model | 0.0495 | 0.0393 | 0.8683 | 0.0055 |
| Traditional model | 0.0935 | 0.0751 | 1.6544 | 0.0103 |

deflator equation is derived.

Quarterly data in Taiwan from 1978.1 to 1993.2 are used. Unit root tests, cointegration tests, ordinary least squares, and two-stage least squares estimation methods are applied to estimate the GDP deflator equation. The empirical results support the theoretical model to a great extent. Decreases in import prices (considering NT dollar appreciation and import decontrol) can result in decreases in the GDP deflator with a one-period time lag. Stock trading had a strong influence on the demand for money in its feverish period 1986–91. Therefore, stock trading can explain price stabilization to some degree. Comparing the predictive power of our model with the traditional model, we also find that our model performs better.

Our results have not only provided theoretical and empirical support for the idea that import price affects the GDP deflator but also indicated that in a developing country with a fast-growing financial or stock market, it may not be proper to analyze the impact of money supply on domestic prices by following the quantity theory of money or the traditional money demand theory, without incorporating the element of money demand for asset transactions.

There are some limitations in our research. The impact of financial liberalization policies, such as interest rate deregulation in the 1980s and bank entry decontrol in the early 1990s, on the demand for money in Taiwan have not been considered.[7] Real estate trading and inflation expectation factors are omitted because pertinent data are unavailable. The lag patterns of the effects of money supply and import prices have not been well dealt with. A general-equilibrium

7. Since World War II, Taiwan's financial system has been strictly controlled. Although financial liberalization has been demanded by the public, its speed was not accelerated until the late 1980s. The government in Taiwan has controlled bank interest rates and blocked the new entry of banks for a long time. Most banks were government-owned. Since the promulgation of the new Banking Law on July 19, 1989, both the ceiling and floor limits for interest rates on deposits and loans have been abolished, and interest rate liberalization has finally been completed. In June 1991, 15 new banks were approved. By April 1993, 17 new banks were established and operating.

macromodel has not been set up to analyze all endogenous economic variable behaviors. All these problems will need further study in the future.

## References

Allen, S. D., and R. A. Connolly. 1989. Financial market effects on aggregate money demand: Bayesian analysis. *Journal of Money, Credit and Banking* 21(2): 158–75.

Chen, C. N., and S. K. Chen. 1989. Quantity theory of the price index in an open economy: The case of Taiwan (in Chinese). *Taiwan Economic Review* 17(2): 189–95.

Chiu, Paul C. H., and T. C. Hou. 1993. Prices, money and monetary policy implementation under financial liberalization: The case of Taiwan. In *Financial opening: Policy issues and experiences in developing countries,* ed. Helmut Reisen and Bernhard Fischer, 173–200. Paris: Organisation for Economic Co-operation and Development.

Dornbusch, R. 1980. *Open economy macroeconomics.* New York: Basic Books.

Engle, Robert F., and C. W. J. Granger. 1987. Co-integration and error correction: Representation, estimation, and testing. *Econometrica* 55(2): 251–76.

Field, A. J. 1984. Asset exchanges and the transactions demand for money, 1919–29. *American Economic Review* 74(1): 43–59.

Friedman, M. 1988. Money and stock market. *Journal of Political Economy* 96(2): 221–45.

Granger, C. W. J., and P. Newbold. 1974. Spurious regressions in econometrics. *Journal of Econometrics* 26:1045–66.

Huang, P. Y., and C. D. Ouyang. 1989. An empirical study of the stock market, money supply and prices in Taiwan (in Chinese). *Taipei City Bank Monthly* 20(11): 21–32.

Liang, F. C. 1989. Money supply, stock price and inflation in Taiwan (in Chinese). *Quarterly Review of the Bank of Taiwan* 40(4):1–27.

Lin, T. Y., and J. C. Lee. 1989. The relationship between the income velocity of money and the stock market (in Chinese). *Central Bank of China Quarterly* 11(4):38–45.

Ou, S. H. 1991. A comparison of the impacts of money supply and import prices on domestic prices in a highly-open economy: Taiwan experience 1970 I–1990 IV (in Chinese). *Central Bank of China Quarterly* 13(3):34–57.

Shea, J. D. 1983. The income elasticity of money demand in Taiwan (in Chinese). *Academic Economic Papers* (Academia Sinica, Taipei) 11(2): 13–30.

Shih, Y. 1990. An empirical study on the term structure of deposit interest rate and the impact of stock exchange on money demand in Taiwan (in Chinese). *Central Bank of China Quarterly* 12(3):45–64.

Tsiang, S. C. 1977. The monetary theoretic foundation of the modern monetary approach to the balance of payments. *Oxford Economic Papers* 29(3):319–38.

Wenninger, J., and L. J. Radecki. 1986. Financial transactions and the demand for M1. *Federal Reserve Bank of New York Quarterly Review* 11(2):24–29.

Wu, C. S. 1989. Transactional money and prices in Taiwan (in Chinese). Discussion Paper no. 7801. Taipei: Institute of Economics, Academia Sinica, May.

Wu, C. S., and J. D. Shea. 1993. An analysis on the relationship between stock, real estate and money markets in Taiwan in the 1980s. Discussion Paper no. 9322. Taipei: Institute of Economics, Academia Sinica, September.

## Comment Kenjiro Hirayama

The focus of Yang and Shea's paper is the combination of high money growth and low price inflation in Taiwan in the 1980s. The authors' approach is to modify the traditional specification of money demand by including the trading value of stocks and import prices. They solve the money market equilibrium condition for the price level and estimate this price equation by two-stage least squares, with generally satisfactory results. The authors also report the dynamic forecasting performances of the modified model and of a traditional model estimated by ordinary least squares. Again, the model with the trading value of stocks and import prices has a better forecasting performance. The theoretical framework is reasonable, and the empirical results lend strong support to Yang and Shea's hypothesis.

Despite the empirical success of focusing on stock trading and import prices, the feature I find difficult to understand is their use of a price equation rather than a straightforward money demand function. Their premise is that price is the equilibrating variable in the money market. I do not deny the role of price adjustment in equilibrating the money market. However, the bulk of any price adjustment would be a response to conditions in the goods market. It would be the interest rate that the money market determines in equilibrium.

A more standard approach to analyzing the combination of high money growth and low inflation would be to ask, Was the high money growth absorbed by the concomitant rise in the demand for money? The reverse case of missing money was extensively studied in the United States. The same line of research might be more appropriate as a first step in answering the question. For example, one can run structural break tests to see whether there was a significant shift in money demand that can explain the low inflation with high money growth.

Arguments traditionally specified in the money demand function are income, interest rate(s), and wealth. Income is included to capture the transactions demand for money. This represents settlement needs for transactions in goods and services, but not for asset trading. In light of a phenomenal rise in stock trading in Taiwan in the 1980s, it seems appropriate that the authors incorporate the trading value of stocks in the demand for money function, which is vindicated clearly by the empirical results. However, they do not utilize a wealth variable in their specification. Their portfolio demand for money as given by equation (2) includes an interest rate only. Without a wealth variable, the trading value might be proxying for this wealth. In the case of Japan, where there was also a stock market rally in the 1980s, for instance, Ueda (1988) and Corker (1990) find that a wealth variable can explain the apparent upward shift in the money demand function.

Although the authors devote little attention to the interest rate variable, there

Kenjiro Hirayama is professor of economics at Kwansei Gakuin University.

are potentially important issues involved in the choice of this variable. They have chosen the three-month deposit rate as the interest rate variable, but this is partly the own rate of return on money. One should probably search for the interest rate on an asset that is most likely to be the alternative to money holding. Trials with a few different interest rates might be informative.

## References

Corker, Robert. 1990. Wealth, financial liberalization, and the demand for money in Japan. *IMF Staff Papers* 37(2):418–32.

Ueda, Kazuo. 1988. Financial deregulation and the demand for money in Japan. Discussion Paper no. 66. Osaka: Osaka University.

# Comment Muthi Samudram

This paper surveys the role of money and prices in Taiwan during the period 1960–93. Episodes of past excessive growth of money supply with low inflation, particularly during the period 1960–80, have been explained by the high income elasticity of demand for money. The paper indicates that similar reasons for the behavior of money and prices in later periods did not hold. There has been evidence that because of strong stock market growth, demand for transaction balances has been significant during the 1980s and 1990s. Yang and Shea believe that in spite of the excessive growth of the money supply, prices have been very low and that the traditional demand for money function cannot explain this phenomenon.

The authors derived the price equation from the demand for money equation, where demand for money was disaggregated into transactions and portfolio demand. The final price equation was derived from the transactions demand for money, taking into consideration the role of the interest rate in the demand for overall money balances.

In deriving the price equation from the transactions demand for money, one is led to believe that developments in the labor market, such as wages and employment, and fiscal policy measures, such as tax cuts, subsidies, and deficit spending, are not relevant in determining the overall GDP deflator. Even if all these factors are subsumed into money supply, one would have expected a significant but large coefficient. Even the real GDP variable is not significant in the two-stage least squares estimation procedure.

Given the large data set available, cointegration analysis would have enabled the authors to determine not only the functional form of estimation but also whether a long-run relationship exists between prices and other variables. In

Muthi Samudram is senior research fellow at the Malaysian Institute of Economic Research.

the present context of the formulation, the money supply variable should have been an excess supply/demand variable rather than money supply itself.

A similar phenomenon of low prices in the face of strong money growth has occurred in Malaysia in the 1990s. We believe that the effect of a significant rise in transactions can be explained by a bullish stock market and the concomitant rise in M1. But this did not affect prices at all. This episode happens to be a one-off event, and therefore prices need not reflect that increase. Similarly in Taiwan's case, there was a significant increase in M1 in 1986 and a slow decline to the trend of growth by 1991.

Therefore the derivation of the price equation in this paper is not complete without the labor market. Even the results do not significantly support the hypothesis of strong monetary effects, with the estimated coefficient being no more than 0.2.

# 9 Financial Liberalization: The Korean Experience

Won-Am Park

## 9.1 Introduction

Korea has achieved remarkable economic growth through an export-oriented growth strategy but has had pervasive government intervention in its credit markets. Korea's high growth was attained through the government's active role in financing industrial development. Policy loans made at preferential interest rates and direct credit control were the main tools used by the government.

Although it is certain that government intervention in the credit market played a role in accelerating Korean development, this strategy has not been without significant costs, borne mainly by financial institutions and depositors. Financial repression created an inefficient banking system, a weak corporate financial structure, and high inflation tax burdens. The benefits and costs of heavy government intervention in the financial sector have been, and still are, hotly debated topics in Korea.

This paper explores changes in financial markets and financial policies and their effects on and consequences for Korea since financial deregulation started in the early 1980s. Finding the causes for changes in financial markets and assessing the impact of financial policies is a very difficult task. The causes and consequences of any specific financial policy are often so multifarious and intertwined that we cannot easily identify them. Nonetheless, this paper will investigate Korea's experiences with financial deregulation since the early 1980s.

Section 9.2 provides an overview of Korea's financial deregulatory process

Won-Am Park is professor of economics at Hong-Ik University and a research associate of the Korea Development Institute.

since the early 1980s and its future plans. Section 9.3 investigates the effects of financial deregulation on the structure of the financial system, behavior of financial intermediaries, and monetary and exchange rate policies. Section 9.4 tests capital mobility in Korea by focusing on saving-investment correlations and interest parity conditions. Section 9.5 analyzes the movements of Korea's nominal and real exchange rates. Concluding remarks are provided in section 9.6.

## 9.2 Overview of Korea's Financial Deregulation since the Early 1980s

When Korea embarked on a policy of outward-oriented growth in the early 1960s, the government began to intervene heavily in financial markets to direct insufficient domestic savings toward investment in export industries. The government's intervention was intensified in the 1970s as its industrial policy shifted to the heavy and chemical industry drive. Bank interest rates were controlled at below the market-clearing level. Credit was also allocated by lending directives set up by the government.

Toward the end of the 1970s, the government's promotion of heavy and chemical industries gave rise to severe distortions in resource allocations and to internal and external imbalances in the economy. To make things worse, the oil price hike, social and political turmoil, and a bad rice crop during 1979–80 brought about serious stagflation in the Korean economy. This poor performance and great imbalances in the Korean economy provided momentum for reevaluating the industrial and financial policies implemented in the 1970s and for pursuing a new policy in the 1980s.

The new policy package aimed at achieving economic balance through economic liberalization. To correct the overinvestment in heavy and chemical industries and distortions created by the strong protectionist policies in the 1970s, the government had respect for the market mechanism and competition and as a result limited government intervention. The import liberalization ratio rose from 68.6 percent in 1979 to 91.6 percent in 1986. The average nominal tariff rate for all commodities declined from 35.7 percent in 1978 to 18.1 percent by 1988. The incentive system for strategic industries, such as preferential credit and tax treatment, was realigned into a system of more indirect and functional support. The tax reform of 1981 substantially reduced the scope of special tax treatment for key industries. This new industrial incentive system culminated in the Industrial Development Law effective from July 1986 that defined some areas of market failure in which the government might intervene for industrial rationalization. The financial deregulatory process that we will review was only part of the new policy package.[1]

1. See Nam (1992), Cho and Kim (1993), and Park (1994) for a recent review of Korea's financial deregulation and financial opening.

### 9.2.1 Domestic Financial Deregulation

Financial deregulation commenced with the removal of various restrictions on bank management and the privatization of commercial bank ownership in the early 1980s. Regulations on commercial banks in the spheres of the organization, budget, branching, and business practices were greatly loosened. During 1981–83, the government sold its shares in all nationwide commercial banks. To prevent bank ownership from being concentrated among Korea's large conglomerates, the *chaebol,* ownership by a single shareholder was restricted to 8 percent of the total. The government also chartered two joint-venture commercial banks with Korean and foreign partners and loosened regulations on chartering nonbank financial institutions (NBFIs) such as investment, mutual savings, and finance companies. In addition, it has continued to broaden and diversify services supplied by financial institutions.

The government's management of credit and interest rates has improved. Although the government continued to set ceilings for bank loans and deposits, it decided to switch from direct credit controls to indirect ones. Most preferential interest rates applied to various policy loans were abolished in June 1982, and further policy loans were restrained. In early 1984, financial institutions were allowed to set their own lending rates within a given range according to the creditworthiness of the borrowers. This action has been followed by a series of measures deregulating interest rates in the organized financial sector. Such measures include the lifting of the upper limit on call rates in 1984, the decontrol of yields on convertible bonds and debentures with bank payment guarantees in 1985, and the freeing of interest rates on certificates of deposit (CDs) and issuing rates for debentures with bank payment guarantees and financial debentures issued by deposit money banks in 1986.

This series of interest rate deregulations culminated in the decontrol of bank and nonbank lending rates in December 1988. These measures were a significant step toward financial deregulation. As interest rates rose after they were decontrolled, however, the government revoked the plan. Furthermore, economic slowdown and labor disputes in 1989 hindered progressive liberalization toward the end of the 1980s. Not until August 1991 did the government release the four-phase schedule for the full liberalization of interest rates in the domestic financial market.

The restructuring of the financial industry has been of concern as the new financial instruments that cross between banking and securities promote competition among financial intermediaries. Korea has not had any formal legal restrictions against a universal banking system since the decision was delegated to the Monetary Operation Board, but Korea generally has maintained a specialized banking system. Banks are limited in dual operations, but some are already in the securities business and involved in short-term financing through the acquisition of subsidiaries. In March 1991, Korea's eight short-term finance companies were changed into two banks and five securities companies. Table 9.1 summarizes major events in Korea's financial deregulation since the early 1980s.

### 9.2.2 Financial Market Opening

Domestic financial deregulation since the early 1980s has been accompanied by a gradualist approach to financial opening. While deregulation in the domestic financial market proceeded faster than financial opening in the first half of the 1980s, the latter went faster in the latter half of the 1980s because the current account ran surpluses during 1986–89 after chronic deficits in the previous years.

Prior to Korea's current account surplus in 1986, some measures were implemented to open domestic financial markets gradually. The basket-peg exchange rate system was adopted in 1980. The forward exchange market was

**Table 9.1 Highlights of Korea's Financial Deregulation since the Early 1980s**

| | |
|---|---|
| *Financial liberalization program* | |
| Introduction of corporate paper | 1981 |
| Privatization of nationwide commercial banks | 1981–83 |
| Abolition of beneficial interest rates on policy loans | 1982 |
| Alleviation of government intervention in the internal operation of banks | 1984 |
| Introduction of negotiable CDs | 1984 |
| Introduction of a band for bank loan rates | 1984 |
| Indirect opening of the stock market through the Korea Fund | 1984 |
| Introduction of cash management accounts by short-term finance companies | 1987 |
| Introduction of bond management funds by securities companies | 1987 |
| Relaxation of entry barriers to financial industry, including banks, life insurance, lease, and investment trust | 1988 |
| Opening of the life insurance industry to foreign firms | 1988 |
| Announcement of phased deposit and loan rate deregulation | Dec. 1988 |
| Opening of the securities industry to foreign firms | 1991 |
| Announcement of a four-step interest rate liberalization plan | 1991 |
| Conversion of some short-term finance companies to securities companies or banks | 1991 |
| Opening of purchase of individual equity stocks on the Korea Stock Exchange to foreign investors | 1992 |
| *Foreign exchange and capital account liberalization* | |
| Switch to a basket-peg exchange rate system from a dollar-peg | 1980 |
| Foreign exchange forward transaction implemented | 1981 |
| Interest rate swap allowed | 1984 |
| Switch to a negative system in foreign direct investment policies | 1984 |
| Issuance of convertible bonds (CBs), warrant bonds (WBs), and depository receipts (DRs) | 1985 |
| Financial futures allowed | 1987 |
| Transition to an IMF article VIII country | 1988 |
| Foreign exchange call market established | 1989 |
| Switch to the Market Average Exchange Rate System | 1990 |
| Switch to a negative system in foreign exchange management | 1992 |

created in 1980 as well. Interest and currency swaps were introduced in 1984. The Korea Fund, a closed-end mutual fund for foreigners who want to invest in Korean stocks, was established and listed on the New York Stock Exchange in 1984.

The current account surpluses in 1986–89 provided further impetus to deregulate foreign exchange transactions in areas such as position management, documentation requirements, and the international use of the won. By deregulating a substantial portion of current account transactions, Korea accepted the obligations of the IMF's article VIII in November 1988. Furthermore, investments by foreigners in domestic securities were permitted and facilitated through the issuing of beneficiary certificates for foreigners and equity-linked overseas securities (CBs, WBs and DRs) by domestic firms, as well as through the additional establishment of overseas country funds—the Korea Europe Fund in 1987 and the Korea Asia Fund in 1991. The watershed was the introduction in March 1990 of the so-called Market Average Exchange Rate System for the determination of exchange rates, whereby rates were allowed to fluctuate daily in accordance with the changes in market supply and demand.

In promoting liberalization of capital account transactions, the government sought first to deregulate foreign direct investment in Korea and Korean direct investment in foreign countries. Since 1984, when the positive list system for approving foreign direct investment was replaced by a negative list system, the government has progressively liberalized Korea's foreign direct investment system by shortening the list of nonpermissible categories of business for foreign investments.

The significant step toward financial opening was taken in 1991. Effective from January 1992, foreigners are allowed to purchase Korean stocks, up to 3 percent of the outstanding shares of each company for each individual; no more than 10 percent of a company may be foreign-owned, however. The government also authorized the operation of foreign securities companies in Korea. In addition, the Foreign Exchange Management Act was revised in 1991 so that the positive system, whereby all foreign exchange activities are initially deemed prohibited unless stipulated otherwise, has been replaced by a negative system which permits in principle all activities except those specified. Table 9.1 also summarizes major events in the financial market opening since the early 1980s.

### 9.2.3 Blueprint for the Liberalization and Opening of the Financial Sector

The current account surplus in the latter half of the 1980s not only stimulated financial opening but also aroused trade and financial conflicts with the United States. Accusing Korea of "manipulating" its exchange rate, the United States demanded that Korea advance its trade and financial liberalization programs and make the liberalization programs more transparent. Korea and the United States, to settle pending issues in their financial conflicts, agreed in August 1989 to hold financial policy talks as needed. Having had several discussions since 1989, both parties agreed to set out the three-stage Blueprint for the Liberalization and Opening of the Financial Sector. The first-stage and second-stage blueprints were announced in March and June 1992, respectively. Extending these, the third-stage blueprint was announced in June 1993.

The third-stage blueprint covers crucial areas such as interest rate liberalization, control of bank loans to *chaebols,* short-term finance, and foreign exchange and capital account liberalization. Table 9.2 outlines the third-stage blueprint, which will be the cornerstone for Korea's financial liberalization. It aims to achieve substantial liberalization of Korea's financial sector by 1997.

## 9.3 Effects of Financial Liberalization

Korea's financial liberalization since the early 1980s can be characterized as cautious and slow in terms of its order and speed. The influence of government

**Table 9.2 Third-Stage Blueprint for the Liberalization and Opening of the Financial Sector (announced June 1993)**

| Schedule | Items |
|---|---|
| Phase I (1993) | 1. Liberalize all bank and nonbank lending rates (except for policy loans) and long-term deposits over two-year maturity. |
| | 2. Issue Monetary Stabilization Bonds and government bonds of close to market interest rates. |
| | 3. Operate M2 targets flexibly. |
| | 4. Liberalize call markets. |
| | 5. Widen the daily won-dollar trading margin from 0.8 to 1.0 percent. |
| | 6. Switch to the notification system for foreign direct investment into Korea. |
| Phase II (1994–95) | 1. Liberalize all lending rates and rates for short-term marketable instruments. |
| | 2. Establish indirect monetary controls. |
| | 3. Deregulate loans to large conglomerates. |
| | 4. Develop short-term financial markets. |
| | 5. Further widen the daily won-dollar trading margin. |
| | 6. Further ease requirements for underlying documentation prior to foreign exchange transactions. |
| | 7. Expand limits on foreign investment in the stock market. |
| | 8. Allow foreign participation in primary markets for some bonds. |
| | 9. Ease requirements for opening branches of foreign securities companies. |
| Phase III (1996–97) | 1. Liberalize all deposit rates except for demand deposits (allow money market certificates and money market funds). |
| | 2. Utilize open market operations as main monetary policy tool. |
| | 3. Operate the Loans Management System as a prudential regulation. |
| | 4. Introduce free-floating exchange rate system. |
| | 5. Eliminate requirements for underlying documentation for the usual foreign exchange transactions. |
| | 6. Allow foreign borrowing through commercial loans. |
| | 7. Allow foreign financial institutions to hold stock of domestic banks. |

diminished gradually in financial markets as its industrial policies were not easily separated from financial policies. The cautious approach to financial opening was preferred to prevent external factors from creating additional disturbances in the process of domestic financial liberalization. Despite the slow pace of financial liberalization, Korea's financial market and financial policies have changed greatly since the early 1980s.

### 9.3.1 Changing Structure of the Financial System

The financial liberalization since the early 1980s stimulated financial intermediation as shown in figure 9.1. As economies grow, there is a tendency for the ratio of financial institutions' assets to GNP to increase. However, financial deepening stagnated in the 1970s as the ratio of domestic financial assets to GNP rose only modestly from 212 percent in 1970 to 240 percent in 1980. In contrast, the ratio doubled during 1980–93 with financial liberalization.

Financial deepening since the early 1980s has been driven by the growth of NBFIs. While the ratio of banks' financial assets to GNP has stagnated since the early 1980s, the ratio of the NBFI sector's financial assets to GNP has jumped remarkably (see table 9.3). The rapid growth of NBFIs can also be confirmed by the composition of financial savings in table 9.4. The share of bank deposits among the total financial savings declined from 46 percent in 1980 to 24 percent in October 1993. In contrast, the share of nonbank deposits increased from 38 percent to 68 percent during the same period.

The growth of NBFIs was possible because they operated under relatively free conditions with respect to interest rate control, burden of policy loans, entry barriers, and ownership regulation in order to absorb informal market funds into the organized financial market. The growth of NBFIs contributed to deepening the financial market, but it resulted in another disequilibrium in the financial market, that is, lack of competition between banks and nonbanks and slow progress toward a universal banking system.

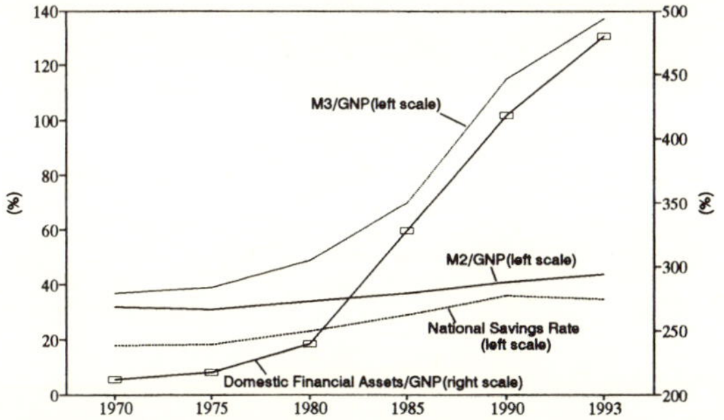


**Fig. 9.1 Trend of financial deepening**
*Source: Economic Statistics Yearbook* (Seoul: Bank of Korea, various issues).

**Table 9.3** **Ratio of Financial Assets to GNP (%)**

| Year | Financial Sector[a] | Deposit Money Banks | Life Insurance and Pension Funds | Other[b] | Nonfinancial Sector (domestic) |
|---|---|---|---|---|---|
| 1975 | 72.7 | 53.3 | 2.7 | 16.7 | 136.4 |
| 1980 | 100.6 | 64.0 | 6.0 | 30.6 | 139.7 |
| 1981 | 107.6 | 64.8 | 7.1 | 35.7 | 147.6 |
| 1982 | 122.6 | 71.8 | 8.5 | 42.3 | 165.2 |
| 1983 | 129.2 | 73.2 | 10.0 | 46.0 | 165.7 |
| 1984 | 134.0 | 71.3 | 11.5 | 51.2 | 170.3 |
| 1985 | 144.9 | 74.8 | 12.8 | 57.3 | 172.8 |
| 1986 | 145.1 | 71.9 | 14.7 | 58.5 | 177.0 |
| 1987 | 150.7 | 70.5 | 16.4 | 63.8 | 185.4 |
| 1988 | 157.5 | 67.7 | 18.4 | 71.4 | 186.4 |
| 1989 | 183.7 | 73.5 | 21.4 | 88.8 | 212.0 |
| 1990 | 191.5 | 74.8 | 23.3 | 93.4 | 214.9 |
| 1991 | 198.2 | 75.0 | 24.4 | 98.8 | 214.2 |
| 1992 | 213.1 | 78.8 | 25.8 | 108.5 | 223.5 |
| 1993 | 226.3 | 79.6 | 26.5 | 120.2 | 234.2 |

*Sources: Flow of Funds* (Seoul: Bank of Korea, various issues); *National Accounts* (Seoul: Bank of Korea, various issues).

[a]Excludes the Bank of Korea.

[b]Includes nonmonetary financial institutions and securities companies.

**Table 9.4** **Composition of Financial Savings (period end; %)**

| Period | Bank Time and Savings Deposits Including CDs[a] | Nonbank Deposits | Securities | Intersectoral Transactions |
|---|---|---|---|---|
| 1972 | 70.0 (82.2) | 22.2 | 13.2 | −5.4 |
| 1975 | 60.2 (65.8) | 27.6 | 15.6 | −3.4 |
| 1980 | 45.9 (51.5) | 37.8 | 21.8 | −5.4 |
| 1985 | 36.3 (42.3) | 53.6 | 24.4 | −14.3 |
| 1990 | 25.6 (38.8) | 60.3 | 29.9 | −15.8 |
| 1991 | 25.3 (38.9) | 59.5 | 30.1 | −15.0 |
| 1992 | 24.7 (40.9) | 64.2 | 27.9 | −16.7 |
| Oct. 1993 | 23.6 (42.0) | 67.8 | 26.5 | −17.9 |

*Source: Fiscal and Financial Statistics* (Seoul: Ministry of Finance, various issues).

[a]Numbers in parentheses are bank time and savings deposits including both CDs and money in trust (the latter being formally classified as nonbank deposits).

### 9.3.2 Behavior of Financial Intermediaries

Deregulation also affected the behavior of financial institutions. First, financial deregulation resulted in the reduction of policy loan burdens, causing the share of policy loans in total domestic credit to decline markedly from 47 percent in 1980 to 25 percent in 1991 (table 9.5). This fall was mainly achieved

**Table 9.5** **Share of Policy Loans (ratio to domestic credit; %)**

| | Monetary Institutions | | | | | | Other Financial Institutions | Total |
|---|---|---|---|---|---|---|---|---|
| Year | Subtotal | Government Funds | Credit to KDB and KEXIM | Foreign Currency Loans | Trade Financing | Housing Loans | | |
| 1973 | 48.2 | 5.3 | 3.4 | 6.6 | 11.5 | 3.1 | 52.8 | 49.3 |
| 1975 | 40.9 | 3.5 | 1.8 | 8.6 | 8.5 | 2.8 | 52.4 | 43.5 |
| 1980 | 49.1 | 3.0 | 1.5 | 15.5 | 10.3 | 5.6 | 43.9 | 47.4 |
| 1981 | 45.7 | 2.9 | 1.5 | 12.6 | 10.0 | 4.2 | 41.1 | 44.1 |
| 1982 | 40.3 | 3.0 | 1.0 | 11.5 | 8.3 | 5.7 | 38.8 | 39.7 |
| 1983 | 41.2 | 3.2 | 1.0 | 9.8 | 8.2 | 6.3 | 36.6 | 39.4 |
| 1984 | 40.7 | 3.5 | 1.0 | 8.7 | 7.7 | 6.4 | 31.7 | 36.8 |
| 1985 | 39.3 | 3.5 | 0.9 | 7.7 | 7.4 | 5.9 | 30.2 | 35.3 |
| 1986 | 40.6 | 3.6 | 1.0 | 7.5 | 7.0 | 5.5 | 24.1 | 33.1 |
| 1987 | 45.7 | 3.5 | 5.8 | 9.7 | 4.2 | 5.5 | 20.5 | 33.6 |
| 1988 | 46.4 | 3.6 | 7.9 | 8.9 | 1.9 | 8.2 | 17.3 | 31.9 |
| 1989 | 46.4 | 3.8 | 7.9 | 8.2 | 1.7 | 6.6 | 14.1 | 29.2 |
| 1990 | 46.3 | 3.6 | 7.7 | 8.5 | 2.0 | 7.0 | 12.7 | 27.8 |
| 1991 | 41.9 | 3.7 | 6.9 | 8.8 | 1.9 | 7.1 | 12.0 | 24.9 |

*Source: Korean Economic Indicators* (Seoul: National Statistical Office, various issues).

by the swift development of NBFIs such as investment and insurance institutions whose loans were not directed by the government and the shrinkage of some NBFIs such as development institutions whose loans are mostly policy-related. In contrast, the portion of policy loans by deposit money banks in total domestic credit showed a slight decrease. That figure declined from 49 percent in 1980 to 39 percent in 1985, but rose again to 46 percent during the latter half of the 1980s. The jump in the share of policy loans during 1987–90 stems from increased credit to development institutions such as the Korea Development Bank (KDB) and the Korea Export Import Bank (KEXIM) and increased agricultural and housing loans, which more than offset the drastic decline of export financing.

Second, while financial deregulation encourages banks to manage their assets and liabilities more carefully, we do not find any significant changes in the composition of bank assets as shown in table 9.6. The loans and discounts of banks continued to occupy almost 50 percent of total assets which exclude acceptances and guarantees, securities about 10 percent, and so forth. The sectoral composition of bank loans extended each year also did not change distinctively in the way that is expected with financial deregulation (table 9.7). Although more than half of all bank loans extended went to the business sector, there is no clear evidence that the business sector received a larger or smaller share of bank loans with the progress in financial liberalization. Rather, the sectoral composition varied each year according to macroeconomic conditions and financial policies.

Table 9.6 **Accounts of Deposit Money Banks (%)**

| Year | Domestic Assets: Cash | Due | Securities | Loans and Discounts | Loans in Foreign Currency | Foreign Assets | Other | Total |
|---|---|---|---|---|---|---|---|---|
| 1970 | 3.7 | 14.9 | 2.4 | 49.3 | 6.9 | 13.8 | 9.0 | 100.0 |
| 1975 | 3.7 | 14.4 | 2.6 | 41.8 | 4.9 | 9.4 | 23.1 | 100.0 |
| 1980 | 8.0 | 7.1 | 7.8 | 46.4 | 9.9 | 11.4 | 9.5 | 100.0 |
| 1981 | 11.0 | 4.7 | 9.8 | 46.8 | 8.1 | 10.4 | 9.2 | 100.0 |
| 1982 | 10.5 | 7.2 | 8.3 | 48.0 | 7.5 | 8.3 | 10.1 | 100.0 |
| 1983 | 9.3 | 3.7 | 10.9 | 48.9 | 6.3 | 8.4 | 12.4 | 100.0 |
| 1984 | 12.0 | 5.3 | 10.2 | 47.0 | 5.3 | 7.9 | 12.3 | 100.0 |
| 1985 | 9.9 | 9.9 | 6.8 | 49.4 | 4.8 | 7.4 | 11.9 | 100.0 |
| 1986 | 8.4 | 9.0 | 7.9 | 51.3 | 4.9 | 6.5 | 12.1 | 100.0 |
| 1987 | 11.7 | 8.3 | 8.3 | 47.8 | 6.1 | 5.8 | 12.0 | 100.0 |
| 1988 | 13.6 | 8.9 | 8.1 | 46.6 | 5.4 | 5.6 | 11.7 | 100.0 |
| 1989 | 12.3 | 6.8 | 8.5 | 50.1 | 5.2 | 4.3 | 12.8 | 100.0 |
| 1990 | 14.9 | 5.5 | 9.1 | 46.7 | 5.2 | 4.3 | 14.3 | 100.0 |
| 1991 | 13.2 | 5.7 | 9.6 | 47.8 | 5.5 | 4.4 | 13.9 | 100.0 |
| 1992 | 10.2 | 5.9 | 10.3 | 48.7 | 4.9 | 4.8 | 15.3 | 100.0 |
| 1993 | 7.5 | 6.0 | 11.6 | 49.5 | 4.5 | 5.6 | 15.3 | 100.0 |

*Source: Monthly Bulletin* (Seoul: Bank of Korea, various issues).
*Note:* Figures are ratios to total assets excluding acceptances and guarantees.

Table 9.7 **Sectoral Composition of Bank Loans Extended (%)**

| Year | Financial Sector | Government | Business | Individuals |
|---|---|---|---|---|
| 1970 | 0.0 | 0.6 | 63.5 | 35.9 |
| 1975 | 1.5 | 3.7 | 68.1 | 26.7 |
| 1980 | 2.5 | 0.8 | 63.4 | 33.1 |
| 1981 | 6.9 | 0.0 | 52.5 | 40.6 |
| 1982 | 1.4 | 2.2 | 61.9 | 34.4 |
| 1983 | 1.1 | 4.2 | 49.8 | 44.9 |
| 1984 | 4.9 | 0.9 | 66.9 | 27.3 |
| 1985 | −0.9 | 3.4 | 76.3 | 21.1 |
| 1986 | −0.5 | −1.2 | 75.9 | 25.8 |
| 1987 | 11.4 | −1.0 | 49.0 | 40.6 |
| 1988 | 12.9 | −1.2 | 52.5 | 35.8 |
| 1989 | 31.9 | 0.7 | 40.6 | 26.8 |
| 1990 | −6.3 | 2.7 | 60.9 | 42.6 |
| 1991 | −1.1 | 1.8 | 66.2 | 33.1 |
| 1992 | 14.7 | 1.0 | 57.8 | 26.4 |
| 1993 | 3.1 | 1.6 | 64.9 | 30.4 |

*Source: Flow of Funds* (Seoul: Bank of Korea, various issues).
*Note:* Figures are ratios to the total bank loans made each year.

Third, financial deregulation did not bring about a rapid expansion in lending, as shown in figure 9.2. This result is in contrast with experiences of other countries in which bank loans grew rapidly as the activities of financial institutions were decontrolled. The boom-bust cycles due to eased credit with financial liberalization are well documented even in the case of advanced countries such as the Scandinavian countries (Åkerholm 1994) and Australia (Lowe 1994).

The mechanism for boom-bust cycles is as follows. Financial liberalization eases credit via the removal of most quantitative restrictions on bank lending, interest rate decontrol, the relaxation of control over foreign capital inflows, and a scramble for market share among financial intermediaries. The eased credit goes to households as well as to businesses. The boom in lending, which happens to coincide with the boom in the economy, soon turns into an asset boom as lax credit is used to finance consumption and asset purchases, which in turn can be used as collateral against which to borrow. An excessive consumption boom and soaring asset prices make an economy highly vulnerable to adverse changes in economic conditions. A credit-supported boom must end in crisis as the authorities adopt tight monetary policy to control rampant inflation and the asset bubble explodes. The longer and more substantial the boom is, the more deep and damaging the crisis.

In Korea, there was close correlation between the growth in financial loans and increases in land prices. Thus credit-supported boom-bust cycles after financial liberalization could have been possible, if the financial repression of the 1970s had been followed by rapid and drastic financial liberalization in the early 1980s. In fact, the cautious and gradual approach to financial liberalization hindered financial intermediaries from engaging in excessive loans to households or investments in asset markets. The actual asset market boom in Korea in the latter half of the 1980s is attributable to the yen and won appreciation vis-à-vis the U.S. dollar rather than to credit expansion.[2]

### 9.3.3 Monetary Policy

The Korean government supplied a large amount of loans to priority sectors to sustain high growth and at the same time tried to control inflationary pressure caused by these loans. To achieve the conflicting goals of economic growth and inflation control, the government had to intervene directly in financial markets by using direct interest rate controls, preferential credit to priority sectors, high reserve requirements, and other direct controls on monetary aggregates and domestic credit.

Until the 1970s, the underdeveloped financial market limited the effectiveness of indirect monetary controls. The rediscount policy was ineffective because rediscounts were almost automatically approved and supplied at preferential rates. The reserve requirements were quite high until 1980, but the high

2. See Park and Park (1994) for a discussion of this issue.

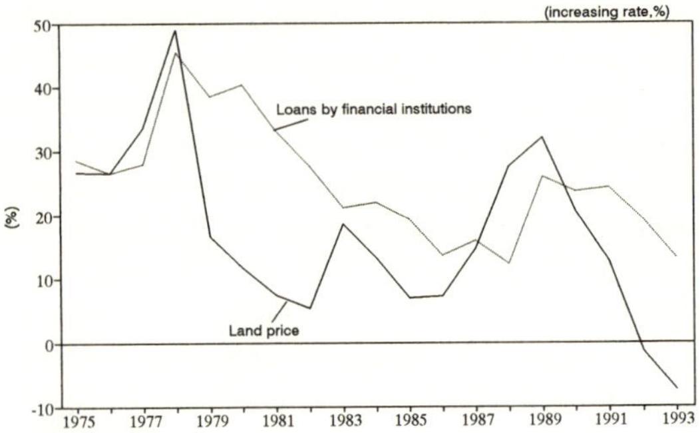


**Fig. 9.2 Loans and land price**
*Sources: Economic Statistics Yearbook* (Seoul: Bank of Korea, various issues); *Land Price Trends* (Seoul: Ministry of Construction, various issues).

reserve requirement ratio was not effective because the reserve deficiencies of the banks were replenished with their borrowings from the central bank. Instead of controlling monetary expansion, the high reserve requirements decreased the profitability of banks. Open market operations, the most important tool for indirect monetary control, were carried out in a limited way because the fiscal deficits were financed through money creation rather than through bond issues and, moreover, interest rates for bonds were significantly below the market-clearing level.

Financial liberalization brought with it important changes in monetary policy from direct monetary controls to indirect ones. First, in 1982, the authorities replaced direct control over bank lending with an indirect reserve control system. Since 1982, there has been no formal direct control of bank credit except for measures to restrict loans to large conglomerates.

Second, efforts were made to restore such traditional central bank policies as the rediscount policy, reserve requirement policy, and open market operations. The emphasis of the rediscount policy has been on setting the rediscount ratios and changing the eligibility criteria of bills presented to the Bank of Korea. The reserve requirement ratio was lowered markedly during 1980–82 because the authorities recognized the ineffectiveness of the high reserve requirement policy and the increased financial burdens of banks caused thereby. The authorities also tried to use open market operations more frequently by financing fiscal deficits more through bond issues and offering Monetary Stabilization Bonds at interest rates close to market rates.[3]

Third, even with financial liberalization, the authorities have been using M2 growth as the intermediate target variable since 1979. The practice of monetary targets had both good and bad aspects in Korea. Monetary targeting certainly

3. See Kang (1993) and Ro (1993) for the details of Korea's monetary policy.

served to curb inflationary pressure when the economy was on the verge of overheating. At the same time, however, rigid monetary targets encouraged the government to rely on direct monetary controls. Sometimes the M2 amount was managed by adjusting the balance sheets of financial institutions.

The progress toward indirect monetary controls was interrupted by huge current account surpluses in the latter half of the 1980s, since the monetary expansion through the foreign sector created additional burdens in controlling the money supply (see table 9.8). On one hand, the excessive money supply necessitated more rapid foreign exchange and capital account liberalization and even a floating exchange rate system. Thus monetary policies in the latter half of the 1980s were concerned mainly with the balance of payments and exchange rates. The current account surpluses accelerated the progress in financial opening and exchange rate floating, leading to the won's appreciation.

On the other hand, the monetary expansion from the foreign sector hindered the deregulation of domestic financial markets. For instance, the measure deregulating lending rates in December 1988 was revoked quickly for fear of a rise in interest rates in the process of monetary contraction. Also the Bank of Korea has had to issue such large amounts of Monetary Stabilization Bonds as to assign them to NBFIs at interest rates below market rates. Furthermore, the money growth targets became more important than any other indicators that could be used to assess domestic economic conditions and the stance of policies.

### 9.3.4 Exchange Rate Policy

Korea maintained a de facto dollar-peg system until 1980 although the system was officially named the unified floating exchange rate system. Under this system, Korea's real exchange rate tended to appreciate. Recognizing the adverse effects of real appreciation on its trade account, Korea adopted the Multiple Currency Basket Peg System in February 1980. The new system was insti-

**Table 9.8** **Sectoral Increases in the M2 Supply (end of year; billion won)**

| Year | Government Credit | Private Credit | External Sector | Other | Total |
|---|---|---|---|---|---|
| 1985 | 40 | 6,462 | −1,595 | −1,047 | 3,860 |
| 1986 | 170 | 6,765 | 2,424 | −4,091 | 5,268 |
| 1987 | −1,656 | 6,115 | 9,030 | −7,043 | 6,446 |
| 1988 | −2,174 | 8,642 | 10,212 | −8,021 | 8,659 |
| 1989 | −1,993 | 16,871 | 2,365 | −7,543 | 9,699 |
| 1990 | −1,458 | 19,068 | 118 | −7,660 | 10,070 |
| 1991 | 778 | 20,840 | −3,117 | −3,463 | 15,038 |
| 1992 | −271 | 14,060 | 4,066 | −5,342 | 12,513 |
| 1993 | −1,919 | 18,136 | 5,397 | −5,654 | 15,961 |

*Source: Monthly Bulletin* (Seoul: Bank of Korea, various issues).

tuted to stabilize the real effective exchange rate of the won. Indeed, the real effective exchange rate has tended to depreciate since 1980 (figure 9.3). Overall, it could be said that Korea's exchange rate policy evolved from a nominal anchor approach in the 1970s into a real target approach in the 1980s.

The real target approach helped to reduce the current account deficit and the huge external debt in the early 1980s. Many international institutions, such as the International Monetary Fund, supported Korea's real depreciation because they thought that real depreciation was required to prevent financial liberalization from being stalled in its beginning stages by the expanded current account deficits and the aggravated external debt problem. However, once the current account began to show surpluses starting in 1986 due mainly to enormous yen appreciation, the situation developed in a different way. Many international institutions including the U.S. Treasury accused Korea of "manipulating" its exchange rates. In response to foreign pressure and an excess supply of foreign exchange, real appreciation of the won occurred during 1988–90.

Korea adopted a new exchange rate system called the Market Average Exchange Rate System in March 1990 to make exchange rates better reflect market fundamentals. Under the new system, the won-dollar exchange rate changes to reflect the demand and supply of foreign exchanges, albeit within a daily trading margin. The daily won-dollar trading margins have been widened several times, from the initial 0.4 percent above and below the base exchange rate to 1.0 percent in October 1993. Under the Market Average Exchange Rate System, the real effective exchange rate of the won tended to depreciate.

Figure 9.3 also shows that Korea was lucky to face sustained improvement in the terms of trade during its financial deregulation. In fact, the improvement in the terms of trade was substantial enough to offset the won's real depreciation.

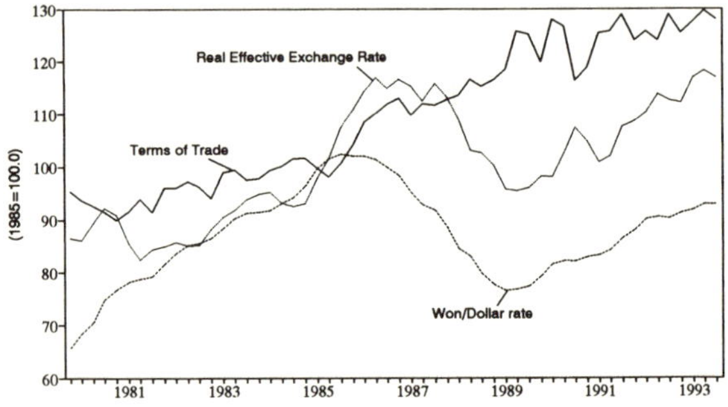


**Fig. 9.3 Exchange rates and terms of trade**

*Source: International Financial Statistics* (Washington, D.C.: International Monetary Fund, various issues).

*Note:* Dotted curve shows won's real effective exchange rate with Korea's seven major trading partners (the United States, Japan, Germany, the United Kingdom, France, Canada, and the Netherlands). Higher values mean real depreciation.

## 9.4 Tests of Capital Mobility in Korea

As reviewed in the previous section, Korea's financial liberalization was extended to financial opening to make it more comprehensive. The package of financial market opening policies includes the liberalizing of foreign exchange transactions, opening of domestic capital markets, and floating of exchange rates.

Table 9.9 shows developments in Korea's capital account since the early 1980s. The capital account was in surplus in the first half of the 1980s to accommodate the large current account deficit. Public and commercial loans were the major source of capital inflows during this period. As the current account registered massive surpluses in the latter half of the 1980s, however, public and commercial loans served as the major source of capital outflows causing capital account deficits. Entering the 1990s, the capital account once again began to register surpluses as capital account liberalization brought in large portfolio investments from abroad. As stated in section 9.2, foreigners were allowed to invest in the Korean stock market starting in 1992.

Table 9.9 raises at least two questions regarding Korea's capital mobility. One is how open Korea's financial markets are in a weak or strong sense. The other is whether the degree of financial openness increased with financial liberalization even though Korea's financial markets are not completely opened. The casual answers to the two questions can be inferred from figure 9.4. Since ex post differences in won returns between won deposits in Korea (measured by corporate bond yields) and dollar deposits abroad (measured by LIBOR) are substantial, one can easily conclude that uncovered interest parity does not hold in Korea and consequently that Korea's financial markets are not completely opened.[4] Regarding degree, Korea's financial opening seemed to deteriorate in the latter half of the 1980s as ex post differences in won currency returns between domestic and foreign assets widened but the capital account registered net outflows during the same period. This stems from the huge current account surplus which in turn led to the won's appreciation vis-à-vis the U.S. dollar and active capital account policy for net outflows, such as advance payments of foreign loans.

Rather than depending on casual empiricism, this section intends to measure and test international capital mobility in Korea. One can measure capital mobility by investigating asset price arbitrage conditions, risk diversification,

4. The interest rate differentials here incorporate the problem of measurement errors. The returns on won deposits are represented by the yield on corporate bonds of three-year maturity while the won currency returns on dollar deposits are represented by the three-month LIBOR plus the won's annual depreciation vis-à-vis the U.S. dollar. These measurement errors were inevitable because (uncontrolled) three-month interbank loan rates are not available in a long series and corporate bond yields used to represent market interest rates in Korea. A one-year horizon for the won's depreciation was chosen arbitrarily by considering the difference in maturity of Korea's corporate bonds and dollar deposits at the London interbank market.

**Table 9.9 Korea's Capital Account (annual average; million U.S. dollars)**

| Item | 1981–85 | 1986–90 | 1991–93 |
|---|---|---|---|
| *Current account* | −2,232 | 6,301 | −4,269 |
| *Capital account* | 1,596 | −1,807 | 6,440 |
| Long-term | 1,702 | −2,673 | 6,739 |
| Liabilities | 2,250 | −1,771 | 7,328 |
| Public loans | 981 | −907 | −1,001 |
| Commercial loans | −81 | −741 | −720 |
| Direct investments | 117 | 676 | 728 |
| Portfolio investments | 315 | 131 | 6,646 |
| Assets (increase, −) | −540 | −902 | −589 |
| Short-term | −106 | 866 | −299 |
| Liabilities | −133 | 1,043 | 499 |
| Assets (increase, −) | 27 | −176 | −799 |

*Source: Balance of Payments Statistics* (Seoul: Bank of Korea, various issues).

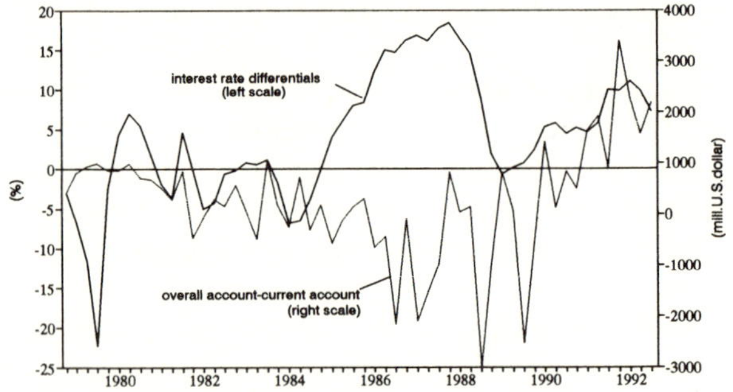


**Fig. 9.4 Interest rate differentials and capital flows in Korea**
*Note:* Korea's corporate bond yield − dollar LIBOR.

saving-investment correlations, or effectiveness of sterilized invention.[5] Among them, this section concentrates on the saving-investment correlations and asset price arbitrage conditions.

### 9.4.1 Saving-Investment Correlations

Feldstein and Horioka (1980) proposed saving-investment correlations as a barometer of capital mobility. They argued that if domestic savings are free to flow to their most productive uses in the world, a change in domestic savings will seldom affect domestic investment. However, this approach raised many questions concerning interpretation and econometric estimation (Obstfeld 1993; Montiel 1993).

5. A good survey on capital mobility is provided in Obstfeld (1993) for advanced countries and Montiel (1993) for developing countries.

Despite many challenges to the Feldstein-Horioka approach, saving-investment correlations are still one of the ways to measure international capital mobility. Table 9.10 presents the regression results of investment ratios with respect to saving ratios in Korea, using quarterly data for 1980.1–1992.4. This time-series estimation has the crucial limitation that it captures only the short-run relationship between national saving and domestic investment without explaining the true long-run relationship. The long-run relationship can be captured by estimating cross-sectional data averaged over a sufficiently long period. Despite these limitations, the saving-investment correlation coefficient was estimated to be small or even slightly negative in table 9.10.

Although the estimates are insignificant, little correlation between saving and investment might suggest high capital mobility in Korea. However, the interpretation and econometric problems involving the Feldstein-Horioka approach could be applied to Korea's saving-investment correlations. Considering that Korea was able to finance its very high investment with foreign funds, one may obtain small estimates even if Korea's financial markets are not sufficiently integrated with world financial markets. The time-series results of only small correlations between national savings and domestic investment should not be interpreted to mean that only small fractions of increases in national savings remain at home or that the saving retention coefficient is low in Korea.

### 9.4.2 Interest Rate Parity Conditions

The degree of financial integration has typically been measured by the extent to which asset price arbitrage takes place. Numerous studies have examined covered or uncovered interest rate parity conditions, but only a few have investigated the Korean case. This lack of interest seems to stem from the observation that uncovered interest parity does not hold in Korea, as shown in figure 9.4.

Rather than testing whether uncovered interest parity holds, Reisen and Yeches (1991) directly estimated the degree of capital mobility following the method of Haque and Montiel (1990), which takes the influence of foreign

**Table 9.10** **Saving-Investment Correlation in Korea**

| | $\hat{\beta}$ | | |
|---|---|---|---|
| Period | Level-OLS | Level-IV | Difference-OLS |
| 1980–92 | 0.15 (1.85) | 0.18 (2.12) | −0.07 (−1.20) |
| 1980–85 | −0.22 (−1.89) | −0.26 (−2.13) | −0.23 (−1.63) |
| 1986–92 | 0.12 (0.31) | 0.45 (0.96) | −0.09 (−0.60) |

*Notes:* "Level" estimates are based on the OLS regression $(I/Y)_t = \alpha + \beta(S/Y)_t + u_t$. IVs are ratio of government consumption to GNP. "Difference" estimates are based on the OLS regression $\Delta(I/Y)_t = \alpha + \beta\Delta(S/Y)_t + \Delta u_t$. Seasonal dummies are included. Numbers in parentheses are *t*-values.

interest rates on domestic interest rates as a barometer of capital mobility. Reisen and Ỳeches (1991) show that the degree of capital mobility was low and declined gradually in the second half of the 1980s in Korea. Their results were challenged by Jwa (1994), who shows that their results could change depending on how one specifies the counterfactual interest rates in the absence of capital mobility. On the other hand, Faruqee (1991) obtained the same results as Reisen and Ỳeches (1991) by employing the autoregressive conditional heteroskedasticity (ARCH) technique of Engle (1982).

We also examine Korea's capital mobility by applying the ARCH technique to interest rate differentials between domestic and foreign assets. Using monthly data for Korea's three-year corporate bond yields and dollar LIBOR for three-month deposits over January 1980-December 1993, the ARIMA (1,1,0) specification was chosen as the appropriate time-series representation for the interest rate differentials. To correct for conditional heteroskedasticity, an ARCH three-lag model was implemented. The results are contained in table 9.11 and figure 9.5.

Figure 9.5 shows that the conditional variance of shocks to interest rate parity declined drastically after it peaked in 1982. But it rose again during 1988–89, indicating that the degree of Korea's capital mobility declined to a certain degree toward the end of the 1980s. The results are little affected by whether the expected rate of the won's depreciation vis-à-vis the U.S. dollar is assumed under perfect foresight to be the actual depreciation rate or the won-dollar exchange rate follows a random walk (expected rate of the won's depreciation is zero). Thus we can conclude on the basis of the ARCH test on interest parity conditions that, although Korea's capital mobility increased significantly in the latter half of the 1980s compared to the early 1980s, it declined more or less in the latter half of the 1980s compared to the period of 1983–86.

**Table 9.11 ARCH Estimation for Interest Rate Differentials (model: ARIMA (1,1,0))**

| | | | ARCH Lag | | | |
|---|---|---|---|---|---|---|
| rd[a] | Constant | $\Delta rd_{t-1}$ | $\alpha_0$ | $\alpha_1$ | $\alpha_2$ | $\alpha_3$ |
| $i - i^* - (\log S_{t+12} - \log S_t)$[b] | 0.10 | 0.43 | 0.20 | 0.43 | 0.32 | 0.06 |
| | (2.57) | (9.58) | (11.74) | (5.97) | (5.63) | (6.19) |
| $i - i^*$ | −0.01 | 0.38 | 0.21 | 0.61 | 0.17 | 0.21 |
| | (−0.14) | (4.63) | (3.95) | (3.31) | (1.42) | (2.14) |

*Note:* Numbers in parentheses are *t*-values.

[a]rd, interest rate differentials; *i*, Korea's corporate bond yields (three-year maturity); $i^*$, dollar LIBOR (three-month deposits); *S*, won-dollar exchange rate.

[b]One-year horizon for the won's depreciation has been chosen arbitrarily considering the difference in maturity of Korea's corporate bonds and dollar deposits at the London interbank market.

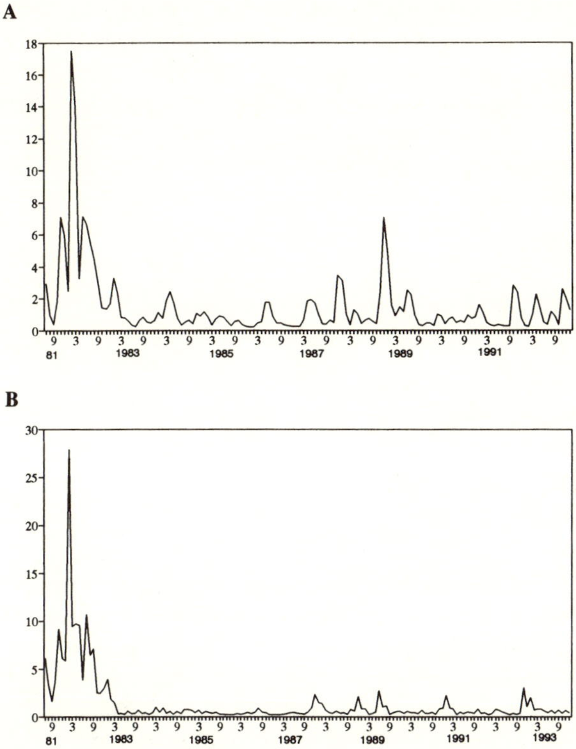


**Fig. 9.5 Deviations from interest rate parity (ARCH variance): (*A*) ex-post interest difference in won currency; (*B*) nominal interest differentials**

## 9.5 Korea's Nominal and Real Exchange Rate

As shown in figure 9.3, Korea's nominal and real exchange rates have fluctuated under different regimes since financial deregulation began in the early 1980s. In this section, we present a very simple model to explain the movements of Korea's real exchange rate and also pay attention to the volatility of the won-dollar exchange rate under the different regimes of the basket-peg and market average rate systems.

### 9.5.1 A Model for Korea's Real Exchange Rate

We formulate a two-sector general equilibrium model to explain changes in Korea's real exchange rate, particularly under the Multiple Currency Basket Peg System during 1980–89. The model is modified from that of Calvo and Rodriguez (1977) and much simpler than that of Edwards (1988). The model assumes a variant of a dual exchange market, where the official exchange rate is separated from the market exchange rate. For simplicity, the model assumes full employment, purchasing power parity, rational expectations, and two assets of domestic and foreign money. We further assume that real transactions take place at the official exchange rate and financial transactions take place at the market exchange rate.

The real exchange rate ($q$) is defined by the relative price of tradable goods ($EP^{T*}$, for $E$ the official exchange rate and $P^{T*}$ the foreign currency price of traded goods) and home goods ($P^{H}$):

(1) $$q = \frac{EP^{T*}}{P^{H}}$$

Production ($Y$) and consumption ($C$) for both goods are specified as functions of the real exchange rate ($q$) and real wealth ($a$):

(2) $$\begin{aligned} Y^{T} &= Y^{T}(q),\ Y^{T}_{q} > 0; \\ Y^{H} &= Y^{H}(q),\ Y^{H}_{q} < 0; \\ C^{T} &= C^{T}(q,a),\ C^{T}_{q} < 0,\ C^{T}_{a} > 0; \\ C^{H} &= C^{H}(q,\ a),\ C^{H}_{q} > 0,\ C^{H}_{a} > 0; \end{aligned}$$

where a subscript denotes differentiation with respect to that variable.

The real wealth of the public in terms of tradable goods comprises domestic money ($M$) and foreign money ($F$):

(3) $$a = \frac{1}{P^{T*}}\left(\frac{M}{E} + \frac{\delta}{E}\right) = \frac{1}{P^{T*}}(m + \rho F)\ ,$$

where $\delta$ represents the market exchange rate, $m = M/E$, and $\rho = \delta/E$.

Equilibrium in the market for home goods ($Y^{H} = C^{H}$) requires a negative relationship between the real wealth of the public and the real exchange rate:

(4) $$a = V(q),\ V_{q} < 0.$$

We assume that domestic money changes according to changes in international reserves or the current account balance, which is more likely in the Korean case of a foreign exchange concentration system:

(5) $$M = EP^{T*}\ (Y^{T} - C^{T}) = EP^{T*}f(a),\quad f_{a} < 0.$$

The demand for each asset depends on the expected relative rates of return on the two monies:

(6) $$\dot{\rho} = \rho L\left(\frac{m}{\rho F}\right),\quad L' < 0.$$

The system can be represented by the state variables of the real balance $m$ and the difference between the market exchange rates and the official exchange rate $\rho$. Figure 9.6 portrays the phase diagram. When $\dot{m} = 0$, equation (5) deter-

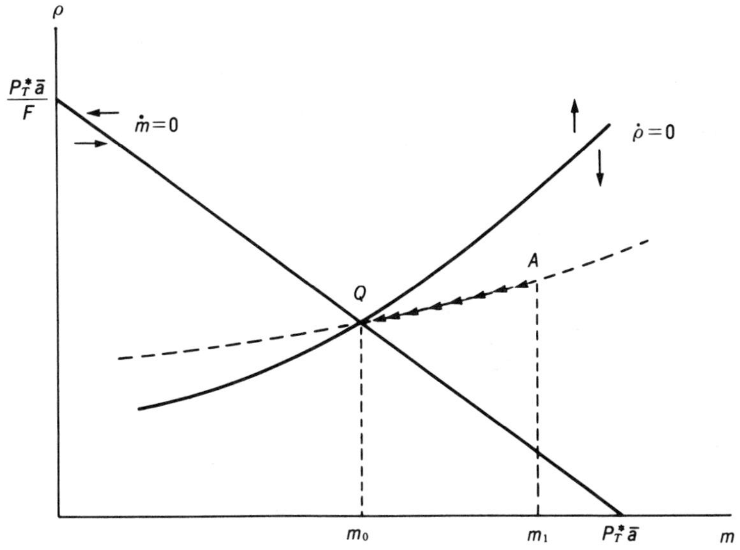


**Fig. 9.6 Impact of money increase and won appreciation**

mines the unique steady state value of real wealth at $\bar{a}$. We know from equation (3) that $P^{T*}\bar{a} = m + \rho F$. Thus the $\dot{m} = 0$ locus is downward sloping. The $\dot{\rho} = 0$ locus is upward sloping from equation (6). The saddle path should be upward sloping in figure 9.6.

We now consider the impact of domestic monetary expansion and nominal appreciation of the domestic money using figure 9.6. Either the increased supply or the nominal appreciation of domestic money raises the real balance of domestic money. The market exchange rate depreciates immediately to point A on the saddle path, thereby increasing real wealth and causing real appreciation if the official exchange rate does not adjust.

Figure 9.7 illustrates the impact of an increase in the foreign currency price of traded goods ($P^{T*}$). With an increase in $P^{T*}$, $\dot{m} = 0$ shifts upward. The market exchange rate depreciates immediately to point B on the new saddle path. As the economy moves toward the new steady state, the market exchange rate continues to depreciate, but the official real exchange rate starts to appreciate. Although this exercise uncovers many interesting points related to changes in the foreign price of traded goods, it has a crucial limitation in that the model assumes the law of one price for traded goods or no changes in the terms of trade. Once the model is extended to the three-sector model of exportables, importables, and nontradables (Edwards 1988), then the shift of the $\dot{m} = 0$ locus depends on how much the production and consumption of traded goods are affected by changes in the terms of trade. Thus the initial impact of changes

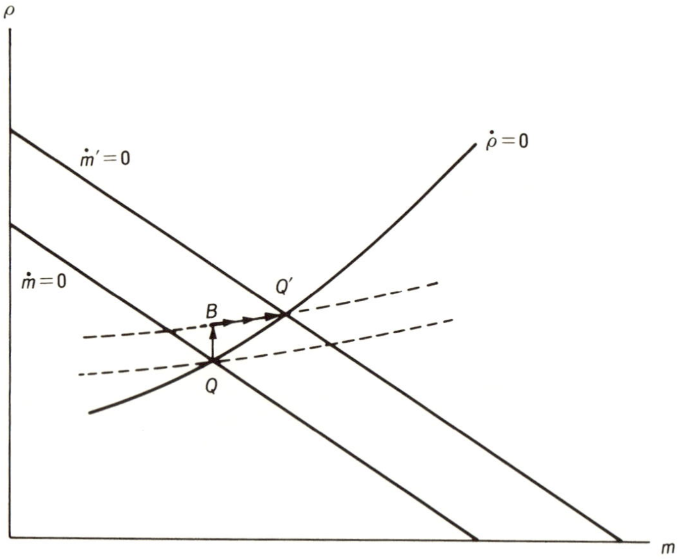


**Fig. 9.7 Impact of an increase in foreign currency price of traded goods and fiscal expansion**

in the terms of trade on the real exchange rate are generally uncertain (Edwards and van Wijnbergen 1987). The same conclusion can be reached in the case of tariff changes.

Figure 9.7 can also be used to show the impact of increased government spending. As government expenditures give rise to additional demand for traded goods and increases in domestic credit, the steady state is achieved with real appreciation. Thus steady state real wealth ($\bar{a}$) must increase, shifting the $\dot{m} = 0$ locus upward. With increases in government spending, the real exchange rate appreciates immediately.

9.5.2 Determinants of Korea's Real Exchange Rate

According to the model of the real exchange that was presented in section 9.5.1, the movement of the real exchange rate shows saddle-path stability. In the short run, the real exchange rate is affected by both real and monetary variables, but in the long run only the real variable affects the real exchange rate. Dynamic changes of the real exchange rate could be formulated as follows:

$$\text{(7)} \qquad \log q_t - \log q_{t-1} = \theta(\log q_t^* - \log q_{t-1}) + \lambda\, x_t\,,$$

where $\theta$ is the coefficient for the adjustment speed, $q_t^*$ equilibrium real exchange rate, and $x_t$ initial disturbance. According to equation (7), the impact of the monetary disturbances $x_t$ must disappear in the long run. But in the estimation we do not emphasize the long-run neutral effects of monetary determinants for the real exchange rate because the monetary and real determinants are correlated and because the impact of monetary disturbances can last a long time if monetary disturbances occur when the actual real exchange rate deviates greatly from the equilibrium level. Thus the estimation equation runs as follows:

$$\begin{aligned} \log \text{REER}_t = {} & \beta_0 + \beta_1 \log \text{TOT}_t + \beta_2 \log \text{GEDP}_t + \beta_3 \log \text{TFF}_t \\ & + \beta_4 \text{RGDP}_t + \beta_5 \text{CAP}_t + (1 - \theta) \log \text{REER}_{t-1} \\ & + \beta_6 \text{RM2}_{t-1} + \beta_7 \text{REX}_t + \beta_8 \text{REFX}_t , \end{aligned} \tag{8}$$

where REER is the won's real effective exchange rate with Korea's seven major trading partners (the United States, Japan, Germany, the United Kingdom, France, Canada, and the Netherlands). We have chosen terms of trade (TOT), ratio of government consumption to GDP (GEDP), tariff (TFF), real GDP growth (RGDP), and capital account balance (CAP) as real determinants. M2 growth (RM2), the won's depreciation against the U.S. dollar (REX), and the dollar's depreciation against Korea's seven major trading partners (REFX) are the monetary determinants for real exchange.

Table 9.12 shows the estimation results. The unique features in Korea's real exchange rate adjustments are in order. First, the terms of trade improvement or the tariff increase caused real depreciation in the 1980s. This result contrasts with experiences of other developing countries in which a terms of trade improvement or a tariff increase induced real appreciation. Second, the real appreciation impact of real GDP growth, representing the Ricardo-Balassa ef-

**Table 9.12** **Determinants for Korea's Real Effective Exchange Rate, 1980.1–1989.4**

| Variable | OLS | | IV[a] | |
|---|---|---|---|---|
| Constant | 1.40 | (2.44) | 0.64 | (0.83) |
| log TOT | 0.14 | (1.73) | 0.15 | (1.77) |
| log GEDP | −0.19 | (−3.24) | −0.16 | (−2.45) |
| log TFF | 0.11 | (3.08) | 0.09 | (2.26) |
| RGDP | −0.17 | (−1.06) | −0.02 | (−0.10) |
| CAP | −0.015 | (−3.09) | −0.012 | (−1.75) |
| log $\text{REER}_{-1}$ | 0.36 | (2.98) | 0.55 | (3.22) |
| $\text{RM2}_{-1}$ | −0.10 | (−1.29) | −0.08 | (−1.00) |
| REX | 0.16 | (1.69) | 0.25 | (2.19) |
| REFX | −0.60 | (−4.35) | −0.37 | (−1.84) |
| $R^2$ | 0.98 | | 0.98 | |
| D-W | 1.70 | | 1.75 | |

*Notes:* Seasonal dummies are included. RGDP, RM2, REX, and REFX are the ratios, not the percentages. CAP is in billion U.S. dollars. Numbers in parentheses are *t*-values.

[a]The instrumental variables are the constant, seasonal dummies, four lags of each explanatory variable except for TFF and REFX, and log TFF.

fects of real growth, was not significant in Korea, quite contrary to expectations. Third, monetary and fiscal expansion and capital inflows caused real appreciation as expected. Last, 10 percent nominal depreciation of the won vis-à-vis the U.S. dollar was estimated to have caused real depreciation of 2 percent in the current quarter and 4 percent within one year under the Multiple Currency Basket Peg System in the 1980s.

With the institution of the Market Average Exchange Rate System, the nominal exchange rate better reflects the market conditions. Accordingly, the relevance of the model diminishes as the official rate is not separated from the market rate. Considering these aspects, we reestimated equation (8) without REX variables over 1980.1–1992.4. But the qualitative results were unaffected when we assumed that the won-dollar exchange rate is determined by other real and monetary factors.

### 9.5.3 Exchange Rate Volatility

As financial markets are gradually opened and the volume of capital flows increase under the floating regime of the Market Average Exchange Rate System, it is generally expected that exchange rate volatility will increase compared to that under the basket-peg regime. To compare exchange rate volatility between the two different regimes, we applied the ARCH technique to the monthly won-dollar exchange rate. The ARIMA (1,1,0) model with ARCH four lag was chosen, respectively, to investigate exchange rate movement during the basket-peg period of March 1980-February 1990 and the market average period of March 1990-December 1993. Quite surprisingly, figure 9.8 shows that won-dollar exchange rate volatility declined under the market average system when measured either by movements of ARIMA residuals or by the conditional variance of ARIMA residuals.

One might interpret this result as evidence that under the Market Average Exchange Rate System the Bank of Korea intervened in the foreign exchange market in order to prevent capital flows from appreciating the won (Park 1994). On the other hand, the less volatile movements of dollar-yen exchange rates during 1990–93 may be one reason for the less volatile movements of won-dollar exchange rates during the same period. In the latter case, the less volatile movements of won-dollar exchange rates do not necessarily imply less free-floating won-dollar exchange rates.

## 9.6 Concluding Remarks

Korea's financial deregulation since the early 1980s has brought about great changes in the financial market and in financial policies. This paper has reviewed the deregulatory process and examined the effects of financial liberalization. Despite a series of deregulatory measures, Korea's financial market still has structural problems and is expected to face difficulties when the market is fully liberalized.

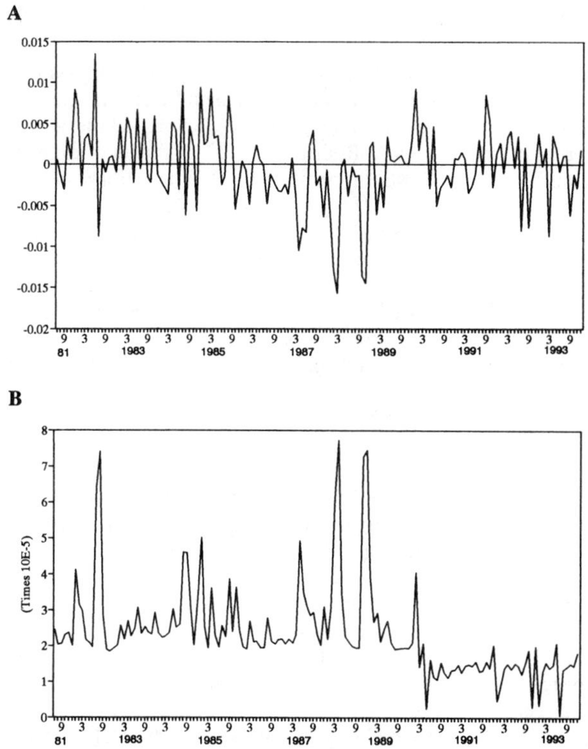


**Fig. 9.8 ARCH variance in won-dollar exchange rate: (*A*) ARIMA (1,1,0) residuals; (*B*) ARCH variances**

Since domestic financial liberalization was mostly based on the deregulation of NBFIs, the reform of the banking sector is still an urgent goal. A gradual shift to a universal banking system seems inevitable to promote competition among financial institutions and to enhance the efficiency of Korea's financial markets.

Both the test of capital mobility and the investigation of Korea's nominal and real exchange rates revealed that Korea still has a long way to go toward the goals of free mobility of capital and floating of exchange rates. Although Korea's cautious approach to financial liberalization succeeded in avoiding the unexpected pitfalls of deregulation and in reaping good results, efforts must yet be made to further deregulate the domestic financial market and increase the scope of financial opening.

# References

Åkerholm, Johnny. 1994. Financial deregulation and economic imbalances in the Scandinavian countries. Paper presented at conference on Financial Opening: Policy Lessons for Korea held at Korea Institute of Finance, Seoul, February 21–22.

Calvo, Guillermo A., and Carlos A. Rodriguez. 1977. A model of exchange rate determination under currency substitution and rational expectations. *Journal of Political Economy* 85:617–26.

Cho, Yoon Je, and Joon-Kyung Kim. 1993. Credit policies and industrialization of Korea. Washington D.C.: World Bank, July. Manuscript.

Edwards, Sebastian. 1988. Real and monetary determinants of real exchange rate behavior: Theory and evidence from developing countries. NBER Working Paper no. 2721. Cambridge, Mass.: National Bureau of Economic Research, September.

Edwards, Sebastian, and Sweder van Wijnbergen. 1987. Tariffs, the real exchange rate and the terms of trade: On two popular propositions in international economics. NBER Working Paper no. 2365. Cambridge, Mass.: National Bureau of Economic Research, August.

Engle, Robert. 1982. Autoregressive conditional heteroscedasticity with estimates of the variance of United Kingdom inflation. *Econometrica* 50(4):391–407.

Faruqee, Hamid. 1991. Dynamic capital mobility in Pacific Basin developing countries: Estimation and policy implications. IMF Working Paper. Washington, D.C.: International Monetary Fund, November.

Feldstein, Martin, and Charles Horioka. 1980. Domestic savings and international capital flows. *Economic Journal* 90 (June):314–29.

Haque, Nadeem U., and Peter Montiel. 1990. Capital mobility in developing countries: Some empirical tests. IMF Working Paper. Washington, D.C.: International Monetary Fund, December.

Jwa, Sung Hee. 1994. Capital mobility in Korea since the early 1980s: Comparison with Japan and Taiwan. In *Macroeconomic Linkage,* ed. T. Ito and A. O. Krueger, 123–63. Chicago: University of Chicago Press.

Kang, Moon-Soo. 1993. Monetary policy implementation under financial liberalization: The case of Korea. In *Financial Opening,* ed. H. Reisen and B. Fischer, 201–26. Paris: Organisation for Economic Co-operation and Development.

Lowe, Phillip. 1994. Financial liberalization: The Australian experience. Paper presented at conference on Financial Opening: Policy Lessons for Korea held at Korea Institute of Finance, Seoul, February 21–22.

Montiel, Peter. 1993. Capital mobility in developing countries. Working Paper Series, no. 1103. Washington, D.C.: World Bank, February.

Nam, Sang-Woo. 1992. Korea's financial reform since the early 1980s. KDI Working Paper no. 9207. Seoul: Korea Development Institute.

Obstfeld, Maurice. 1993. International capital mobility in the 1990s. NBER Working Paper no. 4534. Cambridge, Mass.: National Bureau of Economic Research, November.

Park, Daekeun. 1994. Financial opening and capital inflow: The Korean experience and policy issues. Paper presented at conference on Financial Opening: Policy Lessons for Korea held at Korea Institute of Finance, Seoul, February 21–22.

Park, Yung Chul, and Won-Am Park. 1993. Capital movement, real asset speculation, and macroeconomic adjustment in Korea. In *Financial Opening,* ed. H. Reisen and B. Fischer, 93–115. Paris: Organisation for Economic Co-operation and Development.

Reisen, Helmut, and Helen Ỳeches. 1991. Time-varying estimates on the openness of

the capital account in Korea and Taiwan. Technical Paper no. 42. Paris: Organisation for Economic Co-operation and Development.
Ro, Sung-Tae. 1993. *Korea's monetary policy (1962- 1992).* Seoul: First Economic Research Institute, September.

## Comment Shin-ichi Fukuda

Won-Am Park has written an interesting paper. After surveying Korea's financial deregulatory process since the early 1980s, the paper empirically examines the effects of Korean financial deregulation on the financial structure, capital mobility, and exchange rates. The paper is informative and contains a lot of interesting results on the Korean financial market liberalization. I have three comments.

My first comment is on the interpretation of saving-investment correlations in Korea. Using quarterly time-series data from 1980 to 1992, Park estimates Feldstein-Horioka-type equations which regress investment ratios on saving ratios. His result is striking because it shows little correlation between saving and investment. If we follow the Feldstein-Horioka–type interpretation, this weak correlation implies high official capital mobility in Korea in the 1980s. However, as Park notes, this interpretation is probably not correct.

One possible interpretation is that the weak correlation was caused by high capital inflows from foreign countries but not by capital outflows to foreign countries. This interpretation might be partly true because regressions for different sample periods showed that saving-investment correlation was lower when the capital account was in surplus than when it was in deficit. However, I think that this paradoxical correlation comes from short-term current account fluctuations. By the statistical identity, low correlation between saving ratios and investment ratios implies that domestic investment has a strong negative correlation with the current account. Since high investment usually implies a boom in the economy and a boom in the economy implies the rise of imports, it is quite possible that low correlation between saving and investment comes from a high negative correlation between a high national output level and current account surplus.

My second comment is on the empirical study of interest rate parity conditions. The paper first looks at interest rate differentials between domestic and foreign assets and then applies the autoregressive conditional heteroskedasticity (ARCH) technique to examine the degree of Korea's capital mobility. The estimation result of the ARCH model shows that the conditional variance of

Shin-ichi Fukuda is associate professor at the Institute of Economic Research, Hitotsubashi University.

shocks to interest parity declined after 1982 but rose again during 1988–89. The paper interprets this result as indicating that the degree of Korea's capital mobility declined at the end of the 1980s. However, I am skeptical about this conclusion. In fact, when I look at figure 9.4, I find a sharp structural change at the end of the 1980s. That is, figure 9.4 clearly shows that at the end of the 1980s, interest rate differentials dropped sharply from 20 to −20 percent. I think that the rise of conditional variance in the ARCH model during this period is caused by this sharp drop of interest rate differentials.

My final comment is on the similarity between the Japanese and Korean experiences with controls on cross-border capital flows. In Japan, the liberalization of international capital controls happened in the 1970s. Let me briefly summarize several characteristics of Japan's experience during the liberalization process. First, the process of capital market liberalization was not monotone. In Japan, regulations that were relaxed were reregulated again several times. The main reason for this reregulation was current account fluctuation. That is, current account deficits (surpluses) led to more restrictions on capital outflow (inflow), which were then relaxed when the current account turned to surplus (deficit). Second, Japan's economic environment in the late 1970s was helpful for capital market liberalization. In this period, huge budget deficits created the need to develop a market for government bonds. This led to the liberalization of many domestic interest rates and helped to establish a precondition for free international capital movements. In addition, except for the two oil shock periods, Japan was starting to record large structural current account surpluses. These surpluses relatively reduced the governments' concern about the effects of capital account opening on the balance of payments. Third, there was political pressure from the United States to open Japanese markets. This so-called *gai-atsu* accelerated the capital market liberalization in Japan. I think that contrasting these Japanese experiences with Korean experiences may provide some interesting lessons for understanding the process of capital market liberalization in Korea.

## Comment Huw Pill

Park's very interesting and informative paper describes the twin processes of financial liberalization and financial opening in Korea and the interactions between them. In the light of the earlier failed liberalization attempt of the mid-1960s, this program is shown to have been both gradual and cautious. Something akin to McKinnon's "optimal" order of economic liberalization was followed; fiscal stabilization preceded deregulation of the domestic banking sys-

Huw Pill is assistant professor of business administration at Harvard Business School.

tem and capital markets, which, in turn, preceded the opening of the capital account of the balance of payments.

The paper also attempts to measure the degree of "financial openness" on a number of criteria. Somewhat surprisingly given the descriptive section of the paper, it is suggested that capital mobility through Korea was reduced in the latter part of the 1980s despite the liberalization program.

The paper's tenor is to suggest that the Korean liberalization program, although only partial, should be judged successful. The comments offered are in the form of assessing the success of the program and wondering how exportable it may be to other countries.

Park notes that the role of directed credit and other "financially repressive" measures in the Korean development process is the subject of considerable ongoing controversy. It has been argued that "a little financial repression may be a good thing," citing the Korean experience as an example. The paper remains agnostic on this issue.

However, it is difficult to assess the success or otherwise of the program if one does not take a stand on this issue. Liberalization has not led to loss of macroeconomic control—as has been common in other countries and previously in Korea—because of the gradualism of the program adopted. Yet one can only assess the optimality of the program if one can compare this benefit with the cost of reaching the desired liberalized state less rapidly than may have been possible.

The paper discusses only the financial consequences of liberalization. There is no assessment of the real effects. Has the program been successful in allocating resources more efficiently? Has it improved the growth potential or performance of the real economy? Such an assessment is required to genuinely evaluate whether the program has been successful.

Moreover, it is unclear what the desired liberalized state is. The paper notes that deregulation of the banking system and the capital account of the balance of payments remains partial. These have been the problematic issues in many other countries. Are the potential gains from such liberalization worth the risk of incurring potentially large costs? Is Korea voluntarily extending liberalization to these areas or is it being coerced into so doing by the United States?

If we agree that the program adopted by the Korean authorities has been successful, can it be exported to other countries? In assessing this, one issue stands out where the Korean experience appears exceptional. A common feature of financial liberalization in other countries has been that, once initiated, it creates a momentum of its own. The British experience is instructive, although not unique. The abolition of capital controls allowed dis-intermediation from the domestic banking system to evade controls on the size of onshore banks' balance sheets. Because they were essentially unenforceable, these direct controls were abolished. This allowed banks to expand their domestic activities, notably through aggressive entry into the market for mortgage loans.

The building societies (mutually owned thrifts) which had previously dominated the market for home loans were more strictly regulated than banks and thus felt they were subject to unfair competition—they demanded deregulation for themselves. Thus the process generated a self-sustaining momentum.

How did the Korean authorities prevent these internal pressures for deregulation from emerging and maintain the gradualistic nature of the liberalization program? Presumably, the sequencing of reform is important. An important part of the British experience was the early abolition of capital controls, which was avoided in Korea. However, many countries have found administrative controls of the international movement of capital hard to implement once current account convertibility is established. For example, importers and exporters can manipulate the timing of trade invoicing and payments to generate sizable capital flows in the form of trade credit (which is exempt from restriction under the convertibility clause of IMF article VIII).

Moreover, the paper describes in detail how the main effect of financial deregulation thus far has been to expand the nonbank financial sector at the expense (relatively) of the banking system. The latter remains much more heavily regulated than the former, putting it at a disadvantage in competing for funds. Why have the commercial deposit banks been content to tolerate the consequent erosion of market share? How have the Korean authorities been able to withstand the pressure from the banking system for deregulation to "level the playing field"? Only when these issues have been addressed will it be possible to assess whether the Korean gradualistic approach is genuinely applicable in other contexts.

# 10 The Principal Transactions Bank System in Korea and a Search for a New Bank-Business Relationship

Sang-Woo Nam

## 10.1 Introduction

Korea has a particular form of bank-enterprise relationship that links each large business group to a particular bank (the principal transactions bank) in the context of the credit control system. The major functions of principal transactions banks include monitoring and reporting to the Office of Bank Supervision and Examination the financial situation and investment activities of the corporations, as well as implementing government credit control over the corporate sector.

The nature of credit control has changed, reflecting the emerging challenges faced by the Korean economy. The system was first utilized to encourage large corporations to finance their growth through the stock market. In the 1980s it was used as a means to ease the concentration of economic power by curbing real estate acquisitions and debt-financed business diversification. Despite such changes in the goals pursued, the credit control system remains a regulatory framework to bolster the government's control over the corporate sector. It is far from being an autonomous bank-customer relationship.

However, in the process of opening up the Korean economy, which calls for immense restructuring efforts on the part of corporations, there has been increasing concern that the credit control system poses a serious impediment to the structural adjustment of the economy. As such, the principal transactions bank system must be transformed into a normal bank-customer relationship rather than be allowed to retain its regulatory role of controlling large business groups.

This paper describes the role of the principal transactions bank system in

Sang-Woo Nam is a senior fellow at the Korea Development Institute.
The author thanks Dong-Won Kim of the University of Suwon, Korea, for valuable information and discussions and Yoonsuh Kim of the Korea Development Institute for his research assistance.

Korea and evaluates the costs that accompany such a system. Section 10.2 examines the evolution of the principal transactions bank system in accordance with the shifts in the government's development objectives. Section 10.3 reviews the structure of the present system, which will be followed by a performance evaluation in section 10.4. Section 10.5 will discuss the issues involved in developing a desirable bank-client relationship in Korea with emphasis on comparing Korea's principal transactions bank system with the Japanese main bank system.

## 10.2 Evolution of the Principal Transactions Bank System

The role of financial institutions as mobilizers of savings in Korea was recognized by the government only after the interest rate reform in September 1965 which contributed significantly to the deepening of the financial market. The military coup in the early 1960s led to the nationalization of commercial banks, and a number of new financial institutions were established in the 1960s to perform specialized activities, such as financing small and medium-sized firms and housing and foreign exchange business.

Throughout the 1970s, the Korean financial system was subject to increasing repression with rigid interest rate controls despite accelerating inflation and extensive government intervention in credit allocation. Consequently, financial development was rather slow. However, with the Presidential Emergency Decree in 1972, which froze the unorganized curb loan market, short-term finance companies and mutual savings and finance companies were established, contributing to the diversification of Korea's financial market. The capital market also has grown rapidly since 1972 as the result of strong promotional measures by the government.

Promotion of the heavy and chemical industries in the 1970s by way of providing subsidized bank loans to these industries created several side effects: inefficient investment allocation, weak capital structure of large corporations, limited access of small and medium-sized firms to bank credit, concentration of economic power, and managerial inefficiency of banks.

This experience of excessive government intervention in resource allocation and its serious consequences gave rise to the need for financial liberalization in the early 1980s. The liberalization effort started with the lifting of many restrictions on bank management and the lowering of entry barriers to various financial services in order to promote competition and efficiency. In addition, the government divested its equity shares in all nationwide commercial banks. Most preferential interest rates applied to various policy loans were abolished and more recently interest rates have been partially deregulated.[1]

1. "Policy loans" are loosely defined as those provided at preferential interest rates or earmarked for specific sectors or industries. Such loans include export financing, the National Investment Fund supplied mainly to the heavy and chemical industries, loans for small and medium-sized

Korea's principal transactions bank system started as part of a credit control system on business groups. The evolution of the credit control system must first be analyzed in order to understand the principal transactions bank system because the role of the principal transactions banks and their relationship with the corporate sector were defined within the structure of the credit control system.

### 10.2.1 Introduction of Credit Control and the Principal Transactions Bank System

The principal transactions bank and credit control systems were introduced in 1974 with a view to improving the capital structure of large corporations by encouraging direct financing through public offerings of equity shares while holding down borrowing from financial institutions.

The sharp increase in bank lending after the interest rate reform in 1965 and the large-scale, though tightly controlled, introduction of foreign capital in 1966 resulted in excessive dependence on borrowing and insolvency for many corporations despite rapid economic growth. Because of domestic bank guarantees on foreign borrowing, defaulted foreign loans were turned into loans by domestic banks. Between 1965 and 1970, the equity ratio of manufacturing firms showed a significant decline from 51.6 to 23.3 percent. The Korean government undertook the restructuring of insolvent companies between 1969 and 1971 and the Presidential Emergency Decree of 1972 attempted to address fundamentally the problem of Korea's worsening corporate capital structure and excessive financial burden. The government adopted a credit control system as an institutional tool to promote the sound capital structure of corporations. Together with replacing short-term bank loans with long-term loans, the decree required all curb loans outstanding to be reported to the National Tax Administration; most of these loans were either rescheduled to be repaid over several years at low interest rates or converted into equity capital.

Under the administrative guidance of the government, for the purpose of implementing the credit control system, banks agreed to designate the bank with which the principal company of a business group (whose total credit from banking institutions exceeded a certain amount) had major business relationships as the principal transactions bank for all the member companies of that group. The main functions of a principal transactions bank included reviewing and monitoring its client corporations' plans for improving their capital structure, setting credit ceilings for operating capital, and providing business information and managerial guidance to client corporations. When nonprincipal

firms, housing, agriculture, and fisheries, loans in foreign currency, credit to the Korea Development Bank (KDB) and the Korea Export Import (EXIM) Bank, and special loans for facility investment. In recent years, export financing and loans to specific industries have been phased out significantly, even though credit from deposit money banks to the KDB and EXIM Bank as well as loans for housing, agriculture, and small and medium-sized firms have expanded substantially.

banks extended new credit to a corporation, they had to consult with the corporation's principal transactions bank.

### 10.2.2 Evolution of the Credit Control System

A noteworthy change in the credit control system in the early 1980s was the shift in the central objective of the system from the improvement of corporate capital structure to the restriction of real estate acquisitions and investment in other companies. This shift was geared to support the September 27 Measure of 1980, which was undertaken with a view to reinforcing corporate competitiveness by checking business expansion financed by debt. In the early 1980s, Korean companies suffered from a severe recession caused by the second oil shock as well as political and social unrest following the assassination of President Park. The government seems to have believed that the weakening international competitiveness of Korean companies was fundamentally attributable to their imprudent investment behavior, such as real estate acquisitions and ill-planned business expansion into new industries. The September 27 Measure forced business firms to repay their borrowing from banking institutions by selling their nonoperating real estate as well as the real estate held by business owners and managers, while coercing 26 business groups with too many member companies or weak capital structure to dispose of some of their member companies.[2]

Meanwhile, the credit control system, based on the assumed collusion among banking institutions, was found to be illegal under the Monopoly Regulation and Fair Trade Act. For this reason, the system was reformed into an official regulatory system following the revision of the General Banking Act at the end of 1982. The act states that the Monetary Board may restrict, by fixing ceilings, the aggregate volume of outstanding loans, guarantees, or assumptions of obligations of a banking institution for any individual business group.

The credit control system has undergone significant changes in its objectives and characteristics since 1984, reflecting the progress in financial liberalization as well as political and social changes. These changes resulted in concentration of credit control mainly on the 30 largest business groups while control on other corporations eased.

The credit control system was reformed for three reasons. First, by the early 1980s, an excessive number of groups and companies were subject to credit control (table 10.1). In addition, since the amount of available credit for a company was decided on the basis of its past credit requirements, small but

2. As a result of the September 27 Measure, 309.9 billion won (2.7 percent of the broadly defined money supply) of borrowing from banking institutions was repaid by selling real estate, and 166 member companies of large business groups were severed from their groups by the end of 1984. Of the real estate that was sold, 56 percent (in terms of value) was purchased by individuals and companies not subject to credit control, and the rest was sold to the Land Development Corporation, a government-invested corporation.

**Table 10.1** **Number of Corporations Subject to Credit Control**

| Corporate Type | End 1984 | March 1985 | End 1987 | End 1988 | October 1989 | June 1991 | March 1993 |
|---|---|---|---|---|---|---|---|
| Business groups | 161 | 63 | 50 | 50 | 48 | 50 | 30 |
| Member corporations | 1,459 | 696 | 807 | 845 | 913 | – | 1,014 |
| Companies not belonging to business groups | 280 | – | – | – | – | – | – |

*Source:* Office of Bank Supervision and Examination (1992).

*Notes:* Criteria for selecting corporations to be subject to credit control:

July 1984: (1) Business groups which have more than 20 billion won in total credit (loans plus payment guarantees) from banks and their member corporations. (2) Corporations that do not belong to a business group but that have more than 10 billion won in total credit or more than 5 billion won of loans.

March 1985: Business groups that have more than 100 billion won in total credit and their member corporations.

January 1987: Business groups that have more than 150 billion won in total credit and their member corporations.

June 1991: The 50 largest business groups selected on the basis of loans from banking institutions (excluding loans of major corporations) and their member corporations.

February 1993: The 30 largest business groups selected on the basis of loans from banking institutions (excluding loans of major corporations) and their member corporations.

quickly growing companies were in dire need of credit. In order to correct such inefficiencies, the number of business groups subjected to credit control was reduced, and basket credit control was adopted which regulated the share of large business groups in the total credit of banking institutions.

Second, the extensive nature of credit control hampered the credit evaluation capability of banking institutions and unduly limited corporate activities. Thus, with the progress in financial liberalization during the 1980s, the major emphasis of the credit control system was placed on discouraging real estate acquisition and investment in other companies.

Third, the objective of easing the concentration of economic power and promoting fair access to bank credit gained importance in the credit control system. The government seemed to believe that promoting economic development by depending heavily on large business corporations might no longer be efficient. At the same time, people became more concerned about allocative equity and more critical of large corporations after the democratic reform in 1987. As a result, the credit control system assumed a rather complicated nature, reflecting certain political and social considerations. Consequently, a strong basket control system was adopted in 1988, which led to a steady reduction of the shares of the 5 largest and 30 largest business groups in total bank credit.

Finally, credit control also played an important role in monetary management because the monetary expansion caused by the foreign sector was enormous as a result of the large current account surpluses between 1986 and 1989.

As exports stagnated and the current account returned to deficit in 1990, there was renewed concern about the growth potential of the economy as well as about the international competitiveness of the manufacturing sector. In this connection, the credit control system was criticized for impeding the capability of corporations to respond flexibly to the changing economic environment and to strengthen their competitiveness.

As a result, the tight credit regulations of the 1980s began to be relaxed in 1991. The criterion for selecting business groups subject to credit control was changed from those with total bank credit of more than 150 billion won to the 50 largest borrowers from banking institutions. This criteria was further relaxed in 1993 to the 30 largest business groups. Also, to encourage specialization, each of the 30 largest business groups was allowed to select, from among its member companies, up to three "Major Corporations," to be exempt from credit control.

## 10.3 Structure of the Current Principal Transactions Bank System

### 10.3.1 Basket Credit Control on Business Groups

Control of bank credit in Korea started as an integral part of monetary (M2) targeting. By setting a ceiling on the share of large business groups in banks' total credit, the government has tried to ensure credit availability for small and medium-sized enterprises under a given M2 growth target. Currently, credit control is imposed on the 30 largest business groups selected annually by the Office of Bank Supervision and Examination on the basis of the average end-of-month outstanding borrowings from banking institutions in the previous year. The Office of Bank Supervision and Examination sets a ceiling on the share of the business groups that are subject to basket control in each banking institution's total loans. A bank should not let the collective shares of the 5 largest and the 30 largest business groups in its total loans exceed the levels set by the office.[3] However, the office does not set ceilings on individual business groups. Loans to Major Corporations and "Corporations with Highly Dispersed Ownership" are exempt from basket control. Loans extended by overseas branches and postshipment export financing are also exempt.

### 10.3.2 Selection of the Principal Transactions Banks

The principal transactions bank system applies only to corporations that are subject to credit control as designated by the Office of Bank Supervision and Examination. The bank with which the principal corporation of a business group has major business usually becomes the principal transactions bank for

3. E.g., the credit ceilings for the 5 largest and the 30 largest business groups in 1991 were 5.8 and 10.81 percent of total bank loans. The actual shares of the 5 largest and the 30 largest business groups at the end of 1991 were 5.44 and 9.81 percent. Loans from nonbank financial intermediaries and the issuance of bank-guaranteed corporate bonds are not subject to such ceilings.

all the member firms of the group.[4] Although any banking institution is eligible, only the five major nationwide commercial banks and the Korea Exchange Bank have been selected as principal transactions banks for the 30 largest business groups (table 10.2). Corporations try to meet their financing requirements through their principal transactions bank as much as possible before they approach other banks. Therefore, the principal transactions banks are better positioned than other banks to earn fee income. However, principal transactions banks sometimes lend as much to other business groups of comparable size. When necessary, the Office of Bank Supervision and Examination can change a business group's principal transactions bank, and business groups can also ask for a change, though this has rarely happened in the past.

### 10.3.3 Role of the Principal Transactions Banks

#### *Handling of Information about Credit and Business Activities of Corporations*

The principal transactions bank supervises the overall credit situations of its client corporations, including local financing by their overseas offices. Information about the client corporations collected by nonprincipal banks is supposed to be transmitted to the principal transactions bank.

In reality, principal transactions banks obtain this information from the computer network of banking institutions in which data concerning corporations with more than 2 billion won in bank loans are stored with a separate code for each company. However, as information about most nonbank loans is not entered into this network, a clear financing picture of a client group is available only from the report of the group.

#### *Provision of Loans*

The principal transactions bank sometimes takes the initiative, with or without government intervention, to organize a loan consortium when large-scale loans and guarantees (such as those related to overseas construction projects) are to be provided to its client group. In this case, the principal transactions bank monitors overall performance of the project and corporation on behalf of other participating banks. However, the fact that principal transactions banks' credit supply to their client corporations is typically inadequate limits the influence of the principal transactions banks over their clients.

Each year principal transactions banks require their client corporations to submit their annual investment and financing plans. A favorable evaluation of the investment plan, however, does not necessarily lead to the bank's financing of the major portion of its client's needs. Likewise, even if a principal transactions bank objects to the investment plan, the corporation may continue with

4. The principal corporation is chosen by the Bank Supervisory Board in consideration of the company's position in the group, which depends on asset size and influence on other companies.

Table 10.2 **Status of the 30 Largest Business Groups (end of 1991)**

| Business Group | Sales (billion won) | Debt/ Equity (%) | Number of Companies Subject to Credit Control | Number of Companies Satisfying Guided Capital Ratio | Principal Transactions Bank | Share in Principal Transactions Bank's Equity |
|---|---|---|---|---|---|---|
| 1. Samsung | 21,169 | 323.6 | 49 | 27 | Hanil | 4.9[a] |
| 2. Daewoo | 9,938 | 298.1 | 19 | 9 | Korea First | – |
| 3. Hyundai | 23,401 | 443.4 | 38 | 19 | Exchange | – |
| 4. Hanjin | 3,838 | 1,411.3 | 17 | 7 | Hanil | – |
| 5. Lucky-Goldstar | 12,196 | 355.1 | 53 | 17 | Korea First | 3.2[b] |
| 6. Sunkyung | 6,813 | 244.2 | 29 | 17 | Korea First | – |
| 7. Kia | 4,144 | 328.7 | 8 | 3 | Korea First | – |
| 8. Hanil | 759 | 529.3 | 12 | 5 | Hanil | – |
| 9. Ssangyoung | 5,685 | 173.4 | 20 | 11 | Chohung | 1.7[c] |
| 10. Kumho | 1,402 | 238.6 | 25 | 12 | Chohung | – |
| 11. Korea Explosives | 2,277 | 290.6 | 21 | 8 | Hanil | – |
| 12. Daelim | 1,953 | 436.4 | 12 | 7 | Hanil | 3.7[d] |
| 13. Doo san | 1,839 | 260.8 | 23 | 10 | Commercial | – |
| 14. Hyosung | 2,177 | 317.0 | 14 | 7 | Hanil | – |
| 15. Kukdong Oil Refining | – | – | 4 | 1 | Commercial | – |
| 16. Dongkuk Steel Mill | 1,447 | 158.6 | 11 | 4 | Seoul Trust | 1.5[e] |
| 17. Lotte | 1,384 | 330.9 | 29 | 12 | Commercial | – |
| 18. Halla | 578 | 372.5 | 9 | 3 | Exchange | – |
| 19. Kohap | 884 | 422.6 | 7 | 3 | Hanil | – |
| 20. Dongbu | 1,749 | 288.5 | 7 | 0 | Seoul Trust | – |
| 21. Kukdong Engineering and Construction | 330 | 267.5 | 6 | 4 | Chohung | – |
| 22. Dong-Ah Construction | 1,609 | 1,044.7 | 13 | 5 | Commercial | – |
| 23. Kolon | 1,876 | 252.6 | 20 | 11 | Hanil | – |
| 24. Sammi | 1,223 | 280.4 | 15 | 6 | Commercial | – |
| 25. Byucksan | 765 | 507.2 | 15 | 4 | Commercial | – |
| 26. Samyang Co. | 753 | 217.5 | 5 | 3 | Commercial | 1.1[f] |
| 27. Jinro | 301 | 421.8 | 19 | 5 | Commercial | – |
| 28. Oriental Chemical | 720 | 352.0 | 9 | 6 | Hanil | – |
| 29. Hatai | 644 | 483.1 | 8 | 1 | Chohung | – |
| 30. Woosung Construction | 720 | 539.6 | 6 | 0 | Korea First | – |

*Source:* Office of Bank Supervision and Examination (1992).

[a]Holdings of Sumsung Insurance Co.

[b]Holdings of Lucky Securities and Lucky Fire and Marine Insurance Co.

[c]Holdings of Ssangyoung Cement Co.

[d]Holdings of Daelim Industries.

[e]Holdings of Dongkuk Steel Mill.

[f]Holdings of Samyang Co.

its plan in many cases. In practice, the KDB exerts the most influence on corporations' investment plans (even though it does not serve as a principal transactions bank for any business group), as it provides most of the large, long-term funds for facility investment. In tight credit situations, with corporations badly in need of working capital, the opinion of the principal transactions banks has more impact on the corporations.

*Guidance for the Improvement of Corporate Capital Structure*

The principal transactions bank provides guidance on external financing and its uses to client corporations, urging them to improve their capital structure on the basis of the "guided equity ratio" set by the Office of Bank Supervision and Examination for each industry. If necessary, principal transactions banks must take appropriate measures, such as restricting new credit and urging repayment of loans by corporations not in compliance through the selling of their holdings of securities or real estate. More specifically, business groups are put under special management guidance when their equity ratio, calculated semiannually, declines more than 30 percent from the end of the previous year to below the guided ratio or when the equity ratio falls short of 70 percent of the guided ratio.

However, the principal transactions banks' leverage in corporate management guidance is usually weak because of their limited capacity to meet the credit demands of client corporations under the chronic excess demand conditions in the market. As shown in table 10.2, only 227 (43 percent) of the 523 companies under credit control satisfied the guided equity ratio at the end of 1991, indicating that principal transactions banks' guidance for the improvement of corporate capital structure was not very effective.

*Dealing with Troubled Firms*

When large corporate borrowers are in financial difficulty, the creditor banks usually play only a minor role in deciding whether these companies will be bailed out. Restructuring or liquidation of a large corporation could cause successive bankruptcies of other companies that have business relationships with this corporation and, as a result, threaten the employment stability of the economy. In addition, bankruptcies of large corporations could have a serious impact on the credibility of Korean companies and banks in international financial and export markets. Therefore, decisions concerning the restructuring of large corporations are usually made at the government level (with the Industrial Policy Deliberation Committee and the Ministry of Finance playing major roles), and the principal transactions banks simply carry out the restructuring plan.

During 1986–88, for instance, as many as 78 corporations, largely selected by the Ministry of Finance, were involved in restructuring. Among the 78 corporations, 21 were restructured as a supplementary measure to earlier restructuring of shipping and overseas construction industries (table 10.3). Most of

Table 10.3 **Financial Assistance to the 78 Restructured Corporations (trillion won)**

| Assistance | Shipping Industry Rationalization | Overseas Construction Rationalization | Other | Total |
|---|---|---|---|---|
| Grace period for principal repayment | 0.8 | 0.5 | 0.4 | 1.6 |
| Long-term loans with interest subsidy | – | – | 4.2 | 4.2 |
| Send money: loans for loss compensation | – | – | 0.5 | 0.5 |
| Write-off of principal | – | – | 1.0 | 1.0 |
| Total assistance (principal) | 0.8 | 0.5 | 6.0 | 7.3 |
| Total credit from financial institutions | 1.8 | 1.1 | 6.8 | 9.8 |

*Source:* Office of Bank Supervision and Examination, internal data.

the remaining 57 companies were formally designated targets for rationalization by the Industrial Policy Deliberation Committee and were entitled to receive tax benefits such as an exemption from corporate income tax and acquisition tax in connection with the sale of real estate or subsidiaries.

The principal transactions banks selected candidate companies that might take over problem corporations and negotiated the terms with them. The terms of the financial support package were then examined and coordinated by the Office of Bank Supervision and Examination before they were confirmed by the Ministry of Finance through consultation with other involved ministries and agencies.

In the restructuring process, financial support played a critical role and was given in the form of (1) grace periods of up to 30 years for principal repayment, (2) subsidized long-term loans, (3) the combination of the previous two, or (4) the write-off of principal. To ease the burden of financial support borne by banks in the course of restructuring, sizable subsidized credit was extended by the Bank of Korea.

Before this massive restructuring, in 1985, the Kukje group, which was the sixth largest business group in terms of total sales at the end of 1983, with 23 member corporations, was completely broken up. Before the break-up, Korea First Bank, the group's principal transactions bank, and several other banks provided substantial emergency credit. Continuing emergency credit to a large business group would have had grave impact on the reserve management of the banks and on the monetary control of the authorities. Thus, the decision to provide or to stop emergency credit could not be made solely by the bank without consulting the monetary authorities. In addition, providing substantial emergency credit required the formation of a loan consortium to relieve the principal transactions bank of the financial burden. However, without leadership strong enough to organize and lead the consortium, a principal transactions bank usually needs tacit support from the government. Together with its decision to stop providing emergency credit, the principal transactions bank formed an inspection team with other creditor banks to examine the financial situation of the group and to search for prospective buyers. Eventually, each member corporation of the Kukje group was taken over by another corporation.

*Restrictions on Real Estate Acquisitions and Investment in New Business*

Until 1993, business groups had to obtain prior approval from their principal transactions bank when they wanted to invest in new business (i.e., establishing a subsidiary, buying an existing company, equity participation, and merger) or acquire real estate. The restrictions were intended to induce specialization of business groups and discourage debt-financed expansion of business areas and acquisition of nonoperating real estate. In most cases, approval was given on the condition that the business group make "self-help efforts" worth 200–600 percent of the investment amount. Self-help effort included such activities as raising new capital by selling real estate or securities holdings, issuing new stocks, and disposing of shares of large shareholders. The required level of self-help effort varied depending on the purpose of the investment and whether the investing corporation and the business group satisfied their guided equity ratios.

However, entering 1994, the restrictions on investment in real estate and new business were relaxed significantly. They were completely abolished for the eleventh to thirtieth largest business groups. For the 10 largest groups, ex post reporting largely replaced prior approval from the principal transactions bank, and the burden of self-help effort was lightened to 100–200 percent of the investment amount.

## 10.4 Evaluation of the Principal Transactions Bank System

### 10.4.1 Performance of the Credit Control System

The role of Korean principal transactions banks is defined within the credit control system imposed on business groups, which began as an institutional mechanism designed to alleviate the side effects of strong government support for business groups through intervention in credit allocation in earlier years. Thus, an evaluation of the credit control system should be based on its contribution to alleviating such side effects—that is, how effectively it (1) improves large corporations' capital structure, (2) alleviates concentration of economic power and corrects disproportionate credit allocation, and (3) strengthens the manufacturing industry's competitiveness.

1. The credit control system does not seem to have contributed to the improvement of the capital structure of large corporations in any significant way.

No separate data are available on the changes in capital structure of subject companies since the introduction of the credit control system in 1974. However, the capital structure of large manufacturing firms worsened during the 1970s, and these companies faced severe financial difficulties after making large investments in heavy and chemical industries. The equity ratio of the 30 largest business groups rose from 17.4 to 20.8 percent between 1986 and 1990 (table 10.4). This improvement, however, was mainly attributable to the stock market boom between 1987 and 1989. As corporations faced difficulties in direct financing due to the downturn of the stock market in the early 1990s, their capital structure worsened again with increased borrowing from banks.[5]

2. With respect to reducing the concentration of economic power and providing more equitable access to credit, the credit control system seems to have been successful. As a result of introducing basket credit control in 1984, the share of the 30 largest business groups' bank loans that were subject to credit control fell from 25.3 percent of total bank loans in 1986 to 13.5 percent in 1990, on a year-end basis. Including loans not subject to credit control, their share in total bank loans fell from 28.6 percent in 1986 to 19.4 percent at the end of 1990 (table 10.5).[6]

It is noteworthy, however, that the large business groups' share in total credit of nonbank financial institutions (NBFIs) such as short-term finance companies, merchant banking corporations, and insurance companies, whose credit is not subject to credit control, has substantially increased. In other words, the credit control system has, to a large extent, shifted the financing demand of business groups from the banking sector to NBFIs.[7]

Furthermore, the credit control system appears to have been unsuccessful in discouraging business diversification. Between 1986 and 1991, 20 of the 30 largest business groups increased their number of member corporations in spite of the burden of self-help financing effort (table 10.6). Of course, the number of member firms is not an accurate measure of business diversification, and diversification activity might have been more pronounced without credit control.

3. Concern over the deteriorating competitiveness of the manufacturing industry resulted in the exemption of Major Corporations from credit control in

5. Corporate capital structure seems to be determined mainly by a corporation's financing needs. The equity ratios of the major Japanese manufacturing firms declined steadily during the postwar high-growth period from a 40 percent level in 1955 to below 19 percent during 1974–76.

6. The share of the 30 largest business groups in manufacturing sales and value-added began to decline in 1984 at the same time as the start of basket credit control. However, basket credit control was only one of the reasons for this decline. In the mid-1980s, the manufacturing sector showed strong growth accompanied by a large increase in the number of business establishments, which reduced the relative importance of the large business groups. Reinforced fair trade regulations also checked the expansion of these corporations. On the other hand, as the economy became more mature, business groups started to attach greater importance to service industries such as finance and information.

7. The share of the 30 largest business groups in total equity of all financial institutions other than nationwide commercial banks was 45 percent at the end of 1991 (*Maeil Kyungje,* October 16, 1992).

**Table 10.4** **The Equity Ratio of Korean Corporations (%)**

| Year | Manufacturing: Total | Manufacturing: Large Corporations | Corporations Subject to Credit Control |
|---|---|---|---|
| 1974 | 24.0 | 23.7 | – |
| 1975 | 22.8 | 22.1 | – |
| 1976 | 21.5 | 21.2 | – |
| 1977 | 22.2 | 22.3 | – |
| 1978 | 21.4 | 21.6 | – |
| 1979 | 21.0 | 20.9 | – |
| 1980 | 17.0 | 16.5 | – |
| 1981 | 18.1 | 18.1 | – |
| 1982 | 20.6 | 20.9 | – |
| 1983 | 21.7 | 21.7 | – |
| 1984 | 22.6 | 22.7 | – |
| 1985 | 22.3 | 22.5 | – |
| 1986 | 22.2 | 21.9 | 17.4 |
| 1987 | 22.7 | 23.1 | 19.8 |
| 1988 | 25.3 | 26.0 | 24.7 |
| 1989 | 28.2 | 29.4 | 23.8 |
| 1990 | 25.9 | 26.7 | 20.8 |
| 1991 | 24.4 | 25.6 | 19.4 |
| 1992 | 23.8 | 24.8 | – |

*Source:* Bank of Korea (various issues).

**Table 10.5** **Share of the 30 Largest Business Groups in Bank Loans and in GDP (%)**

| | 1986 | 1987 | 1988 | 1989 | 1990 | 1991 |
|---|---|---|---|---|---|---|
| Share in bank loans | | | | | | |
| Loans subject to credit control | 25.3 | 21.6 | 18.6 | 14.7 | 13.5 | 8.8[a] |
| Total loans | 28.6 | 26.3 | 24.2 | 20.7 | 19.4 | 18.9 |
| Share in NBFI credit | – | 37.9 | 36.5 | 42.1 | 43.6 | – |
| Share in GDP | – | 14.6 | 13.5 | 14.1 | – | – |
| Equity ratio | 17.4 | 19.8 | 24.7 | 23.8 | 20.8 | 19.4 |

*Sources:* Korea Investors Service, Inc. (1988, 1989, 1990); Management Efficiency Research Institute (1987); *Maeil Kyungje* (March 31, 1992); Min (1991, 117).

[a]Excluding credit to Major Corporations, Corporations with Highly Dispersed Ownership, loans extended by overseas bank branches, and postshipment export financing.

1991. Due to this relaxation, in 1991 bank loans to 76 Major Corporations of the 30 largest business groups rose by 38.1 percent over the previous year. This increase contrasts with those of total bank loans (23.6 percent increase) and loans to non–Major Corporations in the 30 largest business groups (8.6 percent increase). It is still too early to evaluate the impact of this inducement to specialization on the strengthening of manufacturing competitiveness. No such

**Table 10.6** **Number of Member Companies of the 30 Largest Business Groups**

| Business Group | 1981 | 1986 (A) | 1987 | 1988 | 1989 | April 1991 (B) | (B) − (A) |
|---|---|---|---|---|---|---|---|
| Samsung | 21 | 31 | 31 | 41 | 42 | 48 | +17 |
| Daewoo | 25 | 25 | 28 | 28 | 30 | 24 | −1 |
| Hanjin | 13 | 12 | 16 | 16 | 18 | 22 | +10 |
| Hyundai | 30 | 43 | 30 | 36 | 37 | 42 | −1 |
| Lucky-Goldstar | 30 | 43 | 30 | 36 | 37 | 42 | −1 |
| Sunkyong | 16 | 13 | 16 | 21 | 22 | 26 | +13 |
| Hanil | 6 | 10 | 11 | 12 | 14 | 13 | +3 |
| Ssangyong | 13 | 16 | 21 | 21 | 21 | 22 | +6 |
| Kia | 12 | 7 | 10 | 10 | 10 | 10 | +3 |
| Daelim | 9 | 12 | 13 | 13 | 13 | 14 | +2 |
| Kumho | 10 | 5 | 8 | 13 | 14 | 22 | +17 |
| Hyosung | 27 | 19 | 12 | 12 | 14 | 14 | −5 |
| Doosan | 14 | 19 | – | 20 | 21 | 23 | +4 |
| Korea Explosives | 16 | 20 | 21 | 25 | 25 | 27 | +7 |
| Dongkuk Steel Mill | – | 12 | 13 | 13 | 13 | 14 | +2 |
| Kukdong Oil | – | – | – | 4 | 4 | 4 | – |
| Kukdong Engineering and Construction | 15 | 12 | 16 | 16 | 16 | 16 | +4 |
| Dong-Ah Construction | 15 | 12 | 16 | 16 | 16 | 16 | +4 |
| Lotte | 16 | 26 | 26 | 31 | 31 | 32 | +6 |
| Dongbu | 7 | 11 | 12 | 13 | 14 | 11 | 0 |
| Sam Yang | – | 3 | – | 7 | 6 | 6 | +3 |
| Kolon | 16 | 10 | 18 | 16 | 18 | 21 | +11 |
| Sammi | 4 | 5 | 9 | 11 | 14 | 15 | +10 |
| Byuksan | – | 6 | – | 14 | 20 | 21 | +15 |
| Woosung Construction | – | – | – | 7 | 7 | 6 | – |
| Kohap | 5 | 4 | 5 | 7 | 7 | 7 | +3 |
| Halla | – | – | 5 | 6 | 6 | 9 | +4 |
| Cho Yang Shipping | – | – | – | – | – | 10 | – |
| Jinro | – | – | – | – | 18 | 20 | – |
| Oriental Chemical | – | – | – | – | 11 | 13 | – |

*Sources:* Office of Bank Supervision and Examination (1992); *Maeil Kyungje* (May 7, 1991).

impact would be expected to the extent of credit diversion from the Major Corporations to other firms of a business group.

### 10.4.2 Problems with the Credit Control System

While the credit control system has had only limited success in achieving its goals, it has incurred heavy regulatory costs to both banks and subject corporations. Our interest here is to review the nature and the magnitude of these costs.

Since its launch, the credit control system has been a source of continuous conflict between the government and the corporate sector. The corporate sector's resistance to the system was not apparent in the beginning but grew stronger in the 1980s as credit control became in essence a way to regulate business activities. This problem became more serious as government support for the corporate sector was largely reduced and stronger private sector initiative became necessary to meet successfully the challenge of intensified global competition.

The credit control system also has seriously hampered autonomous bank management. With the right of prior approval over various corporate activities and the authority to penalize client companies, principal transactions banks are positioned as subordinate organizations of the Office of Bank Supervision and Examination. They are obligated to collect information and report to the Office of Bank Supervision and Examination in connection with the implementation of credit control. They are subject to penalties such as restricted access to central bank credit and penalty interest rates in the event of violating relevant regulations or neglecting their duties as principal transactions banks.

The credit control burden of commercial banks is known to be so substantial as to require one-third of their loan officers. There are also many difficulties in evaluating whether real estate is nonoperating or not for tax purposes. The many unnecessary and trivial items that need the approval of principal transactions banks have been a major source of inefficiency and conflict between banks and their client corporations.[8]

The bank-enterprise relationship in the framework of the credit control system is that of the supervisor and the supervised. Autonomy in bank management and a cooperative bank-enterprise relationship are seriously impaired under the current system, in which control over corporate clients carried out on behalf of the government constitutes a substantial part of banking business. The current system of credit operation, which focuses on conformity to rules and regulations, should be replaced by one that nourishes a spontaneous and cooperative relationship between banks and their clients. To the extent that the government-bank-enterprise partnership constitutes a critical superstructure in determining industrial competence in the global economy, Korean corporations seem to be handicapped.

The current credit control system pursues two conflicting objectives: strengthening manufacturing competitiveness and reducing the concentration of economic power. This conflict makes the government's policy choices challenging. By exempting the Major Corporations from credit control, the govern-

8. Despite substantial operative inefficiency inflicted on banks and corporations, it is questionable whether overall allocative efficiency was as seriously hampered as operative efficiency. Because large corporations can utilize other financing sources, such as NBFIs, capital markets, and foreign capital, as well as fund diversion among firms within a group, their total financing capacity does not seem to be seriously diminished by limited bank credit. Even though some delay and additional costs are inevitable in financing, it is doubtful that a member firm of a large business group would have given up a promising investment project because of credit control regulations.

ment has given priority to strengthening the international competitiveness of industries at the cost of more equitable access to credit and reduced concentration of economic power.

The problem, however, is that the system might produce results that defeat its goal of strengthened manufacturing competitiveness. For instance, business groups tended to select those firms with large financing requirements as their Major Corporations rather than those with good prospects of gaining international competitiveness. For example, each of the five largest business groups have chosen as one of their Major Corporations a petrochemical company.

The relaxation of credit control on Major Corporations may bring about credit diversion from Major to non-Major Corporations to circumvent credit control. If such diversion actually occurs, the credit control system can no longer correct the concentrated access to credit. Loans to Major Corporations and Corporations with Highly Dispersed Ownership, which are not subject to credit control, accounted for 53.6 percent of total loans to the 30 largest business groups at the end of 1991. Accordingly, the share of loans to the 30 largest business groups under credit control declined to 8.8 percent of total bank loans outstanding at the end of 1991.

Under the Operational Bylaw on Credit Control over Business Groups, principal transactions banks are required to submit quarterly monitoring reports to the Office of Bank Supervision and Examination concerning loans to Major Corporations and to revoke the designation of Major Corporation in the event of diversion of credit to other uses. Despite this severe penalty, room for diversion always exists because monitoring the use of bank loans is practically difficult in the case of operating capital and banks have to make judgments mainly on the basis of data presented by the Major Corporations themselves.

In addition, repayment guarantees issued by the Major Corporations for other member companies, roughly equivalent to three times their equity capital, represent de facto credit diversion. At the end of June 1992, payment guarantees for corporations belonging to the 30 largest business groups amounted to four times their equity capital (table 10.7). To redress such problems, the government revised the Monopoly Regulation and Fair Trade Act, forcing busi-

**Table 10.7 Equity Capital and Payment Guarantees of the 30 Largest Business Groups (end of June 1992; billion won)**

| Groups | Equity Capital (A) | Outstanding Cross-Payment Guarantees (B) | B/A |
|---|---|---|---|
| Groups 1–5 | 16,315 | 77,821 | 4.8 |
| Groups 6–30 | 15,087 | 47,831 | 3.2 |
| Total | 31,402 | 125,652 | 4.0 |

*Source:* Office of Bank Supervision and Examination (1992).

ness groups to limit their cross-payment guarantees to a maximum of 200 percent of their equity capital within three years from April 1993. The task of mitigating economic concentration by business groups, one of the major objectives of the credit control system, has been passed on to the domain of fair trade policy.

## 10.5 A Search for a Desirable Bank-Business Relationship

### 10.5.1 Comparison of the Principal Transactions Bank System with the Japanese Main Bank System

Characteristics of the principal transactions bank system become clearer when it is compared with the Japanese main bank system. First, the principal transactions bank system in Korea is officially defined by the regulations of the Monetary Board, while the Japanese main bank system is defined by the conventional customer relationship between banks and their client corporations. Principal transactions banks in Korea, in effect, function as a substructure, or subordinate organizations, of the Office of Bank Supervision and Examination, controlling credit supply to client corporations and gathering and reporting information on their financial and credit situations.

Second, the main bank system in Japan represents a rather broad-based bank-enterprise relationship, with about 30 percent of corporations having such a relationship with their banks (Horiuchi 1990, 1). The principal transactions bank system in Korea, however, applies only to corporations belonging to the 30 largest business groups in terms of borrowing from banks. At the end of April 1992, the number of companies belonging to the 30 largest groups under direct credit control of their principal transactions banks was 591. Other corporations also have banks with which they have closer business relationship than with other banks. These banks, however, do not seem to play special roles which deserve general definition.

Third, the relationship between corporations belonging to Japanese business groups and their main banks is based on mutual equity ownership. In Korea, however, no such relationship is found. Only a few business groups hold equity shares in their principal transactions banks (table 10.2). In some of these cases, the shares just represent shareholding by their securities or insurance affiliates as part of their portfolio management. Also, the level of shareholding by those business groups is far lower than the 8 percent limit that a stockholder can have in the nationwide commercial banks. This lack of interest in holding shares of principal transactions banks might result from the tight credit control over the business groups and the government's influence over bank management, such as the appointment of top managers. On the other hand, there are some cases in which a principal transactions bank holds shares in its client corporations. Such holdings are, however, only for the purpose of asset management and do not represent part of the principal transactions bank relationship. While banks in the Japanese main bank system often play roles as both lender and shareholder, the role of their Korean counterparts is limited to that of lender. A cooperative relationship between banks and their corporate clients, in which both parties share mutual benefits by reducing information asymmetry, is rarely found in Korea.

Fourth, although both Korea and Japan relied heavily on government-initiated industrial policies, such as government intervention in credit allocation, the passive or subordinate role of Korean banks has led to inefficiency in resource allocation. In Japan, the main-bank-enterprise relationship has provided a double-check mechanism regarding the prospect of planned projects. But Korean industrial policy has left little room for principal transactions banks to evaluate the major industrial projects whose undertaking and undertakers were decided by the government, making it difficult for a principal transactions bank to refuse the loans. When a loan consortium is formed by several banks to meet a large investment requirement, the share of each bank in the consortium has usually been allocated by the government. As a result of this lack of autonomy, banks have been more concerned about securing collateral than undertaking credit evaluation, which in turn has led corporations to hold more real estate to offer as collateral. This difference in the role of main banks in the evaluation of projects and borrowers' creditworthiness must have led to the different investment performances of the two countries.

Finally, the role of a principal transactions bank as an overall financial supervisor and a delegated monitor of its client corporations is much weaker than that of a Japanese main bank. Unlike Japanese main banks, Korean principal transactions banks perform these functions only in special circumstances, as when a large client corporation is insolvent. This limited role seems to reflect primarily the fact that a principal transactions bank neither necessarily accepts a disproportionate share of the cost of rescuing or liquidating troubled firms nor takes strong leadership in forming loan consortiums. It may also represent moral hazard behavior in the belief that the government will take responsibility in the worst-case scenario given the government initiative at the planning stage. Moral hazard might also result from the practice of cross-repayment guarantees among member firms of a group. In fact, except for the Kukje case, in which a whole group was broken up and taken over by other firms, member firms of large business groups have rarely been liquidated or rescued from serious financial difficulty by their principal transactions banks.

Another reason for the relative passivity of principal transactions banks is the ownership concentration of large corporations. In 1991, 14 percent of the total shares of the 30 largest groups were held by the group chairmen and their families and another 33 percent were held by member firms of the group. These combined holdings decreased only to 43 percent in 1993. Because the chairman, who has absolute management control of a business group, tends to be very cautious about revealing management information to outsiders, the function of principal transactions banks as monitor and supervisor has inevitably been weak. Corporate clients' lack of confidence in their principal transactions banks as serious evaluators of the clients themselves or their investment projects might also be partly responsible for the weak role of the banks.

### 10.5.2 Directions for a New Bank-Business Relationship

*The Japanese Main Bank System as a Model*

In the search for a more desirable bank-client relationship in Korea, a useful starting point may be an evaluation of the efficiency of the Japanese main bank system. First, the main bank system seems to be efficient in reducing information asymmetry. A Japanese main bank has responsibilities as the leader of loan syndication and as the delegated monitor for other creditor banks. It also takes on a special degree of exposure if necessary and bears loss beyond its exposure if a client defaults on loans. With these responsibilities in a market in which information about borrowers is limited and costly to obtain, main banks make continuous investments in monitoring, which enables them to accumulate information about borrowing firms at lower cost.

This close monitoring may also improve corporate performance by eliminating any motivation to shirk and by reducing other agency costs of external finance. Borrowing firms have incentives to reveal confidential information to their main banks because it helps them to overcome the liquidity constraints of relying on internal finance and to reduce the cost of reorganizing and restructuring in the worst cases of distress. Those main banks or corporate borrowers that have not met their implied obligations and, thus, are perceived to be unreliable partners, suffer serious damage to their reputations. This potential penalty discourages credit diversion or other opportunistic behavior by borrowing firms and makes main banks willingly assume additional risk or loss when their corporate clients are in distress.

Mutual shareholding between main banks and their corporate clients is an important feature of the Japanese main bank system. Main bank ownership of shares of borrowing firms (up to a 5 percent limit) makes the relationship and monitoring close and effective. Bank shares are also frequently held by friendly industrial firms with which they have a main bank relationship. Bank ownership of corporate shares in Japan contrasts with U.S. legislation and British custom, which prohibits such ownership.

The main bank relationship, however, has elements of inefficiency and unfairness as well. The relationship is basically a secretive and exclusive one. Main banks' insider access to information about their client firms and the related nontransparency may create opportunities for fraud or exploitation for the benefit of the banks and involved individuals. The exclusive insider system with barriers to entry by outsiders may result in oligopolistic behavior. More important, the close main bank relationship may tend to bail out firms that should have been liquidated.

Given the overall evaluation, the main bank system would likely serve a useful function in Korea as well. Korean financial markets are far from perfectly competitive and complete. Systems for corporate accounting, auditing, disclosure, and credit rating are yet to be firmly established in Korea. In a still-shallow securities market, insider trading, price manipulation, and other unfair transactions are not effectively regulated. As a result, information asymmetry is large, the search for accurate information is costly, and incentives for fraud or abuse of conflicts of interest are strong. In this world of incomplete and asymmetric information, the role of banks as credit analysts and monitors of corporate borrowers is critical. This function of banks, however, has been largely neglected owing to the heavy intervention of the government in the allocation of bank credit and the prevalent practice of collateral requirement for bank loans.

However, the drawbacks of the main bank system mentioned above make the question of who will monitor the main banks very important. First of all, the role of the Office of Bank Supervision and Examination would become more important. The office is advised to shift its major effort from controlling credit to securing the soundness of bank management and preventing unfair practices. In Korea, the government is also considering a few alternatives to make banks more responsible for their own management. One of them is to have banks set up a Council of Large Stockholders, composed of five to ten major shareholders who own more than 1 percent of the bank's stock. The council will monitor bank management. Another alternative is to allow an individual to hold up to, say, 15 percent of a bank's stock on the condition that the person does not own any nonfinancial firms. The existence of an owner with management control will make bank management more accountable.

*Inducing Autonomous Relationship Banking*

The next question is, How can Korean banks and their corporate clients be encouraged to establish close relationships similar to the Japanese main bank system? This task should first be approached by eliminating the institutional constraints and improving the policy environment that have suppressed the incentives for credit evaluation and close monitoring of corporate borrowers. In this respect, the current system of credit control and principal transactions banks should be transformed to a more autonomous bank-client relationship, with less emphasis on the supervisory function of banks. In fact, credit control procedures are being simplified, and the current system of approval by the principal transactions banks for corporate investment in other businesses and real estate is being phased out. Easing of excessive concentration of economic power and specialization of business groups may better be induced with the provisions of the Monopoly Regulation and Fair Trade Act and the Industrial Development Law. Likewise, speculation in real estate may be addressed by strengthening related tax laws and their implementation. Ultimately, the credit control system will have to focus on maintaining prudence and soundness in corporate banking operations.

Moreover, commercial banks should gradually be relieved of the burden of extending policy loans. Policy loans by banks still account for a substantial portion of their loan portfolios. They include loans to development institutions, the housing and agricultural sectors, and small and medium-sized firms and foreign currency loans mainly for capital goods imports. Until commercial banks are freed from the obligation of supplying policy loans, financial liberalization will be limited and an autonomous, cooperative bank-client relationship will be inhibited. Preferential policy loans may be needed in order to alleviate market imperfections, as is the case for risky projects with long gestation periods and anticipated positive externalities for the economy. Subsidized credit may also be provided out of social considerations. This obligation, however, should be fulfilled from the government budget rather than by commercial banks.

Finally, the practice of requiring collateral should be improved to serve as a complement to, rather than a substitute for, costly credit analysis and monitoring. The majority of bank loans in Korea are secured by collateral, whose value exceeds the loan amount by at least 30–50 percent. All the costs of insuring, registering, and disposing of the collateral are also borne by borrowers. In addition, borrowers are required to provide a surety liable jointly and severally for their borrowing. Fully protected from default risk, banks have little incentive to begin serious credit evaluation, monitoring, and investment on information by relationship banking. Banks may actually be better off when borrowing firms go bankrupt and heavy penalty interest is collected for the delay in repayment. This incentive structure is likely to result in adverse selection, which may be even worse when banks are allowed to charge differential interest rates depending on the creditworthiness of borrowers.

The bargaining power of borrowing firms is, however, improving, as the excess demand situation in the bank loan market is eased with the deregulation of interest rates, increase in loanable funds, and diversification of corporate financing sources for larger firms. Even before pressures from the changing market correct the situation, it may be advisable to regulate the irrational practices related to securing bank loans. For instance, security or subrogation by a surety may be limited up to the loan amount.

With a view to encouraging a binding relationship between a bank and its corporate clients, mutual equity holding may be considered. Given Korea's industrial organization and the realities of corporate governance, however, this arrangement may still be premature. As entry into banking is restricted and bank loans have a subsidy element, allowing large business groups to hold controlling shares of banks would be an unjustifiable favor to the business groups. Even when financial markets are competitive with free entry, a mix of financial and nonfinancial products within a business group increases the probability of abuses as long as the member firms have market power in the nonfinancial products. Given the highly oligopolistic Korean market structure, where large business groups have market-dominating power (table 10.8), the

**Table 10.8 Share of the 5 and 30 Largest Business Groups in Manufacturing Sales and Employment**

| | 1977 | 1982 | 1987 | 1989 |
|---|---|---|---|---|
| Sales | | | | |
| 5 Largest | 15.7 | 22.6 | 22.0 | 21.3 |
| 30 Largest | 34.1 | 40.7 | 37.3 | 35.4 |
| Employment | | | | |
| 5 Largest | – | 8.9[a] | 9.9 | 9.9 |
| 30 Largest | – | 18.6[a] | 18.1 | 16.8 |

*Sources:* Jung and Yang (1992, 40–41); Korea Development Institute, Seoul, and other unpublished survey data at Korea Development Institute.

[a]Figure for 1983.

room for abusing conflicts of interest through tie-in sales, for instance, is potentially great.

On the other hand, banks may enhance their role as shareholders of client corporations. As both a lender and a shareholder, a bank representative may serve as an outside member of the board, with access to corporate inside information. However, corporate management, including that of business groups, is typically very concentrated, with its major owner the central figure. In this management structure, outside board members are not expected to be well utilized as management supervisors. Only when management and ownership are largely separated in Korean business firms may banks be able to play a significant role as shareholders and corporate insiders.

*Major Clients for Relationship Banking*

As has been the case in Japan for some time, Korea's large business groups will rely less on bank loans because they will borrow increasingly from abroad at low cost and utilize less-expensive securities finance. With the development of such practices as accounting, auditing, securities analysis, and credit rating, which reduce information asymmetry and increase relevant information at low cost, large corporations will find it easier and cheaper to finance in the securities market. However, the role of banks is not confined to lending but includes diverse financial services. Because the number of banks with such capacity is limited, very large healthy business corporations are likely to develop close relationships with several nationwide city banks according to the major strength of each bank.

These relationships between fairly large corporations and their banks will resemble those of Japanese core banks. This relationship will basically be a rather competitive one. The client corporations will not wish to commit themselves to a binding relationship with any one bank but will rather maintain financial transactions with several banks, keeping them at arm's length. Banks will compete with one another to secure better clients and consolidate existing client relationships, which will improve banking services and enhance banks' capabilities. As the relationship is not an exclusive or binding one, it will always be subject to change depending on the results of competition through repeated transactions.

On the other hand, with the increasing supply of loanable funds relative to demand, banks are expected to form much closer and binding (main bank) relationships with the smaller large corporations and medium-sized firms that have good growth prospects. For small and medium-sized firms, it is difficult to utilize the capital market. This difficulty is due mainly to high transactions costs for small-scale financing, as well as the high cost of information arising from poor bookkeeping and lack of transparency in management. Thus, such firms rely heavily on bank and nonbank borrowing (table 10.9).

Although the major firms of large business groups may opt out of close and binding relationships with banks, many large firms will remain. This is so because the expected returns on continuous investment in monitoring are higher in the case of larger firms. As business firms grow, they typically need wide-ranging consulting and banking services regarding corporate finance and treasury. In return for entering into a special relationship, they have much lucrative financial business to offer to their banks, including transactions deposits, foreign exchange business, trusteeship, and other fee-generating business. Entering a binding relationship with small firms with all the implied commitments is in general too risky for banks, given these firms' uncertain prospects, lack of operational transparency, and paucity of expected banking business.

## 10.6 Conclusion

The principal transactions bank system in Korea was introduced in order to correct the skewed allocation of bank credit, which was the result of

**Table 10.9** **Sources of Funds for Manufacturing Firms (%)**

| | Large Firms | | Small and Medium-sized Firms | |
|---|---|---|---|---|
| Source | 1984–88 | 1989–92 | 1984–88 | 1989–92 |
| Internal financing | 44.8 | 39.9 | 38.4 | 30.3 |
| External financing | 55.2 | 60.1 | 61.6 | 69.7 |
| Direct financing | 14.9 | 15.0 | 9.8 | 8.1 |
| (Capital increases) | (8.7) | (5.0) | (7.0) | (6.7) |
| (Corporate bonds) | (6.2) | (9.9) | (2.8) | (1.5) |
| Borrowing | 19.4 | 27.9 | 25.7 | 38.9 |
| (From banks) | (14.8) | (19.0) | (23.7) | (30.6) |
| Other | 21.0 | 17.2 | 26.1 | 22.8 |
| Total | 100.0 | 100.0 | 100.0 | 100.0 |

*Source:* Bank of Korea (various years).

government-led economic development. Now, two decades after its introduction, there seems to be broad agreement that the current system of credit control and principal transactions banks needs to be redefined in light of the huge challenges of successfully liberalizing and opening the economy.

The regulatory mechanism of the system unduly restricts corporate activity and imposes operational burdens on the principal transactions banks. An autonomous and close bank-business relationship cannot be fostered because the banks have functioned as de facto suborganizations of the supervisory authorities. Korea's principal transactions banks have not assumed the implicit obligations of the Japanese main banks, such as a disproportionate burden in rescuing or liquidating troubled firms. With its role as a delegated monitor very much limited, the banking sector as a whole is not efficient in generating information and reducing information asymmetry about borrowing firms. Furthermore, the current credit control system seems to be ineffective in serving the two conflicting objectives of strengthening industrial competitiveness and mitigating the concentration of economic power.

As envisaged by the government, credit control and other restrictions on corporate investment and financing should be phased out. Such concerns as excessive concentration of economic power and speculation in real estate may be addressed under the Monopoly Regulation and Fair Trade Act and relevant tax laws. Reduction of government intervention in the loan portfolios of commercial banks, such as the obligation to provide policy loans, also will help nourish close and autonomous bank-business relationships. Moreover, the prevalent practices of repayment guarantees by other member firms of a business group and collateral requirements for loans should be discouraged. They largely nullify any need for serious credit evaluation or monitoring on the part of banks.

Excessive collateral requirements, however, are expected to be eased gradually with the deregulation of interest rates, increase in loanable funds, and diversification of corporate financing sources, including access to the capital market. These structural changes in the financial market will also induce the largest and leading business firms to rely less on bank credit and to maintain rather competitive relationships with several "core" banks. Banks are likely to develop closer and more binding relationships with slightly smaller business firms. Attracted by large potential contributions to bank profitability, banks will be willing to enter into exclusive relationships with these firms. Such relationships will most probably imply an understanding that the firm allows the bank to supply a substantial portion of its lucrative banking services, to share its inside information, and to conduct close monitoring in return for the expectation of emergency loans and other rescue operations in situations of financial distress.

## References

Aoki, Masahiko, and Hugh Patrick, eds. 1994. *The Japanese main bank system.* New York: Oxford University Press.

Bank of Korea. Various issues. *Financial statements analysis.* Seoul: Bank of Korea.

Cole, D. C., and Y. C. Park. 1983. Financial development in Korea, 1945–1978. Cambridge: Council on East Asian Studies, Harvard University.

Horiuchi, Toshihiro. 1990. Management structure of Japanese banks and their optimal relationship with firms as mainbank. Discussion Paper no. 309. Kyoto: Kyoto Institute of Economic Research, Kyoto University.

Jung, Byung-hyu, and Young-sik Yang. 1992. *Hanguk Chaebol Bumun ui Kyungje Bunsuk* (The economic analysis of chaebols in Korea). Seoul: Korea Development Institute.

Kim, Dong-Won. 1992. *Unhaeng Daechul Shijang eseoui Jungbu, Unhaeng, Guiup Gwange ui Jaemosaek* (Reconsideration of the relationship between government, bank and corporation in the bank loan market). Seoul: Korea Economic Research Institute.

Korea Investors Service, Inc. 1988, 1989, 1990. *Chaebol Bunsuk Bogoseo* (Chaebol analysis report). Seoul: Korea Investors Service, Inc.

*Maeil Kyungje* (daily economic newspaper). May 7, 1991; March 31, 1992; October 16, 1992.

Management Efficiency Research Institute. 1987. *Hanguk 50 Daegiup Group Jaemu Bunsuk Jaryojib* (Analysis of financial statements: Fifty major business groups in Korea). Seoul: Management Efficiency Research Institute.

Min, Byong-Kyun. 1991. Keyulgiupgun Yushingwanrijedo Kaisun Bangan (Improving the credit control system on business groups). In *Kumyung ui Kukjehwa wa Kyujewan hwa* (Internationalization and deregulation of finance). Seoul: Korea Economic Research Institute.

Nam, Sang-Woo. 1991. Korea's financial policy and its consequences. Paper presented at workshop on Government, Financial Systems and Economic Development: A Comparative Study of Selected Asian and Latin American Countries, East-West Center, Honolulu, October 18–19.

———. 1992. Korea's financial reform since the early 1980s. Working Paper no. 9207. Seoul: Korea Development Institute.

Office of Bank Supervision and Examination. 1992. Data submitted to the National Assembly (unpublished).

Smith, Roy C., and Ingo Walter. 1992. Bank industry linkages: Models for Eastern European economic restructuring. Paper presented at conference on The New Europe: Evolving Economic and Financial Systems in East and West, Berlin, October 8–10.

## Comment Akiyoshi Horiuchi

Nam gives an overview of the principal transactions bank system in Korea. He describes the evolution of this system, introduced in 1874, evaluates its impact

Akiyoshi Horiuchi is professor of economics at the University of Tokyo.

on corporate behavior in Korea, and compares it with the Japanese main bank system. His explanation in this paper is excellent. Although I am not an expert on the Korean economy, I have some knowledge of the relationships between Korea's major banks and major corporations and the government policy stance toward credit allocation. I would like to comment on his argument about the workings of the principal transactions bank system and then proceed to discuss briefly his comparison between this system and the Japanese main bank system.

Nam emphasizes that because the principal transactions bank system was introduced on the government's initiative, it has played the subordinate role of implementing credit control designed by the government. According to Nam, this role has been a major reason for the unsatisfactory performance of this system since the 1980s. Since principal transactions banks have not been able to determine credit allocation to the major corporations, they have had little incentive to pursue serious credit evaluation, monitoring, and investment on information concerning major borrower firms. Nam suggests that this attitude on the part of the banking sector produced inefficiency in corporate management.

One of the Korean government's most important goals in introducing the credit control system, through the principal transactions banks, was to improve the soundness of the corporate sector. This policy reminds me of the Japanese government's concern for the soundness of Japan's corporate sector in the first stage of the high-growth period. Like the Korean government, the Japanese government worried about the "abnormally" low equity ratio levels of the major companies. The government, particularly the monetary authorities, urged in vain companies and major financial institutions to improve companies' equity ratios. On the other hand, Japanese banks did not seem to cooperate with the monetary authorities. Rather they actively helped their major client firms increase their leverage ratios. Thus, during the high-growth period, the Japanese main banks contributed to industrial development by making it possible for the corporate sector to decrease equity ratios without incurring substantial increases in bankruptcy costs. In this sense, as Nam points out, the Korean principal transactions bank system is very different from the Japanese main bank system.

In my understanding, the Korean economy has a deep and wide curb capital market. In contrast, there is no comparable curb capital market in Japan. The existence of an informal capital market might influence the performance of credit control policy designed by the government. Nam does not explain explicitly the influence of the curb capital market on the efficiency of government credit control policy.

Nam strongly argues that the Korean economy should have much more autonomous bank-enterprise relationships, like Japanese main bank relationships. I fundamentally agree with his argument that the Korean banking sector should be much freer from government control. But I would like to emphasize that the main bank relationship in Japan is not almighty in financially promoting industrial development. The main bank can be an efficient monitor of its client firms' managers so as to prevent inefficient management. But Japan's capital markets have not yet resolved the problem of who can efficiently monitor the monitor. Furthermore, major companies have gradually extended their fund-raising opportunities outside the bank loan market. If capital markets outside bank loan markets are not efficient enough, this expansion of firms' fund-raising power may weaken banks' power to control corporate management. This structural change may threaten development potential in the Japanese economy. The recent experience in the Japanese corporate sector clearly suggests the need for a well-developed capital market competitive with banking in order to preserve efficient industrial evolution.

We have observed both in Japan and Korea the progress of securitization in major firms' finance. The weight of banking business has thus shifted gradually from big-company finance to small-scale enterprise finance. But some scholars worry that the full-scale development of capital markets might prevent banks from cultivating relationships with small-scale enterprises. This is because developed capital markets would give rise to a problem of time inconsistency in the sense that, while in their infancy borrower firms are eager to receive financial support from their main banks, after establishing their own status in financial markets, such firms would wish to sever relations with their main banks. If this is a possibility, banks would hesitate to develop intimate main bank relationships with newly established enterprises. Thus, a well-developed capital market outside the banking sector ironically may hinder main bank relationships with small-scale enterprises, as suggested a few years ago by Colin Mayer (1988).

### Reference

Mayer, Colin. 1988. New issues in corporate finance. *European Economic Review* 32: 1167–89.

## Comment Shang-Jin Wei

A well-written paper is a discussant's enemy, and this paper is my enemy. In this smoothly constructed paper, Sang-Woo Nam has presented a clear description of the main features of the current principal transaction bank (PTB) system, its shortcomings, and a proposal for reform. I have no ground to dispute the factual description.

Shang-Jin Wei is assistant professor of public policy at the Kennedy School of Government, Harvard University, and a faculty research fellow of the National Bureau of Economic Research.

A discussant's job is not complete if he does not quibble. I have two quibbles on this paper. First, I will express my idiosyncratic view on where Nam's analysis of the PTB system may be modified. Second, I will suggest that Nam's reform proposal needs more justification that he has offered so far.

Let me start with my first comment. The PTB system in Korea has three salient features: (1) The government designates, or induces the banking sector and firms to self-designate, a PTB for each large business group (according the borrowing volume of the main firms in a group). (2) Other banks do not lend to a business group without first consulting with and presumably obtaining some tacit approval from the relevant PTB. (I may be reading too much into the paper on this point.) (3) A PTB is to undertake monitoring of investment and other financial transactions for all firms in the business group, to enforce credit control (later on to discourage real estate transactions), and to report to the Office of Bank Supervision and Examination. Later, each group can designate a few firms to be exempted from credit control.

A few implications are immediately clear from this setup. First, the PTB-firm relationship is a government-fostered creature, as opposed to a market-generated institution. Second, there is an anticompetitive element in the system for Korea's banking sector. That is, the PTB system enables the five large banks to divide up the banking business of large business groups and then maintain a quasi-monopolistic position in the relevant segment of the market. Third, the PTBs operate as an extension of a government regulatory agency, namely, the Office of Bank Supervision and Examination. These features are important in one's evaluation of the system.

I agree with Nam's evaluation of the PTB system with one exception. Let me explain this exception. Nam argues that the system has been successful in reducing the concentration of economic power and providing equitable access to credit. As supportive evidence, he cites data on the share of large business groups' loans (which fell from 25.3 percent in 1986 to 13.5 percent in 1990). I think that he may be too generous on this point. As Nam realizes, there was a great deal of substitution of borrowing from nonbank financial institutions for borrowing from the banks. Taking into account this substitution, the actual constraint the PTB system places on the large business groups is substantially more limited than their numerical share in total bank loans may imply. Second, as far as concentration of economic power is concerned, it seems that a better indicator might be the shares of the large business groups in total output, total employment, or total manufacture sales. Nam's paper does report some statistics on the share in manufacture sales (table 10.8). Indeed, during the period 1977–89, there was no evidence that the large business groups' share was declining. On the contrary, the top five groups' share increased from 15.7 percent in 1977 to 21.3 percent in 1989. One reason that the large groups were still able to expand rapidly despite the PTBs and the associated credit crunch, I believe, was the large groups' ability to substitute among financing sources.

Another aspect of the PTB system which Nam has not sufficiently investigated is the magnitude of the efficiency loss. The restriction on large groups' credit access appears to be entirely motivated by equity or redistribution considerations. There is a nonnegligible amount of efficiency loss due to this administrative, and to a large extent arbitrary, restriction. It would be interesting to see whether there is a way to quantify the magnitude of this efficiency loss. Such a quantification seems to me to be an important element in any evaluation of the system. (Of course, if one believes that there is inherent market failure in the banking sector, and less access to loans by firms outside the large business groups is a consequence, then there will be certain efficiency gains in the PTB system resulting from correcting the market failure. This can offset the efficiency loss associated with the administrative credit crunch. I see no convincing argument for the existence of market failure. Hence, the effect of the PTB system is probably negative on pure efficiency grounds.)

My second comment is on Nam's reform proposal. Nam says that the Japanese main bank system, despite its many problems, is a model for Korea's banking sector. I do not necessarily disagree with this. But I think that more careful justification may be needed. Broadly speaking, there are two models of bank-business relationships in capitalist economies. One is the Anglo-Saxon system, in which the stock market plays a significant role in corporate governance. Shareholder meetings as well as the possibility of takeovers injects discipline into the management of publicly listed firms. Banks, for the most part, act more as passive fund providers than as active monitors of firms' management. The alternative model is the so-called German-Japanese model, in which banks play an active role in monitoring, managing, and strategic planning or other operations of the firms. (There may be other variants of the two models, or a mixture of these features with others. For example, McKinnon might suggest a third category, say the Taiwanese model, in which the informal financial market is large in magnitude. For our discussion, we focus on the dichotomy of relative roles of banks vs. equity markets in corporate governance.)

I am not aware of any conclusive evidence favoring one particular system over the alternative in the long run. This is probably a result of my ignorance of the relevant literature. But it seems that each system has its advantages and disadvantages. For example, Nam has argued that one advantage of the Japanese model is that it may reduce information and agency costs between banks and firms. But at the same time, the Japanese model can also *raise* agency costs between banks and depositors. As a bank's involvement with a firm is more than proportional to its loans, there is also greater scope for moral hazard. Contrary to depositors' interests, banks may extend loans to a firm that should be liquidated.

From a global and historical perspective, there are successful economies with either financial model. Indeed, there is a bit of mutual convergence between the two systems. Financial reforms in Japan have given impetus to the development of its capital market, making it several notches closer to the Anglo-Saxon system. On the other hand, the pending deregulation of the banking sector in the United States is making it more like the German-Japanese financial system. To summarize, it appears that either model can be compatible with the successful development of a market economy.

If the long-run economic effects of the two model systems are comparable, is there any short-run reason to favor one model over the other? There may be two reasons for an affirmative answer. First of all, there is substantial initial cost to the development of a capital market. Given the small size of the equity market, the closer bank-firm relations within the main bank system are desirable because they at least provide some external discipline to firm management. The second reason is of the hysteresis type. Given that Korea already has a PTB system, it may be more efficient and less costly to reform it to a main bank system than to dismantle it and foster a parallel capital market. The question is whether these benefits are large enough to overcome the moral hazard problem associated with closer bank-firm relationships. My position is not that a PTB or main bank system is undesirable for Korea, but that more explicit investigation might be useful before proposing a particular bank-business relationship.

# 11 Monetary Autonomy in the Presence of Capital Flows: And Never the Twain Shall Meet, Except in East Asia?

Wing Thye Woo and Kenjiro Hirayama

In a recent OECD report, Fischer and Reisen declared that Southeast Asia is a contradiction of standard open economy macroeconomics. Specifically:

> . . . In the debate on the European Monetary System, the co-existence of exchange stability, free movement of capital, and monetary autonomy has consequently been called the triad of incompatibilities, or the impossible trinity.
>
> However, Singapore and its neighbouring countries, Malaysia and Indonesia, have been largely (though not continuously) successful in reconciling exchange rate stability at competitive levels and a fair amount of monetary independence with an open capital account.
>
> . . . The success of East Asian countries in achieving the impossible trinity challenges . . . the Mundell-Fleming framework on which most macroeconomic analysis of the open (or opening of the) capital account is based. The answers are deeper than suggested by research which has not taken into account the role of institutions such as public pension funds, state banks or public enterprises. . . . To protect the money supply and external competitiveness from movements in their private capital account, they have to rely on positive public savings or mandatory private savings. Once "fiscal complicity" is given, the art of central banking in Southeast Asia has been shown . . . to retain some monetary autonomy, in spite of free capital flows. (1993, 67, 76–77)

Wing Thye Woo is professor of economics and head of the Pacific Studies Program at the Institute of Governmental Affairs at the University of California, Davis. Kenjiro Hirayama is professor of economics at Kwansei Gakuin University.

The authors thank Menzie Chinn for extraordinary support in analysis and data; Jeffrey Frankel, Takatoshi Ito, Basant Kapur, Anne Krueger, Ronald McKinnon, Helmut Reisen, Jeffrey Sachs, and two referees for helpful comments; and Chun-Chien Kuo for excellent research assistance. Wing T. Woo is grateful to the Institute of Governmental Affairs at UC–Davis for financial support. Kenjiro Hirayama acknowledges financial support from Kansai University that enabled him to visit UC–Davis in 1993–94 and work on this paper.

Given the attention that this viewpoint has aroused (e.g., Frankel 1993), do we have yet another proof of East Asian exceptionalism?

We think not. To anticipate the analysis, our first conclusion is that substantial monetary autonomy exists in Indonesia, Malaysia, and Singapore despite their "open capital account policies." The second conclusion is that the monetary autonomy in these countries comes from the exchange risk premium created by the general lack of access to foreign funds, the strong influence that the governments have over the arbitrage activities of their domestic banks, and the readiness of the monetary authorities to change the rules of the game and to engineer perverse exchange rate movements to "cane the speculators." The exchange risk premium consists of more than the conventional portfolio risk premium, it also includes the nonzero covered interest differential generated by the preceding list of factors. The third conclusion of our analysis is that monetary authorities should eschew setting up "market-compatible" forward foreign exchange arrangements to encourage foreign investments, even those guided by theoretical arbitrage conditions, because of the operational difficulties of choosing the correct interest rates.

The paper is organized as follows: Section 11.1 defines the concept of monetary autonomy that we will use. Section 11.2 decomposes the interest rate differential into three analytical components to assess their relative contributions. Section 11.3 uses correlation methods to assess the empirical importance of the exchange risk premium by examining the accuracy of the interest rate differential in predicting exchange rate movements. Section 11.4 is a case study of Indonesia's attempt to establish a neutral-incentive forward exchange facility for "nonspeculative investments." Section 11.5 analyzes three national experiences with speculative attacks on their currencies. Section 11.6 concludes the paper.

## 11.1 Defining Monetary Autonomy

Monetary autonomy refers to the extent to which the monetary authorities can maintain the money supply at any arbitrary target level that they choose. Under a fixed exchange rate regime, full monetary autonomy is identical to having an independent interest rate policy. An independent interest rate is one that differs from the sum of the world interest rate and the expected rate of currency depreciation by a nonzero risk premium that is manipulable by policies such as capital controls, foreign exchange market interventions, and open market operations. A zero risk premium means that bonds denominated in different currencies have the same expected rate of return because they are perfect substitutes for each other, that is, the perfect capital mobility case.[1]

1. Under the floating exchange regime, a country automatically has full monetary autonomy, but it will not have an independent interest rate if foreign bonds are perfect substitutes for its bonds. In short, monetary autonomy does not always imply interest rate autonomy because it

The imperfect capital mobility (imperfect asset substitutability) case has an upward sloping balance of payments (BP) curve and allows the equilibrium interest rate to be any level provided that the IS and LM curves intersect at that point of the BP curve.[2] We find the assumption that $r$ can deviate any amount from $r^* + \hat{e}$ under imperfect capital mobility to be implausible, especially under the fixed exchange rate regime without capital controls. If, as is likely, the amount of capital inflow increases disproportionately with an increase in the interest differential, then there is an interest differential beyond which capital inflows will overwhelm the ability to conduct sterilized interventions.

One simple way to amend the imperfect capital mobility case is to add the condition:

$$\text{maximum domestic interest rate,} \quad r_{\max} = r^* + \hat{e} + \frac{1}{k_r},$$

$$\text{minimum domestic interest rate,} \quad r_{\min} = r^* + \hat{e} - \frac{1}{k_r},$$

where $k_r$ is the responsiveness of net private capital flows to a deviation of $r$ from $r + \hat{e}$; that is, $k_r$ evaluated at $r = r^* + \hat{e}$ is

$k_r = \infty$ for perfect capital mobility,
$k_r = 0$ for zero capital mobility,
$k_r = \sigma$ finite positive number, for imperfect capital mobility.

With this amendment, we have a natural way of comparing degrees of monetary autonomy under fixed exchange rate for different countries. Consider the situation of the money stock being decreased by a one-time open market operation. If the resulting interest rate is above $r_{\max}$, then the resulting capital inflow will be so massive that it will overcome sterilized intervention to keep the money stock at the new level and increase the money stock to the level that is compatible with $r_{\max}$.

This situation is summarized in figure 11.1. An open market operation shifts LM from $LM_0$ to $LM_A$, and the irresistible capital inflows push LM to $LM_B$. If LM had originally been shifted to $LM_C$, then sterilized intervention would be able to keep it there.

Figure 11.2 illustrates our concept of monetary autonomy. A country with high capital mobility ($BP_1$) has monetary autonomy within the range of money stocks that generate $LM_1$ and $LM_2$. Whereas a country with low capital mobility ($BP_2$) has monetary autonomy within the range given by $LM_3$ and $LM_4$. So

depends on the exchange rate regime, whereas interest rate autonomy always implies monetary autonomy regardless of the exchange rate regime.

2. Imperfect capital mobility produces an important asymmetry. Sterilized intervention can maintain an IS-LM intersection to the left of the BP curve (i.e., when the balance of payments is surplus) for a long time, while it can keep an IS-LM intersection to the right of the BP curve only until foreign reserves run out.

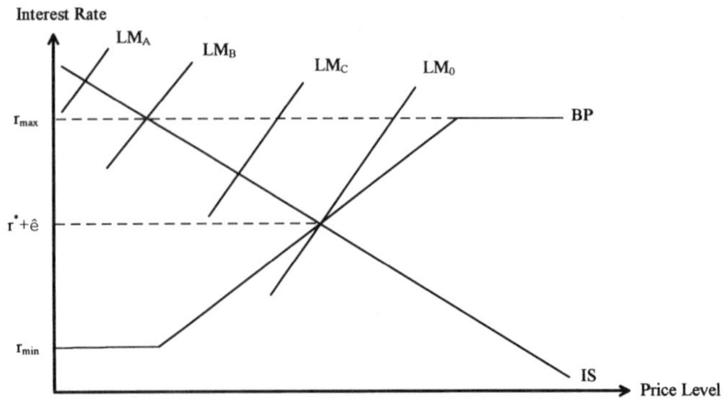


**Fig. 11.1 Constraining of monetary policy by capital flows**

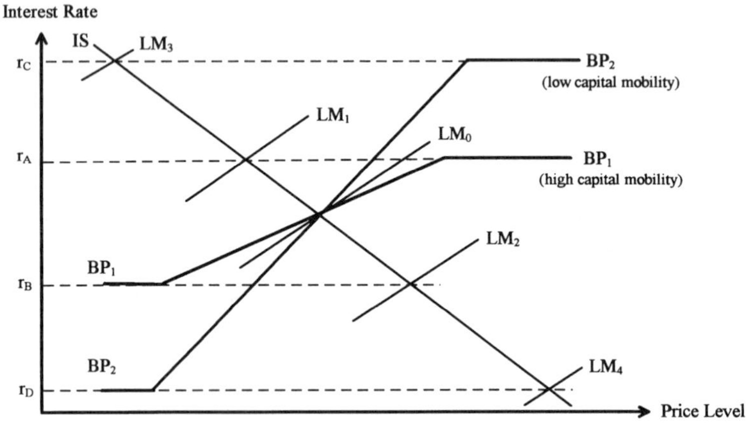


**Fig. 11.2 Defining the degree of monetary autonomy**

a natural measure of the degree of monetary autonomy is the range over which LM can be exogenously set.

## 11.2 An Accounting Framework

One way to examine the source of interest autonomy is to adopt an accounting framework for the deviation of the domestic interest rate from the world interest rate. The deviation can be decomposed into the following three factors; using the 90-day frequency, Indonesia and the United States as the example:

$$\frac{1+r}{1+r^*} \equiv \left[\left(\frac{1+r}{1+r^*}\right)\left(\frac{s}{f}\right)\right]\left[\left(\frac{f}{s}\right)\left(\frac{s}{e}\right)\right]\left[\frac{e}{s}\right], \tag{1}$$

$r =$ 90-day Indonesian interest rate,
$r^* =$ 90-day U.S. interest rate,
$s =$ spot exchange rate expressed as rupiah per dollar,
$f =$ 90-day forward rate,
$e =$ expected value of spot exchange rate 90 days thence.

Taking the natural logarithm of equation (1), we arrive at

$$\begin{aligned}\ln(1+r) - \ln(1+r^*) \equiv & \left[\ln(1+r) - \ln(1+r^*) - \ln\left(1+\frac{f-s}{s}\right)\right] \\ (2) \qquad & + \left[\ln\left(1+\frac{f-s}{s}\right) - \ln\left(1+\frac{e-s}{s}\right)\right] \\ & + \left[\ln\left(1+\frac{e-s}{s}\right)\right].\end{aligned}$$

Using the approximation of $\ln(1+x) \cong x$ when $x$ is small, we obtain

$$\begin{aligned}(3) \quad r - r^* &= \left[r - r^* - \left(\frac{f-s}{s}\right)\right] + \left[\left(\frac{f-s}{s}\right) - \left(\frac{e-s}{s}\right)\right] + \left[\frac{e-s}{s}\right] \\ &= \left[r - r^* - \left(\frac{f-s}{s}\right)\right] + \left[\frac{f-e}{s}\right] + \left[\frac{e-s}{s}\right].\end{aligned}$$

We now define

$\left(\frac{f-s}{s}\right) \equiv d$ the forward discount on the rupiah vis-à-vis the dollar

$\left(\frac{f-e}{s}\right) \equiv \lambda$ the portfolio risk premium

$\left(\frac{e-s}{s}\right) \equiv \hat{e}$ the expected depreciation of the rupiah vis-à-vis the dollar

$(r - r^* - d) \equiv \alpha$ the covered interest differential (country risk premium)

The final result is

$$\begin{aligned}r - r^* = & \text{ [the covered interest differential, } \alpha] \\ (4) \qquad & + \text{ [the portfolio risk premium, } \lambda] \\ & + \text{ [the expected currency depreciation, } \hat{e}],\end{aligned}$$

and we define

$$(5) \qquad \alpha + \lambda = \text{exchange risk premium.}$$

*The covered interest differential, α.* Since $\alpha$ is the result of riskless arbitrage, the expectation is that $\alpha = 0$ in the absence of capital controls, political risks, and transaction costs. With negligible capital controls on the major European currencies and the U.S. dollar since the late 1970s, the nonzero value of $\alpha$ is commonly deemed to reflect the costs of currency transactions and borrowing and lending interest rate spreads. Furthermore, with increasing financial innovations, $\alpha$ is expected to decrease over time. However, if risk-averse speculators fear a possible reimposition of capital controls in the future, then there will be a nonzero $\alpha$ that reflects a country risk premium; and a fluctuating $\alpha$ may reflect the changing probabilities of capital controls being reimposed.

*The portfolio risk premium,* $\lambda$. In a simple two-country case and assuming that a covered interest differential holds ($\alpha = 0$) (e.g., Dornbusch 1983), we have the portfolio-balance equation:

$$(6) \qquad \lambda = \phi\left(\frac{B}{eB^*}\right),$$

where

$B$ = stock of outside bonds denominated in rupiah,
$B^*$ = stock of outside bonds demoninated in dollars,
$\phi$ = a coefficient whose magnitude depends on the degree of risk aversion and the variance and covariance matrix of $r$ and $r^* + \hat{e}$.

The existence of $\lambda$ is controversial. Frankel (1982) and Rogoff (1983) did not find it, while Dominguez and Frankel (1992) and Woo (1987) did.

Table 11.1 decomposes the interest rate differential (of Australia, Canada, Japan, and Singapore vis-à-vis the United States) into three components. The values of $\alpha$, $\lambda$, and $\hat{e}$ do not add up because all terms were calculated by log approximations. Component $\hat{e}$ is calculated from the expected values of the currencies in three months' time as reported in the *Currency Forecaster's Digest.* The dates are arbitrarily chosen to be the beginning and middle of the year, and end-of-month data were used (except for the *Currency Forecaster's Digest* data, a point that will be discussed later).

As $\alpha = 0$ is the zero-profit condition for taking risk-free positions in the foreign exchange markets, it is reassuring that, in absolute terms, the covered interest differential was always very much smaller than the portfolio risk premium and the expected depreciation rate. The largest absolute value of covered interest differential was 1.1 percent (Canada in February 1990) compared to 14.1 percent for portfolio risk premium and 17.4 percent for currency appreciation (both for Japan in August 1989).

There are several (not mutually exclusive) explanations for why $\alpha$ does not equal zero in table 11.1. The first explanation is the match-up error in timing. Our data match only by day and not by time within the same day. This can be a serious problem because financial markets respond to news very quickly. The second explanation is the match-up error in exchange rates. We used the exchange rate that is the average of the ask and bid rates, whereas the arbitrage relationship requires that the ask and bid rates be used according to the direc-

**Table 11.1 Decomposition of the Interest Rate Differential**

| Country and Date | Local Interest Minus Eurodollar Interest Rate $r - r^*$ | Covered Interest Differential[a] $\alpha$ | Portfolio Risk Premium[b] $\lambda$ | Expected Depreciation of Local Currency[c] $\hat{e}$ | Error from Approximation |
|---|---|---|---|---|---|
| *Australia* | | | | | |
| 1988:Feb | 3.8410 | −0.1024 | −5.4407 | 10.1414 | −0.7573 |
| 1988:Aug | 4.5357 | −0.1743 | −2.6628 | 6.4398 | 0.9330 |
| 1989:Feb | 5.7884 | 0.0220 | 2.4956 | 2.4316 | 0.8392 |
| 1989:Aug | 7.9062 | −0.4706 | −2.0192 | 12.2269 | −1.8308 |
| 1990:Feb | 7.0550 | −0.4159 | 0.6527 | 7.6345 | −0.8163 |
| 1990:Aug | 5.2487 | −0.1586 | −3.0633 | 9.2406 | −0.7699 |
| 1991:Feb | 4.5189 | 0.0897 | −2.1782 | 6.2550 | 0.3524 |
| Average | 5.5563 | −0.1729 | −1.7451 | 7.7671 | −0.2928 |
| *Canada* | | | | | |
| 1988:Feb | 1.6721 | −0.2407 | 0.4247 | 0.9460 | 0.5422 |
| 1988:Aug | 1.4517 | −0.1901 | 1.8302 | 0.3248 | −0.5132 |
| 1989:Feb | 1.7532 | −0.0261 | 4.5698 | −2.6846 | −0.1058 |
| 1989:Aug | 3.0400 | −0.1898 | 5.6859 | −2.3861 | −0.0701 |
| 1990:Feb | 4.0507 | −1.1193 | 5.6644 | −1.0844 | 0.5900 |
| 1990:Aug | 3.8330 | −0.7125 | 2.4005 | 1.4085 | 0.7365 |
| 1991:Feb | 2.6538 | −0.2916 | 1.0321 | 2.4190 | −0.5057 |
| Average | 2.6364 | −0.3957 | 3.0868 | −0.1510 | 0.0963 |
| *Japan* | | | | | |
| 1988:Feb | −2.8024 | −0.0222 | 5.6238 | −8.4742 | 0.0702 |
| 1988:Aug | −4.2358 | −0.6608 | −8.3151 | 3.5715 | 1.1685 |
| 1989:Feb | −5.6342 | −0.0251 | 9.6304 | −15.1814 | −0.0582 |
| 1989:Aug | −3.7671 | −0.3581 | 14.0820 | −17.4005 | −0.0905 |
| 1990:Feb | −1.8311 | −0.8417 | 7.6950 | −7.3994 | −1.2850 |
| 1990:Aug | −0.6479 | −0.7916 | 11.6379 | −9.7328 | −1.7614 |
| 1991:Feb | 0.7871 | −0.4380 | 9.5207 | −8.0004 | −0.2953 |
| Average | −2.5902 | −0.4482 | 7.1250 | −8.9453 | −0.3217 |
| *Singapore* | | | | | |
| 1988:Jul | −3.2781 | −0.3783 | 2.3315 | −3.9604 | −1.2709 |
| 1989:Jan | −3.4931 | −0.3232 | −0.6259 | −2.0779 | −0.4660 |
| 1989:Jul | −2.8608 | −0.1331 | −3.7937 | 0.0000 | 1.0660 |
| 1990:Jan | −1.8003 | −0.9624 | −5.8753 | 6.3662 | −1.3288 |
| 1990:Jul | −0.1739 | −0.5052 | −1.9733 | 4.3957 | −2.0911 |
| 1991:Jan | −2.2399 | −0.7334 | −2.7810 | 0.6935 | 0.5811 |
| Average | −2.3077 | −0.5059 | −2.1196 | 0.9028 | −0.5849 |

*Source:* Calculations provided by Menzie Chinn from raw data in various issues of the *Currency Forecaster's Digest.*

[a] Calculated from $\ln(1 + d) = \ln(1 + r) - \ln(1 + r^*) - \ln(f/s)$.

[b] Calculated as $(f - e)/s$.

[c] Calculated from the expected value of the spot exchange rate three months thence.

tion of the capital flow (Ito 1986). The third explanation is the existence of transaction costs that make a nonzero α consistent with zero profits in arbitrage (Keynes 1924). The fourth explanation is that the interest rates used may not have the same risk characteristics. The fifth explanation is the differences in tax treatment of foreign funds and in tax rates across countries. The sixth explanation could be the existence, or expected future existence, of capital controls.

Most studies on covered interest arbitrage have focused on the existence of transaction costs to explain the nonzero α. The reason for this appears to be that these authors limited themselves to the currencies of the industrialized countries and they regarded existing (if any), and the probability of future, capital controls in the industrialized countries to be insignificant. Branson (1969) estimated the transaction cost to be 0.18 percent per annum, while Keynes (1924) "guesstimated" it to be 0.5 percent per annum.[3] As some transaction costs (e.g., telephone charges) have fallen since Keynes's time, it may be reasonable to regard any absolute value of α at or above 0.5 percent per annum to indicate the existence of a country risk premium.

Table 11.1 shows that the α values for Australia, Canada, and Japan are consistent with the existence of transaction costs that eliminated the possibility of unexploited arbitrage profits.[4] Only the α value for Singapore, 0.51 percent per annum, is larger than could be justified by normal transaction costs. We will argue in section 11.5 that the high value of α in Singapore could be the result of Singapore's tight control of arbitrage activities by domestic banks and by its unusual policy reactions to past speculations against its currency.

The estimates of the portfolio risk premium and the expected currency depreciation rate in table 11.1 should be interpreted cautiously because of possible large misalignment errors. The survey by the *Currency Forecaster's Digest* on the expected value of the spot rate in 30 days' time is done on the third Thursday of the month, while our forward and spot exchange data are from the last trading day in the month. Since the portfolio risk premium for any one country in table 11.1 is mostly or overwhelmingly in one direction, it appears that the misalignment error, if it exists, may be consistently biased in one direction. In section 11.3, we will point to partial evidence that indicates that the nonzero portfolio premium is not an artifact created by the timing misalignment.

The portfolio risk premium indicates that similar maturity bonds denomi-

3. Frenkel and Levich (1975) estimated the transaction costs in a 90-day covered interest arbitrage transaction to be about 0.15 percent (see their table 2), but it seems that they neglected to take into account the transaction cost of acquiring the foreign security (their $t^*$), which would raise the total transaction cost to 0.17. Because Frenkel and Levich's estimate cannot be easily made comparable to the annualized α estimates in our table 11.1, in Branson (1969), and in Keynes (1924), we have not used their estimate in our discussion.

4. The value of 0.45 percent per annum for Japan places it at the upper end of transaction costs. This may explain why Bonser-Neal and Roley (1994), unlike Ito (1986), rejected covered interest parity for Japan.

nated in the Canadian dollar and Japanese yen have to pay higher interest rates than U.S. dollar–denominated bonds while those denominated in the Australian dollar and Singapore dollar pay lower interest rates. For Canada and Singapore, the portfolio risk premium was the biggest contributor to the interest rate differential. For Canada, the average absolute size of the portfolio risk premium was 3.1 percentage points, while the average absolute expected depreciation was 0.2 percentage point. For Singapore, they were 2.1 and 0.9 percentage points respectively.

## 11.3 Looking for the Risk Premium

The existence of monetary autonomy depends on the existence of a risk premium that could be due to a country risk premium (a nonzero covered interest differential) *and/or* a portfolio risk premium. We will look for the risk premium using standard correlation analysis under the maintained hypothesis that agents are rational. In the absence of a risk premium, the interest rate differential is a good predictor of the subsequent exchange rate change; to see this, set $\alpha = \lambda = 0$ in equation (4). The converse is that poor predictive capability is consistent with the existence of the risk premium.

In the following three tests, there is decreasing stringency in the criteria of what constitutes adequate predictive power. For a zero risk premium, we expect a systematic relationship between the magnitudes of the two variables in the regression analysis, a systematic relationship between the ranking of the magnitudes in the Spearman correlation coefficient test, and a systematic agreement in signs in the sign test. The interest rate differentials and actual subsequent exchange rate movements for Indonesia, Japan, and Malaysia are shown in figures 11.3, 11.4, and 11.5, respectively.

Panel A of table 11.2 reports the regression results. Regressions are run with and without the constant term, corresponding to the assumption of no risk premium or a constant risk premium. If the predictive power is perfect, we would expect the coefficient on the interest rate differential to be equal to unity. The negative coefficients for Japan and Malaysia clearly reject the interest rate differential as an acceptable predictor of future exchange rate changes. The results for Indonesia are somewhat encouraging but the positive relationship may merely reflect the well-known government policy since 1986 of depreciating the exchange rate by 3–5 percent each year (unless an unexpected large external shock happens).

We now relax the stringency of the link between the change in the value of the currency and the interest rate differential. Spearman rank coefficients were computed for this pair of variables to look into a possible loose correlation (panel B of table 11.2). Only Indonesia exhibits a fair degree of theoretically expected correlation. The *t*-statistics indicate Malaysia's rank correlation coefficient to be zero and Japan's rank correlation coefficient to be significantly negative!

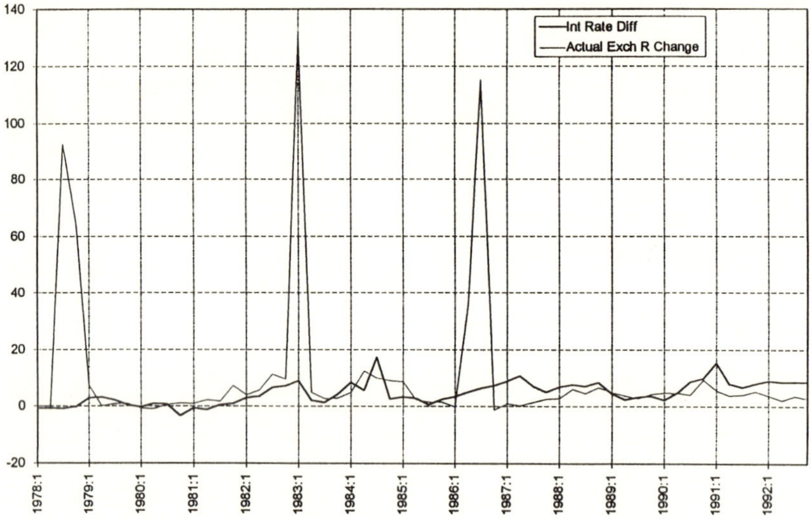


**Fig. 11.3 Indonesia: interest rate differential and actual exchange rate change**

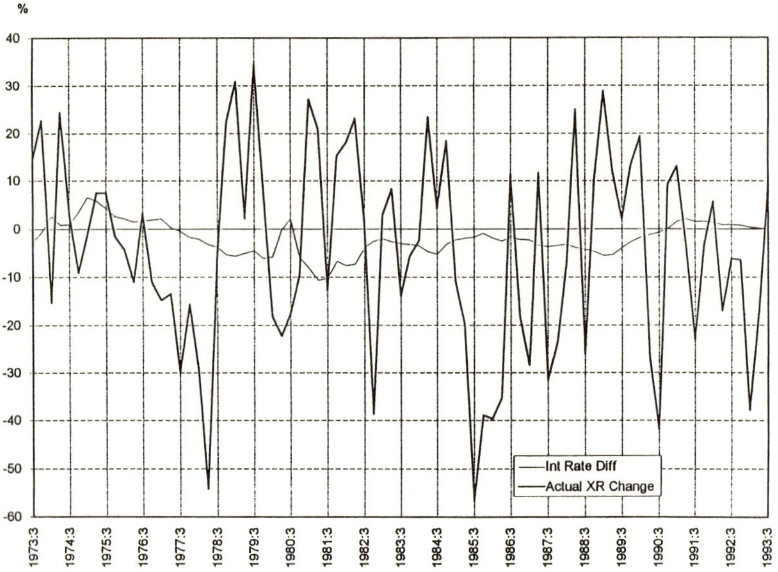


**Fig. 11.4 Japan: interest rate differential and ex post exchange rate change**

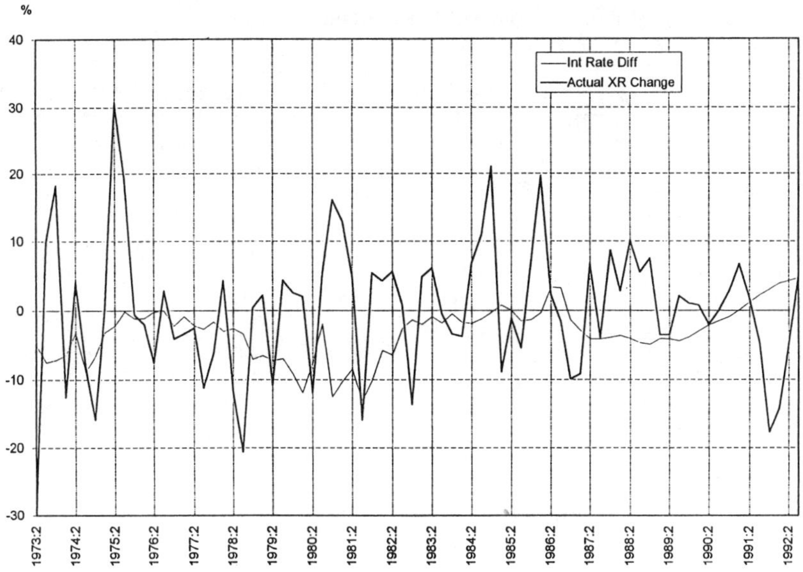


**Fig. 11.5 Malaysia: interest rate differential and ex post exchange rate change**

Panel C of table 11.2 reports the sign test of the two variables. A successful prediction occurs when both variables have the same sign. Under the null hypothesis of the two series being random, these predictions would be correct half the time. Indonesia has an unusually high rate of success (50 out of 58), and the null hypothesis is rejected. The results for Japan and Malaysia are dismal. Sample success rates are only 0.44, and the $p$-values are quite small.

The results in table 11.2 suggest the presence of a risk premium for Japan and Malaysia, and possibly the absence of one for Indonesia.[5] More important, since table 11.1 suggests that covered interest parity holds for Japan, this means that the Japanese risk premium found here reflects a nonzero portfolio risk premium, indicating that the nonzero portfolio risk premium in table 11.1 is not an artifact of the timing misalignment between the survey data and the forward rates.

## 11.4 Indonesia's Experience with Using the Covered Interest Parity Condition

Indonesia removed all controls on capital account transactions in 1971 in recognition of the fact that there was no effective way to administer capital controls in an economy of 13,000 islands, most of which are within a short

5. Our results are consistent with the finding of Hansen and Hodrick (1980, 1983) that risk premia exist in the U.S. dollar exchange rate with the currencies of Canada, West Germany, France, Britain, Switzerland, Japan, and Italy.

**Table 11.2 Predictive Power of Interest Rate Differential**

| Test | Indonesia 1978:3–1992:4 | Japan 1973:3–1993:3 | Malaysia 1973:2–1992:3 |
|---|---|---|---|
| A. *Regression of Rate of Actual Currency Depreciation on Interest Rate Differential* | | | |
| Equation | (1) | (2) | (3) |
| Coefficient on $r - r^*$ | 1.43 | −0.6 | −0.11 |
| ($t$-statistic) | (2.52) | (0.99) | (0.48) |
| Durbin-Watson | 1.34 | 1.27 | 1.53 |
| Adjusted $R^2$ | −0.07 | −0.03 | 0 |
| Equation | (1′) | (2′) | (3′) |
| Constant term | 10.37 | −7.17 | −0.38 |
| ($t$-statistic) | (1.92) | (2.80) | (0.26) |
| Coefficient on $r - r^*$ | 0.15 | −1.49 | −0.16 |
| ($t$-statistic) | (0.17) | (2.25) | (0.53) |
| Durbin-Watson | 1.53 | 1.4 | 1.53 |
| Adjusted $R^2$ | 0.00 | 0.05 | −0.01 |
| B. *Spearman Rank Coefficient between Rate of Actual Currency Depreciation and Interest Rate Differential* | | | |
| Spearman rank coefficient | 0.25 | −0.29 | −0.08 |
| ($t$-statistic) | (1.92) | (2.73) | (0.72) |
| C. *Sign Test for Correct Prediction of the Direction of Change* | | | |
| $N$ | 58 | 81 | 78 |
| Number of matching signs | 50 | 36 | 34 |
| Proportion of matching signs | 0.86 | 0.44 | 0.44 |
| ($p$-value) | (1.00) | (0.19) | (0.15) |

*Notes:* The data are quarterly and the interest rate is money market rate for Indonesia, call rate for Japan, money market rate for Malaysia, U.S. federal funds rate for the common foreign interest rate (these are all line 60B of *International Financial Statistics* [Washington, D.C.: International Monetary Fund, various issues]).

The exchange rate is number of local currency units per U.S. dollar.

boat ride of Singapore, a major international commercial and financial center. With capital controls, the ease of smuggling would quickly create a huge black market for illegal export proceeds already banked in Singapore. Not only would the controls be futile, their very existence would increase the uncertainty perceived by investors and hence increase capital flight.

In order to encourage foreign investment, Indonesia sought to reduce the exchange rate risk by introducing a swap mechanism in January 1979 to supplement its slowly developing private forward exchange market. The swap arrangement had the central bank, Bank Indonesia, simultaneously buying foreign currencies at the current spot exchange rate and entering into a contract to sell the same amount of foreign currencies at a specified future point in time at the current spot exchange rate. Bank Indonesia would charge a swap margin for entering into such an arrangement.

Bank Indonesia initially set the swap margin at 2.5 percent per annum, with the maturity of the swaps ranging from 30 to 180 days. But this meant that whenever the domestic interest rate was more than 2.5 percentage points above the Eurodollar interest rate, there was an opportunity for unlimited profits with no risk for the private agents who contracted swap arrangements with Bank Indonesia. The resulting enormous periodic demands for swaps forced Bank Indonesia to control its exposure to foreign exchange risk by introducing ceilings on the size of individual transactions, adopting an aggregate swap ceiling, and raising the swap margin.

The swap margin was increased to 4.5 percent in March 1983 and to 8 percent in October 1986. Expecting the swap margin of 8 percent to be high enough to inhibit short-term speculative movements, the authorities removed the individual and aggregate swap ceilings to give long-term investors the full benefit of the swap mechanism. But the high demand for swap transactions reappeared after several months when Indonesian interest rates rose relative to international interest rates. The swap margin was raised to 9 percent in the second quarter of 1987.

The government, very sensitive to its laggardness in adjusting the swap margin in response to capital inflows, wanted to avoid any delay in lowering the swap margin if the interest differential were to drop. An excessive swap margin would militate against the objective of the swap mechanism to induce (nonspeculative) investments. With these concerns in mind, the government decided in October 1988 to adopt the covered interest parity condition as the basis for pricing swap transactions.

The swap margin was "market determined" in that Bank Indonesia set it equal to the difference between the average deposit rate for rupiah deposits in the Indonesian banking system and the deposit rate for dollar deposits in international banks in Singapore. This pricing formula for the swap margin was thought to render foreign speculators indifferent between putting their money in foreign banks or putting them in the Indonesian banks, and thus to be neutral in its effects on speculative capital flows. In October 1988, the government also extended the maturity of the swap to three years as an added incentive to foreign companies to undertake long-term physical capital investments in Indonesia.

One of the present authors pointed out in late 1990 that this covered interest parity pricing formula in Indonesia was not neutral in its effect on capital flow. It, in fact, subsidized capital inflows.[6] Neutrality was possible only if the interest rates used in the pricing were lending rates rather than deposit rates. The swap subsidy was the result of the spread between the lending rate and the deposit rate being larger in Indonesia than in Singapore.

To see the subsidy element in the "market-determined" pricing formula, let

$$S = r_d - r_d^*, \tag{7}$$

$$W = r_l - r_l^*, \tag{8}$$

6. This point was also made independently by Nasution (1991). The basis of his analysis and his definition of subsidy are different from ours.

where

$r_d$ rupiah deposit interest rate in Indonesia,
$r_d^*$ dollar deposit interest rate offshore,
$r_l$ rupiah lending rate in Indonesia,
$r_l^*$ dollar rate offshore.

If $S$ is the swap margin, a depositor will be indifferent about whether her funds were dollar deposits in a Singapore bank or rupiah deposits in an Indonesian bank. If the swap margin is smaller than $S$, there will be an inflow of deposits from Singapore. On the other hand, if the swap margin is larger than $S$, it will not induce a capital outflow because the swap mechanism is a one-way mechanism: it guarantees a future exit rupiah-dollar rate for dollars entering Indonesia now, but not a future reentry rupiah-dollar rate for rupiahs leaving Indonesia now.

If the swap premium were set less than $W$, then an Indonesian who had to borrow for a transaction inside Indonesia would be better off borrowing offshore and using the swap mechanism to cover her position. Again because the swap mechanism is one way, a swap premium greater than $W$ will not cause a capital outflow.

Now, defining

(9) $$r_l = r_d + m ,$$

(10) $$r_l^* = r_d^* + m^* ,$$

where

$m$ = intermediation cost in Indonesia (including the profit margin),
$m^*$ = intermediation cost offshore (including the profit margin),

and subtracting equation (1) from equation (9), we get

(11) $$r_l - r_l^* = (r_d^* - r_d) + (m - m^*) ,$$

(12) $$W = S + (m - m^*) .$$

As we know that $m > m^*$, we have

(13) $$W > S .$$

Since the swap premium was set to be $S$, there was neutrality only for depositors but a positive incentive for spenders to borrow from abroad. Specifically, the swap rate set by equation (7) gave a subsidy ($x$) to spenders who borrowed from abroad:

(14) $$x = r_l - (r_l^* + S) ;$$

swap subsidy to borrowers,

(15) $$x = m - m^* .$$

There are two reasons why $m$ is greater than $m^*$. The first is that the greater inefficiency of the Indonesian banking system translates into higher operating costs. The second is that the state banks that dominate the banking system do not compete aggressively enough among themselves, and the result is that banks could have a higher markup over the cost of their deposits.

In terms of the theoretical discussion of section 11.1, the existence of the swap subsidy ($x$) means that the actual cost of external funds is lower than $r^* + \hat{e}$. So with the swap mechanism in place, we have

$$r_{\max} = (r^* + \hat{e} - x) + \frac{1}{k_r}.$$

The value of the floor on the domestic interest rate remains unchanged at

$$r_{\min} = r^* + \hat{e} - \frac{1}{k_r}$$

because the swap mechanism is a one-way mechanism.

This narrowing of the permissible interest rate band by the decline in $r_{\max}$, as shown in figure 11.6, is a reduction in monetary autonomy, as defined earlier in figure 11.2.

The loss in monetary autonomy caused by the swap subsidy was brought home forcefully from the second quarter of 1991 onward. The government decided to reduce money growth to cool the economy. However, they found their credit-tightening efforts significantly attenuated by capital inflows.

This reduction of monetary autonomy was not the only consequence of the swap mechanism. We also attribute to it the nondevelopment of the private market for forward foreign exchange in the 1980s despite the drastic deregulation of the financial system since 1983. The nondevelopment of private forward

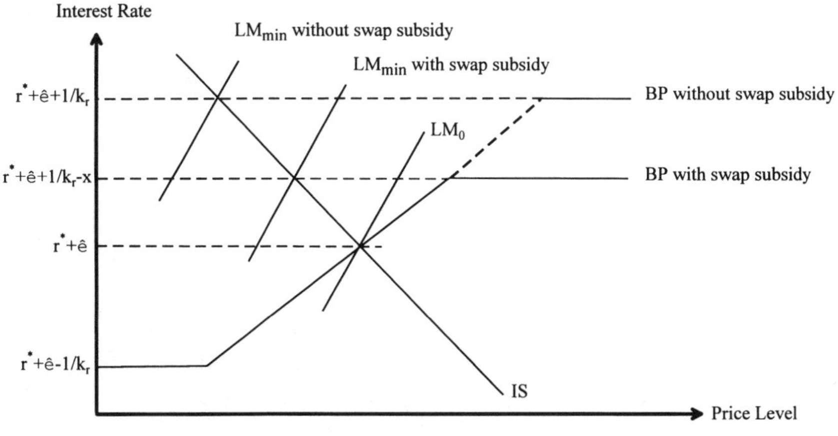


**Fig. 11.6 Effect of the swap subsidy ($x$) on monetary autonomy**

foreign exchange activities had less to do with the incapacity of the private sector to create a sophisticated forward exchange market than with the existence of a subsidized swap mechanism paid for by public funds. The veracity of the proposition that the swap mechanism had suppressed the growth of a private forward market can be seen in the quick growth of the private forward market after the swap mechanism was suddenly eliminated in November 1991.

The swap mechanism was terminated after its abetment of capital inflows was pointed out and confirmed by the huge capital inflows that occurred in 1991, when the swap subsidy ($x$) ranged from 2 to 6 percentage points. There were two reasons why the government decided to abandon the swap mechanism completely rather than to reset the formula using lending rates instead:

1. Just as the pedagogical device of a single interest rate glosses over the distinction between the deposit rate and the lending rate, there is no single lending rate. Getting the appropriate loan rate to use is a particularly serious problem because it is much harder to identify loans to projects with comparable risks across countries than to identify deposits in banks with comparable risks across countries. Using the prime rates of different countries is one possibility, but prime rates tend to be rather rigid and hence not good indicators of current credit conditions.

2. Indonesia has a history of occasional large discrete devaluations (the last one was 35 percent at the end of 1986), and the swap contracts caused major financial losses to Bank Indonesia. Such losses are inevitable with any state-sponsored swap mechanism, and the use of a different interest rate does not solve this basic problem.

## 11.5 Can Caning the Speculators Avoid the Impossible Trinity?

As will be seen, we agree with the primary conclusion in Fischer and Reisen (1993) that Malaysia and Singapore have been able to undertake sterilized intervention to a greater extent than the countries in the European Monetary System, but we differ with them on the applicability of standard macroeconomic theory to these countries. In particular, we view the Southeast Asian experiences as confirming, rather than refuting, the impossible trinity proposition that in the absence of effective capital controls, money growth cannot be set at any arbitrary rate without undermining the exogenously preset level (or depreciation rate) of the exchange rate. The case for our view can be seen in the following three episodes of policy responses to speculative attack on the local currency.

The first episode is Singapore in the last quarter of 1985, when GDP fell 5.5 percent on an annualized basis. A major contribution to the sharp slowdown was the excessive real wage growth in the previous years. At the beginning of the decade, the government had decided to restructure the industrial sector toward high value-added industries by ordering high annual real wage increases to eliminate the low-wage labor-intensive industries. The big push toward more capital-intensive and technology-intensive modes of production caused Singapore's wages to increase by more than 60 percent in U.S. dollars over the 1980–84 period while Hong Kong's wages hardly changed. The outcome was a major loss in competitiveness which together with the economic stagnation in the industrialized countries resulted in a steady decline in growth rates during 1984. In 1985, Singapore had its first negative growth experience since it became independent in 1965.

The Singapore dollar had depreciated quite steadily during 1984 with the slowdown in export earnings and economic growth (see fig. 11.7). When the negative growth in 1985 became obvious in mid-1985, foreign exchange market participants, sensing a possible big devaluation of the Singapore dollar to restore Singapore's competitiveness, began a run on the currency. The end-of-period exchange rate went from S$2.19 per U.S. dollar in July 1985 to S$2.27 per U.S. dollar in August 1985.

The government reacted to Singapore's loss of international competitiveness by cutting labor cost through reductions in the hefty payroll tax and social security contributions instead of through currency depreciation as anticipated by the speculators because it viewed the latter as importing inflation. More interesting, simultaneous with the shift in fiscal policy to correct the balance-of-payments problem, Singapore used its ample foreign reserves to appreciate the Singapore dollar. The exchange rate was S$2.13 per U.S. dollar in September and October, S$2.09 per U.S. dollar in November, and S$2.11 per U.S. dollar in December. The exchange rate averaged S$2.18 per U.S. dollar in 1986. In the bottom-line language of the business community, as headlined in

**Fig. 11.7 Singapore dollar/U.S. dollar exchange rate**

the financial press, the chairman of the Monetary Authority of Singapore had "caned the speculators."

This "caning" episode confirms the impossible trinity. Exchange rate stability was maintained without resort to capital controls, but it involved a fiscal policy adjustment and a massive buying of the Singapore dollar by the monetary authorities, which meant shrinking the money supply to accommodate the speculative drop in money demand. At least U.S.$400 million of reserves were sold between September 13 and 18, and this massive shrinkage of liquidity caused the interbank overnight rate to reach 120 percent (on an annualized basis) on September 17. Monetary autonomy was certainly compromised in order to peg the exchange rate (see fig. 11.8).

The second episode is Malaysia in January 1994. For Malaysia, 1993 was another boom year; economic growth was 8 percent as in the year before. This sustained high-growth performance attracted capital flows that appreciated the ringgit from 2.61 per U.S. dollar in January 1992 to 2.55 per U.S. dollar in December 1993. The final months of 1993 saw large capital inflows and forward buying of the ringgit in anticipation of further ringgit appreciation.

On January 11, 1994, the government responded with two measures to quell the speculation. The first was to raise the reserve requirement on time deposits held by foreigners. The banks, to protect their profit margins, immediately lowered the deposit rate on foreign funds. The second measure was to limit the amount of foreign funds that could be placed in interest-earning accounts. The result of this discrimination against foreign funds was a capital outflow that plunged the ringgit to 2.73 per U.S. dollar on January 17.

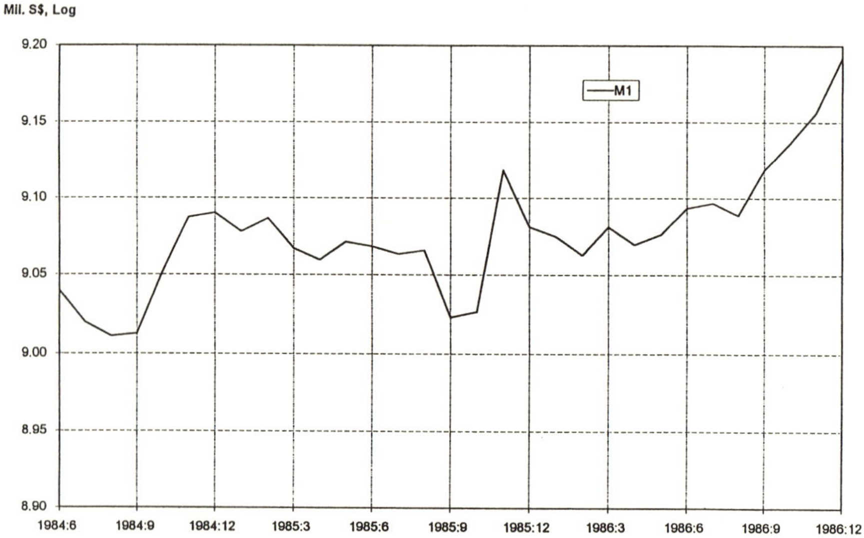


Fig. 11.8 Singapore: M1

When the government followed up with a ban on the sale of money market instruments to foreigners on January 24, the ringgit fell to 2.76 per U.S. dollar. We thus have another example of a government engineering an opposite movement of the currency in order to inflict losses on the currency speculators.

If we regard the prohibition of capital movements as an extreme form of discrimination against foreign capital, then the legal requirement in Malaysia of paying a lower (or no) interest rate on foreign deposits is a moderate form of capital control. The no-interest-payment policy is a form of capital control that uses price to discourage capital inflow as compared with the traditional practice of using a quantity quota to contain the volume of inflow. So while Malaysia had caned the speculators without compromising monetary autonomy, it had to interfere with the free flow of capital in order to do so.

The third episode is Indonesia in June 1987 and February 1991. In both instances, the government halted the run on the rupiah by ordering state enterprises to withdraw the bulk of their funds from the banking system and purchase central bank certificates.[7] In both cases, the high interest rates created by the liquidity squeeze convinced speculators of the government's resolve to support the exchange rate, and capital held abroad returned to Indonesia. With this, the overnight interbank rate that had jumped from 17.6 percent in January 1991 to 26.9 percent in March 1991 fell to 11.3 percent in May 1991. These two Indonesian monetary shock therapies are clearly cases of compromising monetary autonomy to maintain the value of the exchange rate and confirm the impossible trinity.

The actions by Malaysia and Singapore to move the exchange rate in the counterintuitive direction are rare events in international experience. Italy widened its exchange rate band to accommodate the greater and more frequent speculative bouts on the lira, and Britain devalued by leaving the Exchange Rate Mechanism when the pound was under attack. The different national reactions suggest many interesting possibilities.

One is that counterpunches used to punish speculators may hurt the economy in the process, but the economic cost of these counterpunches may be lower in East Asia. While such a possibility is hard to assess definitively because different governments may have different thresholds for economic distress, we think that an important reason for the different national responses to speculative attacks is that it is technically easier for Indonesia, Malaysia, and Singapore than for European countries to influence their foreign exchange markets.

We see three factors that make it technically easier for these Southeast Asian countries to face down the speculators. The first is that private capital flows into and out of these Asian countries (not counting the pure offshore transactions in Singapore) are much smaller than those of Western Europe. Most busi-

7. For details of the two episodes, see Woo, Glassburner, and Nasution (1994).

nesses (especially in Indonesia) do not meet the creditworthiness criteria of international banks and hence do not have access to foreign credit. Furthermore, Malaysia and Indonesia have carefully limited the entry and activities of foreign banks.

The second factor is the great influence that the governments have on banks either through regulation or through ownership. Singapore requires banks to submit daily reports on their foreign exchange transactions and to get approval for large transfers of foreign currencies. Quasi state banks and state banks dominate the Malaysian and Indonesian financial sectors and foreign exchange dealing, and their managers understand that respecting the wishes of the central bank may be more important than profit maximization.

It is well known that the two largest Malaysian banks (Malayan Banking and Bank Bumiputra; the government is the major shareholder in both), which dominate the money market, coordinate their transactions with the central bank. The close relationship between the central bank and these banks is well illustrated by the recent appointment of the president of Malayan Banking to the governorship of the central bank. So if the central bank is intervening to push the exchange rate against the tide, it would be career termination for bank managers to take a speculative position opposite to that of the government even though it would be likely to enhance bank profits. The usual outcome under this career constraint is that the large banks would start assuming positions that support the government's actions and slow down the processing of foreign exchange transactions.

In short, given that profitability is not the sole objective of the large Southeast Asian banks, their response to changes in interest rate differentials is predicated on the government's view of how their funds should be invested. In the absence of profit-maximizing actions by the biggest players in the foreign exchange markets, it is not necessary for the government to introduce explicit capital controls to slow down capital flows.

Finally, the third factor that makes sterilization easier in Southeast Asia than in Europe comes from the willingness of the Southeast Asian governments to take extreme measures, such as massive monetary contractions and alterations of the rules on interest payments, in order to bring the fundamentals in line with the existing value of the exchange rate. These actions, backed by large foreign reserves, have created large risk premia that international speculators need to be compensated for if they are to speculate against the Southeast Asian currencies.

All of these three factors make it easier for the Indonesian, Malaysian, and Singapore governments to influence the exchange rate because they lower capital mobility. It is our conjecture that the risk premium generated by these factors consists of a country risk premium as well as the conventional portfolio premium. This may be why covered interest parity did not hold for Singapore in table 11.1. In brief, these factors create a risk premium that widens the span between $r_{max}$ and $r_{min}$ and gives greater monetary autonomy to the government.

## 11.6 Conclusion

Our simple empirical investigations suggest that interest rate linkages may be loose enough that it is possible to conduct independent monetary policy, at least within a limited range. A necessary condition for independent monetary policy is the existence of risk premia, and we found evidence of them (1) in the decomposition of the interest rate differential and (2) in the failure of the interest rate differential to predict even the sign of the subsequent exchange rate change correctly, under the maintained hypothesis of rational expectations.

Our examination of Indonesia's use of the covered interest parity condition to formulate an incentive-neutral swap mechanism to cope with capital flows shows that it actually subsidized capital inflows. The result was a reduction in Indonesia's monetary autonomy. The subsidy element could be removed by using lending rates instead of deposit rates in the pricing of swaps. But the difficulty of deciding which lending rate to use renders the fix nonoperational.

The analysis of three episodes of speculative attacks suggests that the ability of the Indonesian, Malaysian, and Singapore monetary authorities to turn the tables on the speculators comes from the thinness of their foreign exchange markets and the domination of these markets by domestic banks whose arbitrage activities are closely supervised by their governments. We think that the combination of the governments' influence on the foreign market transactions of the domestic banks, the governments' readiness to change the rules of the game, and the governments' willingness to shock their own economies in order to punish currency speculators is the reason for the large and persistent deviations from covered interest arbitrage for Malaysia and Singapore noted in Chinn and Frankel (1994).

To see this, consider a foreign investor who invested her funds in a time-deposit account in Malaysia and had covered her position with a forward sale of ringgit. Assuming that the covered interest differential was zero at the time of the contract, the investor was in a zero-loss situation. But if the Malaysian government (as it did in January 1994) were then to ban the payment of interest to foreigners, the investor would suffer a loss.

If the investor had assumed nonzero probability of such an action by the Malaysian government from the very beginning, then the covered interest differential that would emerge would be nonzero even in the absence of transaction costs. Furthermore, if the investor were risk averse, the fact that a time deposit is no longer a riskless asset means that a portfolio risk premium would also be present.

We end this paper with some words of caution. We have taken it for granted that monetary autonomy is desirable because it confers flexibility on the government's macroeconomic management. But we have seen that this monetary autonomy is sometimes the result of possible microeconomic inefficiency, for example, the state bank's compromising its maximization of profits to allow the government to cane the speculators and the government's willingness to impart interest rate shocks to the domestic economy in order to execute the punishment. Clearly, we must not be so obsessed with monetary autonomy that we do not consider the microeconomic costs of obtaining it.

Even more important, we want to avoid giving the impression that the Southeast Asian governments can always succeed in caning the speculators. They succeeded in the past only because they interfered with capital flows and/or changed their macroeconomic policies to bring the fundamentals back in line with the value of the exchange rate. The successful caning of speculators came from the heavy influence that the governments had on the fundamentals that affected the values of their exchange rates and *not* from the governments' ability to anticipate the future better than private speculators. This point is demonstrated by the large losses suffered by the Malaysian central bank in 1992 when it speculated on Britain's staying in the European Exchange Rate Mechanism. The Malaysian central bank was caned by private speculators because it did not possess better information on the fundamentals that determined the value of the pound vis-à-vis the currencies of the other industrialized countries. Or to put it differently, the Malaysian central bank lost in this speculation because it did not possess the same means to influence the pound-dollar exchange rate as it does the ringgit-dollar exchange rate.

## References

Bonser-Neal, Catherine, and V. Vance Roley. 1994. Are Japanese interest rates too stable? *Journal of International Money and Finance* 13(3): 291–318.

Branson, William. 1969. The minimum covered interest differential needed for international arbitrage activity. *Journal of Political Economy* 77(6): 1028–35.

Chinn, Menzie D., and Jeffrey Frankel. 1994. Financial links around the Pacific Rim: 1982–1992. In *Exchange rate policy and interdependence: Perspectives from the Pacific Basin,* ed. R. Glick and M. Hutchison. Cambridge: Cambridge University Press.

Dominguez, Kathryn, and Jeffrey Frankel. 1992. Does foreign exchange intervention matter? Disentangling the portfolio and expectations effects. Working Paper no. C92–001. Berkeley: Center for International and Development Economics Research, University of California, February.

Dornbusch, Rudiger. 1983. Exchange risk and the macroeconomics of exchange rates determination. In *The internationalization of financial markets and national economic policy,* ed. R. Hawkins, R. Levich, and C. Wihlborg. Greenwich, Conn.: JAI.

Fischer, Bernhard, and Helmut Reisen. 1993. *Liberalising capital flows in developing countries: Pitfalls, prerequisites and perspectives.* Paris: Development Studies Centre, Organisation for Economic Co-operation and Development.

Frankel, Jeffrey. 1982. In search of the exchange risk premium: A six-currency test assuming mean-variance optimization. *Journal of International Money and Finance* 1(3): 255–74.

———. 1993. Sterilization of money inflows: Difficult (Calvo) or easy (Reisen)? Work-

ing Paper no. 93–024. Berkeley: Center for International and Development Economics Research, University of California, October.
Frenkel, Jacob, and Richard Levich. 1975. Covered interest arbitrage: Unexploited profits? *Journal of Political Economy* 83(2): 325–38.
Hansen, Lars, and Robert Hodrick. 1980. Forward exchange rates as optimal predictions of future spot rates: An econometric analysis. *Journal of Political Economy* 88(5): 829–53.
———. 1983. Risk averse speculation in the forward foreign exchange market: An econometric analysis of linear models. In *Exchange rates and international macroeconomics,* ed. Jacob Frenkel. Chicago: University of Chicago Press.
Ito, Takatoshi. 1986. Capital controls and covered interest parity between the yen and the dollar. *Economics Study Quarterly* 37(3): 223–41.
Keynes, John. 1924. *Monetary reform.* New York: Harcourt, Brace.
Nasution, Anwar. 1991. Swap facility and implicit government guarantees on foreign borrowings by private sector are germs of Indonesia's own destruction. University of Indonesia, May. Manuscript.
Rogoff, Kenneth. 1983. On the effects of sterilized intervention: An analysis of weekly data. Working Paper no. DM/83/41. Washington, D.C.: Research Department, International Monetary Fund.
Woo, Wing Thye. 1987. Some evidence of speculative bubbles in the foreign exchange markets. *Journal of Money, Credit and Banking* 19(4): 499–514.
Woo, Wing Thye, Bruce Glassburner, and Anwar Nasution. 1994. *Macroeconomic crises and long-term growth: The case of Indonesia, 1965–1990.* Washington, D.C.: World Bank Press.

## Comment Ronald I. McKinnon

Do international capital flows limit national monetary autonomy? In answering this most interesting question, the authors divide their paper into two parts which are only loosely related.

The first, and least successful, part applies high-powered econometrics to a large database in search of "the" elusive risk premium in interest differentials. A bit dubiously, they want to use estimates of the risk premium as a measure of monetary autonomy in the country in question.

The second part (sections 11.4 and 11.5) is a fascinating discussion of how the monetary authorities in Indonesia, Malaysia, and Singapore lean on domestic banks and other institutions associated with international capital flows to give their central banks a measure of independence in formulating monetary policy—of which the exchange rate itself is an important part. As long as the fundamentals for the exchange rate were right, the government could even use its massive weight in the market to "cane" speculators for trying to move the rate in the wrong direction.

In the Indonesian case, a further dilemma arises in setting forward rates of

Ronald I. McKinnon is the William Eberle Professor of International Economics in the Department of Economics, Stanford University.

exchange when the capital account is open on the one hand but the domestic financial system remains somewhat repressed with a substantial wedge between deposit and loan rates of interest on the other. Although the authors show that the Indonesian authorities may have stumbled a bit in handling the problem, students of development finance will recognize it as a fundamental dilemma when a country inverts the optimum order of economic liberalization (McKinnon 1993). If a country decides (perhaps because it has no choice) to open the capital account of the balance of payments before fully liberalizing its domestic banking system, problems of foreign exchange management can be acute.

## The Elusive Risk Premium

In the first part of the paper, the authors borrow a large, impersonal database with survey data on expected exchange rate changes "matched" with forward rate and short-term interest rate quotations against the U.S. dollar for Australia, Canada, Japan, and Singapore monthly from February 1988 to February 1991. The fact that covered interest differentials are not zero, however, suggests that these forward and interest rate quotations are not precisely matched—through time or in the relevant offshore or onshore market.

More important to the authors, however, is to measure "the" risk premium, roughly the extent by which the domestic interest rate exceeds the U.S. dollar rate by more than the domestic currency is expected to depreciate, for each of the four countries. "The existence of monetary autonomy depends on the existence of a risk premium that could be due to a country risk premium . . . *and/or* a the portfolio risk premium" (sec. 11.3). Unfortunately, their complex econometric analysis does not seem very robust. But the remarkably high risk premium of 3.1 percentage points estimated for Canada seems consistent with political risk: Canada could break up with the secession of Quebec.

The general problem with the authors' approach, however, is that most risk premia vary through time rather than being a single number that reflects political risk of long standing—such as Canada's. Indeed, implicit in the authors' analysis is a second, distinctly different concept of the risk premium: the interest differential varying with the short-run ebb and flow of domestic monetary policy relative to America's. As long as capital is imperfectly mobile, a relatively tight domestic monetary policy will force domestic interest rates above U.S. levels, generating a positive risk premium in the short run, and with easy money "the" risk premium becomes negative. But there is no one number to estimate from a multiyear data series, and whether the terminology "risk premium" is at all appropriate for this second concept is questionable. Better to call it just the "monetary residual" in the interest differential.

In short, I think the authors should try to measure the degree of capital mobility, that is, their $\sigma$ parameter, more directly rather than reducing the problem to the estimation of a single-valued risk premium.

## Indonesia's Swap Margin

In order to encourage foreign investment—or, more accurately, short-term foreign borrowing by Indonesians—Bank Indonesia simultaneously bought foreign currencies at the current spot exchange rate and entered into a contract to sell the same amount of foreign currencies at a specified future point in time at the then-current spot exchange rate. According to the authors, Bank Indonesia initially set the swap margin too low, at 2.5 percentage points per annum, with the maturity of the swaps ranging from 30 to 80 days.

The high demand for such swaps was due to the fact that the borrowing rate in Indonesia was much higher than the deposit rate. So even though 2.5 percentage points fairly reflects the gap between the deposit rate in rupiahs versus that in dollars, illiquid Indonesians facing a much higher borrowing rate would still want to borrow "too much"—particularly if they could cover forward with the government's swap facility. But if the swap rate was made much higher to deter borrowers as the authors wanted (probably correctly), the implicit forward rate would no longer be an unbiased estimate of the spot rate expected in the future. The rupiah would be overly discounted, and importers would not want to use such a rate to buy dollars forward.

In general, as long as there is a big wedge between the deposit and loan rates of interest, no forward exchange rate will clear the market properly. No one forward rate will more or less accurately reflect the spot rate expected in the future without "penalizing" one group or another. Thus, a cost to the Indonesian economy of operating with a repressed domestic banking system, one with with a large wedge between deposit and loan rates, is a missing market, that is, a well-functioning, thick market in forward exchange.

If the government contracts forward with one group or another to partially fill this gap, possibly creating windfall profits and/or losing monetary control, moral hazard is very high indeed. Perhaps the government should simply stay out of the forward exchange market altogether as the authors suggest. More positively, this forward exchange dilemma is another reason why the Indonesian authorities should liberalize domestic finance. By eliminating onerous bank reserve requirements and subsidized loans to favored borrowers, the wedge between deposit and free market loan rates can be reduced toward levels prevailing on world markets.

## Reference

McKinnon, Ronald I. 1993. *The order of economic liberalization: Financial control in the transition to a market economy,* 2d ed. Baltimore: Johns Hopkins University Press.

## Comment Basant K. Kapur

Woo and Hirayama have written an interesting and wide-ranging paper, exploring a number of issues relating to capital flows and monetary autonomy in various East Asian countries. My comments will deal, first, with certain central theoretical considerations in their argument and, second, with more specific aspects of some of their country studies. At the theoretical level, I would like to begin by making three observations:

1. As is well known, the IS-LM-BP framework that the authors employ is a short-term, flow-oriented construct and—unless considerably elaborated—cannot do full justice to stock adjustment dynamics.

2. There is a curious dichotomy in the literature between the view, prevalent in open economy macroeconomics, that asset markets adjust instantaneously and the common empirical finding of a lagged adjustment in the market for money, which has been given a plausible theoretical underpinning in, among others, the "buffer stock" approach advanced by Milbourne (1987), Laidler (1984), and others. Unless monetary disequilibria are reflected entirely in opposite goods-market disequilibria, which is unlikely, adjustment lags in the money market will entail lags in other asset markets as well.

3. As Woo and Hirayama correctly point out, portfolio balance models generally incorporate stocks of "outside bonds," the supplies of which (particularly in the case of domestic bonds) are exogenous. However, their empirical work uses interest rates on domestic vis-à-vis offshore bank deposits, which are not outside assets. An excess demand for domestic bank loans can, for example, through incipient loan and deposit interest rate movements induce reserve flows and thereby domestic deposit expansion.

What is the implication of the three foregoing observations? Woo and Hirayama are correct, in my view, in ascribing a significant part of the interest differential in various countries between domestic and foreign assets to the existence of a portfolio risk premium. This was, in fact, also the conclusion from a study on Singapore conducted a few years ago (Ariff, Kapur, and Tyabji, in press), which also found that the Singapore-U.S. exchange rate could be modeled as a random walk without drift. However, Woo and Hirayama jump too easily from the demonstration of the existence of a portfolio risk premium to the conclusion that there exists some—limited—monetary autonomy in the countries concerned. The time dimension is, in my view, crucial. In the very short run, owing to the adjustment lags I have discussed under point 2 above, there may indeed be some monetary autonomy. However, beyond the very short run—in other words, beyond a period of, probably, six months at the most—reserve flows are likely to occur (point 3 above) to serve to reequilibrate asset supplies and demands at the same risk premium as had prevailed previously.

Basant K. Kapur is associate professor and head of the Department of Economics and Statistics, National University of Singapore.

The monetary autonomy is therefore not only limited but also temporary, and it is questionable whether such temporary monetary autonomy is of much use to policymakers from a macroeconomic standpoint.

The foregoing discussion also implies, from an analytical standpoint, that a distinction should be drawn between "temporary" imperfect capital mobility—based on asset adjustment lags—and "permanent" imperfect capital mobility—based genuinely on imperfect asset substitutability. One could even have a combination of the two, or of their consequences: there could exist a portfolio risk premium, implying imperfect asset substitutability, and yet at the same time the resulting interest differential would not be capable of manipulation by monetary authorities outside of the very short run because the supplies of the assets concerned are endogenous.

Finally, some more specific points:

1. It is doubtful whether in Singapore there does exist any deviation, even a small one, from covered interest parity, as the authors claim. Empirical studies on Singapore have failed to uncover any such deviation,[1] and the authors' findings may, as McKinnon has said, well be the result of measurement error.

2. In the Indonesian case, an examination of how widespread the access (of Indonesians) to the swap facility was would certainly be useful, since imperfect access could well imply some flexibility in the rupiah deposit rate around its covered interest parity value.

## References

Ariff, M., B. K. Kapur, and A. Tyabji. 1995. Money markets in Singapore. In *Asian Money Markets,* ed. D. C. Cole, H. S. Scott, and P. A. Wellons. New York: Oxford University Press.

Laidler, D. 1984. The buffer stock notion in monetary economics. *Economic Journal* 94 (Suppl.): 17–34.

Milbourne, R. 1987. Re-examining the buffer-stock model of money. *Economic Journal* 97 (Suppl.): 130–42.

1. See, e.g., Tse and Tan, chap. 12 in this volume.

# 12 Interest Parity and Dynamic Capital Mobility: The Experience of Singapore

Tse Yiu Kuen and Tan Kim Song

## 12.1 Introduction

The questions of international capital mobility and financial market integration have long attracted the attention of both researchers and policymakers, and understandably so. A high degree of capital mobility not only affects the independence of domestic monetary and fiscal policies, it also adds to the complexity of managing saving and investment problems in a country.

The issue is of particular interest to Asia-Pacific countries, many of whom have embarked on large-scale financial market liberalizations since the early 1980s. In Japan, Taiwan, South Korea, as well as ASEAN countries such as Malaysia and Thailand, various capital and exchange controls were dismantled during the past decade. Whether these liberalization measures have resulted in a greater degree of capital mobility, and how they might have affected the implementation of monetary and exchange rate policies in these countries, have been the subject of various studies (see Ito 1988; Glick and Hutchison 1990; Reisen and Yèches 1993; among others).

This paper seeks to shed some light on the extent of international capital mobility in Singapore. On first thought, such a question might appear to be rhetorical. Most of the capital and exchange controls in Singapore were effectively abolished by the late 1970s. There has been virtually no barrier to the flow of foreign currency funds held either by domestic or foreign residents. Neither is there any substantive restriction on the movement of funds between the domestic banking system and the offshore Asian dollar market. Singa-

Tse Yiu Kuen is associate professor in the Department of Economics and Statistics, National University of Singapore. Tan Kim Song is a senior correspondent at the Straits Times Editorial, Singapore Press Holdings.

The opinions expressed in this paper are those of the authors alone. They do not represent the views of the institutions to which they belong.

poreans (and foreigners), if they so desire, can hold any well-diversified portfolio of assets denominated in Singapore and foreign currencies. Indeed, in the few empirical studies that have been conducted on the subject so far, the evidence generally points to a high degree of international capital mobility in Singapore (see Edwards and Khan 1985; Frankel 1991; Faruqee 1992; among others).

It is also this belief in high capital mobility that underlies the focus of the Monetary Authority of Singapore (MAS) on the management of exchange rate, rather than that of interest rate or some monetary aggregate, when pursuing its objective of domestic price stability. As Teh and Shanmugaratnam (1992) pointed out, the lack of control on capital flows had resulted in quick, cross-country movements of capital whenever there were small changes in the differential between domestic and foreign (especially U.S.) interest rates. Such capital mobility, they added, "makes it difficult to target either money supply or interest rates in Singapore" (see Teh and Shanmugaratnam 1992, 291–92).

The purpose of this paper is not to question the openness of Singapore's capital market and its integration with the rest of the financial world. Rather, we hope to achieve a better understanding of how the linkage has changed over time. A study of dynamic capital mobility, we believe, can serve several useful purposes. First, even in the absence of capital and exchange controls, there are presumably periods when capital flows more smoothly than others. An analysis of these changes will add to our understanding of the underlying forces that drive the movement of capital across borders. Second, from a policy perspective, it pays to know whether the Singapore capital market has indeed, over time, become more closely linked with those of other countries. An increase in capital mobility not only reflects on the impact of the various liberalization measures taken to promote Singapore as a financial center, it also has obvious implications for the management of exchange rate. The tremendous problems faced over the last two years by some Southeast Asian central banks, such as Bank Negara in Malaysia, in sterilizing their capital inflows point to the policy dilemma in a financially open economy.

The basic benchmark used to measure international capital mobility in this paper will be the deviation from interest rate parity. Deviations from both covered and uncovered interest parities will be discussed, although covered interest parity, as we shall see later, is considered by many economists to be a more generic test of capital mobility.

The paper is organized as follows: Section 12.2 provides a brief discussion of some of the works on capital mobility, with particular focus on studies about Singapore. Section 12.3 explains the methodology followed in this paper. Section 12.4 presents and interprets the results of our findings. Section 12.5 concludes.

## 12.2 Interest Parity and International Capital Mobility

Feldstein and Horioka (1980) created a stir among economists more than a decade ago when they argued that, based on the close correlation between domestic saving and investment rates that they observed in many countries, international capital might not be as mobile as economists typically assumed.

Since then, research on this issue has developed in two directions: one that follows the Feldstein-Horioka approach, focusing on the link between domestic savings and investment, and another that looks at the parity between domestic and foreign interest rates.[1] But as some economists have pointed out, the Feldstein-Horioka approach is really more suited to the study of how efficiently savings and capital are allocated globally, rather than how closely integrated capital markets are. To equate a zero correlation between domestic saving and investment with perfect capital mobility, a number of preconditions must first be satisfied. Not only must there be parity of real interest rates, but investment behavior must also respond in a particular way to interest rate changes. In practice, neither of these two conditions can be easily met (see Frankel 1991; Obstfeld 1994).

Even for tests of interest rate parity, opinions differ on the correct yardstick to be used. Of the two most commonly used parity concepts, covered interest parity (CIP) is often deemed to be a better indicator of financial openness than uncovered interest parity (UIP). Deviations from CIP suggest that there exist some risk-free arbitrage opportunities that might have arisen from capital and exchange controls, differential tax treatments for capital returns in different countries, the possibility of future controls and regulations, and other country-specific transaction costs such as differences in languages and business practices. These are generally considered barriers to capital movement in a generic sense.

Deviations from UIP, on the other hand, can occur even if CIP holds—that is, even if the forward market is efficient and there is no hindrance to the arbitrage process—as long as a certain exchange risk premium exists. In fact, it is well known that a test of UIP amounts to a joint test of CIP and zero risk premium. But risk premium, as Frankel (1991) pointed out, has more to do with the currency in which the interest rate is denominated than the institutional restrictions on capital flow imposed by individual governments. In other words, while an adherence to UIP would suggest a capital market well integrated with the international economy, the failure of UIP need not necessarily imply a lack of capital mobility.[2]

1. Obstfeld provides a simple definition of international capital mobility. Capital is freely mobile, he said, if "residents face no official obstacles to the negotiation and execution of financial trades anywhere and with anyone in the world, and face transaction costs that are no greater for parties residing in different countries than for parties residing in the same country" (1994, 2).

2. Ito (1988) argued that it was possible for UIP to hold without CIP, as was the case for the Japanese market in the late 1970s.

The different implications of CIP and UIP on international capital mobility were brought out clearly in Frankel's own study of 25 developed and developing countries. Frankel found that, when measured by the size and variability of the *covered* interest differentials, most industrial countries (including Canada, Germany, the Netherlands, Switzerland, the United Kingdom, Austria, Belgium, Sweden, and Japan) and certain Asia-Pacific economies such as Hong Kong and Singapore displayed few barriers to capital movement during the 1980s (1982–88).[3] However, the picture looked very different when *uncovered* interest parity was used as the benchmark for capital mobility instead. Few of these supposedly "open" economies attained any form of UIP. A significant amount of currency risk (including exchange risk premium and expected real depreciation) was observed in almost all the economies.

While the relevance of UIP as a measure of capital mobility may be limited in static analysis, the situation is somewhat different in a dynamic setting. Here changes in the extent of deviation from UIP do provide some information about changing capital mobility. As capital markets become more integrated, one possible outcome is that assets denominated in different currencies become more substitutable. This will reduce the risk premium and narrow the uncovered interest differentials. In other words, a sustained narrowing of uncovered interest differentials over time could itself indicate an increased level of capital mobility.

Faruqee (1992) applied such an argument in his study of dynamic capital mobility in four Asian economies, including Singapore.[4] He first examined the differentials between the LIBOR rate on yen deposits and some domestic interest rates in Singapore, Malaysia, Thailand, and South Korea from 1978 to 1990. A generalized autoregressive conditional heteroskedasticity (GARCH) structure was then fitted on these differentials. Both the size of the differential bands and the conditional variances of the differentials in these countries were used to illustrate the dynamic changes of capital mobility in these countries. A smaller band and a reduced variability of the differentials are said to reflect more financial openness.

For Singapore, a declining variability of uncovered interest differentials throughout the sample period was observed, pointing to a consistent trend toward greater capital mobility. Such a trend contrasted sharply with the "epi-

3. On the other hand, substantial barriers to capital flow appeared to remain in countries like France, Italy, Ireland, and EC members that adopted a timetable for capital account liberalization in accordance with the single European program set out in the Single European Act of 1987 (see Obstfeld 1994, 11).

4. Faruqee's study is the only one that provides a detailed analysis of dynamic interest parity in Singapore. Previous studies, including that of Frankel (1991), examined the issue from a static perspective. Edwards and Khan (1985), e.g., reached the same conclusion of high capital mobility by comparing the relative importance of interest parity and domestic monetary conditions in determining the domestic interest rates in Singapore. They found that the Singapore interest rates during the period from 1976 to 1983 were largely influenced by their parity with the prevailing Eurodollar rates.

sodic" developments in the other three countries, which oscillated between periods of high and low financial openness. Simulation of impulse responses to domestic monetary shocks were also conducted for all four countries. The results showed that the Singapore interest rate returned to its parity condition within a much shorter time than those in other countries. This again was evidence of greater capital mobility in Singapore.

In this paper, we shall provide another perspective on dynamic capital mobility in Singapore. The time-series properties of the interest differentials from 1977 to 1993 will be examined. Unlike Faruqee, however, both covered and uncovered interest differentials will be studied, in order to give better insight into the various forms of barriers to capital movement. A GARCH model is then fitted to the residuals. The parameters of the model are estimated simultaneously using the maximum likelihood estimation (MLE) method, instead of the (less efficient) two-stage method used by Faruqee. We then offer some explanation for the particular trends taken by deviations from CIP and UIP and try to relate them to the prevailing monetary and financial conditions. We also discuss briefly the efficient market hypothesis in the context of Singapore.

## 12.3 Methodology

To examine the interest rate and exchange rate relationships, the following notation is used:

$F_1$ = one-month forward exchange rate (S$ per U.S.$)
$F_3$ = three-month forward exchange rate (S$ per U.S.$)
$S$ = spot exchange rate (S$ per U.S.$)
$f_1$ = logarithm of one-month forward exchange rate (S$ per U.S.$)
$f_3$ = logarithm of three-month forward exchange rate (S$ per U.S.$)
$s$ = logarithm of spot exchange rate (S$ per U.S.$)
$R_1^S$ = one-month yield of Singapore dollar
$R_3^S$ = three-month yield of Singapore dollar
$R_1^U$ = one-month yield of U.S. dollar
$R_3^U$ = three-month yield of U.S. dollar

Consider investments over a one-month horizon. Lack of risk-free arbitrage opportunities requires that the principal plus interest for a unit U.S. dollar investment is equal to the principal plus interest on an equivalent amount of Singapore dollar investment, when the latter is converted to U.S. currency at the forward rate of exchange. Using continuous compounding, the following relationship holds at time $t$:

$$\exp R_{1,t}^{U} = \frac{S_t \exp R_{1,t}^{S}}{F_{1,t}}, \tag{1}$$

which implies

$$R^{U}_{1,t} + f_{1,t} - s_t - R^{S}_{1,t} = 0\,. \tag{2}$$

Equation (2) is known as CIP. A similar argument for the three-month investment horizon implies

$$R^{U}_{3,t} + f_{3,t} - s_t - R^{S}_{3,t} = 0\,. \tag{3}$$

We denote the left-hand sides of equations (2) and (3) by $C_{1,t}/1200$ and $C_{3,t}/400$, respectively. Thus, $C_1$ and $C_3$ represent deviations from CIP in annualized percentage terms. Note that if $C_i > 0$ for $i = 1, 3$, a risk-free opportunity is available by selling Singapore dollars for U.S. dollars, with a synchronized long forward contract to buy Singapore dollars.

As pointed out by Ito (1988), CIP is an arbitrage condition without any theoretical hypothesis about the financial market. In an economy with free capital mobility, the validity of CIP is a matter of fact. On the other hand, UIP is a hypothesis that can be tested irrespective of capital mobility. It states that the interest rate spread between two currencies is equal to the difference between the expected future (logarithmic) exchange rate and the current (logarithmic) exchange rate.[5] Using the above notation, UIP is defined as the hypothesis that

$$\mathrm{E}_t\,(s_{t+i}) = s_t + R^{S}_{i,t} - R^{U}_{i,t}, \tag{4}$$

where $i = 1, 3$ denotes the horizon of the yield and $\mathrm{E}_t$ denotes the expectation conditional on information at time $t$.

A direct test of UIP is difficult because the hypothesis involves the unobservable expectation of the future spot exchange rate. Analysis may be simplified, however, with additional assumptions. For example, under the hypothesis that the spot exchange rate follows a random walk (RW) that is, $\mathrm{E}_t(s_{t+i}) = s_t$, equation (4) can be written as $R^{S}_{i,t} - R^{U}_{i,t} = 0$. Thus, denoting $U_{1,t} = (R^{S}_{1,t} - R^{U}_{1,t}) \times 1200$ and $U_{3,t} = (R^{S}_{3,t} - R^{U}_{3,t}) \times 400$ as deviations from UIP(RW) in annualized percentage terms, a test of UIP may be constructed by examining whether $U_1$ and $U_3$ are significantly different from zero.

An alternative approach to modeling the expected future spot rate is to assume rational expectations (RE). If we assume expectation is formulated rationally with perfect foresight, that is, $\mathrm{E}_t(s_{t+i}) = s_{t+i}$, deviations from UIP(RE) may be calculated as $U^{*}_{1,t} = (R^{S}_{1,t} - R^{U}_{1,t} + s_t - s_{t+1}) \times 1200$ and $U^{*}_{3,t} = (R^{S}_{3,t} - R^{U}_{3,t} + s_t - s_{t+3}) \times 400$. Both UIP(RW) and UIP(RE) will be examined in this paper.

Using equations (2) and (3), equation (4) can be written as

$$\mathrm{E}_t\,(s_{t+i}) = f_{i,t}\,. \tag{5}$$

Thus, UIP and CIP together imply that the forward exchange rate is an unbiased predictor of the future spot rate. This is referred to as the efficient market hypothesis without risk premium.

5. From here onward we shall simply refer to the logarithmic data as exchange rate.

Recently, Faruqee (1992) examined the changing degree of capital mobility by capturing the time-varying structure of UIP deviations. He argued that a sustained narrowing in deviations of interest rate differentials from an appropriate measure of interest rate parity indicates an increased level of capital mobility. The banding structure of deviations is examined using a GARCH framework. If we denote $y$ generically as deviations from either UIP or CIP, a time-series model that captures autoregressive (AR) structure in both mean and variance can be written as follows:

$$y_t = \alpha_0 + \alpha_1 y_{t-1} + \ldots + \alpha_p y_{t-p} + \varepsilon_t,$$

(6) $$\varepsilon_t \sim N(0, h_t^2),$$

$$h_t^2 = \beta_0^2 + \beta_1 h_{t-1}^2 + \beta_2 \varepsilon_{t-1}^2.$$

Thus, $y_t$ follows an AR ($p$) process with a conditional variance equation described by a GARCH (1, 1) process. Parameters of the model can be estimated simultaneously using the MLE method. The estimated conditional standard deviation $\hat{h}_t$ gives an indication of the changing conditions of capital mobility.

## 12.4 Empirical Results

The data used in this paper were extracted from various issues of the *Business Times.* For interest rate data, we use interbank offer rates of one-month and three-month duration on both the Singapore dollar and the U.S. dollar. The foreign (U.S.) interest rates, referred to as SIBOR, are quotes from the Asian Currency Units.[6] End-of-month data were compiled from January 1977 through September 1993, totaling 201 observations.

Table 12.1 summarizes some statistics of the unconditional distributions of the exchange rate and interest rate data. Two sets of autocorrelation statistics are presented: $\hat{\rho}_{1,i}$ is the $i^{\text{th}}$ sample autocorrelation coefficient of the series, and $\hat{\rho}_{2,i}$ is the $i^{\text{th}}$ sample autocorrelation coefficient of the square of the deviation from mean of the series; $Q_j$ (24), $j$ = 1,2, are the Box-Pierce portmanteau statistics based on autocorrelation coefficients of order up to 24. On the null hypothesis of white noise, $Q$ is approximately distributed as a $\chi^2$ with 24 degrees of freedom. To the extent that these statistics may be affected by nonnormality we also calculate the nonparametric runs tests. Thus, $R_1$ is the runs test statistic for the series, and $R_2$ is the runs test statistic for the square of the series. On the null hypothesis of white noise, $R_1$ and $R_2$ are approximately distributed as standard normal.

It can be seen that all seven series exhibit high autocorrelation in mean as well as in variance. The autocorrelation functions of the raw data decline very

6. SIBOR is used in preference to LIBOR as the data can be conveniently extracted from a single source. Also, synchronous trading in domestic and foreign interbank markets facilitates arbitrage activities.

Table 12.1 Summary Statistics of Exchange Rate and Interest Rate Data

| Statistic | $f_1$ | $f_3$ | $s$ | $R^S_1$ | $R^S_3$ | $R^U_1$ | $R^U_3$ |
|---|---|---|---|---|---|---|---|
| Mean | 0.709 | 0.706 | 0.711 | 0.005 | 0.015 | 0.007 | 0.023 |
| S.D. | 0.113 | 0.111 | 0.112 | 0.002 | 0.007 | 0.003 | 0.009 |
| Minimum | 0.462 | 0.462 | 0.462 | 0.001 | 0.004 | 0.002 | 0.006 |
| Maximum | 0.901 | 0.904 | 0.902 | 0.011 | 0.034 | 0.017 | 0.049 |
| Skewness | −0.779 | −0.746 | −0.785 | 0.899 | 0.851 | 0.866 | 0.746 |
| Kurtosis | 2.774 | 2.768 | 2.772 | 3.625 | 3.510 | 3.737 | 3.283 |
| $\hat{\rho}_{1,1}$ | 0.977 | 0.977 | 0.977 | 0.956 | 0.967 | 0.950 | 0.957 |
| $\hat{\rho}_{1,2}$ | 0.956 | 0.956 | 0.956 | 0.907 | 0.923 | 0.901 | 0.909 |
| $\hat{\rho}_{1,3}$ | 0.934 | 0.933 | 0.934 | 0.855 | 0.871 | 0.855 | 0.863 |
| $\hat{\rho}_{1,4}$ | 0.913 | 0.911 | 0.914 | 0.817 | 0.830 | 0.815 | 0.828 |
| $Q_1$ (24) | 3072 | 3052 | 3082 | 2054 | 2193 | 2076 | 2156 |
| $R_1$ | −13.7 | −13.4 | −13.7 | −12.2 | −12.8 | −12.5 | −12.4 |
| $\hat{\rho}_{2,1}$ | 0.964 | 0.964 | 0.964 | 0.888 | 0.902 | 0.820 | 0.850 |
| $\hat{\rho}_{2,2}$ | 0.931 | 0.930 | 0.931 | 0.753 | 0.765 | 0.657 | 0.713 |
| $\hat{\rho}_{2,3}$ | 0.898 | 0.896 | 0.899 | 0.600 | 0.602 | 0.550 | 0.619 |
| $\hat{\rho}_{2,4}$ | 0.865 | 0.861 | 0.867 | 0.509 | 0.487 | 0.490 | 0.546 |
| $Q_2$ (24) | 2052 | 2009 | 2069 | 844 | 873 | 786 | 925 |
| $R_2$ | −13.9 | −13.9 | −13.9 | −11.7 | −12.0 | −12.5 | −12.8 |

slowly with the lag order, suggesting strongly that the series may be nonstationary and integrated. Table 12.2 summarizes similar statistics for the first difference of the data. For the exchange rate data, autocorrelations in mean and variance seem to have been eliminated.[7] Thus, there is evidence to support the hypothesis that both forward and spot exchange rates may be treated as random walks. For the interest rate data, all $Q$ statistics are significant, indicating that there is autocorrelation in mean as well as in variance. Thus, it may be appropriate to model the differenced interest rate data as an autocorrelated time series with time-varying conditional variance. Table 12.2 also presents the standardized statistics of skewness and kurtosis.[8] It is found that both exchange rate and interest rate data exhibit higher kurtosis than that of a normal distribution. This result, however, may be due to autocorrelation in variance. To ascertain the nonstationarity of the raw data, we calculate the Dickey-Fuller (DF) and augmented Dickey-Fuller (ADF) tests. Results are summarized in table 12.3. It can be observed that the null hypothesis of nonstationarity cannot be rejected for all cases.

Deviations from CIP, $C_1$ and $C_3$, are calculated, and their summary statistics

7. For $\Delta f_3$, $Q_1$ is marginally significant at the 5 percent level. Otherwise, all other $Q$ statistics are insignificant at the 5 percent level.

8. These statistics are approximately standard normal if the data are normally distributed. Their validity, however, depends on the assumption that the data come from a random sample. Thus, these statistics are not presented in table 12.1, as the exchange rate and interest rate data are highly autocorrelated.

**Table 12.2** **Summary Statistics of Differenced Exchange Rate and Interest Rate**

| Statistic | $\Delta f_1$ | $\Delta f_3$ | $\Delta s$ | $\Delta R_1^S$ | $\Delta R_3^S$ | $\Delta R_1^U$ | $\Delta R_3^U$ |
|---|---|---|---|---|---|---|---|
| Mean | −0.002 | −0.002 | −0.002 | 0.000 | 0.000 | 0.000 | 0.000 |
| S.D. | 0.014 | 0.014 | 0.014 | 0.001 | 0.002 | 0.001 | 0.002 |
| Minimum | −0.063 | −0.067 | −0.062 | −0.003 | −0.008 | −0.005 | −0.014 |
| Maximum | 0.045 | 0.045 | 0.045 | 0.003 | 0.007 | 0.003 | 0.008 |
| Skewness | −0.305 | −0.358 | −0.407 | 0.314 | 0.356 | −0.926 | −0.901 |
| St. skewness | −1.763 | −2.066 | −2.347 | 1.812 | 2.056 | −5.348 | −5.199 |
| Kurtosis | 5.999 | 6.423 | 6.454 | 6.683 | 8.762 | 12.119 | 10.557 |
| St. kurtosis | 8.659 | 9.882 | 9.972 | 10.633 | 16.633 | 26.324 | 21.816 |
| $\hat{\rho}_{1.1}$ | −0.036 | −0.061 | −0.036 | 0.045 | 0.165 | 0.068 | 0.157 |
| $\hat{\rho}_{1.2}$ | 0.028 | 0.082 | 0.020 | 0.039 | 0.110 | −0.053 | −0.046 |
| $\hat{\rho}_{1.3}$ | −0.030 | −0.021 | −0.051 | −0.180 | −0.177 | −0.064 | −0.134 |
| $\hat{\rho}_{1.4}$ | −0.108 | −0.134 | −0.068 | −0.106 | 0.220 | −0.217 | −0.224 |
| $Q_1$ (24) | 32.60 | 36.51 | 28.38 | 77.95 | 110.60 | 80.15 | 72.69 |
| $R_1$ | −2.13 | −1.84 | −1.84 | 0.12 | −1.56 | 0.50 | −0.52 |
| $\hat{\rho}_{2.1}$ | 0.289 | 0.282 | 0.282 | 0.281 | 0.215 | 0.473 | 0.486 |
| $\hat{\rho}_{2.2}$ | −0.036 | −0.031 | −0.010 | 0.100 | 0.084 | 0.167 | 0.221 |
| $\hat{\rho}_{2.3}$ | −0.057 | −0.055 | −0.040 | 0.105 | −0.023 | 0.066 | 0.108 |
| $\hat{\rho}_{2.4}$ | −0.048 | −0.035 | −0.054 | 0.191 | 0.217 | 0.070 | 0.160 |
| $Q_2$ (24) | 34.06 | 31.83 | 32.47 | 108.27 | 127.42 | 139.14 | 158.38 |
| $R_2$ | −0.57 | −0.55 | −0.97 | −2.44 | −1.78 | −5.91 | −5.20 |

*Notes:* St. skewness = standardized skewness, and St. kurtosis = standardized kurtosis. Skewness is standardized with respect to mean zero and standard deviation $\sqrt{6/n}$, while kurtosis is standardized with respect to mean 3 and standard deviation $\sqrt{24/n}$.

**Table 12.3** **Unit Root Tests**

| Variable | DF | D-W | ADF | $\chi_1^2$ |
|---|---|---|---|---|
| $f_1$ | −0.3052 | 2.065 | −0.2895 | 0.0376 |
| $f_3$ | −0.3764 | 2.113 | −0.3139 | 1.1134 |
| $s$ | −0.2945 | 2.065 | −0.2672 | 0.0195 |
| $R_1^S$ | −1.9857 | 1.869 | −2.0889 | 0.5471 |
| $R_3^S$ | −1.6541 | 1.646 | −2.0292 | 2.3948 |
| $R_1^U$ | −2.1224 | 1.798 | −2.0119 | 0.1053 |
| $R_3^U$ | −1.9800 | 1.618 | −1.9726 | 1.0271 |

*Notes:* DF = Dickey-Fuller statistic, D-W = Durbin-Watson statistic of the associated regression of the DF test, ADF = augmented Dickey-Fuller statistic, $\chi_1^2$ = Lagrange multiplier test for residual correlation of the ADF regression. The (lower-tail) critical values of the DF and ADF tests at 5 and 1 percent levels are, respectively, approximately −2.88 and −3.46.

are presented in table 12.4. We can see that $C_1$ has larger volatility than $C_3$. The $Q$-statistics show that $C_1$ is a white noise, while $C_3$ is an autocorrelated series. This agrees with the well-known result that if the sampling interval is shorter than the length of the forward contract, serial correlation is induced. The covered interest differential for the whole period was 1.045 percent for the one-month interest rate, while that for the three-month interest rate was

Table 12.4 Summary Statistics of CIP and UIP Deviations

| Statistic | $C_1$ | $C_3$ | $U_1$ | $U_3$ | $\Delta U_1$ | $\Delta U_3$ |
|---|---|---|---|---|---|---|
| Mean | 1.045 | 0.944 | −2.876 | −2.902 | −0.011 | −0.012 |
| S.D. | 2.569 | 1.120 | 1.751 | 1.679 | 1.170 | 0.998 |
| Minimum | −6.135 | −4.374 | −9.375 | −8.500 | −4.563 | −3.875 |
| Maximum | 16.988 | 6.175 | 1.729 | 1.794 | 5.750 | 4.688 |
| $\hat{\rho}_{1,1}$ | 0.083 | 0.249 | 0.759 | 0.804 | −0.118 | −0.065 |
| $\hat{\rho}_{1,2}$ | −0.034 | 0.136 | 0.585 | 0.652 | −0.211 | −0.161 |
| $\hat{\rho}_{1,3}$ | −0.017 | 0.135 | 0.507 | 0.555 | −0.134 | −0.266 |
| $\hat{\rho}_{1,4}$ | −0.054 | 0.074 | 0.490 | 0.553 | 0.041 | 0.060 |
| $Q_1$ (24) | 31.51 | 116.66 | 563.18 | 713.83 | 60.24 | 79.40 |
| $R_1$ | −2.00 | −4.71 | −8.83 | −9.68 | 1.95 | 0.58 |
| $\hat{\rho}_{2,1}$ | −0.039 | −0.023 | 0.422 | 0.509 | 0.434 | 0.391 |
| $\hat{\rho}_{2,2}$ | −0.034 | −0.029 | 0.287 | 0.317 | 0.145 | 0.182 |
| $\hat{\rho}_{2,3}$ | 0.195 | 0.111 | 0.127 | 0.200 | 0.106 | 0.137 |
| $\hat{\rho}_{2,4}$ | 0.046 | 0.020 | 0.198 | 0.226 | 0.073 | 0.175 |
| $Q_2$ (24) | 17.78 | 14.59 | 170.60 | 175.81 | 160.05 | 169.51 |
| $R_2$ | 0.65 | −0.77 | −7.89 | −9.19 | −2.22 | −4.62 |

*Note:* Deviations from CIP and UIP are measured in annualized percentages.

smaller, at 0.944 percent. Taking account of the usual bid-offer spread and thus the transaction costs in the market, these figures represent mild deviations from CIP.[9]

Figure 12.1 presents $C_1$ and $C_3$ graphically, from which the higher fluctuations in $C_1$ are evident. Note that deviations from CIP were mostly positive in the sample period. This indicates that if there was any transaction cost limiting the flow of capital, it was in the form of outward "restrictions," that is, restrictions on Singapore residents' purchase of foreign assets. The restriction has, however, become less and less important over the years. By late 1991, they had nearly all disappeared, as can be seen by the near-zero deviations.

The higher covered interest differential from late 1980 to the end of 1981 might have to do with the additional adjustment cost that arose from the change in the monetary and exchange rate regime. Until then, the MAS had focused on the management of domestic interest rates and money supply to ensure price stability. In 1981, however, it decided to switch its focus to exchange rate man-

9. These deviations, however, may be large compared to studies on other countries (see, e.g., the post-1981 results for the Japanese market in Ito [1988]). It should be pointed out that to capture the effects of transaction costs adequately, it may be more appropriate to consider *one-way arbitrage.* Thus, using the subscripts B to denote bid price and O to denote offer price, arbitrage opportunity exists if

$$R^{U}_{B,t} + f_{B,t} - s_{O,t} - R^{S}_{O,t} > 0 \quad \text{or} \quad R^{U}_{O,t} + f_{O,t} - s_{B,t} - R^{S}_{B,t} < 0.$$

This approach was used by Ito (1986) in his study on the yen-dollar relationship. Although it explicitly takes transaction costs into account, it requires bid-offer data that are exactly synchronized. Research following this approach will be left to future studies.

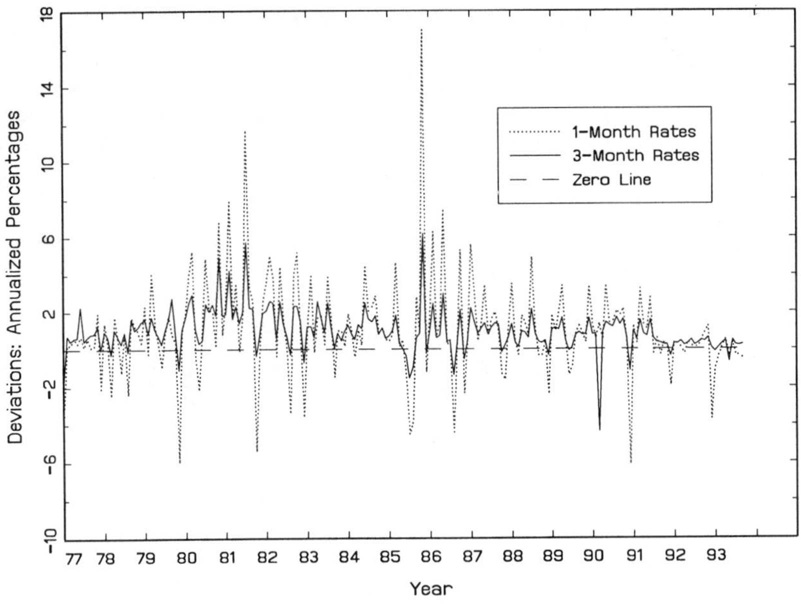


**Fig. 12.1 Deviations from CIP**

agement, that is, to rely on a strong Singapore dollar to keep the domestic inflation rate low. This change came about as the MAS increasingly recognized the small and open nature of the Singapore economy, and its need to maintain a liberal financial environment, so as to promote the country as a regional financial center. Much of the exchange rate management was carried out through swap operations between the U.S. dollar and Singapore dollar. In fact, there was a substantial increase in the volume of swap transactions in 1981. The need to keep the Singapore currency strong, and hence the emphasis on more capital inflow than outflow, could be one reason why the domestic interest rate seemed to enjoy a greater advantage. This indicates that some arbitrage opportunity was present during this period of regime change.

Table 12.4 also presents summary statistics of the interest rate differentials, $U_1$ and $U_3$, as well as their differences, $\Delta U_1$ and $\Delta U_3$.[10] Unlike the $C_i$, the $U_i$ exhibit autocorrelation in mean and in variance.[11] UIP deviations, as is well known, result from a certain expectation about exchange rate changes as well

10. As pointed out in section 12.3, the interest rate differential measures UIP deviations conditional on the assumption that spot exchange rates follow a random walk, which is an acceptable hypothesis based on results in tables 12.2 and 12.3.

11. The autocorrelations in the $U_i$ are surprisingly high. The DF statistics for $U_1$ and $U_3$ are, respectively, −5.3176 and −4.9913. The corresponding D-W statistics are 1.993 and 1.979. Thus interest rate differentials are stationary. This implies that $R^U$ and $R^S$ are cointegrated.

as the presence of risk premium. But, if as we found earlier the exchange rate follows a random walk, then the differential can be interpreted as the time-varying risk premium.

The graphs in figure 12.2 show that the $U_i$ are negative almost throughout the whole sample period. Overall, the uncovered interest differentials exhibit a broad trend similar to covered interest differentials, with the gap becoming negligible from about 1991 onward. The mean values of $U_1$ and $U_3$ for the whole period are 2.876 and 2.887 percent, respectively. The risk premium, however, was much larger in the early 1980s, especially from mid-1979 to late 1983. At its height, it reached about 8 percent above the UIP level, notably in the first quarters of 1980 and 1982. Such a high premium was again a result of the changes in monetary and exchange rate conditions in that period. One reason could be the fear of inflation and the tight monetary policy conducted by the U.S. Federal Reserve Board during that period. High interest rates in the United States and the uncertainty surrounding inflation had added to the volatility and hence the riskiness of the U.S. dollar. The uncertainty was compounded by a worsening of the world debt problem and the doubt it cast on the U.S. banking system. The latter was reflected in the slowdown in Asian Dollar Market activities. By 1983, for example, the gross size of the market increased by only 8 percent, which paled in comparison to the 20 and 58 percent increases in 1982 and 1981, respectively. That the SIBOR rate was far higher

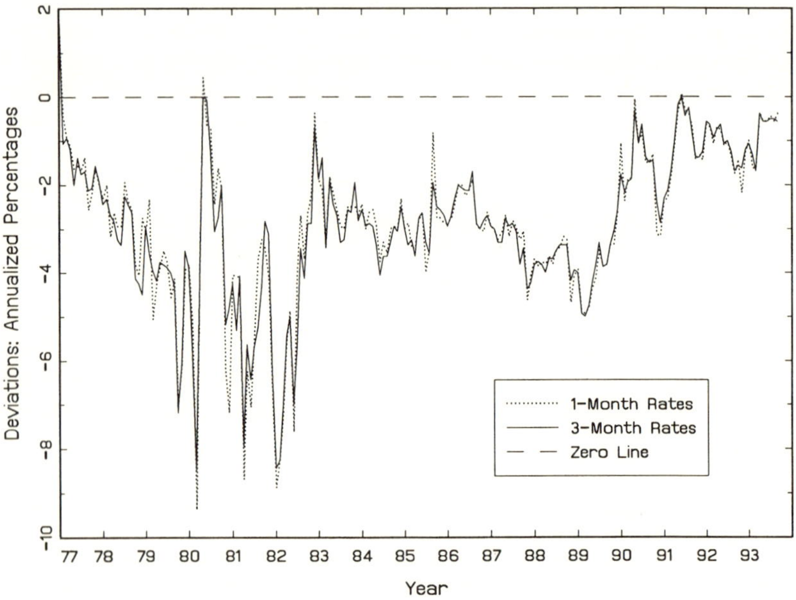


**Fig. 12.2 Deviations from UIP(RW)**

than the Singapore dollar interest rate was itself an indication of the strong preference for assets denominated in the Singapore dollar.

But as Marston (1993) pointed out, uncovered interest differentials need not be equal to zero even in the absence of any risk premium. The market, for example, might be learning about changes in regimes that have occurred. If so, the forecast error for exchange rate movement might be systematically positive or negative, even though the market might be processing information in a rational manner. This could have been the case in 1981 and 1982, after the MAS switched its modus operandus from interest rate and money supply management to exchange rate management, in its rationalization exercise. Another aspect of the MAS's rationalization process, which might also have added to the adjustment cost, was the policy initiated in 1981 of relying on greater "self-regulation" by financial institutions. This change was intended to maintain a liberal environment. It was felt that anticipations of strict penalties for noncompliance with legislation and administrative guidelines under this freer environment would not only help to ensure the success of the policy but also provide more opportunities for self-improvement by the financial institutions.

The band of interest deviations is not the only indicator of changing capital mobility. As Faruqee (1992) argued, another way to measure such mobility is to look at the conditional variance of such deviations. With greater capital mobility, not only the band but also the variance would decline over time. A preferred model with well-known success in financial research is the GARCH model. For CIP deviation, however, the results in table 12.2 show that there is no significant correlation in conditional variance. To give some indication of the time-varying volatility, we compute standard deviations of CIP deviations over subperiods of 20 observations each. The series of sample standard deviations is plotted in figure 12.3. As we can see, there is no discernible trend in the volatility, although the standard deviation of $C_1$ is generally greater than that of $C_3$.

For the UIP(RW) deviations, the results in table 12.2 show that there is significant serial correlation and conditional heteroskedasticity for both one-month and three-month data. Thus we fit an autoregressive process with GARCH residuals for both $U_1$ and $U_3$. The results are summarized in table 12.5. It is found that $U_1$ is driven by an AR(2) process while $U_3$ follows an AR(1) process. Parameter estimates of the variance equation are very similar.[12] Residual diagnostics using the $Q$ and $R$ statistics show that the model adequately captures autocorrelations in both mean and variance. To study the changing degree of capital mobility we calculate the conditional standard deviation, $\hat{h}_t$, and plot the series in figure 12.4, which largely confirms our earlier finding. That is, except for the period from late 1979 to late 1983, volatility has been very small, not exceeding 1 percent. At its height in 1980, the conditional

12. As in many other studies of financial data, the values of $\hat{\beta}_1 + \hat{\beta}_2$ in the model are very close to unity, implying that conditional variance is highly persistent.

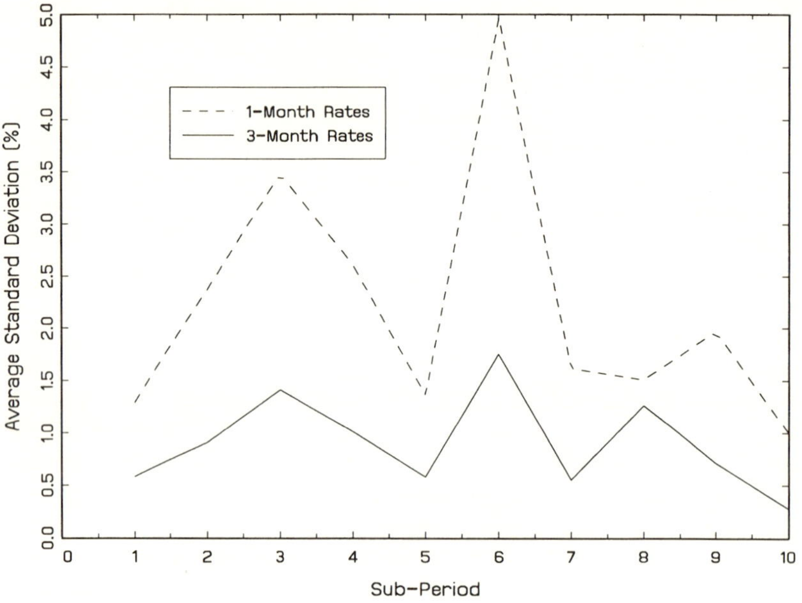


**Fig. 12.3 Average standard deviations, CIP**

standard deviation reached 2.4 percent. Since then it has been decreasing, indicating an increasingly higher degree of capital mobility.

Comparing our findings with those of Faruqee, we see that Faruqee failed to capture the large volatility in the first few years of the 1980s. This could be explained by the larger sample size used in our study and the fact that we use a more efficient simultaneous estimation method. Furthermore, the slight reversal in increasing volatility in late 1989 found by Faruqee proved to be temporary. The volatility had since then returned to a downward trend until the second half of 1993, when the Singapore stock market was swept by an unprecedented bull run. The bull run, fueled by, among other things, the listing of Singapore Telecom in an effort to encourage Singaporeans to own shares and a series of pro-business policies, had led to a tremendous inflow of capital. This in turn had caused some instability in the domestic interbank market, which was reflected in the volatility of the UIP deviations.

To consider an alternative assumption about the expectation of the future spot rate, we consider UIP(RE). Figure 12.5 plots the deviations from UIP(RE). It can be observed that the deviations are much larger than those of UIP(RW). The fact that some of the deviations from UIP(RE) are exceedingly large, reaching over 60 percent in annualized terms, may be an indication that the perfect foresight assumption is inappropriate. Serial correlation analysis shows that the deviations do not exhibit conditional heteroskedasticity. Similar to CIP, we consider the average standard deviations for the deviations from

**Table 12.5 Estimation Results of GARCH Models for UIP Deviations (eq. [6])**

| | Parameters | | | | | | Residual Diagnostics | | | |
|---|---|---|---|---|---|---|---|---|---|---|
| Dependent Variable | $\alpha_0$ | $\alpha_1$ | $\alpha_2$ | $\beta_0$ | $\beta_1$ | $\beta_2$ | $Q_1$ | $R_1$ | $Q_2$ | $R_2$ |
| $U_1$ | −0.2360 | 0.7549 | 0.1698 | 0.2403 | 0.7336 | 0.2277 | 36.03 | 0.930 | 34.53 | 0.213 |
| | (−1.932) | (8.667) | (2.003) | (5.801) | (27.736) | (6.668) | | | | |
| $U_3$ | −0.2093 | 0.9015 | | 0.1718 | 0.8188 | 0.1345 | 24.26 | 0.359 | 21.56 | 0.462 |
| | (−2.012) | (25.224) | | (3.605) | (28.973) | (5.664) | | | | |

*Notes:* Numbers in parentheses are *t*-values. $Q_1$ and $R_1$ test for residual serial correlation. $Q_2$ and $R_2$ test for conditional heteroskedasticity. If residuals are white noise, $Q_1$ and $Q_2$ are approximately distributed as a $\chi^2_{24}$, and $R_1$ and $R_2$ are approximately distributed as a standard normal.

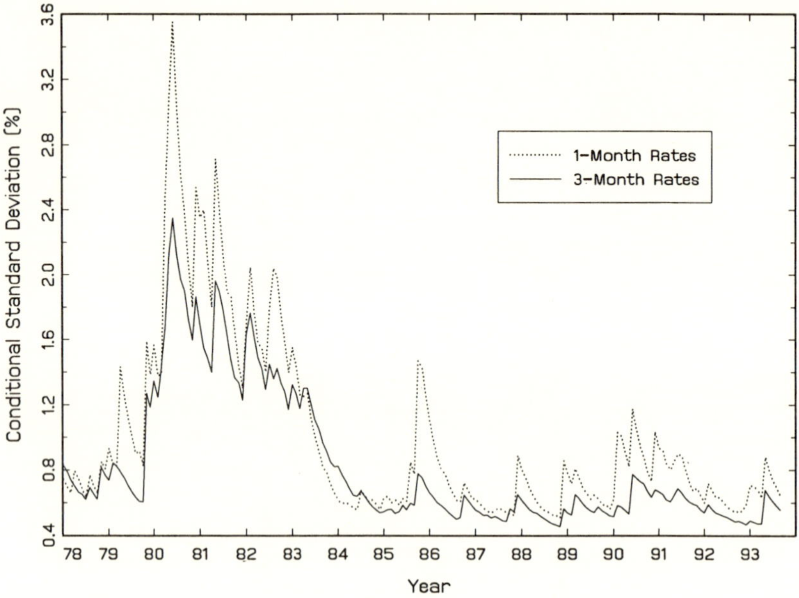


**Fig. 12.4 Conditional standard deviations, UIP(RW)**

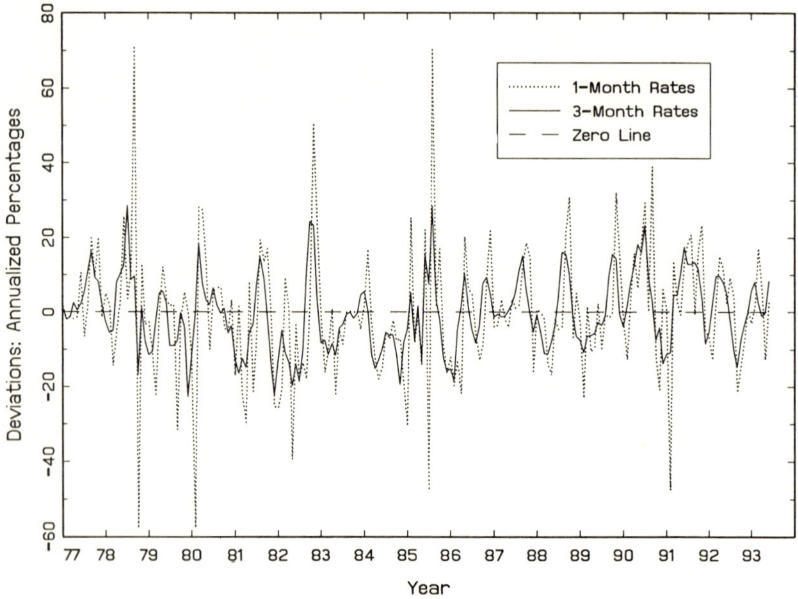


**Fig. 12.5 Deviations from UIP(RE)**

UIP(RE) over 10 subperiods. Results are plotted in figure 12.6. Although there is no obvious trend in the volatility, the standard deviations of the one-month data show a slight declining tendency.

Finally, we follow the Hansen-Hodrick (Hansen and Hodrick 1980) approach to examine the orthogonality of the prediction error of the spot exchange rate (using the forward exchange rate) on some information variables, including past prediction errors and forward premium. If the market is efficient, these information variables should be orthogonal to future forecast errors. To avoid the problem of serial autocorrelation in residual errors, we rely on quarterly data when three-month forward rates are used. The results of the tests are summarized in table 12.6.

For the monthly data, we notice that the $F$ statistics in all three equations in table 12.6 suggest that the forward rate is statistically no different from the (ex post) actual spot rate, whether we use forward premium or past prediction errors (both for the immediate past month and past two months) as the information variable. This implies that there is no evidence of inefficiency in the market.

For the quarterly data, the results are less clear-cut. The market passes the efficiency test when past forecast errors are used as the information variable but fails when forward premium is used. This, together with the fact that the marginal significance level is higher when forward premium is used as the information variable in the quarterly data equation, may be a reflection more

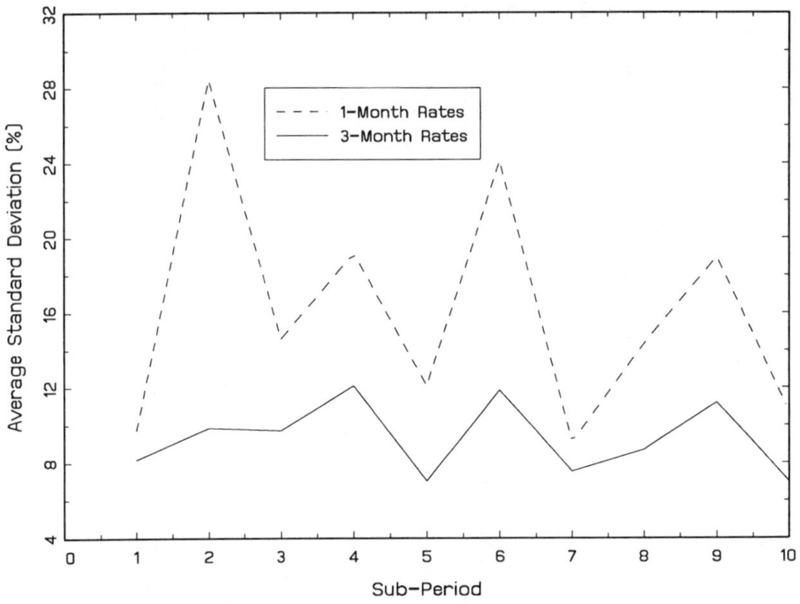


**Fig. 12.6 Average standard deviations, UIP(RE)**

**Table 12.6** **Tests of UIP Using Hansen-Hodrick Approach**

| | | | Regression Parameters | | | | | Residual Diagnostics | | |
|---|---|---|---|---|---|---|---|---|---|---|
| Dependent Variable | Sampling Interval | Sample Size | Constant | Lag−1 Dependent Variable | Lag−2 Dependent Variable | Forward Premium | $F$ ($p$-value) | D-W | $Q_1$ | $Q_2$ |
| $s_t - f_{3,t-1}$ | Quarterly | 65 | −0.0019 (−0.5963) | −0.0530 (−0.4215) | | | 0.178 (0.675) | 2.022 | 35.63 | 30.74 |
| $s_t - f_{3,t-1}$ | Quarterly | 65 | −0.0128 (−2.8463) | | | 2.3584 (3.2259) | 10.406 (0.002) | 2.248 | 40.87 | 31.73 |
| $s_t - f_{1,t-1}$ | Monthly | 199 | −0.0007 (−0.6713) | −0.0154 (−0.2159) | | | 0.047 (0.829) | 1.996 | 32.02 | 34.04 |
| $s_t - f_{1,t-1}$ | Monthly | 198 | −0.0007 (−0.6480) | −0.0146 (−0.2046) | 0.0521 (0.7275) | | 0.288 (0.750) | 1.996 | 31.41 | 33.66 |
| $s_t - f_{1,t-1}$ | Monthly | 200 | −0.0017 (−1.4400) | | | 0.6986 (1.6082) | 2.586 (0.109) | 2.060 | 29.43 | 33.80 |

*Notes:* Numbers in parentheses are $t$-values. The $F$-statistic tests that all regression parameters, apart from the constant, are jointly zero.

of the existence of some risk premium than of the inability of the market to exploit possible arbitrage opportunity.

### 12.5 Conclusion

This paper examines the dynamic changes in the degree of international capital mobility in the context of Singapore. Our concern here is not so much with the financial openness in Singapore relative to other countries, but with the changes in this openness over time. The issue is important not only because it reflects the impact of various liberalization measures taken over the years but also because of its relevance to the conduct of independent domestic monetary policy.

Both the band and the variability of deviations from covered and uncovered interest parities are used to measure changing capital mobility. We have found that, except for a brief period in the early 1980s, both the band and the variability of the deviations have been declining over time, implying that capital has indeed become increasingly mobile. In the 1990s, the deviations have virtually disappeared, suggesting almost perfect capital mobility. In addition, we found that, for the sample period as a whole, there is no reason to reject the efficient market hypothesis.

Like Frankel and other researchers, we found that, whatever barriers to capital movement exist seem to take the form of currency-related risks, as shown by the larger deviations from uncovered interest parity. Country-specific transaction costs, which deviations from covered interest parity are supposed to capture, are rather negligible. This finding is consistent with the fact that, since the late 1970s, all capital and exchange controls have effectively been abolished, even though the system is not immune to external economic shocks. It also implies that the effort to promote Singapore as an international financial center by removing unnecessary restrictions is indeed bearing fruit.

The results nevertheless suggest that the central bank's ability to conduct independent domestic monetary operations will be severely hampered. Any attempt to fix the domestic interest rate at a level different from the world interest rate (the U.S. rate in particular) is likely to be foiled. Exchange rate management, rather than domestic monetary policy tools, will more than ever be the key to maintaining domestic price stability.

## References

Edwards, S., and M. S. Khan. 1985. Interest rate determination in developing countries: A conceptual framework. *IMF Staff Papers* 32:377–403.

Faruqee, H. 1992. Dynamic capital mobility in Pacific Basin developing countries. *IMF Staff Papers* 39:706–17.

Feldstein, M., and C. Horioka. 1980. Domestic saving and international capital flows. *Economic Journal* 90:314–26.
Frankel, J. 1991. Quantifying international capital mobility in the 1980s. In *National saving and economic performance,* ed. D. Bernheim and J. Shoven, 227–60. Chicago: University of Chicago Press.
Glick, R., and M. Hutchison. 1990. Financial liberalization in the Pacific Basin: Implications for real interest linkages. *Journal of the Japanese and International Economies* 4:36–48.
Hansen, L. P., and R. J. Hodrick. 1980. Forward exchange rates as optimal predictors of future spot rates: An econometric analysis. *Journal of Political Economy* 88:829–53.
Ito, T. 1986. Capital controls and covered interest parity between the yen and the dollar *Economic Studies Quarterly* 37:223–41.
———. 1988. Use of (time-domain) vector autoregressions to test uncovered interest parity. *Review of Economics and Statistics* 70:296–305.
Marston, R. 1993. Determinants of short term interest differentials between Japan and the United States. *Bank of Japan Monetary and Economic Studies* 11:33–61.
Obstfeld, M. 1994. International capital mobility in the 1990s. CEPR Discussion Paper no. 902. London: Centre for Economic Policy Research.
Reisen, H., and H. Ỳeches. 1993. Time varying estimates on the openness of the capital account in Korea and Taiwan. *Journal of Development Economics* 41:285–305.
Teh, K. P., and T. Shanmugaratnam. 1992. Exchange rate policy: Philosophy and conduct over the past decade. In *Public policies in Singapore,* ed. M. H. Toh and L. Low. Singapore: Times Academic.

## Comment Ngiam Kee Jin

The paper by Tse and Tan examines whether there were deviations from covered and uncovered interest parity in Singapore during the period 1977–93. Deviations from covered interest parity (CIP) were found to be generally small during the sample period but large during the early 1980s. Similarly, deviations from uncovered interest parity (UIP) were found but became smaller and less variable over time. Based on these findings, it is then claimed that capital has tended to be more mobile in Singapore over time because of the various liberalization measures taken by the authorities over the years.

One way to test whether CIP holds is to find out whether the following inequality is satisfied:

$$|R^{U} + F - S - R^{S}| < C, \quad (1)$$

where $C$ is the cost of carrying out the transaction, and the left-hand side is the absolute value (ignoring the sign) of the gap between the Eurodollar rate ($R^{U}$) and the onshore Singapore interest rate ($R^{S}$), adjusted for the forward premium or discount ($F - S$). Hence, contrary to the claim made in the paper, deviations from CIP do not necessarily imply that risk-free arbitrage opportunity is avail-

Ngiam Kee Jin is senior lecturer in the Department of Economics and Statistics, National University of Singapore.

able. Arbitrage profits arise only if the deviations are greater than the transaction costs.

In testing whether CIP holds for the Singapore and U.S. dollars, the biggest problem is deciding what Singapore interest rate should be used. There is no problem with the U.S. interest rate because the LIBOR (or SIBOR) can be used. As for the Singapore interest rate, the domestic interbank rate is commonly used. This paper is no exception. In the Singaporean context, the correct domestic interest rate is the effective cost of funds (EC) because it is used by foreign exchange traders to calculate the Singapore-U.S. dollar forward exchange rate or the swap points. The EC can be obtained by adding the reserve cost to the nominal cost of borrowing (NC). In the simplest form, the EC is expressed by the following:

$$(2) \qquad x\,\mathrm{CR} + (1 - x)\,\mathrm{EC} = \mathrm{NC}\,,$$

where CR represents the interest on cash reserves held by the bank (which, for simplicity, are assumed to earn zero interest) and $x$ is the ratio of cash reserves against the liabilities base.

Rearranging equation (2) gives

$$(3) \qquad \mathrm{EC} = \frac{\mathrm{NC} - x\,\mathrm{CR}}{1 - x}\,.$$

It is clear that the EC is always greater than the NC, which is actually the weighted average of the CR and EC. Moreover, a given change in the NC will lead to a more than proportionate change in the EC. This merely shows that the reserve cost is higher (lower) when the interest rate is higher (lower). For many banks in Singapore, especially foreign banks, which normally have a low deposit base, the domestic interbank rate is their nominal cost of funds. However, the minimum rate at which they can lend is not NC but EC, which takes into account the reserve cost.

Tse and Tan find that the left-hand side of equation (1) is always positive and that in the early 1980s the positive deviations were larger than usual. It should be noted that during the early 1980s, the domestic interbank rate soared to a yearly average of 11.48 percent in response to the surge in the U.S. interest rate. Consequently, the increase in EC would have been greater than the rise in NC. If EC rather than NC were used to proxy the Singapore interest rate, most of the positive deviations in the sample period, including the early 1980s, would be substantially reduced in size and may even disappear altogether. The argument in the paper that the smaller deviations from CIP in subsequent years is due to the various liberalization measures taken by the Singapore government is not convincing. This is because Singapore had completely liberalized its exchange control as early as June 1978. Since then, Singaporeans have been allowed to borrow and lend freely in all currencies as well as to deal freely in foreign exchange.

The test for UIP is more fruitful and interesting and may involve testing the following equation:

$$S^e - S = a + b(F - S) + u, \tag{4}$$

where $S^e$ is the expected spot rate in the $i$th period ahead, $F - S$ is the forward premium or discount, and $u$ is the error term. The problem with testing equation (4) is that $S^e$ is unobservable and has to be estimated. There are several ways to solve this problem. One approach is to use survey data on the expectations of the Singapore-U.S. dollar exchange rate, which fortunately can be obtained from the *Currency Forecaster's Digest.* Another way is to use an exchange rate model to generate the exchange rate expectations. Last, but not least, the actual exchange rate movements that occur over time can be used if there is perfect foresight. However, the paper tests for UIP by simply assuming that the Singapore-U.S. dollar exchange rate follows a random walk, which means that $S^e = S$. Thus, the UIP holds only if

$$R^U - R^S = 0\,. \tag{5}$$

Moreover, if the CIP holds, then

$$S^e = F\,, \tag{6}$$

which implies that there is no risk premium in the case of the Singapore-U.S. dollar exchange rate.

The assumptions made in the paper for testing UIP are arbitrary and tend to oversimplify. Figure 12.2 shows that the Singapore interest rate has been consistently below the U.S. interest rate and that there has been significant deviation between the two rates. Can one then conclude that UIP is not supported? The answer is obviously no. The failure of the data to accord with equation (5) above can be explained by the fact that UIP does not hold (probably because of the existence of a risk premium) or that the assumptions about exchange rate expectations are at fault, or both. This is really a test of the joint hypothesis.

Suppose that the Singapore-U.S. interest rate differential can be decomposed into two parts as follows:

$$R^U - R^S = (S^e - S) + \mathrm{RP}, \tag{7}$$

where $S^e - S$ is the expected change of the exchange rate and RP is the risk premium. In order to test adequately whether UIP holds, one must be able to measure anticipated exchange rate changes. Otherwise, how can one tell whether a risk premium or discount exists? The existence of a risk premium cannot be easily dismissed in the case of Singapore. Over the entire decade of the 1980s, the Singapore-U.S. interest rate differential averaged 3.5 percent. During the same period, the Singapore dollar appreciated against the U.S. dollar by 2.3 percent on average. This difference might suggest that the market perceived Singapore dollar deposits to be less risky than U.S. dollar deposits and therefore would require a risk premium in order to induce investors to hold the U.S. dollar–denominated assets. Finally, it is useful to remember that the test of UIP is not a test of the degree of capital mobility. Failure of UIP may simply reflect the fact that Singapore and U.S. assets are not perfect substitutes but move freely. The question of capital mobility can only be deduced from CIP which, I believe, is valid in the case of Singapore.

# 13 Singapore as a Financial Center: New Developments, Challenges, and Prospects

Ngiam Kee Jin

Since the late 1960s a number of international financial centers have emerged in Asia. These centers are major meeting places for internationally mobile funds. The rapid economic growth in many Asian countries combined with their various stages of economic development has increased the flow of funds across countries. This in turn has induced internationally renowned banks to establish branches in Asia to facilitate the cross-border flow of funds. Singapore has had a head start on other Asian centers as it was the first to allow a foreign bank to operate an offshore banking unit, as far back as 1968.[1] This unit, also known as the Asian Currency Unit (ACU) or the Asian Dollar Market, was created by removing the withholding tax on interest paid to nonresidents for the placement of foreign currency deposits.[2] Since then, other banks in Singapore have followed suit by setting up their own ACUs. Like Singapore, Hong Kong has gradually evolved into an international financial center. The transformation of Hong Kong gained momentum after 1978 when the government lifted its moratorium on the issuance of new banking licenses. In 1986, Tokyo set itself up as a global financial center with the establishment of the Japan Offshore Market. Other latecomers in international financial markets are Taipei, Bangkok, and Labuan.

Singapore is currently a major financial center, serving not only its domestic economy but also its region and beyond. The financial services provided by Singapore have contributed significantly to its economic development. Over

Ngiam Kee Jin is senior lecturer in the Department of Economics and Statistics, National University of Singapore.

The author thanks Christopher Lee for able research assistance and Soon Teck Wong for helpful comments.

1. The unit was operated by the Bank of America.

2. It was only five years later, in January 1973, that the tax on bank profits from the ACUs was cut from 40 to 10 percent.

the past seven years, the financial sector has been the best-performing sector of the economy, averaging 20 percent growth per annum, or twice the annual rate of growth of the entire economy. In 1993, the financial sector grew at 20.8 percent compared with 9.9 percent for the whole economy. Today, financial and business services contribute about one-quarter of the country's gross domestic product. They now constitute a larger sector of the economy than the manufacturing industry. The outlook and future role of Singapore as an international financial center are subjects of great interest.

This paper is organized as follows: Section 13.1 analyzes the major developments in the Singapore financial scene in recent years. Section 13.2 addresses the challenges from the other financial centers in Asia, especially Hong Kong and Tokyo. Section 13.3 provides the outlook and future directions for Singapore as an international financial center. Finally, section 13.4 gives the conclusions.

## 13.1 Recent Developments in Singapore Financial Markets

The role of Singapore financial markets as a conduit for the international flow of funds is shown schematically in figure 13.1. Global funds can be channeled through Singapore via either of two routes: direct finance and indirect finance. In indirect finance, lenders and borrowers go through the Asian Dollar Market with the ACUs acting as intermediaries. A financial institution operating in the Asian Dollar Market must maintain an ACU separate from its domestic banking unit (DBU). The ACU of a bank deals only with claims denominated in non-Singapore currencies and does not need to maintain any reserves against deposits. In contrast, the DBU of a bank deals mainly with deposits and loans denominated in Singapore dollars and has to observe cash and liquid reserve requirements.[3] In direct finance, borrowers obtain funds directly in financial markets by selling claims (equities, Asian commercial paper, or Asian dollar bonds) to lenders. The role of the foreign exchange market and the Singapore International Monetary Exchange is basically to bind together the various segments of the Asian Dollar Market—Eurodollar, Euroyen, Euromark, and so forth.

Recognizing the importance of financial services as an independent growth area, various measures were undertaken in the 1970s and 1980s to turn Singapore into an international financial center. Listed below are some of the concrete steps toward deregulation and liberalization:[4]

| | |
|---|---|
| September 1970 | Policy toward admission of foreign banks is liberalized. |
| July 1972 | Cartel system for fixing exchange rates is abolished. |

3. Currently, the minimum cash balance and liquid assets ratio are 6 and 18 percent, respectively, of the bank's liabilities base.

4. For more details, see MAS (1989).

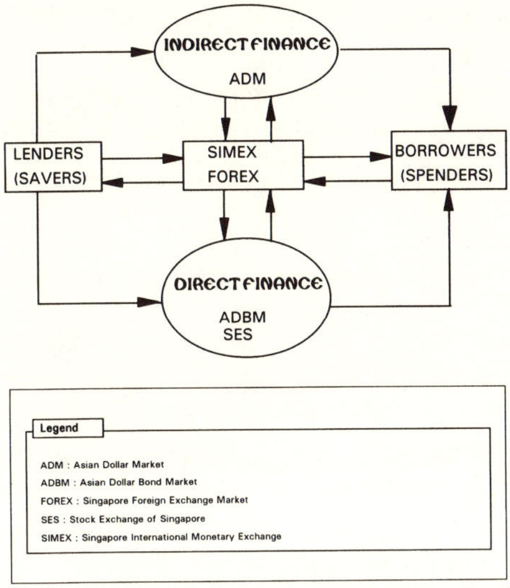


**Fig. 13.1 Flow of international funds through the Singapore financial system**

| | |
|---|---|
| July 1973 | Floating of the Singapore dollar is instituted. |
| August 1973 | Dealings in the gold market are completely liberalized. |
| July 1975 | Cartel system for fixing interest rates is abolished. |
| June 1978 | Exchange control is completely liberalized. |
| March 1987 | The stockbroking industry is opened to local banks and foreign financial institutions. |

Certain regulations are still vigorously enforced by the authorities. The opposition of the Monetary Authority of Singapore (MAS) to the internationalization of the Singapore dollar (through limits on lending overseas and borrowing by nonresidents) is perhaps the most controversial.[5] This regulation has been defended on the grounds that internationalization would render the conduct of monetary policy more difficult. The cost is that domestic money and capital markets in Singapore will not be fully developed. Prior to 1980, Japan similarly had opposed the internationalization of the yen.[6] However, as both domestic and international pressure increased to open Japan's capital markets, the Bank of Japan withdrew its opposition. The large growth of Japanese capital markets in the past decade and the rapid progress made in liberalization has resulted in wider use of the yen in international transactions. Nothing thus far has occurred that would support the fear that Japan would lose control of its money supply.

5. Other controversial regulations include the restrictive trading rules of the Stock Exchange of Singapore, discussed in section 13.3.
6. For a discussion of the internationalization of the yen in the early 1980s, see Frankel (1984).

### 13.1.1 Asian Dollar Market

Much of Singapore's growth as an international financial center in the early years resulted from the rapid growth of its Asian Dollar Market (ADM), which is the Asian counterpart of the Eurodollar market, rather than from the growth of its domestic financial system. The ADM is essentially an international money and capital market in foreign currencies. The major currencies are the U.S. dollar, deutsche mark, yen, pound sterling, and Swiss franc. Since its inception in 1968, the growth rate of the ADM has been phenomenal, as illustrated in figure 13.2. Its current size, as is evident from the value of assets in the ACUs, has dwarfed that of other banking and financial institutions. As shown in table 13.1, the ACUs accounted for 66.2 percent of total assets of the financial sector in 1993. This is an enormous jump from the 0.1 percent accounted for by the first ACU during its first year of operation. Commercial banking activities, while increasing absolutely, constituted only 18.3 percent of banking activities in 1993. It is clear that the financial sector has been transformed from a predominantly domestic operation conducted mainly through commercial banks into a global financial market channeled through ACUs.

The characteristics of ACUs have undergone some significant changes over the years. As shown in table 13.2, the share of funds going to nonbank customers rose to 35.4 percent in 1992 from 25.3 percent in 1976.[7] The share of interbank lending, while still dominant, declined from 72.7 percent in 1976 to 55.5 percent in 1992. The composition of the sources of funds has remained relatively constant, although deposits of nonbank customers have increased marginally at the expense of interbank deposits.[8] Interbank deposits predominate, accounting for 80.0 percent of total funds in 1992. Most of these interbank deposits come from outside Singapore.

Although statistics on the sources and uses of ACU funds by country or region are confidential, a few salient features can be deduced from published works. According to Bryant (1989), Singapore was a net creditor to the rest of the world as it had a positive net claim (total external assets exceeding total external liabilities) against all other countries. Singapore has always been a net creditor to the other Asia-Pacific region economies (including Hong Kong) but a net debtor vis-à-vis Europe and the Middle East. With the rapid development in the Asia-Pacific region in recent years, Singapore might have played an even larger role as a net creditor to China and the ASEAN countries since 1987. In its first annual report, in 1993, the Hong Kong Monetary Authority reported that the colony borrowed some S$24 billion from Singapore in 1993 compared with about S$20 billion in 1992. One factor might be that Singapore residents were placing their funds in Hong Kong rather than Singapore to avoid paying

7. Nonbank borrowers include multinational corporations, Singapore companies, and foreign governments.

8. Nonbank depositors include nonresident private individuals, multinational corporations, and regional central banks.

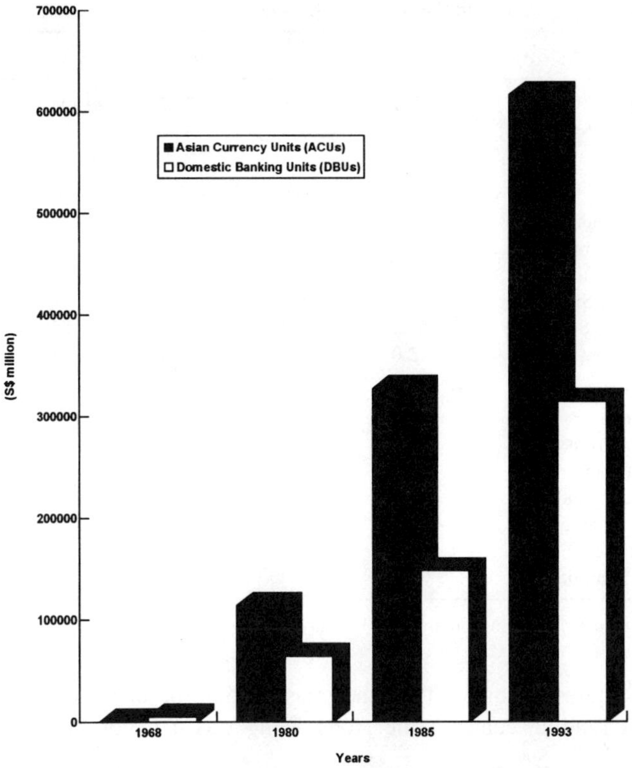


**Fig. 13.2 Growth of the financial sector in Singapore (ACU and DBU assets)**
*Source: Annual Report* (Singapore: MAS, various issues).

**Table 13.1 Total Assets of the Financial Sector (million Singapore dollars)**

| Assets | 1968 | 1980 | 1985 | 1993 |
|---|---|---|---|---|
| ACUs[a] | 60 (0.1) | 113,870 (64.5) | 327,062 (68.9) | 616,143 (66.2) |
| Commercial banks | 3,674 (74.2) | 33,316 (18.4) | 70,618 (14.9) | 170,250 (18.3) |
| Merchant banks | – | 13,300 (7.4) | 28,207 (5.9) | 42,205 (4.5) |
| POSB | 43 (0.1) | 2,757 (1.5) | 9,193 (1.9) | 20,310 (2.2) |
| CPF | 540 (10.9) | 9,551 (5.3) | 26,834 (5.7) | 52,334 (5.6) |
| Discount houses | – | 950 (0.5) | 2,469 (0.5) | – |
| Finance companies | 431 (8.7) | 3,075 (1.7) | 6,936 (1.5) | 14,994 (1.6) |
| Insurance companies | 199 (4.0) | 1,242 (0.7) | 3,527 (0.7) | 14,470 (1.6) |
| Total | 4,947 (100) | 178,061 (100) | 474,846 (100) | 930,706 (100) |

*Source: Annual Report* (Singapore: MAS, various issues).
*Note:* Numbers in parentheses are percentages.
[a]The figures for ACUs are converted from U.S. dollars to Singapore dollars using the yearly average exchange rate given in the MAS *Annual Reports*.

Table 13.2 Uses and Sources of ACU Funds (%)

| | 1976 | 1980 | 1985 | 1990 | 1992 |
|---|---|---|---|---|---|
| Total assets (million U.S.$) | 17,354.1 | 54,392.6 | 155,374.2 | 390,395.5 | 355,378.6 |
| *Uses of funds* | | | | | |
| Total assets | 100.0 | 100.0 | 100.0 | 100.0 | 100.0 |
| 1. Loans to nonbank customers | 25.3 | 22.8 | 24.1 | 32.2 | 35.4 |
| 2. Interbank funds | 72.7 | 72.7 | 67.5 | 61.3 | 55.5 |
| a. Within Singapore | 19.4 | 20.3 | 20.4 | 11.1 | 11.5 |
| b. Outside Singapore | 53.3 | 52.4 | 47.2 | 50.2 | 44.0 |
| 3. Other assets | 2.0 | 4.5 | 8.4 | 6.6 | 9.1 |
| *Sources of funds* | | | | | |
| Total liabilities | 100.0 | 100.0 | 100.0 | 100.0 | 100.0 |
| 1. Deposits of nonbank customers | 11.3 | 17.0 | 18.0 | 17.1 | 16.2 |
| 2. Interbank funds | 86.8 | 75.2 | 77.3 | 79.3 | 80.0 |
| a. Within Singapore | 21.6 | 20.7 | 20.1 | 11.9 | 13.0 |
| b. Outside Singapore | 65.2 | 54.5 | 57.2 | 67.4 | 67.0 |
| 3. Other liabilities | 1.9 | 7.8 | 4.7 | 3.6 | 3.8 |

*Source: Annual Report* (Singapore: MAS, various issues).

taxes on interest income.[9] The other reason could be that Singapore was an important funding center while Hong Kong was a major loan syndication center.

As in the London market, ACU transactions (including loans and deposits) are typically short-term and are pegged to the Singapore Interbank Offered Rate (SIBOR).[10] As shown in table 13.3, transactions with maturity of less than one month constitute the largest categories of both assets and liabilities. In 1992, about 20 percent of the ACU loans have maturity of more than one year, up from 16.7 percent in 1976. The trend toward longer maturity in loans may reflect the increased importance of medium-term syndicated loans. In contrast, the maturity structure of ACU deposits remained quite stable over the years, with deposits of longer than one year accounting for only 3–5 percent of the liabilities.

### 13.1.2 Asian Dollar Bond Market

The Asian dollar bond market began in 1971 with the issue of U.S.$10 million by the Development Bank of Singapore. To encourage its development, the stamp duty on Asian dollar bonds was abolished in April 1980. Since then,

9. Nonbank deposits in Hong Kong rose rapidly after 1982 when Hong Kong exempted nonresidents from the withholding tax on deposits.

10. Nowadays, banks seldom quote the London Interbank Offered Rate (LIBOR). With the globalization of financial markets, there should be no difference between LIBOR and SIBOR.

Table 13.3 **Maturity Structure of ACU Assets and Liabilities (%)**

| | 1976 | 1980 | 1985 | 1990 | 1992 |
|---|---|---|---|---|---|
| *Maturity of Assets* | | | | | |
| Total assets | 100.0 | 100.0 | 100.0 | 100.0 | 100.0 |
| Less than 1 month | 35.1 | 32.6 | 40.8 | 39.5 | 40.4 |
| 1–3 months | 27.3 | 26.8 | 21.8 | 26.2 | 22.4 |
| 3–12 months | 20.9 | 21.6 | 18.5 | 17.3 | 18.0 |
| Over 12 months | 16.7 | 19.0 | 18.9 | 17.0 | 19.2 |
| *Maturity of Liabilities* | | | | | |
| Total liabilities | 100.0 | 100.0 | 100.0 | 100.0 | 100.0 |
| Less than 1 month | 49.2 | 44.4 | 52.5 | 52.4 | 56.4 |
| 1–3 months | 28.0 | 30.1 | 26.1 | 26.8 | 26.2 |
| 3–12 months | 19.4 | 20.5 | 18.3 | 15.7 | 14.3 |
| Over 12 months | 3.4 | 5.0 | 3.1 | 5.1 | 3.1 |

*Source: Annual Report* (Singapore: MAS, various issues).

Table 13.4 **Asian Dollar Bond Issues (million U.S. dollars)**

| Year | Number of Asian Dollar Bond Issues | New Issues in Asian Dollar Bond Market (A) | New International Bond Issues (B) | (A)/(B) |
|---|---|---|---|---|
| 1971 | 1 | 10 | 7,110 | .001 |
| 1972 | 2 | 51 | 11,320 | .005 |
| 1973 | 3 | 70 | 9,910 | .007 |
| 1974 | 0 | 0 | 12,310 | 0 |
| 1975 | 3 | 47 | 22,820 | .002 |
| 1976 | 9 | 266 | 34,310 | .008 |
| 1977 | 14 | 368 | 36,090 | .010 |
| 1978 | 12 | 403 | 37,480 | .011 |
| 1979 | 8 | 358 | 37,330 | .010 |
| 1980 | 18 | 659 | 39,400 | .016 |
| 1981 | 22 | 1,238 | 49,000 | .025 |
| 1982 | 16 | 1,018 | 71,700 | .014 |
| 1983 | 16 | 1,145 | 72,000 | .016 |
| 1984 | 8 | 864 | 108,400 | .008 |
| 1985 | 4 | 235 | 164,500 | .002 |
| 1986 | 15 | 785 | 221,700 | .001 |
| 1987 | 18 | 1,482 | 177,000 | .008 |
| 1988 | 12 | 1,273 | 226,300 | .006 |
| 1989 | 18 | 3,500 | 262,800 | .013 |
| 1990 | 5 | 300 | 241,400 | .001 |
| 1991 | 6 | 749 | 316,700 | .002 |
| 1992 | 12 | 965 | n.a. | |
| Total | 222 | 15,786 | 2,159,580 | .007 |

*Source: Annual Report* (Basel: BIS, various issues).

the market has grown rapidly, although the level of activity fluctuates from year to year as can be seen in table 13.4. At the end of 1992, 222 issues had been floated, totaling some U.S.$15.8 billion. Most of the borrowers were from outside Singapore and comprise banks, multinational corporations, and government. As in the Eurobond market, most of the Asian dollar bonds are denominated in U.S. dollars. Other currencies include the yen, Australian dollar, deutsche mark, and European Currency Unit (ECU). In addition to straight fixed-rate issues, floating-rate notes, convertible bonds, and bonds with warrants are issued in the Asian dollar bond market. Despite its impressive growth, it still forms less than 1 percent of the international bond market.[11]

In recent years, Singapore has played an important role in the region for raising funds for infrastructural and capital development (see MAS 1992, 48). The growth in regional demand for funds has also been reflected in higher syndicated loan and "dragon bond" activity in the Singapore capital market. In 1992, a record 112 applications, amounting to U.S.$6.8 billion, were approved under the tax exemption scheme for syndicated offshore credit and underwriting facilities. Almost all the syndicated facilities raised were denominated in U.S. dollars. In addition, Singapore banks have played an active role as lead managers for the launching of dragon bonds, which are debt instruments issued in Asia but outside Japan. These bonds are listed in at least two of the three regional centers—Singapore, Hong Kong, and Taiwan. Since the launch of the first dragon bond by the Asian Development Bank in November 1991, 12 more issues (with one issue from China) have been launched. The outstanding amount in the dragon bond market now stands at more than U.S.$3 billion.

### 13.1.3 Foreign Exchange Market

The development of the foreign exchange (forex) market in Singapore can be traced back to the abolition of all foreign exchange controls in 1978.[12] Further impetus to the market was given by the entry of new foreign banks and international money brokers into Singapore.[13] It was also helped by deregulatory measures taken by Japan in 1984 and 1985 that had the effect of increasing foreign exchange transactions in Japan and elsewhere.[14] As shown in figure 13.3, the market has expanded nearly sevenfold, from a daily turnover of around U.S.$12 billion in 1985 to about U.S.$81 billion in 1992. Growth accelerated after 1985. As a result, Singapore is currently ranked fourth in terms of average daily foreign exchange turnover, after London, New York, and Tokyo.[15]

11. The international bond markets consist of two broad groups: foreign bonds and Eurobonds.

12. In June 1978, residents were finally allowed to borrow and lend freely in all currencies as well as deal freely in foreign exchange.

13. Currently, there are 115 foreign banks with either full, restricted, or offshore banking licenses. Eight international money brokers now operate in Singapore.

14. In 1984, Japanese dealers were allowed to make forward contracts freely and to deal with any parties outside Japan. In 1985, direct interbank dealings among banks in Japan were allowed.

15. The ranking was done in 1992 by the Bank for International Settlements (BIS).

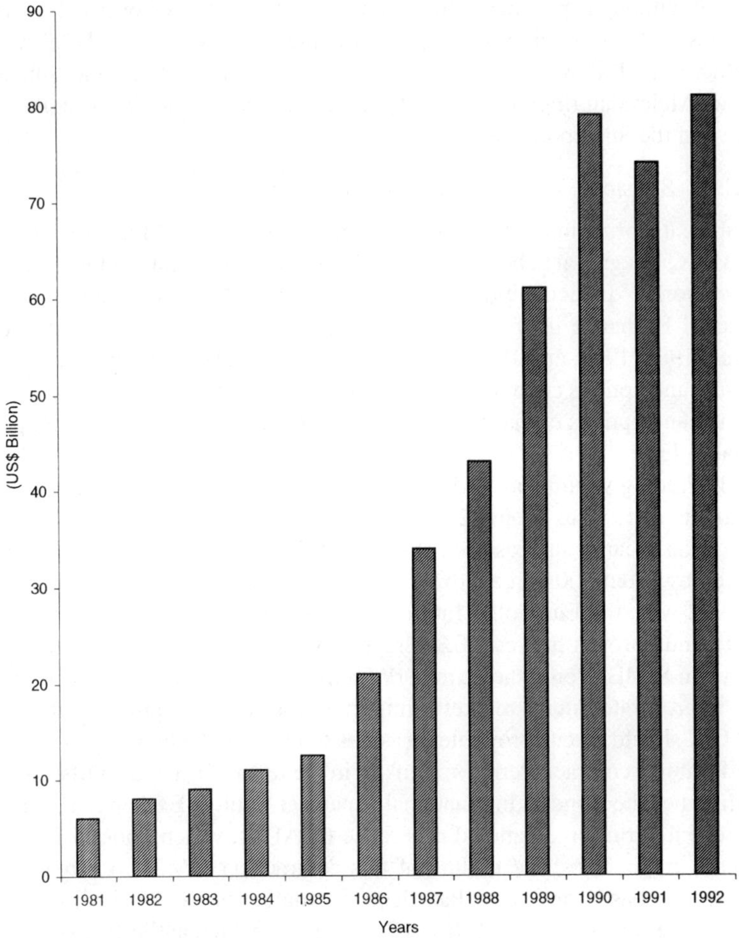


**Fig. 13.3 Average daily foreign exchange turnover in Singapore**
*Source: Annual Report* (Singapore: MAS, various issues).

A major characteristic of Singapore's forex market is that it deals almost exclusively in U.S. dollars rather than Singapore dollars against all major currencies. This is not surprising, especially in view of its close link with the ADM and the MAS's desire to discourage the internationalization of the Singapore dollar. In 1990, U.S. dollar–deutsche mark and U.S. dollar–yen transactions accounted for 31 and 29 percent of total transactions, respectively.[16] The share of Singapore-U.S. dollar tradings was only 5 percent. In recent years, both the swap and forward markets have been growing faster than the spot

16. These are the latest statistics.

market, although spot market transactions still account for over half of forex business.[17] In addition, cross-currency trading of the yen, deutsche mark, and British pound as well as trading of regional currencies (e.g., the Singapore dollar, Malaysian ringgit, Thai baht, and Indonesian rupiah) has become more active in the Singapore market.

### 13.1.4 Singapore International Monetary Exchange

Since its formation in 1984, the Singapore International Monetary Exchange (SIMEX) has grown to become one of the major futures and options exchanges in the world.[18] In recognition of its achievements, SIMEX was named the International Exchange of the Year by the *International Financing Review* three times (1989, 1992, and 1993). As of March 1993, SIMEX offered a total of 16 futures and options contracts, which makes it the most diversified international futures and options exchange in Asia. The products it offers can be grouped as in table 13.5.

The trading volume on SIMEX has grown spectacularly from only 538,829 contracts in 1985 to about 12.2 million contracts in 1992, as shown in figure 13.4. The greatest increase occurred in 1992 when SIMEX's trading volume soared by about 100 percent over the previous year. The most active contracts in 1992 were the Eurodollar futures (46.1 percent), Nikkei futures (27.5 percent), and Euroyen futures (20.4 percent). Among the interest rate futures contracts on SIMEX, only the Euromark futures contract is inactive. Since an active interest rate futures market is important for the development of the ADM, SIMEX should take appropriate measures to improve the liquidity of the Euromark futures contract. Perhaps, a linkup in the form of a Mutual Offset System with either the London International Financial Futures Exchange (LIFFE) or Marché à Terme International de France (MATIF), which trade in Euromark futures, might boost the trading of this contract on SIMEX. Currently, four contracts—based on Eurodollar, deutsche mark, yen, and British pound futures—are traded on the SIMEX-CME (Chicago Mercantile Exchange) Mutual Offset System, established in 1984 as the first such system between two exchanges in the world. This innovative system, which straddles two time zones, allows trades initiated on either exchange to be liquidated in or transferred to the other.

### 13.1.5 Stock Exchange of Singapore

One of the most significant developments in equity markets in the 1980s was the growing trend toward the trading of equities across frontiers. Singapore is no exception, as the Stock Exchange of Singapore (SES) started secondary listings of foreign shares in the late 1980s. As a result, the total market capital-

17. Over-the-counter currency options trading is well developed in London but still in its infancy in Singapore.
18. SIMEX is still ranked seventeenth in the world in terms of volume of business.

**Table 13.5 SIMEX Products (as of March 1993)**

| Product Category | Futures Contracts | Options Contracts |
|---|---|---|
| Interest rate | Eurodollar (1984) | Eurodollar (1987) |
| | Euroyen (1989) | Euroyen (1990) |
| | Euromark (1990) | |
| Currency | Yen (1984) | Yen (1987) |
| | Deutsche mark (1984) | Deutsche mark (1987) |
| | British pound (1986) | |
| Stock index | Nikkei (1986) | Nikkei (1992) |
| | MSCI HK[a] (1993) | |
| Commodity | HSFO[b] (1989) | |
| | Gasoil (1991) | |
| | Gold (1984) | |

*Note:* Year in which contract was introduced is given in parentheses.
[a]Morgan Stanley Capital International Hong Kong index.
[b]High-sulfur fuel oil future.

ization on the main board of the SES has been increasing, as can be seen in figure 13.5.[19] By 1992, it reached S$99.2 billion, which represented 1.3 times the size of Singapore's GNP.[20] Foreign counters accounted for only about 20 percent of total market capitalization over the period 1988–92.

All secondary listings of foreign stocks other than Malaysian stocks on the SES are denominated in non-Singapore currencies. Malaysian stocks traded on the SES are allowed to be denominated in Singapore dollars. Recently, the SES has been actively encouraging the listing of Singapore depository receipts (SDRs), which are the local equivalent of American depository receipts (ADRs).[21] This move is designed to increase the breadth of stocks available on the SES and to promote it as a regional securities market. However, except for the Malaysian and a few non-Malaysian foreign counters, the trading of secondary listings on the SES is practically nonexistent. In contrast, shares of local companies listed on the SES are actively traded, which can be attributed to a number of measures taken by the authorities to help Singaporeans own shares of Singapore companies. The euphoria created by the biggest privatization issue of Singapore Telecom, the liberalization of the CPF Investment

19. Companies on the main board are larger companies, while those listed on the second board, Sesdaq, are smaller. In 1990, the SES introduced an over-the-counter market, known as CLOB International, to allow investors to trade in a number of foreign securities listed on foreign stock exchanges.

20. The figures for 1993 look even more impressive as the public issues of shares (excluding rights issues and private placements of listed shares) amounted to a record S$6.84 billion. Singapore Telecom accounted for about 60 percent of total funds raised.

21. PT Gadjah Tunggal, an Indonesian manufacturing firm, was the first to list its SDRs on CLOB International in 1992. The latest to list its SDRs is Daimler-Benz, Germany's largest industrial conglomerate.

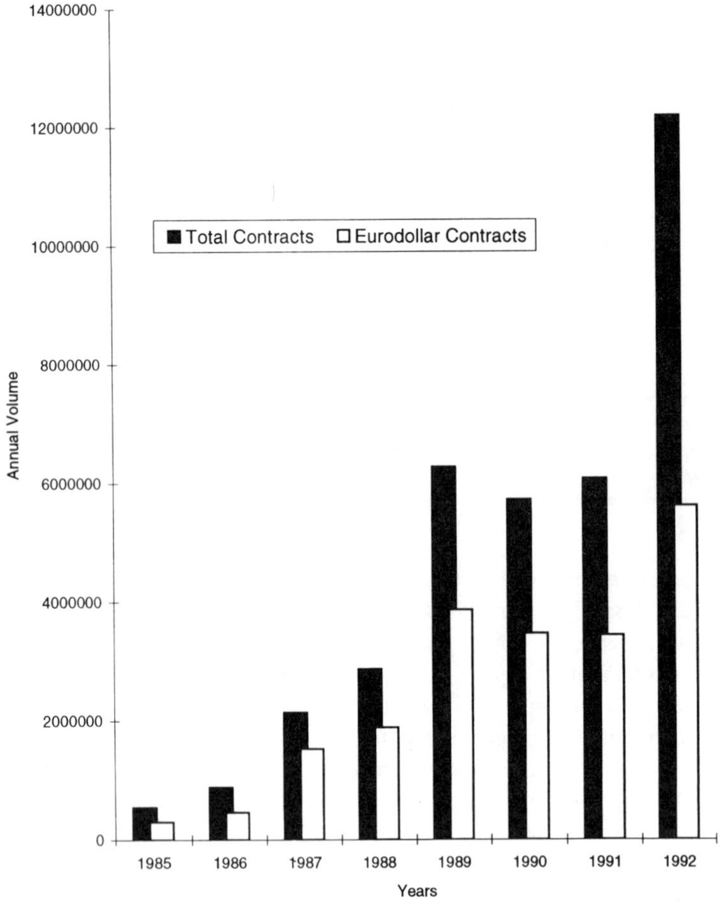


**Fig. 13.4 Annual turnover on SIMEX (total and Eurodollar contracts)**
*Source: Annual Report* (Singapore: SIMEX, various issues).

Scheme, and the unprecedented bull run in 1993 attracted many small investors to the local stockmarket.[22] The SES was capable of handling such a huge volume of trade mainly because it had implemented a scripless trading system.[23]

In recent years, the SES has been following the worldwide trend by allowing greater use of equity derivatives such as warrants, covered warrants, convertible bonds, and stock options. Currently, there are 37 warrants and only 2 covered warrants listed on the SES. The trading of warrants is significantly more

22. According to the latest survey conducted by the SES, in 1991 Singaporeans held 89.9 percent of the shares listed on the local bourse.

23. The use of automated teller machines to purchase initial public offerings has helped to speed up the whole process of raising equity capital in Singapore.

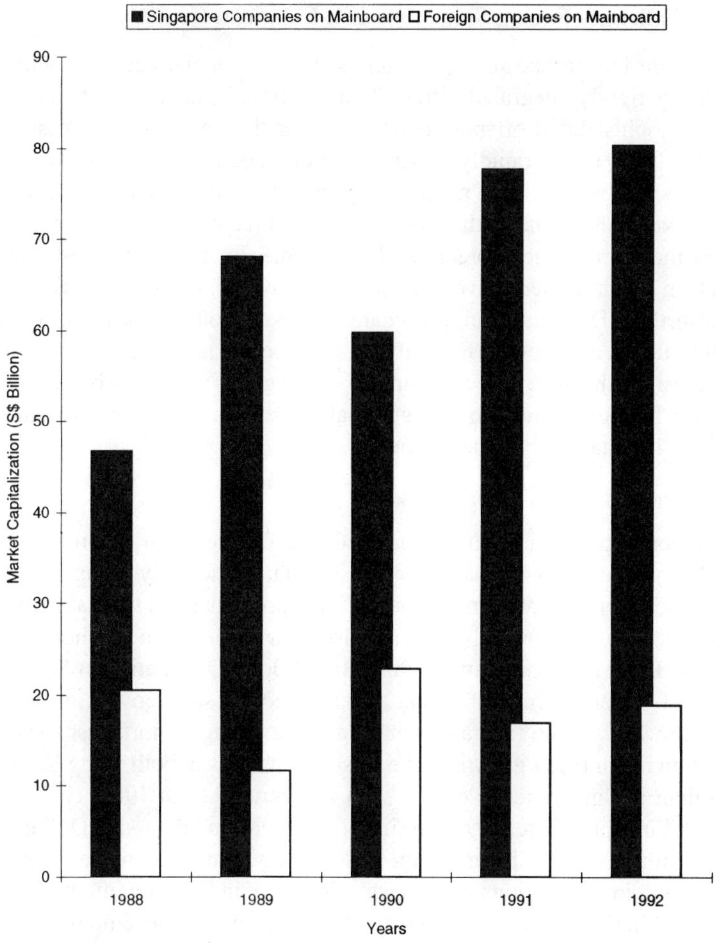


**Fig. 13.5 Market capitalization in the Singapore stock market**
*Source: SES Journal* (May 1993).

active than the trading of covered warrants because under existing SES regulations warrants can be traded by any investor whereas covered warrants can be traded only by certain investors.[24] The trading of stock options made its reappearance on the SES in March 1993.[25] By the end of that year, options on four local stocks were traded. However, the volume of trade in these options is still very anemic.

24. Apart from financial institutions, only investors with net assets of S$5 million or an annual income of S$200,000 are allowed to trade in covered warrants.

25. The SES started stock option trading in 1977 but terminated it in early 1980 because of lack of interest.

## 13.2 Challenges Facing Singapore as a Financial Center

Singapore has earned its reputation as Asia's financial center by building four strong, tightly integrated "pillars." First, it has already established its position as a sophisticated offshore banking center that meets the increasing demand for loans to the rapidly expanding Asian countries by borrowing from outside Asia as well as from neighboring countries. In particular, Singapore is well known as the home of the ADM. Second, it has overtaken Switzerland to become the fourth-largest foreign exchange center in the world. Third, SIMEX has set up dynamic derivative markets that thrive principally on instruments traded in the ADM and foreign exchange market. Fourth, the SES, which is probably the weakest of the four pillars, has recently taken some major initiatives to establish Singapore as a hub for the region's securities business. The challenge for Singapore is to strengthen all four pillars in order to enhance its role as an international financial center.

### 13.2.1 Pillar 1: Asian Dollar Market

Singapore's position as the home of the ADM has been vigorously challenged in recent years by many centers in Asia, particularly Hong Kong and Japan. The external environment facing Singapore changed dramatically during the 1980s, as evidenced by the establishment of the Japan Offshore Market (JOM) in 1986, the signing of the Sino-British Joint Declaration in September 1984, and the emergence of China as an economic superpower in the latter half of the 1980s. The favorable conditions prevailing in northeast Asia have resulted in much faster growth of the offshore markets in both Hong Kong and Japan than in Singapore, as can be seen in figure 13.6. In 1986, Hong Kong overtook Singapore in terms of the size of the ADM and the Asian Dollar Bond issues. With the establishment of the JOM, Hong Kong has enjoyed a tremendous growth in transactions with Japan, especially in Euroyen interbank transactions. China's insatiable demand for funds to fuel its development should lead to more loans from Hong Kong to nonbank customers in China. However, Hong Kong's return to China in 1997 is still a cloud on the horizon. How Hong Kong will fare as a financial center depends very much on how China reestablishes its relationship with the outside world as well as on how the Sino-British Joint Declaration is carried out.

Currently, Hong Kong and Singapore are regarded as two of the major offshore centers in Asia. Despite the large size of the JOM, Tokyo does not seem to enjoy the same status. Singapore is popularly known as the "funding center" and Hong Kong as the "lending center". With positive encouragement from its government, Singapore has also emerged as an important center for loan syndication.[26] In the Singapore market, developed under the close supervision of the MAS, there is a clear distinction between domestic and offshore transactions in order to insulate the domestic financial market from outside distur-

26. In 1983, ACUs were granted a 10-year tax holiday for all income derived from syndicated offshore loans arranged in Singapore.

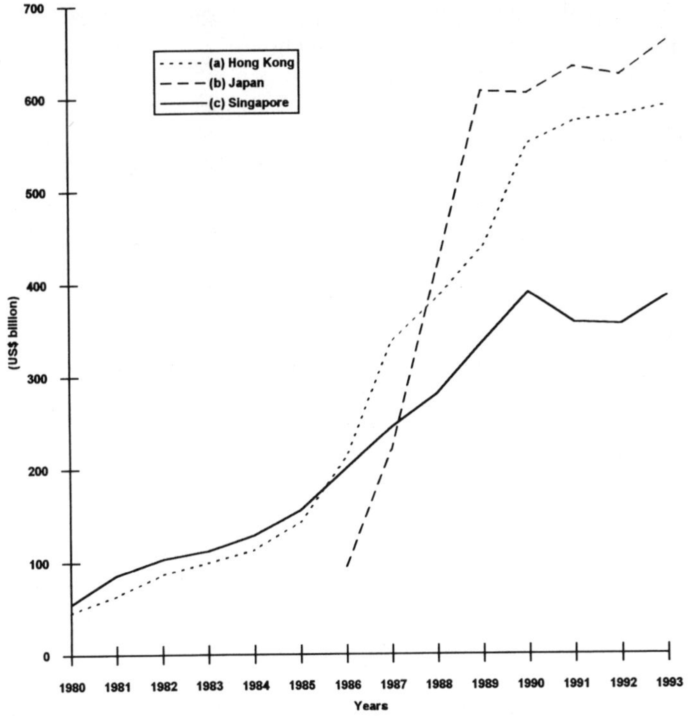


**Fig. 13.6 Size of major offshore markets in Asia**

*Sources:* (a) *Monthly Digest of Statistics* (Hong Kong: Census and Statistics Department, various issues); (b) *Monthly Bulletin* (Tokyo: Bank of Japan, various issues); (c) *Annual Report* (Singapore: MAS, various issues).

bances. The profits from offshore banking are taxed at a concessionary rate of 10 percent as opposed to the 27 percent tax on profits from domestic banking. In contrast, Hong Kong, which has until recently followed a laissez-faire policy,[27] has no separation between offshore and domestic banking businesses. In Hong Kong, all profits, whether from domestic or offshore business, are currently subject to a 16.5 percent tax.[28] In this sense, Hong Kong is not a typical offshore market.

With its enormous economic and financial strength, Tokyo should be the natural financial center of the Asia-Pacific region. Within two years of its establishment in 1986, the JOM overtook Singapore and now occupies the world's number-two spot behind London. The JOM may have caused a slowdown in the growth of Singapore's offshore market, but the Singapore foreign exchange

27. Departing from its traditional laissez-faire principles, Hong Kong took measures to strengthen its financial institutions by introducing net worth ratio requirements (September 1988) and regulations on foreign exchange positions (July 1990).

28. The offshore banking profits of financial institutions were not taxed in Hong Kong until 1978.

market has certainly benefited from Japan's financial liberalization. In the long run, Japan should not be a threat to Singapore because Singapore has its own market niche, unless further deregulation takes place in the JOM.[29] Japan has a comparative advantage in long-term financing, especially in fulfilling China's financial needs, while Singapore's advantage lies in short- to medium-term financing for Southeast Asia. Barring serious political uncertainties, Hong Kong should remain unchallenged in short- to medium-term financing to northeast Asia, including China.

### 13.2.2 Pillar 2: Foreign Exchange Market

In recent years, Singapore has consolidated its position as an active and liquid forex center apart from its already established reputation as a major ADM. Although Singapore is currently the world's fourth largest forex trading center, with an average daily turnover of over U.S.$80 billion, it is still a long way behind London, New York, and Tokyo. However, as shown in figure 13.7, Singapore and Hong Kong are slowly chipping away at Tokyo's position as Asia's top forex center. The volume on the Tokyo market has hardly increased since the bubble economy years in Japan ended in 1990, despite the fact that the world's forex turnover jumped by some 45 percent between 1989 and 1992. Meanwhile, the daily forex turnover in Singapore increased by 40 percent and in Hong Kong by 22 percent over the same period. Japan's protracted recession coupled with the booming economies in other parts of Asia are increasingly inducing American and European banks to locate their forex operations in Singapore and Hong Kong.

Looking ahead, Singapore is likely to face keener competition from Hong Kong than from Tokyo. Unlike Tokyo, which is dominated by dollar-yen trading, business in both Singapore and Hong Kong is more diversified.[30] Moreover, the cost of doing banking business is lower in Singapore and Hong Kong than in Tokyo. In view of these factors, Singapore should continue to play a key forex role in Asia despite Tokyo's bigger forex market and its emergence as a world financial hub. To stay ahead of Hong Kong, Singapore must step up the trading of regional currencies and derivative products such as futures, forward rate agreements, interest rate swaps, and options.[31] It should have no difficulty in staying ahead in this game given its success in launching the SIMEX, ADM, and forex cash market.

29. Currently, the JOM has too many restrictions. Only nonresidents and overseas subsidiaries can deposit and borrow in the offshore market. Securities businesses are prohibited. Offshore accounts, while not subject to withholding tax, still incur stamp duties and municipal taxes. Moreover, offshore banking income still faces a stiff corporate tax rate of about 48 percent.

30. Japan's development is still lopsided as over 50 percent of the transactions in the JOM are denominated in yen.

31. On January 25, 1994, the *Business Times* reported that two major European banks—Crédit Suisse and Société Générale—had made Singapore their regional center for trading currency options.

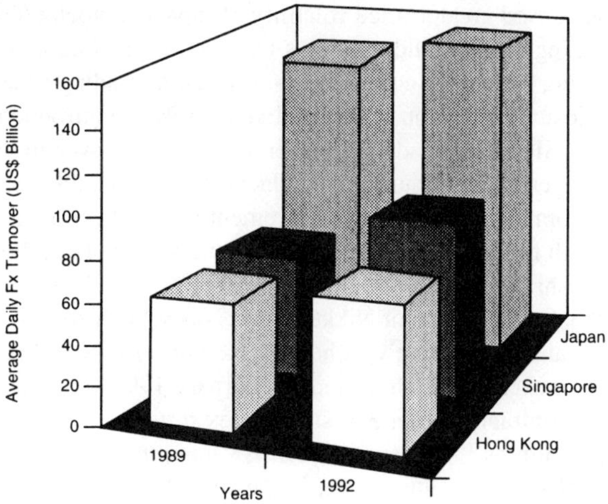


**Fig. 13.7 Size of major forex markets in Asia**
*Source: Central Bank Survey of Foreign Exchange Market Activity* (Basel: BIS, March 1993).

### 13.2.3 Pillar 3: Singapore International Monetary Exchange

After experiencing slow growth in its first decade of operation, SIMEX has become the fastest-growing futures and options exchange. SIMEX is now "Asia's one and only truly international derivative supermarket" (see International Financing Review 1993). However, its path to the top was not unobstructed as SIMEX had to face stiff competition from other exchanges and new technology developments such as Globex. The success of SIMEX in the face of these challenges is a testimony to its competitiveness, efficiency, and inventiveness.

Currently, there are 15 official financial and commodities futures exchanges in the Asia-Pacific region. Like SIMEX, most of these regional exchanges, such as the Sydney Futures Exchange (SFE), Tokyo International Financial Futures Exchange (TIFFE), Tokyo Stock Exchange (TSE), Osaka Stock Exchange (OSE), and Hong Kong Futures Exchange (HKFE), have enjoyed record trading volumes since 1988. These exchanges have been competing for a market share of the contracts traded at SIMEX.[32] For example, TIFFE trades in both Eurodollar futures and Euroyen futures, which are among the three most popular contracts traded at SIMEX. Nikkei 225 futures, the second most active contract on SIMEX, is traded at OSE.[33]

In March 1992, the Japanese authorities introduced several measures to curb derivatives trading, particularly index-linked arbitrage activity, which was be-

32. The only exception is the HSFO contract which is traded only at SIMEX.
33. SIMEX launched the Nikkei 225 in September 1986. Two years later, the OSE followed suit, and the TSE launched futures for the broader Tokyo Stock Price Index (Topix).

lieved to have caused greater price volatility of Japanese stocks. The measures include tightening rules on index futures and options, raising margin requirements, increasing brokerage commissions, shortening trading times, and forcing more disclosure of data on arbitrage. Even before the introduction of these new measures, SIMEX already had several advantages over the OSE. First, SIMEX has longer trading hours and conducts trading on public holidays. Second, brokers' commissions, margin requirements, and other charges at SIMEX are lower.[34] With the new Japanese measures, the daily volume for Nikkei futures in Osaka shrank to about 50,000 contracts from nearly 100,000 in 1991. In contrast, the daily volume for Nikkei futures on SIMEX rose to about 7,000 contracts from about 2,500 the year before (*Business Times* 1992). The rivalry between the two exchanges intensified in February 1994 when the OSE introduced another contract, Nikkei 300 stock index futures, to eventually replace the Nikkei 225 futures.[35] In response, SIMEX announced in June 1994 that it would launch Nikkei 300 futures later in the year (*Business Times* 1994).

SIMEX has adopted the open outcry system that is currently used in the major futures exchanges in the world. In fact, the top six futures exchanges in 1992 (which include three in the United States, one in the United Kingdom, one in France, and one in Brazil) use this system. The system's main drawback is that it can be abused by floor traders.[36] For instance, it can give rise to "syndicated trading," in which traders collude to widen spreads ahead of customer orders (see *Straits Times* 1993). The physical organization of open outcry trading, in which the exact time sequencing of all trades is not known ex post, makes it difficult for surveillance systems to detect any violations of rules. Trades executed during volatile market periods are especially susceptible to abuse. On the positive side, this system ensures that prices of futures contracts respond sensitively to relevant new information. Equilibrium prices are quickly established. Thus, the futures markets resemble closely the Walrasian auction system, in which no recontracting is allowed.

Globex, the Chicago-based electronic trading system, has emerged as an alternative to futures trades conducted through the open outcry system. Launched in mid-1992, the 24-hour trading that Globex offers could take some business away from the open outcry system. How much of SIMEX's business will eventually be diverted depends on whether Globex is able to provide uninterrupted service, security, and superior liquidity. Critics contend that it will never be able to give the liquidity that is provided by the open outcry system. Only time will tell. Globex trading is already taking place in the Asian time

34. E.g., in the case of calendar spreads (such as buying the March contract and simultaneously selling the June contract), charges are levied on both contracts at the OSE but on a netted basis at SIMEX.

35. While the Nikkei 225 represents the simple average of 225 component index stocks, the Nikkei 300 is a weighted index—based on market capitalization—which tracks the performance of 300 stocks listed on the TSE.

36. For a comprehensive treatment of the abuses, see General Accounting Office (1989).

zone as Globex terminals can be found in trading rooms in Tokyo and Hong Kong. However, Globex trading has thus far been very sluggish. For instance, the daily Eurodollar futures turnover by Globex is currently between 1,000 to 2,000 lots. In contrast, the daily average volume of Eurodollar futures on SIMEX was around 31,000 lots in February 1994.

SIMEX should continue to play a key role in enhancing Singapore's role as a financial center as long as it remains cost effective, responsive to market needs, and innovative in introducing new products. The new products it plans to offer should reinforce the other three pillars that give support to Singapore's position as a financial center. In this sense, SIMEX should concentrate on three core groups: interest rates, currencies, and stock indexes.[37] There is tremendous scope for SIMEX to introduce futures on long-term debt instruments, regional currencies, and regional stock indexes.[38] This is partly because the increasing deregulation of financial markets in this region should result in an enlarged customer base for SIMEX.

### 13.2.4 Pillar 4: Stock Exchange of Singapore

Once a major stock market in Southeast Asia, the SES has recently been dwarfed by its counterpart in Malaysia. Thailand is also catching up fast as an important stock market in the region. Table 13.6 shows that among the Asian economies outside Japan, Hong Kong occupies the top spot with a market capitalization of U.S.$293 billion, followed by Taiwan (U.S.$202 billion), Malaysia (U.S.$170 billion), South Korea (U.S.$139 billion), and Singapore (U.S.$125 billion). The SES is expected to raise U.S.$2.5 billion worth of new funds in 1994, which represents only 2.0 percent of its market capitalization. All the other regional markets listed, with the exception of the Philippines, are expected to raise more equity capital than Singapore in 1994.

With economies growing faster in Asia than in other parts of the world, capital markets in the region can be expected to experience strong growth with the tapping of foreign capital. Keen competition among regional exchanges to convince regional companies to use their markets to raise capital is expected to intensify. With its strategic location and excellent infrastructure, Singapore is well placed to act as a capital market for the ASEAN region. At the moment, Singapore has a head start in this regional game plan on at least three counts. First, the SES has already put in place a high-technology settlement system, which is essential for playing the role of a regional market. Second, Singapore has been recognized as a center for the listing and trading of foreign stocks. Third, the membership of the SES includes several foreign stockbroking firms

37. Perhaps the trading of commodity futures should be left to the newly created Singapore Commodity Exchange (SICOM), which currently trades only in rubber but will soon be launching Asia's first coffee contract.

38. Currently, SIMEX trades the Japanese government bond futures contract as well as in MSCI Hong Kong index futures, which mirror closely the widely watched Hang Seng index futures.

**Table 13.6 Market Capitalization and Estimated New Issues in Asian Stock Markets (billion U.S. dollars)**

| Market | Market Capitalization in 1993 | Expected New Issues in 1994 | New Issues as Percentage of Market Capitalization |
|---|---|---|---|
| Hong Kong | 293 | 8.1 | 2.8 |
| Taiwan | 202 | 5.1 | 2.5 |
| Malaysia | 170 | 4.0 | 2.4 |
| South Korea | 139 | 7.0 | 5.0 |
| Singapore | 125 | 2.5 | 2.0 |
| Thailand | 110 | 5.8 | 5.3 |
| Philippines | 35 | 2.0 | 5.7 |
| Indonesia | 28 | 3.5 | 12.5 |

*Source:* Salomon Brothers, as reported in the *Straits Times* (May 28, 1994).

that have helped raise the level of sophistication of the Singapore securities market.

While more counters and derivatives are certainly needed on the local bourse, the SES must simultaneously seek an active trading environment for securities that are already listed. To add depth to the local bourse, the SES should reassess brokerage fees and existing regulations, which might have discouraged trading in the Singapore market. Currently, brokerage fees in Singapore rank among the highest in the world. Singapore brokers impose graduated commission rates of between 0.5 (for transactions above S$1 million) and 1 percent (for transactions below S$250,000). This compares unfavorably with negotiable fees in London and a fixed 0.5 percent in Hong Kong.

While rules may, under certain circumstances, be needed to safeguard the interests of investors, they cannot be so strict that they stifle innovation and impede the growth of Singapore as a regional market. The requirement that foreign stocks other than Malaysian stocks listed on the SES be denominated in non-Singapore currency might have discouraged many local investors who would have to contend with foreign exchange risk. Another restrictive rule is that covered warrants on the SES can be traded only by financial institutions and individuals with high net worth. Covered warrants thrive in other financial centers, such as Hong Kong, mainly because there are no restrictions on their trading. Relaxing this rule can only enhance Singapore's regional role because it may pave the way for the introduction of covered warrants on regional stocks. Thus, unless remedial actions are taken, the inactivity of these securities can undermine Singapore's efforts to become a regional market, as foreign companies considering the SES may be discouraged from seeking secondary listings on the SES. Worse still, foreign companies now on the SES may be tempted to delist.

Any new instruments introduced by the SES should not only be in demand by investors but also help to consolidate Singapore's position as a center for securities business. In this respect, the SES or SIMEX should launch a futures contract on a local stock index and, at a later stage, a stock index options contract.[39] Hong Kong has been successful with the trading of futures and options on its Hang Seng index. By providing a useful hedging mechanism to investors, such futures and options contracts should make Singapore a more attractive place for investors and fund managers.[40] The task of underwriters of stocks would become easier and safer because they can use these derivative instruments to hedge the market risk.[41]

## 13.3 Prospects for Singapore as a Financial Center

The rapid developments in the Asia-Pacific region in the past decade greatly enhanced the importance of Singapore and Hong Kong as leading financial centers in Asia. These two city-states have benefited from the opening-up of China, the growing prosperity in the ASEAN economies, and the increased flow of funds from advanced countries (the United States, Japan, and Europe) to the Asia-Pacific region. Hong Kong has played a vital role as the gateway to China, and Singapore to ASEAN. As the ASEAN economies are expected to continue growing and to further liberalize their financial markets, there is tremendous scope for Singapore to play an even greater role as a major financial center. Although new financial centers in this region (Bangkok, Taipei, and Labuan) have been trying to secure a share of the offshore banking business, Singapore's position in the next decade should not be adversely affected as it still will have certain advantages, which include political stability, a well-developed infrastructure, a highly skilled workforce, and a strategic location. The challenge for Singapore is to maintain its competitive edge in the longer term.

The kind of financial services provided by Singapore may, however, undergo some changes in view of the changing external environment and the judicious effort Singapore has made to carve specific niches for itself. For example, ACU growth will probably be constrained on account of two external developments. First, banks throughout the world are required to adopt a common capital adequacy requirement,[42] which tends to favor the flow of funds through direct finance rather than indirect finance (see figure 13.1). Second, the other regional financial centers are providing direct competition to Singapore with attractive tax packages to boost their share of ACU business.[43]

However, Asia's booming economies coupled with their need to build mas-

39. Only stock index options rather than options on individual stocks can complete the market.

40. Since short selling is disallowed in Singapore, the only way an investor can hedge his stock portfolio is through the futures and options markets.

41. Because of the absence of a suitable hedging device in Singapore, underwriters can resort to a "force majeure" clause which allows them to withdraw their commitments under adverse market conditions.

42. Under BIS guidelines, banks are required to have capital equivalent to at least 8 percent of their assets.

43. Taiwan went even further than Singapore by granting tax exemption to bank profits from ACU business.

sive infrastructural and manufacturing projects will provide new opportunities for regional financial centers such as Hong Kong, Singapore, and Japan.[44] According to the Asian Development Bank, Asia's developing countries will grow by 7.2 percent in 1994 and 1995, while global growth will be only 1.8 percent in 1994 and 3 percent in 1995. Estimates of infrastructure spending in Asia seem to be clustered around U.S.$1.5 trillion over the next 10 years.[45] As a result, there will be an increase in demand for such services as fund raising, fund management, and risk management, which Singapore is well equipped to provide.

With the viability and depth of its financial markets, Singapore could play a particularly useful role in mobilizing the large amounts of funds required by the Asian countries. In this respect, the bond market in Singapore is likely to be the main beneficiary for two reasons. First, with its strategic location, Singapore will be an important supplier of funds through Asian dollar bonds to countries in Southeast Asia and the Indian subcontinent. Second, as China's needs may be too enormous for Hong Kong to meet, Singapore should enjoy a "spill-over" effect because of its close link with China, especially at the governmental level. The development of industrial parks in China by the two governments should help strengthen existing ties between the two countries.[46] There is thus tremendous scope for Singapore to serve as the second gateway to China. After the successful launching of Singapore's dragon bonds worth U.S.$300 million in October 1993, China may increasingly turn to this source of finance for its major infrastructural projects.

However, Asia's companies may find Singapore an unattractive place to raise equity capital in view of the general lack of interest in the foreign (non-Malaysian) shares listed on the SES. The fact that such shares must be denominated in non-Singapore currency might have deterred many local investors, and probably some fund managers, from trading in them because they involve a currency risk in addition to the risk associated with equity investment. In contrast, Malaysian shares listed on the SES are actively traded partly because they are denominated in Singapore dollars.[47] Similarly, the H shares of Chinese state enterprises listed on the Hong Kong stock exchange, which are denominated in Hong Kong dollars, have a liquid market. Encouraged by the initial

44. Recently, the Singapore government took the lead by investing U.S.$250 million in the U.S.$1 billion AIG (American International Group) Asian Infrastructure Fund.

45. The Economic and Social Commission for Asia and the Pacific estimated that Asia will require approximately U.S.$140 billion per year to develop its infrastructure. The International Finance Corporation calculated that third-world nations will need about U.S.$150 billion annually for private infrastructure projects in the 1990s.

46. Currently, two joint ventures in China have been agreed upon. The Suzhou township will cover 70 sq. km. and is a 35:65 joint venture between the Suzhou government and a Singapore consortium led by the Keppel Group. The Wuxi Industrial Park, which will cover 1,000 hectares, is being developed by a 30:70 joint venture between the Wuxi government and a Singapore consortium led by the Singapore Technologies Industrial Corporation.

47. The other reason may be that Singaporeans are familiar with the Malaysian counters.

success of these H shares, more Chinese state enterprises will soon be listing their shares in Hong Kong.

After many years of official encouragement, Singapore has finally become a major fund management center like Switzerland and Hong Kong. Singapore has several attractions for the fund management industry. First, it is situated in a fast-growing region that should continue to attract funds from the United States and Europe for higher returns and diversification. Second, it has a thriving market for regional stocks, particularly Malaysian shares listed on the SES and Thai shares, which are unlisted.[48] Third, it provides a broad range of derivative products for fund managers to hedge their exposure in this region. SIMEX currently trades in futures and options on the Nikkei 225 as well as futures on the MSCI Hong Kong Index and will be expanding the range of derivative products to include other Asian equity index futures contracts. Fourth, it provides generous fiscal incentives whereby fees earned by approved fund managers are taxed at only 10 percent.[49] As a result, the amount of funds managed in Singapore has increased fivefold over the last four years. In 1993, the total pool of funds managed by the 82 approved fund managers in Singapore reached a record high of S$61.8 billion (see *Straits Times* 1994). Nevertheless, there is still scope for growth as this sum represents only a small fraction of the total funds handled by fund managers worldwide.[50]

Several measures taken by Singapore in recent years to increase the sophistication and diversity of its financial market should enhance its role as a risk management center. First, incentives are available for multinational corporations (MNCs), including banks, to set up operational headquarters (OHQ) in Singapore. Several MNCs with operations in the region have already used Singapore to carry out their regional treasury activities under the OHQ scheme.[51] Second, the introduction of derivatives of more regional debt and equity products should provide corporations with additional tools for managing their financial risk. Finally, the MAS has introduced tax incentives to encourage financial institutions to undertake financial engineering and financial R&D in Singapore.[52] Collectively, these measures are powerful attractions to ensure that Singapore will remain a leading center for risk management in the region.

48. The trading of unlisted regional stocks in Singapore amounted to some S$41.5 billion in 1993.

49. In addition, all income earned by nonresidents is exempt from tax.

50. The amount of funds invested in the Asia Pacific region, excluding Japan, is estimated at only 5 percent of the total funds managed by international fund managers.

51. Under this scheme, income derived from trading in foreign exchange, financial futures, and other treasury support activities conducted by an MNC for a group of companies in the region will be taxed at a concessionary rate of 10 percent.

52. Introduced in June 1992, the tax incentives are in the form of double tax deduction for qualifying expenses relating to the establishment and development of new skill and knowledge-intensive financial activities in Singapore.

## 13.4 Conclusions

Singapore has become a major financial center of international repute. Its foreign exchange market is now the fourth-largest and SIMEX is among the fastest-growing futures and options exchanges in the world. However, ACU business in Singapore has not been growing as rapidly as in Hong Kong and Tokyo. Looking ahead, ACU business, which is basically conventional banking service, will face greater competition from such emerging financial centers in the region as Taipei, Bangkok, and Labuan. However, with flexibility and innovativeness, Singapore should be able to face the challenges and stay ahead. Singapore's status will be similar to that of London, which continues to be the financial capital of Europe despite the development of Frankfurt and other cities.

The robust Asian economies coupled with the enormous financial requirements of their infrastructure and investment projects should provide a tremendous potential for the growth of the financial centers in the region. With its strategic location and well-developed financial market, Singapore is well poised to provide the more sophisticated financial services, particularly in fund-raising, fund management, and risk management. However, it must watch developments in other financial centers to ensure that it is not hamstrung by its own regulations. The most contentious regulation has always been the restriction on the issuance of Singapore dollar–denominated securities by foreigners or by Singaporeans who intend to use the proceeds outside Singapore. This restriction is supposed to prevent the internationalization of the Singapore dollar, which can have a destabilizing effect on the domestic money supply or exchange rate. The cost is that the domestic (or onshore) financial markets in Singapore will not be as fully developed as in, say, Switzerland, which has allowed the Swiss franc to be internationalized.

# References

*Business Times*. 1992. SIMEX drawing Nikkei futures trade: Dealers. April 3.
———. 1994. SIMEX likely to launch Nikkei 300 in September. June 9.
Bryant, Ralph. 1989. The evolution of Singapore as a financial centre. In *Management of success: The moulding of modern Singapore,* ed. K. S. Sandhu and P. Wheatley. Singapore: Institute of Southeast Asian Studies.
Chan, Kenneth S., and Ngiam Kee Jin. 1992. Currency interchangeability arrangement between Brunei and Singapore. *Singapore Economic Review* 37 (October): 21–33.
Chin, Anthony, and Ngiam Kee Jin, eds. 1994. *Outlook for the Singapore economy.* Singapore: Trans Global.
Foley, Bernard J. 1992. *Capital markets.* London: MacMillan.
Foundation for Advanced Information and Research. 1991. *Japan's financial markets.* Tokyo: Foundation for Advanced Information and Research.
Frankel, Jeffrey. 1984. *The yen/dollar agreement: Liberalizing Japanese capital mar-*

*kets,* Policy Analyses in International Economics, no. 9. Washington D.C.: Institute for International Economics.
Freris, Andrew F. 1991. *The financial markets of Hong Kong.* London: Routledge.
Giddy, Ian H. 1994. *Global financial markets.* Lexington, Mass.: Heath.
Ho, Yan-Ki. 1992. Hong Kong, Singapore, and Taiwan as new financial centers. In *The future of Asia-Pacific economies: Emerging role of Asian NIEs and ASEAN,* ed. Fu-Chen Lo and Narongchai Akrasanee. New Delhi: Allied Publishers.
Hu, Richard. 1992. Keynote address, SES/SIMEX Seminar on International Investment and Risk Management, Tokyo, September 29.
International Financing Review. 1993. *Year in review 1993.* London: IFR Publishing.
Lee, Sheng Yi. 1992. Taipei as a financial centre. *Singapore Economic Review* 37 (October): 89–100.
Lim, Chong Yah, and Associates. 1988. *Policy options for the Singapore economy.* Singapore: McGraw-Hill.
Luckett, Dudley, David Schulze, and Raymond Wong. 1994. *Banking, finance and monetary policy.* Singapore: McGraw-Hill.
MAS (Monetary Authority of Singapore). 1989. *The financial structure of Singapore.* Singapore: Monetary Authority of Singapore.
———. 1992. *Annual report 1991/1992.* Singapore: Monetary Authority of Singapore.
McKenzie, Colin, and Michael Stutchbury. 1992. *Japanese financial market and the role of the yen.* Sydney: Allen and Unwin.
Ministry of Trade and Industry. Economic Committee. 1986. *The Singapore economy: New directions.* Singapore: Ministry of Trade and Industry.
Sarver, Eugene. 1990. *Eurocurrency market handbook.* New York: Institute of Finance.
*Straits Times.* 1993. Open outcry system at SIMEX can attract abuse. May 20.
———. 1994. Funds managed in Singapore grew by 65% to S$62b in 1993. March 7.
Tan, Augustin H. H., and Basant Kapur, eds. 1986. *Pacific growth and financial interdependence.* Sydney: Allen and Unwin.
Thorn, Richard S. 1987. *The rising yen.* Singapore: Institute of Southeast Asian Studies.
U.S. General Accounting Office. 1989. Chicago futures market: Initial observations on trade practices abuses. GAO/GGD-89-58. Washington, D.C.: General Accounting Office.
Walter, Ingo. 1993. *High performance financial systems: Blueprint for development.* Singapore: Institute of Southeast Asian Studies.

## Comment Sang-Woo Nam

This paper provides a lot of factual information about the financial center of Singapore. I agree that a well-trained workforce together with accumulated expertise, credible supervisory capability, and political stability are the important advantages of Singapore as a financial center. I am also convinced that the Singapore financial market is likely to find a niche as a risk management and fund management center as well as a fund supplier through Asian dollar bonds to countries in Southeast Asia and the Indian subcontinent.

Sang-Woo Nam is a senior fellow at the Korea Development Institute.

My first comment is about the future of Singapore as a financial center. First of all, we cannot help comparing Singapore with Hong Kong. Hong Kong will continue to play the major role in taking care of the financing needs of northeast Asia, including China, Vietnam, and Korea, while Singapore will do more business with the ASEAN countries. Since the northeast Asian economies are likely to grow much faster than the ASEAN countries, the potential demand for financial services to be met by Hong Kong's financial center is also going to grow much faster than that for Singapore's. Although Singapore's financial center may aim to become "the second gateway" to China, this role may be limited.

Of course, the future of Hong Kong is uncertain. However, recent developments seem to indicate that this uncertainty has been substantially reduced, at least in the short and medium run. Two-way investment between Hong Kong and China is enormous, including real estate purchases. Their interests have been interlocked by taking each other hostage. In the long run, Shanghai or Hainan might share the role of Hong Kong as a financial center, which may not have any significant impact on the Singapore financial market.

In addition, deregulation in the Japan Offshore Market (JOM) will affect the growth of Singapore's financial center. As the author notes, the JOM is only for nonresidents, and securities businesses are prohibited. Furthermore, the tax burden on offshore accounts and offshore banking income in the JOM is fairly heavy. With continued progress in domestic financial liberalization in Japan, the JOM may see gradual deregulation in business boundaries and in other respects. This will tend to divert some business from Singapore and Hong Kong to the JOM.

My second comment concerns the long-run underlying trend for offshore financial activities in general. With continued financial liberalization, which relaxes many of the regulations on banking activities, and the global integration of financial markets where foreign banks operate in a much freer environment, local (onshore) banks are likely to absorb much of current offshore activities. Moreover, with the development of computers and telecommunication technologies, the physical location of an international financial center is not as important as it has been in the past. The gravity of a financial center is becoming functional rather than locational.

My final comment is related to the impact of increasing external capital flows on the macroeconomic stability of a country. With the liberalization of capital transactions and the introduction of the Asian Currency Unit market, Singapore must have faced increasing capital mobility. I wonder to what extent it undermined Singapore's monetary independence and macroeconomic stability. As a means of insulating the domestic financial market from outside disturbances, Singapore banks are required to make a clear distinction between domestic and offshore transactions. With transferrable deposit instruments and other innovations, the separation might have been incomplete. The experience of Singapore with capital account liberalization might provide a valuable lesson for other countries such as Korea, which is in the process of seriously opening the capital account.

## Comment Pakorn Vichyanond

From my viewpoint, Ngiam's paper is truly impressive in that, given its length, it provides a very comprehensive picture of developments in Singapore as a financial center. Essential facets, or pillars as he calls them, are well contained. Nevertheless, let me add a few points.

First, we should probably be cautious before claiming that deregulation or financial liberalization will definitely encourage cross-border capital flows or strengthen the prospects of any city like Singapore as a financial center. The key point is what we are referring to in the term "deregulation" or "financial liberalization." If we mean fewer capital or exchange controls, its contribution to the development of an international financial center may be positive. But if we mean *less stringent* controls on access to local markets, that is, that tapping local funds from local capital markets is *easier* than before (which is applicable to Thailand), then chances are *slimmer* that local companies will tap funds from abroad or an international financial center like Singapore. The primary reason for reverting to home markets is exchange risk.

Risk aversion to exchange rate variations is well known and also endorsed by Ngiam. That is, local investors in Singapore are generally reluctant to buy securities issued by foreigners on the Stock Exchange of Singapore mainly because those securities must be denominated in non-Singapore currency. The same feeling is true on the other side of the coin. That is, when foreign borrowers such as the ones in Thailand can choose between tapping funds from either the Stock Exchange of Thailand in baht or Singapore's Asian Dollar Market in nonbaht currencies, Thai borrowers are ordinarily tempted to tap funds from local sources, especially their stock market. Therefore, an increasing degree of deregulation or financial liberalization does not necessarily lead to the prosperity of international financial centers. Its largely depends on specific aspects of such deregulation or liberalization.

Evidence from several markets supports my viewpoint, that is, that deregulation can lead to more direct financing and less dependence on offshore money markets. An example is the case of corporate bonds covered by Horiuchi amid the widespread issuances of notes and warrants on the Stock Exchange of Thailand after the newly established Securities and Exchange Commission (1992) implemented several relaxing measures for the stock market. (If my concern is taken into account, there are some implicit paradoxes in Ngiam's paper.)

My second point concerns offshore rivals of Singapore, such as Thailand's

Pakorn Vichyanond is a senior research fellow at the Thailand Development Research Institute.

Bangkok International Banking Facilities and Malaysia's Labuan. Because of their proximity, they represent formidable challenges to Singapore as banking centers accommodating the financial needs arising from the emergence of the economic quadrangle among Thailand, China, Burma, and Laos.

Finally, I would like to investigate the genuine intention of the Monetary Authority of Singapore (MAS) in preventing the internationalization of the Singapore dollar. Ngiam is correct that such a shut-in policy is costly in hindering Singapore's development as an international financial center. But our second thoughts easily support the MAS, since such restriction will help preserve financial stability and minimize disturbances from external sources. In other words, avoiding the internationalization of the Singapore dollar may help retain the current degree of MAS autonomy or independence, if there is indeed any such thing.

# Contributors

Jonathan Eaton
Department of Economics
270 Bay State Road, Room 501
Boston University
Boston, MA 02215

Shin-ichi Fukuda
Institute of Economic Research
Hitotsubashi University
Kunitachi, Tokyo 186
Japan

Kenjiro Hirayama
School of Economics
Kwansei Gakuin University
Nishinamiya-shi, Hyogo 662
Japan

Akiyoshi Horiuchi
Faculty of Economics
University of Tokyo
Hongo 7-3-1, Bunkyo-Ku
Tokyo 113
Japan

Bor-Yi Huang
Department of Finance
Shih Chien College
3 Lane 62 Ta-Chih Street
Taipei, Taiwan
R.O.C.

Takatoshi Ito
International Monetary Fund
Research Department
Washington, DC 20431

Basant K. Kapur
Department of Economics and Statistics
National University of Singapore
10 Kent Ridge Crescent
Singapore 0511

Toshihiko Kinoshita
Research Institute for International Investment and Development
Export-Import Bank of Japan
4-1 Ohtemachi, Chiyoda-ku
Tokyo 100
Japan

Akira Kohsaka
Osaka School of International Public Policy
Osaka University
1-7 Machikaneyama
Toyonaka-shi, Osaka 560
Japan

Anne O. Krueger
Department of Economics
Stanford University
Stanford, CA 94305

Hsiu-Yun Lee
Graduate Institute of International Economics
National Chung Cheng University
Chia-Yi, Taiwan
R.O.C.

Kenneth S. Lin
Department of Economics
National Taiwan University
21, Hsu-Chou Road
Taipei 10020, Taiwan
R.O.C.

Ronald I. McKinnon
Department of Economics
Stanford University
Stanford, CA 94305

Francisco de Asis Nadal De Simone
Reserve Bank of New Zealand
P.O. Box 2498
2 The Terrace
Wellington
New Zealand

Chong-Hyun Nam
Department of Economics
Korea University
1, 5-Ga, Anam-dong, Sungbuk-ku
Seoul 136-701
Korea

Sang-Woo Nam
Korea Development Institute
Chongnyang, P.O. Box 113
Seoul 130-012
Korea

Ngiam Kee Jin
Department of Economics and Statistics
National University of Singapore
10 Kent Ridge Crescent
Singapore 0511

Won-Am Park
Department of International Trade
Hong-Ik University
#72-1 Sangsoo-Dong
Mapo-Gu, Seoul 121-791
Korea

Huw Pill
BGIE Group
Morgan Hall
Harvard Business School
Soldiers Field
Boston, MA 02163

V. V. Bhanoji Rao
Department of Economics and Statistics
National University of Singapore
10 Kent Ridge Crescent
Singapore 0511

Muthi Samudram
Malaysian Institute of Economic Research
9th Floor, Block C
Bangunan Bank Negara Malaysia
Jalan Kuching
P.O. Box 12160
50768 Kuala Lumpur
Malaysia

Jia-Dong Shea
Institute of Economics
Academia Sinica
Nankang, Taipei, Taiwan
R.O.C.

Tan Kim Song
Department of Economics and Statistics
National University of Singapore
10 Kent Ridge Crescent
Singapore 0511

Akiko Tamura
Department of Economics
Boston University
270 Bay State Road
Boston, MA 02215

Tse Yiu Kuen
Department of Economics and Statistics
National University of Singapore
10 Kent Ridge Crescent
Singapore 0511

Amina Tyabji
Department of Economics and Statistics
National University of Singapore
10 Kent Ridge Crescent
Singapore 0511

Pakorn Vichyanond
Thailand Development Research Institute
565 Soi Ramkhamhaeng 39
Wangthonglang, Bangkapi District
Bangkok 10310
Thailand

Shang-Jin Wei
Kennedy School of Government
Harvard University
79 JFK Street
Cambridge, MA 02138

Wing Thye Woo
Department of Economics
University of California
Davis, CA 95616

Ya-Hwei Yang
Chung-Hua Institution for Economic Research
75 Chang-Hsing Street
Taipei 10671, Taiwan
R.O.C.

# Author Index

Åkerholm, Johnny, 257
Alesina, Alberto, 210
Allen, S. D., 231n3
Amirahmadi, Hooshang, 79t
Aoki, Masahiko, 189n19
Ariff, M., 332
Asian Development Bank (ADB), 124t
Association of Securities Underwriters, Japan, 176t

Bade, Robert, 210
Balassa, Bela, 208n10
Bank for International Settlements (BIS), 107, 132t, 366n15, 375f
Bank of Japan, 135–36, 138f, 139f, 169, 173t
Bank of Korea, 253f, 254t, 256t, 258f, 259t, 289t, 299t
Berg, L., 9
Bernanke, B. S., 12, 20
Blinder, A. S., 12, 20
Bonser-Neal, Catherine, 314n4
Boot, Arnoud W., 190
Bosworth, Barry, 8
Brainard, S. Lael, 64n7
Branson, William, 314
Brealey, Richard A., 179
Bryant, Ralph, 362
*Business Times,* 376

Calder, Kent E., 171n5
Calvo, Guillermo, 10, 43, 138n15, 265
Census and Statistics Department, Hong Kong Monetary Authority, 134t
Central Bank of China, Taiwan, 198f
Chan, Vei-Lin, 197
Chen, C. N., 233, 234n5
Chen, S. K., 233, 234n5
China Ministry of Foreign Economic Relations and Trade, 80t, 81t
China State Statistics Bureau, 77, 79t, 91
Chinn, Menzie, 327
Chiu, Paul C. H., 231
Cho, Yoon Je, 248n1
Church, K., 12
Claessens, Stijn, 138n15
Conley, J. P., 11, 17, 21, 30
Connolly, R. A., 231n3
Corbo, V., 138n15
Corker, Robert, 244
Cukierman, Alex, 206t, 207, 226

Daveri, F., 10
Deardorff, Alan V., 59n6
de Castro, Sergio, 11
De Gregorio, Jose, 197n4
Dervis, Kemal, 195, 199, 210n12, 225
Dixit, Avinash, 53
Dollar, David, 197
Dominguez, Kathryn, 312
Dornbusch, Rudiger, 7, 8, 234n5, 312
Drysdale, Peter, 59n6

Eaton, Jonathan, 51, 52n1, 53, 64, 67, 107
Edwards, Alexandra, 8

Edwards, Sebastian, 8, 265, 267, 268, 336, 338n4
Engle, Robert F., 236, 264

Faruqee, H., 264, 336, 338, 341, 347
Federation of Bankers Associations of Japan, 167n2
Feldstein, Martin, 90n9, 262, 337
Fernandez-Arias, Eduardo, 120
Field, A. J., 231n3, 234n4
Fischer, Bernhard, 9, 12, 307, 322
Fischer, Stanley, 195, 197n4, 198t, 200, 205, 225, 226
Frankel, Jeffrey A., 18, 59n6, 107, 138n15, 140n16, 147, 167n1, 308, 312, 327, 336, 337, 338n4, 361n6
Frenkel, Jacob, 314n3
Friedman, M., 231n3
Froot, Kenneth, 90n9
Fukuda, Shin-ichi, 151, 155n4

Gandolfo, Giancarlo, 47
Garnaut, Ross, 59n6
Gertler, M., 12
Ghosh, Atish R., 120
Giavazzi, F., 9
Gilchrist, S., 12
Giovannini, Alberto, 149n1, 151
Glassburner, Bruce, 325n7
Glick, Reuven, 140n16, 335
Gooptu, Sudarshan, 120
Granger, C. W. J., 236, 237
Grossman, Gene M., 56n2

Hamada, Koichi, 149
Hansen, Lars, 317n5, 351
Haque, Nadeem U., 140n16, 263
Helpman, Elhanan, 52n1, 56n2
Hernandez, L., 138n15
Hines, James, Jr., 83n4
Ho, Corrinne, 107
Hodrick, Robert, 317n5, 351
Horioka, Charles, 262, 337
Horiuchi, Akiyoshi, 149, 293
Hoshi, Takeo, 168n4, 172–73n7, 185, 189n19
Hou, T. C., 231
Hsiao, Cheng, 84
Huang, P. Y., 231, 233
Hufbauer, Gary, 84n5
Hutchison, Michael, 140n16, 335

International Finance Corporation (IFC), 107
*International Financing Review,* 368, 375
International Monetary Fund (IMF), 79t, 107, 113–14t, 115–17t, 123t, 124t, 133n10, 138n15, 198f, 260f
Ito, Takatoshi, 149, 157n9, 314, 335, 337n2, 340, 344n9

Japan External Trade Organization, 128
Japan Securities Research Institute, 185t
Japan Tariff Association, 155, 162
Jensen, Michael, 179, 181
Ji Cong, 151, 155n4
Jung, Byung-hyu, 298t
Jwa, Sung Hee, 264

Kang, Moon-Soo, 258n3
Kashyap, A. K., 12, 20, 172–73n7, 189n19
Kawai, Masahiro, 149
Keynes, John M., 28, 314
Khan, M. S., 336, 338n4
Kim, Joon-Kyung, 248n1
King, M. A., 10
Kinoshita, Toshihiko, 87
Kiyotaki, Nobuhiro, 150
Kohsaka, Akira, 107
Kortum, Samuel, 51
Krugman, P., 13, 16, 56n2, 149n1, 150
Kueh, Y. Y., 78, 79n1
Kurz, M., 26
Kydland, Finn E., 210
Kyriacou, George, 59

Labán, R., 8
Laidler, D., 332
Lakdawalla, Darius, 84n5
Lardy, Nicholas R., 88, 96
Lattimore, R., 9
Leamer, Edward E., 52n1, 59n6
Lee, J. C., 231
Leiderman, Leonardo, 138n15
Levich, Richard, 314n3
Levine, Ross, 200, 226
Lian, Peng, 92n11
Liang, F. C., 231n3
Lichtenberg, Frank R., 189n19
Lin, Ching-Yuan, 193
Lin, Kenneth, 197
Lin, T. Y., 231
Lipsey, Robert E., 90n9
Lowe, Phillip, 257
Lucas, Robert E., Jr., 83n3, 85

McKinnon, Ronald I., 7, 9, 12, 13, 15, 20, 23, 30, 31, 151n2

Malani, Anup, 84n5
Maloney, W. F., 11, 17, 21, 30
Markusen, James R., 52n1
Marston, Richard, 149n1, 347
MAS (Monetary Authority of Singapore), 360n4, 366
Mathieson, Donald J., 138n15
Matsui, Akihiko, 150
Matsuyama, Kiminori, 150
Mayer, Colin, 303
Meckling, William, 179, 181
Milbourne, R., 332
Miller, M., 10
Min, Byong-Kyun, 289t
Ministry of Construction, Korea, 258f
Ministry of Finance, Japan, 132, 177t
Ministry of Finance, Korea, 254t
Montiel, Peter, 140n16, 262, 263
Morck, Randall, 189n19
Muellbauer, J., 27
Mundell, Robert, 50, 52n1
Murphy, A., 27
Mussa, M., 10
Myers, Stewart C., 179

Nakamura, Masao, 189n19
Nam, Sang-Woo, 50, 248n1
Nasution, Anwar, 319n6, 325n7
National Statistical Office, Korea, 255t
Newbold, P., 237
Nomura Research Institute, 169f, 174t, 178t, 185t

Obstfeld, Maurice, 262, 337, 338n3
Office of Bank Supervision and Examination, Korea, 281t, 284t, 286t, 290t, 292t
Ohno, Kenichi, 149n1
Organisation for Economic Co-operation and Development (OECD), 127–28t
Ostry, Jonathan, 120
Ou, S. H., 233
Ouyang, C. D., 231, 233
Ozeki, Yuzuru, 149, 162t

Padoan, Pier Paolo, 47
Park, Daekeun, 248n1
Park, Won-Am, 257n2
Park, Yung Chul, 257n2
Parkin, Michael, 210
Patrick, Hugh, 189n19
Petri, Peter A., 107, 195, 199, 210n12, 225
Pill, Huw, 9, 12, 13, 15, 27, 28
Piñera, Jose, 11
Poyhonen, Pentti, 59n6
Prescott, Edward, 210
Prowse, Stephen D., 172–73n7, 189n19
Purvis, Douglas D., 52n1
Pushner, George M., 189n19

Radecki, L. J., 231n3, 234n4
Reddy, J. Mahender, 88n8
Reinhart, Carmen M., 10, 138n15
Reisen, Helmut, 9, 12, 263, 264, 307, 322, 335
Renelt, David, 200, 226
Ro, Sung-Tae, 258n3
Rodriguez, Carlos, 265
Rogoff, Kenneth, 312
Rojas-Suarez, Liliana, 138n15
Roley, V. Vance, 314n4
Romer, P., 15n1
Roubini, Nouriel, 199n5

Sachs, Jeffrey, 104
Sala-i-Martin, Xavier, 199n5
Sargent, Thomas, 210
Saxonhouse, Gary, 107, 149n1, 164
Schadler, S., 8, 9, 12, 13, 14t, 138n15
Scharfstein, David, 172–73n7, 189n19
Schmidt-Hebbel, K., 11
Shanmugaratnam, T., 336
Shaw, E. S., 20
Shea, Jia-Dong, 199n6, 230n2, 231
Sheard, Paul, 189n19
Shih, Y., 231
Shiller, R. J., 22
Smith, P., 12
Sokoloff, Kenneth, 197
Spaventa, L., 9
Stein, J. C., 12, 20
Stein, Jeremy C., 179, 181
Stiglitz, Joseph, 45, 53
*Straits Times,* 376, 378t
Summers, Lawrence H., 210
Sutherland, A., 10

Taguchi, Hiroo, 149
Takeda, Masahiko, 149, 176n9
Tamura, Akiko, 52n1, 53, 64, 67
Tavlas, George S., 149, 162t
Teh, K. P., 336
Tinbergen, Jan, 59n6
Tsiang, S. C., 230n2
Turner, Philip, 149, 176n9
Tyabji, Amina, 332

Ueda, Kazuo, 244
United Nations, 80, 81, 83–84
U.S. General Accounting Office (GAO), 376n36

van Wijnbergen, Sweder, 268
Végh, C. A., 10, 43

Wallace, Neil, 210
Wallis, K., 12
Walters, A. A., 9
Wei, Shang-Jin, 59n6, 90, 92n11, 96, 107, 147
Weiss, Andrew, 45
Wenninger, J., 231n3, 234n4
White, Halbert, 60
Wilcox, D. W., 12, 20
Willard, Kristen, 83n4
Woo, Wing Thye, 312, 325n7
World Bank, 23, 84, 85n6, 107, 108, 109, 119–20t, 125n6, 126, 131n8, 138n15
Wu, C. S., 231
Wu, Weiping, 79t

Yang, Ya-Hwei, 199n6
Yang, Young-sik, 298t
Yeches, Helen, 263, 264, 335
Young, Alwyn, 195n2, 197n3
Yuan, Tsao, 107

# Subject Index

ACUs. *See* Asian Currency Units (ACUs)
ADM. *See* Asian Dollar Market (ADM)
ANIEs (Asian newly industrialized economies). *See* Newly industrialized economies (NIEs)
Arbitrage: in deviations from covered interest rate parity, 337, 340, 355
ASEAN4: FDI in Pacific Asia (1982–93), 128–31
Asian Currency Units (ACUs), 359–60
Asian Development Bank: dragon bond issue, 366, 380
Asian dollar bond market, 364–66
Asian Dollar Market (ADM): creation, 359–60; Eurodollar, Euroyen, Euromark, etc. segments of, 360; growth of, 362–63
Asia-Pacific countries, FDI share, 80–90

Balance of payments: capital account, Asia and Western Hemisphere (1973–93), 112–14; capital account averages, Asia and Western Hemisphere, 112–14; capital accounts in Pacific Asia (1982–92), 114–18; capital account transactions in Indonesia, 317; capital account without restrictions, 18–19; current account behavior, Taiwan and South Korea, 215–22; Japan's long-term capital account, 134–38; Korean capital account transaction liberalization, 251, 275; Korean current account surpluses (1980s and 1990s), 251, 261; long-term capital account, Pacific Asia, 114–18
Bangkok International Banking Facilities, 386
Banking system, Japan: compared with Korean principal transactions banks, 293–95; dominance in Pacific Asia, 132; as model of bank-business relations, 295–96, 305
Banking system, Korea: with abolition of capital controls, 275–76; deregulation, 249, 275; evaluation of principal transactions bank system, 287–93; evolution of principal transactions bank system, 278–82; proposals for bank-business relations, 295–99, 305; role in credit control, 279–82; shift to universal, 271; structure and role of principal transactions bank system, 282–87
Banking systems: effect of capital inflows on newly liberalized, 22; with financial reform and economic stabilization, 42–48; with liberalization and financial innovation, 22–25; loan flow in international, 131–34; in overborrowing model, 19–21; Pacific Asia cross-border interdependence, 131–34; with policy response to overborrowing, 28–35
BIAC. *See* Bond Issue Arrangement Committee (BIAC), Japan
Bond Issue Arrangement Committee (BIAC), Japan, 171–72, 176, 178
Bond markets: Asian dollar bond market, 364–66; with internationalization of financial markets, 168, 170, 174–78; Japanese corporate, 168–78, 183–85; liberalization of Japanese, 188–91

Bond markets, international: Asian dollar bond market in, 364–66; dragon bond market in, 366
Business groups, Korea: basket credit control, 282, 287–88; proposals for bank-business relations, 295–99, 305; subject to credit control, 280–81

Capital: absence of controls in Indonesia, 317–18; model of consequences in China of foreign, 90–99
Capital flows: amendment to imperfect capital mobility, 309–10; in and out of Asia, 112–18; to China, 78–79; components of, 108; components of official, 126; in domestically liberalized economy, 15; effect of inflows on banking sector risk, 22; implications of covered and uncovered interest parity on, 337–38; from industrial to developing countries (1990–93), 1; international mobility of Korean, 261–65, 271, 273; Japanese-Korean cross-border, 274; long-term capital flows between Japan and Pacific Asia, 134–37; macroeconomic consequences of large inflows, 12–14; market-determined and government-determined, 142; mobility with uncovered interest parity deviations, 341; in model of Singapore interest rate–exchange rate relationship, 347–53; net resource flows to developing countries (1982–94), 109–12; perfect and imperfect capital mobility, 308–9; role of Singapore financial markets in international, 359–60; shift in pattern to developing countries, 108–9; using covered interest parity swap pricing, 319–22; volume and mobility, 1
Capital flows, Pacific Asia: changing pattern in, 108, 138–40; inflows, 118–20; interdependence with, 125–34
Capital markets: borrowing from international, 18–19; government role in Korea, 278; response to reform and stabilization programs, 10–11; short-term in Japan, 150; Singapore syndicated loans and dragon bonds, 366, 380
Caribbean, 109–12
Central bank, Korea: credit system, 212–15; financial sector regulation, 214; index of independence, 206–7, 226; role in export-led growth, 206–10
Central bank, Taiwan: credit system, 211–15; currency appreciation, 218–19; export financing, 211–12; index of independence, 206–7, 226; role in export-led growth, 206–10
Central banks: differences in role in developed and developing countries, 194; role in swap mechanism in Indonesia, 318–19
Chicago Mercantile Exchange. *See* SIMEX-CME Mutual Offset System
China: attraction for FDI compared to other countries, 87–90; consequences of foreign capital in, 90–99; as host country for FDI, 77–79, 82–87; joint ventures with Singapore, 380; model of consequences of foreign capital in, 90–99; relation of output growth to foreign investment, 92–94
Cities, China: analysis of output growth in, 92–94, 103–4; relation of human capital, output, and foreign investment, 94–96, 103–4; with special economic status, 94–96, 103–4
Consumption: in domestically liberalized economy, 15–18; Fisherian two-period model of intertemporal, 13–15, 49–50; in internationally liberalized economy, 18–19; with overborrowing, 11–12
Corporate bonds, Japan: control of issues, 171; convertible bond issues, 168–70, 176–78; convertible bond issues with market liberalization, 178–88; domestic market for, 174–78; eligibility for issues, 173–74; hypothesis for surge in convertible issues, 178–79; issuance overseas, 174–78; liberalization of markets for, 170–78; response of stock prices to issues of convertibles, 183–85
Corporate finance: evidence to support hypothesis related to Japanese convertible bond issues, 183–86; hypothesis related to Japanese convertible bond issues, 179–81; model of hypothesis of Japanese convertible bond issues, 181–83; standard theory of convertible bond issues, 179
Corporate finance, Japan: changes in, 168–69; securitization of, 168; structural change (1980s), 178
Corporate governance, Japan: evidence to support hypothesis related to, 183–86; hypothesis related to, 178–79; model of hypothesis related to, 181–83; questions related to, 189–90
Corporations, Korea: application of principal

transactions bank system to, 282–83; behavior with credit control system, 287–93; exemptions from credit control of Major Corporations, 287–93; subject to credit control, 280–81
Countries: destination countries for Japanese and U.S. FDI, 58–65; destination country in model of trade, investment, and growth, 53–58; FDI to developing countries, 80–90; Japan and United States as source countries in FDI analysis, 58–65; source country in model of trade, investment, and growth, 53–58; sources of FDI to China, 81
Countries, host: determinants of foreign investment, 121–25; factors in rise and fall of FDI in, 142–46
Countries, investor: factors in rise and fall of FDI from, 142–46
Covered interest: differential between domestic and world interest rates, 311–14
Covered interest parity: deviations of Singapore data from, 342–53; Indonesia, 317–22; in model of Singapore interest rate–exchange rate relationship, 340–41; of price swap transactions in Indonesia, 319
Credit control, Korea. *See* Credit system, Korea
Credit markets: domestically liberalized economy, 15–18; internationally liberalized economy, 18–19
Credit system: foreign loans to Asian countries, 112–14; liberalization of credit controls in Korea, 249; South Korea, 213, 226, 247–48; Taiwan, 211–12, 226. *See also* Finance, external; Overborrowing; Overborrowing episodes
Credit system, Korea: credit control, 277, 282, 287–93; evolution of credit control, 279–82; with financial deregulation, 255–59; subsidized bank loans to industry, 278. *See also* Principal transactions bank system, Korea
Currencies: composition in East Asian external debt, 161–62; East Asian currency links, 147–48; tying to U.S. dollar of East Asian, 155; U.S. dollar as dominant invoicing currency, 142. *See also* Exchange rates; Invoice currencies

Data sources: analysis of FDI in China, 91–92; for FDI in China, 78, 83–84; invoice currency analysis, 155, 160, 162; relation between Japanese-U.S. direct foreign investment and exports, 70; response of stock prices to convertible bond issues, 184, 185; Singapore interest rate–capital mobility analysis, 341; Taiwan money and price analysis, 242
DBU. *See* Domestic banking unit (DBU)
Debt, external: currency composition of East Asian, 161–62; Pacific Asia, 118–20; Taiwan and South Korea, 216, 222, 227
Derivatives, Singapore markets, 381
Development institutions, Korea, 255
DFI (direct foreign investment). *See* Foreign direct investment (FDI)
Distance: relation to FDI, Japan and United States, 58–65, 67–70, 73–75; relation to FDI in China, 84
Dixit-Stiglitz production relationship, 53
DLE. *See* Domestically liberalized economy (DLE)
Domestically liberalized economy (DLE): effect of market failure, 23–24; features with reform, 15; in intertemporal model with perfect certainty, 15–18; solving for outcomes of, 36–37
Domestic banking unit (DBU), 360

East Asia: changes in capital flows to, 109–14
Economic growth: influence of FDI on, 101–2, 103–4; link to macroeconomic policy, Taiwan and South Korea, 195–205; role of government in Korea for, 247–48
Economic policy, China, 78
Economic shocks, Taiwan and South Korea, 218, 222
Economy: domestically liberalized reform economy, 15; financially repressed prereform economy, 15–16; internationally liberalized reform economy, 15
Efficient market hypothesis, 340
Eicker-White standard errors, 60
Euromarkets, 175–77
European Community (EC): FDI in Pacific Asia (1982–93), 128–31; investment income flows between ANIEs and (1983–93), 137–38
Exchange rate policy, Korea, 216–18; Market Average Exchange Rate System, 251, 260, 270; Multiple Currency Basket Peg System, 259–60, 265, 270
Exchange rate policy, Taiwan, 216–18

Exchange rates: in choice of invoice currency, 151; in FDI, 101; influence on uncovered interest parity deviations, 345–46; model of relation to interest rates in Singapore, 339–53; monetary autonomy with fixed exchange rate policy, 308; regression of Japanese export prices on, 156–57; risk avoidance of Japanese trading companies, 150–51
Exchange rates, Korea: basket-peg system, 250; determinants of real, 268–70; fluctuation of nominal and real, 265, 271; model for real, 265–68; volatility, 270
Export-led growth: role of central bank, Taiwan and South Korea, 205–10; role of fiscal policy, Taiwan and South Korea, 205–10
Export prices: choice of Japanese invoice currency, 155–57, 164; determinants of, 164. *See also* Invoice currency ratios
Export promotion: FDI as, 102; Taiwan, 211, 215
Exports: differences in Japan's invoice currencies for, 152–56, 161; with foreign investment in China, 96–98; Japan's reliance on exports to United States, 150; relation to direct foreign investment in country receiving technology, 56–58; relation to foreign investment in China, 96–98; relation to outward FDI positions, Japan and United States, 58–65

Factor endowments, Japanese-U.S. trade and investment, 58–65, 73–75
Finance, external: conditions for sustained, 125; to developing countries, 108; official capital flows in Pacific Asia, 126–28; to Pacific Asia, 108, 138–40; Taiwan and South Korea, 214
Financial centers, international: challenges for Singapore as, 372–79; future locations, 384; Hong Kong as, 133, 384; prospects for Singapore as, 379–81, 384; transformation of Singapore into, 133, 360
Financially repressed economy (FRE): prereform economy as, 15–16
Financial markets: cross-border claims and liabilities, 133–34; diversification in Korea, 278; internationalization, 168, 170, 174–78, 188–89; with uncertainty, 22–25
Financial sector, Korea: central bank regulation, 214; deregulation and liberalization, 249–52, 278; performance with liberalization, 252–60, 270–71, 275–76
Financial sector, Singapore: ACU as proportion of total assets, 362
Financial services, Singapore, 359–60; deregulation and liberalization, 360–64, 385; future of, 379–81. *See also* Asian Currency Units (ACUs); Asian Dollar Market (ADM)
Financial systems: international liberalization, 189; liberalization of Japanese, 167–68
Firms: with foreign investment in China, 96–98; growth of nonstate Chinese, 98–99. *See also* Foreign-invested firms (FORs), China; Individual-owned firms (INDs), China; Township and village enterprises (TVEs), China
Fiscal policy: associated with large capital inflows, 12–14; role in developing countries, 194; role in export-led growth, Taiwan and South Korea, 206–10, 225; tax reform in Korea (1981), 248
Foreign direct investment (FDI): China as host country for, 77–79, 82–87; determinants, 72; factors influencing, 101; factors in rise and fall of, 142; as form of capital flow to developing countries, 109–13; forms in China of, 79; geographic distribution in Pacific Asia, 128–31; gravity and factor endowment specifications, 59, 72; industrialized and developing countries worldwide, 80–90; model of distribution to China, 82–87; predictions for China, India, and four NIEs, 87–90; relation of distance and regional effects, Japanese-U.S., 58–65, 67–70, 73–75; relation to exports in country receiving technology, 56–58; share in foreign capital inflows in Pacific Asia, 118–20
Foreign Exchange and Foreign Trade Control Law (1948), Japan, 174–75
Foreign exchange markets: relation with Singapore International Monetary Exchange, 360; Singapore, 366–68, 373–74, 380
Foreign exchange reserve policy, Taiwan and South Korea, 218–21
Foreign-invested firms (FORs), China, 92–93, 98–99
Foreign Investment Law (1950), Japan, 174
Forward exchange markets: Korea, 250–51; with swap mechanism in Indonesia, 318–22

Forward exchange rate: implication for future spot rate, 340
Fund management, Singapore, 381
Futures exchanges: Singapore, 368; Asia-Pacific, 375

Germany, 81–82
Globex, 376–77
Government role, Korea: in credit control system, 291–93; in credit market, 247–48, 257, 278; with financial liberalization, 252–60; in principal financial bank system, 304; in resource allocation, 212
Gradualism in Japanese financial liberalization, 168, 189

Hong Kong: FDI in Pacific Asia (1982–93), 128–31; as offshore banking center, 372–73; role as international financial center, 131–34, 379; as source of FDI to China, 81
Hong Kong Futures Exchange, 375
Hong Kong Monetary Authority, 362
Human capital: influence on exports and FDI, 64; measure of stock of Chinese, 94–96

ILE. *See* Internationally liberalized economy (ILE)
Imports: differences in Japan's invoice currencies for, 156–59, 165; protection, Taiwan, 220–21
Income per capita, Japan-U.S. trade and investment, 58–65, 72–74
India, 88
Individual-owned firms (INDs), China, 92–93
Industrial targeting policy: Korea, 197, 214–15, 225, 247–48, 278; Taiwan, 195, 197, 225
Inflation: Korean government control of, 257–59; Taiwan and South Korea (1973–87), 206, 217, 225
Innovation, technological: dissemination through direct foreign investment, 51; dissemination through export of new products, 51; in model of trade, investment, and growth, 53–58
Interest rate parity: covered and uncovered, 337–39; deviations from uncovered, 337
Interest rates: deviation of independent domestic rate from world rate, 310–15; independence with monetary autonomy, 308, 310–15; liberalization in Japan, 167–68; model of relation to exchange rate in Singapore, 339–53
Interest rates, Korea: control in, 257–59; covered and uncovered interest rate parity, 262f, 263–65, 273–74; deregulation in, 249, 278; relation to capital flows, 261–62
Internationally liberalized economy (ILE): effect of market failure in, 24–25; features with reform, 15; in intertemporal model with perfect certainty, 18–19; solving for outcomes of, 37
Investment: country's ability to absorb technology, 56–58; financing in domestically liberalized economy, 15; Fisherian two-period model of intertemporal, 13–15, 49–50; foreign investment in China, 78–99; non-FDI foreign investment in China, 78; privileges in FDI, 101; relation to macroeconomic policy, Taiwan and South Korea, 197–99. *See also* Portfolio investment
Investment income flows, Japan and ANIEs (1983–93), 137–38
Invoice currencies: determinants of Japan's export, 149–51; determinants in Japan's imports, 156–59; hypothesis related to choice of foreign or domestic, 151–53; Japan's use of yen when exporting to East Asia, 149–50; U.S. dollar as, 150
Invoice currency ratios: differences in Japan's exports to United States and East Asia, 152–56; factors to increase yen-denominated, 159–61, 165; of Japanese exports and imports, 147–48; Japanese exports in yen-denominated, 150; for Japan's imports, 157–58; of OECD domestic, 147–49

Japan: FDI in Pacific Asia (1982–93), 128–31; financial role in Pacific Asia, 134–38, 140; invoice currency ratios of exports and imports, 152–59; Japan Offshore Market, 359, 372–73, 384; role in capital flow interdependence, 126–28; as source of FDI to China, 81–82, 87; trends in outward FDI, 143–46
Japan Offshore Market, 132, 359, 372, 384

Korea Asia Fund, 251
Korea Development Bank (KDB), 255
Korea Europe Fund, 251

Korea Export Import Bank (KEXIM), 255
Korea Fund, 251
Korea Planning Board, 212–13

Labor cost, production facilities location, 101
Labuan, Malaysia, 386
Latin America: changes in capital flows to, 109–12; investment ratio compared to Asia, 122–25
Legal system, China, 82, 88

Macroeconomic development, Pacific Asia, 118–25
Macroeconomic policy: link to long-term growth, Taiwan and South Korea, 195–205, 224–25; role in export-led growth, 205–10; stability as condition for attracting foreign investment, 122–25, 139. *See also* Credit system; Fiscal policy; Industrial targeting policy; Monetary policy
Market failure: formal model of deposit insurance–induced, 37–38; relation to optimistic expectations, 27; welfare comparison with, 31–33, 38–40
Ministry of Finance (MOF), Japan, 171
Monetary autonomy: defined, 308–10; dependent on risk premium, 315; relation to capital mobility, 309–10; with swap subsidy in Indonesia, 321–22, 327
Monetary policy: constrained by capital flows, 309–10; in Korea with financial liberalization, 257–59; South Korea, 217; Taiwan, 217–18. *See also* Exchange rate policy
Money demand: estimates of traditional equation, 239–41; portfolio demand in Taiwan model, 234–35, 244, 245; transactions demand in Taiwan model, 234, 245
Money supply: equated with money demand in Taiwan model, 235; with monetary autonomy, 308
Multinational institutions: role in Asian capital flow interdependence, 126–28

Newly industrialized economies (NIEs): FDI in Pacific Asia (1982–93), 128–31; FDI policies, 89; local capital outflow in Asian, 114–18; long- and short-term capital flows between Japan and Asian, 136–40; market liberalization and deregulation, 2; savings and capital flows in Asian, 123–25
Nonbank financial intermediaries (NBFIs), Korea: charters, 249; deregulation, 271; financing of business groups, 288, 304; growth, 253; investment, insurance, and development institutions, 254–55
Nonstate sector, China, 98–99, 104

Official development assistance (ODA): factors influencing levels of, 142–46; as official capital flow, 126; Pacific Asia, 126–28
Offshore financial activities: growth, 133; Hong Kong and Singapore, 372–73; Japan Offshore Market, 359, 372, 384; long-run trend, 384
Openness of economy: Chinese open coastal cities, 96; Hong Kong, Korea, Singapore, Taiwan, 88–89; of Japan to U.S. exports, 65–70; Korea, 277; of Oceania and East Asia to Japanese and U.S. exports, 65–70; open door policy in China, 78, 79; relation to foreign capital inflows, 122
Options exchange, Singapore, 368
Osaka Stock Exchange, 375
Other official flows (OOF): factors influencing levels of, 142–46; as official capital flow, 126; Pacific Asia, 126–28
Output and input: relation of foreign investment to growth in China, 92–94
Overborrowing: conditions for, 19–21, 27; policy responses to, 28–35; rational expectations and rational beliefs, 25–28
Overborrowing episodes: features of, 12–13; in liberalizing and industrialized economies, 7–10

Pacific Asia: changes in capital flows to, 109–14; investment ratio compared to Latin America, 122–25; long-term capital flows between Japan and, 134–36; net official capital flows, 126–28
Plaza Accord (1985), 120
Population: effect on exports and FDI, Japanese-U.S. trade and investment, 58–65, 73–74
Portfolio investment: of ANIEs in Japan, 137; conditions for external, 120–21; as form of capital in Pacific Asia, 138; in Korea, Malaysia, and Thailand (1990s), 118–20
Price stability: central bank maintenance of, 194

Pricing-to-market (PTM): behavior of Japanese exporters, 149; as explanation of Japanese choice of invoice currency, 155–56
Principal financial bank system, Korea, 304
Principal transactions bank system, Korea: comparison with Japanese banking system, 293–95; evaluation, 287–93; evolution, 278–82; structure and role of, 282–87
Private sector, China, 98–99, 104
Production location: in model of trade, investment, and growth, 53–58
PTM. *See* Pricing-to-market (PTM)

Rational beliefs concept, 25–28
Rational expectations, 25–28
Reform programs: Chile, 10–11; China's economic reform (1979), 78; domestically liberalized economy with, 15–18; internationally liberalized economy, 18–19; response to, 11; result of, 11
Regionalization of outward investment, 84
Risk premium: covered and uncovered interest rate parity, 337–39; efficient market hypothesis without, 340; measurement of, 330; model of Singapore interest rate–exchange rate relationship, 346–47; monetary autonomy dependent on, 315; relation of portfolio risk premium to interest rate differential, 312–15; zero and nonzero, 308
Risks with large capital inflows, 22–23

Saving-investment correlations, 262–63, 273
SES. *See* Stock Exchange of Singapore (SES)
SIMEX. *See* Singapore International Monetary Exchange (SIMEX)
SIMEX-CME Mutual Offset System, 368
Singapore: FDI in Pacific Asia (1982–93), 128–31; fund management in, 381; joint ventures with China, 380; as offshore banking center, 372; as risk management center, 381; role as international financial center, 131–34, 379–81
Singapore Commodity Exchange (SICOM), 377n37
Singapore International Monetary Exchange (SIMEX): futures and options exchange, 360, 368, 375, 381
Special economic zones (SEZs), China, 95–96
Stock Exchange of Singapore (SES), 368–71, 377–79
Stock Exchange of Thailand, 385
Stock market, Taiwan: performance (1986–91), 237
Stock prices: index, Taiwan (1985–91), 237; response to convertible bond issues in Japan, 183–86
Subsidies: covered interest parity swap pricing in Indonesia, 319–22
Swap mechanism, Indonesia: covered interest parity to price transactions, 319; forward exchange market with, 318–22; margins, 331; subsidy to capital inflows, 319–22
Sydney Futures Exchange, 375

Taiwan: FDI in Pacific Asia (1982–93), 128–31
Technology: exports and FDI as conduits for transfer, 66; transfer in model of trade, investment, and growth, 53–58
Tokyo International Financial Futures Exchange, 375
Tokyo Stock Exchange, 375
Township and village enterprises (TVEs), China, 92–93, 98–99, 104
Trade dependency, 160–61
Trade flows: determinants of bilateral, 72; gravity and factor endowment specifications, 59, 72; Japan–East Asia, 147; Japanese-U.S. bilateral, 73–75. *See also* Export prices; Exports; Imports; Invoice currency ratios
Transaction costs, foreign investment in China, 82
Triumphalism: effect of, 26–27; with successful reform (1978–82), 10–11

Uncertainty: in Fisherian two-period model, 19–21
Uncovered interest parity: deviations of Singapore data from, 342–45; in model of Singapore interest rate–exchange rate relationship, 340–41
United States: FDI in Pacific Asia (1982–93), 128–31; investment income flows between ANIEs and (1983–93), 137–38; role in Asian capital flow interdependence, 126–28; as source of FDI to China, 81–82
U.S.-Japan Yen-Dollar Committee, 167

Wages: in production location decisions, 53–58